THE LIFE OF DAVID

THE LIFE OF
DAVID HUME

Ernest Campbell Mossner

SECOND EDITION

Be a philosopher; but amidst all your philosophy,
be still a man

CLARENDON PRESS · OXFORD

OXFORD
UNIVERSITY PRESS

Great Clarendon Street, Oxford OX2 6DP

Oxford University Press is a department of the University of Oxford.
It furthers the University's objective of excellence in research, scholarship,
and education by publishing worldwide in

Oxford New York

Auckland Bangkok Buenos Aires Cape Town Chennai
Dar es Salaam Delhi Hong Kong Istanbul Karachi Kolkata
Kuala Lumpur Madrid Melbourne Mexico City Mumbai Nairobi
São Paulo Shanghai Singapore Taipei Tokyo Toronto

and an associated company in Berlin

Oxford is a registered trade mark of Oxford University Press
in the UK and in certain other countries

Published in the United States
by Oxford University Press Inc., New York

© Oxford University Press 1980

First published by Thomas Nelson & Sons Ltd, 1954
Reprinted 1970
Second Edition 1980
First published in paperback 2001

British Library Cataloguing in Publication Data
Data available

Library of Congress Cataloging in Publication Data
Data applied for
ISBN 0-19-924336-0

3 5 7 9 10 8 6 4 2

Printed in Great Britain
on acid-free paper by
Biddles Ltd., Guildford and King's Lynn

1954

To a young David
in the hope that he, too,
will never lose faith
in the dignity
of
human nature

1970

In memory of a young David
who died in combat
in the faith
of the dignity of man

1979

To my wife

PREFACE 1980

" I REMEMBER an Author, who says, that one half of a man's Life is too little to write a Book; and the other half to correct it." So wrote David Hume to his publisher in the last months of his life. I take comfort in the remark in regard to the present book, which was first published in 1954 after nearly twenty years of preparation, reprinted in 1970, and now published as " revised and enlarged " after more than another twenty years. It is truly astonishing that a book which has so frequently been called " definitive "—that much abused word—needs to be " revised and enlarged " after a mere score of years. The study of Hume has prospered mightily in recent times as I became fully aware when I approached the preparation of a new edition. It has taken me nearly two years to examine the new works of and about Hume, to evaluate them, and to incorporate those that rightly belonged to a biography into the present volume. The bibliography, likewise, required much updating; the BM has become the BL.

Norman Kemp Smith in the preface to his monumental study of *The Philosophy of David Hume* (1941) observes : " One day, we may hope, someone equipped with a sufficient range of interest and understanding will treat of Hume in all his manifold activities: as philosopher, as political theorist, as economist, as historian, and as man of letters. Hume's philosophy, as the attitude of mind which found for itself these various forms of expression, will then have been presented adequately and in due perspective, for the first time." That day has not yet arrived nor has that scholar yet identified himself. A friendly warning : he had better be young in years at the outset if " one half of a man's Life is too little to write a book," leaving " the other half to correct it." That much wished for study in Humean synthesis will probably not take the form of a biography, not even an intellectual biography such as this present work professes to be. Were I twenty years younger, or even fifteen, I might be tempted to have a go at it (" The Mind of David Hume ") myself. But alas . . ..

In order to make a new edition possible in 1979 certain restrictions were dictated by the hard economic facts of present-day publication. A complete re-setting of type was out of the question. So the start had to be photographic reproduction of the original edition. Small alterations were permitted within the text itself, while larger alterations were placed in a new Textual Supplement at the end of the volume.

Were I to list all those philosophers and scholars who have been in touch with me since 1954 offering advice, information, and corrections, the question might very well be raised, What have I done myself? To avoid that embarrassment, I will confine my list to a few, leaving the nameless others with my no less sincere thanks and gratitude. Charles P. Finlayson, John V. Price, and the late D. B. Horn, Edinburgh University; Mary Baker, William B. Todd and Ann Bowden Todd, University of Texas; Ian S. Ross, University of British Columbia; Geoffrey Hunter, University of St Andrew's; the late James Osborn, Yale University; Michael Morrisroe, Jr., John Marshall Law School; David Raphael, Imperial College, University of London; Raymond Klibansky, McGill University; Aruc Aruoba, Hacettepe Universitesi, Ankara; Paul E. Chamley, University of Strasbourg; P. H. Nidditch, University of Sheffield; R. W. Connon, Linacre College, Oxford; Mrs Donald F. Hyde, the Donald F. and Mary Hyde Library; A. S. Crockett, Director of Highways, Lothian Regional Council; Duncan Thomson, Scottish National Gallery; William Beattie and Alan S. Bell, National Library of Scotland. Finally, to my wife, who decade after decade, has been my best critic and loyal supporter, my devoted gratitude.

No sooner had I written the above (which was intended to be the conclusion) than a letter from Alan Bell, Assistant Keeper of MSS in the National Library of Scotland, demanded immediate attention: the signed, dated, and place-named covers ostensibly in Hume's hand of a series of historical notes were pronounced forgeries. The nefarious perpetrator of this outrage was none other than Alexander Howland (" Antique ") Smith, the late nineteenth century fabricator of historical documents. " This information," continued Mr Bell with scholarly irony, " may affect some of the topographical and intellectual arguments of your biography." Yes, indeed. It took me well over a fortnight to straighten things out, and there is no estimating what effort it cost the highly competent copy-editor, Mrs

W. E. S. Thomas. Mr Bell's unsolicited updating of MSS in the NLS and in other Edinburgh collections was also much appreciated.

E. C. M.

Austin, Texas
26 April 1978

PREFACE 1954

SINCE the death of David Hume in 1776 the story of his life has hitherto been told at book-length three times—by T. E. Ritchie in 1807, John Hill Burton in 1846, and J. Y. T. Greig in 1931. Ritchie's work was superseded by Burton's substantial two volumes, which still remain the most complete biography, despite the eminently readable and entertaining account by Greig. That James Boswell, who had the inestimable advantage of personal acquaintance with Hume, did not proceed with the original intention of writing his biography is certainly regrettable : the occasional anecdotes about Hume in the *Boswell Papers* have been a boon to the present writer.

A critical problem faces the biographer who has chosen to treat of a man of letters remembered chiefly as a thinker : shall he treat of his subject's thought as well as of the external facts of his life ? This is what both Ritchie and Burton, in some measure, attempted to do for Hume ; Greig relegated the philosophy proper to an introductory chapter which he cavalierly invited the general reader to skip at pleasure. The problem has more recently been pointed by Canon A. A. Luce, who in *The Life of Bishop Berkeley* (1949) expressed the opinion that " the story of the life " and " a study of the thought " do not " mix well," and hence essayed what he termed " *a separate life.*" Dr Luce was willing to concede, however, that the point is arguable.

While recognising that there is a major difference of emphasis between the story of the life and a study of the thought, I am firmly convinced that the biography of a man of letters who devoted himself primarily to matters of the intellect can have no deep significance, perhaps even little human interest, without *some* consideration of the intellectual activities which made him worthy of a biography. The real issue is *how much* consideration ? As I conceive his task, the biographer must present enough of the thinking of his subject to be able to interpret his actions without, at the same time, going so far as to overburden the narrative with *systematic* exposition, making it difficult of comprehension for a reader less interested in the ideas than in the man. Such is the basic plan of this book ; the man predominates, but the ideas provide the rationale of his actions.

The presence of an autobiography may, curiously enough, not be a wholly unmixed blessing for a biographer. In general, I may venture to observe that a long autobiography tends to be helpful, while a short one is troublesome. Hume's five-page *My Own Life*, at any rate, is invaluable in the revelation of character, but at the same time offers difficulties by reason of its high compression and consequent suppression of facts. Hence *My Own Life* is reprinted in its entirety in Appendix A (pp. 611–15, below) for the benefit of the careful reader who may wish to correlate the biography with the autobiography.

The Letters of David Hume (two volumes, ed. J. Y. T. Greig, 1932) and *New Letters of David Hume* (edd. R. Klibansky and E. C. Mossner, 1954), all three volumes published by the Clarendon Press, provide the most important source of information about Hume's day-to-day living. To avoid an excessive number of footnotes in the present work, quotations from the letters which are identifiable by date or by other simple means are undocumented. Original sources are cited whenever possible and in original orthography and punctuation. Nineteenth-century printed versions of such documents have been generally avoided since they are frequently unreliable because of errors of transcription and omissions without indication. Translations from foreign languages are my own except when otherwise noted. Quotations appearing on the title-page and at the chapter headings are Hume's.

The Life of David Hume, I feel bound to acknowledge, has been on the stocks—more or less—since 1936, at which time my study of eighteenth-century British thought turned from *Bishop Butler and the Age of Reason* to focus on Hume. During the ensuing years Hume has continued to hold my attention, as may be attested by a score of articles in historical, literary, and philosophical journals, and by a book. *The Forgotten Hume : Le bon David* (1943) was a preparative for the present work in that its avowed purpose was to determine the character of the man as found through his relations with a selected group of friends, protégés, and rivals. The interruptions in academic and scholarly life caused by World War II have resulted in inevitable delay—but to have done with apologies, I find solace in the sage remark of Dr Johnson that " Every long work is lengthened by a thousand causes that can, and ten thousand that cannot, be recounted."

In the preparation of a work as long as this an author's obligations to scholars and to institutions of learning are necessarily legion. And, in taking this opportunity to make public acknowledgment only to a few, I am not unappreciative of the many that are not specifically identified, particularly the students in my seminars at the universities of Syracuse and Texas. Perhaps I owe most, all in all, to the John Simon Guggenheim Memorial Foundation and the Research Institute of the University of Texas : the one for the grant of a fellowship in 1939-40 and a renewal in 1945-46 ; the other, for research leave in the spring semester of 1950 and for research assistants from 1947 to 1954.

The very notion of a Republic of Letters implies an open exchange of information among scholars, and I am happy to name some of those who have freely offered facts and advice : Professors R. H. Griffith, Oscar E. Maurer, Harry Ransom, and Rudolph Willard of the University of Texas ; Robin Adair of McGill University ; Benjamin Boyce of Duke University ; Edwin Cady of Syracuse University ; James L. Clifford and Norman L. Torrey of Columbia University ; David Daiches and C. R. Fay of Cambridge University ; Alan D. McKillop of the Rice Institute ; Paul H. Meyer of Bryn Mawr College ; James M. Osborn and Frederick A. Pottle of Yale University ; L. F. Powell of Oxford University ; Edward Ruhe of Rutgers University ; and N. Kemp Smith of Edinburgh University. Outside the academic realm, I am especially indebted to the Reverend Alfred McKeachie, Minister at Chirnside, Berwickshire, who so hospitably opened my eyes to the lore of David Hume's home environs ; and to Charles Sandler, M.D., of New York City, who so painstakingly reviewed the evidence and corrected my amateurish diagnosis of the philosopher's last illness.

To name all the libraries and to extol the friendly co-operation of all the librarians whom I have consulted would be to extend this preface overmuch. I must, however, single out the National Library of Scotland and Edinburgh University Library : at the former, Henry W. Meikle, Marryat R. Dobie, William Beattie, and William Park ; at the latter, L. W. Sharp. To these I should add the names of W. S. Haugh, City Librarian at Bristol ; A. N. L. Munby, Librarian at King's College, Cambridge ; and Miss Margaret Wood, Curator at the City Chambers, Edinburgh.

To Yale University and the McGraw-Hill Book Company, Inc., of New York City, I am greatly indebted for permission to quote materials from the " Yale Editions of the Private Papers of James Boswell." Similarly am I indebted to the Royal Society of Edinburgh for permission to use their collection of Hume MSS and to the Royal Irish Academy in Dublin for permission to use the " Anecdotes of Hume " in their collection of Lord Charlemont's MSS. For permission to use microfilms of the Newhailes MSS, I wish to thank Sir Mark Dalrymple, Bt., and the National Library of Scotland ; I wish also to thank Professor David Yalden-Thomson, who made available to me the copies in the library of the University of Virginia.

For careful criticism of the entire work I am deeply obligated to my good friends, Professor Raymond Klibansky of McGill University, Professor W. G. Maclagan of Glasgow University, and Dr Jean Holloway of Fort Worth, Texas. Dr Holloway also compiled the index. R. L. C. Lorimer, philosophical editor of Thomas Nelson and Sons Ltd., has been all that an author could desire of an editor ; and the general interest of Dr H. P. Morrison of Nelsons and Frank H. Wardlaw of the University of Texas Press has proved most stimulating. Dr L. F. Powell, to whom all students of the eighteenth century owe so much, generously read the proofs. To him, and to the publishers' compositors and readers, I owe a special debt.

Finally, it would not be meet to close the biography of so Roman a moralist as David Hume without paying due tribute to the *Lares* and *Penates* of the several places of its composition : the office on the 25th (latterly the 24th) floor of the University of Texas library tower at Austin ; the lodge of " Okaga " at Lake Brownwood, Texas ; and the cottage of " El Descanso " at Cloudcroft, high in the Sacramento Mountains of New Mexico, at the foot of which shimmer the White Sands, birthplace of the Atomic Bomb.

E. C. M.

Austin, Texas
June 1954

CONTENTS

APPENDICES   609

LIST OF ABBREVIATIONS
AND REFERENCES

MANUSCRIPT COLLECTIONS

BL   British Library

EU   Edinburgh University Library

HMC   Historical Manuscripts Commission

NLS   National Library of Scotland

Newhailes   Microfilms of Newhailes MSS deposited in NLS and in University of Virginia Library

PRO   Public Record Office, London

RIA   Royal Irish Academy, Dublin

RSE   Royal Society of Edinburgh

SRO   Scottish Record Office, Register House, Edinburgh

HUME'S WRITINGS

HL   *The Letters of David Hume*, ed. J. Y. T. Greig. Oxford 1932. 2 vols.

NHL   *New Letters of David Hume*, edd. R. Klibansky and E. C. Mossner. Oxford 1954

Phil. Wks.   *The Philosophical Works of David Hume*, edd. T. H. Green and T. H. Grose. London 1874–5. 4 vols. Reprinted 1964. Scientia Verlag. Aalen.

OTHER AUTHORS

Boswell Papers = *Private Papers of James Boswell from Malahide Castle*, edd. G. Scott and F. A. Pottle. [Privately printed.] New York 1928–34. 18 vols.

Caldwell Papers = *Caldwell Papers*, ed. Wm. Mure. Glasgow 1854. 2 vols. [VOL. II in 2 pts.]

Carlyle = *The Autobiography of Alexander Carlyle of Inveresk*, ed. John Hill Burton. London and Edinburgh 1910.

Greig = J. Y. T. Greig, *David Hume*. London 1931.

Hill Burton = John Hill Burton, *Life and Correspondence of David Hume*. Edinburgh 1846. 2 vols.

Home-Mackenzie = *The Works of John Home*, to which is prefixed an account of his life and writings by Henry Mackenzie. Edinburgh 1822. 3 vols.

Johnson = *Boswell's Life of Johnson*, ed. G. Birkbeck Hill ; revised and enlarged by L. F. Powell. Oxford 1934–50. 6 vols. 2nd ed. of vols. V and VI, 1964.

Ramsay = John Ramsay of Ochtertyre, *Scotland and Scotsmen of the Eighteenth Century*, ed. Alexander Allardyce. Edinburgh and London 1888. 2 vols.

Ridpath = George Ridpath, *Diary*, ed. Sir James Balfour Paul. Edinburgh 1922.

Rousseau = Jean-Jacques Rousseau, *Correspondance Générale*. Paris 1924–34. 20 vols.

Walpole Letters = Horace Walpole, *Letters*, ed. Mrs Paget Toynbee. Oxford 1903–05. 16 vols.

Walpole Corr. (Yale) = *The Yale Edition of Horace Walpole's Correspondence*, ed. W. S. Lewis. New Haven 1937. . . .

PART I

STUDENT OF HUMANITY

1711-1744

CHAPTER 1

MAN OF LETTERS

" Almost all my Life has been spent in literary Pursuits and Occupations."

DAVID HUME lived during the Age of Enlightenment amidst that welter of ideas and social forces that was to make the eighteenth century part-and-parcel of modernity. But it was Hume's distinctive, if not his unique, feature that while seeking to revolutionise the study of human nature, he never lost sight of the understanding of the general public. Welding philosophy and learning together with literature, he set himself up, not as specialist, but as man of letters, according to the intellectual ideals of his age. Like his earlier counterpart of the Renaissance, the ideal man of letters of the Enlightenment might still take all knowledge as his province ; but, for the first time in the history of mankind, his circle of readers was enlarged to include the majority of the public. Hume's philosophy proper, to be sure, might necessarily be restricted to the learned ; his studies of government, economics, ethics, religion, and the social sciences in general might interest only the relatively well-educated ; but his national history might, and actually did, appeal to most of those who were capable of reading.

The life of letters was the burning ambition of David Hume, and few men have ever pursued that life with purer and more steadfast devotion. Literary expression was to Hume the fulcrum by which he strove to overturn the rationalistic tradition that had dominated European thought ever since the distant age of Socrates. This intellectual revolution, first proposed in 1739 by Hume when a young man of twenty-seven, was repeatedly prosecuted by him throughout his life in various literary forms. It constituted the prime motivation of his life : " Obscurity, indeed, is painful to the mind, as well as to the eye ; but to bring light from obscurity, by whatever labour, must needs be delightful and rejoicing." Thus it is that the key to Hume's career as man of letters is to be found only on the level of idea. No biography of Hume can make any pretention to depth or solidity that neglects to take notice of his thinking.

Yet with all his devotion to philosophy, Hume was able to follow his own precept : " Be still a man." As a man—and this book is primarily devoted to him as a man—he had many virtues. The French learned to call him *le bon David*, but the epithet cannot readily be translated into one English word. To call Hume *good* would be misleading, for he was certainly no saint. In many ways, however, he *was* good : he was humane, charitable, pacific, tolerant, and encouraging of others, morally sincere and intellectually honest. He was always a loyal friend. He was, however, somewhat inclined to be jealous—jealous of his own reputation, jealous of the integrity of friendship, jealous of the prestige of his native country. Intellectually a citizen of the world, he was emotionally a Scot of Scots. He was, moreover, a worldly man who thoroughly enjoyed the good things of life—food and drink, wit, conversation, rational discourse. A man of unusual self-control, he was yet a man of feeling, a man of passion, a man not unsusceptible to women. He was, to repeat with the French, *le bon David*.

Hume was the first distinguished man of letters in Britain to earn a modest fortune from literature alone. Shakespeare, it is true, had prospered—but chiefly as an actor, manager, and stock-holder. Dryden had endured—but through the patronage of the great. Addison had done well—but through government pensions. Pope had waxed wealthy—but through a third type of patronage, subscriptions prior to publication. Johnson eked out a livelihood by hack-writing for the booksellers—but achieved competency only with a late government pension. Such pensions were the expected rewards of the man of letters of the eighteenth century ; and Hume, in due time, received his share. His basic success, however, came from a broad appeal to the public at large. Never dedicating a work to a patron, never seeking for advance subscriptions, Hume prospered simply through the booksellers.

Although today Hume is generally recognised as the most authentic voice of the Enlightenment, that age itself would hardly have been in agreement. The Age of Enlightenment read his *History* and *Essays* widely enough to ensure the outward success of his career, but remained unreceptive to his philosophy. Yet philosophy, including " religion, which is only a species of philosophy," was always his dominant interest. In England he suffered frustration and humiliation because he was a Scot in a period of strong anti-Scottish feeling and because he was the proponent of unpopular ideas. In his native Scotland he was frequently snubbed socially and constantly attacked by the ultra-orthodox. Only within the small circle of Edinburgh intellectuals was his genius fully appreciated, though not fully approved, and of that intimate group only his closest friend Adam Smith gave the nod of whole-hearted approval. If he was ultimately acclaimed in France as Britain's leading man of letters, not even there was his philosophy completely understood. Society is wont to deal unkindly with those it does not fully comprehend. Hume's life was a constant struggle against odds—against financial straitness, poor health, family ambitions ; against the power of names, the inertia of ideas, the forces of superstition and intolerance.

The " Science of Human Nature " expounded by Hume throughout a long career was either ignored or misunderstood by his own generation, and he did not live to know the more favourable reactions of Kant. In the nineteenth century his philosophy attracted considerable attention, but mainly for purposes of refutation. Only in the twentieth century has it met with sympathy and understanding. Today his ideas are constantly discussed and, whether in approval or disapproval, they always receive respectful attention. Albert Einstein, for instance, has acknowledged that the critical reasoning required for the discovery of the special relativity theory rejecting the absolute character of time was decisively furthered by the reading of David Hume's philosophical writings. Philosophically, Hume is more alive today than ever he was previously.

An amusing and revealing account of Hume's acceptance today is to be found in one of Bertrand Russell's short stories, in the volume entitled *Nightmares of Eminent Persons*. The assertion is made that there is a peculiarly painful chamber in Hell inhabited solely by philosophers who have refuted Hume. " These philosophers," comments Russell dryly, " though in Hell have not learned wisdom." As yet I have not had the opportunity of verifying Russell's Dantesque vision in person, but am more than inclined to think it likely enough.

Hume's all-inclusive " Science of Human Nature " has now become the study of specialists in many fields, including psychology, ethics, religion, government, economics, and the social sciences. Of all the investigators in the present day of specialisation only a few—notably Bertrand Russell and John Dewey—have attempted to retain the universality of the man of letters of the Enlightenment. This universal approach to man was based upon the belief in the essential dignity of his nature, a conviction held by Hume as fundamental to all philosophy.

The life of David Hume, man of letters of the Age of Enlightenment, provides a fitting commentary upon the perennial theme of the dignity of human nature.

CHAPTER 2

THE HUMES OF NINEWELLS

"I was of a good Family."

"*Edinburgh, 26th Aprile 1711* [o.s.]. *Mr Joseph Home of Ninewells, advocat, and Katherine Ffalconer, his lady. A S[on] N[amed] David. W[itnesses] : George, Master of Polwarth, Sir John Home of Blackadder, Sir Andrew Home, advocat, and Mr Alexander Ffalconer Junior, advocat. Born this day.*" So runs the entry in the Edinburgh baptismal Register, and lest there be any doubt concerning the identity of this David, baptised on the day of his birth, an eighteenth-century hand has written in the margin : "The child here registered is the celebrated David Hume Historian and Philosopher." [1]

The unknown annotator of the Register undoubtedly sought to obviate confusion engendered by the variant spellings of the family name. "David *Hume*, son of Joseph *Home*," is indeed a discrepancy to give pause to the careful reader, although one familiar with Scottish philological backgrounds recognises that both surnames are pronounced *Hume*. Actually, these were but two of a score of variant spellings adopted by the several branches of the family from the fifteenth until the eighteenth century, with David in his lifetime deliberately making the shift from *Home* to *Hume*, while his brother and his famous cousin John Home, the dramatist, conservatively clung to the then-accepted spelling.

The Edinburgh dwelling of Joseph Home, where presumably his celebrated son was born, was in a *land* or tenement house fronting on the south side of the Lawnmarket in a neighbourhood then much favoured by Edinburgh lawyers. And the not undistinguished group of country gentry and professional men witnessing the baptism of the child affords some indication of the social status of the family.

Though in reality he was sufficiently modest, David Hume was in later years, largely on the strength of his autobiography, to be accused of overweening family pride. "I was," he states in *My Own Life*, "of a good Family both by Father and Mother. My Father's Family is a Branch of the Earl of Home's

[1] Parochial Registers, Co. of Edinburgh, B. 1708–14, Vol. 685 (i), no. 15, in SRO.

THE HUMES OF NINEWELLS

or Hume's ; and my Ancestors had been Proprietors of the Estate, which my Brother possesses, for several Generations. My Mother was Daughter of Sir David Falconar, President of the College of Justice : The Title of Lord Halkerton came by Succession to her Brother. My Family, however, was not rich. . . ." To these bare particulars Hume added some correct but sketchy details in a letter written to supply information for a book on the Scottish peerage, where an incidental comment on the worth of family histories in general may be taken as reflecting a quiet satisfaction in his own lineage : " I am not of the opinion of some, that these matters are altogether to be slighted. . . . I doubt that our morals have not much improved since we began to think riches the sole thing worth regarding." [1]

Though unremarkable for their wealth, David Hume's forebears were of a moderate affluence, and sufficiently distinguished to warrant some pride of race in their most famous son. The Hume genealogy reflects a strong family personality, its dominant characteristics being clearly discernible in the fragments of documentary evidence which survive. The Humes were, for many centuries, men of spirit, doughty warriors, and, as befitted a family which produced its share of men of the law and married more than its share of advocates' daughters, aggressively litigious men of affairs. They were worldly, and, within the connotations of successive ages, well-travelled, albeit " good Scots," provincial, and loyal to family ties. The blood-lines intermingle, and the families intertwine.

A simple clue to the devious interconnexions of the Hume family tree, as well as historical authority for David's spelling of his surname, is afforded by a long, flat, rectangular tombstone in the graveyard at Hutton, Berwickshire, just beyond and down the Water of Whiteadder from the Ninewells estate. The inscription is still plainly legible :

Here was buried Robert Hume of Hutton Bell, Sone to George Hume of the Ninewells, nephue to Thomas Hume of the Brumhouse, Pronephue to Thomas Hume of Tinningham, brother to the founder of Dunglas. ANN 1564.

When it is borne in mind that in sixteenth-century Scotland *nephew* meant grandson and *pro-nephew* great-grandson, and that Dunglass is the courtesy title of the eldest son of the Earl of Home, the significance of the inscription becomes apparent as validating

[1] HL, I, 276.

David Hume's claim that his father's family was " a Branch of the Earl of Home's or Hume's." [1]

Although the territory of Home in Berwickshire dates at least from 1138, so far as the Humes of Ninewells are concerned, it is only necessary to go back to the early fifteenth century to Sir Alexander Home of Home. That warrior had followed Archibald, fourth Earl of Douglas, to France and was killed in 1424 by the English at the bloody battle of Verneuil. He left behind him a widow—Jean, daughter of Sir William Hay of Locharret or Yester, and several sons. Alexander, the eldest, became Warden of the Marches and " founder of Dunglas " ; his son, also Alexander, was created a Lord of Parliament in 1473 as Lord Home. Thomas, a younger son of the first Alexander, started the Tynninghame line ; but within two generations that Haddingtonshire estate was dissipated by lavish living, and his descendants were then provided with the lands of Ninewells in Berwickshire as patrimony. Thus the sixteenth-century George Hume of Ninewells named on the Hutton tombstone as grandson of Tynninghame was properly the first Hume of Ninewells.

From George, the line descended through Andrew, David, John, Andrew, John, Andrew, David, John, John, to Joseph—and Joseph was the father of John and Katherine, and of their brother David, the historian and philosopher. So David's " several generations " during which " my Ancestors had been Proprietors of the Estate " of Ninewells is clearly an understatement. It is observable, however, that twelve generations within 200 years do not denote a long-lived stock, and this observation is given added weight by the fact that two eldest sons during that period—by coincidence both named David—died before they succeeded to the inheritance.

Living as they did along the Border in the gateway between the ever-warring Scots and English, the early Humes of Ninewells were stalwart and self-reliant. They were also sagacious, retaining and augmenting the family estates. Let a few illustrations sketch in these family characteristics.

The first Andrew Hume, son of the first Laird of Ninewells, apparently jeopardised the family patrimony. In 1539 all his goods were escheat to the Crown for a wilful error in a legal entanglement and were held under " letter of gift " by Henry Lauder, the Lord Advocate. But the records also show that Andrew

[1] For the genealogy of the Humes of Ninewells, see below, Appendix B, p. 616.

was a Baron Baillie to the Prior and Convent of Coldingham—in other words, a man of the law and of some position. Perhaps by legal sagacity, perhaps by influence, Andrew retained the family patrimony. There is no indication that the estate was ever more than technically forfeited.[1]

Andrew's son, David, added to the family heritage. He was interested in the Tweed fishing, which throughout the eighteenth century remained valuable for its salmon, and in 1576 and 1579 he bought at Eyemouth, a few miles north of Berwick on the sea coast, lands amounting to eight acres, with five houses and gardens, and a half-share in a fishing-boat. He was also a depute Baillie at Eyemouth under Alexander Lord Home.

This first David died without issue and was succeeded by his brother John, who had two sons, David and John. The second David also left no issue. The elder John's son Andrew was perhaps more stalwart than sagacious. In 1607 he and his brother Nicholl placed themselves at the head of an armed party of fifty men and invaded the lands of David Home of Godscroft. Burning the turf and carrying away on their horses a quantity of heather, they threatened the very lives of the tenants " with mony horrible and blasphemous aithis." The brothers were summoned to Edinburgh to give an account of themselves, but with what results is unknown.[2] This foray of the Humes of Ninewells was neither the first nor the last. Though in his *History of England* David Hume makes no mention of the martial prowess of his own family, he elsewhere boasts that " in the antient Civil Wars of *Scotland*, we find that the Highland Families were always of little Weight on either Side, and that the Battles were decided entirely by the *Douglasses, Carrs, Humes*, and the other Low-Country Borderers ; who, preserving the same Manners and Institutions with their Countrymen in the Mountains, had acquired a superior Address and Bravery, by their frequent Skirmishes and Battles with the *English*." [3] This passage is in the spirit of tribal bravado of the old Border jingle :

> The haughty Humes,
> The saucy Scotts,
> The cappit Kerrs,
> The bauld Ratherfords.

---

[1] *Accounts of the Lord High Treasurer of Scotland*, III (Edinburgh 1907), 67 ; *Register of the Privy Seal of Scotland*, II (Edinburgh 1921), 451.
[2] *Register of the Privy Council of Scotland*, XIV (Edinburgh 1898), 302.
[3] Hume, *A True Account of the Behaviour and Conduct of Archibald Stewart, Esq ; late Lord Provost of Edinburgh, In a Letter to a Friend* (London 1748), p. 6.

Yet another David, who succeeded Andrew in 1613, improved the financial position of the Humes by a judicious marriage in 1628. The *tocher* or dowry of his bride Helen Belsches, daughter of John Belsches of Tofts, advocate, included 8,000 merks (£444 stg) and certain Tweed fishing-rights.[1] In the following year, David was honoured with the grant of his lands anew, in accordance with the Scottish feudal system, directly from the Earl of Home. In 1636, after David's death, the Earl's uncle Sir John Home married Lady Ninewells, who remained the life-renter of the lands of Ninewells during the minority of her son John. (In addition to John, David also left a natural son, George, who in 1638 was apprenticed to an Edinburgh tailor.)

John Hume, the great-grandfather of our David and the first of the Ninewells family about whom much particularised information is available, is referred to by a nephew in the Home of Wedderburn family as " my unkell, Jhone Hum of Ninholles." During the period of the Civil War, John Hume was on the Committee of War for Berwickshire in 1643, 1646, and 1649. In 1645 he was one of those " gentlemen of Berwickshire " who signed an agreement permitting the Mayor and Baillies of Berwick to erect a dam on the " Water of Whittater " for the purpose of obtaining power to run a mill. The gentlemen were chiefly interested in safeguarding their salmon fishing.[2]

In 1653 John Hume married a neighbour, Margaret Home, eldest daughter of John Home of Blackadder, who came to him with a *tocher* of 6,000 merks (£333 stg). John Hume himself died before 1661, for in that year his widow, " Margaret Hoom, Lady Nyneholls," together with her father and George Home of Wedderburn, " and a great number of their tenants and servants," twice led forays into a fishing village belonging to the city of Berwick. Armed with " swords, pistolls, pitchforks, picks, lances, staffes, battones and other weapons invasive," they violently expelled the tenants, cutting and destroying their nets and cables, and menacing them with the loss of their lives if they ever returned. Legal action was brought against the Humes before the Privy Council of Scotland for damages of " £118 Sterling and upwards," but again the consequences are unknown.[3] Men of the law or not, the Humes of Ninewells sometimes resorted to direct action !

With the next John Home, son of the redoubtable Margaret and grandfather to the philosopher David, the focus may be

[1] HMC, LVII (London 1902), 265.   [2] *Ibid.*, 100, 97.
[3] *Register of the Privy Council of Scotland*, Third Series, I (Edinburgh 1908), 66–7.

shifted from family to individual portraiture. Joseph, the father who died in David's infancy, must remain something of a shadowy personage, but his flamboyant grandfather John, a minor meteor blazing through the last quarter of the seventeenth century, may be taken as the true type of the menfolk of Ninewells, unmellowed as yet by eighteenth-century decorum—or by the pursuits of philosophy.

Three times married, John indulged in the sport of kidnapping ; was stabbed in a brawl over cards ; was for three years Commissioner of Supply for his home county ; sat on the jury which found Renwick, the last of the Covenanters, guilty of the offences for which he suffered martyrdom ; fought for William and Mary as a captain of dragoons ; became Lieutenant-Colonel of the Militia ; and died at a relatively early age.

To start at the beginning, the date of John's birth is unknown ; but he was served heir to his father in 1667. Ten years later he entered upon his first adventure, an essay at kidnapping.[1] The Countess of Home was guardian to the heiress of Ayton, a minor. Colonel John Home of Plendergast, the next male heir of Ayton, was willing to forego his claim to that rich Berwickshire estate if a marriage could be arranged between the heiress and his son. He petitioned the Privy Council for approval of the marriage, and for the attendance of the Countess and her ward at the next meeting of the Council to ratify such an arrangement. But on that very day some local bloods under the leadership of Charles Home, the Earl's brother, rode to the residence of the young lady, and carried her " ower the Border and awa." The conspirators were mostly Homes who did not approve of the tactics of Plendergast—Homes of Linthill, of Kimmerghame, of Polwarth, and of Ninewells—and Johnston of Hilton. And the moving spirit of the conspiracy was the countess-guardian herself.

Holding the heiress as " prisoner and malefactor," the kidnappers debated the most profitable means of disposing of her in marriage. Ninewells was probably the youngest of the group ; for, the decision once taken, he it was who mounted horse and rode to Edinburgh—perhaps fifty miles from the rendezvous— took the " poor young boy, George Home, sone to . . . Cumergeme [Kimmerghame], out of his bed," and brought him back to England. There, on the very day when she was to have

[1] *Register of the Privy Council of Scotland*, Third Series, v (Edinburgh 1912), 30–3 ; Fountainhall, *Historical Notices of Scottish Affairs* (Edinburgh 1848), I, 180–1 ; Chambers, *Domestic Annals of Scotland* (Edinburgh 1859–61), II, 390–1.

appeared before the Council, the girl was forced to marry the boy in a ceremony rendered especially obnoxious by the services of an Anglican rather than a Scottish Presbyterian clergyman. In the meantime, the Countess of Home was dutifully explaining to the Council at Edinburgh the absence of her ward as being " sickly and tender and not able to travell, and not fitt for marriage for many years to come. . . ."

When the true facts became known, the wrath of the Privy Council knew no bounds. The bride and groom, mere puppets in the whole affair, were fined, deprived of their interests *jure mariti* and *jure relictae*, and imprisoned for three months in Edinburgh Castle. Several of the active participants in the plot were assessed large fines, that of John Home of Ninewells amounting to 1,000 merks (£55 10s stg). Such was the humiliating conclusion to an escapade in abduction.

John's next adventure involved murder.[1] During the Christmas holidays of 1683, and in the prolonged absence of her husband, the Earl of Home, the Countess invited a group of gentlemen to a party at the family seat of Hirsel Castle, near Coldstream. The guests included William Home, another of the Earl's brothers, and Sheriff of Berwickshire ; Johnston of Hilton ; and Home of Ninewells. On the day after Christmas, much liquor brought on cards and dice, and gaming brought on a quarrel. William Home lost heavily and exchanged angry words with Hilton, who, in turn, roundly abused him and boxed his ears. The affair subsided and all went to bed amicably. Ninewells was soon aroused from his slumbers, however, by a commotion in Hilton's room. Supposedly, the Sheriff had gone there to demand satisfaction for the affront done him, and the quarrel had been renewed. In a fit of temper, the Sheriff ran Hilton through nine times with his sword as he lay defenceless in bed. And, as John Home entered the room, he also was stabbed. The Sheriff fled into England on Hilton's horse, thus combining theft with murder, and remained in exile for the rest of his life. Hilton soon died, but Ninewells recovered. To his credit, it should be said that he appears to have kept his head throughout and to have been a more or less innocent victim.

John Home's political and religious convictions were, as was inevitable in seventeenth-century Scotland, loosely interwoven. Ostensibly a Presbyterian, he was certainly neither an evangelical

---

[1] Chambers, *Domestic Annals*, II, 454–6 ; Fountainhall, *Historical Observes* (Edinburgh 1840), p. 116.

in belief nor in morals a puritan. During the period of the religious persecution of the Covenanters as political traitors against the Crown, John sat on the Edinburgh jury that condemned James Renwick early in 1688, despite that clergyman's protest against the inclusion of Presbyterians. After conviction, Renwick placed John's in a list of " infamous Names " of those " that call themselves *Presbyterians*, [and who] did not scruple to sit there, or to bring back their Verdict unanimous with the rest (and that more suddenly and hastily than was usual) that *he was guilty.*" [1]

A captain of dragoons, John Home fought in the campaign of 1688–89. Stationed first at Haddington, near Edinburgh, he was ordered to take his troop to Perth. And in July 1689 Captain Home was further ordered, as part of the detachment under the Earl of Argyll, to proceed to the West Highlands and " to prosecute with fyre and sword " the " Viscount of Dundie and all persones whatsomever who are or shall be in the armes for the late King James in oppositione to their Majesties government." [2] In 1689 he is also listed as being Lieutenant-Colonel of Militia and Commissioner of Supply for Berwickshire, the latter being a position he had held in 1683 and held again in 1690.

If the career of this John Home be taken as typical of his family, it is understandable why the Earls of Home, their undisputed chiefs, have borne on their arms the inscription : A HOME. A HOME. JAMAIS ARRIÈRE. Perhaps there is also significance in the fact that towards the close of the seventeenth century the Homes of Ninewells, along with several other cadets of the family, adopted as motto on their altered arms the more cultivated sentiment : TRUE TO THE END.

Be that as it may, the family life of David's grandfather was as chequered as his career. In 1678 he married a daughter of Joseph Johnstone of Hilton. Her Christian name has not been recorded. One of her five children was Joseph, who was to become David's father. Katherine, the eldest child, was born in 1678 ; then came Margaret in 1679, Joseph in 1681 (10 February), Mary in 1683, and Helen in 1685. This good and prolific lady must have died shortly after the birth of Helen about the end of August 1685, because John Home married for the second time on 4 June 1686.[3] The new Lady Ninewells was Agnes Nisbet, who

---

[1] Alexander Shields, " Life of Renwick," in *Biographia Presbyteriana* (Edinburgh 1827), II, 162.
[2] *Register of the Privy Council of Scotland*, Third Series, XIII (Edinburgh 1932), 344, 391, 398, 482–3.
[3] Scottish Record Society, XXVII (Edinburgh 1905), 334.

bore him no children and who did not live very long ; she was interred in the Greyfriars burying-ground at Edinburth on 1 June 1687. The date of John's third marriage is not fixed ; but the lady was Mary, widow of Sir David Falconer of Newton, late Lord President of the Court of Session, and mother, by him, of seven children ; of whom one, Katherine by name, was to become the mother of David Hume.

With this third marriage the household of the philosopher's grandfather became little short of prodigious. To John's five children were added Mary's seven ; and in 1692 Mary bore John Home a son, also named John, who lived, however, only until the following May. Later, another son, Michael, was born to bring the total up to thirteen, which might have been regarded as sizeable, even in that time of large families. How this household was managed, how the children were brought up, and what education they received—these are questions of no inconsiderable import because the Home-Falconer menage at Ninewells included not only the girl who was to become David Hume's mother, but also the boy who was to become his father. It is, therefore, fortunate indeed that these questions can be fairly adequately answered.

At the beginning, financial difficulties arose out of the negligence of the Laird of Glenfarquhar, uncle and " tutor " of the Falconer children, in providing for their maintenance. Lady Home was consequently obliged to seek legal redress by petitioning the Privy Council. A decree [1] of 11 August 1691, specifying the sums ordained by the lords for the support of her seven children, provides important social information and a useful standard for the current value of money. To David—aged ten, eldest son, and heir to his father's estate of 12,565 merks (£698 stg) yearly over and above the widow's jointure—was assigned 1,000 merks (£55 10s stg) yearly for " bed and board, clothing, and other necessaries, and for educating him at schools and colleges as becomes his quality, with a pedagogue and a boy to attend him." To Mistress Margaret—aged twelve-and-a-half, the eldest daughter, with a portion of 12,000 merks (£666 stg)—was assigned 500 merks (£27 15s stg) yearly for " bed and board, clothing, and other necessaries, and for her education at schools and otherwise as becomes her quality." To Mistress Mary—aged eleven, with a portion of 10,000 merks (£555 10s stg)—was assigned 450 merks (£25 stg) yearly for " aliment and education." To Alexander—aged nine, with a

---

[1] Chambers, *Domestic Annals*, III, 55-6.

provision of 15,000 merks (£816 13s stg)—was assigned 600 merks
(£33 6s stg) yearly. To Mistress Katherine, aged eight, and to
Mistress Elizabeth, aged seven, with portions of 8,000 merks
(£444 stg) each, was assigned 360 merks (£20 stg) yearly apiece.
Finally, to George, aged six, was assigned 400 merks (£22 6s stg)
yearly. All payments were to be made to John Home and his
lady as long as the children lived with them.

John Home survived this settlement by fewer than four years.
Not yet aged forty, he died of unspecified causes at Edinburgh on
14 February 1695 ; his will was registered in that city three years
later.[1] His widow was left in charge of a large family in which
our chief interest centres upon her own daughter Katherine
Falconer, and her stepson Joseph Home.

On 3 September 1696, at the age of fifteen, Joseph Home was
served heir to the Ninewells estate. His early education had
probably paralleled that of David Falconer, who was, as we have
seen, to be provided with a " pedagogue and a boy to attend him."
It would seem a reasonable assumption that the pedagogue,
probably " a dominie," thus hired by John Home for David
Falconer would also teach Alexander Falconer and Joseph Home,
who were almost of the same age. It is certain that some five
months after Joseph was served heir, he and these two Falconer
boys were ready for their formal education. The three went up
to Edinburgh University at the same time and signed the Matriculation Book on Regent Row's page on 8 February 1697. They
also paid the standard library fee of £1 10s Scots (2s 6d stg.) [2]
All three were preparing for the law, and, in accordance with a
widespread custom in the Scottish universities, none stayed to
take the bachelor's degree. Their " Regent," John Row, was a
famous Hebrew scholar, but it is hardly to be supposed that the
three boys with law in their minds benefited greatly by that fact.
Yet, as they were later admitted advocates, they must have
studied law after the usual undergraduate preparation.

The atmosphere at Ninewells under John Home, and presumably also under his widow, was clearly not puritanical in the
popular sense ; rather, it was convivial, cultivated, and worldly.
Though not rich, the family was yet well-off. There were servants
enough, and the eight or nine small rooms of the house were
teeming—probably as never before or after—with lively young

[1] Scottish Record Society, xxxi (Edinburgh 1908), 28 ; ii (1898), 200.
[2] EU, MSS entitled (1) " Matriculation Book, 1627–1703 " ; (2) " Library
Accounts, 1697–1765."

folk. The library of a family upwards of two centuries in the same place, though perhaps no scholar's haven, would not have been inadequate for the early education of the children ; and with so many lawyers in and connected with the family, there would also have been a fair number of professional works. Nor is the house [1] in Edinburgh to be overlooked, for it is certain enough that the family stayed there during the winters, and the three boys while attending college classes. If the whole family did not remain in the city with them, the boys would be sure to have been supplied with a servant or two, as well as with a tutor. After completing their studies, the Falconer lads would go their own way. The Falconer girls, however, would stay on at Ninewells at least as long as their mother was alive ; the date of her death is un-recorded. Excepting Katherine, the Falconer girls did not marry.

There is no reason to suppose that the cultivated atmosphere which had prevailed at Ninewells under John and Mary changed appreciably when Joseph became laird, and Katherine his lady. This enlightened spirit at Ninewells seems, in some degree at least, to have been the spirit of the local Berwickshire community. However dour and religiously bigoted Scotland may have been elsewhere—and witches were put to death in Sutherland and Ross as late as 1722 and 1727—Chirnside maintained a due modera-tion. The witch-hunt was never up in Chirnside—possibly because it could get no official sanction. Withered old women with the palsy were not persecuted and were even protected by the local authorities. Whatever the state of popular superstition may actually have been, the Kirk Session Book during the ministry of the Reverend William Miller, 1698-1702, reveals that before the repeal of the Witches Act in 1736, intelligence and understanding were already exorcising superstition and bigotry.

By 1700 Joseph Home would have completed his under-graduate course and would have begun reading law. As there was yet no law faculty at Edinburgh University, he had little choice. He would attend a course in civil law given annually by a member of the Faculty of Advocates, usually in his own home. He would also attach himself in apprenticeship to a practising advocate and would learn procedure by attending the Court of Session. Presumably Joseph thus spent the following two years in Edinburgh, at least during the session. By the autumn of 1702, at any rate, he was ready to complete his legal education abroad,

---

[1] In Edinburgh the word " house " still means " flat " or " apartment " as well as " dwelling-house."

and was inevitably drawn to Holland, where the Dutch jurists offered the best courses in Roman law on the Continent.

But before Joseph left Scotland, he was required to appear before the Kirk Session of Chirnside. The story is an incident of family and community life. Elspeth Burnett, servant to David Home in Ninewells (that is, Joseph's uncle), was cited as being with child. On 22 March 1702 she " compeared " [1] before the Session and confessed her guilt. Asked to name the father of the child, she named Joseph Home of Ninewells. As Joseph was then in Edinburgh, presumably in pursuit of the law, and could not answer the accusation for himself, the case was adjourned until his return. On the 9th of August Joseph himself " compeared " before the Session and denied the charge. But on being questioned as to what he knew about the matter, he told a tale of youthful high jinks.

During one of his respites from study, Joseph had been staying at his uncle's house and had had as his guest a local laird, Archibald Lauder. The two youths retired to sleep in the same bed. In the middle of the night Lauder woke up, got out of bed naked, and went in search of the servant-lass Elspeth : according to Joseph's evidence before the Session, she also was naked. An hour later Lauder returned to his slumbers, and Joseph left it to the Session to draw their own inferences as to what had occurred. He neglected to explain how he knew whether Elspeth was clothed or unclothed, but he named witnesses who (he said) also knew the facts. His evidence suggests that several young people were wandering about the house and grounds throughout the night in various stages of undress.

It was quite properly pointed out to Joseph that he was accusing another man of the sin of fornication and was thus instituting a new case which would also have to be looked into. Joseph, for his part, was firm that he would not be available for any further proceedings before the Session, " being to goe off ye Countrey for Holland this week." So, having insisted on giving his testimony and making his accusation on the spot, " seeing that by reason of my other important affairs & necessary I am at present oblidg'd to goe out of this Kingdome," he withdrew and went his way. As will appear shortly, his way led to the University of Utrecht for the study of law.

What became of the case of Elspeth Burnett is not entirely clear. Joseph himself did not testify again. One of his witnesses

[1] i.e. " appeared in answer to a summons."

refused to " compear " and another who did give evidence denied part of his story. The matter dragged on in the Kirk Session, and was then referred to the Presbytery, until finally, like so many others, it simply disappears from the records. Whether Joseph was innocent or guilty there is no means of knowing beyond his own word, and there seems to be no reason why that should not be accepted. If he was innocent, and the girl did not retract her charge after his denial, he could then (had he been present) have offered to take the Oath of Purgation before the Kirk Session or before the Presbytery, and the matter would have been concluded so far as he was concerned. If he was guilty, there is no apparent reason why he should have implicated Lauder and no particular reason why he should have denied his guilt. The scandal would probably not have damaged his own good name irreparably.

The Kirk Session records reveal that from time to time members of the country gentry, while going their nocturnal rounds, would enjoy an amorous encounter with a servant-girl. Some of these gentlemen were willing to pay the consequences : they would offer to do penance privately from their pews, rather than publicly from the *joug* or iron-collar chained at the Kirk-door and from the pillory or the stool of repentance in front of the pulpit, and to make a reasonable contribution to the Kirk poor-box. The offer—ten shillings seemed reasonable—was usually accepted. The girl in the case, to be sure, normally put on the sackcloth for three Sundays, but was frequently compensated with a gift of money—say another ten shillings—from the gentleman concerned.[1]

By the opening of the eighteenth century, however, it was becoming possible to avoid even such token discipline by the Kirk. A statute of 1690 disallowed the civil consequences of excommunication. When the Kirk was defied, a sentence of the Lesser Excommunication was usually levelled against the offender, sometimes to be followed by that of the Greater. In most cases, that was the end of the affair. Yet throughout the century a man in public office could hardly afford to offend the Kirk. The questions of the legal consequences of fornication and of excommunication were not to be without personal interest in later years to Joseph Home's famous son.

[1] In 1723 Macky cynically remarked : " Church-Censures are said to be very severe here ; but I perceiv'd, the Poor only suffer'd by them : For a Piece of Money will save a Man here from the *Stool of Repentance*, as much as in England " (*Journey through Scotland*, p. 224).

Josephus Home, Scotus. Such is the entry in the books at the University of Utrecht for the year 1704. There is no record of the courses taken, but Joseph would almost certainly have attended the renowned lectures on civil law and on the law of nature and nations. Cornelius Van Eck, the Professor of Law, was University Rector for the year. Exactly what Joseph had meant by " my other important affairs & necessary " seems impossible to determine ; perhaps it was just a young man's way of being impressive about his studies, or perhaps he really did have business affairs to transact in Holland. However that may be, Joseph was back in Scotland again by the spring of 1705, for on the 27th of June of that year he was admitted advocate at Edinburgh. And on 11 September 1706 he was created a burgess of Edinburgh and a guild brother, *gratis*, by Act of the Town Council.[1] An honour reserved for people of distinction and influence which did not carry with it the financial immunities and privileges accorded to genuine tradesmen, this is presumably to be taken as an indication that Joseph Home, following the long-established tradition of the Ninewells family, resided in Edinburgh during the winter months and was actually practising law there.

The career that Joseph had planned for himself would seem to have been that combination of lawyer in the city and gentleman-farmer in the country which was to be carried on so successfully for the last three-quarters of the century by David's friend Henry Home, Lord Kames, and by many others. Both as a laird of twenty-seven and as an advocate with good prospects, Joseph Home was now ready for marriage, and his choice of wife was Katherine Falconer. The fact that Joseph was marrying his step-sister would probably not have raised any adverse comment, either in the family or in the neighbourhood. The young couple were married at Edinburgh on 4 January 1708, little more than a month before Joseph's twenty-eighth birthday and while Katherine was aged twenty-four.[2]

In the five and a half years of wedded life before Joseph's untimely death in 1713, Katherine bore him three children : John, the heir ; Katherine, beloved companion of the two brothers ; and David, the man of letters.

[1] *Album Studiosorum Academiae Rheno-Traiectinae* (Utrecht 1886). p. 106 ; J. P. Wood, " List of Advocates, 1687–1751," NLS, MS 37.2.8 ; Scottish Record Society, LXII (Edinburgh 1930), 100.
[2] Parochial Registers, Co. of Edinburgh, B. 1708–14, in SRO.

CHAPTER 3

BOYHOOD AT NINEWELLS

*" Our Mother . . . devoted herself entirely to the
rearing and educating of her Children."*

NINEWELLS, where the three Home children passed their childhood, is the pleasantest place imaginable. The Merse is that part
of Berwickshire consisting of the valley of the Tweed and its
tributaries, of which the chief is the Whiteadder, the southern
boundary of the Home estate. Half a mile or so down the Whiteadder from Ninewells and beyond Ninewells Mill, just at Allanton
Bridge, the Blackadder flows into it from the south-west. The two
streams are well named and easy to distinguish : the Whiteadder
(" white water ") is the faster running and its clear waters break
into white froth as they tumble over the rocks on the way down
from the hills ; the Blackadder (" black water ") meanders along
dark from its mossy bottom. Beyond the bridge, the Whiteadder
continues its tumultuous course until finally it empties itself into
the Tweed a mile before that " pure Parent-stream " reaches the
historic town of Berwick.

" I have reason to believe," remarks David Hume in a letter [1]
concerning his family, " . . . as Ninewells lay very near Berwick,
our ancestors commonly paid contributions to the governor of that
place, and abstained from hostilities and were prevented from
ravages." Berwick, let it be remembered, after changing hands
many times, was finally ceded to the English in 1482 and was held
thereafter, even to the present time, as the only part of England
north of the Tweed. It is nine miles from Chirnside village on the
outskirts of which lies Ninewells.

The Merse, a low-lying undulating plain enclosed on three
sides by high hills, has sometimes been called " the garden of
Scotland." But before the drainage projects begun in the middle
of the eighteenth century, it was cluttered with bogs and pools,
whence the name, Merse or marsh. According to another interpretation, which also has some authority, Merse means march or
frontier land. During the boyhood of David Hume, at any rate,

---

[1] HL, I, 276.

it was both frontier and marsh with a wide extent of heath or muirland. From Chirnside Hill, along the ridge of which extends the village, the valley of the Tweed opens up for twenty or twenty-five miles. One of the most picturesque views in the Lowlands of Scotland, it is sharply terminated to the south by the bleak English Cheviots and to the north by the wild Scottish Lammermuirs. To the west rises the easy slope of the Teviots, while to the east the valley declines gently towards the Bay of Berwick and the North Sea beyond.

The village and parish of Chirnside—and, in the day of David Hume, the Presbytery as well—is one of the highest in the Merse, rising to some 400 feet above sea level. On the outskirts and along the slopes of the hill, in the early eighteenth century, a common muir provided pasturage for the sheep and cattle of the villagers. Their thatched cottages, made of stone, clay, and wood, were dark, dank, and smoky, and extended in two rows from east to west along the main ridge of the hill. The village took the form of a T because another row of cottages descended in a southerly direction to the Manse with its surrounding glebe-lands, and finally to the Kirk. Some parts of the Kirk date perhaps from the twelfth century; a Norman tower with vaulted chambers dominated the countryside until 1750, and a fine Norman doorway still remains. A square stone inside the Kirk bears the date 1573 and the inscription HELP THE PVR. Beyond the Kirkgate on the Berwick road was the change-house, a hostelry and public house where post-horses were changed or " baited." The village held an annual fair late in the season to dispose of its staple commodity of sacking or bags for grain.

In all that idyllic countryside of the Merse, there is no lovelier situation than the estate of Ninewells. The house itself stands on a bluff some eighty feet above the rushing waters of the Whiteadder. Out of the sloping bank, and descending into the stream, there gush the springs which give the estate its name. The scene was described by Lord Fountainhall on a visit to the Merse in 1670 : " Saw Chirnesyde toune standing a mile of Idingtoun. . . . It will be more than halfe a mile long. At the end of it neir to Whitater stands the Nynewells (corruptly called the Nyneholes), from 9 springs of water besyde it, wheirof on[e] in the fountain is verie great ; are Homes to their name." [1] The Ninewells Beech, to become celebrated in the later eighteenth century and to last through the first quarter of the twentieth, is not mentioned by

[1] Fountainhall, *Journals* (Edinburgh 1900), p. 201.

Lord Fountainhall ; yet it must have been considerably more than a sapling at the time of his visit. Located in a grove a little to the east of the house, it had attained a girth of seventeen feet by 1790. Still farther east beyond the house is the Lady Well, so named, allegedly, after the cure worked by its waters on one of the Ladies Ninewells.

Down the bluff a few yards, and to the south-east of the house, an overhanging rock forms a shallow cave. Here David probably played as a boy, or read a book in solitary majesty ; and here, according to the inevitable local legend, he indulged in profound philosophical meditation. Here also, according to the same source, his great-grandfather hid an Episcopalian poet from a search-party of Covenanters. Along the waterside are other caves, quarries, and freestone rocks. At the southern extremity of Ninewells on the bluff above the town and extending out across the public road are the remains of an old Roman earthwork fort. The trenches and ramparts would have provided the Ninewells boys with a fine playground.

In the stream below the house, David and John would frequently have thrilled to the leap of the mighty salmon as they battled their way upstream from pool to pool. David later had the name of being clumsy, and I do not fancy him as an accomplished sportsman ; yet his publications contain many allusions to hunting and fishing. And he himself writes that, " when I was a Boy, I had a very contemptible Idea, of the bravery of the Edinburgh Trained-Bands, having observed that they customarily shut their eyes when firing their pieces. And I," he continues complacently, " who had at that time been accustomed to fire at Rooks and Magpyes, was very much diverted with their Timorousness." [1] At some time or other David did take lessons in fencing and succeeded only in wrenching his back. John, on the contrary, came to be regarded as an expert in the high and manly art of the " leister " or salmon-spear. As to riding, both lads indulged in what was, indeed, for most of their lives virtually the only means of transportation as well as a sport and healthful exercise. The boys would perhaps ride to Eyemouth, eight miles away on the coast, to watch the fishing-boats set out, and to Berwick to make purchases for their mother. Though mainly passed at Ninewells, their childhood would occasionally have been enlivened by a visit to one of the neighbouring estates in the Merse and by a winter at the family " house " in Edinburgh.

[1] Hume, *Account of Stewart*, p. 15.

The facts reflected by the baptismal records,[1] that John and
David were born in Edinburgh, is added confirmation that
Joseph and his growing family spent a considerable part of each
year there. But during the period of his marriage the young Laird
of Ninewells was by no means neglecting the family estate in
Berwickshire. The indications are that he was attempting to
build it up and to extend it. One of Joseph's legal actions, that
against Johnston of Hilton, was known to his son David, who
writes in his letter on family history : " I have learned from my
mother, that my father, in a lawsuit with Hilton, claimed an old
apprizing upon the lands of Hutton-Hall, upon which there had
been no deed done for 140 years. Hilton thought that it must
necessarily be expired ; but my father was able to prove that,
during that whole time there had not been forty years of majority
in the family. He died soon after, and left my mother very
young. . . ." Another suit was brought by Joseph in 1711 and
again in 1712 against Ninian Home, Minister of the Gospel at
Sprouston, and George Home of Wedderburn.

From the extant papers [2] of Joseph Home it is possible to arrive
at a fairly accurate estimate of his financial resources and of the
extent of the Ninewells holdings. One of these documents shows
that the laird kept twenty-eight shearers who had houses in
Chirnside and shears at Ninewells, the houses being let to them
at £3 10s Scots (5s 6d stg) yearly. These " shearers " were
presumably cottars or other small tenants who in return for their
holdings sheared the laird's sheep with shears provided by him.

Another document discloses the condition of the estate as it
was to be left to the young Lady Ninewells a few months later.
Drawn up in 1713 in Joseph's own hand, the document is divided
into two parts : " List of Ninewell's Debts " and " Rental of
Ninewell's estate as the same is presently gott." The debts are
difficult to analyse but may be divided into (1) a larger group owed
to members of the family, and (2) a smaller group, owed to
business associates. The family items would seem to consist of
the unpaid portions due from the estate to Joseph's brothers and
sisters. For instance :

To Mary Home my sister—£6,666 13s 4d Scots [£556 10s stg].
To Michael Home after his prentice fee—£5,333 6s 8d Scots [£444 6s stg].
To Margaret Home my sister—£2,000 Scots [£166 12s stg].

[1] For John, see Parochial Registers, Co. of Edinburgh, B. 1708–14, in SRO ;
Katherine's baptismal record is to be found neither at Edinburgh nor Chirnside.
[2] Ninewells Papers, in SRO, Bundle 129, Misc. Papers.

The Michael Home mentioned here is Joseph's youngest brother ; and Joseph would seem to have already advanced out of his portion.the fee covering his apprenticeship, presumably to an advocate. The £444 6s stg still due Michael on reaching his majority—if this interpretation is correct—would represent the portion of the youngest male of the Ninewells family. In any event, Joseph's total debts in 1713 amounted to £20,860 5s 6d Scots (£1,738 stg), a rather considerable sum of money according to the prevailing monetary standards.

The rentals on Joseph Home's list are easier to comprehend. Those payable out of the lands of Hornden, Paxtoun, Nineward, the Mains of Ninewells, Hiltoun Mireside, and Chirnside total £2,079 2s Scots (£173 stg). Those from various farmers and a weaver in Chirnside come to £229 Scots (£19 stg). In addition to the above rentals, all apparently payable in money, are those from Chirnside and Eyemouth specified as payable in victuals to the equivalent of £425 Scots (£35 stg). These accounts totalling £227 stg, it is well to remember, reflect only the affairs of the Ninewells estate proper and not of Joseph's possible outside legal and business interests, nor is Katherine's portion of at least £20 stg a year included.

In the statement on his family in *My Own Life*, David Hume remarks, " My Family, however, was not rich ; and being myself a younger Brother, my Patrimony, according to the Mode of my Country, was of course very slender." This statement requires careful examination, because " rich " is an ambiguous word varying with the point of view.

In later years, David was to accumulate a substantial estate through his unprecedented earnings as a man of letters, aided by the usual eighteenth-century reward for public service, government pensions. But in the earlier years of struggle he was not provided by his family with sufficient income easily to enable him to devote all his time to studying and to writing, rather than to earning his living. " Had I been born to a small Estate in Scotland of a hundred a Year," he wrote in 1768, " I shoud have remaind at home all my Life, planted and improvd my Fields, read my Book, and wrote Philosophy. . . ." [1] But in reality he was unable solely to cultivate his garden, for, under a system of primogeniture, the family was not well enough off to provide more than a very modest portion for a younger son, though they could live comfortably and solidly as highly respected country

[1] HL, II, 188.

gentry and educate their children as they desired. Joseph Home was, indeed, not rich, compared with his many friends among the nobility, but he was also far from being poor.

What patrimony did he leave his son David? On 14 June 1712 Joseph drew up his will. Though unfortunately not extant, this document must have specified the portions. Obviously enough, however, David did not receive so much as £100 yearly and, judging by his many and repeated complaints, nowhere near it. But by stringent living he could get along on considerably less. Remember that in 1691, £55 10s stg was deemed sufficient to provide bed, board, clothing, and education for a lad of quality and to provide him as well with a pedagogue and a boy to attend him. And in 1734 David indicates that it was costing him £80 a year to live at Rheims in France [1] ; the fact that he soon removed to a smaller and more provincial town is some evidence that he was living beyond his income at the moment. His patrimony, before any augmentation on his part, probably brought him somewhat less than £50 annually.

To the portrait of Joseph Home as careful householder and substantial man of affairs can be added only one lighter touch— a charming story, garbled in transmission, but which yet has the ring of truth.

Attributed to the authority of his wife Katherine, the story runs that Joseph, at the time of the accession of the House of Hanover, arrived home late in the evening without his shirt and wig, but triumphant. Upon interrogation, he admitted that he had been in the town of Duns nearby when the good news arrived and that he and his cronies had spontaneously, but solemnly, taken off their wigs and shirts and tossed them into a bonfire for sheer joy.

This glimpse of Joseph in *déshabillé*, coupled with the Burnett affair, makes him more credible as the son of the flamboyant John, and prepares the way for some of *his* son's lighter moments. Unfortunately for strict accuracy Joseph died the year before the accession of the House of Hanover. Let me conjecture, however, that Katherine actually had in mind the Union of the Parliaments in 1707, wherein Scotland secured the Protestant succession.[2] Joseph had the reputation of being a Revolution Whig. His lawsuit against George Home of Wedderburn, a Jacobite, was undoubtedly coloured by political feelings. It seems entirely

[1] HL, i, 23.
[2] On 16 January 1707 the Scottish Parliament in Edinburgh voted itself out of existence. The news would have reached Duns within a few hours.

likely that Joseph celebrated the great Whiggish victory of 1707 and perhaps in the manner indicated. George Chalmers, who tells the story, concludes with the statement that "The Humes were all Whigs."[1]

Joseph Home, like his father, died young. Though his will is not available, the "tutors" of the estate are known. They include some familiar Scottish names, reflecting Joseph's high legal and family connexions : Alexander, Lord Polwarth, one of the Senators of the College of Justice ; Sir Andrew Home of Kimmerghame ; Mr George Dalrymple, one of the Barons of Exchequer ; Sir William Purves of that Ilk, Bart. ; Sir Patrick Johnston, late Lord Provost of Edinburgh ; Sir John Home of Blackadder, Bart. ; David Falconer of Newtoun ; Mr Alexander Dundas, Doctor of Medicine ; William Home of Linthill.

On 13 March 1713 Joseph Home docketed anew all his papers. Some time in August of the same year he died, aged thirty-three, but whether by illness or accident is unknown. The Homes of Ninewells had not previously been a long-lived family. David's sole comment in *My Own Life* on the father he never really knew may be taken as that gentleman's epitaph : " My Father, who passed for a man of Parts, dyed, when I was an Infant." There can be little doubt of Joseph Home's right to pass for " a man of Parts."

Having pronounced benediction upon the father who died too early for him to remember, David Hume proceeds, " leaving me, with an elder Brother and a Sister under the care of our Mother, a woman of singular Merit, who, though young and handsome, devoted herself entirely to the rearing and educating of her Children "—perhaps as fine a tribute as a son ever paid to the memory of a beloved mother. Hume was, of course, referring to the fact that his mother, though highly eligible, never remarried ; he would also seem to imply that it was not for lack of opportunity.

Katherine Home, *née* Falconer, was highly eligible from the standpoint of family connexions. The Falconers were an old and respectable family that might—had they desired to go back far enough—have claimed royal blood ; they subsequently became the Earls of Kintore.[2] Sir David Falconer, Katherine's father,

[1] George Chalmers, in EU, Laing MSS, II, 451/2.

[2] *The Scots Peerage* (Edinburgh 1904-14), V, 247 ff. ; Fountainhall, *Journals*, p. 216, comments on the Falconers : " The family is said to be pretty old, and both their name and stile to be taken from the charge they had at the time our Kings of Scotland resided in the Mernes, whosse falconers they were, and their villege was hence called the Halkerstoune." The family name survives in Halkerston's Wynd in the city of Edinburgh.

had had a distinguished public career. Admitted advocate in 1661, he was named Commissary of Edinburgh the same year and a Lord of Session in 1676. Six years later he rose to be Lord President and for 1685–86 sat as a Member of Parliament for Forfarshire. From 1681 to his death in 1685, he compiled the *Decisions of the Court of Session.* He was buried in the Greyfriars at Edinburgh with a Latin inscription extolling his loyalty to king and to country. In 1691 his widow and second wife, Mary, daughter of George Norvell of Boghall, Linlithgowshire, married John Home, the grandfather of David, thus creating the step-relationship between David's two parents.

Widowed at thirty, Katherine Home refused the choice of remarriage accepted by her mother. Opportunities must have offered, by virtue not only of her family connexions, but also of her own attractions. Her portrait has been described by one who saw it as representing " a thin but pleasing countenance, expressive of great intellectual acuteness." [1] It is significant that her son writing in late life quite obviously visualised her through the eyes of boyhood : She was " a woman of singular Merit . . . young and handsome. . . ."

The tender affection in which Katherine Home was held by her children is reflected in a letter of 1745 wherein David mentions " My Mother's Death, which makes such an immense void in our Family." [2] Affectionate of nature, Katherine must also have been independent and firm of mind. She had need to be.

Within a year after the death of Joseph Home, a creditor outside the family circle was demanding payment. And in the following year, 1715, the distinguished " tutors " of John Home of Ninewells, finding that they did not have time to attend to his affairs themselves, appointed " the Lady Nynewells " their commissioner with power to " uplift " all rents and profits of the lands of Ninewells. [3] So the management of the estate fell upon the attractive widow, now aged thirty-two. And although John legally succeeded his father as laird on 23 October 1716, it is hardly to be imagined that Katherine took the occasion to turn entire control over to her seven-year-old son ! The rentals of the Ninewells estate, £192 stg in money, and £35 stg in victuals, would probably have continued unaltered ; but the debts might well have caused Katherine some embarrassment as they became due, from time to time, because of the difficulties of raising cash sums

---

[1] Hill Burton, 1, 294n.   The portrait has since disappeared.
[2] NHL, p. 17.   [3] Ninewells Papers.

from a fixed income. Manage she did, however, and that to the admiration at least of her younger son.

Yet the efficiency with which Katherine discharged the responsibilities of the family did not change the comfortable spirit of the Ninewells household. In maturity, when they were big and robust men, both David and John displayed a fondness for a large and well-prepared meal, for good drink (claret or port), and for the conviviality that good food and good drink in the proper proportions inspire—the witty anecdote, the spicy story, the friendly raillery, the practical joke. It is pleasant to be able to trace this similarity of taste to their boyhood training. Katherine, after all, had been brought up in John Home's household and had been mistress for nearly six years of Joseph's ; and both had been convivial gentlemen. Granted that the tone would change somewhat during her widowhood with no man as head of the house ; yet Katherine would—I should think—want her sons to imbibe as deeply of the traditional family spirit as possible. She would probably go out of her way to plan occasions of good comradeship whenever the opportunity arose and, with a family of such wide connexions, it might arise not infrequently. The lesson was well learned, and both sons later gained the reputation of being genial hosts.

The present Ninewells mansion (in an " Elizabethan " style)[1] was built about 1840 after a disastrous fire. Just a century earlier, another fire had partially destroyed the house in which David Hume spent his childhood. Rebuilt by David's brother in his characteristically cautious manner, the Ninewells house of the later eighteenth century would probably not have been greatly altered from the earlier one. In 1846 a picture of Ninewells was printed in Drummond's *Histories of Noble British Families*, where the building is described as " a favourable specimen of the Scotch laird's houses, by the possession of which they think themselves entitled to modify their family coats of arms, and establish coats of their own." So writes the professional herald. Drummond's sarcasm is directed against the family's incorporation of the nine wells of their estate into their arms, where the wells appear as nine circles, with horizontal etching, in the irregular border surrounding the lion rampant.

The view in Drummond—later copied in Chambers's popular *Book of Days* with the addition of a cow in the yard !—is from the north-west and represents the approach to the house through a

[1] By the 1960s it was a roofless ruin ; by the 1970s everything movable had gone.

fenced-in yard. The house itself fronts the bluff with a southerly exposure overlooking the Merse and the Cheviot Hills in England beyond. Like virtually all Scottish houses put up before 1900, it is built of stone, undoubtedly grey sandstone ; the roof is slated and has gable-ends with three sets of chimneys. Utilitarian in design and sturdy in execution, it is definitely a country farm-house ; but its three stories and basement are commodious and would appear to provide eight or perhaps nine small rooms. Of two outhouses pictured, the larger might be the stables and barn, and the smaller the storeroom for farm implements. The tree to the east of the house and just behind the stables may be taken as the Ninewells Beech as it appeared in the mid-eighteenth century. Whether this picture has any validity at all as Ninewells, there is only the word of Drummond ; but I can hardly believe that it is pure fabrication. If it is authentic, the question still remains as to whether it represents the house previous to the fire of 1740 or after it. Yet even if the latter, that is, if it is the structure as rebuilt by John Home, it would still, I should think, be fairly representative of the house in which David Hume was reared.

Hume himself has little to contribute concerning the house of Ninewells. Some information, however, is to be found in a letter [1] which seems to have been written about 1730, when he was nine-teen years old. Here he is inviting an intimate friend to spend a vacation with him. The friend, Michael Ramsay, had apparently intended to go to the Highlands. David reminds him of " a kind of promise you made me of coming here," and then continues in remonstrance : " Perhaps you was afraid, that you would have no Conveniency in this little House, or that you would disturb us. For my Share, . . . I shall give you my room, & be contented to share one with John. This I can assure you, will be no manner of Loss to me, & I hope it will make you as easy as you cou'd wish." The interesting touch about " this little House " where, it would seem, each of the four members of the family had a separate bedroom, confirms the impression already formed of its size—and also of its hospitality. The littleness was by way of comparison with one of the mansions in the Highlands where Ramsay had also been invited.

To furnish the interior of Ninewells is of necessity even more conjectural than to provide the house itself and, in this connexion, it must be emphasised yet again that, although the family was not " rich," it *was* " good." Certain items of cultivated and genteel

[1] HL, ii, 337.

living would, therefore, surely be present in addition to the heavy and cumbersome furniture of every country house. These household amenities, the symbols of rank that no Lady Ninewells would conceivably be without, would include at the minimum a few hangings or draperies of rich material, some decorative objects of crystal, and a certain amount of silverware to grace the board. Every room was provided with its grate or open hearth—if the Drummond picture does not lie—but the window space, as befits a northern climate, was limited. The main rooms downstairs might be panelled in wood and the Lady's bedchamber upstairs hung with paper and possibly having a carpet on the floor ; other rooms would probably be left unfinished.

And how many and what sort of books on the shelves ? The education of every man begins at home, and the home education of so bold a thinker and so erudite a scholar as David Hume is of the utmost importance. I have already postulated a library at Ninewells sufficient for the elementary education of the children, together with some professional volumes of law. Can any further information be garnered that might throw light upon Hume's early upbringing ? Yes : and to begin with, there is his own statement that he was reading at an extremely young age. Writing at the age of twenty-three a letter [1] containing " a kind of History of my Life," Hume remarks, " You must know then that from my earliest Infancy, I found alwise a strong Inclination to Books & Letters." And in *My Own Life* at the age of sixty-five, he repeats the same thought : " I . . . was seized very early with a passion for Literature which has been the ruling Passion of my Life, and the great Source of my Enjoyments."

Without being fanciful and without attempting to endow him with the literary precociousness of the Admirable Crichton or even of the more recent Bentham-Macaulay-Mill variety, it is yet necessary to provide this " infant " David with home-reading materials in literature beyond the obvious school textbooks, the family Bible and Catechisms and religious works, and the ancestral legal tomes. I have little hesitation, therefore, in furnishing Ninewells wtih a fair range of the Latin classics in prose and poetry, a few of the Greek, a few more of the French, and a miscellaneous lot of the English, including, certainly, Shakespeare, Milton, and Dryden, as well as the more recent *Tatlers* and *Spectators* and Pope. " From my earliest Infancy, I found alwise a strong Inclination to Books & Letters "—yes, beyond all fear of

[1] HL, I, 13.

contradiction, David Hume acquired his passion for literature and nurtured his ambition to become a man of letters at the family home.

In 1726 Hume acquired a three-volume set of Shaftesbury's *Characteristicks*.[1] The following year his first extant letter remarks that " . . . just now I am entirely confind to my self & Library for Diversion," and indicates plainly that he owned a copy of Milton. Later still, he writes about returning " to Books, Leizure, & Solitude in the Country," and again admits " an inward Reluctance to leave my Books & Leizure & Retreat." Most significant of all is the passage in a letter of June 1747, wherein he debates whether to " return to my Studies at Ninewells " or to remain in London, " . . . Tho I confess, that I felt the Solitude in the Country rather too great, especially as I was so indifferently provided of a Library to employ me."[2] Despite his all too restricted income, Hume had certainly augmented the library by purchases of his own, and in 1751 he was to boast of a collection worth £100. The key point in the 1747 letter is not, I think, so much that the Ninewells library was no longer adequate for him, but rather that it should be considered at all. For by that time Hume was deep in the study of history and political science far beyond the possible scope of any private country collection. The passage implies, I believe, not that Ninewells was so very poorly provided with books, but that he knew the collection almost by heart. What he required in 1747 was the richness of the Advocates' Library in Edinburgh, but for that he had to wait another five years.

The boy David was not, to be sure, entirely self-educated. The Homes of Ninewells had previously provided tutors for their sons, and Katherine would probably do the same for John and David. Tutors, frequently young clergymen just out of college, were to be had cheap and sometimes were shared among several families. I am inclined to suspect that this was the case with the Ninewells lads. Such tutors might be either good or bad. Take the case of Henry Home of Kames, for example. His family being temporarily in straitened circumstances, Henry was not sent to Edinburgh University but was taught at home by a private tutor, to whom also came the sons of several neighbouring gentlemen. His first tutor, a non-juring clergyman who whipped the

---

[1] The third edition (1723). Each volume is signed " Da : Home " and dated 1726 ; the later bookplate " David Hume Esq." is also pasted in each volume. The set is now in the library of the University of Nebraska, and was kindly brought to my attention by Professor Benjamin Boyce.

[2] HL, i, 9, 111 ; NHL, pp. 25–6.

boys through Despauter's Latin Grammar, was later replaced by another, more humane, who taught them the rudiments of Greek, Mathematics, and Natural Philosophy.[1]

The problem of teaching the two Ninewells boys was perhaps simplified by the fact that although John was the senior by two years, David was the quicker student. By the time that the two went to college together in 1722, it would appear that David had not only caught up with his brother but had actually advanced beyond him. Not that John, slow and painstaking as he was, was in any sense a dullard. His education was basically sound and well retained, and in later life his wide reading in both ancient and modern literature has been noted, particularly the fact that he " ordinarily enjoyed the evening over a book, Latin or French, as often as English." With his usual acumen, James Boswell was to describe John Home, on first meeting him in 1762, as " a sensible good man, who reads more than usual. He has an anxiety of temper which hurts him. Very different from his Brother." [2]

In religion the Ninewells family were Presbyterians, members of the established Church of Scotland. In politics they were Whigs, strongly approving the Revolution of 1688, the Union of 1707, and the accession of the House of Hanover in 1714 ; and strongly disapproving all varieties of Jacobitism. No Hume close to the Ninewells family was out in the rising of 1715. But some of their neighbours, George Home of Wedderburn and divers others, supported that abortive Stuart movement and subsequently were attainted. In the famous distinction later to be made by the philosopher, the Homes of Ninewells were " Political Whigs " rather than " Religious Whigs." Therefore, although liberals politically, they were unreceptive to the religious " enthusiasms " of the Covenanters and of the Evangelicals in general. At Chirnside, the Kirk was heavily under the domination of the family : the Ninewells pew was the dominant pew and the Ninewells vault was the dominant vault. But though highly influential in the Chirnside congregation, the Homes of Ninewells—so far as I have been able to discover—never produced a clergyman in the family.

The Minister of Chirnside from 1698 to 1702, the Reverend William Miller, was, as has been seen, somewhat enlightened and tolerant. Earlier, however, the parish had had its ups-and-downs.[3] In 1658 the incumbent had confessed himself guilty of immorality

[1] *Boswell Papers*, xv, 268–9.
[2] John Kay, *Edinburgh Portraits* (Edinburgh 1885), II, 93 ; *Boswell Papers*, I, 109.
[3] Hew Scott, *Fasti Ecclesiae Scoticanae* (Edinburgh 1917), II, 32 ff.

and fled the country. In 1689 another was deposed by the Privy Council for failing to pray publicly for William and Mary. His successor, Henry Erskine, a Presbyterian of the " true-blue " school, was imprisoned several times for nonconformity ; he is chiefly remembered as the father of Ralph and Ebenezer Erskine, who were to lead the Secession Movement in the eighteenth century. From 1704 to 1741 the parish was ministered by the Reverend George Home of Broadhaugh, who in 1706 married Katherine Home, sister of Joseph Home of Ninewells.

Nothing specifically is known about the religious beliefs of this uncle of David Hume nor how far he was affected by the evangelicalism of his father, Alexander Home of Kennetsidehead, who had been hanged at Edinburgh in 1682 as a Covenanter after a particularly dubious trial. Consequently, nothing is known about the influence that this uncle may have exerted upon David either at home or at church. George and Katherine raised a family of six children, one of whom became a " baxter " (baker) in the Canongate of Edinburgh. It is reported [1] that David later held aloof from this cousin ; but, if so, whether out of personal dislike or social snobbery remains unsettled ; another cousin, however, the Reverend Abraham Home, who succeeded his father as minister of Chirnside, David liked. As a young boy David had no prepossessions against religion and, therefore, probably no dislike of the Reverend George Home as a minister. How he fancied him as an uncle is again unknown.

The Ninewells family presumably attended church regularly (as they were, in fact, required to do by law) and were regarded as religious and god-fearing people. All surviving comment on Katherine Home indicates that she was sincerely and deeply religious. The rigorous " Scottish Sabbath " of the dawning eighteenth century, however, with its early morning family prayers, its two long services and sermons at the Kirk, and its severe restrictions upon personal freedom, must occasionally have struck even the most godly as depressing and gloomy. That impression, at any rate, is gathered from reading the intimate diaries and personal letters of the period and is confirmed by an English traveller who wrote in 1723 : " Certainly no Nation on Earth observes the Sabbath with that Strictness of Devotion and Resignation to the Will of God : They all pray in their Families before they go to Church, and between Sermons they fast ; after Sermon

---

[1] Hill Burton, I, 198n ; and letter from Joseph Grant to Hill Burton in NLS, MS 3005, f. 211.

every Body retires to his own Home, and reads some Book of Devotion till Supper, (which is generally very good on *Sundays*) ; after which they sing Psalms till they go to Bed." [1] Yet of David's kicking over the sabbatical traces as a boy, there is not the slightest indication. On his own word, he was " religious when he was young," apparently accepting the stern Calvinistic doctrines of Original Sin, the Total Depravity of Human Nature, Predestination, and Election, without a tremor—which is only what was to be expected of a normal boy.

Taking his religion unusually seriously, the young David Hume was attracted to the task of soul-searching. He went to the extent of abstracting a list of the vices catalogued at the end of that widely circulated seventeenth-century book of popular devotion, *The Whole Duty of Man*, and of testing his character against them, " leaving out Murder and Theft and such vices as he had no chance of committing, having no inclination to commit them." This, he later acknowledged, "was strange Work ; for instance, to try if, notwithstanding his excelling his schoolfellows, he had no pride or vanity." [2] The comment was made at the age of sixty-five, very shortly before his death. Strange work it assuredly was, but that it is to be regarded as " wrestling with sin " in the recommended manner of the Evangelicals remains dubious.

The boy David Hume was, it is clear, already beginning to think for himself and to deem moral issues of paramount importance. This earnest and thinking boy it was who, before his twelfth birthday, went up to Edinburgh University to complete his formal education. And there can be no doubt that his mind was so framed as to be receptive to new ideas and new influence.

[1] Macky, *Journey through Scotland*, pp. 3–4.
[2] *Boswell Papers*, xii, 227–8. N. Kemp Smith in his introduction to *Hume's Dialogues Concerning Natural Religion*, 2nd edn. (Edinburgh 1947), pp. 5–6, lists " a few of the vices " enumerated in *The Whole Duty of Man* : " not believing there is a God ; not believing his Word ; not desiring to draw near to him in his ordinances ; placing religion in hearing of sermons, without practice ; resorting to witches and conjurers, i.e., to the Devil ; not arranging any set or solemn times for humiliation and confession, or too seldom ; being puffed up with high conceits of ourselves, in respect of natural parts, as beauty, wit, &c., of worldly riches and honours, of Grace ; making pleasure, not health the end of eating ; wasting the time or estate in good fellowship ; abusing our strength of brain to the making others drunk ; using unlawful recreations ; being too vehement upon lawful ones ; abstaining from such excesses not out of conscience but covetousness ; pinching our bodies to fill our purses."

CHAPTER 4

STUDENT DAYS AT EDINBURGH

" I passed through the ordinary Course of Education with Success."

EDINBURGH was no novel sight to the two Ninewells boys in the winter of 1722–1723, nor the " house " in the Lawnmarket where they resided with their mother and sister during the terms at college. Childhood visits had long since made the metropolis familiar yet perennially fascinating. Familiar as it was, the first view as they reached the crest of the hills to the immediate south after the nearly forty-mile ride on horseback from the Merse would still have been breathtaking. Forty years later the same view evoked from the youthful but already world-weary James Boswell, at the moment also saddle-weary from the same ride— " The roads in the Merse are the worst that I ever saw "—the comment : " The Prospect of the firth of forth, the lomond hills, Arthur-seat and the ancient City of Edina pleased me exceedingly." [1] Even today only the most hardened and cynical of world-travellers fails to respond similarly.

Built along the narrow ridge of a hill sloping from the Palace of Holyrood House at the base to the Castle at the summit nearly 200 feet higher, the city of Edinburgh in the boyhood of David Hume was a mile in length and nearly half a mile in breadth. At the foot of the hill to the north lay an artificial pond, the Nor' Loch ; and a mile or so beyond that Leith, the port of Edinburgh, on the Firth of Forth. Two miles west of the city was Corstorphine Hill ; and, not far to the south of it the Blackford and the Braid Hills. To the north of the lower part of the town rose precipitously the Calton Hill, and, immediately to the south-east, Salisbury Crags, a semicircular grouping of rocks, behind which towered Arthur's Seat, the highest peak in the vicinity.

Against a background of brilliant waters, green vales, and craggy hills, there rose the smoke of " Auld Reekie " to screen alike the grey stone of the houses, the forbidding castellations of the fortress, and the inviting elegance of the palace. A paradoxical city of austerity and homeliness, of isolation and cosmopolitanism, of rusticity and urbanity, of the old world and of the modern, a city

[1] *Boswell Papers*, i, 118.

imbedded in the past and yet with aspirations for the future, Edinburgh was later to call itself with somewhat more than local pride, " the Athens of the North."

Though physically one city, Edinburgh was administratively two : the lower town or independent Burgh of the Canongate and the high town or Edinburgh proper. This latter, walled in the mid-fifteenth century against " the Evil and Skaith of oure Enemies of *England*," was entered from the Canongate at the Netherbow Port. Through this gate ran the city's backbone, a wide and well-paved thoroughfare, extending the whole steep way from Palace to Castle ; in the lower town it was known as the Canongate, and in the high town, as the High Street. Four other major gates to the fortified part of the city were the Cowgate Port in the east wall south of the Netherbow ; the Potter-Row Port in the centre of the southern wall ; the Bristow Port a little beyond to the west ; and finally the West Port off the Grassmarket and directly opposite the Cowgate. At the summit, the Castle had its own gate.

Paralleling the High Street to the south was the narrow Cowgate. Off these two principal thoroughfares ran the " closes " or entries, and, in turn, off the closes, as well as off the streets themselves, the " wynds " or lanes, around which arose the towering grey sandstone tenement-houses locally called " lands." The residential sections of the city were thus localised along the length of the two streets ; beyond them, north and south, the outer layers consisted of garden plots ; and finally along the outskirts were various industrial sections. To the north on the slope of the hill facing the Nor' Loch were located the slaughter-houses of the butchers and the pits of the tanners ; while to the south along the city wall and convenient to several springs were the breweries.

The lands in which the townspeople lived were amazingly tall. Though latterly restricted by law to five storeys fronting the streets, they rose in the rear, because the city was laid out on the spine of a steep ridge, to nine or ten storeys. The tallest block of buildings in Edinburgh, that adjacent to the Parliament Square, stood no fewer than seven storeys in front and twelve in the rear. People of substance owned their own " houses " in these massive piles ; and so close were they built together, after the manner of the old city of Paris, that one set of public stairs sometimes accommodated the " houses " of two different lands. The most fashionable of the lands had a private central organisation or

" parliament " for social as well as for police and sanitary purposes. Hume's Edinburgh thus exhibited urban community-dwelling at its highest and also (for the sake of the record) almost at its lowest.

Citizens of Scotland's capital city lived in a manner curiously akin to that of certain well-to-do New Yorkers today who prefer to own, rather than to rent, apartments in so-called co-operative buildings. The analogy may be extended. The city of Edinburgh, within the framework of eighteenth-century architecture, resembled certain sections of modern Manhattan where restricted ground-space on that tight little island has resulted in the raising of buildings for both dwelling and business to fantastic heights. If Manhattan is overcrowded because it is a narrow island in high residential and commercial demand, Edinburgh was overcrowded because of the narrow area within the city walls, behind which protection all buildings within the Royalty were erected. Those in the Canongate, to be sure, lay outside the fortified walls ; but the fiasco of the defence of the city during the Rebellion of 1745 was to prove that those within the walls were no better off than those without. But this does not alter the fact that the old fortifications were a cramping influence. The frequent efforts of the populace to spill out beyond the walls was to lead to an extension of the Royalty in the second half of the century, an exodus that was to sweep David Hume along with it.

The situation of Edinburgh University when the Ninewells boys were students was little different from that of the present university, at least so far as the Old Quadrangle is concerned. At the southern extremity of the city, just off the Potter-Row Port, the university buildings were clustered around three courtyards or quadrangles. Nearest the city gate was the entrance to the students' courtyard, containing their " apartments " (although most students lodged privately in town), and beyond that, to the east, a second courtyard with the library and administrative buildings. Up a flight of stairs from the students' courtyard was the largest quadrangle, round which were built the Schools and the houses of the principal and the professors. The spacious gardens in the centre were restricted to the faculty. This main courtyard was also entered from the north through a gateway in a lofty bell tower, the finest of the buildings.

In 1768, during a public campaign to raise funds for new and more commodious buildings—not finally erected until 1789— Principal Robertson stated : " A stranger, when conducted to view the University of Edinburgh, might, on seeing such courts and buildings, naturally enough imagine them to be almshouses for the reception of the poor ; but would never imagine that he was entering within the precincts of a noted and flourishing seat of learning." In 1788, the second historian of the city was equally caustic but more pithy : " The College is composed of a set of very mean buildings, neither fit to accommodate, nor suited to the dignity of such an University." [1]

" In studying four Years at this College," wrote John Macky in 1723, " you commence Master of Arts : The Scholars are not in Commons, and kept to strict Rules as in the Colleges in *England*, nor wear Gowns ; they lodge and diet in the Town, as at the Colleges in *Holland*, and are required to attend their several Classes from eight in the Morning till twelve, and from two to four. I wonder," the English traveller shrewdly observed, " how a College in a Town, used to so much Business and Diversion to take off from the Study of Youth, should ever produce a good Scholar." [2] Yet produce good scholars Edinburgh did, whatever the distractions of the town and whatever the condition of its buildings. Indeed, this youngest of the four Scottish universities, which had been established only in 1582, was unquestionably the highest in reputation by 1722. A major reason for this prestige was the change in 1708 from the ancient method of regentships to the modern one of professorships, a move that was to be imitated by Glasgow University in 1727, St Andrews in 1747, and Aberdeen in 1754.[3]

When Joseph Home went to Edinburgh University in 1697, he had matriculated under John Row. Under the system of rotating regents, this meant that during his entire stay he was conducted by that distinguished Hebrew scholar through the classes of Greek, logic, natural philosophy, and moral philosophy. In 1708, however, under the far-seeing leadership of that distinguished Scottish churchman and Whig statesman, Principal Carstares, and undoubtedly from the examples set by the Dutch universities of Leyden and Utrecht, Edinburgh adopted the system of specialisation, each subject being thenceforth taught by a professor. In the basic curriculum of arts and sciences, the first-year class was devoted to the study of Latin under the Professor of Humanity (as that subject is still named in the Scottish universities)

[1] Robertson, in *Scots Mag.*, xxx (1768), 114 ; Hugo Arnot, *History of Edinburgh* (Edinburgh 1788), p. 308.

[2] Macky, *Journey through Scotland*, p. 68.

[3] Sir Alexander Grant, *Story of the University of Edinburgh* (London 1884), i, 263.

and was matriculated in 1710 for the first time. In 1722 the Professor of Humanity was Laurence Dundas. The *Bajan* class —properly first-year, but now second-year in view of the matriculation of the Humanity class—was under the Professor of Greek, William Scot. The *Semi* or third-year class was devoted to logic and metaphysics under Professor Colin Drummond. The *Magistrand* or Senior class in natural philosophy was conducted by Professor Robert Stewart.

Besides these four regular classes, three others might be elected. Professor James Gregory's in mathematics, William Law's in ethics, and Charles Mackie's in history. Private classes, both elementary and advanced, were also offered in most subjects by the different professors. Finally, a series of public lectures, open to students and to townspeople alike, was given annually by the entire faculty. A clearly unexpected result of the adoption of the professorial system was the immediate drop in the proportion of students taking degrees. Under the old system each regent had been under a competitive, as well as a financial, compulsion to laureate as large a class as possible ; now that only the Professor of Natural Philosophy received graduation fees, the competition was lost and few students troubled to take degrees. This practice did not, however, lower college standards or student morale, as has often been thought—rather the contrary. In any event, like their father, John and David did not take degrees.

" The Colledge meittings begins with October " the University Statutes stipulated,[1] but matriculation took place in the spring term. The brothers signed the Matriculation Book on the page set aside for William Scot, the Professor of Greek : David on 27 February 1723, and John on 1 March. David's boyish hand is unmistakable and John's is similar. There is a figure " 2 " next to David's signature but no figure next to John's.

Some additional private evidence about the Hume brothers at the University is provided by their copy of Justin's Latin history (1701). The flyleaf is inscribed "John Home his Book 1721 March 6 Edinburgh " ; the " John " is partly scratched out and is superinscribed " David " and the " 1721 " is raised to " 1723 ". The ostensibly contradictory evidence of the Matriculation Book and the Justin volume remains puzzling, and I am unable to provide a completely convincing explanation.[2]

---

[1] *University of Edinburgh Charters, Statutes, and Acts of the Town Council and the Senatus, 1583–1858*, ed. Alexander Morgan and R. K. Hannay (Edinburgh 1937), p. 157, No. 1. Cited hereafter as Morgan and Hannay.   [2] See Textual Supplement.

Although in the Matriculation Book both lads signed themselves *Home*, in the library-account book of Professor Scot under the date of 27 February, their names are given (in the professor's or the librarian's handwriting) in payment of the fee of £1 10s Scots (2s 6d stg) as *Dav. Hume* and *John Hume*.[1] Little wonder if David was thinking of reverting to the older spelling.

The official records of Edinburgh University provide no further information on the undergraduate career of its most brilliant alumnus; and David Hume himself has nothing to add beyond two brief public statements and two passing comments in personal letters. The statement in *My Own Life* is a classic of the indefinite: " I passed through the ordinary Course of Education with Success "; after which he continues tantalisingly, " and was seized very early with a passion for Literature, which has been the ruling Passion of my Life, and the great Source of my Enjoyments." This passion for literature, though born at Ninewells, was nurtured at the University. Its influence was playfully stressed in a letter near the close of his life: " Had I a Son I shou'd warn him as carefully against the dangerous Allurements of Literature as K[ing] James did his Son against those of Women; tho' if his Inclination was as strong as mine in my Youth, it is likely, that the warning would be to as little Purpose in the one Case as it usually is in the other." [2]

In a second public statement, an advertisement prefixed to the posthumous and authoritative edition of the *Essays and Treatises* of 1777, Hume refers to his *Treatise of Human Nature* as, " A work which the Author had projected before he left College. . . ."— which, if literally true, might indicate a profound collegiate influence upon his thinking. The statement, however, must be tempered by another made many years earlier in a personal letter, wherein he placed the *Treatise*, " as plan'd before I was one and twenty, & compos'd before twenty five." Equally important is a passage from the " kind of History of my Life," written at the age of twenty-three: " . . . our College Education in Scotland, extending little further than the Languages, ends commonly when we are about 14 or 15 years of Age. . . ." [3] Less than ten years after the fact, this second letter would seem to limit, or even slightly belittle his collegiate training.

Collegiate education at Edinburgh in the early eighteenth

---

[1] EU, MSS entitled " Scholarium Matricula ab Anno MDCCIV," under date; and " Library Accounts, 1696–1756," under date.
[2] HL, I, 461.   [3] HL, I, 158, 13.

century was more akin to that of a modern classical high-school than a modern college. Indeed the statutes of the University clearly regard the pupils as children needing strict discipline.[1] Hume entered college at the age of eleven and left at fourteen, if he stayed no longer than the minimum course. A precocious mind might, nevertheless, be profoundly influenced at that stage and Hume found there the stimuli needed for early maturity.

In addition to the required Arts course of Greek, logic and metaphysics, and natural philosophy, it may be conjectured, in the absence of any evidence, that David Hume elected, at the least, the classes in ethics and mathematics. The subject-matter of these classes at that time is unknown but may be reconstructed from evidence of the period immediately following. The intellectual atmosphere prevailing at the University would, however, have been more important and Edinburgh was undoubtedly seething with new ideas of science, philosophy and literature.

" Not to name the school or the masters of men illustrious for literature," pontificated Dr Johnson, " is a kind of historical fraud by which honest fame is injuriously diminished."[2] And in the case of a man of letters illustrious in philosophy—if one may amend the great doctor—not to name all the possible sources of his ideas is a kind of historical fraud by which the philosopher is injuriously made to think *in vacuo*, and *nihil ex nihilo* is sound common-sense as well as elementary Humean philosophy.

First, then, to William Scot, who was certainly no ordinary Professor of Greek. A regent since 1695, Scot was appointed sole Professor of Greek in 1707 by royal patent; this appointment enabled Principal Carstares to extend the professorial system throughout the University. Scot held the chair of Greek—the holder was often called the Professor of Greek and Philosophy—until 1729, when he had the long-awaited opportunity to transfer to that of Ethics. As early as 1706 Scot lectured on the law of nature and nations and had later been an unsuccessful candidate for that chair in the Faculty of Law. For the use of a private class in that subject, moreover, he had edited an abridgment of Hugo Grotius' *De Jure Belli ac Pacis*, a work long established as standard in moral philosophy. From the bent of Scot's mind

---

[1] No. 8 : " All are to be dilligent and painefull in ther studies, neither must any interrupt ane other by entering into his class or chambers, or earnestly harken or listen att dores or windowes except the censors." (The last part of this sentence is " Early Scotch Westergate.") Morgan and Hannay, p. 158.

[2] Johnson's " Life of Addison," at the beginning.

towards ethics, it would seem more than likely that some hints from Grotius were passed on to his students, and Grotius would certainly have provided David Hume with a fruitful field for speculation.

How well did Hume learn Greek in the classroom of Professor Scot ? Clearly he attained no great proficiency, for there is the remark in *My Own Life* that in the period following the publication of the *Treatise* he " recovered the Knowlege of the Greek Language," which he had " too much neglected " in early youth. Yet certain of his reading memoranda, to be dated immediately before the publication of the *Treatise*, indicate that even then he had already recovered some knowledge of Greek.[1] Hume blamed himself and not his professor and rather implied that his original study of Greek had lasted no more than an academic year.

Apart from the classical languages, the remaining " colleges " or series of lectures were elementary " survey courses " teaching little more than a few basic facts about the great books of the ages. The emphasis was always on developing the fluent use of spoken Latin rather than on the contents of the required texts. Under Professor Colin Drummond in 1724 Hume studied logic and metaphysics. Since Drummond was sufficiently interested in the " New Philosophy " four years later to be one of six Edinburgh professors to subscribe to Henry Pemberton's *View of Sir Isaac Newton's Philosophy*, it may be presumed that he took up in his class both Newton and Locke. Like all professors of logic in the Scottish universities at this period, he also took up applied logic in rhetoric and literary criticism. (His successor in 1729, John Stevenson, lectured in this field with great success, his illustrations of Aristotle's *Poetics* and Longinus *On the Sublime* being particularly popular ; he also read much from the prose discourses and prefaces of Dryden, as well as from the *Spectator* papers). However Hume may have reacted to Drummond's metaphysical teachings, he would surely have responded sympathetically to the critical and literary.

Natural philosophy was taught by Professor Robert Stewart, originally a Cartesian but later a Newtonian. As advertised [2] in 1741, his lectures emphasised the new developments in physics, including optics and astronomy, from the works of Newton and

[1] Mossner, " Hume's Early Memoranda, 1729–40 : The Complete Text," in *Journal of the History of Ideas*, IX (1948), 492–518.

[2] By Robert Henderson, Library-keeper and Secretary, in " A short account of the University of Edinburgh, the present Professors in it, and the several parts of Learning taught by them," in *Scots Mag.*, III (1741), 371–4.

his disciples ; and his students were required to have studied at least one year of collegiate mathematics. Stewart's conversion to Newtonianism is undated, but by 1728 he subscribed to Pemberton's interpretation of Newton. It is highly probable that David Hume would have heard from Stewart, at the very least, an explication of the major features of that system which was to play so large a part in his own intellectual development.

The Professor of Mathematics was James Gregory, of the world-famous family of academic Gregorys. His father, also James Gregory, had taught mathematics at Edinburgh from 1674 to 1675. Another son, David, held the chair from 1683 to 1691, when he left to become Savilian Professor of Astronomy at Oxford. When James Gregory " the Second " in his turn inherited the Edinburgh chair of mathematics, he also inherited the Newtonianism which had been introduced into the course by David Gregory shortly after the publication of Newton's *Principia Mathematica* in 1687. Outside Newton's own university, Cambridge, Edinburgh was thus the first institution of higher learning to teach the master's principles. By 1720, however, the second James Gregory was aged and infirm, and had to resort to substitutes to deliver his lectures. During the 1721-22 term, for instance, they were given by Robert Wallace, who was later to become the defender and friend of David Hume. In 1725 Gregory was finally compelled to retire, although retaining his title and salary as long as he lived. His deputy-professor and eventual successor was Colin Maclaurin, who was brought to Edinburgh from Aberdeen University at the personal nomination of Sir Isaac himself. One of the most celebrated of the early followers of Newton, Maclaurin expounded and taught the " New Philosophy " in popular textbooks written in English rather than in Latin. From Gregory himself, or his lecturer, or Maclaurin, David Hume would have received an ample infusion of Newtonianism.

The elective class of " Pneumatical and Ethical Philosophy," as distinguished from the *Semi* class of " Rational and Instrumental Philosophy " (i.e. logic and metaphysics), was taught by Professor William Law. Little is known about Law except that by 1728 he was one of Pemberton's subscribers. The title of the course demands explanation today. In the programme [1] of John Pringle, his successor in 1729, " Pneumatics " is divided into : (1) Metaphysical inquiry into such subtle and material substances as are imperceptible to the senses and known only through their opera-

---

[1] Henderson, *op. cit.*, p. 373.

tions ; (2) Proof of the immortality of the soul ; (3) Nature of immaterial created beings not connected with matter ; (4) Natural Theology, or the demonstration of the existence and the attributes of God. The pneumatics might well have proved strong poison to the young David Hume, but the moral philosophy was surely his meat. In the theoretical part of moral philosophy, Pringle chose his texts from Cicero and Marcus Aurelius among the ancients, and from Puffendorf and Bacon among the moderns. In the practical part, he expounded " the origin and principles of Civil Government, illustrated with an account of the rise and fall of the ancient governments of Greece and Rome, and a view of that form of government which took its rise from the irruptions of the Northern nations." Pringle's students were required to deliver public discourses on prescribed topics. It is likely enough that Pringle—certainly no original genius in philosophy—had taken over the subject-matter and the methods of Professor Law ; and it is, therefore, presumptive that Pringle's account would substantially cover Hume's student period. Some twenty years later, in 1744–45, David Hume was to make a bid to become Pringle's successor by standing candidate for the chair of Pneumatical and Ethical Philosophy. He was unsuccessful. Later still, Pringle was to become Hume's personal physician and friend.

The year 1722 is memorable in the history of Edinburgh University for the inauguration of three new chairs : Civil Law, Scots Law, and History. Strictly speaking, perhaps, only the Scots Law Chair was new ; but the salaries of all three were now burdened to the ale tax. By an Act of the Parliament in London, the City of Edinburgh was permitted to renew the duty of two pennies Scots on each pint of ale brewed and sold within the city and the four adjacent parishes, and out of these proceeds to pay a salary of £100 stg a year to the three designated professors.

Charles Mackie,[1] brother-in-law of Principal Carstares, had been called to the University in 1719 as Professor of Universal History—a title later expanded into Professor of Universal History and Scottish History ! A graduate of Edinburgh, Mackie had studied on the Continent at Groeningen and Leyden Universities, matriculating at the latter in law. On his return he was admitted advocate, and was thus able to fulfil the somewhat curious requirement for the new chair of History that the professor be an advocate.

---

[1] Much of the following information on Mackie is taken from an article by Dr L. W. Sharp, " Charles Mackie : The First Professor of History at Edinburgh University," in *Scottish Historical Review*, XLI (1962) 23–45.

This requirement has led to the mistaken notion that the Professorship of History originally belonged to the Faculty of Law. From the University's public advertisement of 1741, it is clear that Mackie was unconnected with the Law Faculty but was a member of that of Arts and Sciences.

Mackie entered upon his work with an enterprise and enthusiasm that warranted the high success he was to achieve. Universal history, it might be surmised, offered considerable scope, and Mackie was the man to take full advantage of it. He gave two " colleges," one on Roman antiquities, the other on universal history. His general lectures on the history of the world from the beginnings to the modern period included, for example, the decline and fall of the Roman Empire, the errors of history and of historiographers, and Scottish history ; but he also extended himself into literary history, reviewing the lives of the most celebrated writers on all subjects and covering fine letters and criticism generally. The popularity among the students of this new literary approach was an early augury of the full bloom of literature at Edinburgh within the following quarter-century. John Mitchell, a friend of Mackie's, writing from London in 1728 to congratulate him upon this success, was perfectly justified in remarking, " it affords a prospect of the revival, as I may call it, of letters in our country."

What was David Hume doing during this period of literary animation ? Alas, it is not certain. Fastidious and precise, Professor Mackie was a born cataloguer who apparently tabulated everything. So although there was no matriculation in History at the time and although his class-lists are not extant, there is a compilation of his own making : " An Alphabetical List of those who attended the prelections on History and Roman Antiquities from 1719–1744. Collected 3 July 1746." In this fascinating and important document, Mackie records the names of his students, their family, the subsequent station in life when known, the class taken, the year, and the fees paid. During twenty-six years he had an average of nearly thirty students annually, a remarkable record for a non-compulsory class. In the list, sure enough, the name *David Hume* appears for the requisite years, 1725 and 1726. But sad to say, this David is described by the professor as " son to Clerk Home of Edinburgh," and I find it difficult to believe that so careful a compiler as Mackie would have made so fundamental a mistake. Yet Mackie's list includes many of the friends and acquaintances of Hume's, names that will appear frequently in these pages : Mark Akenside, Thomas Blacklock, Alexander Boswell (father of James), George Dempster, Sir Gilbert Elliot, Lord Gardenstone, John Home, James Johnstone of Westerhall, Robert Keith, Sir Andrew Mitchell, James Oswald of Dunnikier, William Robertson, John Stevenson.

The Principal of Edinburgh University during Hume's student days was William Wishart, one of whose duties was to exercise general supervision over the intellectual and spiritual welfare of the students. An Act of 1 November 1723 of the Town Council of Edinburgh was directed towards this latter : " . . . the Town Council appointed the professors and students in the Colledge of this city to be accomodat with seats in the Lady Yesters Church to hear the Word preached. . . ." [1] In regard to intellectual welfare, the Principal presided at all open sessions in the great hall over the library, where the students were required to debate or to read papers. According to the statutes, Saturday forenoon was to be devoted to these exercises, and a special contest was held at Candlemas. Disputations had to be held in Latin, but the requirement that students should speak only Latin within the precincts of the University had been winked at for the past half-century. English was used despite the fact that the University Statutes of 1704 were still in effect during Hume's stay.[2]

What theses the doughty David Hume publicly defended and impugned before Principal Wishart is unknown. Yet among the extant Hume manuscripts there is one that bears all the hall-marks of a student's paper and, although it is written in English, I am convinced that it belongs to Hume's college days. In a boy's precise hand the manuscript is eight pages in length and, at that, incomplete. A fair copy evidently written out with great pains, it is entitled " An Historical Essay on Chivalry and modern Honour." [3] Lacking evidence to the contrary, one might have been inclined to suspect that it was prepared for Professor Mackie's history class, as Mackie certainly ought to have encouraged the writing of essays in English. Curiously enough, however, and

---

[1] Morgan and Hannay, p. 172.

[2] No. 7 reads : " Students are obleidged to discourse allwayes in Latine, as also to speak modestly, chastlie, courteously and in maner uncivily or quarellsome, but to enterteane good profitable and pious conferances, who transgress, especellie such who speik English within the Colledge, are lyable the first tyme in a penie, therefter in two pence." Ibid. p. 158.

[3] RSE, xiv, 4 ; reprinted with introduction by Mossner, " David Hume's ' An Historical Essay on Chivalry and modern Honour '," in *Modern Philology*, xlv (1947), 54–60.

despite pressure to the contrary, he insisted on giving his " prelections " in Latin. In his above-mentioned letter to Mackie
of 1728, John Mitchell wrote : " Give me leave to say that
I wish some method might be fallen upon to teach young gentlemen the English our chief tongue, and that whereby any can make
a figure in affairs at home ; and the want of it is a very great loss
to all who are sent here [London]." Hume's paper, in any event,
could equally well have been intended for Professor Law's class
in ethics or even for Professor Drummond's class in logic.

Wherever the essay was presented, the maturity of the thought
is belied only by the immaturity of the hand. No mental stripling,
this fourteen-year old David ! The thesis is standard for the Age
of Enlightenment : the degeneration of true classical virtue and
the rise of false Gothic chivalry. The method is true Hume :
philosophical and psychological analysis of historical facts. Indeed, the substance of the essay is repeated in abbreviated form
in an appendix to that volume of the *History of England* which was
published in 1762. A true mentor of his own age, Hume never
altered his youthful opinion of the Dark Ages.

The philosophical-historical method, as well as the style, may
be illustrated by a few typical extracts :

> What kind of monstrous Birth this of Chivalry must prove we may learn
> from considering the different Revolutions in the Arts, particularly in Archi-
> tecture, & comparing the Gothic with the Grecian Models of it. The one
> are plain, simple, regular, but withal majestic & beautyful, which when
> these Barbarians unskillfully immitated, they run into a wild Profusion of
> Ornaments, & by their rude Embellishments departed far from Nature & a
> just Simplicity. They were struck with the Beauties of the antient Buildings,
> but ignorant how to preserve a just Mean ; & giving an unbounded Liberty
> to their Fancy in heaping Ornament upon Ornament, they made the whole
> a heap of Confusion, & Irregularity. For the same Reason, when they wou'd
> rear up a new Scheme of Manners or Heroism, it must be strangely over-
> charged with Ornaments, & no part exempt from their unskillful refinements.
> And this we find to have been actually the Case, as may be proven by running
> over the several parts of it.

The boy's thoughts on love deserve notice, especially as the theme
was to be recurrent throughout life. Here he is analysing the
" System of Courtly Love : "

> So that a Mistress is as necessary to a Cavalier or Knight-Errant as a
> God or Saint to a Devotee. Nor woud he stop here, or be contented with a
> submiss Reverence & Adoration to one of the Sex, but wou'd extend in some
> degree the same Civility to the whole, & by a curious Reversement of the
> Order of Nature, make them the superior. This is no more than what is suit-
> able to that infinite Generosity of which he makes Profession. Every thing
> below him he treats with Submission, & every thing above him, with Con-

tumacy. Thus he carries these double Symptoms of Generosity which Virgil makes mention of into Extravagance :

Parcere subjectis & debellare superbos.[1]

Hence arises the Knight-Errants strong & irreconciliable Aversion to all Giants with his most humble & respectful Submission to all Damsels. These two Affections of his, he unites in all Adventures, which are alwise design'd to rescue distrest Damsels from the Captivity & Violence of Giants. As a Cavalier is compos'd of the greatest Warmth of Love, temperd with the most humble submission & Respect, his Mistresses Behaviour is in every point, the Reverse of this, & what is conspicuous in her Temper is the utmost Coldness along with the greatest Haughtyness & Disdain ; untill at last Gratitude for the many Deliverances she has met with, & the Giants & Monsters without Number that he has destroy'd for her Sake, reduces her tho unwilling to the Necessity of commencing a Bride. Here the Chastity of Women, which, from the necessity of human Affairs, has been in all Ages & Countreys an extravagant Point of Honour with them is run into still greater Extravagance, that none of the Sexes may be exempt from this fantastic Ornament.

What honours, if any, Hume won with this essay remain unknown. Obviously he deserved the highest ; but, as an experienced college-professor, I cannot feel sure that he got them. The fact remains, however, that the manuscript was preserved, and that in itself may provide some hint that it was a prize essay.

During David Hume's student-days at Edinburgh, perhaps the strongest unofficial influence towards the cultivation of good English style, soundness of literary taste, and general freedom of thinking was the Rankenian Club.[2] Organised in 1716 or 1717 by a group of the faculty and students of divinity and law, the club took its name from the tavern-keeper in whose house they met. Principal Wishart himself was a member. Other early members included Charles Mackie, Colin Maclaurin, John Smibert, John Stevenson, George Turnbull, and Robert Wallace ; and later, Alexander Boswell, Alexander Cunningham (to become Sir Alexander Dick), Andrew Mitchell, and John Pringle. Undergraduate students apparently were never admitted during its more than sixty years of existence. A literary correspondence was carried on by the club with Dean Berkeley, in which the Rankenian Club " pushed his singular tenets all the amazing length to which they have been carried in later publications." Berkeley is also said to have been greatly pleased " with the extraordinary acuteness and peculiar ingenuity displayed in them, and he has been heard to say, that no persons understood his system better than this set of young gentlemen in North Britain." [3] Berkeley flattered the Rankenians further by offering them a place in his missionary college in the Bermudas, projected in 1725. The club

---

[1] *Aeneid*, vi, 853.　　　[2] See below, Appendix C, p. 617.　　　[3] *Scots Mag.*, xxxiii (1771), 341.

remained chary, however, of this visionary scheme. Yet when Berkeley finally sailed for Rhode Island in 1728, " to follow his western star," John Smibert, the Scottish portrait painter, went along with him as Professor-of-Fine-Arts-to-be. During the voyage, Smibert painted a group portrait of the Berkeley expedition, and, upon the failure of the college to get started, married and settled in Boston to paint many of the leading colonists ; he also tried his hand at architecture and designed Fanueil Hall, later to become known as " the cradle of liberty " in America.

The educational significance of the Rankenian Club lies in the fact that its members were predominately the leading spirits of the faculty, and their Rankenian enthusiasms may legitimately be used to fill out the barren official accounts of the classroom teaching. Their strong literary bent, for instance, may have strengthened David Hume's native passion for literature and directed him towards the important problems of English style. Their equally strong philosophical bent may have centred his attention upon the " New Philosophy " deriving from Newton and Locke. Shaftesbury was received by Robert Wallace, among others, and Berkeley, of course, was known to all. That Clarke and Mandeville, and, in due time, Hutcheson and Butler, were slighted is hardly to be imagined. The philosophical success of the Rankenians is perhaps best attested by Ramsay of Ochtertyre's otherwise somewhat obscure statement : " It is well known that between 1723 and 1740, nothing was in more request with the Edinburgh *literati*, clerical and laical, than metaphysical disquisitions. These they regarded as more pleasant themes than either theological or political controversies, of which, by that time, people were surfeited." [1] Ramsay then proceeds to enumerate Locke, Clarke, Butler, and Berkeley, to whom he should certainly have added Shaftesbury, Mandeville, and Hutcheson.

David Hume may have left Edinburgh University in 1725 or perhaps not until 1726. A possibly influencing factor in this connexion was the destruction by fire of the Ninewells " house " in the Lawnmarket in 1725. Thus burnt-out, the family may have been compelled to return home at once. Yet as they continued to spend the winter months in the city, it would seem likely that they soon acquired another dwelling.

However that may be, it is time to inquire what, after three or four years at the University, Hume took away with him ? Especially, what had become of his already strong passion for literature ? Of his intense moral predilections ? Of his religious beliefs ?

[1] Ramsay, I, 195–6.

Lastly, are there any indications of new developments in his thinking on philosophical subjects ?

Something will be said briefly about each of these questions, but first a general remark concerning his standing as a student. After Hume's death the story began to be circulated that, " In his early years, he was by no means distinguished as a scholar, or by any of those accomplishments which are supposed to qualify youth for the liberal professions," and, more specifically, that he " *got the epithet of the Clod when at school, from his being a dull scholar, & a clumsy Boy.*" [1] That Hume was a tall and ungainly boy, there is no doubt ; but that he was a dull scholar is sheer nonsense. In concocting tales about the childhood of genius, the popular mentality seems to alternate indiscriminately between the impossibly brilliant and the impossibly stupid. Not for a single instant can I believe that David's schoolfellows did not recognise his superior mentality and, to some degree, acknowledge it. Who does not recall that the big and awkward Samuel Johnson, who also was to remain ungainly all his life, was occasionally carried to school on the shoulders of the pupils in honourable tribute to his intellectual attainments ? No, however teachers may sometimes err, students seldom fail to recognise superiority ; and, if David was actually called " the Clod " by his school-fellows, it was probably less in derision than in affection.[2]

Furthermore, I would wish to emphasise the word " success " in the remark already quoted from *My Own Life*, " I passed through the ordinary Course of Education with Success." A man of personal modesty, though with understandable intellectual pride in his achievements, Hume here implies, I believe, that he was recognised as a superior scholar, that perhaps he was formally commended on some occasion or other—and there always remains, of course, the possibility of " An Historical Essay on Chivalry and modern Honour " as a prize essay. Finally, on his deathbed a few months after writing the autobiography, Hume privately admitted " his excelling his schoolfellows." [3]

Without the slightest doubt, also, Hume's passion for literature was intensified while at college. Whatever actual learning he may have acquired in the academic halls, he had shared an unusually keen atmosphere which was soon to stimulate him and many others to literary activity. He had also learned, if indeed he did

---

[1] " An Account of the Life and Writings of the late David Hume," in *Annual Register*, xix (1776), 27 ; MS letter of Alexander Stenhouse to George Chalmers, 22 Mar. 1788, in EU, Laing MSS, ii, 451/2.

[2] Thomas Aquinas, one calls to mind, was affectionately known to his fellow students as the " Dumb Ox."   [3] *Boswell Papers*, xii, 227.

not already know, the inestimable value of a good library. Edinburgh University Library was not at this time, however, pure gold. Most of its 13,000 volumes were locked behind iron screenings, and the reading room was never open for more than two hours daily in the winter and four in the summer. A few volumes, it is true, might be borrowed, but only upon full receipt for their value. An avid reader of modest circumstances would hardly have been happy under these restrictions.

The religious beliefs of David Hume were probably lost while he was at college or shortly thereafter. At the close of his life Hume was to reveal to an inquirer that, " he never had entertained any belief in Religion since he began to read Locke and Clarke." [1] The immediacy of the reaction may perhaps be suspect but, as an item of intellectual autobiography, the fact itself remains incontestable. Hume had certainly heard both Locke and Clarke " prelected " upon at college ; but he may well have read their works somewhat later. This was the case with Longinus, whose treatise *On the Sublime* Hume did not begin reading until 1727. He then found that Longinus " does really answer the Character of being the great Sublime he describes "—reminiscent of Pope's couplet :

> Whose own example strengthens all his laws ;
> And is himself that great Sublime he draws.[2]

Whether Hume returned to Ninewells in 1725 or 1726 with religious convictions or not, those convictions were waning and were certainly lost in the next few years.

As to new developments in his philosophical thinking, I am convinced that he left college with a strong metaphysical leaning in addition to the original literary and moral. The rudiments of the New Philosophy, so often extolled in so many different classes, could hardly have failed to take seed in his mind. How these Newtonian, Lockian, and Berkeleian principles were to be fertilised with those of the moral philosophy, both ancient and modern, and applied specifically to the " Science of Human Nature," eventually to come forth after due travail as the product of original genius will provide the substance of the next several chapters. For the present, it remains only to be said that the earnest and reflective boy who had gone up to Edinburgh University in 1722, returned home in 1725 or 1726 a deep-thinking, inquiring, and extraordinarily ambitious youth, dedicated to the life of letters.

[1] *Boswell Papers*, XII, 227.   [2] *Essay on Criticism*, 679–80.

Chapter 5

LAW *VERSUS* LITERATURE

" While . . . [my Family] fancyed I was poring over Voet and Vinnius,
Cicero and Virgil were the Authors which I was secretly devouring."

AFTER leaving Edinburgh University in 1725 or 1726, without
taking his degree, David Hume settled down to a prolonged course
of private study which lasted until 1734. This critical period in
his intellectual development is summarily dismissed in *My Own
Life* : " My studious Disposition, my Sobriety, and my Industry
gave my Family a Notion that the Law was a proper Profession
for me : But I found an unsurmountable Aversion to every thing
but the pursuits of Philosophy and general Learning ; and while
they fancyed I was poring over Voet and Vinnius, Cicero and
Virgil were the Authors which I was secretly devouring." This
retrospective account, however, oversimplifies the situation. For
the eight-year period falls into two distinct parts : the first, to the
spring of 1729, while he studied law and read general literature ;
and the second, from the spring of 1729 to the spring of 1734,
while he enthusiastically followed an independent programme of
philosophical and scholarly research directed towards the formu-
lation of a new system of philosophy and criticism.

According to the mode of the day in Scotland, the careers open
to a younger son of the landed gentry were limited. David Hume
might, of course, have remained at Chirnside, acquired a piece
of land, and lived out his days as a small laird. That he would
have been willing to do so had he inherited an estate of as much
as £100 a year has already been noted ; but, even then, he would
have been no ordinary farmer, for he insists that he would have
read his book and written his philosophy. The qualifications are
important because they indicate that the career of letters was ever
before his mind. With a portion of somewhat under £50 annually,
however, such a choice was not really available.

The professions were open to a youth of ambition : army,
church, law, medicine, politics, teaching ; and, in addition, there
was always commerce. I doubt whether as a youth Hume even
considered the army. Whether in 1726 he would have said categorically, as he was to say twenty years later while still discussing

the choice of a career, " the Church is my Aversion,"[1] is not certain. Nevertheless, the loss of his religious beliefs had already passed beyond the point where, without hypocrisy, a career in the church would still be open. Of the pretensions of medicine, he early became sceptical. As to a tutorship, he was still too young, and further studies would be required. Commerce would be ruled out at the start, not on the grounds of social snobbery (for several of the younger sons of the Homes of Ninewells had entered trade), but of the attitude and the desire of the lad to continue his studies. Against all these choices weighed the paramount consideration that the Homes of Ninewells had long been men of the law. So in the considered opinion of his mother and brother, and probably also with the approbation of his uncle, the Reverend George Home, law would be the obvious solution. And law would automatically open up politics if his ambitions and aptitudes chanced to turn in that direction.

What did the lad himself want? Above everything else he wanted time, time to continue reading, time to think, time to prepare for the life of letters. He was, I am inclined to believe, sated with educational courses as such, courses, moreover, under professors whose mental endowments—with all due justice—he could not help but realise were inferior to his own. Such is not infrequently the unenviable position of the superior student! Task-reading he had learned to hate. Likely enough, too, he had begun to be irked by the air of piety in the college classes, by the constant requirement of praying before learning. One of the first requests made by his later friend Adam Smith on becoming Professor of Logic at Glasgow University in 1751 was to be relieved of this duty—but without success. The young David Hume's growing independence of mind demanded that he should be left alone ; and, if the family could hardly be expected to understand that desire fully at the moment, he might be able to educate them into it in the course of time. In this more or less neutral spirit, he was willing to try the law. It would, at least, have the tonic effect of requiring his presence at Edinburgh during the winters, where he would have the benefit of adequate library facilities.

Accordingly, from 1726 to the spring of 1729, Hume made a trial of the law. " As our College Education in Scotland, extending little further than the Languages, ends commonly when we are about 14 or 15 Years of Age, I was after that left to my own Choice in my Reading, & found it encline me almost equally to

[1] NHL, p. 26.

Books of Reasoning & Philosophy, & to Poetry & the polite Authors." So he wrote in 1734 in the highly significant " kind of History of my Life." [1] The very phraseology, " I was . . . left to my own Choice in my Reading," would seem to imply that his mother was of an understanding nature and also that David himself was somewhat less than enthusiastic about the law. Yet pursue it he did. But how and to what extent ?

Since the time of Joseph Home, the study of law had become more regularised. In 1707 Edinburgh University had instituted a chair of Public Law, in 1710 a chair of Civil Law, and in 1722 a chair of Scots Law. But the older informal method of apprenticeship also remained in use and was frequently combined with the newer. As Professor of Scots Law at Edinburgh University at the end of the eighteenth century, Baron David Hume, the philosopher's nephew, commented on the then totally out-moded system of apprenticeship : " And no doubt, at long run, following this course, a man of unremitting industry, and sound parts, would become an able lawyer. But surely, even to him, the difficulties could not but be great ; and to those of inferior capacity and strength of mind, they must have been unsurmountable." [2] Unremitting industry and sound parts, the professor's uncle surely possessed ; but, just as surely, that industry and those parts were not directed wholeheartedly towards the law.

Whether David Hume followed the older or the newer system of studying the law, or a combination of the two, remains unknown. In any event, he would have had to attend the Court of Session in order to learn procedure. That he actually did so seems to be attested by a letter [3] of 1742 addressed to Henry Home of Kames. Already by that time a distinguished advocate and a man of learning, Henry Home could not properly have been called a classical scholar. So, in answer to an inquiry, his young friend provides him with a long disquisition on the merits of Cicero as a lawyer, including a comparison between the ancient and the modern legal methods. " I agree with you," he begins, " that Cicero's Reasonings in his Orations are very often loose, & what we shou'd think to be wandering from the Point ; insomuch that nowadays a Lawyer, who should give himself such Liberties, wou'd be in danger of meeting with a Reprimand from the Judge or at least of being admonish'd of the Point in Question." And

---

[1] HL, i, 12–18.
[2] *Baron David Hume's Lectures, 1786–1822,* ed. G. C. H. Paton (Edinburgh 1939), i, 1–2.　　　[3] NHL, pp. 7–8.

he proceeds, " If you read his Oration [for Milo], you'll agree with me, I believe, that he has scarce spoke any thing to the Question, as it wou'd now be conceivd by a Court of Judicature."

In the essay " Of Eloquence " published in 1742, Hume has much more to say concerning the study of the law in ancient and modern times. The palm is awarded to antiquity :

> The study of the laws was not then a laborious occupation, requiring the drudgery of a whole life to finish it, and incompatible with every other study or profession. The great statesmen and generals among the Romans were all lawyers ; and Cicero, to shew the facility of acquiring this science, declares, that, in the midst of all his occupations, he would undertake, in a few days, to make himself a compleat civilian. . . . But how shall a modern lawyer have leisure to quit his toilsome occupations, in order to gather the flowers of Parnassus ? Or what opportunity shall he have of displaying them, amidst the rigid and subtile arguments, objections, and replies, which he is obliged to make use of ? The greatest genius, the greatest orator, who should pretend to plead before the *Chancellor*, after a month's study of the laws, would only labour to make himself ridiculous.[1]

Here speaks bitter personal experience, clearly indicating that David Hume had found the study of the law incompatible with the life of letters.

In the end, Hume's legal knowledge, both theoretical and practical, was not inconsiderable. The theoretical, forming an integral part of moral philosophy, appears so frequently in his published works as to require no special comment. Of theoretical jurisprudence, Hume was a master. The practical side, however, warrants a few words. It was thought sufficient, for instance, to gain him the commission of Judge-Advocate to a military expedition of 1746 ; and throughout life it enabled him to draw up legal documents of many different types and to offer expert comment on matters pertaining to the law. In short, David Hume was fully qualified to become an advocate ; and his later reiterated disparagement of the legal profession reflects less a lack of knowledge than an eventual alienation.

Law-studies at Edinburgh would have opened up to Hume the privilege of borrowing from the Advocates' Library, not in his own right, to be sure, but through the medium of an advocate friend. The 30,000 volumes, most of which could actually be taken out of the library, far outweighed the highly restricted and much smaller Edinburgh University Library which, furthermore,

---

[1] *Phil. Wks.*, III, 167–8.

was not as yet open to graduates or former students. Twenty years later Hume was still borrowing books from the Advocates' Library through the courtesy of lawyer friends, and not until 1752 did he have free access to its riches with his election to the Keepership.

The lighter side of Hume's reading, the current periodicals and the latest poetry and criticism, would have been available through Scotland's first circulating library, the shop of Allan Ramsay in the Luckenbooths on the High Street.[1] There, in the second " house " above the later shop of William Creech, were to be rented all the latest publications. According to an outraged spokesman for the rigidly righteous, " profaneness is come to a great height ; all the villanous, profane, and obscene books and plays printed at London by Curle and others are got down by Allan Ramsay and lent out for an easy price to young boys, servant boys, servant girls of the better sort, and gentlemen, and vice and obscenity are dreadfully propagated." [2] But David Hume would have been unafraid of this literary vice and obscenity and would have delighted in the shop of the tiny Jacobite wig-maker-turned-bookseller, the very hub of Edinburgh's new literary life. For Ramsay was also Edinburgh's darling poet, having published in 1721 a collection of his own verses and in 1725 *The Gentle Shepherd*, a pastoral drama which was brought on locally with great success and which, as literature, enjoyed as much popularity in England as in Scotland. Besides composing English poetry, Ramsay sought to revive interest in the native Scottish dialect and, to that end, brought out in 1724 *The Evergreen*, a selection of poems from the old Makars. His *Tea-Table Miscellany* (1724–32) contained old English and Scottish songs and a few verses by himself and friends, including Hamilton of Bangour's well-known " Braes of Yarrow." Ramsay's dual interests in English and Scottish poetry were symbolised by the sign outside his shop, the two heads of Ben Jonson and Drummond of Hawthornden.

The bookseller's son, born in 1713 and also named Allan, became the close friend of David Hume probably sometime before 1733 when he went up to London to study art. Later the official portrait painter to the court of George III, this younger Allan Ramsay was destined to play a minor—though unwitting—part in the fantastic *affaire* between Hume and Rousseau. He will also appear in 1754 as one of the founders, along with David Hume,

[1] Known as the " Goose Pie ".   [2] Robert Wodrow, *Analecta* (Glasgow 1853), III, 515.

of the important Select Society at Edinburgh. A man of letters as well as a painter, Allan Ramsay the younger became a distinguished exemplar of the Enlightenment.

The literary circle to which David Hume belonged during his Edinburgh sojourns included Henry Home of Kames, to whom reference has already been made. Aged thirty, and David's senior by fifteen years, Henry Home was an advocate of three years' standing in 1726. The estate of Kames was located in Berwickshire only ten miles from Ninewells, and the two families could have " called cousins " in the pleasantly elastic Scottish mode. For many years to come they exchanged visits, and as a boy David would probably have looked up to Henry as a learned and intellectual man. Educated at home by a tutor because he was unable to afford college, Henry was indentured at the age of sixteen to a W.S. at Edinburgh,[1] where he also attended the lectures in civil law given by Professor Craig. Many years later, being a man of outspoken language, Henry was to term Wingate, his first tutor at Kames, " a Blockhead and a barbarous fellow " ; Craig, " a very dull man " ; and the apprenticeship to Dickson, the solicitor, " the worst education." [2]

After two years in Dickson's chambers, Henry switched over to the broader prospects of an advocate. It was the richer intellectual interests that allured him, as he was to prove in two early publications, one on the scholarship of law, *Remarkable Decisions of the Court of Session 1716–1728* (1728), the other on the philosophy of law, *Essays upon several Subjects in Law* (1732). His intellectual interests included metaphysics, and he had entered a classical club in 1722 or 1723 with the deliberate intention " to puzzle and make mischief " among the divinity students, and later admitted that he had " succeeded but too well with many, making them Deists." [3] In 1723 Henry Home's free-thinking philosophical proclivities led him into correspondence with both Samuel Clarke and Andrew Baxter.

Later the author of *An Enquiry into the Nature of the Human Soul* (1733) and, later still, the somewhat incongruous friend of the infidel statesman John Wilkes, Andrew Baxter was in 1723 tutor to William Hay of Drumelzier and residing at Duns Castle near both Kames and Ninewells. In the first half of that year Henry

---

[1] Society of Writers to H.M. Signet, so called because its members were in former days clerks in the office of the King's Secretary and responsible for the preparation of all warrants for grants and charters to be passed under the King's signet.
[2] *Boswell Papers*, xv, 268–70.   [3] *Ibid.*, xv, 284.

Home corresponded with Baxter on the theory of causation, a subject which had been brought to his attention by the chapter on " Power " in Locke's *Essay concerning Human Understanding.* It " crucified " him, Home was to tell Boswell.[1] Now by way of reaction to John Keill's *Introduction to Physics,* a work based on Newtonian principles, the young advocate sought to maintain the Aristotelian principle that matter requires a constant and continual cause to keep it in motion. The young tutor, on the contrary, upheld the Newtonian *vis inertiae* or the tendency of matter to continue in the state it is in, whether motion or rest. Henry Home's scientific heterodoxy finally led Baxter to complain, " When you are pleased to write to my comprehension, I shall answer you always frankly honestly and ingenuously." [2] The exchange ended amicably, and the two agreed to return and then to burn their letters—a bargain which was not kept, on the advocate's part at least.

Samuel Clarke's Boyle Lectures *On the Being and Attributes of God* (1704–1705) had established him as the undisputed head of the rationalist school of English philosophy which sought to deduce moral laws from logical necessity. A disciple of Newton, Clarke emphasised the mathematical aspects of his master's teaching at the expense of the experimental. In 1713 the student Joseph Butler, later the distinguished Anglican bishop, upheld the empirical or Lockian position against Clarke's *a priori* in a series of calm and ably reasoned letters. In 1717 another student, Frances Hutcheson, of great distinction later as Professor of Moral Philosophy at Glasgow University, did likewise. And in August 1723, after having puzzled over Clarke's metaphysics for seven years, so did Henry Home. This last exchange, however, amounted to no more than a single letter apiece and covered but a few of the points originally made by Butler. With admirable forbearance, Clarke answered all the letters of these young doubting Thomases, but failed to convert any of them.

David Hume's friendship with Henry Home had probably begun early in life, likely enough as cousins and neighbours in the Merse—but of that we have no definite information. During his period of law study at Edinburgh, David would have been attracted by Henry's philosophical interests. Yet the first extant letter between them is rather late, that of David writing from London on 2 December 1737. That it refers, however, to previous

[1] *Boswell Papers,* xv, 273.
[2] Baxter, MS letter, 13 June 1723, in SRO, Abercairny Papers, GD 24.

correspondence is certain ; and, as David had left Scotland in the beginning of 1734 and had not returned at the time of writing, the friendship is pushed back at least to 1733. Furthermore, the tone of the letter is deeply intimate and suggests a relation of long standing. When it is called to mind that Hume was addressing a man fifteen years his senior and whom he had not seen for over four years, a passing remark [1] towards the close of the letter, distinctly indelicate, is proof as positive as could be wished that the two had been bosom companions. The deference due an older person combines with the assurance of an equal who feels entitled to take certain liberties with the proprieties to argue the companionship of men-about-town. This inference is corroborated by an incidental comment in a letter to Henry Home by James Oswald of Dunnikier : " You will Remember," reminisces Oswald, writing from London in 1742 as M.P. for Kirkcaldy, " how your friend David and you used to laugh at a most sublime Declamation I one night made, after a Drunken Expedition to Coupar, on the Impotency of Corruption in certain Circumstances. . . ." [2]

The picture evoked by this evidence is of a Henry Home in his mid-thirties taking a group of aspiring young law students under his wing and introducing them to the extra-curricular activities of Edinburgh and neighbouring towns—the coffee houses, the oyster-cellars, the taverns, the assemblies. All his life an ardent patron of the arts and sciences, and especially of the deserving youth of both sexes, Henry Home was a past master of the social amenities, as was early attested by the verses of his friend, William Hamilton of Bangour, " To H[enry] H[ome] in the Assembly " :

> While crown'd with radiant charms divine,
> Unnumber'd beauties round thee shine, . . .
> Say, youth, and canst thou keep secure
> Thy heart from conqu'ring beauty's pow'r ?
> Or, hast thou not, how soon ! betray'd
> The too believing country maid ?
> Whose young and unexperienc'd years
> From thee no evil purpose fears ;
> And, yielding to love's gentle sway,
> Knows not that lovers can betray.
> How shall she curse deceiving men ?
> How shall she e'er believe again ?

[1] See below, p. 111.
[2] James Oswald, MS letter to Henry Home, 6 Mar. 1742, in SRO, Abercairny Papers, GD 24.

The Jacobite poet was also the friend of David Hume, but that David was a frequenter of the dancing assemblies is rather to be doubted. It is quite possible, however, that he was developing an eye for " country maids." Another friend of Henry's, and probably also of David's, was Colonel James Forrester of the Guards, dilettante author of *The Polite Philosopher* (1734). In 1738 Forrester was tutor to the " mad " Marquis of Annandale, a position that David Hume was to inherit seven years later, although not directly from Forrester. James Ferguson, subsequently to become a Scottish judge under the title of Lord Pitfour, was another friend of David's during this period.

Of all the Edinburgh group of young men of letters, Michael Ramsay of Mungale was Hume's most intimate friend. A curiously fleeting figure, this Michael Ramsay inspired or repelled according to the personality of those who met him. On the one hand, Alexander Cunningham (later Sir Alexander Dick), who knew both Henry Home and Michael Ramsay well, describes Ramsay as " a very debauched, licensious Creature, who took pleasure in corrupting all the Youth of families that came in his way, by carrying them to lewd women, drunken companions who like himself neither feared God nor Man." And Sir Alexander confesses that he always inwardly thought of " this wretch " as " Michael the Arch Divel." Henry Home, on the other hand, commented that Michael Ramsay was " a harmless creature, and [that] Sir Alexander Dick misunderstood his character." Nor did Henry follow Dick in blaming Ramsay for his own debt of £300 incurred during this period of " pretty riotous and expensive society." Henry blamed no one but himself. Upon becoming aware of his financial plight, he had wisely withdrawn from the circle and attempted to carry " Willy " Hamilton along with him, but the poet always remained wedded to high life.[1]

" Arch Divel " or " harmless creature " ? The one Michael Ramsay is the estimate of the puritanically-minded, the other of the man of the world. There can be little question that Ramsay was a gay young blade. That he was also ambitious, intellectual, and literary is equally clear from his intercourse with David Hume, in which there is no hint of the " Arch Divel." Yet when that man of the world, James Boswell, met Ramsay in 1762, he was at once struck with his " disagreable roughness of behaviour." At that moment, however, Boswell was in the depths of one of his habitual fits of depression and admitted hating everyone. Con-

[1] *Boswell Papers*, xv, 315–16.

ceding that Ramsay " is a good scholar and an accurate man of business and is very much disposed to oblige," Boswell found his wife " a lowbred chattering Woman, and his sons blackguard dogs." [1]

Little is known about Ramsay's career beyond the fact that, after an early inclination to take orders in the Church of England, he travelled abroad as tutor to the families of the Earl of Home and the Earl of Eglintoun and later became Chamberlain to the Duke of Roxburgh. Throughout life he had a happy facility for friendship, attracting such disparate characters as Laurence Sterne and Charles Burney. More important, Michael Ramsay was always the good friend of the entire Ninewells family and was the recipient of David Hume's first extant letter. The two continued to exchange reading materials and literary compositions for many years. After their death, Michael Ramsay the younger wrote to David Hume the younger concerning these two friends, " whose correspondence proceeded from the purest friendship, & the strongest attachment. Nor do I believe there ever were two Companions upon earth, more respectable for their constancy, & mutual esteem for one another." [2]

The convivial spirit of the Edinburgh fraternity of young men centring about Henry Home is portrayed in the lines [3] of their poet laureate, Hamilton of Bangour :

> For me at *Keith's*
> Awaits a bowl, capacious for my cares. . . .
> There was a time we would not have refus'd
> *Macdougal's* lowly roof, the land of ale ;
> Flowing with ale, as erst is Canaan said
> To flow with honey : There we often met,
> And quaff'd away our spleen, while fits of mirth
> Frequent were heard : nor wanted amorous song,
> Nor Jocund dance ; loud as in Eden town,
> Where the tir'd *writer* pens the livelong day, . . .
> Spent with his toil when the thirsty twilight falls,
> He hies him gladsome, to the well-known place
> *Bull-cellar*, or O *Johnstoun's* thine ! where fond
> Of drink, and knowledge, erst philosophers
> Have met ; or *Couts's* dark cymmerian cell,
> Full many a fathom deep : from far he hears
> The social clamour through the dome resound ;
> He speeds amain to join the jovial throng.
> So we delighted once. . . .

[1] *Boswell Papers*, I, 109.   [2] RSE, VIII, 27.
[3] Hamilton of Bangour, " To a Gentleman going to travel."

There is no indication that David Hume's association with Henry Home and the Edinburgh circle led him into debauchery or debt. His natural sobriety would have prevented any indulgence beyond a general acquaintance with the society and the manners of the town, and his constant endeavour to secure financial independence would have kept him out of debt. Hume's letters of 1738 and 1739 to Henry Home reflect the more serious side of the fraternity, the " philosophical Evenings " and the " Papers of your Friends." The personal relations between the two men are made clear when David Hume in 1745 expresses " the Regret that I shou'd have so little Prospect of passing my Life with you, whom I always regarded as the best Friend, in every Respect, I ever possess." [1]

In his brief career as a student of the law, David Hume may have been guided by the advice of Henry Home of Kames, or he may not. If he was, he would surely have welcomed the opportunity to discuss metaphysics with his friend, and his attention might very well have been thus directed to the subject of causation. Not improbably it was with Henry's connivance that David began to neglect his law studies, with the already mentioned result that, while the family " fancyed I was poring over Voet and Vinnius, Cicero and Virgil were the Authors which I was secretly devouring." Ultimately, again with Henry's encouragement, David might have dropped the pretence and have persuaded the family, perhaps by his friend's influence, to permit him to pursue his own course. The nature of that course is foreshadowed in a letter to Michael Ramsay from Ninewells of 4 July 1727.

" Just now," exults David, " I am entirely confind to my self & Library for Diversion. . . . I take no more of them than I please, for I hate task-reading, & I diversify them at my Pleasure ; sometimes a Philosopher, sometimes a Poet. . . . I live like a King pretty much by my self. . . ." He quotes from Virgil and Cicero, refers to Longinus and Milton, and delights in a high Virgilian " peace of mind, in a Liberty & Independancy on Fortune, & Contempt of Riches, Power & Glory." The *Georgics*, he takes occasion to argue, provide " nothing short of the Instruction of the finest Sentence in Cicero. And is more to me," he adds significantly, " as Virgils Life is more the Subject of my Ambition, being what I can apprehend to be more within my power." Here in his earliest letter is Hume's rejection of politics, the forensic life of Cicero, from which he disqualifies himself apparently by

[1] NHL, p. 17.

reason of a bashful temperament, lack of ease in public-speaking, and, no doubt, the physical awkwardness of which he was ever conscious. Here also is his clear and definite choice of the career of man of letters.

The letter shows further that Hume already regarded philosophy as part-and-parcel of literature. To be a philosopher is to be a man of letters : the proposition was received by Hume and the eighteenth century as axiomatic. Hume is reading, he informs Ramsay, " sometimes a Philosopher, sometimes a Poet " ; but both philosopher and poet supply grist for the philosophical mill that has already begun to grind. Proposing to make a contribution of his own in the realm of philosophy, Hume is diffidence itself in referring to it. " Would you have me send in my loose, uncorrect thoughts? Were such worth the transcribing? " he somewhat rhetorically inquires. " All the progress that I made is but drawing the Outlines, in loose bits of Paper ; here a hint of a passion, there a Phenomenon in the mind accounted for, in another the alteration of these accounts ; sometimes a remark upon an Author I have been reading, And none of them worth [any thing] to any Body & I believe scarce to my self."

This first letter of Hume's provides his first statement of the importance of style—but not his last. The primary requisite of a serious thinker with original thoughts, he always maintained, is to present his thoughts so that they may be understood by others. Hardly writing as yet for a public, the youthful David Hume was no more than preparing a series of memoranda on the basis of which a system might later be constructed. The course of reading which provided the materials for these memoranda is described in the autobiographical letter of 1734 :

> I was after that [that is, after college] left to my own Choice in my Reading, & found it encline me almost equally to Books of Reasoning & Philosophy, & to Poetry & the polite Authors. Every one, who is acquainted either with the Philosophers or Critics, knows that there is nothing yet establisht in either of these two Sciences, & that they contain little more than endless Disputes, even in the most fundamental Articles. Upon Examination of these, I found a certain Boldness of Temper, growing in me, which was not enclin'd to submit to any Authority in these Subjects, but led me to seek out some new Medium, by which Truth might be establisht.[1]

These " Books of Reasoning & Philosophy " and of " Poetry & the polite Authors " necessarily led Hume to the study of French, in which language so many of them were composed. So he

---

[1] HL, I, 13.

mastered French ; and requests to borrow the French historians and philosophers soon begin to appear in his letters.

About this time also Hume lost, or rather completed losing, his religious beliefs. The process was one of rational education. Religion he gave up slowly and reluctantly, even against his will, as it were, in the face of what he regarded as ineluctable logic. For to him, as previously to Butler, Hutcheson, and Home, the *a priori* argument of Clarke held no validity. But Hume now pressed on beyond these other inquirers to question even the argument from probability based on the empirical philosophy of Locke and Newton. This empirical argument, however, always remained for Hume the only philosophical argument concerning religion worthy of serious consideration. So in 1751 he was to request a friend to help him strengthen the empirical side of the *Dialogues concerning Natural Religion*, which he was then beginning to compose. The sceptical side, he acknowledged, needed no bolstering. " Any Propensity," he continued, " you imagine I have to the other Side [that is, the sceptical], crept in upon me against my Will : And tis not long ago that I burn'd an old Manuscript Book, wrote before I was twenty ; which contain'd, Page after Page, the gradual Progress of my Thoughts on that head. It begun with an anxious Search after Arguments, to confirm the common Opinion : Doubts stole in, dissipated, return'd, were again dissipated, return'd again ; and it was a perpetual Struggle of a restless Imagination against Inclination, perhaps against Reason." [1] From this it is abundantly clear that the youthful Hume relinquished his religious beliefs gradually over the course of years rather than immediately upon reading Locke and Clarke. And it is also clear that those religious beliefs were relinquished under philosophical pressure—that Hume *reasoned* himself out of religion.

An interesting feature of this reverse-conversion, and one that had evidently played no small part in bringing it about, was Hume's change in ethical standards. As a boy, it will be recalled, he had tested his moral fibre against the stern catalogue of vices in the pietistic *Whole Duty of Man*. Still intensely earnest concerning personal morals, he now progressed—or retrogressed—to the more humane evaluations of the pagan philosophers, Cicero in particular. As he later observed to Frances Hutcheson, " I desire to take my Catalogue of Virtues from *Cicero's Offices*, not from the *Whole Duty of Man*." Smitten with the " beautiful Representations of Virtue & Philosophy " that he found in Cicero, Seneca, and

[1] HL, I, 154.

Plutarch, the earnest young student " undertook the Improvement of my Temper & Will, along with my Reason & Understanding. I was continually fortifying myself with Reflections against Death, & Poverty, & Shame, & Pain, & all the other Calamities of Life." [1] Some of the curious psychological consequences of this revised classical programme of soul testing and character building will shortly become apparent.

In this youthful period Hume's moral fibre was tested at a dinner party given by Lady Dalrymple in Edinburgh. Lady Anne Lindsay relates the story as told by her grandmother.

> You know the Truthfulness of his Honest Nature . . . as a Boy he was a fat, stupid, lumbering Clown, but full of sensibility and Justice,—one day at my house, when he was about 16 a most unpleasant odour offended the Company before dinner . . . " O the Dog . . . the Dog," cried out everyone " put out the Dog ; 'tis that vile Beast Pod, kick him down stairs . . . pray."—
>
> Hume stood abashed, his heart smote him . . . " Oh do not hurt the Beast " he said . . . " it is not Pod, it is Me ! "
>
> I think this is capable of being made a very good proverb of, " It is not Pod, it is me."
>
> How very few people would take the evil odour of a stinking Conduct from a guiltless Pod to wear it on their own rightful Shoulders. [2]

In the spring of 1729 after three arduous years of study and reflection, Hume's new-found " Boldness of Temper " was suddenly rewarded with an important discovery. No longer were his reading and thinking desultory. At once everything became pointed and details began to fall into place. A system was emerging. The transformation is described by Hume himself : " After much Study, & Reflection on this [new Medium, by which Truth might be establisht], at last, when I was about 18 Years of Age, there seem'd to be open'd up to me a new Scene of Thought, which transported me beyond Measure, & made me, with an Ardor natural to young men, throw up every other Pleasure or Business to apply entirely to it. The Law, which was the Business I design'd to follow, appear'd nauseous to me, & I cou'd think of no other way of pushing my Fortune in the World but that of a Scholar & Philosopher." [3] The study of law was fast abandoned, and Hume was never called to the bar. In 1729, once and for all, the die was cast. Man of letters he would be, " a Scholar & Philosopher."

---

[1] HL, I, 34, 14.
[2] Memoirs of Lady Anne Lindsay, Crawford Muniments, II, 107 (1773), John Rylands Library, Manchester. First published by Geoffrey Hunter, " David Hume : Some Unpublished Letters, 1771–1776," in *Texas Studies in Literature and Language*, II, 1960, p. 135, n. 15.   [3] HL, I, 13.

CHAPTER 6

DISEASE OF THE LEARNED

"I had no Hopes of delivering my Opinions with such Elegance
& Neatness as to draw to me the Attention of the World."

THE precipitous abandoning of the law in the spring of 1729 gave
David Hume the needed opportunity to exploit the " new Scene
of Thought " which had so suddenly and so excitingly opened up
to his vision. In practical terms, this decision meant that the
young man of eighteen was deliberately flouting potential
security and resigning himself, for a minimum of ten years, to
almost certain insecurity. It may well have been this decision
that prompted his mother's famous remark—a remark unfortunately that has no documentary basis—that " Our Davie's a fine
good-natured crater, but uncommon wake-minded." [1] The good
Lady Ninewells may easily be forgiven for her seeming obtuseness
in view of her son's mental and physical anguish of the following
five years and of his financial problem of the following fifteen
years.

The ardour with which Hume threw himself into his studies
in the spring of 1729 burned unabated for six months until the
beginning of September, when it seemed " in a moment to be
extinguisht, & I cou'd no longer raise my Mind to that pitch, which
formerly gave me such excessive Pleasure." Mutely accusing
himself of " a Laziness of Temper," he redoubled his application,
but after some nine months began to be troubled by certain physical
symptoms accompanying the mental. At the age of eighteen,
David Hume was " tall, lean, & rawbon'd " and looked as if he
were on the verge of consumption. For the first time in his life
he now became acutely conscious of the precarious state of his
health. [2]

The course of character-improvement that Hume had been
putting himself through on the basis of moral maxims from the
ancient pagan philosophers he came to recognise, too late, as a
contributory factor to the ruining of his health. These " Reflec-

[1] Hill Burton, I, 294n.
[2] All otherwise unannotated quotations from Hume in the present chapter come
from the autobiographical letter of 1734 in HL, I, 12–18.

66

tions against Death, & Poverty, & Shame, & Pain, & all the other Calamities of Life," he was to confess, " no doubt are exceeding useful, when join'd with an active Life ; because the Occasion being presented along with the Reflection, works it into the Soul, & makes it take a deep Impression, but in Solitude they serve to little other Purpose, than to waste the Spirits, the Force of the Mind meeting with no Resistance, but wasting itself in the Air, like our Arm when it misses its Aim." Morbid introspection may become a variety of auto-intoxication and is curable only by extraordinary effort on the part of the diseased. Hume, apparently, made that effort and regained self-mastery.

Unwilling to admit that he might be afflicted with the " vapors " or lowness of spirits, a disease of the mind which he vainly imagined was restricted to the idle rich, Hume became worried over some scurvy spots which broke out on his fingers. " A very knowing Physician " prescribed anti-scorbutic juices (the product of citrus fruits), which brought partial relief. But by April 1730 Hume was forced to consult his physician a second time, now to complain of " a Ptyalism or Watryness in the mouth." The doctor was, indeed, very knowing for he immediately recognised the symptoms : " he laught at me, & told me I was now a Brother, for that I had fairly got the Disease of the Learned." A " Course of Bitters, & Anti-hysteric Pills " were recommended to Hume by the doctor, together with an " English Pint of Claret Wine every Day " and a long horseback ride. Finally convinced against his will that he was genuinely a victim of the " vapors," the " spleen," lowness of spirits, or hypochondria or melancholia— the name changes but the disease persists—Hume submitted to the regimen, following it with his usual determination and earnestness for the next seven months to the beginning of winter, 1730.

Somewhat relieved to discover that his difficulty " proceeded not from any Defect of Temper or Genius, but from a Disease, to which anyone may be subject," Hume began to indulge himself a little, studying more moderately and only when so inclined, and no longer forcing himself when fatigued. His " Spirits very much recruited," he passed the winter of 1730–1731 in Edinburgh and was even " able to make considerable Progress in my former Designs." Regularity guided his diet and way of life, and he made it " a constant Rule to ride twice or thrice a week, & walk every day." So that with the approach of summer, 1731, and the consequent return to Ninewells, he felt that he had every reason to expect accelerated improvement and perhaps even the final shaking-off of the distemper. But in these hopes he was cruelly disappointed.

May 1731 brought Hume " a very ravenous Appetite, & as quick a Digestion," which seemingly healthful symptoms, however, were accompanied with " a Palpitation of Heart." Within six weeks' time the " tall, lean, & rawbon'd " young man had metamorphosed into the " most sturdy, robust, healthful-like Fellow you have seen, with a ruddy Complexion & a chearful Countenance." The unnatural appetite wore off gradually but " left me as a Legacy, the same Palpitation of the heart in a small degree, & a good deal of Wind in my Stomach, which comes away easily, & without any bad Gout, as is ordinary." More important, " Those who live in the same Family with me, & see me at all times, cannot observe the least Alteration in my Humor, & rather think me a better Companion than I was before, as choosing to pass more of my time with them."

During the winters Hume continued to reside at Edinburgh, at least for some time, and during the warmer weather at Ninewells. In March 1732 he invited Michael Ramsay for a visit to Ninewells, adding, " I am in pretty good Health Just now & I think in better health these two months than for two Years before." In the summer of 1733 he " undertook a very laborious task, which was to travel 8 Miles every Morning & as many in the Forenoon, to & from a minerall Well of some Reputation." Duns Spa would seem to fit Hume's description ; but whatever the spa, there is concrete evidence in Hume's manuscript memoranda [1] of his interests in the properties of mineral waters. Of nine notes on " Natural Philosophy," presumably belonging to the period 1729–1734, the fifth and the sixth deal with that subject and are apparently the result of some research on Hume's part. These two notes read as follows :

Tis probable that mineral Waters are not form'd by running over beds of Minerals ; but by imbibing the Vapours which form these Minerals ; since we cannot make Mineral Waters with all the same Qualitys.

Hot Mineral Waters come not a boiling sooner than cold Water.

The final note of the same section is also pertinent to Hume's experience of these years and affords a strong presumption that he

[1] RSE, IX, 14. See Mossner, " Hume's Early Memoranda, 1729–40 : The Complete Text," in *Journal of the History of Ideas*, IX (1949), 492–518 ; esp. 494, 499–500. Hume's notes are cited hereafter as " Early Memoranda," and are referred to as they are catalogued in the above article.

was developing a healthful scepticism regarding the pretensions of physicians and their medicines :

> This seems to be a strong Presumption against Medicines, that they are mostly disagreeable, & out of the common Use of Life. For the Weak & Uncertain Operations of the common Food &c is well known by Experience. These others are the better Objects of Quackery.

Quackery or not, however, Hume continued to be a good patient and to take his medicine as prescribed : " I renew'd the Bitters & Anti-hysteric Pills twice, along with Anti-scorbutic Juices last Spring [1733], but without any considerable Effect, except abating the Symptoms for a little time." Although disabused of any real faith in physicians thus early in life, Hume was always to be a believer in moderate exercise. In 1775 he found himself in the unusual position of having to counsel his nephew, David Home, aged eighteen, against overstudy :

> . . . I cannot forbear saying, that every day, fair or fou[l, you] ought to use some Exercise : Relaxation for Amusement you may use [or not] as you fancy, but that for Health is absolutely necessary. When I was [of your] Age, I was inclind to give in to Excesses of the same kind ; and I remember [a Story] told me by a Friend, the present Lord Pitfour : A man was riding, with [great] Violence, and running his Horse quite out of Wind : He stopt a moment to a[sk when] he might reach a particular Place. In two Hours, reply'd the Countreym[an, if you] will go slower : In four, if you be in such a Hurry. Bad Health, be[sides other] Inconveniences, is the greatest Interruption to Study in the World.[1]

The successful man of letters of sixty-four had not forgotten his own ill-health between the ages of eighteen and twenty-three, and the causes of it. He might have taken the occasion to quote from one of his favourite poems, *The Art of Preserving Health* by his poet-friend John Armstrong :

> I tame my youth to philosophic cares,
> And grow still paler by the midnight lamps.

During the four years following the onset of ill health in 1729, Hume was no ordinary valetudinarian nursing ills, real and imaginary. He was, on the one hand, a scholar, putting himself through a rigorous and extensive course of reading and study ; and he was, on the other hand, a philosopher, undergoing the most creative period of his life and laying the foundations for all of his future speculations. The scholar was reading " most of the cele-

---

[1] HL, II, 305–6.

brated Books in Latin, French & English, & acquiring the Italian";
the philosopher was investigating "a new Scene of Thought," a
"new Medium, by which Truth might be establisht." This
scholar-philosopher was a decidedly sick man, displaying many
of the symptoms of a deep-set emotional and physical disorder.
So, despite his having scribbled in the three-year period, 1731–
1733, "many a Quire of Paper, in which there is nothing contain'd but my own Inventions . . . the rude Materials for many
Volumes," Hume was forced to concede : "my Disease was a
cruel Incumbrance on me."

His own analysis of the respects in which the disease was a cruel
incumbrance on him reveals his ideal of a man of letters. "I
found that I was not able to follow out any Train of Thought,
by one continued Stretch of View, but by repeated Interruptions,
& by refreshing my Eye from Time to Time upon other Objects."
Furthermore, in reducing notes and memoranda to words, "when
one must bring the Idea he comprehended in gross, nearer to him,
so as to contemplate its minutest Parts, & keep it steddily in his
Eye, so as to copy these Parts in Order, this I found impracticable
for me, nor were my Spirits equal to so severe an Employment.
Here lay my greatest Calamity. I had no Hopes of delivering my
Opinions with such Elegance & Neatness, as to draw to me the
Attention of the World, & I wou'd rather live & dye in Obscurity
than produce them maim'd & imperfect." Thus again did Hume
express clearly and indelibly his conviction of the necessary union
of philosophy with art.

How was a man so afflicted to "endure the Fatigue of deep
& abstruse thinking" and to express his thoughts so as to draw
to him the attention of the world ? "Tis a Weakness rather than
a Lowness of Spirits which troubles me," Hume's self-analysis
proceeds, "& there seems to be as great a Difference betwixt
my Distemper & common Vapors, as betwixt Vapors & Madness."
He then offers an extraordinary, yet pertinent, comparison :

I have notic'd in the Writings of the French Mysticks, & in those of our
Fanaticks here, that, when they give a History of the Situation of their Souls,
they mention a Coldness & Desertion of the Spirit, which frequently returns,
& some of them, at the beginning, have been tormented with it many Years.
As this kind of Devotion depends entirely on the Force of Passion, & consequently of the Animal Spirits, I have often thought that their Case & mine
were pretty parralel, & that their rapturous Admirations might discompose
the Fabric of the Nerves & Brain, as much as profound Reflections, & that
warmth or Enthusiasm which is inseparable from them.
However this may be, I have not come out of the Cloud so well as they

commonly tell us they have done, or rather began to despair of ever recovering. To keep myself from being Melancholy on so dismal a Prospect, my only Security was in peevish Reflections on the Vanity of the World & of all humane Glory ; which, however just Sentiments they may be esteem'd, I have found can never be sincere, except in those who are possest of them.

The problem of reconciling his literary ambitions with a practical career troubled Hume constantly and contributed to his anguished state. Insight into his feelings on that subject may be found in his manuscript memoranda of reading from the Abbé Dubos's *Réflexions critiques sur la poésie et sur la peinture*, a two-volume work which had first appeared in 1719, and which was to go through several editions and translations and to exert considerable influence on the world of the Enlightenment. The first three of Hume's notes under the heading of " Philosophy " are taken from Dubos and probably belong to the present period. The second and the third of these notes pertain to the relation between genius and education and were made by Hume seemingly to bolster up his personal beliefs and also possibly to be used as authority in debate with his mother and brother on the subject of his career. The notes read :

Too careful & elaborate an Education prejudicial ; because it learns one to trust to others for one's Judgement. L'Abbe de Bosse.

For a young Man, who applys himself to the Arts & Sciences, the slowness with which he forms himself for the World is a good sign. Id.

Here were comforting thoughts, indeed, for a scholar-philosopher afflicted with the " vapors " and struggling desperately to express his original ideas artistically !

From Dubos's treatment of the problem of genius, Hume must have derived both consolation and hope. Defining genius as " an aptitude, which man has received from nature to perform well and easily, that which others can do but indifferently, and with a great deal of pains," Dubos develops the thesis that nature will prevail. " Whatever is proposed to him [the man of genius] as the object of his application, can never fix him, unless it be that which nature has allotted him. He never lets himself be diverted from hence for any length of time, and is always sure to return to it, in spite of all opposition, nay sometimes in spite of himself. Of all impulses, that of nature, from whom he has received his inclinations, is much the strongest." Two further thoughts of Dubos concerning genius must have appealed strongly to the intransigent Hume, first and last : " 'Tis in vain . . . to attempt to persuade young people, pressed by emulation, excited by the fire and activity of youth, and spurred on by the impatience of their genius to the pursuit of fame, to defer making their appearance in public, till they have discovered their kind of talent, and sufficiently improved it " ; and, again, " Genius is the last thing that grows old in man." [1]

Practical advice concerning Hume's own distemper was also to be had from Dubos. " The soul hath its wants no less than the body," maintains the *philosophe*, " and one of the greatest wants of man is to have his mind incessantly occupied." Three methods, he suggests, may be employed to occupy the mind : external exercise, sensible impressions (such as the art-gallery and the theatre), and reflection or meditation. Reflection, the most important of these in the final analysis, presents its own problems : the mind, ultimately fatigued with close application, seeks to unbend itself, " and a dull heavy pensiveness, unattended with the enjoyment of any one particular object, is the fruit of the efforts it has made for its amusement." After four years of intense meditation Hume knew all about this " dull heavy pensiveness," and he would have been in perfect accord with Dubos's psychology of the passions :

> Thus we are led by instinct, in pursuit of objects capable of exciting our passions, notwithstanding those objects make impressions on us, which are frequently attended with nights and days of pain and calamity : but man in general would be exposed to greater misery, were he exempt from passions, than the very passions themselves can make him suffer.[2]

Early in 1734 when Hume finally decided to take desperate measures to combat his emotional and physical distemper, he reverted, it would seem, to the above analysis of Dubos. " I found," he admits, " that as there are two things very bad for this Distemper, Study & Idleness, so there are two things very good, Business & Diversion. . . . For this reason I resolved to seek out a more active Life, & tho' I cou'd not quit my Pretensions in Learning, but with my last Breath, to lay them aside for some time, in order the more effectually to resume them." But before following Hume into the " more active Life " in 1734, it is meet to return briefly to 1729 and to attempt to trace the main lines of his investigations into the " new Scene of Thought."

> Having now Time & Leizure to cool my inflam'd Imaginations, I began to consider seriously, how I shou'd proceed in my Philosophical Enquiries.

---

[1] J.-B. Dubos, *Critical Reflections on Poetry, Painting and Music*, Engl. transl. by Thomas Nugent (London 1748), ii, 5, 18, 64, 66.   [2] *Ibid.*, i, 5–6, 9.

I found that the moral Philosophy transmitted to us by Antiquity, labor'd under the same Inconvenience that has been found in their natural Philosophy, of being entirely Hypothetical, & depending more upon Invention than Experience. Every one consulted his Fancy in erecting Schemes of Virtue & of Happiness, without regarding human Nature, upon which every moral Conclusion must depend. This therefore I resolved to make my principal Study, & the Source from which I wou'd derive every Truth in Criticism as well as Morality. I believe 'tis a certain Fact that most of the Philosophers who have gone before us, have been overthrown by the Greatness of their Genius, & that little more is requir'd to make a man succeed in this Study than to throw off all Prejudices either for his own Opinions or for this [sic] of others.

So writes Hume in the autobiographical document of 1734 that has already provided the substance of the account of the psychosomatic disorder of the previous four years. The passage demands explanation from the point of view of making explicit what he had earlier referred to so cryptically as " some new Medium, by which Truth might be establisht."

By way of background, it will be useful to review Hume's three statements[1] concerning the *Treatise of Human Nature*, extended treatment of which has been postponed until this point. These three statements represent that that work was *projected* before he left college (aged fourteen or fifteen), was *planned* before he was twenty-one, and was *composed* before he was twenty-five. Translated into dates, this would mean that the *Treatise* was *projected* before 1725 or 1726, *planned* before 1732, and *composed* before 1736. There seems to be no good reason why these statements should not be taken seriously, although it is perhaps not necessary to take them literally. In general, then, how may they be reconciled with other known facts, and how may they be interpreted in terms of development of thought ?

Hume had left college by 1726 at the latest, determined to make original studies in moral philosophy, a field which in the eighteenth century still included, not only ethics and psychology, but also politics and government, history, all the social studies, and aesthetics and criticism. He was already provided with the scientific method which had been so brilliantly used by Newton in the realm of Natural Philosophy and he was undoubtedly inspired—as were so many other thinkers during the Age of Enlightenment—by Newton's own hint, dropped at the close of the *Opticks* : " If natural Philosophy in all its Parts, by pursuing this Method, shall at length be perfected, the Bounds of Moral

Philosophy will also be enlarged." The examples set by Locke, Shaftesbury, Mandeville, Hutcheson, and Butler in the experiential approach to the study of human nature were ever before his mind. During the period 1726–9, post-collegiate studies had deepened his conviction that man is the measure of all things, that all knowledge derives, in greater or lesser degree, from the Science of Man. Such, I should argue, represents the stage of development of Hume's thinking covered by the term *projected*.

The succeeding stage, the period when the work was *planned*, and, in part, attempted, begins in 1729 and extends to 1732, according to his date—although I am myself inclined, from the evidence of the autobiographical account of 1734, to think that it continued on into 1733. The third and final stage, the period when the work was *composed*, coincides with his residence in France from 1734 to 1737. In *My Own Life* Hume remarks tersely : "During my Retreat in France, first at Reims, but chiefly at La fleche in Anjou I composed my *Treatise of Human Nature*." The first two books, to be published in 1739, were unquestionably completed, though not finally polished, in France. The third book, to be published in 1740, was completed in Scotland.

The period 1729–1733, then, is the crucial one when Hume pressed his investigations into "a new Scene of Thought" so ardently as to ruin his health. In what way and within what limits is this new scene to be delineated? Here we may turn to the *Treatise* itself and to Hume's own *Abstract* of it to determine what is new there beyond what we know to have been in his fertile mind before 1729. "An Attempt to introduce the experimental Method of Reasoning into Moral Subjects" (the sub-title to the *Treatise*) implies the author's sense of innovation ; yet that innovation is one of degree only. The experimental method itself may be said to be Newton's, and Hume specifically names Locke, Shaftesbury, Mandeville, Hutcheson, and Butler as among those "who have begun to put the science of man on a new footing," that is to say, to "attempt to introduce the experimental method of reasoning into moral subjects." The main difference between those earlier philosophers and Hume is that he is utterly fearless as a thinker and applies the method systematically and relentlessly, whatever the consequences.

The method of Hume is Newton's. Yet how is this fact to be reconciled with Note 4 of the manuscript memoranda on "Natural Philosophy," which seems to belong to this pre-*Treatise* period? This note reads : " A Proof that natural Philosophy has no Truth in it, is, that it has only succeeded in things remote, as the heavenly Bodys, or minute as Light." How could Hume, in other words, simultaneously believe that natural philosophy has no truth in it and yet be an avowed disciple of Newton ? Furthermore, it will have been observed that the note limits the success of natural philosophy to astronomy and to light, that is, as it were, to Newton's two major works, the *Principia* and the *Opticks*.

What Hume is objecting to in the note becomes clear in his later comment on Boyle in the *History of England* : " Boyle was a great partizan of the mechanical philosophy ; a theory, which, by discovering some of the secrets of nature, and allowing us to imagine the rest, is so agreeable to the natural vanity and curiosity of men." What Hume held to be true scientific method appears in the subsequent passage on Newton :

In Newton this island may boast of having produced the greatest and rarest genius that ever rose for the ornament and instruction of the species. Cautious in admitting no principles but such as were founded on experiment ; but resolute to adopt every such principle, however new or unusual ; from modesty, ignorant of his superiority above the rest of mankind, and thence, less careful to accommodate his reasonings to common apprehensions ; more anxious to merit than acquire fame ; he was, from these causes, long unknown to the world ; but his reputation at last broke out with a lustre which scarcely any writer, during his own life-time, had ever before attained. While Newton seemed to draw off the veil from some of the mysteries of nature, he showed at the same time the imperfections of the mechanical philosophy, and thereby restored her ultimate secrets to that obscurity, in which they ever did and ever will remain.[1]

The sceptical and positivistic aspects of the Newtonian methodology appealed strongly to Hume and were adopted by him as well as the experimental. Like the poet Donne a century earlier, Hume was convinced that " new Philosophy calls all in doubt."

To return to the problem of the " new Medium by which Truth might be establisht." Hume's real innovation in philosophy does not, we have seen, lie in introducing " the experimental method of reasoning into moral subjects." Nor yet does his real innovation lie in founding ethics on sentiment, rather than on reason, contrary to much contemporary thinking though that was. Even this fundamental principle is more Hume's in phraseology than in origin : " We speak not strictly and philosophically when we talk of the combat of passion and of reason. Reason is, and ought only to be, the slave of the passions, and can never pretend to any other office than to serve and obey them." [2]

---

[1] Hume, *History of England* (Edinburgh 1792), VIII, 334.　　　[2] *Phil. Wks.*, II, 195.

One of the manuscript memoranda,[1] for instance, makes the point of his debt to ancient " sentimentalists " perfectly clear : " The Moderns have not treated Morals so well as the Antients merely from their Reasoning turn, which carry'd them away from Sentiment." Shaftesbury, Dubos, Butler and, above all, Hutcheson are among the modern " sentimentalists " to whom he is indebted. Two slim volumes by Hutcheson appeared anonymously, the first in 1725,[2] and the second in 1728.[3] They probably came to his attention and, if so, helped to clarify his state of mind. When in the *Philosophical Essays concerning Human Understanding* (1748) Hume made the following observation, he was merely overstating the case as a compliment to Hutcheson, whom he then knew personally :

> That Faculty, by which we discern Truth and Falshood, and that by which we perceive Vice and Virtue had long been confounded with each other, and all Morality was suppos'd to be built on eternal and immutable Relations, which to every intelligent Mind, were equally invariable as any Proposition concerning Quantity or Number. But a late Philosopher [" Mr. Hutcheson," added as a note] has taught us, by the most convincing Arguments, that Morality is nothing in the abstract Nature of Things, but is entirely relative to the Sentiment or mental Taste of each particular Being ; in the same Manner as the Distinctions of sweet and bitter, hot and cold, arise from the particular feeling of each Sense or Organ. Moral Perceptions therefrom, ought not to be class'd with the Operations of the Understanding, but with the Taste or Sentiments.[4]

Hume was more thorough than Hutcheson and the other " sentimentalists " in applying this principle and in excluding the idea of the supernatural from the realm of human nature. Under the influence of the physical sciences, Hume was convinced that " the Science of Man " could be reduced to relatively few simple principles. As the poet of the *Essay on Man* had only recently put it, he would

Account for moral, as for nat'ral things.

Hume's unique contribution to the philosophy of human nature may be stated in the form of just such a principle : *the extension of sentiment or feeling beyond ethics and aesthetics* (to which it was

[1] Early Memoranda, III, 257.
[2] *An Enquiry into the Original of our Ideas of Beauty and Virtue ; In Two Treatises.*
[3] *An Essay on the Nature and Conduct of the Passions and Affections. With Illustrations on the Moral Sense.*
[4] *Phil. Wks.*, IV, 10n. N. Kemp Smith has somewhat overstated Hume's debt to Hutcheson, e.g. he omits Dubos. But Kemp Smith's insight is sound that in Hume's thinking morals antedates metaphysics, but it remains to be proved in actual date of composition. See his *Philosophy of David Hume : A Critical Study of Its Origins and Central Doctrines* (London 1941), pp. 14–20, 24.

limited by Hutcheson etc.) *to include the entire realm of belief covering all relations of matter-of-fact.* " Belief " is further defined as " A lively idea related to or associated with a present impression "; and this definition is regarded by Hume as a momentous discovery : " This operation of the mind, which forms the belief of any matter of fact, seems hitherto to have been one of the greatest mysteries of philosophy ; tho' no one has so much as suspected, that there was any difficulty in explaining it." [1] Hume applies this discovery to the principle of cause and effect. Why do we believe that the future will conform to the past ? Why do we believe that when one billiard ball hits another, the second will be put into motion ? When in 1740 Hume saw fit to print *An Abstract of a Book lately Published ; Entituled, A Treatise of Human Nature, &c.*, which was designed to illustrate and to explain further " The Chief Argument of that Book," he centred upon the analysis of cause and effect.[2]

The intense excitement with which Hume greeted his discovery concerning the extension of sentiment and the nature of causation in the spring of 1729 is explainable in terms of its implications. This was not a mere metaphysical notion with no practical consequences ; it was, on the contrary, a matter to be considered by every man interested in the very foundations of knowledge. Causation, it was argued by Hume, is the basis, not only of natural philosophy, but of moral philosophy, that is, of all matters of fact, of all sciences other than logic and mathematics. Now if causation is no more than belief, and if belief is no more than " a lively idea related to or associated with a present impression," then what becomes of the vaunted certainty of knowledge upon which the modern world had so much prided itself ? It is certainly not fantastic to ask whether any matter of fact can ever have absolute certainty ? The very question might suggest to the questioner that he was starting a Copernican or a Newtonian Revolution—or a Humean Revolution !

A revolution implies a substitution of something new and more useful in place of the old and outworn. So in the Introduction to the *Treatise*, Hume pointed out both the destructive and the constructive elements in his thinking :

There is no question of importance, whose decision is not compriz'd in the science of man ; and there is none, which can be decided with any certainty, before we become acquainted with that science. In pretending,

---

[1] *Phil. Wks.*, 1, 396–7.   [2] See below, pp. 125 ff.

therefore, to explain the principles of human nature, we in effect propose a compleat system of the sciences, built on a foundation almost entirely new, and the only one upon which they can stand with any security.[1]

No wonder the callow philosopher of eighteen trembled at the import of his thinking as he forced himself to work out the details and to make application to the multifarious aspects of the Science of Man ! The sustained and intense intellectual excitement brought on, as we have seen, a psychosomatic disorder which was to last more than four years. The really amazing thing, after the brilliance of the discovery itself, is how much Hume was able to accomplish during that time and under such difficult conditions.

At this point it may be helpful to turn once more to the manuscript memoranda and to name some of the more important authors that Hume was dealing with and being influenced by in this important period of creation. First, it must be emphasised that he was studying the ancients—all of them—and that much of his thinking—much more, I am inclined to believe, than has generally been suspected—originates from that source. Perhaps the most appropriate motto to express his intellectual attitude was found by Hume in Epicharmus and copied out in the manuscript memoranda : *Keep sober and remember to be sceptical.*[2] Among the moderns, five names from the " Philosophy " section will be commented on briefly, not because I wish to make claims for any of them as " sources " for Hume, rather, on the contrary, because I wish to stress the danger of looking for the unique source by indicating the wide range of influences to which he was deliberately subjecting himself. These five names form a somewhat odd reading-list : Bayle, Cudworth, Dubos, Fénelon, and King.

Bayle, we know, was being consulted by Hume in 1732 ; and careful scrutiny proves further that Hume, at one time or another, was familiar with both the *Dictionnaire historique et critique* (1697) and the *Œuvres diverses* (1727-1731). The great French sceptic knew how to publish his scepticisms without getting himself into trouble with the authorities. Amazing compendiums of Enlightenment those works are, where no important intellectual subject is untouched, yet where none is taken up in proper alphabetical order as befits an encyclopedia, but remains buried as a

---

[1] *Phil. Wks.*, I, 307.

[2] *Early Memoranda*, II, 40, n17. It is worth noting that this line of Epicharmus was taken by F. H. Jacobi as the motto on the title-page of his *David Hume über den Glauben, oder Idealismus und Realismus, Ein Gespräch* (Breslau 1787). See also p. 296, below.

footnote or a sub-footnote to the purported biography of an other-wise long-forgotten monk ! What treasures are to be found in Bayle, but what effort to dig them up ! Proper source for a twenty-one-year-old burning with intellectual curiosity, Bayle is definitely to be avoided by the elderly who have little spare time on their hands. It is worth remarking on the surprising absence of Montaigne from the Early Memoranda. Though many of the scepticisms of the *Apologie of Raymond Sebond* are repeated in Bayle, I am confident that Hume knew Montaigne at first-hand in this pre-*Treatise* period. His name first appears in print in an essay of 1742.[1]

The True Intellectual System of the Universe : The First Part ; Wherein, All the Reason and Philosophy of Atheism is Confuted ; and Its Impossibility Demonstrated (1678) of Ralph Cudworth, distinguished Cambridge Platonist, paradoxically afforded Hume a simpler " Primer of Atheism " than Bayle. For Cudworth religiously combed the atheistical arguments of the ages, ancient and modern, in order to refute them, and was moreover so careful a scholar as to quote them at length. Hume, however, is not quite satisfied with all of Cudworth's summaries and pens a note to the following purport :

> Four kinds of Atheists according to Cudworth, the Democritic or Atomical, the Anaximandrian or Hylopathian, the Stratonic or Hylozoic, the Stoic or Cosmo-plastic. To which he might have added the Pyrrhonian or Sceptic. And the Spinozist or Metaphysical. One might perhaps add the Anaxagorian or Chymical.[2]

Whether Hume knew Cudworth's posthumous continuation, *A Treatise concerning Eternal and Immutable Morality* (1731), I am not sure, but would hazard the guess that he did.

Dubos has received sufficient comment already except perhaps to emphasise his importance as a Hutchesonian before Hutcheson. Mainly interested in aesthetics, Dubos erects a system completely on sense or the direct reactions of the feelings, rather than on reason. His defence of the Ancients in the Ancient and Modern controversy and his insistence on the paramount importance of physical, particularly climatical, causes upon the formation of national characters were to be long remembered by Hume and later to be challenged by him. The early pre-*Treatise* influence of Dubos upon Hume, however, seems curiously to have gone unnoticed.

The third Frenchman on the list of five moderns is François

---

[1] *Phil. Wks.*, iii, 230n.   [2] Early Memoranda, ii, 40.

de Salignac de La Mothe Fénelon, famous Archbishop of Cambray and philosopher of Quietism. His *Traité de l'existence et des attributs de Dieu* (1713) instigated Hume to make three memoranda :

> Some pretend that there can be no Necessity according to the System of Atheism : Because even Matter cannot be determin'd without something Superior to determine it. Fenelon.
> Being, & Truth & Goodness the same. Id.
> Three Proofs for the Existence of a God. 1. something necessarily existent, & what is so is infinitely perfect. 2. The Idea of Infinite must come from an infinite Being. 3. The Idea of infinite Perfection implys that of actual Existence. Id.[1]

Within a few years Hume was to meet and to have some philosophical conversations with one of Fénelon's disciples, the Chevalier Ramsay; but the two did not hit it off very well.[2]

The translation of 1731 from the Latin of William King's *De Origine Mali* (1702) is, in a sense, three works in one. The anonymous translation was made by Dr Edmund Law with copious explanatory notes, forming in themselves a separate work ; and the independent and anonymous " Dissertation concerning the fundamental principle and immediate criterion of virtue," prefixed to the translation, was by Dr John Gay. Scrutiny of Hume's five notes on " King " indicates that he was using the 1731 translation and was, therefore, exposing himself to the ideas of Law and Gay, as well as of King. This fact is of importance, for example, because Gay's short dissertation is the earliest known reconcilement of ethical utilitarianism with psychological associationism, two doctrines that were to be employed by Hume himself.

But it is necessary now at last to return from the consideration of Hume's reading and thinking in this critical period of development to the tenor of his outward life. Early in 1734 he had reached a determination to take drastic action to regain his health : " . . . I began to rouze up myself ; & being encourag'd by Instances of Recovery from worse degrees of this Distemper, as well as by the Assurances of my Physicians, I began to think of something more effectual, than I had hitherto try'd." The proposed expedient was the trial of " a more active Scene of Life." His intention is announced in the same long letter from which we have already drawn so much, perhaps the longest letter Hume ever wrote and certainly the most interesting, written at London while he was on the road to Bristol. Hume had left Ninewells the latter part of February 1734 determined to rid himself at long last of the " Disease of the Learned."

¹ Early Memoranda, II, 35–7.   ² See below, pp. 93 ff.

CHAPTER 7

RECOVERY THROUGH CATHARSIS

"I was tempted or rather forced to make a very feeble Trial for
entering into a more active Scene of Life."

SHORTLY after David Hume left Ninewells, presumably taking
ship at Berwick for London, a local scandal broke out in Chirnside.
On 5 March 1734, one Agnes Galbraith, presented herself before
the Reverend George Home and confessed that she was with child.
A meeting of the Session of Chirnside was immediately called
pro re nata. According to the record :

> The Minister represented that Agnes Galbraith had this day come to him
> and Confessed her being with Child, whereupon he had Called the Session
> to hear her Confession, and whom she would give the Child to, as Father.
> She being called, Compeared and confessed her being with Child, and that
> Mr David Home, brother to Ninewells, is the Father of her Child. She being
> rebuked for her Sin and Scandal, and dealt with to be ingenuous in her
> Confession which the Session had some ground to suspect, in respect that it
> was Notour [notorious] to the Country, and well known to herself, that, that
> Gentleman was going off the Country, and also in respect she did not Compear
> when Cited, about three weeks ago, when he was in the Country, and had
> come this day without being Cited, when he was gone.[1]

The scepticism of the Session about this story of Agnes's is
obvious ; it was, no doubt, somewhat augmented by the embarrassment of the minister over the accusation against his nephew. Agnes
Galbraith was making her third confession of fornication ; moreover, she had deliberately defied the Kirk authorities in waiting
three weeks to reply to their citation. The inferences seemed clear
enough : she was not one to be believed, and she was employing
subterfuge in naming a man who could not possibly be present to
answer the accusation. "Finding it a matter of Difficulty," the
Session recommended it to the minister that he seek the advice of
the Presbytery. The case was duly presented to the Presbytery of
Chirnside on 26 March, and their officer was appointed " to cite
the said Agnes to the first Ordinary meeting of the Presbyterie to
be in this place." That meeting was held on 25 June.

---

[1] Extract from the minutes of the Session of Chirnside in the " Minutes of the
Presbyterie of Chyrnside (1713-1734)," in possession of the Clerk of the Presbytery
of Duns.

[Agnes] being called, Compeared, and being Charged by the Moderator with the guilt of Fornication for the third time, She adhered to her Confession formerly emitted before the Session of Chirnside, Declaring that Mr David Home brother German to John Home of Ninewells, is the father of her Child. Whereupon the Moderator rebuked her gravely and Exhorted her to be Ingenuous, and Confess if any other person was the father of her Child, but she still insisted that no other person was guilty with her. Then she was removed, and the Presbyterie having Considered the affair, and being Informed that the said David Home was gone out of this Kingdom, they remitted her to the Session of Chirnside, to make satisfaction according to the Rules of this Church.

The language of the Moderator would seem to imply that the child had already been born, an inference that is substantiated by the following cryptic entry[1] in the " Chirnside Parochial Register " : " May 5th [1734]—John Galbraith in Chirnside had a —— Baptized named ——." One might perhaps have expected an entry of " Agnes Galbraith, fornicatrix . . ." ; but it was the custom to put the entry always in the name of the man. I should, therefore, assume that the Reverend George Home, taking for granted the innocence of his nephew, had assigned the custody of Agnes Galbraith's third child out of wedlock to a man in her family, likely enough her father.

In due course, Agnes must have appeared in sackcloth before the Kirk of Chirnside, both at the " joug " and at the pillory, for the customary three Sundays. But that she underwent no permanent reformation is proved by the reappearance of her name in the Kirk Session Records of Chirnside in 1739. This time Agnes named her then master as the guilty man and testified further that he had given her a present of seven shillings. He denied it and offered to take the oath of purgation before the Presbytery, but not before his own church at Ayton. This defying of the authority of the local kirk caused quite a scandal. David Hume, who was back at Ninewells by that time, undoubtedly knew of the affair and noted that Agnes was up to her old tricks.

But what of David Hume and the Galbraith *affaire* of 1733–34 ? Was he the father of her child ? Had his departure from Scotland been hastened by the impending event ? Had he connived with the woman over her delay in answering the citation of the Session of Chirnside ? No further facts are known : we are left to such inferences as may legitimately be drawn from the evidence already presented. To begin with, it is patent that neither the minister, nor the Session, nor the Presbytery took much stock in Agnes's story. This disbelief derived no doubt from her bad record, but

[1] In SRO.

also perhaps from the local reputation of David Hume as a serious, sober, and studious young man, and (what would also be of import in a small community) as the brother of the Laird of Ninewells. *Beware to attack the Deil and the laird's bairns* is an old Scottish saying with more than one application.

So far as the family at Ninewells were concerned, they would have been loyal in any event. If David was not guilty, they would have been shocked at the wanton accusation. If he was guilty, he had unquestionably taken them into his confidence, and it was probably at the urging of his mother and brother that he had left the country in order to escape some part of the inevitable notoriety. The mother and sons were always on terms of intimacy. And Katherine Home, now aged fifty, would have recalled with a sigh an almost parallel incident in the youth of David's father. Whatever the facts of the Galbraith *affaire*, David Hume in later life, in Italy, and France, and Scotland, was to prove a man of normal sexual desires.

Meanwhile, in London early in March, and before proceeding to Bristol, the anguished and frustrated Hume paused for final reconsideration of his plans for the future. Friends and acquaintances he would meet in London ; but the problem of his health could not profitably be discussed with James Oswald, who was completing his legal studies at Lincoln's Inn, nor with the several Scottish M.P.s to whom, doubtless, he carried letters of introduction. Lonely as he was and morbidly preoccupied with his own problems, he was sorely tempted to take someone into his confidence. Was he employing the best means to a complete and permanent cure ? At one and the same time sure of himself, and yet curiously unsure, he felt the need for confirmation of his own diagnosis—if the right physician could be found. Was there in all this strange and vast metropolis, he asked himself, was there a physician, a brother-Scot, famous and skilful in his profession, familiar with chronic and mental diseases ; a man, moreover, of keen intellect and learned beyond mere medicine ; a man of letters and intimate with men of letters and their ways ; a person of great humanity, good-natured, witty, candid, and wise ? If such a paragon of a physician there was, and one furthermore who was a complete stranger to Hume, he must also be agreeable to diagnose the case of a man so shy as to be unwilling to present himself for personal consultation and so reticent as even to be unwilling to sign the very letter requesting advice.

In addition to these specified requirements, two others of

importance may be inferred from the general tone of the letter that he wrote to the physician, and from certain incidental remarks. It is obvious from his apologetic and deferential tone that Hume was taking considerable pains to ingratiate himself with the physician while requesting so considerable and so extraordinary a favour. After all, he himself was as yet totally unknown, while the physician was a man of high reputation. Hume would, therefore, be studious to exclude everything which might conceivably give offence. Yet he actually goes out of his way, to some extent, to condemn all hypothetical and systematic schools of natural and moral philosophy : " I found that the moral Philosophy transmitted to us by Antiquity, labor'd under the same Inconvenience that has been found in their natural Philosophy, of being entirely Hypothetical, & depending more upon Invention than Experience." It would, therefore, seem evident that his physician was not known as a subscriber to any of the current hypothetical and systematic philosophies. It would also seem evident from Hume's rather derogatory references to " the French Mysticks " and " our Fanatics here " that his physician was known to be neither a fanatic nor a religious mystic.

David Hume knew his man—and I think that I have been able to identify him—Dr John Arbuthnot, the only candidate perfectly fulfilling all the qualifications laid down and implied in the letter.[1] John Gay had sung his praises :

> Arbuthnot there I see, in physic's art,
> As Galen learned or fam'd Hippocrate ;
> Whose company drives sorrow from the heart
> As all disease his med'cines dissipate.

Swift had appraised him dispassionately : " more wit than we all have, and more humanity than wit." Dr Johnson was later to name him the " first man " among the writers of his day : " He was the most universal genius, being an excellent physician, a man of deep learning, and a man of much humour."

The mind that scorned pedantry in all forms was itself unpedantically learned in both the medical and outside fields. In addition to his classic *John Bull*, *Martinus Scriblerus*, and other

---

[1] See Mossner, " Hume's Epistle to Dr. Arbuthnot, 1734 : The Biographical Significance," in *Huntington Library Quarterly*, vii (1944), 135–52, for the full evidence concerning the Arbuthnot identification and the disqualification of the hitherto generally accepted candidate, Dr George Cheyne (Hill Burton, i, 42–3 ; HL, i, 12, *n2*). In brief, Cheyne is definitively disqualified, first, because he was no longer practising medicine in London and, second, because he would almost certainly have taken offense at Hume's remarks on philosophy and religion.

politico-satirical works, Arbuthnot wrote on a wide range of subjects : the laws of chance and the general usefulness of mathematics, the weights and coins of the ancient world, the Treaty of Union (1707), the meaning of the apparently constant ratio between male and female births. Scholar and wit, Arbuthnot was also an expert precisely where Hume required an expert. In 1731 he had published an *Essay concerning the Nature of Aliments, and the Choice of Them, according to the Different Constitutions of Human Bodies*, and, two years later, a continuation in an *Essay concerning the Effects of Air on Human Bodies* ; but death early in 1735 cut short his programme of writing also on the influence of rest and motion on human bodies.

It was one thing for Hume to decide to write to Arbuthnot and quite another actually to write to him. To put one's own case-history into concise form is never easy, and it was certainly far from easy for David Hume. His letter to the physician is at once the most intimate and the strangest that he ever wrote, partaking of the candour of the consulting-room and perhaps even of that of the confessional. It opens :

Sir

Not being acquainted with this hand-writing you will probably look to the bottom to find the Subscription, & not finding any, will certainly wonder at this strange method of addressing to you. I must here in the beginning beg you to excuse it, & to perswade you to read what follows with some Attention, must tell you, that this gives you an Opportunity to do a very good-natur'd Action, which I believe is the most powerful Argument I can use. I need not tell you, that I am your Countryman, a Scotchman ; for without any such tye, I dare rely upon your Humanity, even to a perfect Stranger, such as I am. The Favour I beg of you is your Advice, & the reason why I address myself in particular to you need not be told. As one must be a skilful Physician, a man of Letters, of Wit, of Good Sense, & of great Humanity, to give me a satisfying Answer, I wish Fame had pointed out to me more Persons, in whom these Qualities are united, in order to have kept me some time in Suspense. This I say in the Sincerity of my Heart, & without any Intention of making a Complement : For tho' it may seem necessary, that in the beginning of so unusual a Letter, I shou'd say some fine things, to bespeak your good Opinion, & remove any prejudices you may conceive at it, yet such an Endeavour to be witty, woud but ill suit with the present Condition of my Mind ; which, I must confess, is not without Anxiety concerning the Judgement you will form of me. Trusting however to your Candor & Generosity, I shall, without further Preface, proceed to open up to you the present Condition of my Health, & to do that the more effectually shall give you a kind of History of my Life, after which you will easily learn, why I keep my Name a Secret.

There follows the " full account of the Condition of my Body," together with the narrative of " how my Mind stood all this time, which on every Occasion, especially in this Distemper, have a very near Connexion together," that provided so much of the substance of the preceding chapter. Although not written in modern technical terminology, Hume's case-history of his psychosomatic disorder is as clear as could possibly be penned by any highly intelligent person today, and, as such, is diagnosable by modern psychiatrists.

Whether, having completed this remarkable letter, Hume actually dispatched it to Arbuthnot's London residence at Cork Street, Burlington Gardens, is quite another matter. There is no positive evidence one way or the other, and arguments from the lack of evidence can never be final. Only the letter itself exists, preserved among the Hume documents ; it is unaddressed and unsigned, but a fair copy suitable to be sent. No reply is extant. It is, to be sure, possible that one was received but not preserved, although that hardly seems consonant with Hume's expressed attitude of hero-worship towards the physician. It would, therefore, appear more likely that no answer was received. There may have been no answer either because Arbuthnot refused to be a party to " this absurd Method " of procuring medical advice or because he never received the letter. In the eighteenth century it was not at all uncommon for physicians to attempt diagnosis by post, although presumably not customarily for otherwise unknown patients. That Arbuthnot refused to answer the youthful, earnest, and somewhat pathetic appeal—no matter how absurd—would seem most unlikely from his justly renowned humanity. It is, however, conceivable that he was unable to answer or to suggest a face-to-face consultation because of his illness at this time, an illness from which he never recovered. It is also conceivable that the letter was not dispatched by Hume because at the last moment he had learned of the doctor's illness.

Yet a simpler hypothesis than all these suggests itself, one which, moreover, is entirely in keeping with the psychological indications of the letter itself and indeed with all known information regarding the character of the writer. Hume's reluctance to consult at all, his disinclination to a personal interview, his retreat into anonymity, may not unnaturally have eventuated in total suppression of the letter once he had completed it. The very act of putting his symptoms into writing may in itself have provoked a psychological catharsis. As an unintentional consequence of writing the letter, Hume may have come to the realisation that all that could be done had been done, that the break from the contemplative to the active life had been made. The trip from Berwick to London may already have wrought a sea-change, and the intensive review in the letter of the last several years may have dated the whole distemper definitely as of the past. Now, to push on at once to Bristol with high hopes for the future !

" The Questions I wou'd humbly propose," as Hume had written in conclusion, suddenly appeared absurdly simple. At the outset Hume had wanted professional advice upon which to lean ; but now, upon completion of the letter, he no longer required such confirmation. Self-confidence had been completely restored. Why, he could provide the answers himself, just as well as any physician, no matter how expert ! And, as a matter of fact, he could and did ; for the desired, and basically sound, responses are all patently suggested in the very wording of the questions themselves.

Question one : " Whether among all these Scholars, you have been acquainted with, you have ever known any affected in this manner ? " Answer : *Yes, many.* Question two : " Whether I can ever hope for a Recovery ? " Answer : *Assuredly, you can.* Question three : " Whether I must long wait for it ? " Answer : *No, not under favourable circumstances.* Question four : " Whether my Recovery will ever be perfect, & my Spirits regain their former Spring and Vigor, so as to endure the Fatigue of deep & abstruse thinking ? " Answer : *Most probably.* Question five : " Whether I have taken a right way to recover ? " Answer : *Certainly ; keep it up.* And the letter closed with Hume's tacit recognition that his ailment was basically mental rather than physical : " I believe all proper Medicines have been us'd, & therefore I need mention nothing of them." *No, indeed ; you are cured because you have the confidence that you are cured.*

Presumably never dispatched, this " Epistle to Dr Arbuthnot " was yet preserved by Hume throughout life. It was preserved, not because of its self-revelation, but in spite of its self-revelation. It was preserved, I believe, because it became to Hume the symbol of self-mastery. A crisis had arisen which he had met successfully. Never again did Hume feel the necessity of consulting authority over the direction of his career. That career, which had long since been dedicated to the life of letters, was never again to be diverted by adversity.

The letter to Dr Arbuthnot had explained that, " in order the more effectually to resume them," Hume was temporarily laying aside his " Pretensions to Learning." He was making a trial of the active life. Of two types that seemed open to him, he had disqualified himself from that of a travelling tutor because of his lack of " Confidence & Knowledge enough of the World. . . . I therefore fixt my Choice," he continued, " upon a Merchant ; & having got Recommendation to a considerable Trader in Bristol, I am just now hastening thither, with a Resolution to forget myself, & every thing that is past, to engage myself, as far as is possible, in that Course of Life, & to toss about the World, from the one Pole to the other, till I leave this Distemper behind me." By mid-March David Hume had reached Bristol. The post road from London ran 115 miles through Middlesex, Buckinghamshire, Berkshire, Wiltshire, and Gloucestershire, and was one of the six principal roads in the kingdom, affording a pleasant relief from the choppy waters of the North Sea. Hume's " Recommendation to a considerable Trader "—in *My Own Life* he was to claim " some Recommendations to eminent Merchants "—was duly presented, and he was given his position. The trader by whom he was employed was Mr Michael Miller, who lived and traded at 15, Queen Square.[1] A sugar-merchant importing from the West Indies, Miller, in all likelihood, was also involved in the slave-trade in accordance with the customary practice of the lucrative triangular voyage, Africa—West Indies—England.

So Hume, despite his romantic anticipation in the letter to Dr Arbuthnot of the life of a supercargo—" to toss about the World, from the one Pole to the other "—became just another clerk in a counting-house in the homeland. Whether this was by his own choice or not cannot be ascertained ; but, in later years at least, he acknowledged himself such a poor sailor as to be unable to cross even the Firth of Forth without getting seasick. Perhaps the coastal voyage to London had already given him some inkling of that weakness.

Bristol, in the eighteenth century, was the chief port for the West India trade, and, though small after London, was customarily reckoned the second city in England ; it was densely populated within a small walled area, and dirty, with prosperity crowding its dark narrow streets. Apart from the teeming waterfront of the Avon and Frome Rivers and the " Floating Harbour," the centre of its commercial life was the Old Market nearby. Yet Bristol was also a centre of culture ; the City Library, one of the first of its kind in Britain, had been founded early in the seventeenth century. The list of subscribers in 1728 to Henry Pemberton's *View of Sir*

---

[1] John Latimer, *Annals of Bristol in the 18th Century* (Bristol 1893), pp. 189–90.

Isaac Newton's Philosophy includes no fewer than twenty-five residents of Bristol, certainly affording some indication of its cultural status.

In his new surroundings, Hume soon found good company. For, when not deep in his studies, he was a sociable lad ; " the most sturdy, robust, healthful-like Fellow you have seen, with a ruddy Complexion & a chearful Countenance," he had described himself to Arbuthnot. He might have added with equal truth that he was tall, just under six feet, infallibly gave the impression of being country-bred, and, from his talk could never have been taken for anything but a Scot.

Of Hume's friends at Bristol, three can be named with certainty. The first, and apparently most intimate, the " dear Jemmy " of his letter from France later in the year, was employed at the Old Market. James Birch, freeholder in St Philip and Jacob Ward, Bristol, was evidently a young man of no great fortune, who, like David, had some aspirations of going over to France for " Study & Diversion." " Will Yonge will give you my Direction," wrote Hume to Birch in the aforesaid letter. This reference may possibly be to the later Sir William Young, who became Lieutenant-Governor of Dominica in 1763—but that is admittedly a guess. Hume's letter to Birch concludes : " Make my Complements to Mr Peach, and all Friends." Although the friends remain undesignated, Mr John Peach was a linen-draper in Maryleport Street, Bristol, wealthy and at the same time learned and wise. In later years he became the good friend of the young Hannah More and instructed her in literary criticism. According to her,[1] Peach also long remained the friend of David Hume, even into the 1750s. To him, it is said, Hume sent his *History of England* for correction, that is, so far as detecting Scotticisms was concerned ; the story proceeds that Peach found over 200 such words and expressions.

Birch, Peach, and Yonge are the only Bristol friends actually named by Hume. Many years later Dr Josiah Tucker, then Dean of Gloucester and Rector of St Stephen's in Bristol, told Lord Hailes that Hume, while at Bristol, had become acquainted with Thomas Morgan, the Whiggish and deistical writer ; but his lordship, for some reason, remained dubious.[2] The question is

[1] Wm. Roberts, *Memoirs of the Life and Correspondence of Mrs. Hannah More* (London 1834), I, 16 ; Mary A. Hopkins, *Hannah More and Her Circle* (New York 1946), p. 26.
[2] " A volume of anecdotes, etc. collected by Lord Hailes," HMC, Fourth Report (London 1874), p. 532. In 1742 Hume alluded disparagingly to Morgan's *Moral Philosopher* ; see *Phil. Wks.*, III, 189.

merely of academic importance, however, for there is little in the writings—and probably no more in the personality—of Morgan that could have influenced the already mature mind of Hume.

Two events of the Bristol sojourn are worthy of mention. It must surely have been in Bristol that David, recognising the futility of getting Englishmen to pronounce *Home* as *Hume*—" thae glaekit English bodies, who could not call him aright ! "—changed the spelling of his surname to conform to the pronunciation.[1] A second event was David's quarrel with his master at the counting-house. The quarrel was over matters literary : David's corrections of grammar and style in Miller's letters. Exasperated at the repeated criticisms from his young clerk, Miller is said to have told him that he had made £20,000 with his English and would not have it improved. The story in itself is sufficiently convincing, for Hume could touch no writing without—as he had informed Arbuthnot—attempting to express himself with " Elegance & Neatness."

As a result of the quarrel, David left Bristol harbouring deep resentment. Part of this spleen was worked off in the *Treatise of Human Nature*, composed in France shortly thereafter. " A mere soldier," Hume avers, " little values the character of eloquence : A gownman of courage : A bishop of humour "—then the thrust home !—" Or a merchant of learning." [2] Many years later, Hume's still smouldering resentment inspired him to a delicious piece of irony in his account in the *History of England* of James Naylor. That seventeenth-century " enthusiastic " Quaker who fancied himself as a second Christ is described as entering Bristol mounted on a horse—" I suppose," observes Hume dryly, " from the difficulty in that place of finding an ass." On the basis of this long-continued resentment on the part of Hume, a resentment quite out of character, I should surmise that his feelings had been terribly hurt, that he had perhaps been subjected to ridicule because of his nationality and speech, that he had been snubbed because of his learning, in short, that he had been ignominiously discharged from his post in the counting-house.

Yet so far as the early leaving of Bristol is concerned, it must be recalled that Hume's letter to Arbuthnot makes it certain that he regarded the whole experiment as a last expedient, that he never had any intention of remaining long there, or anywhere else, away from his studies and writings. If my interpretation of that

---

[1] Quoted by G. F. Black, *The Surnames of Scotland* (New York 1946), p. 362, but without citation of authority.   [2] *Phil. Wks.*, II, 115.

letter is substantially correct, it follows that no extended trial of the business world was needed psychologically. Hume's own comment on the Bristol episode in *My Own Life* perhaps gives the proper perspective : " . . . my Health being a little broken by my ardent Application, I was tempted or rather forced to make a very feeble Trial for entering into a more active Scene of Life. In 1734, I went to Bristol with some Recommendations to eminent Merchants ; but in a few Months found that Scene totally unsuitable to me." After perhaps four months in the world of commerce, Hume was fully prepared to return to his studies once more ; and by mid-summer he was in Paris. In retrospect there, he might well have felt that, despite the lingering ill-will towards his former master, the Bristol experiment had not been unsuccessful, that the " more active Scene of Life " had accomplished its purpose.

CHAPTER 8

TRANQUILLITY IN FRANCE

*" I went over to France with a View of prosecuting
my Studies in a Country Retreat."*

SCOT that he was, David Hume must have experienced poignant emotions on first setting foot on French soil. The national, cultural, and sentimental ties of many centuries which bound Scotland to France would not have been repudiated by the young Revolution Whig, and indeed would rather have been augmented by his admiration for the literature of the period of Louis XIV and by his respect for French philosophy. And it is most unlikely that his Protestantism was sufficiently strong for him to have echoed with any sincerity the remark of his countryman, Lord Fountainhall : " We landed in France the land of graven images." [1] Hume's love for France, indeed, as expressed in an essay of 1741, was virtually unbounded :

> . . . the French are the only people, except the Greeks, who have been at once philosophers, poets, orators, historians, painters, architects, sculptors, and musicians. With regard to the stage, they have excelled even the Greeks, who far excelled the English. And, in common life, they have, in a great measure, perfected that art, the most useful and agreeable of any, *l'Art de Vivre*, the art of society and conversation. [2]

During his stay in France, 1734 to 1737, Hume composed the *Treatise of Human Nature* and studied *l'Art de Vivre*.

The two most popular routes to France were from Dover to Calais and from Rye to Dieppe. In either case, the trip to Paris in the crowded *diligence* or public coach might have taken upwards of a week, during which time the traveller had ample opportunity to become acquainted with the French character. On the basis of his experiences while travelling in France and Italy in 1736, one of Hume's friends advised another :

> Be sure, dear Dempster, when you go to bed,
> To lay your breeches snug beneath your head ;
> Throw them not off with a neglectful ease,
> If you regard your money or your keys :
> For many a thief will rob them on a chair,
> Who to disturb your pillow would not dare.

---

[1] Fountainhall, *Journals*, p. 2.   [2] *Phil. Wks.*, III, 159.

Think you at Inns that you have noght to fear ?
Have Ostlers then antipathies at beer ?
Has the brisk Waiter got no paramour ?
Has Boot-catch ta'en a vow of being poor ? [1]

No Scotsman of the eighteenth century had need to remain long solitary in France, for that kingdom was literally teeming with his fellow-countrymen, many of them exiles along with the royal Stuarts. And Hume, as always, came armed with letters of introduction, one of which may have been written by the Earl of Stair, that distinguished Scottish soldier-diplomat and former ambassador to France.

In Paris, Hume was received " with all imaginable Kindness," as he took occasion to inform " Jemmy " Birch, by the Chevalier Ramsay, a cousin of Hume's boyhood friend, Michael Ramsay of Mungale.[2] Hume's pleasant reception in Paris attests the politeness and amiability of both the Chevalier and himself, for surely two more different characters could scarcely be found. Andrew Michael Ramsay, then somewhat more than twice the age of Hume, was a Scot who had been lured away from Presbyterianism to Roman Catholicism of the mystical variety of Quietism. In short, he had become the disciple of Fénelon and later his literary inheritor. Through the Archbishop's influence, Ramsay was given the post of tutor to the Duc de Château-Thierry and the Prince de Turenne. In 1724 he held a similar post at Rome with the two sons of the Pretender, Prince Charles Edward Stuart and his brother Henry.

In England in 1730, by special permission of the government, Ramsay was awarded the honorary degree of LL.D. at Oxford University, then a hotbed of sentimental Jacobitism. Ramsay was also a well-known man of letters, who had published in French a life of Fénelon, a discourse on epic poetry, an essay on civil government and, in English, a volume of poems. His chief literary fame, however, rested upon the *Voyages de Cyrus* (1727), composed in avowed imitation of his master's *Télémache*. In 1748–49, after Ramsay's death, his *Philosophical Principles of Natural and Revealed Religion, Unfolded in a Geometrical Order*, was published in two volumes at Glasgow.

The meeting of the opinionated, dogmatic, and mystically religious Ramsay with the enthusiastically sceptical Hume produced reactions that were long remembered by both. In 1757

[1] Alexander Dick, "Journal of a Tour, 1736," in *Gent.'s Mag.*, N. S. xxxix (1853), 162. [2] G. D. Henderson, *Chevalier Ramsay* (Edinburgh 1952), p. 7.

Hume writes of " an author of taste and imagination, who was surely no enemy to Christianity. It is the Chevalier Ramsay, a writer, who had so laudable an inclination to be orthodox, that his reason never found any difficulty, even in the doctrines which free-thinkers scruple the most, the trinity, incarnation, and satisfaction." The irony is plain enough ; but Hume hastens to make some amends by recalling Ramsay's " all imaginable Kindness." He proceeds : " His humanity, alone, of which he seems to have had a great stock, rebelled against the doctrines of eternal reprobation and predestination." [1]

Written in 1742, the Chevalier's recollections of David Hume are more pointed and more picturesque. Dr John Stevenson, an eminent Edinburgh physician, had evidently recommended Hume as translator for some " Chinese Letters " that Ramsay was writing. Ramsay replies : " The gentleman you mention to whom you intend to intrust the Translation of the Chinese letters, would no doubt acquit himself very well of that commission, but I am affrayed he wont undertake it. If I don't mistake his Character, or if it be not changed since I had the honor to see him, he is too full of himself, to humble his pregnant, active, protuberant Genius to drudge at a translation." Yet he adds magnanimously, " If he will out of friendship to you undergo that Slavery, I am sure he will do it finely." [2]

The Chevalier appraised Hume correctly as his radical antagonist in philosophy, and it is not difficult to see why. " By the litle I heard from & read of that young Gentleman," the letter continues, " he seems to me far from being a True master of metaphysicks, which as mathematicks their companion or rather branch, is the apex of humane reason. That bright Ingenious young Spark does not seem to me to have acquir'd a sufficient Stock of solid Learning, nor to be born with a fund of noble Sentiments, nor to have a genius capable of all that Geometrical attention, penetration and Justness, necessary to make a True Metaphysician. I am affrayd his spirit is more lively than solid, his Imagination more luminous than profound, and his heart too dissipated with material objects & spiritual Self-Idolatry to pierce into the sacred recesses of divine Truths." The rambling discursive letter comments on Hume's " superficial learning and Studys," and finally comes to

---

[1] *Phil. Wks.*, IV, 355n.
[2] Ramsay, MS letter, 24 Aug. 1742, in EU, Laing MSS, II, 301 ; the letter is unaddressed but is in a group written to Dr John Stevenson. That this Stevenson was not the Professor of Logic and Metaphysics at Edinburgh University seems clear from Henderson, *op. cit.*, pp. 204–5.

a philosophical comparison : " He [Hume] seems to me one of those philosophers that think to spin out Systems, out of their own brain, without any regard to religion, antiquity or Tradition sacred or profane ; but Descartes is a melancholy example that such Cobwebbs are of no use, & yet that philosopher was one of the Greatest Genii of his age, & far superiour to your thin, superficial, meagre lean Skeleton Lock."

Ramsay, it is fair to say, had not read the *Treatise* when thus summarily he rejected Hume's philosophy : " The Gentleman we speak of sent me his Essay upon *humane Nature* about fifteen Months ago by one Sir John Ramsay a Countryman of ours now at Angers. I have neither had time nor health to peruse such an obscure, dark, intricate performance. I shall however read it when I go to Boulogne. So if you have sent it, it will furnish me perhaps with some materials for my great work, & oblidge me to dissipate the objections made by that author against the Zenonian or privation Scheme of Liberty & prescience in opposition to the fatalistical necessitarian systeme." This was neither the first nor the last time that Hume was damned after a glance at the table of contents. The Chevalier, however, was courteous enough to add, by way of apology to Stevenson, " Pardon the freedom with which I talk of your friend." Ramsay's posthumous *Philosophical Principles of Natural and Revealed Religion, Unfolded in a Geometrical Order*, was obviously uninfluenced by Hume's *Treatise*.[1]

One unavoidable topic of conversation, between Hume and the Chevalier Ramsay, may have been the recent miracles of the Abbé Pâris, which Hume probably knew about before going to France, as they had been reviewed and ridiculed in the London *Historical Register* for 1731 :[2] " the Story [of the early miracles performed at the tomb of the Abbé] took so well, that in some Time the City of Paris was fill'd with Miracles of the same Kind, by the Credulity of the Parisians, who are very great Bigots in the Roman-Catholick Way." In Paris, Hume learned much more about the alleged miracles from common talk and from carefully reading and documenting the more important of the many publications on the subject. His initial Protestant-bred scepticism would have been intensified by his studies in scientific method and by his interests in history.[3] The problem of miracles

---

[1] See Textual Supplement.   [2] *Historical Register*, xvi (1731), 317–17.
[3] To " Of Miracles," Section X of *Philosophical Essays concerning Human Understanding* (1748), Hume appends a footnote of some three pages in derisive treatment of "such despicable materials."

was to remain quiescent in his mind until a later incident in France crystallised his thinking.

Though there was no likelihood of a true meeting of minds, the Chevalier Ramsay was personally kind to his young visitor. Possibly he introduced Hume to some of the *philosophes* of Paris— Dubos, for example, would have been a man that Hume would want to talk with. Certainly the Chevalier would be free with advice to a youth at the outset of a career as man of letters. Paris, it was by now all too apparent to Hume, was an expensive place for a highly restricted income. And although Hume loved it first and foremost—" a place of the World I have always admird the most," he wrote in 1763 on the eve of returning there as Britain's greatest man of letters—in 1734 he could ill afford the luxury. Was there, Hume wanted to know, a provincial town well endowed with men of intellect and with good library facilities, where one could live inexpensively and have opportunity to study and to write ? Whether the Chevalier suggested Rheims or not is unknown ; but, once decided upon, he it was who provided his compatriot with three letters of introduction to dignitaries in that city.

Situated about a hundred miles north-east of Paris in the province of Champagne, " an easy days Journey by Post " as Hume remarked, Rheims at first impressed him as an ideal place in which to settle down. The modern tourist in this " very famous & antient Town & University " would perhaps be inclined to look first at the renowned Cathedral of Notre-Dame, dating from 1211. Little interested in cathedrals, however, Hume was more concerned with the practical fact that no more than thirty families in a city of 40,000 inhabitants kept their own coaches, and not one of the thirty had an income of as much as £500 a year. The houses of these " People of Fashion " were built off the streets and entirely concealed except from those who were fortunate enough to gain entrée.

The letters provided by the Chevalier Ramsay gave Hume immediate entrée to " two of the best Families in Town." " I am every Day," he writes, " in some of their Houses, they make Parties of Diversion to show me more Company, & if I cou'd but speak their Language perfectly I wou'd immediately be acquainted with the whole Town." The names of these hospitable people are unavailable, but one, we may conjecture, was the Godinot family. Jean Godinot was a Doctor of Theology and Canon of the metropolis of Rheims. Having doubled his fortune by prudent cultivation of the grapes of the Vesle Valley, he determined to return his gains to the city and the district which had helped to produce them. A few years after Hume's sojourn at Rheims, Godinot completed the installation of a new system of water-supply and sewage-disposal. The home of such a public-spirited citizen would always be open to the stranger.

On 12 September 1734, when Hume wrote to Michael Ramsay and James Birch, he had not yet delivered the third introduction. The gentleman to whom it was addressed, he remarked, " is not at present in Town, tho' he will return in a few days." Hume's air of impatience is transparent; he envisages great things from this " man, who they say, is one of the most learned in France." He writes expectantly about the possibility of contracting a friendship with him and is interested in his " fine Library," but fails to mention his name. This man turns out to be the Abbé Noel-Antoine Pluche, as in a letter of 29 September to Michael, Hume is enthusiastic about his good fortune in being admitted to the Abbé's excellent library. This letter moreover proves that just before composing the *Treatise*, Hume was *rereading* Locke and Berkeley : " It is my Pleasure to read over again today Locke's *Essays* and The Principles of Human Knowledge by Dr Berkeley which are printed in their original state and in French copy." [1]

The Abbé Pluche was indeed a learned man, a Jansenist and an anti-Cartesian, having held the chairs of Humanity and Rhetoric in the University of Rheims. He is particularly noteworthy for his *Spectacle de la Nature* (1732), a series of dialogues on natural theology. Translated into English as *Nature Displayed* (1735), the work was popular in Britain far into the next century.

Another renowned scholar of Rheims was Louis-Jean Lévesque de Pouilly, but there is no evidence that Hume met him.[2] Pouilly had been one of the earliest interpreters of Newtonianism in France, later visiting England, where he became the friend of Sir Isaac himself. He was also the friend of Lord Bolingbroke, and in 1720, during that statesman's exile in France, had guided him through a course of study in philosophy.

---

[1] See Textual Supplement for letter of 29 September 1734. See Michael Morrisroe, Jr., " Did Hume read Berkeley ? A Conclusive Answer," in *Philological Quarterly*, 52 (1973), pp. 314–15. The newly found letter settles the controversy but Morrisroe rightly concludes that the more important question of " the influence that Berkeley's works had upon the young Hume may now be raised anew."

[2] Fernand Baldensperger, " La première relation intellectuelle de David Hume en France : une conjecture," in *Modern Language Notes*, LVII (1942), 268–71. This conjecture, though acute, is proved incorrect by Hume's letter of 29 September 1734.

Bolingbroke's *Substance of some Letters, Written originally in French, about the Year 1720, to Mr de Pouilly* was not published, however, until 1754. For his part, Pouilly published in 1736 a letter, originally written to Bolingbroke, under the title of *Théorie des sentiments agréables*. This aesthetic and ethical work in the tradition of Shaftesbury, Dubos, and Hutcheson would certainly have been agreeable to David Hume; and it is worth noting that the manuscript would have been in the final stages of completion at the time of Hume's stay in Rheims. Also agreeable to Hume would have been the fact that Pouilly had scandalised the French Academy of Inscriptions by expressing doubts of the authenticity of the accepted history of France during the first centuries. Finally, Pouilly was the friend and correspondent of most of the leading men of letters of France.

It is not known whether Pouilly invited the young Scotsman to live with him. We know only that on 12 September Hume's address was : *Monsieur David Hume, Gentilhomme Ecossois, chez Monsieur Mesier, au Peroquet verd proche la porte au feron. Rheims.* Luckily David had already changed the spelling of his name in Bristol. His pride in his social standing as a gentleman is not to be overlooked ; it was beginning to open doors to him in an age of accentuated social distinctions. In his youth he never forgot that, though " not rich ", his family was " good ".

Even in later life, Hume's conversational French was not fluent, and he always retained a Scottish burr which either disgusted or delighted the listener. The ladies, generally, were delighted with it and with David himself. Some slight indication at this early date of Hume's interest in the French girls is perhaps to be found in the quotation in one of his letters of some verses from La Fontaine in their praise. Judging by the letters from Rheims, however, Hume's chief interests lay in the manners and the character of the French, subjects to which the Chevalier had directed his attention. Ramsay had advised him " to observe carefully & imitate as much as possible, the manners of the French. For (says he) tho' the English, perhaps, have more of the real Politeness of the Heart, yet the French certainly have a better way of expressing it." Upon due consideration, " in my humble Opinion," writes Hume, " it is just the Contrary, viz that the French have more real Politeness & the English the better Method of expressing it." Somewhat shamefaced at holding such positive opinions on so difficult a subject after no more than a couple of months in the country, Hume explains the principle of national characters : " you'll please to observe that 'tis with Nations as with particular Man [*sic*], where one Trifle frequently serves more to discover the Character, than a whole Train of considerable Actions." He illustrates this by the different use of, in English, " humble servant," which is omitted upon intimacy, and, in French, " the Honour of being your most humble servant," which is never forgotten. " This Phraze of the Honour of doing or saying such a thing to you goes so far, that my Washing Woman to day told me, that she hopt she shou'd have the Honour of serving me, while I stay'd at Rheims." It is characteristic of Hume that his philosophy is not restricted to the study but partakes of everyday activities. As he himself remarks, " Even to be acquainted with the language of the common people, is a great relief in every country, and supplies many scenes of observation and amusement to a person of a philosophical turn."

David Hume spent a year at Rheims, learning the language, meeting the people, and living a pleasant social life, but he found the city too expensive. Living was costing him £80 a year, he informed Birch, nearly twice his regular income. Leaving Rheims in 1735, Hume journeyed to La Flèche in Anjou, 150 miles south-west of Paris, where the major part of the composition of the *Treatise* was completed. " During my Retreat in France, first at Reims, but chiefly at La fleche in Anjou," he wrote in *My Own Life*, " I composed my *Treatise of human Nature*." La Flèche, it is certain, better suited his avowed purpose " of prosecuting my Studies in a Country Retreat." And it was presumably there that he laid down and began to carry out " that Plan of Life, which I have steddily and successfully pursued : I resolved to make a very rigid Frugality supply my Deficiency of Fortune, to maintain unimpaired my Independency, and to regard every object as contemptible, except the Improvement of my Talents in Literature."

But why La Flèche, it may be legitimate to inquire ? Situated on the Loire River in a hilly wine-growing country, La Flèche was a small and quiet country town with a population not over 5,000, and with nothing to attract the travelling intellectual except a " College of a hundred Jesuits." This college,[1] moreover, was remarkable for having educated René Descartes (who called it " one of the most celebrated schools in all Europe ") and was still in 1735 a centre of Cartesianism—perhaps the ideal place for an anti-Cartesian to rusticate. Of greater importance was the

[1] Described by Sir Andrew Balfour, *Letters Writ to a Friend* (Edinburgh 1700), p. 30.

" cheapness " of the place, which, Hume told " Jemmy " Birch, " has formerly made it so much frequented by our Countreymen, that there was once 30 Englishmen boarded in this small Town." On a later occasion he was even more specific : " I remember, when I lived in Anjou, there came there an English Catholic Lady, Mrs Gage with her two Sons. She took up House there ; and assurd me, that all Provisions were there at a third of the Price, which they were in Suffolk, where she usually liv'd." [1] At La Flèche " the best lodging was *Au quatre Vents* ", wrote Sir Andrew Balfour in 1700 ; but Hume lived elsewhere.

On the vine-covered slopes of Saint-Germain-du-Val, cradled in a slight declivity, lies the manor-house of Yvandeau ; and there, according to local tradition,[2] David Hume dwelt for two years while composing his philosophical masterpiece. A considerable estate, Yvandeau included a little out-of-doors theatre and a subterranean chamber popularly styled " Hell's Mouth," which is said—no doubt with pardonable local pride— to resemble the catacombs of Rome. Hume's own apartment, it may be inferred from a section in the *Treatise* which contains several autobiographical details, was a combined bedroom and study, provided with table, bookcases, fireplace, and windows. It overlooked " a great extent of fields and buildings," " mountains, and houses, and trees." Service included a porter—see, now he opens the door to deliver a letter. " I receive a letter, which upon opening it I perceive by the hand-writing and subscription to have come from a friend, who says he is two hundred leagues distant . . . the whole sea and continent between us. . . ." [3] Roughly figured, Hume's 200 leagues is 600 miles : the letter, therefore, came from a friend in Scotland. From the happy abode at Yvandeau, Hume descended into the town to consult the library at the college, which, at its dissolution by Louis XV in 1762, numbered some 40,000 volumes. According to local tradition and despite the vast differences in their philosophies, Hume maintained cordial relations with the resident Jesuits.

Some years previously, Hume's countryman Lord Fountainhall had had an experience with the Jesuits at Orléans, which may be

---

[1] " Hume at La Flèche, 1735 : An Unpublished Letter," ed. Mossner, in The University of Texas *Studies in English*, xxxvii (1958), p. 32 ; Hume-Elibank, p. 446.
[2] R. de Linière in *Les Annales Fléchoises et la Vallée du Loir*, ix (1908), 244–5. The earliest known reference to Hume at Yvandeau is in F. R. F. Marchant de Burbure, *Essais historiques sur la ville et le collège de la Flèche* (Angers 1803), pp. 25–6.
[3] *Phil. Wks.*, i, 481, 484, 485, 486.

suggestive of the difficulties involved in maintaining cordial relations.[1] " I went also to the Jesuits Colledge," writes Fountainhall, " and discoursed with the *praefectus Jesuitarum*, who earnestly enquiring of what Religion I was, for a long tyme I would give him no other answer but that I was *religione christianus*. He pressing that he smeled I was a Calvinist, I replied that we regarded not these names of Calvin, Luther, Zuinglius, yea not their very persons, but in whow far they hold the truth. After much discourse on indifferent matters, at our parting he desired me to search the spirits, etc."

David's own relations with the Jesuits remained on a better footing. Normally reluctant to indulge in abstract disputation with mere acquaintances, he occasionally broke down.[2] " I was walking in the cloisters of the Jesuits' College of La Flèche," he reveals, " a town in which I passed two years of my youth, and engaged in conversation with a Jesuit of some parts and learning, who was relating to me, and urging some nonsensical miracle performed in their convent, when I was tempted to dispute against him ; and as my head was full of the topics of my *Treatise of Human Nature*, which I was at that time composing, this argument [in the essay " Of Miracles "] immediately occurred to me, and I thought it very much gravelled my companion ; but at last he observed to me, that it was impossible for the argument to have any solidity, because it operated equally against the Gospel as the Catholic Miracles ;—which observation I thought proper to admit as a sufficient answer." The argument that had momentarily gravelled the learned Jesuit was directed, not against the possibility of miracle, but against the proofs of miracle : " That no testimony is sufficient to establish a miracle, unless the testimony be of such a kind, that its falsehood would be more miraculous than the fact, which it endeavours to establish : And even in that case there is a mutual destruction of arguments, and the superior only gives us an assurance suitable to that degree of force, which remains, after deducting the inferior." [3]

Whoever Hume's " Jesuit of some parts and learning " may have been, he most certainly was of a different class from Père Jean-Baptiste-Louis Gresset. Called from the Jesuit College at Tours where he had been teaching the humanities, Gresset in 1735 was temporarily sequestered at La Flèche.[4] Still a scant twenty-

[1] Fountainhall, *Journals*, p. 12.   [2] HL, I, 361.

[3] *Phil. Wks.*, IV, 94.   See also Ch. 22, below.

[4] L. F., " Gresset et Frédéric II," in *Les Annales Fléchoises et la Vallée du Loir*, II (1904), 232–5.

six years old but already a Jesuit for ten years, Gresset had recently attracted the attention of the public, as well as of men of letters, by his deliciously naughty verses on the parrot of Nevers, *Vert-Vert*. The Society of Jesus became disturbed over Gresset, and Gresset became unhappy in the Society of Jesus. At La Flèche he soon petitioned for release from his exile, and, after due time, it was granted him on condition that he resigned from the order. He was delighted to do so and went to Paris, where he made a name for himself as a dramatist. Gresset's story could hardly have failed to reach Humes's ears and it is pleasant to imagine that the two young men may have met and exchanged badinage. In 1752, in his capacity of Keeper of the Advocates' Library in Edinburgh, Hume ordered two items signalising his youthful residence at La Flèche and at Rheims, Gresset's collected works and Pouilly's *Théorie des sentiments agréables*.

Among others, Hume may well have met Francois-Michel de la Rue du Can, mayor of La Flèche in 1735. Many years later he remembered " the agreeable experience of the polite hospitality, by which . . . [France] is distinguished " and the " provincial town, where I enjoyed the advantages of leisure for study, and an opportunity of learning the language. . . ." Perhaps the highest compliment he ever paid La Flèche was the comment of 1756, written at Edinburgh: " Were I to change my habitation, I would retire to some provincial town in France, to trifle out my old age, near a warm sun in a good climate, and amidst a sociable people." [1]

When " Jemmy " Birch wrote to inquire about the advisability of studying under " a celebrated Professor " in France, Hume's reply was sardonic, possibly in remembrance of some of the Edinburgh faculty; it was also a declaration of intellectual independence.[2]

Most likely it was at La Flèche that Hume read in the excellent library of the college many of those French works to which he refers in his publications and which seem so astonishing for a foreigner to have consulted, for instance, Nicolas de Malezieu's *Eléments de Géométrie de M. le duc de Bourgogne*. He would also, in order to be able to converse intelligently with the local faculty, have acquired a first-hand acquaintance—if indeed he did not have it already—with the works of Descartes and Malebranche, Arnauld and Nicole. It is also easy to imagine the vivacious yet searching questions put by the learned Jesuits to the visiting

[1] HL, I, 344–5, 232.   [2] See Textual Supplement for Hume's letter, 1735.

foreigner regarding the recently published *Lettres philosophiques sur les Anglais* by " M. de V——" Everyone knew, of course, that it was the work of Voltaire and was based upon his residence in England, 1726–1729. But had not Voltaire, perhaps suggested Hume's interrogators, exaggerated the extent of freedom in England, especially in matters pertaining to religion and government? What was the truth about the Anglicans? Those odd people, the Quakers? The Presbyterians, who were really no better than Calvinists? What did Hume think of Voltaire's estimates of Descartes and Newton? Of Pope and Swift?

Another incident of Hume's residence in France deserves to be related, although it is not a real incident at all, but only fictional. It is, however, sufficiently true to character to have taken in Adam Smith momentarily : Smith wondered that his good friend had never mentioned it to him while reminiscing of his youth. The incident was published in *The Mirror* during 1779–1780 under the title of " The Story of La Roche," [1] and came from the pen of Henry Mackenzie, who was proud to remember that he had once been David Hume's " literary page." The story opens : " More than forty years ago, an English philosopher, whose works have since been read and admired by all Europe, resided at a little town in France. Some disappointments in his native country had first driven him abroad, and he was afterwards induced to remain there, from having found, in this retreat, where the connections even of nation and language were avoided, a perfect seclusion and retirement highly favourable to the development of abstract subjects, in which he excelled all the writers of his time."

The real significance of Mackenzie's story lies not, however, in the sentimental account of the Swiss Protestant pastor, La Roche, nor of his lovely daughter, but in the character portrayal of David Hume. Mackenzie knew only the older Hume, and his estimate is to be contrasted with that given by the Chevalier Ramsay so far as the latter may be discerned through the screen of prejudice. Both Ramsay and Mackenzie acknowledge the brilliance, liveliness, and inquiring nature of Hume's mind, his ambitious drive, his anti-religious sentiment, and his humanity : but there they part company. The youthful Hume, as seen by Ramsay, was " full of himself," " dissipated with material objects & spiritual Self-Idolatry." The older Hume, as seen by Mackenzie, was character-ised by " the mildness of his manners "—" though he felt no devotion, [he] never quarrelled with it in others "—by " a degree of simplicity and gentleness," " by nothing of that self-importance, which superior parts, or great cultivation of them, is apt to confer." " Of all men I ever knew," writes Mackenzie, " his ordinary conversation was the least tinctured with pedantry, or liable to dissertation." Yet it is not difficult to reconcile the two characterisations, to see the same man in both, for the second is but the mellowing of the first.

But to return to La Flèche. By the middle of 1737, after nearly three years of intensive writing, the *Treatise of Human Nature* was substantially completed. The ideas which earlier in Scotland had proved so intractable had finally fallen into place. " Alone in perfect tranquillity in France," Hume was sanguine that he had been able to deliver his opinions " with such Elegance & Neatness, as to draw to me the Attention of the World." The ultimate testing of any man's systematic thought, however, necessitates its presentation to the world of his peers. In short, it was high time to return to London and to publish.

First to Paris. En route at Tours, on 26 August 1737, Hume wrote to his old friend Michael Ramsay of Mungale, to assure him of his friendship, and to prepare him for the reading of the manuscript of the *Treatise*, by asking him:

. . . to read once over le Recherche de la Verité of Pere Malebranche, the Principles of Human Knowledge by Dr Berkeley, some of the more metaphysical Articles of Bailes Dictionary; such as those [of] Zeno, & Spinoza. Des-Cartes Meditations would also be useful but don't know if you will find it easily among your Acquaintances. These Books will make you easily comprehend the metaphysical Parts of my Reasoning and as to the rest, they have so little Dependence on all former systems of Philosophy, that your natural Good Sense will afford you Light enough to judge of their Force and Solidity.[1]

Hume's brief list of influential thinkers is comprised of two orders: the rationalists (Descartes and Malebranche) to be refuted; the sceptics (Bayle and Berkeley) to be confirmed. Important though it is, the list is rather confirmation than disclosure: all names are mentioned in Book I, " Of the Understanding ", of the *Treatise of Human Nature*,[2] that is, " the metaphysical Parts of my Reasoning." Of greater importance is Hume's firm conviction that the truly original parts of the *Treatise* are to be found, not in the metaphysical, but in the

[1] Hume–Poland, pp. 133–4. See Textual Supplement for full letter of 26 August 1737.
[2] Descartes not by name but implied in " Cartesians ". Publication of the above letter settled the controversy over whether Hume had read Berkeley in the original.

moral " which have so little Dependence on all former systems of Philosophy." This conviction has not been generally shared by his readers in the history of his philosophical works.

Expecting " nothing but Cavilling " from the Chevalier Ramsay, Hume was no doubt relieved to find him unavailable in Paris.

" After passing three years very agreeably in that Countrey," Hume wrote in *My Own Life*, " I came over to London in 1737."

CHAPTER 9

FEVER OF PUBLICATION

"The Nearness & Greatness of the Event . . . made me
more difficult to please."

BACK in London by mid-September 1737 Hume began to seek a
publisher. Buoyant and confident, he was yet feverish with
expectancy in "that dangerous Situation, in which I have
placed myself." By 2 December he could inform Henry Home
at Edinburgh that he had been "alwise within a Week of
agreeing with Printers, & you may imagine I did not forget the
Work itself during that Time, where I began to feel some Passages
weaker for the Style & Diction than I cou'd have wisht. The
Nearness & Greatness of the Event rouz'd up my Attention, &
made me more difficult to please than when I was alone in
perfect Tranquillity in France."[1]

In London from September 1737 to February 1739 David
Hume was neither alone nor in perfect tranquillity. There were
three different worlds in the metropolis that he now had the time
and the opportunity to investigate. And despite his concern over
making an early contract with a publisher, he did learn something
of the great world of court, parliament, and high society ; of the
world of pleasure ; and of the world of letters and learning.
Although Hume, at one time or another during his life, was to
spend upwards of five years in London, he never found it wholly
congenial. Perhaps he was alienated by London contempt for
provincials and Scotsmen. In such an atmosphere he missed the
cosmopolitanism of Paris and France, and even of Edinburgh.

The Scottish politicians and men of letters had already since
the Treaty of Union of 1707 begun the invasion of London, establishing there an outpost that later in the century, for a while,
almost gave them control—at any rate, that was strong enough
to create considerable friction with the English. Hume's Scottish
contacts opened up to him the three worlds of London in so far
as he was interested in entering them. He had little interest, however, in the "great world." Yet there were his neighbours from
the Merse, Lord Polwarth (later third Earl of Marchmont) and
his twin brother Alexander Hume-Campbell. Both were M.P.s.

[1] NHL, pp. 1-2.
106

Lord Polwarth supplied Hume with franked letters, as also did Alexander Brodie, member for Caithness, and, likely enough, other Scottish members. Lord Islay, to become the third Duke of Argyle in 1743, was Keeper of the Great Seal and very close to Queen Caroline ; he prided himself that he might be approached by any gentleman of North Britain. That Hume attended one of his levees, and probably at this time, is certain, and he later acknowledged him to be " undoubtedly a Man of Sense & Learning."

Important events happening in court circles were common gossip, and intimate titbits would be passed on to the young man by his friends and acquaintances in high society. On 12 September 1737 Frederick, Prince of Wales, with his wife Augusta, and their family, was banished from St James's Palace as the result of a protracted feud with his father and mother, the King and Queen. Crowds of Londoners lining the streets dissolved in tears as the royal carriages passed by on their way to Kew. Frederick became, for a while, the focus of union of all those who opposed the power of the Prime Minister, Sir Robert Walpole, and of those who disliked their still half foreign King and Queen for maintaining such close ties with Hanover. Caroline the Illustrious, as she was fondly known by admirers, martyr to George II's irascibility of temperament and to his German mistresses, and patron of philosophers and theologians, scientists, and men of letters, died painfully and unhappily at ten o'clock on Sunday night, 20 November 1737. Rumour had it that she had refused all religious consolations and, with her dying breath, had urged the King to retain Walpole as Prime Minister and to promote Dr Joseph Butler, her Clerk of the Closet. She was duly rewarded with her husband's sobbing resolve never to marry again but only to keep mistresses.

One of Hume's essays of 1742 throws some light upon his activities in London in the worlds of pleasure and of letters.[1] " We are told," he remarks, " that, when Demosthenes was to plead, all ingenious men flocked to Athens from the most remote parts of Greece, as to the most celebrated spectacle of the world. At London you may see men sauntering in the court of requests, while the most important debate is carrying on in the two houses ; and many do not think themselves sufficiently compensated, for the losing of their dinners, by all the eloquence of our most celebrated speakers. When old Cibber is to act, the curiosity of

[1] *Phil. Wks.*, III, 165–6.

several is more excited, than when our prime minister is to defend himself from a motion for his removal or impeachment." Law courts, Parliament, and theatre, these are fitting scenes for the student of law, of eloquence, and of the arts—and for the student of human nature.

Hume knew his theatre, both French and English, and vastly preferred the classical simplicity of the former to the Shakespearean complexities of the latter. In the essay just referred to, he comments that the English " in general are not remarkable for delicacy of taste, or for sensibility to the charms of the muses. . . . Hence their comic poets, to move them, must have recourse to obscenity ; their tragic poets to blood and slaughter. . . ." We have no record of Hume's theatrical attendance during the seventeen months in London, 1737–1739, yet he had the opportunity of seeing at Covent Garden and Drury Lane theatres no fewer than sixteen different plays of Shakespeare, several of Ben Jonson, and many of the Restoration and earlier eighteenth-century dramatists. The recent Licensing Act influenced theatrical managers to revive old plays rather than to risk putting on new ones. At the Haymarket Theatre Hume had the choice of half-a-dozen Italian operas.

New plays by David Mallet and James Thomson, both Scots and former students of Edinburgh University, we may presume Hume went to see. Mallet, who had preceded him at Edinburgh by one term, he probably knew already ; Thomson had given up the study of divinity at about the time that Hume entered. Thomson's *Agamemnon* was put on at the Drury Lane Theatre 6 April 1738 and ran for nine nights with Quin in the leading role and Mrs Cibber as Cassandra. Andrew Mitchell, a classmate of Hume's at Edinburgh, had been in London since 1735, being called to the English bar in 1738. Later distinguished as British Envoy to the court of Frederick the Great, Mitchell was a good friend of James Thomson and provided the inquisitive Boswell with anecdotes concerning the dramatist's first nights. On such occasions Thomson, on the authority of Mitchell, was wont to sweat so much " that when he came and met his friends at a tavern in the Piazza, his wig was as if it had been dip'd in an Oil-pot." [1] It is by no means unlikely that David Hume was in the group that

[1] *Boswell Papers*, III, 37. In a letter to Hume of 27 July 1764, Sir Alexander Dick writes : " This comes to your hand by . . . Mr. Sargent, who I dare say you will remember a great while ago in the days of Mr. Thomson and Mr. Mitchel the ambassador with whomme we used to associate in those days " (RSE, IV, 75). John Sargent was a linen draper near Mercer's Chapel in London.

fêted Thomson after the *première* of *Agamemnon* and drank toasts in his honour. A similar occasion was provided by Mallet's *Mustapha*, 13 February 1739, on the eve of Hume's departure for Scotland.

Dr John Armstrong, another Edinburgh man already known to David Hume and a close friend of Thomson, had been in London since 1735 building up a medical practice. He was succeeding well in 1736 when he had the temerity to publish verses on *The Oeconomy of Love*, which offered practical advice to young men on the *art d'amour*. His medical career nearly wrecked as a result, Armstrong sought to make amends the following year with a professional *Synopsis of the History and Cure of Venereal Diseases*. His *Art of Preserving Health* of 1744 was " truly classical," David Hume informed Boswell many years later ; his *Oeconomy of Love*, " very poetical." On another occasion, according to Boswell, " Mr. Hume said that Armstrong's *Art of Preserving Health* was the most classical Poem in the english language, that Thomson's *Seasons* had more luxuriance or splendour, but that it had not order and the transitions were rude." [1]

Michael Ramsay of Mungale, Hume's boyhood companion, was in London during the latter part of 1738 and, man of the world that he was, would have made ideal company for the theatre and for visits to Vauxhall Gardens. Still London's main highway, as in the days of Shakespeare, the Thames afforded the approach to Vauxhall, the city's boast by way of outdoor entertainment. Symmetrically formal gardens flanked with semicircular dining pavilions provided strange contrasts of classic, Gothic, and Chinese motifs in design and architecture. The thickly planted groves, according to the description in a contemporary guide-book, " are the verdant abode of nightingales, blackbirds, thrushes, and other feathered minstrels, who, in the most delightful season of the year, ravish the ears of the company with their harmony." In the shadows of the gardens, amorous couples strolled ; in the open spaces, ballad-singers warbled ; in the pavilions, ladies and gentlemen dined and wined. Despite the air of delicious scandal that always pervaded Vauxhall—perhaps because of it—everyone went there.

" Notwithstanding all the Pleasures of the Town," Hume wrote to Henry Home early in 1738, upon learning of his possible visit to London, " I woud certainly engage you to pass some philosophical Evenings with me, & either correct my Judgement,

[1] *Boswell Papers*, i, 127 ; xi, 40.

where you differ from me or confirm it where we agree." The indications are that David devoted most of his evenings, not to the pleasures of the town, but to philosophical conversation, probably often at the Rainbow Coffeehouse, where he joined another Edinburgh University man, Alexander Cunningham (later Sir Alexander Dick) and resided for upwards of a year after March 1738. At the Rainbow in Lancaster Court there gathered a not undistinguished group of exiled French Protestants, one of whom at least, Pierre Desmaizeaux, became Hume's acquaintance. Himself a man of letters, the biographer and literary executor of Pierre Bayle and once a friend of such liberal spirits as Anthony Collins, Lord Shaftesbury and Addison, Desmaizeaux was surely a proper adviser for a young man at the opening of his literary career. He was also the London correspondent of certain Continental periodicals, and some interesting consequences of this fact and of his acquaintance with Hume were to become apparent after the publication of the *Treatise*.

But to return to that work. At the request of an unnamed gentleman in London, Hume had in vain attempted to make an abridgment of it so that its purport could more easily be comprehended ; nor did he succeed even at a similar request from Henry Home. As the months crept past, Hume toyed with the notion of going down to Scotland to visit Henry and other friends and to " have your Advice concerning my philosophical Discoveries." But curiously a new frustration set in : " a certain Shamefacedness I have to appear among you at my Years without having yet a Settlement or so much as having attempted any." No established career at the advanced age of twenty-six ! The humour of the situation or, at least, its irony did not entirely escape the earnest young man. " How happens it that we Philosophers cannot as heartily despise the World as it despises us ? I think in my Conscience the Contempt were as well founded on our Side as on the other." [1]

Now that publication seemed imminent, a second frustration began to harass Hume. Was he being sufficiently prudent ? Was there anything in the manuscript which, " even as the World is dispos'd at present," might land him in trouble with the authorities ? Could a proper balance be maintained between courage and prudence ? It was one thing in France to uphold Voltaire's account of the unlimited freedom of the English press ; it was quite another in England to publish original thoughts with

[1] NHL, p. 2.

daring implications and to face the possible consequences. The "Jesuitical" analysis of miracles, for example, was almost certain to give offence. It would hardly do to let even Dr Butler see it, and yet Hume was greatly interested in learning Dr Butler's opinion of his philosophy. He had already written to Henry Home about Butler and was pleased to find that Henry too held the same high opinion of that divine ; David was further delighted to find out that Henry had met Butler personally and would gladly furnish a letter of introduction.

The name of Joseph Butler had long been familiar to Hume. Under the unpromising title of *Fifteen Sermons preached at the Rolls Chapel* (1726), Butler had actually made an important contribution to the study of ethics, one that shuns inquiry into " the abstract relation of things " and begins with " matter of fact, namely, what the particular nature of man is, its several parts, their economy or constitution ; from whence it proceeds to determine what course of life it is which is correspondent to this whole nature." [1] On Hume's return from France, he would immediately have heard of a new book of Butler's published within the year. This was the *Analogy of Religion, Natural and Revealed, to the Constitution and Course of Nature* (1736), a dispassionate and well-reasoned work, designed to convince the Deists by empirical arguments that their refutations of Christianity were equally valid against their own Religion of Nature. The *Analogy* was to remain the one theological work of the century that Hume was to deem worthy of serious consideration and whose author was always to be highly respected by him.[2]

In the spring of 1737 Henry Home, on a visit to London, was anxious to meet Butler, then Clerk of the Closet to Queen Caroline and Dean of St Paul's. Applying to Lord Islay, Home was told, " I know not how to get you introduced but by introducing You to the Queen, and She will introduce You to her favourite Chaplain." [3] Discouraged by this prospect, Home finally went to Butler's residence and brazened an entrance. He was courteously received and offered a dish of chocolate. After two hours of pleasant conversation, the Scottish lawyer-philosopher left, to return later for a second interview. On the basis of this short and forced acquaintance, Henry provided David with a letter of introduction which, the latter was afraid, stretched " the Truth in Favour of a Friend. I have call'd upon the Dr," he wrote, however, in March

---

[1] Butler, Preface to *Sermons*.
[2] The *Analogy*, though unnamed, is discernible in Cleanthes' empirical arguments in Hume's *Dialogues*.   [3] *Boswell Papers*, xv, 292-3.

1738, " with a Design of delivering him your Letter ; but find he is at present in the Countrey. I am a little anxious to have the Dr's Opinion. My own I dare not trust to, both because it concerns myself, & because it is so variable, that I know not how to fix it. Sometimes it elevates me above the Clouds : At other times it depresses me with Doubts & Fears ; so that whatever be my Success I cannot be entirely disappointed."

Before attempting to meet Butler, Hume submitted his manuscript to drastic surgery, a section on miracles which he had composed at La Flèche being cut out. " I am at present castrating my Work," he had informed Henry Home the previous December, " that is, cutting off its noble Parts, that is, endeavouring it shall give as little Offence as possible ; before which I cou'd not pretend to put it into the Drs hands." The letter proceeds, " This is a piece of Cowardice, for which I blame myself ; tho I believe none of my Friends will blame me. But I was resolv'd not to be an Enthusiast, in Philosophy, while I was blaming other Enthusiasms." Although he was to print on the title-page of the *Treatise* a motto from Tacitus pointing out the rare felicity of the times when a man could think freely and publish freely, Hume retained a characteristic caution. The excised " Reasonings concerning Miracles " he sent to friend Henry with the request for a candid opinion both as to argument and to style. " I beg of you show it to no Body, except to Mr Hamilton, if he pleases ; & let me know at your Leizure that you have receiv'd it, read it, & burnt it. I wou'd not even have you make another nameless Use of it, to which it wou'd not be improper, for fear of Accidents." What Willy Hamilton thought of the performance, if he actually saw it, remains unknown ; but Henry Home advised total suppression. It was not restored to its original place in the *Treatise*.

During the 1730s London was in a ferment of philosophical-religious controversy. It was a period of easy publication ; and, seemingly, almost everyone who could write rushed into print. The Deists, adherents of the Religion of Nature (or Religion of Reason), as opposed to the Christian Religion of Revelation, were taking advantage of the freedom of publication to press their case. Matthew Tindal's *Christianity as old as the Creation : Or, the Gospel, a Republication of the Religion of Nature*, which had appeared in the first year of the decade, was at once received as " the Deist's Bible." The implications of the sub-title, though never fully exploited by the learned Fellow of All Souls himself, were yet generally recognised and drew replies from more than 150 of the more orthodox, of which Butler's *Analogy* was but the foremost. On a somewhat different level, Pope's brilliant philosophical poem, the *Essay on Man*, was calling forth answer after answer in dull and heavy prose. Finally, in 1739, the strongest concerted effort of orthodoxy, the Boyle Lectures, were published under the title of *A Defence of Natural and Revealed Religion*. Into this atmosphere of controversy, Hume would inevitably have been plunged had he insisted upon retaining the section " Of Miracles." His decision not to do so is an indication that what he was counting on was serious consideration of his philosophy as philosophy, rather than as religious controversy. The decision— little perhaps did he realise it at the moment—was momentous : it was to dictate the turn of his career.

His philosophy, Hume was confident, would put an end to all such controversies as that between the Deists and the Christians by proving that both sides were wrong, that rationalistic proof of matters of fact is as invalid as authoritarian proof, that the scope of analogy is strictly delimited. The publication of the *Treatise*, he felt certain, would cause a tremendous stir in the intellectual world. " My Principles," he informed Henry Home with perhaps pardonable pride, " are . . . so remote from all the vulgar Sentiments on this Subject, that were they to take place, they wou'd produce almost a total Alteration in Philosophy. . . ." [1] No wonder he was eager to publish ! The chief wonder is that he took so long, somewhat more than a year, to reach an agreement with a publisher. Three determinations of his own, in this regard, proved obstacles and require explanation.

First, Hume was determined to be absolutely independent and not to seek the patronage of " the great," whether by soliciting subscriptions or by making a public dedication to some great man. Second, he was determined to publish anonymously, in accordance with a well-established contemporary practice. Locke, for instance, had published the first edition of his *Essay concerning Humane Understanding* (1690) without his name on the title-page but, inconsistently, had signed the Epistle Dedicatory ; the second edition was acknowledged. Within the early lifetime of Hume, the philosophical works of Baxter, Hutcheson, Mandeville, and Wollaston, to mention but a few of many, had all appeared anonymously ; Hutcheson, in particular, never put his name to any of his English writings. Third, Hume was determined to sell the rights to a first edition only, reserving for himself the rights to any

[1] NHL, p. 3.

future edition ; he also refused to contract in advance for any further volume or volumes that might be added to the *Treatise*. These three terms spelt difficulty and ultimately required corresponding concessions on Hume's part when he and John Noon signed articles of agreement on 26 September 1738.[1]

John Noon, at the White Hart, near Mercer's Chapel in Cheapside, was a publisher of some importance in the realms of general learning, philosophy, and religion. In addition to an interminable number of sermons, his list includes the several encyclopaedias for students by Benjamin Martin, translations from the Greek, an index of Greek manuscripts, controversial works against Baxter, Butler, and Wollaston, a " defence " of Christianity by the Deist Thomas Morgan, and various studies in surgery. In 1740 and 1741 Noon brought out two works of George Turnbull, *Principles of Moral Philosophy*, in two volumes, and a translation of Heineccius' *Methodical System of Universal Law*, also in two volumes.[2] Turnbull, who held an LL.D. from Edinburgh, was Professor of Moral Philosophy at Marischal College, Aberdeen, and had been the teacher of Thomas Reid, who was to become Hume's most important philosophical antagonist in Scotland.

How Hume met John Noon is not known. One might think that he would have approached Andrew Millar, a Scot but four years his senior, who had already published Thomson's *Seasons*. Perhaps he did, but without reaching an agreement ; it is probable that the two became acquainted at this time, because in 1742 Millar was one of three to handle the London sales of Hume's *Essays*, and six years later became his chief London publisher. But in 1738, according to the terms of the contract, Hume assigned to Noon all rights for a first edition of the *Treatise of Human Nature* in two volumes octavo, the said edition to be limited to 1,000 copies, for the sum of £50 payable in six months, and twelve bound copies of the work upon publication. Upon penalty of £50 Hume, for his part, agreed not to publish a second edition unless he bought from Noon at the standard booksellers' price all unsold copies of the first edition. The agreement, then, carries out Hume's notions concerning publication but at the cost of some restriction upon a

---

[1] MS " Articles of Agreement . . . Between David Hume of Lancaster Court . . . and John Noone of Cheapside . . .," in RSE, IX, 5.

[2] A list of twenty-one books published by Noon is printed at the end of Turnbull's 1740 publication and a list of eighty-three, at the end of his 1741 publication. Hume's *Treatise* is included in the first list only.

second edition. Noon's investment was safe ; and although he can hardly have made a large profit, he never regretted the bargain, and in 1740 was quite willing to bring out a third volume. Hume, however, was convinced almost from the beginning that he had conceded too much in the matter of limitations upon a second edition. By 1740 he could say, " I concluded somewhat of a hasty Bargain with my Bookseller from Indolence & an Aversion to Bargaining, as also because I was told that few or no Bookseller[s] wou'd engage for one Edition with a new Author."

" I have found by Experience," admitted Hume late in life, " that nothing excites an Author's Attention so much as the receiving the Proofs from the Press, as the Sheets are gradually thrown off." Thus the closing months of 1738 were probably among the most exciting in Hume's career, for a first book is always the most important to an author. Finally, in the last week of January 1739, John Noon published *A Treatise of Human Nature : Being an Attempt to introduce the experimental Method of Reasoning into Moral Subjects.* " Book I, Of the Understanding. Book II, Of the Passions. Ten Shillings." The third volume " Of Morals," the manuscript of which was still in the process of revision, did not appear until early November 1740, and then by a different publisher, Thomas Longman. During 1739, however, Hume's anxiety was that of a new parent. His revolutionary thoughts had been placed before the learned world. Would they produce the anticipated " total Alteration in Philosophy " ? And what, in fact, had they produced in the realm of Hume's own beliefs and feelings ?

In a mood of " philosophical melancholy " in the conclusion to Book I, Hume had given poignant expression to his doubts and fears :

I am first affrighted and confounded with that forelorn solitude, in which I am plac'd in my philosophy, and fancy myself some strange uncouth monster, who not being able to mingle and unite in society, has been expell'd all human commerce, and left utterly abandon'd and disconsolate. Fain wou'd I run into the crowd for shelter and warmth ; but cannot prevail with myself to mix with such deformity. I call upon others to join me, in order to make a company apart ; but no one will hearken to me. Every one keeps at a distance, and dreads that storm, which beats upon me from every side. I have expos'd myself to the enmity of all metaphysicians, logicians, mathematicians, and even theologians ; and can I wonder at the insults I must suffer ? I have declar'd my dis-approbation of their systems ; and can I be surpriz'd, if they shou'd express a hatred of mine and of my person ? When I look abroad, I foresee on every side, dispute, contradiction, anger, calumny and detraction. When I turn my eye inward, I find nothing but doubt and ignorance. All the world conspires to oppose and contradict me ; tho' such is my weakness, that I feel all my opinions loosen and fall of themselves, when unsupported by the approbation of others. Every step I take is with hesitation, and every new reflection makes me dread an error and absurdity in my reasoning.

But the melancholy mood was soon dispelled :

> Most fortunately it happens, that since reason is incapable of dispelling these clouds, nature herself suffices to that purpose, and cures me of this philosophical melancholy and delirium, either by relaxing this bent of mind, or by some avocation, and lively impression of my senses, which obliterate all these chimeras. I dine, I play a game of backgammon, I converse, and am merry with my friends ; and when after three or four hours' amusement, I wou'd return to these speculations, they appear so cold, and strain'd, and ridiculous, that I cannot find in my heart to enter into them any farther.[1]

That nature will prevail is central in the Humean teaching. " Be a philosopher ; but amidst all your philosophy, be still a man," he cautioned himself as well as others. Hume's ability to follow his own precept was soon to be put to the acid test.

---

[1] *Phil. Wks.*, 1, 544–5 ; 548–9.

CHAPTER 10

A TREATISE OF HUMAN NATURE

"Never literary Attempt was more unfortunate. . . . It fell
dead-born from the Press."

AT the close of his life David Hume had no lingering doubts about
the vitality of the first offspring of his intellect ; he was convinced
that it had never been alive. " Never literary Attempt was more
unfortunate than my Treatise of Human Nature," he wrote in
My Own Life ; " It fell *dead-born from the Press* [1] ; without reaching
such distinction as even to excite a Murmur among the Zealots."
The issue might seem settled once and for all by this unequivocal
statement, yet there is evidence to the contrary. First, the *Treatise*
was sufficiently alive in 1745 to lose for Hume the Professorship
of Ethics and Pneumatical Philosophy at Edinburgh University.
Secondly, after a quiescent period of more than a decade, the
" Murmur among the Zealots " began to rise in the 1750s, reaching
something like a roar in the 1770s. Thirdly, before the end of the
eighteenth century, the ideas of the *Treatise* began to filter through
to important thinkers, until, in the twentieth century, that work
has finally been recognised as Hume's supreme philosophical
effort. While the world has not really been willing to let the
Treatise die, an author must write primarily for his own age and
only secondarily for posterity. Though Hume's statement in *My
Own Life* by no means tells the whole story, the immediate reception of the *Treatise* was certainly not such as to lend him encouragement.

Under no illusion about the likelihood of popular sales, Hume
was not at all interested in sales merely for their own sake. A
fortnight after publication, he wrote to Henry Home : " In
looking over your Letters I find one of a twelve-month's Date,
wherein you desire me to send down a great many Copys to
Scotland. You propos'd no doubt to take the Pains of recom-
mending them, & pushing the Sale. But to tell the Truth there
is so little to be gain'd that way in such Works as these, that I

---

[1] All, all but truth, drops dead-born from the press,
Like the last Gazette, or the last Address.

Pope, *Epil. Sat.*, II, 226–7.

wou'd not have you take the Trouble." The essential point, he recognised, is not how *many* people read the philosophy, but *who* reads it. So Hume inquires whether his friend knows anyone " that is a Judge. . . . Tis so rare to meet with one, that will take Pains on a Book, that does not come recommended by some great Name or Authority, that, I must confess, I am as fond of meeting with such a one, as if I were sure of his Approbation." He realises, of course, that the learned world is not apt to react hastily and that he must be patient. " I thought it wou'd contribute very much to my Tranquillity," he naïvely confesses, " & might spare me many Mortifications, to be in the Countrey, while the Success of the Work was doubtful." [1] So the anxious philosopher decided to go back to his family at Ninewells.

For over three weeks in February Hume was detained in London by " contrary Winds, which . . . kept all Berwick-Ships from sailing." This storm, which immediately followed an eclipse of the moon, did severe damage to the eastern seaboard of Scotland, extending into the Merse and Chirnside, and possibly to Ninewells. [2] During the forced stay in London, copies of the *Treatise* were presented to friends in that city. One was given to Pierre Desmaizeaux, another to Dr Butler. " I have sent the Bishop of Bristol a Copy," Hume informed Henry Home ; " but cou'd not wait on him with your Letter after he had arriv'd at that Dignity : At least I thought it wou'd be to no Purpose, after I begun the Printing." Hume also sent a copy to Alexander Pope, with an anonymous inscription. [3] On reaching Ninewells early in March, other copies were distributed to his family and friends.

Just before leaving London, Hume had clarified his position to Michael Ramsay : " As to myself, no Alteration has happen'd in my Fortune, nor have I taken the least Step towards it. I hope things will be riper next Winter ; & I wou'd not aim at any thing till I cou'd judge of my Success in my grand Undertaking, & see upon what footing I shall stand in the World. I am afraid, however, that I shall not have any great Success of a sudden. Such Performances make their way very heavily at first, when they are not recommended by any great Name or Authority." Sound common sense this, to wait a year in order to determine his standing in the world.

Patience hardly characterised Hume while waiting. Everyone was so slow in reading the *Treatise* and in making up his mind about it ! You could hardly expect to hear from the Bishop of

[1] NHL, pp. 4, 3.   [2] *Gent.'s Mag.*, IX (1739), 45.   [3] See Textual Supplement.

Bristol, but surely you could from your friends. There was Harry Home, for instance, who had previously been so interested in metaphysics. " I shall present you with a Copy as soon as I come to Scotland," David had written from London, " & hope your Curiosity as well as Friendship will make you take the Pains of perusing it." Yet at first, Henry had positively refused so much as to read the two volumes. In 1778 the then Lord Kames related the incident to Boswell, who thus reports it :

About a Month after, David came back and begged he would read them to oblige him, Said My Lord : " I'll do any thing to oblige you. But you must sit by and try to beat your Book into my head." He did so. Yet My Lord had no more than a glimmering of what was his meaning. Some time after this, My Lord, who had a farm in the country and had got up at six in a may Morning when there was nothing to do in the fields, took up David's Book, and as a proof that thoughts ripen in the Mind imperceptibly, he read it, to his astonishment, with the clearest understanding. And he sat down and wrote Observations upon it. David, who used to come frequently to him, came soon after. " Well, David, I'll tell you News. I understand your book quite well." He shewed him his Objections, and David, who was not very ready to yield, acknowledged he was right in every one of them.[1]

Henry Home's observations on the *Treatise* are not extant, but he was to speak his mind in print at a later period. According to Boswell, " He said he Never did think as David does in that Treatise."

As early as April 1739 the impatient Hume had written to Pierre Desmaizeaux " at Chaugnion's Bookseller in the Strand London," to inquire about his opinion of the *Treatise* :

Whenever you see my Name, you'll readily imagine the Subject of my Letter. A young Author can scarce forbear speaking of his Performances to all the World : But when he meets with one, that is a good Judge, & whose Instruction & Advice he depends on, there ought some Indulgence to be given him. You were so good as to promise me, that, if you cou'd find Leizure from your other Occupations, you woud look over my System of Philosophy, & at the same time ask the Opinion of such of your Acquaintance as you thought proper Judges. Have you found it sufficiently intelligible ? Does it appear true to you ? Do the Style & Language seem tolerable ? These three Questions comprehend every thing ; & I beg of you to answer them with the utmost Freedom & Sincerity.

No direct reply to this charmingly eager letter has survived ; but there are signs of an indirect reaction. Desmaizeaux was the London correspondent of a French periodical published at Amsterdam, the *Bibliothèque raisonnée des ouvrages des savans de*

---

[1] *Boswell Papers*, xv, 273-4.

l'Europe. In the issue for the second quarter of 1739 in the "Literary News from London" appeared a brief notice opening, "A Gentleman, named Mr. *Hume*, has published *A Treatise of Human Nature* . . .," and closing, "Those who demand the new will find satisfaction here. The author reasons on his own grounds ; he goes to the bottom of things and traces out new routes. He is very original." [1]

Here was reason for Hume to be both pleased and dismayed —pleased with the complimentary tone and dismayed at the public release of his name. Already in February Hume had remarked in a letter, " . . . I have endeavour'd all I cou'd to conceal my Name ; tho' I believe I have not been so cautious in this respect as I ought to have been." Thirteen months later he was finally to concede, " I was also determin'd to keep my Name a Secret for some time tho I find I have fail'd in that Point." Desmaizeaux was one of the few, except close personal friends, who were in the secret ; and it seems likely that it was Desmaizeaux who revealed it. If so, it was also he who wrote the friendly puff in the *Bibliothèque raisonnée*, which, in the event, was to prove the only friendly comment ever published during his lifetime.

The honour of the first notice of Hume's *Treatise* in a learned journal belongs, however, not to the *Bibliothèque raisonnée*, but to the *Neuen Zeitungen von gelehrten Sachen*, published at Leipzig. Dated 28 May 1739, this notice is so short and its tone so typically hostile that it may be given here in full :

A new free-thinker has published an exhaustive *Treatise of Human Nature*, 2 volumes, octavo. In it he attempts to introduce the correct method of philosophising into moral matters, examining and explaining, first of all, the characteristics of the human understanding and then the effects. The author's evil intentions are sufficiently betrayed in the sub-title of the work, taken from Tacitus : *Rara temporum felicitas, ubi sentire, quae velis ; & quae sentias, dicere, licet.*

More friendly was the notice in the *Nouvelle bibliothèque, ou histoire littéraire des principaux écrits qui se publient*, appearing at The Hague in October 1739. The reviewer comments : " Although the ideas of the author approach closely in some places to those of Dr *Hutcheson* on the moral sentiment and on the human passions, there are yet many original things in this new treatise, which, however, is only the commencement of a more extended and more complete work." But another periodical of The Hague, the

[1] For fuller text and discussion of this and other Continental reviews following, see Mossner, " The Continental Reception of Hume's *Treatise*, 1739-1741," in *Mind*, LVI (1947), 31-43.

Bibliothèque britannique, ou histoire des ouvrages des sçavans de la Grande-Bretagne, was severe in its notice in the issue for the last quarter of 1739 : " This is a system of logic, or rather of metaphysics, as original as can be, in which the author claims to rectify the most ingenious philosophers, particularly the famous Mr *Locke*, and in which he advances the most unheard-of paradoxes, even to maintaining that the operations of the mind are not free."

None of the accounts of the *Treatise*, so far mentioned, were genuine reviews. The custom of the learned journals of the day was to print a descriptive notice as soon as possible after publication, and to return later, if the work was deemed sufficiently important, for a full-scale review. So the Continental journals reviewed the *Treatise* only in 1740.

In the meanwhile, what was happening in England? Practically nothing, because 1739–1740 was a most unfortunate period for the reviewing of books. The *Gentleman's Magazine* of London and its counterpart and rival in Edinburgh, the *Scots Magazine*, did not go in for reviewing at all, resting content with mere lists of the publications of the month. Thus both magazines name the *Treatise* in their numbers for January 1739. Before the establishment of the great reviews of the later eighteenth century, the *Monthly* and the *Critical*, Hume could expect the *Treatise* to be given serious consideration only in the *History of the Works of the Learned*. Each month, therefore, during the summer he eagerly scanned the pages of that London periodical. When in October silence still reigned, he resolved to take measures himself.

At least twice already Hume had failed in attempts to prepare an abstract of the *Treatise*. Now in October and November he tried once more, and this time successfully. The effort was to take the form of an anonymous letter to the editor of the *History of the Works of the Learned*, commenting on and explaining the main contributions to thought of the *Treatise of Human Nature*—a puff, if you please, of a neglected book. The practice of an author's puffing his own work or of having it puffed by his friends has had a long and honourable history. But before Hume could send his abstract up to London, the November issue of that journal had appeared. There, finally, was the long-awaited review, and so extensive was it as to require continuation in the December issue ; in all, it came to forty-six pages.[1]

The stated boast on the masthead of the *History of the Works of the Learned* was that it contained " Impartial Accounts and

[1] *History of the Works of the Learned* (1739²), 353–90 ; 391–404.

Accurate Abstracts of the most valuable Books published in *Great-Britain* and Foreign Parts." How true this was may be verified immediately. The reviewer begins : " I do not recollect any Writer in the *English* Language who has framed a System of human Nature, morally considered, upon the Principle of this Author, which is that of Necessity, in Opposition to Liberty or Freedom." Like most eighteenth-century reviews, this one is composed largely of quotations from the original, interlarded with editorial comments. These latter reveal the deep-set personal animus of the writer : " Our Author has sufficiently (he says) explained the Design of this Work of his in the Introduction. Perhaps he expects we should understand it by the following Passages. . . . Here the Reader has all that I can find in the Introduction to this Work, which can in the least give him any Idea of the Design of it : How far he will be thereby instructed in it, must be left to his own Judgment. . . ."

The rancour of the reviewer is undisguised, and few opportunities to display it are let slip. A footnote gibes : " This Work abounds throughout with *Egotisms*. The Author would scarcely use that Form of Speech more frequently, if he had written his own Memoirs." Frequent ironical thrusts are directed at " Our author " : "agreeable to his Sagacity" ; "the superior Capacity of our Author" ; "he goes on, full as wisely as he begun " ; " this extraordinary Philosopher " ; " our Author's superlative Modesty " ; " he assumes the Air of a Sphinx, only not attended with the horrible Cruelty of that Monster " ; " the Depth of this great Mathematician's Erudition " ; " this incomparable Arguer " ; " so profound and accurate a Genius " ; and so on *ad nauseam*, as it must have seemed to Hume.

The treatment of the philosophy, rather than of the philosopher, is all of a piece : raillery and falsification. The raillery may be illustrated by a passage dealing with Hume's principle " that all our Ideas are copied from our Impressions " :

I have afore hinted the mighty Value of this Discovery, the Honour of which is intirely due to our Author, but it cannot be too often inculcated. I verily think, if it were closely pursued, it would lead us to several inestimable *Desiderata*, such as the *perpetual Motion*, the *grand Elixir*, a *Dissolvent of the Stone*, &c. Many Wonders have been done in the Republick of Letters by a single and very simple Principle ; tho' I question if any may compare with the above-mentioned, except that of *M. Leibnitz*. Every one has heard, what an immense Field of Knowledge he opened by his *sufficient Reason*, and how much wiser the World is by it, at this Day. Such Benefactors to Mankind will always be the Admiration of Posterity.

Perhaps the best illustration of the reviewer's deliberate falsification (and one that was to plague Hume throughout life by repeti-
tion on the part of other opponents) is to be found in that passage
dealing with Part III, Section XV, of Book I of the *Treatise*.
There Hume had written :

> According to the precedent doctrine, there are no objects, which by the
> mere survey, without consulting experience, we can determine to be the
> causes of any other ; and no objects, which we can certainly determine in
> the same manner not to be the causes. Any thing may produce any thing. Crea-
> tion, annihilation, motion, reason, volition ; all these may arise from one
> another, or from any other object we can imagine.

Omitting the qualification, " without consulting experience," the
reviewer reprints the next two sentences, and seizes upon the
opportunity presented to sneer : " A most charming System indeed ! one can hardly conceive the Uses it may be put to, and
the different Purposes it will serve : It is to be hoped, the inimitable
Inventor will one Day give us a large and ample Account of them."
The reviewer then proceeds to elaborate upon " our Author's
Doctrine, ' That *any thing* may produce any thing.' "
The second instalment of the review ends on a note so completely different as to invite comment. The passage will be
presented in full :

> Perhaps I have already and sufficiently answered the End of this Article,
> which is to make the Treatise it refers to more generally known than I think
> it has been ; to bring it, as far as I am able, into the Observation of the
> Learned, who are the proper Judges of its Contents, who will give a Sanction
> to its Doctrines, where they are true and useful, and who have Authority to
> correct the Mistakes where they are of a different Nature ; and lastly, to hint
> to the ingenious Writer, whoever he is, some Particulars in his Performance,
> that may require a very serious Reconsideration. It bears indeed incontestable
> Marks of a great Capacity, of a soaring Genius, but young, and not yet
> thoroughly practised. The Subject is vast and noble as any that can exercise
> the Understanding ; but it requires a very mature Judgment to handle it as
> becomes its Dignity and Importance ; the utmost Prudence, Tenderness and
> Delicacy, are requisite to this desirable Issue. Time and Use may ripen
> these Qualities in our Author ; and we shall probably have Reason to consider
> this, compared with his later Productions, in the same Light as we view the
> *Juvenile* Works of *Milton*, or the first Manner of a *Raphael*, or other celebrated
> Painter.

This final passage, it may be inferred, is the product of another
hand, likely enough that of the editor of the periodical himself,
weary with the prolonged abuse heaped upon the anonymous
author. Who, then, wrote the main body of the review ? There
is no direct evidence, but it may be conjectured that it was William

Warburton, later the Bishop of Gloucester, the colossus of eighteenth-century controversy.[1] It is as certain as can be, however, that Warburton did not know that the author of the *Treatise* was David Hume, for we find him in 1749 inquiring into the identity of that philosopher.[2]

The affair of the Warburtonian review—if it may justly be so called—would be incomplete without reference to the well-known apocryphal anecdote of Hume's violent reactions to it. This account first appeared in the *London Review* a year after Hume's death as part of a comment on *My Own Life*, and was apparently written by the editor, Dr William Kenrick. In a fit of " violent rage " over the treatment of the *Treatise* in the *History of the Works of the Learned*, Hume is said to have demanded satisfaction from Jacob Robinson, the printer, and " during the paroxysm of his anger," to have kept him at sword's point trembling behind the counter of his shop, " lest a period should be put to the life of a sober critick by a raving philosopher." [3] The anecdote, frequently repeated and frequently denied, seems unlikely. It is entirely out of keeping with the character of Hume and with other known facts. At the time of the supposed assault, Hume was in Scotland and was to be absent from London for the subsequent five years. His only known comment, made in March 1740, was certainly mild enough, describing the article merely as " somewhat abusive." It will, however, be observed shortly that this was probably deliberate understatement on the part of Hume and that, in reality, he had been quite put out. The review is further remarkable, no matter by whose hand, in that it set the standard for the public misinterpretation of the *Treatise* throughout most of the eighteenth century in the three basic respects of restricting itself entirely to Book I, " Of the Understanding " ; of deliberately misrepresenting the text ; and of eschewing refutation by argument for ridicule and abuse.

After the appearance of the " somewhat abusive " article in the *History of the Works of the Learned*, Hume decided not to submit his own abstract to the editor of that periodical. So he had it published separately by Charles Corbet " at Addison's Head, over-against St. Dunstan's Church, in Fleet-street," London. This anonymous sixpenny pamphlet was announced in the *Daily Advertiser* of 11 March 1740 as *An Abstract of a late Philosophical Performance, entitled A Treatise of Human Nature, &c. Wherein the*

---

[1] See below, Appendix D, p. 617.   [2] See below, pp. 289 ff.
[3] *London Review*, v (1777), 200.

chief Argument and Design of that Book, which has met with such Opposition, and been represented in so terrifying a Light, is further illustrated and explain'd. The title, so highly coloured emotionally, may indicate Hume's immediate indignation over the manifest unfairness of the review in the *History of the Works of the Learned.* Characteristically Hume soon cooled off, for the title on the six extant copies of the pamphlet reads simply, *An Abstract of a Book lately Published ; Entituled, A Treatise of Human Nature, &c. Wherein The Chief Argument of that Book is farther Illustrated and Explained.*[1]

Under the first title, the pamphlet was noticed by the *Bibliothèque britannique* for the first quarter of 1740, where, together with the *Treatise of Human Nature*, it was attributed to a " Mr. Thurnbull," clearly Professor George Turnbull of Aberdeen University. Under the revised title, the pamphlet was noticed in Desmaizeaux's *Bibliothèque raisonnée* for the second quarter of 1740 : " Some people having found that the *Treatise of Human Nature* of Mr. *Hume* was a little too abstract, a brochure has been published to help them understand it." This was the second time that Hume's name was publicly put to the *Treatise* and, if due to Desmaizeaux, he was not in the secret of the *Abstract*, or else determined to keep it.

Possibly also Hume knew of other reviews. If, for instance, he had come across the three-page item in the *Göttingische Zeitungen*, dated 7 January 1740, his heat would have been intense. After a sketch of the methodology of the *Treatise*, the reviewer proceeds :

Thus all ideas originate in impressions which consequently correspond exactly to them. So the author hopes at one stroke to do away with the existence of innate or inherent ideas. His conceptions of abstract ideas, of the ideas of memory and imagination, of the association of ideas, of the concept of substance and modes are so abstract, not to say confused, that one can scarcely hope that he will shed more light on moral truths than has been done heretofore. The author agrees with Dr Berkeley, whose theories he considers irrefutable in all respects, that all supposedly general ideas are but particular ones associated with certain words that give them a wider meaning so that, on occasion, they can convey other single related conceptions. If the reader will accept these beliefs as completely as their author does, then he will no doubt be convinced of their validity ; yet we fear that this will not be the case should the reader not accept the evidence here presented.

Then comes the standard charge, the cruellest blow of all :

[1] *An Abstract of a Treatise of Human Nature, 1740 : A Pamphlet hitherto unknown by David Hume*, reprinted with an Introduction by J. M. Keynes and P. Sraffa (Cambridge 1938). The editors were unaware of Hume's first title. W. B. Todd argues against my surmise that " . . . the more provocative title may have been devised by the publisher to enhance his sales, a not uncommon practice." See " David Hume. A Preliminary Bibliography," in *Hume and the Enlightenment* (Edinburgh and Austin 1974), p. 204, n. 5.

His conceptions of certainty and probability are peculiar. He has a great talent for presenting in confused terms what others have stated clearly. The lucidity of the idea that all that comes into existence must have a cause is matched by the obscurity of the author's examination of it. The necessity of these causal concepts exists with him only in theory and not in the existing object itself, as all necessity of cause-and-effect consists only in the propensity of the mind always to think of two objects together. Oddly enough we shall not even think of the consequences the author derives therefrom !

To turn, for a moment, from the tissue of misunderstanding of the *Treatise* being fabricated by the English and Continental learned world to the *Abstract* written by its author is to see clearly and forcefully what Hume had intended to be " The Chief Argument of that Book." The preface to the thirty-two page pamphlet points out the revolutionary nature of the thinking :

> The book seem'd to me to have such an air of singularity, and novelty as claim'd the attention of the public ; especially if it be found, as the Author seems to insinuate, that were his philosophy receiv'd, we must alter from the foundation the greatest part of the sciences. Such bold attempts are always advantageous in the republic of letters, because they shake off the yoke of authority, accustom men to think for themselves, give new hints, which men of genius may carry further, and by the very opposition, illustrate points, wherein no one before suspected any difficulty.

The opening pages of the text emphasise the systematic and constructive aspects :

> Beside the satisfaction of being acquainted with what most nearly concerns us, it may be safely affirmed, that almost all the sciences are comprehended in the science of human nature, and are dependent on it. *The sole end of logic is to explain the principles and Operations of our reasoning faculty, and the nature of our ideas* ; morals and criticism *regard our tastes and sentiments ; and* politics *consider men as united in society, and dependent on each other.* This treatise therefore of human nature seems intended for a system of the sciences. The author has finished what regards logic, and has laid the foundation of the other parts in his account of the passions.

To summarise Hume's own summary of the *Treatise* may seem a thankless task, yet it is necessary to provide the reader of his biography with some notion of both the revolutionary and the constructive sides of his thinking. Only so can Hume's natural disappointment at the failure of the learned world to understand him be sympathetically felt ; and it was this failure to understand his first philosophical effort that altered the course of his career.

 In the Age of Reason, Hume set himself apart as a systematic anti-rationalist. Most of what passes for knowledge, he taught, is not achieved by the faculty of reason but by custom and habit ;

and most knowledge is not perfectly certain but, at best, probable. The realm of reason is, therefore, restricted to the relations of ideas, as in pure logic and pure mathematics, and it is only in that realm that absolute certainty is achievable. All other knowledge belongs to the realm of matter of fact : " all our reasonings in the conduct of life " ; " all our belief in history " ; " all philosophy, excepting only geometry and arithmetic." And all our knowledge of matter of fact is determined by our inferences from cause to effect. This relation, then, provides the key to the remainder of the *Treatise*, and is the only idea extensively treated in the *Abstract*.

The discussion opens with a simple illustration : " Here is a billiard-ball lying on the table, and another ball moving towards it with rapidity. They strike ; and the ball, which was formerly at rest, now acquires a motion. This is as perfect an instance of the relation of cause and effect as any which we know, either by sensation or reflection. Let us therefore examine it." Hume's analysis indicates that there are but three circumstances which determine the relation between cause and effect ; these are conti-guity, priority, and constant conjunction, determinants which are discoverable only by experience. Prior to experience, anything *may* be the cause of anything. There is, in short, no metaphysical necessity between the cause and the effect. " All reasonings con-cerning cause and effect, are founded on experience, and . . . all reasonings from experience are founded on the supposition, that the course of nature will continue uniformly the same." But the uniformity of nature " is a point, which can admit of no proof at all, and which we take for granted without any proof. We are determined by *Custom* alone to suppose the future comfortable to the past. . . . 'Tis not, therefore, reason, which is the guide of life, but custom."

Why do we have a belief in the uniformity of nature ? " What then is this *belief*? And how does it differ from the simple con-ception of any thing ? Here," interpolates Hume triumphantly, " is a new question unthought of by philosophers." Analysis indicates that belief adds nothing new to the mere conception of an object, and is no more than a different manner of conceiving it. The argument may be resumed in Hume's own words : " No matter of fact can be proved but from its cause or its effect. Nothing can be known to be the cause of another but by experience. We can give no reason for extending to the future our experience in the past ; but are entirely determined by custom, when we conceive an effect to follow from its usual cause. But we also

believe an effect to follow, as well as conceive it. This belief joins
no new idea to the conception. It only varies the manner of conceiving, and makes a difference to the feeling or sentiment. Belief,
therefore, in all matters of fact arises only from custom, and is an
idea conceived in a peculiar *manner*." This peculiar manner is
difficult to express in words. Sometimes it is described as " a
stronger conception, sometimes a more *lively*, a more *vivid*, a *firmer*,
or a more *intense* conception. And indeed, whatever name we
may give to this feeling, which constitutes belief, our author thinks
it evident, that it has a more forcible effect on the mind than fiction
and mere conception. This he proves by its influence on the
passions and on the imagination ; which are only moved by truth
or what is taken for such. Poetry, with all its art, can never cause
a passion, like one in real life. It fails in the original conception
of its objects, which never *feel* in the same manner as those which
command our belief and opinion."

Hume's emphasis upon feeling and the passions, rather than
upon reason with its supposed certainty, was, of course, sceptical
in tendency yet not sceptical to the exclusion of all knowledge.
The *Abstract* stresses both the destructive and the constructive
elements in his thinking :

> By all that has been said the reader will easily perceive, that the philosophy
> contain'd in this book is very sceptical, and tends to give us a notion of the
> imperfections and narrow limits of human understanding. Almost all reasoning
> is there reduced to experience ; and the belief, which attends experience,
> is explained to be nothing but a peculiar sentiment, or lively conception
> produced by habit. Nor is this all, when we believe any thing of *external*
> existence, or suppose an object to exist a moment after it is no longer perceived,
> this belief is nothing but a sentiment of the same kind. Our author insists
> upon several other sceptical topics ; and upon the whole concludes, that we
> assent to our faculties, and employ our reason only because we cannot help it.
> Philosophy wou'd render us entirely *Pyrrhonian*, were not nature too strong for it.

The constructive element is indicated briefly at the close of the
Abstract in the principle of the association of ideas, which is analysed
into the three subordinate parts of resemblance, contiguity, and
causation. The work closes :

> 'Twill be easy to conceive of what vast consequence these principles must
> be in the science of human nature, if we consider, that so far as regards the
> mind, these are the only links that bind the parts of the universe together, or
> connect us with any person or object exterior to ourselves. For as it is by
> means of thought only that any thing operates upon our passions, and as these
> are the only ties of our thoughts, they are really *to us* the cement of the universe,
> and all the operations of the mind must, in a great measure, depend on them.

In brief, Hume is pointing out in the *Abstract* that Book I of the *Treatise* elucidated a notion of cause and effect which would deprive all our knowledge of matter of fact of absolute certainty. He is also pointing out that his thinking does not end in scepticism but proceeds to build up a new world, naturalistic rather than supernaturalistic, empirical rather than rationalistic, based upon the clearer understanding of the manner in which the mind of man really functions. As, fundamentally, a *feeling* rather than a *reasoning* creature, man is yet capable of philosophy. The science of human nature, which Hume anticipates he may be able to complete in all its parts, will continue with the study of the passions, of morals, of criticism, and of politics, the last including both social relations and history.

It is time now to return to the learned world of 1739-40, to note the further reactions to the *Treatise*, and to see whether any fuller comprehension of the impact of Hume's thought developed after the appearance of the *Abstract*. In the April-May-June 1740 number of the *Bibliothèque raisonnée*, exactly a year after the original notice, appeared the first section of a forty-nine page review of the *Treatise*. Though purporting to cover the original two volumes, the first instalment deliberately restricts itself to the reasonings on cause and effect, and " Of the Passions " is no more than mentioned in the final paragraph.

Opening with a wide preliminary survey of the contemporary state of metaphysics, the reviewer proceeds to comment on the *Treatise* :

> This entire work, in general, is filled with original thoughts, which have all the merit of singularity. Perhaps it will be found that in wishing to investigate the inmost nature of things, the anonymous writer sometimes uses a language a little unintelligible to his readers. Again I fear that his paradoxes favour Pyrrhonism and lead to consequences that the author appears to disown. Metaphysics has its stumbling blocks as well as the other sciences. When it passes certain limits, it obscures the objects that it searches out. Under pretence of yielding only to evidence, it finds difficulties in everything.

In connexion with Hume's reasonings concerning cause and effect, the reviewer observes that, " This is pretty close to the manner in which *Sextus Empiricus* formerly reasoned in his *Hypotyposes*, Book III, Chap. III " ; and again on the same subject, he ventures to take issue with his author, by repeating over and over again that the resemblance of the future to the past is a matter of fact, that the effect is infallible because what operates in the same manner must produce the same effect. On Hume's reduction of belief to " a lively idea, related to or associated with a present impression," he exclaims in utter exasperation : " This is the definition which the author himself gives. It would be perfectly unintelligible if the entire course and connexion of the propositions which we have just reviewed had not been mastered. I do not know whether even with all that it will appear very evident and it ought not to be said here, *Fiat Lux*."

Finally the reviewer reverts to a theme which must have become depressingly familiar to Hume :

> There would be a hundred things to remark in our author, whether on the taste for Pyrrhonism which reigns in his manner of philosophizing ; whether on the inconsistency of so many of the singular propositions that he has been pleased to accumulate ; whether finally on the pernicious consequences that could be drawn from his principles. What is most offensive is the confidence with which he delivers his paradoxes. Never has there been a Pyrrhonian more dogmatic. It is not by doubting that he dares to substitute his specula-tions for the opinion of the greatest philosophers on the most abstract matters, as on the nature of our ideas, on extension, on space, on the vacuum, on identity, etc. It is not by doubting that he proceeds to maintain, for example, that it is false that everything which exists must necessarily have a cause of its existence ; that we have no proof *a priori* of the existence of God ; that the most ingenious mathematicians have no certainty of the truth of their dis-coveries until the learned public has approved them ; and a number of other propositions as bold, to say nothing stronger. The author is on all this as positive as can be. The Lockes and the Clarkes are often, to his eyes, but paltry and superficial reasoners in comparison with himself ; and, if it be permitted to speak his language here, it is easy to see that habit and custom have already so framed him to believe that he believes nothing except in a very lively manner. It is good, however, for the public to know that it is a young philosopher to whom they are indebted for the essays with which we have just entertained them. What cannot we expect from a genius so subtle and so profound when once age will have ripened his taste, and he will have had time to meditate anew the matters that he has rough-hewn ?

The article continues with a half-promise to proceed at a later date to Book II, which, concedes the reviewer, seems to have " more clarity." " While waiting," he continues, " we ask pardon from the learned and ingenious author for the errors which have slipped by us in our desire to abridge his reasonings." And he closes on an ironical note, commenting that the author

> has burst through the bounds of a *prudent scepticism* and has made too frequent use of those means of speaking so commonly used inappropriately, *'tis evident*, *'tis certain*, *'tis undeniable :* but he expressly declares that, if this has happened to him, it is inadvertently in consequence of the lively impression that objects have made on him and not at all through egotism or a taste for *dogmatic philosophy*, from which he is, he says, *very remote*. And, in truth, one would have to be madly Pyrrhonian to refuse to believe him.

One final Continental review must be mentioned briefly. The *Nouvelle bibliothèque* at The Hague returned to the *Treatise* in July and September 1740, in a forty-six page article. Though more moderate and dispassionate than most, this writer follows the usual pattern of restricting himself almost exclusively to the analysis of cause and effect. Again, like the other reviewers, he fails to make use of the *Abstract* in order to comprehend that central doctrine. A certain, almost begrudging, admiration of the author of the *Treatise* is admitted : " Allow me to remark in passing, that if the principles of the author on impression, belief, and custom are not solid, it must at least be admitted that he uses them skilfully to clarify several intellectual phenomena equally important and difficult to explain."

Apart from notices and reviews, the *Treatise* met its first formal refutation in the form of an unsigned letter to the editor of the Whig political periodical, *Common Sense : or the Englishman's Journal*, for Saturday, 5 July 1740.[1] The writer proclaims himself the author of the recent *Essay towards demonstrating the Immateriality and Free-Agency of the Soul*. Reviewed in the same issue of the *History of the Works of the Learned* as contained the second article on Hume's *Treatise*, this work fared much better : " Our Author has handled his Subject with a Perspicuity that one does not very often find in Treatises of this Nature. We can every-where understand him, if we cannot in all Things agree with him ; tho' I think he is throughout a rational as well as a clear Writer."

Though termed by the editor of *Common Sense*, a dissertation, the letter is more modestly described by its author as " a short Answer to a long Book lately published, intitled a Treatise of Human Nature. . . ." Attacking Hume's doctrines of necessity and of cause and effect, as well as his discussion of mathematics, the writer deliberately puffs his own *Essay*, to which he refers in all cases for fuller refutation. Hume's " Novel Sort of Diction " is stigmatised and, as usual, his unintelligibility. " . . . Indeed, I should have taken no Notice of what he has wrote," the comment goes, " if I had not thought his Book, in several Parts, so very abstruse and perplex'd, that, I am convinced, no Man can comprehend what he means ; and as one of the greatest Wits of this Age has justly observed, this may impose upon weak Readers, and

---

[1] This item was brought to my attention through the kindness of Professor A. D. McKillop of Rice University. For a full discussion, see Mossner, " The First Answer to Hume's *Treatise*: An Unnoticed Item of 1740," in *Journal of the History of Ideas*, XII (1951), 291–4.

make them imagine, there is a great Deal of deep Learning in it, because they do not understand it." So Hume's *Treatise* met its first refutation on the grounds that it was so incomprehensible as to delude weak readers into accepting it as important philosophy ! So far as philosophy is concerned, the writer of the " short Answer " was as deficient as the writers of the several reviews. Hume had reason only to congratulate himself that his anonymity had not been penetrated, that it might be said, " I can upon my Honour declare, I never had the least Intimation, who he is. . . ."

That Hume was acquainted with the comment on the *Treatise*, both English and Continental, goes almost without saying. After all, just what was he awaiting during those anxious months following publication ? Good sales, yes, as an indication of general interest ; but good reviews, much more so. For better or for worse, he had placed himself before the learned world ; and reviews are the chief means of ascertaining their approval or disapproval or, what is worse from the point of view of the author, their indifference. In a day given to controversy by means of the pamphlet, he might also have expected reaction in that form ; yet with " Of Miracles " excised, the abstract thinking of the *Treatise* would not be likely to attract the attention of the theological pamphleteers. It may be assumed that Hume made some effort to keep up with the periodicals. It is certain, of course, that he knew of the article in the *History of the Works of the Learned*. His relations with Desmaizeaux, as well as his personal knowledge of the learned world of the Continent, would have made him aware of the articles in the French journals. His acquaintance with the German articles is somewhat questionable, to be sure, as is his knowledge of that language, although he would undoubtedly have been interested had they been brought to his attention. By November 1742 Hume was well enough informed to be able to refer sportively, in a letter to a friend, to his " being accus'd of being unintelligible in some of my Writings."

What, then, did Hume find in the periodicals that, in retrospect, might have led to his remark that the *Treatise* fell dead-born from the press ? He found that the critics displayed little understanding of, and no sympathy for, his proposed intellectual revolution ; that they boggled at the analysis of cause and effect in Book I and rarely got beyond that point. Their minds were totally unprepared for a Newton of Moral Philosophy, as Hume sanguinely imagined himself. They were, moreover, timorous of the applications of his system of naturalism to religion and to practical morality. Hume found that his youthful ebullience over his great discoveries was universally interpreted as dogmatic and egotistical ; and he must have been utterly dismayed to discover that he was inevitably charged with being abstruse to the point of unintelligibility.

Hume could not, therefore, have meant by his remark on the *Treatise* being born dead, as has customarily been thought, that it was totally ignored. A writer signing himself " Eumenes " in the *Weekly Magazine, or Edinburgh Amusement* for 1771, denying the allegation that the *Treatise of Human Nature* " has either been read by few, or is intirely forgotten," states that, " I was in Edinburgh soon after the original publication, and well remember how much and how frequently it was mentioned, in every literary conversation. . . ." [1] An anonymous writer in the *Annual Register* for 1776 is somewhat more qualified in his estimate, if not in his enthusiasm : " This work [the *Treatise*], though not inferior to any thing of the moral or metaphysical kind in any language, was entirely overlooked, or decried at the time of its publication, except by a few liberal-minded men, who had courage to throw aside their popular and literary prejudices, and to follow sound reasoning without being afraid of any dangerous conclusion, or fatal discovery ; of seeing errors unveiled, however sanctified by years, or supported by authorities. . . ." [2] Even at that, the " few liberal-minded men," whoever they may have been, refrained from publicising their approbation.

By no means totally ignored, the *Treatise* was yet totally misunderstood and badly misrepresented by all who dealt with it publicly and, what was worse, it failed to stimulate comment from any of the minds competent to deal with it. Bishop Berkeley and Bishop Butler maintained severe silence. Hutcheson, the only other thinker still alive of those in the empirical tradition with which Hume had deliberately associated himself, made no known comment to Hume himself ; but he did respond to Henry Home, who had sent him through an intermediary the first two books of the *Treatise*.[3] Hutcheson was soon to become Hume's friend and adviser, only to turn enemy later on the question of a professorship at Edinburgh. The substance of their relations will form part of the story of the succeeding chapters.

---

[1] *Weekly Magazine, or Edinburgh Amusement* (1771³), 99–100.
[2] " An Account of the Life and Writings of the late David Hume," in *Annual Register*, xix (1776), 28.
[3] See Textual Supplement for Hutcheson's letter to Henry Home.

CHAPTER 11

ESSAYS MORAL AND POLITICAL

*" I very soon recovered the Blow, and prosecuted with
great Ardour my Studies in the Country."*

" IN the End of 1738," wrote Hume in *My Own Life*, " I published
my Treatise ; and immediatly went down to my Mother and my
Brother, who lived at his Countrey house and was employing
himself, very judiciously and successfully, in the Improvement of
his Fortune." Then after telling how the *Treatise* fell dead-born
from the press, he continued, " But being naturally of a
cheerful and sanguine Temper, I very soon recovered the Blow,
and prosecuted with great Ardour my Studies in the Country."
The very simplicity of this statement, however, is misleading.
Despite the failure of the *Treatise*, Hume had no intention of
abandoning the life of letters. The fault, he freely acknowledged,
was his own, and might have been avoided with more caution.
His immediate literary programme included the publication of
Book III of the *Treatise*, and the attempt to find a new vehicle
for his thoughts better suited to the public taste. He also began
to cast about for a professional career which might enable him to
afford the luxury of a life of letters, seemingly incapable of supporting itself. Having previously found the life of a merchant
insufferable, he wondered how happy he would be as a tutor—or
as a professor.

Francis Hutcheson, whose personal conduct and whose
philosophy Hume so much admired, was the man who might be
expected to be of most help to him on both literary and professional
counts. So one of Hume's first efforts was to get in touch with the
Professor of Moral Philosophy at Glasgow University, whose own
efforts to meet Hume during the vacation had failed. It is to
be assumed, naturally, that Henry Home had shown David
Hutcheson's letter on the two published books of the *Treatise*.
By September 1739 Hume had certainly sent Hutcheson the
manuscript of Book III, " Of Morals," inviting criticism. The
professor was kind enough to return it with some reflections on
the principles there developed. Hutcheson's reflections on the
manuscript are unfortunately not extant, but their main thrust
may be observed in Hume's reaction.

" What affected me most in your Remarks," replied Hume with noticeable chagrin, " is your observing, that there wants a certain Warmth in the Cause of Virtue,[1] which, you think, all good Men wou'd relish, & cou'd not displease amidst abstract Enquirys." His defence certainly is not lacking in warmth :

I must own, this has not happen'd by Chance, but is the Effect of a Reasoning either good or bad. There are different ways of examining the Mind as well as the Body. One may consider it either as an Anatomist or as a Painter ; either to discover its most secret Springs & Principles or to describe the Grace & Beauty of its Actions. I imagine it impossible to conjoin these two Views. Where you pull off the Skin, & display all the minute Parts, there appears something trivial, even in the noblest Attitudes & most vigorous Actions : Nor can you ever render the Object graceful or engaging but by cloathing the Parts again with Skin & Flesh, & presenting only their bare Outside. An Anatomist, however, can give very good Advice to a Painter or Statuary : And in like manner, I am perswaded, that a Metaphysician may be very helpful to a Moralist ; tho' I cannot easily conceive these two Characters united in the same Work. Any warm Sentiment of Morals, I am afraid, wou'd have the Air of Declamation amidst abstract Reasonings, & wou'd be esteem'd contrary to good Taste. And tho' I am much more ambitious of being esteem'd a Friend to Virtue, than a Writer of Taste ; yet I must always carry the latter in my Eye, otherwise I must despair of ever being servicable to Virtue. I hope these Reasons will satisfy you ; tho at the same time, I intend to make a new Tryal, if it be possible to make the Moralist & Metaphysician agree a little better.

Hume's answer is sincere and to the point. So, too, is his disagreement with Hutcheson's use of the term *natural* : " Tis founded on final Causes ; which is a Consideration, that appears to me pretty uncertain & unphilosophical. For pray, what is the End of Man ? Is he created for Happiness or for Virtue ? For this Life or for the next ? For himself or for his Maker ? " If the reviewers of the *Treatise* had noted with sufficient truth that Hume was the follower of Hutcheson so far as sentiment was concerned, they might just as truly have added that he parted company with Hutcheson in excluding theological reasonings from his strictly naturalistic system.

It is eminently to the credit of Hutcheson that he was sufficiently broadminded to correspond on terms of equality with a man who was seventeen years his junior and as yet unknown to the world, and whose thinking was of that radical disposition which was most likely to incur the enmity of the rigidly righteous —if they would take the pains to read him. But then Hutcheson

---

[1] The same charge had been brought earlier against Butler's famous sermons " Upon Human Nature ".

had been prosecuted in 1737 for teaching the heresy that we can have knowledge of good and evil without, and prior to, a knowledge of God.[1] The professor clearly had a way with his students, who learned to love as well as to respect him; Adam Smith later characterised him as "the never to be forgotten Hutcheson." His warmth in teaching was such that it has been said he *preached* his philosophy. Hume remarked upon Hutcheson's "Good-Nature & friendly Disposition," and the two got along famously when they met in the winter of 1739–1740, probably on a trip of Hume's to the West of Scotland especially for that purpose.[2]

The friendly relations between the two philosophers during this period, despite certain differences in ethical doctrine, may be taken as illustrative of the principle of sympathy, which both regarded as one of the strongest in the constitution of human nature and one of the foundation stones of ethics. So in the manuscript of Book III of the *Treatise,* Hutcheson would have read with approbation :

> . . . So close and intimate is the correspondence of human souls, that no sooner any person approaches me, than he diffuses on me all his opinions, and draws along my judgment in a greater or lesser degree. And tho', on many occasions, my sympathy with him goes not so far as entirely to change my sentiments, and way of thinking ; yet it seldom is so weak as not to disturb the easy course of my thought, and give an authority to that opinion, which is recommended to me by his assent and approbation. . . .
>
> This principle of sympathy is of so powerful and insinuating a nature, that it enters into most of our sentiments and passions, and often takes place under the appearance of its contrary. For 'tis remarkable, that when a person opposes me in any thing, which I am strongly bent upon, and rouzes up my passion by contradiction, I have always a degree of sympathy with him, nor does my commotion proceed from any other origin.[3]

On three related problems of publication, the younger man consulted the elder, whether by letter or in person. These problems concerned the *Abstract,* a second edition of the first two volumes of the *Treatise,* and the bringing out of the third. The *Abstract* had been read by Hutcheson in manuscript ; and it is not, perhaps, too fanciful to suggest that he may have been responsible for urging Hume to prepare it as a simple introduction to the *Treatise.* In any event, he did advise Hume to send a copy to

---

[1] John Rae, *Life of Adam Smith* (London 1895), pp. 12–13.
[2] W. R. Scott, *Francis Hutcheson : His Life, Teaching and Position in the History of Philosophy* (Cambridge 1900), Chs. 4–6, passim.
[3] *Phil. Wks.,* II, 349–50.

John Smith, " at the Philosopher's Head on the Blind Quay," Dublin.[1]

This Smith, in partnership with Hutcheson's cousin, was the Irish publisher of Hutcheson's own works. Hume also sent to Smith the two printed volumes of the *Treatise* in the hope that he might become interested in bringing out a " pirated " edition, which would have the effect of providing the author with a second and corrected edition. England and Scotland, at this date, were bound by the Copyright Act, but not Ireland. And Hume was further personally restricted, as he reminded Hutcheson, by a clause in the contract with John Noon, " which may prove troublesome, viz, that upon printing a second Edition I shall take all the Copys remaining upon hand at the Bookseller's Price at the time. . . . I wait with some Impatience for a second Edition," he went on, " principally on Account of Alterations I intend to make in my Performance. This is an Advantage, that we Authors possess since the Invention of Printing & renders the *Nonum prematur in annum* [2] not so necessary to us as to the Antients. Without it I shoud have been guilty of a very great Temerity to publish at my Years so many Noveltys in so delicate a Part of Philosophy : And at any Rate I am afraid, that I must plead as my Excuse that very Circumstance of Youth, which may be urg'd against me." But John Smith, although a notorious literary " pirate," was as uninterested in any part of the *Treatise* as in any abstract of it. In 1755, however, he did bring out a Dublin edition of the first volume of Hume's *History of the Stuarts*.

Despite the two setbacks of the *Abstract* and the *Treatise*, the third problem, that of Book III of the *Treatise*, was solved by Hutcheson to Hume's satisfaction. In March 1740 Hume had asked the professor for two favours : " to tell me what Copy-Money I may reasonably expect for one Edition of a thousand of this Volume, which will make a four Shillings Book ; And, if you know any honest Man in this Trade, to send me a Letter of Recommendation to him that I may have the Choice of more than one Man to bargain with," that is, with someone in addition to John Noon, who yet " is very willing to engage. . . ." Hume was careful to point out his reluctance to embarrass Hutcheson over " a Book that may give Offence to religious People. . . . I assure you, therefore, that I shall not take [it] in the least amiss,

---

[1] The identification of Hume's " Mr Smith " with the Irish bookseller is made by Keynes and Sraffa in the introduction (pp. xviii–xxiii) to their edition of Hume's *Abstract*.   [2] Horace, *Ars Poetica*, 388.

if you refuse me." Far from refusing, Hutcheson was willing to write to his own publisher in London, Thomas Longman, " at the Ship in Paternoster-Row." The offer was accepted, and Longman agreed to publish; but the contract terms are not known. In the spring of 1740 Hume was in London to see his third volume through the press. In late May and early June he was on holiday in nearby Richmond with William Mure of Caldwell and other Scottish friends. Stopping *en route* to the University of Leyden to continue his legal studies, Mure, then twenty-two, gave his sister Agnes a vivid account of David Hume at the age of twenty-nine, in a letter dated " Richmond June 5th 1740." [1]

" Of Morals " duly appeared as Volume III of the *Treatise* on 5 November 1740. The price was four shillings. The concluding section of the work reflects the exchange of letters with Hutcheson and reiterates Hume's defence of his position as an anatomist of the mind. " An Appendix. Wherein some Passages of the foregoing Volumes are illustrated and explain'd," was Hume's compromise over the failure to bring out a second and corrected edition of the first two volumes; [2] several of his emendations had already been anticipated in the *Abstract*. The " Advertisement " prefixed to the third volume expressed optimism tinged with cynicism on the part of the still unnamed author : " I think it proper to inform the public, that tho' this be a third volume of the *Treatise of Human Nature*, yet 'tis in some measure independent of the other two, and requires not that the reader shou'd enter into all the abstract reasonings contain'd in them. I am hopeful it may be understood by ordinary readers, with as little attention as is usually given to any books of reasoning. . . ."

The third volume of the *Treatise*, however, so far from buoying up the earlier two, attracted even less attention. The sole review, in the spring 1741 issue of the *Bibliothèque raisonnée*, was hardly encouraging. Beginning in a somewhat conciliatory manner, the writer soon returned to his more normal critical position :

> Such is the general plan of morality that our author has formed. It is, in our opinion, rather an outline of principles of the art of good living than a system complete and connected in its parts. He could have more order in it, more clarity, more detail ; but also he could not have more paradoxes in it, more singular associations of ideas and of words which no one had yet taken it into his head to bring together ; more passages calculated to excite the

---

[1] See Textual Supplement.
[2] For evidence that Hume was revising and correcting the *Treatise* for a desired second edition, see P. H. Nidditch, *An Apparatus on Variant Readings for Hume's Treatise of Human Nature* (Sheffield 1976).

curiosity of people who do not like the beaten path, and, to sum up, more new and original thoughts. We must make allowances to the subtle and ingenious anonymous author for these things. *Non omnis fert omnia tellus.*[1]

Hume, according to the reviewer, is pure Hutcheson in regard to sentiment and pure Hobbes in regard to the origin of justice and of property rights. " Here, as you can see, is the system of Hobbes dressed up in a new taste. If that philosopher had produced it in this fashion I doubt if he would have had such a reception in the world." Yet the reviewer closes in a more friendly manner, deprecating his inability to follow the thoughts of the author and to render them intelligible to his readers. " The surer plan is to send directly to the work those readers curious for subtleties and for metaphysical abstractions. If the author wished to add a glossary to it, he would save them much work."

As late as February 1756, the remnants of the first edition of the *Treatise* were still cluttering up the publishers' shelves.[2] Their fate remains unknown and Hume did not live to see a second edition.

In 1739 and 1740 Hume was not devoting himself exclusively to his first publication, but was actively laying plans to reach a more popular audience. Within a few months after his return to Ninewells and while awaiting the verdict of the learned world on the *Treatise*, he began exchanging newly composed papers with Henry Home. The original intention was to bring these papers out in a weekly periodical " to comprehend the Designs both of the *Spectators* & *Craftsmen*," that is, the world of society and letters, on the one hand, and that of politics, on the other. But one feature always insisted on by Hume, as distinguished from most other writers in a period of intense political feeling, was that politics was to be approached from the point of view of a non-partisan philosopher :

> . . . The Reader may condemn my Abilities, but must approve of my Moderation and Impartiality in my Method of handling *Political Subjects.* . . . Public Spirit, methinks, shou'd engage us to love the Public, and to bear an equal Affection to all our Country-Men ; not to hate one Half of them, under Pretext of loving the Whole. This *Party-Rage* I have endeavour'd to repress, as far as possible ; and I hope this Design will be acceptable to the moderate of both Parties ; at the same Time, that, perhaps, it may displease the Bigots of both.

The original design of periodical essays, however, was shortly

---

[1] Virgil, *Eclogues*, IV, 39.
[2] Between 7 Dec. 1754 and 10 Feb. 1756, a period of notoriety over the first volume of Hume's *History of the Stuarts* and the suppression of his " Five Dissertations," the *Treatise* was advertised in various London newspapers.

dropped, " partly from Laziness, partly from Want of Leisure " ; and the collected items were brought out at Edinburgh early in 1741[1] as a small duodecimo volume of *Essays Moral and Political*. This half-crown book was printed by R. Fleming and A. Alison for Alexander Kincaid, Edinburgh's leading publisher. Describing the anonymous writer as a " new Author," the preface affords the first outward sign that Hume was already beginning to dissociate himself from the *Treatise*. That possibility, after all, had been a point in the original anonymity ; and now that the work seemed definitely unsuccessful, Hume was entitled to make full use of it. But that is not to say that he had, in any sense, given up philosophy. No, the *Treatise* was a failure, he argued, because of its style and form. Since the time of Addison and Steele the essay had established itself as the most popular literary form and, as early as 1725 Dr Isaac Watts, the Nonconformist minister and hymn-writer, had lamented that fact : " Now we deal much in Essays, and most unreasonably despise systematic Learning, whereas our Fathers had a just Value for Regularity and Systems ; then Folio's and Quarto's were the fashionable Sizes, as Volumes in Octavo are now."[2]

The *Essays Moral and Political*, therefore, are to be regarded as a literary experiment towards the possible recasting of the philosophy of the ill-fated *Treatise*. Having failed to reach the public in the more learned form, perhaps he could do better in the more popular form. " I had always entertained a Notion," writes Hume in his autobiography, " that my want of Success, in publishing the Treatise of human Nature, had proceeded more from the manner than the matter ; and that I had been guilty of a very usual Indiscretion, in going to the Press too early." The original notion of periodical essays was dropped when he came to recognise that he would be tied down and perhaps kept from more serious studies. And it was during this post-*Treatise* period that Hume " recovered the Knowlege of the Greek Language, which I had too much neglected in my early Youth." He was also intensifying his historical studies. Another reason for giving up the idea of a periodical was that he would be compelled to write frivolous essays, from time to time, in order to retain public attention ; and his deep and abiding interests were always in philosophy and its practical applications.

---

[1] 1742, however, is the date on the title-page.
[2] Watts, *Logick : Or, The Right Use of Reason in the Enquiry after Truth* (ed. of London 1729), p. 219.

The experiment in essay-writing was successful, and Hume was now certain through the approbation of the public that he was really master of the pen. " In 1742," he relates in *My Own Life*, with evident satisfaction, " I printed at Edinburgh the first part of my Essays : The work was favourably received, and soon made me entirely forget my former Disappointment." The second volume of *Essays Moral and Political* appeared at Edinburgh in January 1742. Hume was jubilant. Writing to Henry Home on 13 June, he said :

> The Essays are all sold in London ; as I am inform'd by two Letters from English Gentlemen of my Acquaintance. There is a Demand for them ; & as one of them tells me, Innys the great Bookseller in Paul's Church Yard wonders there is not a new Edition, for that he cannot find Copies for his Customers. I am also told that Dr Butler has every where recommended them. So that I hope they will have some success. They may prove like Dung with Marle, & bring forward the rest of my Philosophy, which is of a more durable, tho of a harder & more stubborn Nature. You see, I can talk to you in your own Style.[1]

After mid-year appeared a " Second Edition, Corrected," of the first volume.

The last remark in the letter to Henry Home refers to his having adopted new methods for the cultivation of crops on his estate of Kames. But what is the meaning of the previous, and rather cryptic, sentence ? How was the publication of some anonymous essays to fertilise, as it were, and to " bring forward " the rest of Hume's philosophy, that is, the equally anonymous *Treatise* ? I suspect that what Hume had in mind was not so much the possibility of the success of the *Essays* in stimulating the sale of the *Treatise*, as the possible adaptability of the essay form to philosophical subjects.

The twenty-seven essays in the two volumes of *Essays Moral and Political* cover a variety of subjects. A few are definitely " frivolous," and for that reason were later withdrawn by the author. The essays withdrawn are " Of Impudence and Modesty," " Of Love and Marriage," " Of the Study of History," " Of Avarice," " Of Essay Writing," " Of Moral Prejudices," " Of the Middle Station of Life." These essays attempt the light vein of the Addisonian tradition ; but Hume was not destined to receive the title of the " Scottish Addison," which was later acquired by his young friend, Henry Mackenzie. He could, however, achieve a certain lightness of style, but the effort seemed not worth the candle to a man whose mind was teeming with world-shaking ideas. In " Of Essay Writing," for instance, the Addisonian imitation is manifest :

> . . . I cannot but consider myself as a Kind of Resident or Ambassador from the Dominions of Learning to those of Conversation ; and shall think it my constant Duty to promote a good Correspondence betwixt these two States, which have so great a Dependence on each other. I shall give Intelligence to the Learned of whatever passes in Company, and shall endeavour to import into Company whatever Commodities I find in my native Country proper for their Use and Entertainment. . . .
>
> As 'twou'd be an unpardonable Negligence in an Ambassador not to pay his Respects to the Sovereign of the State where he is commission'd to reside ; so it wou'd be altogether inexcusable in me not to address myself, with a particular Respect, to the Fair Sex, who are the Sovereigns of the Empire of Conversation. I approach them with Reverence ; and were not my Countrymen, the Learned, a stubborn independent Race of Mortals, extremely jealous of their Liberty, and unaccustom'd to Subjection, I shou'd resign into their fair Hands the sovereign Authority over the Republic of Letters. . . .
>
> . . . In a neighbouring Nation, equally famous for good Taste, and for Gallantry, the Ladies are, in a Manner, the Sovereigns of the *learned* World, as well as of the *conversible* ; and no polite Writer pretends to venture upon the Public, without the Approbation of some celebrated Judges of that Sex.[1]

But in adding that, " The Balance of Trade [between the two dominions] we need not be jealous of, nor will there be any Difficulty to preserve it on both Sides," Hume was clearly wrong. The balance of trade leaned heavily on the side of the learned world, and the attempt to preserve it equal was soon dropped. The several attempts at literary allegory were feeble from the start.[2]

The serious essays may be classed as criticism, philosophy, or politics, of which the last won the greatest popularity. Criticism includes such typically Humian performances as " Of the Delicacy of Taste and Passion," " Of Eloquence," " Of the Rise and Progress of Arts and Sciences," " Of Simplicity and Refinement." Philosophy includes " Of Superstition and Enthusiasm," " Of the Dignity of Human Nature," and the " characters " of four typical philosophers : Epicurean, Stoic, Platonist, Sceptic.

" Of the Dignity of Human Nature " might well have been sub-titled " The Thinker of Scientific Method in the Realm of Human Nature " ; Hume there depicts that ideal man.[3]

This passage from " The Sceptic " shows the popularization of some of Hume's philosophical principles from the *Treatise* :

> If we can depend upon any principle, which we learn from philosophy, this, I think, may be considered as certain and undoubted, that there is nothing,

---

[1] *Phil. Wks.*, IV, 368–70.
[2] Norah Smith's study of " Hume's ' Rejected ' Essays " corroborates my conclusions : *Forum for Modern Language Studies*, VIII (1972), 354–71.
[3] *Phil. Wks.*, III, 152.

in itself, valuable or despicable, desirable or hateful, beautiful or deformed ; but that these attributes arise from the particular constitution and fabric of human sentiment and affection.   What seems the most delicious food to one animal, appears loathsome to another : What affects the feeling of one with delight, produces uneasiness in another. . . .

Desire this passionate lover to give you a character of his mistress : He will tell you, that he is at a loss for words to describe her charms, and will ask you very seriously if ever you were acquainted with a goddess or an angel ? If you answer that you never were : He will then say, that it is impossible for you to form a conception of such divine beauties as those which his charmer possesses ; so complete a shape ; such well-proportioned features ; so engaging an air ; such sweetness of disposition ; such gaiety of humour. You can infer nothing, however, from all this discourse, but that the poor man is in love ; and that the general appetite between the sexes, which nature has infused into all animals, is in him determined to a particular object by some qualities, which give him pleasure.   The same divine creature, not only to a different animal, but also to a different man, appears a mere mortal being, and is beheld with the utmost indifference.[1]

Here is an eloquent and powerful voice speaking ; here is food for thought ; and here is direct application of prime theses from the neglected *Treatise*.   Yet, despite Hume's fondest hopes, it was not such philosophical essays that caught the public eye at first, but rather the political.

Among the more notable of the political essays are " Of the Liberty of the Press," " That Politics may be reduc'd to a Science," [2] " Of the first Principles of Government," " Of the Independency of Parliament," " Of the Parties of Great Britain." These essays, and others like them, were gradually to build up Hume's great reputation as man of letters.   But in January 1742, when the second volume of *Essays Moral and Political* appeared, it was " A Character of Sir Robert Walpole " that attracted immediate attention and that was reprinted in many of the newspapers of the kingdom and in such leading monthlies as the *Gentleman's Magazine*, the *London Magazine*, and the *Scots Magazine*. And though the author's name was not put to the " Character ," Hume could inform William Mure of Caldwell with pardonable pride and with certain truth that he had " publish'd to all Britain my Sentiments on that Affair."

The timeliness of the " Character of Sir Robert Walpole " was partly intentional and partly fortuitous.   From London the previous December, James Oswald, the Scottish M.P. and friend of Hume, wrote to Henry Home :   " . . . I dont think for [myself] that there could be a more proper opportunity of our friend Davids Character seeing the Light." [3] Oswald points out

---

[1] *Phil. Wks.*, III, 216.   [2] See Textual Supplement for Hume's denial of Pope.
[3] Oswald to Home, MS letter, 17 Dec. 1741, in SRO, Abercairny Papers, GD 24.

that the House of Commons was just investigating the evidence concerning the Westminster Election, in which Walpole was notoriously implicated, an investigation that was to prove the immediate occasion of his fall in the first days of February 1742. In the " Advertisement " prefixed to the second volume, Hume was already more inclined to lenity than he had been in the " Character " itself. He writes there :

> The character of *Sir Robert Walpole* was drawn some months ago, when that Great Man was in the Zenith of his Power. I must confess, that, at present, when he seems to be upon the Decline, I am inclin'd to think more favourably of him, and to suspect, that the Antipathy, which every true born *Briton* naturally bears to Ministers of State, inspir'd me with some Prejudice against him. The impartial *Reader*, if any such there be ; or Posterity, if such a Trifle can reach them, will be best able to correct any Mistakes in this Particular.

Posterity has generally agreed that the " Character " is a fine example of the dispassionate moderation sought after by Hume. The conclusion affords a particularly good specimen :

> During his [Walpole's] time trade has flourished, liberty declined, and learning gone to ruin. As I am a man, I love him ; as I am a scholar, I hate him ; as I am a *Briton*, I calmly wish his fall. And were I a member of either house, I would give my vote for removing him from *St. James's* ; but should be glad to see him retire to [his estate of] *Houghton-Hall*, to pass the remainder of his days in ease and pleasure.

In the next edition of the *Essays* after Walpole's fall, that of 1748, the " Character " was degraded to a footnote with an even more placatory preface ; in 1770 it was finally omitted from the collected edition of Hume's works.

The widespread circulation of the " Character of Sir Robert Walpole " led Hume into a minor, yet curious, literary exploit.[1] The *Newcastle Journal* of 13 February 1742 responded with critical remarks on it and a list of ten questions addressed to the author. The *Scots Magazine* for March,[2] amongst several periodicals, printed the list of " queries proposed to the consideration of the author, who," states the editor, " having favoured us with his answers, we shall insert them. . . ." The answers thus attributed to Hume, and never publicly or privately denied by him or by his publisher, sound remarkably like him. The queries and answers corresponding to the passage from the " Character " quoted above will be given by way of illustration :

---

[1] R. C. Elliott, " Hume's ' Character of Sir Robert Walpole ' : Some Unnoticed Additions," in *Journal of English and Germanic Philology*, XLVIII (1949), 367–70.
[2] *Scots Mag.*, IV (1742), 119 ; *Gent.'s Mag.*, XII (1742), 82, 265.

Query 6 Will the author of the character attribute the flourishing of trade to the measures of the Prime Minister ?

Answer Yes : so far as the administration has been pacific, and private property has been preserved inviolate, by keeping parties from the courts of judicature. I speak with regard to England.

Q. 7 What instances have we of the declension of liberty ?

A. There are many instances, tho', I hope, none fatal ; such as, the increase of the civil list, votes of credit, and too large a standing army, etc.

Q. 8 Is learning really gone to ruin ?

A. To a great degree. What successor have Addison, Congreve, Prior, Newton, etc. left in Britain ? Who are to succeed Pope, Swift and Bolingbroke ?

Q. 9 Are a *man*, a *scholar*, and a *Briton*, so distinct things, and opposite in their natures, as that what is the object of love in one, is the object of hate in another ?

A. The same person may, without any inconsistency, be considered in several different views.

Q. 10 Would not a plain honest answer to the above queries greatly illustrate and confirm the justice of the character ?

A. The character seemed as clear as was consistent with its brevity.

If the answers are really by Hume—as there is sufficient reason to believe that they are—this was to be one of the few times during a long career as man of letters that he took public notice of any reactions to his publications. It is worth adding that even this notice was made anonymously.

Some part of the success of *Essays Moral and Political* was doubtless due to puffing by loyal friends of the author. At Edinburgh Henry Home was hard at work, and at London James Oswald. Following the publication of the second volume, James wrote to Henry about his efforts in behalf of David. This highly informative account of the contemporary state of letters corroborates Hume's own estimate :

Nothing [writes Oswald] can be more agreable to me than either to recommend our Friend Hume or his book. In either of these Cases the Person who Recommends does himself in my opinion an honour as he becomes a Sharer of that Merit which is in both. But you cannot imagine what a Difficult matter it is here at present to fix any Mans Attention but for a Moment upon any general Subject. Every thing must be Particular and for that Precise Reason any thing that I have seen come out since I have been here is extremely bad. All Declamation. But such is the general Indolence of Mind here that one Flashy Lively thing whether in thought or Expression tho in the midst of Trash is more greedily swallowed than the most elegant piece of Reasoning. That Attention of Mind which is absolutely necessary in some degree at least to relish the beauty of such writing is rarely to be found. They cry this is Cold and that Dry always in general without daring from their indolence to come to Particulars and almost Constantly point out as faults in a writing what is entirely the effect of their own Disgust and vitiated habit of mind. However, I am convinced Mr Humes things will make their way & Nothing shall be left on my Part to lett them be known as far as I can. I know some of the young People about the Prince who seem to have a very good Taste. I go to no Court myself. But as I have an opportunity of seeing some of these Gentlemen sometimes I shall do what I can to excite their Curiosity and shall afterwards let you hear their Sentiments.[1]

How Oswald and Hume fared with the coterie of Prince Frederick is unknown, but that prince generally proved a disappointment to those who put their trust in him.

The sale of *Essays Moral and Political* was handled in London, according to an advertisement in the *Daily Advertiser* of 1 March 1742, " by J. and P. Knapton, in Ludgate-Street ; C. Hitch, in Pater-noster Row ; and A. Millar, over-against St. Clement's Church in the Strand." Though an undoubted success, a third edition was not called for until six years later, at which time Millar became Hume's chief London publisher. For original editions of the customary 1,500, rather than of the 1,000 of the *Treatise*, Hume may be presumed to have ultimately benefited to the extent of from £150 to £200. This sum would have been a welcome addition to his still inadequate income of little more than £50 annually, on which he could live independently in Scotland as a professional man of letters but could hardly save money.

At Ninewells David could always recoup his finances. His brother, the laird, was, as David observed, " employing himself, very judiciously and successfully, in the Improvement of his Fortune." Like Henry Home at Kames nearby, John was one of the pioneers in introducing modern methods of farming into Scotland. In 1740 he was also rebuilding the Ninewells house, which had been partially burned out by fire, a disaster possibly connected with the terrible storms of January and February 1739. With his customary caution, however, he is said to have rebuilt it only on a limited scale, meaning, I should assume, that he repaired the old building rather than put up an entirely new one. In November 1740 John Home also lost a legal suit over the payment of land purchased from Ninian Home of Billie.[2] John, it would seem, had cited the forfeiture clause from the Clan Acts, passed after the '15, as reason for non-payment.

During this period when Hume was making his headquarters

---

[1] Oswald to Home, MS letter, [Jan. 1742], in SRO, Abercairny Papers, GD 24.
[2] *Decisions of the Court of Session (1733-1754)*, ed. Patrick Grant of Elchies (Edinburgh 1813), I, APPENDIX II, " Forfeiture," under date 14 Nov. 1740.

at Ninewells, there is no sign that he took any interest in Dr Stevenson's proposal that he should translate the Chevalier Ramsay's " Chinese Letters." And, without specific evidence, it seems best to accept the opinion of the Chevalier that Hume was " too full of himself, to humble his pregnant, active, protuberant Genius to drudge at a Translation." Not all of his time was employed in composition, however, and he took many social trips. He was constantly back and forth to Edinburgh, occasionally visited Glasgow and the West of Scotland, got to Kirkcaldy in Fife, rode over to Berwick frequently, and was, of course, a common visitor to his neighbours in the Merse and the Border country—Henry Home at Kames, the Humes of Marchmont at Red-braes Castle, the Stewarts at Allanbank, the Elliots at Minto. In all these places, David was a prime favourite with the ladies, old and young : Lady Jane at Red-braes Castle ; the Edinburgh circle of " very fine ladies " of Mrs Home of Kames, " the widow," " my Flame Betty Dalrymple " ; the Glasgow and Caldwell set, Lady Mure and her daughters Agnes, Betty, and Nancy, and Miss Dunlop. " Tell your Sister Miss Betty (after having made her my Compliments)," he banters Mure, " that I am as grave as she imagines a Philosopher shou'd be : Laugh only once a fortnight : Sigh tenderly once a Week : But look sullen every Moment. In short, none of Ovid's Metamorphosis ever show'd so absolute a Change from a human Creature into a Beast ; I mean from a Gallant into a Philosopher." His letters are full of playful gallantry but nowhere reveal any serious amorous attachment. They do, however, express a strong preference for the gay and sprightly Scottish women over the " dry & reserv'd . . . foolish English women."

When William Mure of Caldwell, Hume's intimate friend, was elected M.P. for Renfrewshire in 1742, Hume wrote with delicious irony : " as you are my Disciple in Religion & Morals, why shou'd you not be so in Politics ? I entreat you to get the Bill about Witches repeal'd, & to move for some new Bill to secure the Christian Religion, by burning Deists, Socinians, Moralists, & Hutchinsonians." The humour lies in the fact that the early seventeenth century " Witches Act," which made witchcraft a capital offence, had been repealed in 1736 by an enlightened parliament—much to the mortification of the bigots. The Hutchinsonians, I hasten to add, were not followers of the Glaswegian philosopher, but were members of a minor radical religious sect.

Mure's former tutor, William Leechman, became Professor of Divinity at Glasgow late in 1743. As Leechman had graduated from Edinburgh in 1724, he and Hume may possibly have been acquainted even then ; if not, they met now through Mure. Leechman's sermon " On the Nature, Reasonableness, and Advantages of Prayer," recently published, was attracting considerable attention. Intimate friend of Hutcheson's that he was, and a liberal in theology, Leechman was charged by the Glasgow Presbytery, on the occasion of his election to the divinity professorship, with heresy ; but he was acquitted by the Synod of Glasgow and Ayr. His acquittal was hailed by the student body at the university as the defeat of the over-zealous and the triumph of the liberals. Hume's comments on the sermon take the form of a long letter, dated 30 June 1743, to Mure and designed to be read by Leechman. The letter opens with a paradox :

I have read Mr Leechman's Sermon with a great deal of Pleasure, & think it a very good one ; tho' I am sorry to find the Author to be a rank Atheist. You know (or ought to know) that Plato says there are three kinds of Atheists. The first who deny a Deity, the second who deny his Providence, the third who assert, that he is influenc'd by Prayers or Sacrifices. I find Mr Leechman is an Atheist of the last kind.

Continuing with a long list of stylistic suggestions, Hume generalises concerning Leechman's style : " . . . in my humble Opinion he does not consult his Ear enough, nor aim at a Style that may be smooth & harmonious ; which, next to Perspicuity is the chief Ornament of Style. Vide Cicero, Quinctilian, Longinus, &c., &c. If this Sermon were not a popular Discourse, I shoud also think it might be made more concise."

Hume then proceeds to an " Objection both to Devotion & Prayer, & indeed to every thing we commonly call Religion, except the Practice of Morality, & the Assent of the Understanding to the Proposition *that God exists*." The argument, which Leechman is asked to consider, and which is revealing of Hume's personal religious position, is that, " from this Circumstance of the Invisibility & Incomprehensibility of the Deity [a man, no matter how perfectly moral] may feel no Affection towards him." Even were devotion admitted, prayer must still be excluded, for it is only a kind of rhetorical figure, which is ultimately dangerous and leads to impiety and blasphemy. " Tis a natural Infirmity of Men to imagine, that their Prayers have a direct Influence, & this Infirmity must be extremely foster'd & encouragd by the constant Use of Prayer. Thus all wise Men have excluded the Use of Images &

Pictures in Prayer ; tho they certainly enliven Devotion ; because tis found by Experience, that with the vulgar these visible Representations draw too much towards them, & become the only Objects of Devotion." Leechman's answer, if any was forthcoming, is unknown. As Principal of Glasgow University in 1764, however, he delivered a sermon warning his students against Voltaire, Rousseau, Bolingbroke, and Hume, whom he distinguished as " the most celebrated men in some species of writing that are perhaps in Europe at present." [1]

Hume's relations with Professor Hutcheson continued cordial during this period. When Hutcheson's *Philosophiae moralis institutio compendiaria* was published at Glasgow in December 1742, a copy was dispatched by the author to Hume. The latter wrote in thanks for " your very agreeable Present ; for which I esteem myself much oblig'd to you." " I have subjoined," he adds, " a few Reflections which occurd to me in reading over the Book. By these I pretend only to show you, how much I thought myself oblig'd to you for the Pains you took with me in a like Case, & how willing I am to be grateful." A major reflection points to a central issue of ethics : " You seem here," comments Hume, " to embrace Dr Butler's Opinion in his Sermons on human Nature ; that our moral Sense has an Authority distinct from its Force and Durableness, & that because we always think it *ought* to prevail. But this is nothing but an Instinct or Principle, which approves of itself upon reflection ; and that is common to all of them." Then he adds diffidently, " I am not sure that I have mistaken your Sense, since you do not prosecute this Thought." Concerning a fundamental point of difference, the origin of justice and property, Hume complains, " It mortifies me much to see a Person, who possesses more Candour & Penetration than any almost I know, condemn Reasonings, of which I imagine I see so strongly the Evidence. I was," he adds, " going to blot this out after having wrote it, but hope you will consider it only a Piece of Folly, as indeed it is."

The letter concludes : " I must own I am pleas'd to see such Philosophy & such instructive Morals to have once set their Foot in the Schools. I hope they will next get into the World, & then into the Churches. Nil desperandum Teucro duce & auspice Teucro." [2] Hume's interest in the spread of the modern philosophy from the schools into the world and ultimately into religious

[1] Wm. Leechman, *Sermons*, ed. James Wodrow (London 1789), i, 185.
[2] Horace, *Odes*, i.vii, 27.

practice is important in light of events shortly to develop, the possibility of his becoming a professor of philosophy himself. His relations with Hutcheson and Leechman and his complete candour with them on matters of philosophy and religion were not to be without influence in that regard.

Before Hume developed aspirations of becoming a professor of philosophy, however, he had expressed interest in the somewhat less dignified position of a tutor. In November 1739, when his career as a man of letters seemed at an ebb, he had requested a friend to investigate a tutorship to the young Lord Haddington and his brother. " There are many inviting Circumstances," wrote Hume, " with regard to these young Gentlemen, which have engag'd me to make this Step. They have a very good Character ; I have the Honour to be their Relation (which gives a Governour a better Air in attending his Pupils) And I have at present some Leizure to bestow." Nothing came of the overture, as apparently the young men were already provided for. When, however, in the summer of 1744 the position of travelling tutor to the son of Murray of Broughton in Dumfriesshire was offered to Hume, he was not able to accept it. " I coud not positively accept," he informed Mure of Caldwell, " 'till I had seen the End of this Affair, which is so near a Crisis." This critical affair was his candidature for the chair of Ethics and Pneumatical Philosophy at Edinburgh University.

PART II

OBSERVER OF HUMAN NATURE

1744–1749

Chapter 12

ACADEMIC ILLUSION

" Such a popular Clamour has been raisd against me in Edinburgh, on account of Scepticism, Heterodoxy & other hard Names . . . that my Friends find some Difficulty in working out the Point of my Professorship."

It is perhaps a truism that scholars are peculiarly susceptible to returning to the academic societies that nourished their scholarship. If so, David Hume was no exception to the rule. The chance to succeed Dr John Pringle in the chair of Ethics and Pneumatical Philosophy at Edinburgh University occurred in the summer of 1744. Here was a dignified position with a good salary that would give him the opportunity to cultivate his literary and philosophical ambitions. In his eagerness, Hume incautiously forgot his own precept stated to Hutcheson some five years before : " Except a Man be in Orders, or be immediatly concern'd in the Instruction of Youth, I do not think his Character depends upon his philosophical Speculations, as the World is now model'd. . . ." Hume was soon to find through sad experience that the new-modelled world did indeed remain intolerant. He was also to find that the *Treatise* was not dead.

Pringle " was an agreeable lecturer, though no great master of the science he taught," commented one of his students, Alexander Carlyle of Inveresk,[1] later Hume's great friend. Pringle had never taken his chair over-seriously and, since 1742, had been on leave of absence as physician to the army. Soon after being appointed Physician-General to the Forces in Flanders, Pringle wrote from Brussels, on 20 June 1744, to the Lord Provost of Edinburgh : " I take therefore this opportunity to acquaint your Lordship I am ready to do what your Lordship and the Patrons of the university shall judge for the good of that Society, and beg that your Lordship will upon the receipt of this let me know your mind, That if it is necessary, I may send immediately a formall Resignation to allow my Patrons time for chuseing a proper person to succeed before the next winters Session." [2]

[1] Carlyle, pp. 54–5.
[2] This and all otherwise unacknowledged quotations from the Town Council minutes are taken from the MS " Council Records," vols. lxiv, lxv, under dates specified, in the City Chambers, Edinburgh.

The Lord Provost, John Coutts, delighted with the imminent vacancy, immediately asked his young friend, David Hume, if he was interested in standing as a candidate. Hume was, and Coutts mentioned his name to several members of the Town Council, also advising him " to mention myself as a Candidate to all my Friends, not with a View of solliciting or making Interest, but in order to get the Public Voice on my Side, that he might with the more Assurance employ his Interest in my Behalf. I accordingly did so," declares Hume in a letter of 4 August; " & being allow'd to make use of the Provost's Name, I found presently that I shou'd have the whole Council on my Side, & that indeed I shou'd have no Antagonist."

Nevertheless, when Coutts read Pringle's letter before the Town Council on 18 July, other letters from him to individual members of the Council were produced which made it abundantly clear that Pringle was really angling for an extension of leave for a third year. But the majority of the Council were firm and instructed Coutts to demand that Pringle should either return by 1 November or resign immediately : " and in case the Doctor wrytes no Letter signifying that he is to Return or Demitt, the Councill Resolve they will then hold and Declare the office vacant." " But Mr Couts," continues Hume in the above letter, " tho his Authority be quite absolute in the Town, yet makes it a Rule to govern them with the utmost Gentleness & Moderation ; this good Maxim he sometimes pushes even to an Extreme." The actual letter, therefore, that Coutts sent to Pringle on 20 July, with the Council's consent, offered a compromise, which Coutts was certain would be rejected :

I am further commanded by the Councill to say that in order to demonstrate the great Regard they have for you, They would even make a Stretch of Indulgeing you another year, provided they were absolutely certain, That you would return to your Residence here at the end thereof, And that this may not appear to you a bare Compliment, I have the Authority of the Councill to say that you can still command that Indulgence by expressing to me in a Letter by Course of post, that you positively will in any Event make your Residence here before sitting of the Colledge. And that if it be then war, you will Resign your office of Physician to the army or any other office you shall be possest of incompatable with your attendance on the University. . . .

" This last Condition," wrote Hume in the letter of 4 August, " Mr Couts thinks it impossible he [Pringle] will comply with : Because he has a Guinea a day at present as Physician to the Army, along with a good deal of Business, & half pay during Life : And there seems at present to be small Chance for a Peace before the Term here assign'd." But Coutts's desire to placate both sides enabled Pringle to equivocate further. Within two hours of receiving the Council's communication, he penned his reply, dated 15 August, N.S. Seizing the offer of an extension of leave, he "can never think they [the Town Council] intended to burthen their free Gift with a Condition implying ane utter Impossibility of being able to profite of their Good Will, which impossibility I have not as the Words stand been able to separate from the Offer." Were he free, he would return at once ; but a soldier, he reminds them, is not free. "The Council will likewise advert that it is not here in the Active part of War as at home with Civil posts, when a Man may resign or promise to Resign when he pleases ; but whoever is here engaged, is engaged strictly 'till he is dismiss'd. . . ." He, therefore, freely submits a new proposal to the effect that, ". . . as the Council has agreed there may yet ane Indulgence be allowed for another Year on Condition of a Certainty for having a Professor teaching the Year following ; I hereby solemnly engage myself by Aprile next to assure the Council of my returning or not returning by Winter. . . ."

Realising his tactical blunder, Lord Provost Coutts replied to Pringle unambiguously : ". . . I am desir'd [by the Council] to give for Answer, that since they cannot have a Security for your Returning to the Exercise of your profession in this University in terms of their Letter of the 20. Ulte, they think themselves bound in Duty to desire that in Course of post, you will be pleased to send your Resignation. . . ." Pringle could hardly evade this.

But evade it he did. On 17 August, N.S., he accepted the original offer of a year's extension of leave and promised to return then. The promise, however, is vaguely worded : "I can with Assurance acquaint your Lordship, that as my last Engagements were made with Sincerity & Inclination to return, I have now the firm belief of having it in my power to doe it by November 1745, in the terms offered me by the Council." Naturally the Council was dissatisfied and required a direct answer with positive assurances of the terms of their original letter of 20 July.

All these exchanges of letters proved time-consuming, and time was working for the doctor and against David Hume. With the start of the University session in November, no answer had been received from Pringle. So to him went the victory by default. The chair had not been declared vacant and his substitute, a Mr William Cleghorn, was the only person authorised to conduct his classes. At the Town Council meeting on 7 November the newly elected Lord Provost, Archibald Stewart, informed his colleagues that although Pringle had not replied, he had definitely received the Council's ultimatum. His Lordship, who was also Hume's good friend, recommended to the Council " (after a decent time still allowed to the Doctor to send his Answer) That in Case no Answer came, or none to their Satisfaction, That they would take such measures as might tend to Vindicate the Honour and Authority of the Council, and Security to the true Interest of the University whereof they are patrons." The Council agreed to act " as soon as the Nature of the thing will admit."

The nature of the thing admitted of no action until 27 March 1745, when Pringle's letter of resignation was finally produced before the Town Council. Provost Stewart being on official business in London at the moment, the Council was presided over by Baillie Gavin Hamilton, the eminent Edinburgh bookseller. The resignation was accepted and the chair declared vacant. As the University was in session, Mr William Cleghorn, who had been teaching Pringle's classes for nearly three years, was instructed to continue, " so as the Students may have no Cause of Complaint during the Vacancy of the Professorship." In the meanwhile, the Council " may have under their Consideration the Supplying the said office with an able and well qualified person." The continued postponements, together with the loss of the influential Coutts and Stewart as Lords Provost, were not helping Hume's candidacy. The opposition was growing.

As early as August 1744 Hume had informed Mure of Caldwell that, " The accusation of Heresy, Deism, Scepticism, Atheism &c &c &c. was started against me ; but never took, being bore down by the contrary Authority of all the good Company in Town." By April 1745, however, he was forced to admit " that such a popular Clamour has been raisd against me in Edinburgh, on account of Scepticism, Heterodoxy & other hard Names, which confound the ignorant, that my Friends find some Difficulty, in working out the Point of my Professorship, which once appear'd so easy." This letter to Matthew Sharpe of Hoddam, therefore, requests him to use his good offices with his nephew, Lord Tinwald, to bring influence to bear upon certain members of the Council. The philosopher, with tongue in cheek, tells Sharpe, " Did I need a Testimonial for my Orthodoxy I shoud certainly appeal to you. For you know that I always imitated Job's Friends, & defended the Cause of Providence when [you] attackt it, on account of the Headachs you felt after a Deba[uch]."

By the spring of 1745 Hume's friends faced an opposition which included such important figures as Professors Hutcheson and Leechman of Glasgow University as well as William Wishart, the Principal of Edinburgh University. Hume was greatly distressed; he found it " absolutely incredible " that Hutcheson and Leechman " agreed that I was a very unfit Person for such an office." To Mure he complained bitterly:

All my Friends think that he [Hutcheson] has been rendering me bad Offices to the utmost of his Power. And I know, that Mr Coutts, to whom I said rashly, that I thought I coud depend upon Mr Hutcheson's Friendship & Recommendation; I say, Mr Coutts now speaks of that Professor rather as my Enemy than as my Friend. What can be the Meaning of this Conduct in that celebrated and benevolent Moralist, I cannot imagine. I shall be glad to find, for the Honour of Philosophy, that I am mistaken; & indeed, I hope so too: And beg of you to enquire a little into the Matter; but very cautiously, lest I make him my open and profess'd Enemy, which I woud willingly avoid.

Hutcheson presumably deemed Hume unfit for the chair as the University Senatus had imposed on the holder, at Pringle's election in 1734, the duty of reconciling Moral Philosophy with Divinity. The Professor was especially directed to " praelect " every Monday " upon the Truth of the Christian religion."

On 3 April 1745 the Town Council, in the absence of some of Hume's friends, met and elected Francis Hutcheson to the professorship. The Minutes actually read " George Hutchison "! Baillie Hamilton was instructed to convene the Reverend Ministers of the City of Edinburgh for their *avisamentum* or advice. The Ministers declared themselves, " well pleased " but hoped that in future the Honourable Town Council would " order the ministers *avisamentum* to be held prior to any Choice, and that such *avisamentum* should be taken by the whole Councill and not by a Committee as heretofore has been the practice."

On 10 April Baillie Hamilton was chagrined to have to inform the Council that Professor Hutcheson had declined to accept the office. Here was an unexpected blow to the anti-Hume forces! Hutcheson's letter also shows that he had been apprised of the Council's intention " some time agoe," but had been undecided. " . . . . Severall other persons," including David Hume and William Cleghorn, were " named as proper Candidates . . . " but Hume's enemies refused to allow a decision. It was voted to delay action for a month or six weeks and, in the meantime, to take the ministers' *avisamentum*. During this tense period Hume wrote the desperate appeal for help to Matthew Sharpe of Hoddam: " There is no Time to lose. . . . A Word to the Wise."

Although Hutcheson's refusal made it still possible, in theory, for Hume to be elected, political factors intervened. The Principal Secretary of State for Scotland was John Hay, fourth Marquess of Tweeddale, the leader of the " Squadrone Volante," a third force operating between the Argyll–Islay interest and the Jacobites. His office afforded him tremendous powers of patronage and he was receiving almost daily reports from various " informers," notably Alexander Arbuthnot and Thomas Hay.[1] Much of the opposition to Hume, from the Edinburgh ministers and others, was in reality opposition to Coutts and his party, and political intrigue worked against Hume equally with the charges of " Heresy, Deism, Scepticism, Atheism &c &c &c " that he had complained about to Mure of Caldwell.

On 26 May, for instance, Hay told Tweeddale that " Deacon Cuming had declared he was under promise to Lord Elibank to vote for Mr Home because his Lordship had got a Brother of Cumings recommended in the fleet & Mr Arbuthnot said that all he believed it would be practicable to bring Cuming to would be to be absent." Like many laymen concerned, Hay viewed the election in a purely political light, but he was not without a certain ironic awareness of the effect that Hume's " Heresy " and " Atheism " were having on his friends and supporters. " I hardly think," he opined, " that any politic consideration has led Lord Elibank to draw Cuming off. I presume he has meddled out of friendship to Mr Hume for My Lord & he [Cumin] & Provost Couts are all too wise to enter into the vulgar mistakes of Christianity." Hume would surely have appreciated that sally, had he known it, but he was unaware of the political confrontation, as well as of the friendly intervention of his old friend Lord Elibank.

No official record survives of the joint session of the Ministers of Edinburgh (a body quite distinct from the Presbytery of Edinburgh) and the Town Council. The precise function of the *advice* of the ministers remains undefined, that is, whether the ministers could veto any candidate proposed by the patrons of the university, the Town Council, or whether they merely had the opportunity to express their preference. In Hutcheson's case, the ministers were consulted after the election, but urged that in future they should be consulted beforehand. In Hume's case, they were consulted in advance, a fact which spelt his doom.

At the meeting early in May, the attack on Hume was led by the Principal, William Wishart, who had himself been accused

---

[1] All succeeding quotations from letters of the " informers " to Lord Tweeddale are taken from NLS, MS 7076 (part of the Yester Papers).

of heterodoxy a few years before (for not sufficiently stressing the importance of Original Sin). The son of the principal during Hume's student days, and a professor of divinity, he had been elected Principal in 1737. Hume's account of the principal's charge, in a letter to Henry Home, is illuminating:

> The Principal found himself reduc'd to this Dilemma; either to draw Heresies from my Principles by Inferences & Deductions, which he knew wou'd never do with the Ministers & Town Council. Or if he made use of my words, he must pervert them & misrepresent them in the grossest way in the World. This last Expedient he chose, with much Prudence but very little Honesty.[1]

Hume was not, however, entirely undefended by the ministers. "I think," he continues in this letter, "Mr Wallace's Conduct has been very noble & generous; & I am much oblig'd to him." Robert Wallace, once Professor Gregory's substitute in his mathematical class and a member of the Rankenian Club, had in 1733 become minister to the New Greyfriars Church in Edinburgh and in 1739 was translated to the New North Church. He was also charged with church patronage in Scotland, and in 1744 was appointed one of His Majesty's chaplains for Scotland. A man with the courage of his convictions, Wallace had in 1737 defied the national government over the Porteous Riots, and in 1739 the Town Council of Edinburgh over his church translation. In ecclesiastical polity he was one of the leaders of the Moderate Party, whose views he summarized in the title of an early sermon: *Ignorance and Superstition a Source of Violence and Cruelty.* In 1743 he was Moderator of the General Assembly. Robert Wallace was a man of influence and prestige, as well as of liberal principles. The friendly connexions with Hume, his junior by some fourteen years, continued for a long time.

The writer of an unsigned letter to the *London Chronicle*, 5–7 November 1776, soon after Hume's death, was clearly present at the meeting of Ministers and Town Council in 1745:

> . . . it is true that most of the clergy objected to the electing of honest David, grounding their objection on "A Treatise on Human Nature," published in 1739, which had been ascribed to him. All the body, however, did not concur in the measure. The late celebrated Dr. Wallace, faithful to those generous sentiments which he had early imbibed and uniformly professed, with an impartiality as well as dignity becoming them, declared to the counsellors in strong terms, that he did not think himself entitled to give his opinion, on pretext too of a juvenile as well as anonymous performance, which had been little read, and which was less understood, against chusing that ingenious gentleman, more than any of the other candidates. The Doctor's liberal mind

[1] NHL, p. 15.

was elevated far above, and his philosophic indignation was greatly raised at the inquisitorial zeal discovered on this occasion.

But Wallace's sweet reasonableness was brushed aside by the inquisitorial zeal of Wishart and his followers of the " Popular " or Evangelical Party, and twelve of the fifteen ministers of Edinburgh advised against David Hume's election. The three in the minority were Patrick Cumin, Professor of Church History at Edinburgh University; Alexander Webster, minister of the Tolbooth Church ; and of course Robert Wallace. The case was not yet finally lost, however, as the Town Council still had to hold its election and clearly did not consider itself necessarily bound by the minister's *avisamentum*.

When the news of the ministers *avisamentum* reached Hume, at Weldehall near St Albans, he immediately wrote a " hastily compos'd " letter to Coutts, dated 8 May 1745. This reached Henry Home, who rushed it into print as : *A Letter from a Gentleman to his Friend in Edinburgh : Containing some Observations on a Specimen of the Principles concerning Religion and Morality, said to be maintain'd in a Book lately publish'd, intituled, A Treatise of Human Nature, &c.* The anonymous pamphlet was advertised in both the *Caledonian Mercury* and the *Edinburgh Evening Courant* for Tuesday 21 May 1745. This recently discovered item has its bearing on Hume's thought.[1]

A Letter from a Gentleman is more personal in tone than the *Abstract* because Hume is defending his qualifications for a professorship and refuting Principal Wishart's six specific charges against him. Not having a copy of the *Treatise* at hand, he is relying on memory and reason, so that his views on scepticism and causality are stated afresh in accounts as clear and forthright as they are concise. His rejection of the *a priori* in the realm of matters of fact is vigorously put and his " common sense " and " orthodox " attitudes are emphasized. In a few instances, he plays down certain highly unorthodox religious scepticisms, already stated in the *Treatise*, or to be stated later, notably in the *Dialogues concerning Natural Religion.* This was, moreover, Hume's first opportunity since the *Treatise* to defend his system of morality. In addition this letter augments what had been rather neglected in the *Treatise*, though somewhat developed in the *Abstract* : the naming of names and the placing of the author in past and contemporary contexts. For example, the Moderns instanced

---

[1] *David Hume : A Letter from a Gentleman to his Friend in Edinburgh (1745)*, edited, with detailed introduction, by Mossner and J. V. Price (Edinburgh 1967). The NLS acquired the pamphlet in 1966. See Textual Supplement.

include Descartes, *Huet* and Malebranche ; and Berkeley, Clarke, *Cudworth*, Locke, *Newton*, Hutcheson, *Tillotson* and Wollaston. (The italicized names are not mentioned in either the *Treatise* or the Abstract.)

All was in vain. Convinced that defeat was inevitable, Hume wrote to Archibald Stewart in the attempt " to disengage myself from my friends in Edinburgh " ; and Stewart " very frankly and kindly allow'd me my liberty of choice. . . ." So on 1 June Hume asked Henry Home to withdraw his candidacy, provided his supporters agreed. " I can now laugh," he added, " at the Malice of those who intended to do me an Injury, without being able to reach me." But this letter arrived too late for the Council meeting of 5 June, when, according to Hume, " the matter was brought to an issue, and by the cabals of the Principal, the bigotry of the clergy, and the credulity of the mob, we lost it." In the official language of its Minutes, the Town Council, " being satisfied that Mr William Cleghorn merchant burgess of Edinburgh (who has had the Care and Teaching of Doctor Pringles Class these three years past, and is otherwise well Recommended) is sufficiently qualified to discharge the Duty of that office," duly elected the said Mr Cleghorn " to be Professor of Pneumaticks and morale Philosophy in this Citys university *ad vitam aut Culpam*." At the next meeting on 19 June, Cleghorn accepted the post and was sworn in. An academic question was settled.

Four days before Hume had commented to Henry Home : " I have indeed a great Regard as well as Sense of Gratitude for Mr Couts, & am heartily sorry he shou'd have been defeated by a Pack of Scoundrels, tho it was entirely by his own Fault." What Hume was not aware of was that Coutts had been not only inept but actually faithless. Arbuthnot, the " informer " spells out to Tweeddale Coutts's shifting strategy :

The man Mr Coutts first Sett up was Mr Home a Son of Ninewalls ; when he found that he could not carry him then Mr Law whose father [William] had formerly been prophessor [1708–29] was Sett up and when that could not be brought to bear as his Last Shift, he sett up principal Wishart, though he by no means Liked the man, yett he judged him the only person that could defeat his opposers and therefor sett him up but yesterday when the affair came to be determined he had only twelve of the Councill for him and Mr Cleghorn had nineteen . . .

So much for politics—and friendship.

" I never was very fond of this Office of which I have been disappointed, on account of the Restraint, which I forsaw it wou'd have impos'd on me." Hume's last words on the

Edinburgh chair strike me, regrettably, as sour grapes, for he had not really learnt his lesson. Academic life, under a principal who had opposed his election and with an antagonistic clergy denouncing him from the pulpit, could never have been calm or lasting. Astonishingly, Hume was willing to stand in 1751 for the Logic Chair at Glasgow University, but happily for his peace of mind, with the same result. (Edinburgh's greatest non-Professor is now vindicated by the David Hume Tower in George Square.)

After Hume's death, the debate raged in the press over certain events of his career. For the Edinburgh University chair, the affirmative side declared " he was eminently qualified . . . [and in that office] could have been of more service to his country than in any other." The negative side waxed ironical : " Ye illiberal and narrow-minded men of the presbytery of Edinburgh, what hurt did you not do to your country, in depriving it of David Hume for professor of morality ! What a blessed system of ethicks would he have instilled into our youth ! " [1]

The episode of the Edinburgh chair was further evidence that the *Treatise of Human Nature* was never strictly dead. Its reputation branded the author as unfit to teach the young. An ill-fated work, it not only failed to interest thinkers capable of grasping its ideas, but it was beginning to be read by those who, without understanding it, could make trouble for the author. Hume's feelings against the *Treatise* became so intense that, after rewriting some sections of it, he ultimately disowned it publicly. The *Letter to a Gentleman* contains the first disavowal : " I am indeed of Opinion, that the Author had better delayed the publishing of that Book ; not on account of any dangerous Principles contained in it, but because on more mature Consideration he might have rendered it much less imperfect by further Corrections and Revisals."

Baulked at the University, David Hume yet became an educator in 1745—at least, in name. Invited in January to be the tutor to the Marquess of Annandale, he left Edinburgh in February, in secrecy, " which I thought necessary for preserving my Interest there." From Weldehall near St Albans, he directed the final stages of the campaign for the Edinburgh chair and lost it.

[1] " An Account of the Life and Writings of the late David Hume," in *Annual Register*, XIX (1776), 30 ; " Strictures on the Account of the Life and Writings of David Hume," *Weekly Magazine*, XXXVIII (1777), 291.

CHAPTER 13

THE UNFORTUNATE TUTOR

" I have found in this whole affair that some men are
honest and sincere, and others not so."

" IN 1745, I received a Letter from the Marquess of Annandale,
inviting me to come and live with him in England : I found also,
that the Friends and Family of that young Nobleman, were
desirous of putting him under my Care and Direction : For the
State of his Mind and Health required it. I lived with
him a Twelvemonth : My Appointments during that time
made a considerable Accession to my small Fortune." So wrote
Hume in *My Own Life*, giving no hint of any fracas and little more
than a hint about the madness of the Marquess. The complete
story of this unhappy year proves, however, that Hume's brief
account is correctly pointed, that its chief value to him was the
increase in his small fortune.

The year was not, however, entirely unhappy. It started out
well enough in January with the letter from the Marquess of
Annandale inviting Hume to come and live with him in London
and enclosing a bill of £100 to cover immediate expenses. That
David Hume was cautious about this overture is evident both from
his investigations amongst the friends and family of the young
nobleman and from the fact that he signed the receipt for the bill
of £100 at Edinburgh only on 8 February.[1] Consultation with
Ronald Crawfurd, Scottish agent for the Annandale family, revealed that it was his lordship's intention to pay the new companion
£300 annually. Lord Elibank, James Ferguson (later Lord Pitfour), Henry Home, Archibald Stewart—all intimate friends of
Hume's—were connected in one way or another with the
Johnstones of Annandale or, at any rate, knew the full story of that
very old and very wealthy house. Their advice was sought and,
although they were not over-enthusiastic (especially as the
Edinburgh professorship was still hanging fire), they finally
approved.

With the £100 in his pocket, David Hume went up to London

---

[1] Sir William Fraser, *The Annandale Family Book, of the Johnstones, Earls and Marquises
of Annandale* (Edinburgh 1894), I, cccxxxvi.

about the end of February. There he met the handsome twenty-five year old Marquess, whom he found to be eccentric but cordial. Hume must, indeed, have been both surprised and flattered to discover that he owed his good fortune to the young man's having been " charmed " with some of the *Essays Moral and Political*. With this good augury, Hume " took lodgings near him, and saw him every day, till we went out together to Weldehall on the first of Aprile." In the meanwhile Hume also met Sir James Johnstone of Westerhall, brother-in-law to the Dowager Marchioness of Annandale, and Captain Philip Vincent of the Royal Navy, her cousin. These gentlemen, the lady's chief advisers, corroborated the terms already mentioned ; it was not, however, until 1 September that they were put into writing by Vincent at Hume's request. As they were to become subject of dispute, it will be well to observe the exact wording :

> I engaged [wrote Vincent] that my Lord should pay you three hundred pounds Sterling a year, so long as you continued to live with him, beginning from the first of April, one thousand seven hundred and forty five : also, that the said Marques, or his heirs, should be engaged to pay you, or your heirs, the sum of three hundred pounds, as one year's salary, even though the Marques should happen to die any time in the first year of your attendance, or should embrace any new scheme or plan of life, which should make him chuse that you should not continue to live out the first year with him. Another condition was, that, if you should, on your part, chuse to leave the Marques any time in the first or subsequent years, you should be free to do it ; and that the Marques should be bound to pay you your salary for the time you had attended him, and also the salary for that quarter in which you should leave him, in the same manner as if that quarter should be fully expired.[1]

The terms of the contract were designed to afford a modicum of protection to the gentleman-companion from possible vacillations on the part of the Marquess, to which the long string of tutors he had previously had bears mute testimony. Several of Hume's predecessors can be named : Colonel James Forrester, a certain Major Johnstone, Mr Peter Young ; the immediate predecessor was apparently a Mr Grano. Hume was further protected by the contract in that, if he was offered the Edinburgh professorship, he was entitled to resign immediately and to receive full compensation for his services.

For some time all was tranquillity at the country manor in the pleasant hilly country near St Albans, a little less than twenty miles north-west of London. On 25 April Hume could write that, " as my Lord has now taken as strong a Turn to Solitude & Repose

---

[1] Quoted by Thomas Murray in his *Letters of David Hume, and Extracts of Letters referring to him* (Edinburgh 1841), p. 10. Cited hereafter as " Murray."

as he formerly had to Company & Agitation, tis to be hopd that his good Parts & excellent Dispositions may at last being accompanyd with more Health & Tranquillity, render him a Comfort to his Friends, if not an Ornament to his Countrey." Annandale's "good Parts" took a literary bent, to foster which Hume and Captain Vincent chose for him "a very pretty collection of authors." One of Annandale's literary products was a novel of which, Hume tells Johnstone, after fruitless attempts at suppression, they were "oblig'd to print off thirty copies, to make him believe that we had printed a thousand, and that they were to be disperst all over the kingdom"; and in the conclusion of the same letter, "We live," he adds, "extremely well together, without the smallest interruption of good will and friendship, and he has done me the honour of composing some French verses in my praise."

"In the main I am far from being displeasd with my present Situation," Hume reported to Henry Home the middle of June. "I shall pass the Winter in London, & the Summer *en famille* with very agreeable People, & at such a Distance from London that I can be there once a week or fortnight, if I please. My Friend's *Bizarreries* may give me Diversion sometimes, sometimes *l'ennui* but never Trouble. And there is a pretty certain Prospect, that tho his Case will become, perhaps, more melancholy for him, yet it will become every day more easy for me. At all Adventures I shall be able to save Money; & if my Course of Life shoud become tiresome to me, I may give up their Bond of Annuity, & retire to the South of France or home with such a Competency as may satisfy my Wants, & which consequently ought to satisfy my Ambition." Captain Vincent had indeed mentioned to Hume the possibility of securing for him an annuity of £100 a year for life; but the suggestion eventually fell through because of the objections of the Solicitor-General for England, William Murray, later the great Earl of Mansfield. Another disappointment was hinted at in the same letter to Henry Home: "I have Leizure enough for reading; but scarce for writing at present. However I intend to continue these philosophical & moral Essays, which I mention'd to you."

By September, however, difficulties began to arise, both foreseen and unforeseen. The Marquess, as had been anticipated, became more violent and more intractable. He developed the habit of deliberately vomiting after meals and had to be constantly watched. His companion, consequently, was forced to

become more a keeper than a tutor. Yet this " melancholy &
unsociable " life might have remained at least bearable, considering the excellent financial arrangements had it not been for
the downright suspicious actions of Captain Philip Vincent. In
April Hume had described Vincent as " a mighty honest friendly
Man." In October he was complaining to Sir James Johnstone
for his " having yokt me here with a man of the Captain's character, without giving me the least hint concerning it, if it was
known to you, as indeed it is no secret to the world." Finally, by
the end of November, on the authority of Oswald of Dunnikier,
who had become Scottish Commissioner of the Navy in 1744,
Hume spelt out for Johnstone the character of Vincent. The
Captain " was universally regarded as a low, dirty, despicable
Fellow ; and particularly infamous for pimping his wife to another
Peer. That is a Fact," continued Hume, " I have also some
reason to know ; and tallies exactly with what I told you. You
may ask Oswald."

For his part, Captain Vincent also changed his original high
opinion of David Hume. In April Vincent wrote of " Mr Hume
a gentleman born, and of parts and education, as well as of temper
and manners," and, as late as August, referred to him as, " a man
of erudition and letters, whom indeed I think very deserving and
good natured " ; " a very worthy and knowing man " ; and " my
friend Mr Hume." By November, however, Vincent was prepared
to pay Hume off on the spot, and the following spring to cut his
salary in half. Finally, after Hume's dismissal in mid-April 1746,
Vincent expressed regret that he had ever " had any sort of
correspondence or knowledge " of Hume, " which I reckon one
of the misfortunes of my life." [1]

There seems little doubt that Vincent was a highhanded and
unscrupulous adventurer, who, having been placed in charge of
the English affairs of the Annandale estate with the approval
of the complaisant and unbusinesslike Sir James Johnstone, began
to abuse his authority for purposes of his own. In the course of
time, David Hume became convinced that these " dark intricate
designs " included the ousting of Johnstone as family adviser and
eventually the lifting of the estate, or some part of it, from the
Dowager Marchioness herself. Whether this was actually true
to the extent that Hume imagined it or not cannot now be determined, but there was unmistakable evil in the house. The
philosopher-tutor, believing himself to be caught in a mesh of

[1] Murray, pp. 13, 14, 15, 67.

intrigue involving the good name of an ancient Scottish family, sought to resist it.. In so doing he came up against brutality and unscrupulousness and fought a losing battle from the moment of the declaration of hostilities.

The first skirmish occurred when Vincent announced that the Marquess and his companion were to remain at Weldehall during the ensuing winter. Hume rebelled, cautiously at first, and then openly. Vincent was astonished that a mere tutor—to his way of thinking an upper servant—should challenge his decision. He was angered when that tutor could neither be bribed nor bullied and appealed over his head to both Sir James Johnstone and the Marchioness. Hume's arguments against remaining at Weldehall make sound sense : the Marquess needed more society and diversion and a warmer and more habitable house during the cold weather ; such a place, too, might be had in town at a saving to the family of £300–400. There is no doubt, in addition, that Hume was personally desirous of spending the winter in London, for reasons shortly to appear ; and one of his boasts to Henry Home had been that " I shall spend the Winter in London." The Marchioness refused, in however friendly a manner, to step in and settle a dispute between her two advisers. And Sir James Johnstone could never be brought to make a troublesome decision. The skirmish was won by Vincent.

Having made an unanticipated antagonist in David Hume, Vincent determined to get rid of him. Taking advantage of one of the Marquess's many fits of depression during which he expressed the desire to be alone, Vincent somehow induced him to say the same to Hume, then at once informed the Marchioness and Johnstone. A few days later the Marquess told Hume that he was entirely happy with him. Hume at once informed the Marchioness and Johnstone. And so it went back and forth, month after month. Even my Lord's valet, Panaiotty, entered into the fracas, being used as a go-between by all concerned.

During this unhappy period Hume hung on grimly in the " resolution of weathering out all the difficulties and discourage- ments as long as possible. . . ." He vainly tried to get Johnstone to intercede, writing to him, for example, towards the end of October : " God forgive you, Dear Sir, God forgive you, for neither coming to us, nor writing to us. The unaccountable, and, I may say, the inhuman treatment we meet with here, throws your friend [the Marquess] into rage and fury, and me into the greatest melancholy." Another time Hume exclaimed to Johnstone :

" What a scene is this for a man nourished in philosophy and polite letters to entér into, all of a sudden and unprepar'd ! But I can laugh, whatever happens ; and the newness of such practices rather diverts me. At first they caus'd indignation and hatred ; and even (tho' I am asham'd to confess it) melancholy and sorrow." It is certain, however, despite Hume's bravado, that melancholy and sorrow predominated.

Hume himself vacillated in the warfare with Vincent. On one occasion he informed Vincent that he could not possibly stay on with Lord Annandale after the completion of his year, but on another occasion said that he might possibly stay on. Vincent, for his part, having made up his mind that Hume must not stay on, set the salary for a second year as half that for the first. This cut was made in the name of retrenchment and on the pretext that the Marquess required only a companion and not a tutor. It was really made, as Hume at once recognised, not to save money for one of the wealthiest estates in the two kingdoms, but to humiliate him with the name of keeper rather than of tutor and to ensure his consequent resignation. Yet that resignation was not immediately forthcoming. Stubbornly Hume held on and wrote to the Marchioness to say that he would accept the new terms if she agreed that they were just. Hume also, to be sure, appealed to Johnstone, without whom the Marchioness made no decision ; but, with experience of Johnstone's indecisiveness, Hume further appealed to Lord Elibank and to Henry Home to exert pressure upon him. This they did, and in no uncertain terms.

" I take the liberty," wrote Elibank to Johnstone, his brother-in-law, " to send you the enclosed from David Hume, and am persuaded you'll think it for your own interest to comply with the request of it. I own it is my opinion that Vincent's only view in turning off Hume is, that he finds him an obstacle to selfish views of his own, to which even Lady Annandale may in time become a sacrifice. This I say from my personal knowledge of the man." [1] These are pretty strong words, and they afford a complete confirmation of Hume's own interpretation of the case. Henry Home's letter, even more forthright, indicates a deep personal feeling for David Hume and must be presented in full :

Kames, 14th April, 1746.
Sir,
    I had a letter from my friend David Home lately, which surprised me not a little, as if there were a plot formed against him to diminish his salary.

[1] Murray, p. 50.

For my part, I was never hearty in his present situation ; as I did not consider
the terms offered as any sufficient temptation for him to relinquish his studies,
which, in all probability, would redound more to his advantage some time or
other. For this reason, tho' I had a good deal of indignation at the dishonourable behaviour of the author of this motion, yet underhand I was not displeased
with any occasion, not blameable on my friend's part, to disengage him.
I thought instantly of writing him a letter not to stay upon any terms after
such an affront ; but, reflecting upon your interest in this matter, I found
such an advice would be inconsistent with the duty I owe you, and therefore
stopped short till I should hear from you. I'm well apprized of the great
tenderness you have for your poor chief ; and it is certainly of some consequence that he should have about him at least one person of integrity ; and
it should have given me pain to be the author of an advice that might affect
you, though but indirectly. At the same time, I cannot think of sacrificing
my friend, even upon your account, to make him submit to dishonourable
terms ; and, therefore, if you esteem his attendance of any use to the Marquis,
I beg you'll interpose that no more attempts of this kind be made. For I
must be so free to declare that, should he himself yield to accept of lower
terms, which I trust he will not be so mean spirited to do, he shall never
have my consent, and I know he will not act without it. If you find you can
do without him, I shall be glad to receive him home upon fair terms ; otherwise I entreat, for your own sake, you will try to disencumber yourself of that
intolerable shyness which plagues you, and act with that vigour and resolution
which becomes your station, and the near relation you bear to the family.
Do this to oblige me as well as yourself ; for it would be a new and disagreeable
scene to be engaged in any interest against you. Show this letter to the Lady,
and I know she will espouse my friend's quarrel heartily. She hates cunning
and low arts. 'Tis not impossible I may see her this summer, especially if the
Session sit not ; and there appears no great prospect of its sitting this summer.
Till I hear from you, I shall endeavour to keep my friend in suspense.

Yours devotedly,

Henry Home.[1]

Was David Hume being " mean spirited " in offering to submit
to Vincent's " dishonourable terms " ? Under the circumstances,
I think not. In reality he did not submit, stating only that he
would accept the terms if the Marquess and the Marchioness
thought them just and in so saying he of course felt positive that
they would not. Despite all his troubles, Hume was not really
anxious to leave the Annandale family. He had, on the one hand,
a keen sense of responsibility in keeping an eye on the machinations
of Vincent, and he was, on the other, deep in his own literary
pursuits. With a reasonable salary—he informed Johnstone that
£200 might be acceptable—he could well afford to swallow a certain amount of pride. It was all very well for his friend Henry
Home, well meaning—though highhanded—as he was, to express
such keen hopes for his future as a man of letters, but actually

---

[1] Murray, pp. 55–7.

now, at the age of thirty-five, he had no permanent career by which he might support himself. Still, he was most unhappy over the prospects of staying on with Lord Annandale if subject to the authority of Vincent. " My way of living," he told Johnstone the end of March, " is more melancholy than ever was submitted to by any human creature, who ever had any hopes or pretensions to any thing better ; and if to confinement, solitude, and bad company, be also added these marks of disregard, . . . I shall say nothing, but only that books, study, leisure, frugality, and independence, are a great deal better."

In the event, the final decision was not Hume's to make. The Dowager Marchioness again refused to enter into the dispute ; but even before her letter could reach him, a crisis had been precipitated. After a period of relatively good behaviour, Lord Annandale threw a tantrum and peremptorily ordered Hume out of the house. This was nothing new, but it was repeated throughout the course of the following week. My Lord was not to be reconciled. Finally on 16 April Hume moved out bag-and-baggage, not without the approval of Captain Vincent, and not without a final explosion over the payment of his salary. The Captain gave Hume a banker's draft for £200, payable in fifteen days, and a promissory note for another £100, payable in September. Hume demanded a further £75, invoking the clause in the contract which stipulated that he was entitled to full payment for a quarter if he left before the end of the quarter. Vincent refused.

Hume, of course, did not take this refusal lying down, and appealed to Sir James Johnstone, writing to him the following day : " There was a most villainous trick endeavour'd to be play'd me by my old friend, who, after stating justly and fairly the sum due to me, in order to engage me to go away more easily, immediately afterwards pretended to have chang'd his opinion and endeavour'd to defraud me of £75. But I got it under his hand (because I told him I wou'd not trust his word for a farthing), to stand to your award and Lady Annandale's. There is no haste in the determination ; so I shall write you more fully afterwards." [1]

From Edinburgh, Henry Home, as usual, jumped to the rescue. On 9 June he wrote to Johnstone :

I am sorry to find by a Letter from my friend David Home that he has left the Marquess of Annandale, upon a hint as he tells me that there is no longer occasion for his attendance. I am concerned upon his account and partly that I doubt of the Marquess's finding a more faithful or more affectionate Servant.

He acquaints me that there is a dispute about a Quarter's Sallary which is submited to My Lady Marchioness of Annandale and to you, begging that I wóu'd write my Thoughts to you upon this Subject. I cannot decline this Task, because it is the Request of a friend ; and for that Reason you'll pardon me for giving you some trouble.

Of the agreement betwixt the Marquess of Annandale and Mr. Home, one Article is, that the Sallary shall be due for that Quarter in which Mr. Home leaves his Service in the same way as if he had served out the Quarter. This Clause is very equitable, and was well design'd. A Servant who is dropt betwixt Terms is not suppos'd to find ready Imployment ; and therefore unless the Separation be by his fault, he should not be a Loser by it, but his Sallary carried on for some moderate Space of Time, such as may be thought sufficient to get into new Imployment. And here a Quarter is condescended on, the shortest Time commonly allowed in such Cases.

Mr. Home entered to his Service 1st. Aprile 1745 and continued with the Marquess 'till the 16th Aprile 1746. By the tenor of the Agreement he's intitled to a year and a Quarter's Sallary. But it is objected against him that on the 29th of March 1746 Captain Vincent offered him but £150 for another year's attendance and therefore that his Claim for the Quarter in dispute is but in proportion to that offer viz. £37.10sh.

Touching this Circumstance Mr. Home acknowledges the offer was made him and says he gave his Answer on the 3d Aprile that whatever Lord and Lady Annandale decided he would willingly submit to but that instead of concluding the new Agreement, he was dismist altogether upon 16th Aprile.

The Question then is whether he is intitled to £75 for the broken Quarter or only to £37.10sh. The thing is a mere trifle to the Marques of Annandale, but of some importance to a young Gentleman, who has not a large Stock ; and supposing the Claim to be doubtful, I have great confidence in your Generosity, that for a trifle you wou'd not chuse to leave a Grudge in the young Gentleman's mind, of a hardship done him.

But to deal with you after that plain manner which I know you love, I will speak out my mind to you, that in strict Justice and in the direct Words of the agreement, Mr. Home is intitled to £75 : I have inclosed a Copy of it, and the principal is in my hand ready at your Call. Captain Vincent's Words are " I engaged that My Lord should pay you £300 sterling a year so long as you continued to live with him, beginning from the first of Aprile 1745 and that you shou'd have your Sallary for that Quarter in which you shoud leave him, as if the Quarter were fully expired." I subsume directly upon this Clause that Mr. Home continued to live with the Marques for one entire year and sixteen Days of another and therefore is intitled to £300 and a Quarter of that Sum.

Touching the offer of a smaller Sallary, nothing in my apprehension, can be built upon it, because it was a proposal only which was not brought to a Bearing. Mr. Home continued to live with the Marques after the proposal was made, in the same manner as before, and as the proposal was not accepted of, there was no Innovation or Change upon the original Covenant, which subsisted in it's full Strength and Effect 'till the 16th of Aprile 1746 when a final Close was put to it by Mr. Home's dismission.

It is admitted that Mr. Home has a Claim for a broken Quarter. If so it must be upon the footing of the original Covenant, because no other Bargain was struck betwixt the Marques and him. It cannot be upon the footing of a Proposal or offer which never came the length of a Covenant and which therefore never had any Effect.

It will do me a singular Pleasure that you will communicate these things to the Marchioness of Annandale and what further will better be suggested by yourself. Whatever shall be your Opinion will be received with due deference and Respect as becomes

Your obedient Servant
Henry Home

Remember that while Mr Home was with the Marques, the Professorship was lost.[1]

Despite Henry Home's laying down of the law in the case, the £75 was not forthcoming immediately. A long series of accidents intervened. Lady Annandale and Johnstone placed the claim before my Lord's lawyer, who verbally acknowledged the justness of it, but before he could reduce his opinion to writing, suddenly died. In 1746 Captain Vincent also died. Then Hume was out of the country for a couple of years, during which time Lord Annandale was judged to be a lunatic, and to have been one from 12 December 1744. About 1750, on Henry Home's advice, David Hume opened a lawsuit. The heir-at-law, Lord Hopetoun, promised justice when he took over the estate. In 1759 he offered to pay at once if secured by a decision of a Judge of the Outer House of the Court of Session at Edinburgh. Negotiations were still going on in 1761, but presumably were then settled out of court to Hume's satisfaction, for he would never have let the matter drop, no matter how well-off he had become in the meantime. The betterment of his financial situation had nothing to do with the dispute over the Annandale salary. Consider : here was a debt, the justness of which was admitted, dating back fifteen years when the money was really important to him. It was still his whether needed or not. "Justice and equity must be here the same," he had told Johnstone in 1746 ; " for can it be imagin'd that I am in a condition to make the M. of A. a present of £75 that of right belongs to me ? " The accumulated funds of the Annandale estate, tied up in litigation, ultimately rose to the staggering sum of £415,000 ! There seems to be no good reason why a philosopher should not be permitted to collect his debts as well as a businessman.

" I have found in this whole affair that some men are honest and sincere, and others not so. A very slender discovery you'll

[1] Home, MS letter, 9 June 1746, in NLS, MS 2956, ff. 81–2 ; reprinted in Murray, pp. 68–9.

say ; but which, however, may be useful to me, by teaching me not to trust too much to professions and appearances." So wrote Hume plaintively to Sir James Johnstone immediately after the final quarrel with Vincent, and the comment may serve as fitting conclusion to the story of his unfortunate tutorship. But Hume's time during that year was not completely taken up with the affairs of the mad Marquess. There were also several important personal developments.

The first of these, and one that contributed greatly to his despondency, was the death of his mother. In December 1743 Hume had refused to leave Ninewells " because of my Mother's bad State of Health, whom I am unwilling to leave for any time, in her present Condition." Now while he was in England, in the spring of 1745, Katherine Home died. We may easily imagine the remorse and the self-accusation of the fond son for being absent during his mother's hour of need. The exact date of her death is unknown, but it is certain that it took place before 15 June, at which time David wrote to Henry Home : " I receive very melancholy Letters from my Brother, which afflict me very much. My Mother's Death, which makes such an immense void in our Family, along with my Absence, & his Dissappointment in Love, sink him I find very much." [1]

The death of Katherine Home has hitherto been incorrectly dated 1748 or 1749, presumably because of a rather loose statement in *My Own Life* : " I went down in 1749 and lived two Years with my Brother at his Country house : For my Mother was now dead." After Hume's own death several stories were circulated concerning this event which were evidently designed to malign the character of the philosopher.[2] There is no reason at this late date to revive the fabrications of pious zeal only in order to refute them. That story, however, which was told to Alexander Carlyle of Inveresk by the Honourable Patrick Boyle, minister of Irvine, Ayrshire, and the second son of John, Earl of Glasgow, bears every evidence of the truth and was indeed accepted as fact by the philosopher's nephew, Baron David Hume. As related by Carlyle, the story goes as follows :

When David and he [Patrick Boyle] were both in London, at the period when David's mother died, Mr. Boyle, hearing of it, soon after went into his apartment—for they lodged in the same house—when he found him in the deepest affliction and in a flood of tears. After the usual topics of condolence,

[1] NHL, p. 17.
[2] e.g. Robert Chambers, *A Biographical Dictionary of Eminent Scotsmen* (Glasgow 1875), art. " Hume," III, 119–20.

Mr. Boyle said to him, " My friend, you owe this uncommon grief to your having thrown off the principles of religion ; for if you had not, you would have been consoled by the firm belief that the good lady, who was not only the best of mothers, but the most pious of Christians, was now completely happy in the realms of the just." To which David replied, " Though I threw out my speculations to entertain and employ the learned and metaphysical world, yet in other things I do not think so differently from the rest of mankind as you may imagine." [1]

Boyle and Carlyle, David's intimates, fondly persuaded themselves that this reply was an indication that David was a good Christian at heart. It is perhaps the greatest compliment to him that so many others of his friends attempted to persuade themselves similarly. Yet it will not do. David Hume had long since renounced the Christianity of revelation and acknowledged " the character of an infidel." That he retained the characteristics of a good and moral nature is no evidence to the contrary, nor is his remark above, presuming that it has been faithfully reported. Supernaturalism Hume rejected along with the philosophy implicit in what he termed " the religious hypothesis," yet social and family ties always remained strong and, above all, devotion to his mother.

David Hume's ability to inspire love and affection extended beyond his immediate family to a host of friends. Nowhere is this better illustrated than in the case of Henry Home, many of whose acts of kindness and devotion have already been observed. In a letter of 13–15 June 1745 to Henry, David expresses his reciprocal feelings of gratitude in apparent allusion to an offer, extended after the fiasco of the Edinburgh professorship, to return to Scotland and live with him. " The kind Sentiments," writes David, " you express towards me, & of which I never doubted, renew the Regret that I shou'd have so little Prospect of passing my Life with you, whom I always regarded as the best Friend, in every respect, I ever possest, *Mais tel est notre Sort*." It is in the same letter that David remarks, " I intend to continue these philosophical & moral Essays, which I mention'd to you."

The indications are that, during his residence at Weldehall and London, Hume was already working on the *Philosophical Essays concerning Human Understanding*, later known as the *Enquiry concerning Human Understanding*, which constitutes the substantial rewriting of Book I of the *Treatise*. He was also probably working upon *Three Essays, Moral and Political*. As will shortly become evident, between leaving the Marquess of Annandale and

[1] Carlyle, p. 287.

the publication of these new works in 1748, David Hume was too much involved with other affairs to have much freedom left for literary composition.

In the *Philosophical Essays* Hume achieved a new plane of lucid philosophical exposition. " I believe the philosophical Essays contain every thing of Consequence relating to the Understanding, which you would meet within the Treatise," Hume advised Gilbert Elliot of Minto, " & I give you my Advice," he continued, " against reading the latter. By shortening and simplifying the Questions, I really render them much more complete. *Addo dum minuo.*" [1] Gone are the hesitations of the *Treatise*, the intricacies of detail, the tortured analysis—gone, too, inevitably are some fine passages which had shown aspects of modern philosophy in the making, the autobiography, as it were, of a thinker in the act of thinking. The *Philosophical Essays* are a work of art, polished and impersonal. Nowhere perhaps is this new tone better exemplified than in the famous conclusion to the work. Here Hume reviews the basic principles of what he calls " *mitigated* scepticism or *academical* philosophy " : that the certainty of demonstration is limited to the pure realm of idea (the sciences of logic and mathematics), and that all other sciences concerning matter of fact or existence, which are based upon arguments from cause or effect, are reduced to some degree of probability. Triumphantly he asks :

When we run over libraries, persuaded of these principles, what havoc must we make ? If we take in our hand any volume ; of divinity or school metaphysics, for instance ; let us ask, *Does it contain any abstract reasoning concerning quantity or number ?* No. *Does it contain any experimental reasoning concerning matter of fact and existence ?* No. Commit it then to the flames : For it can contain nothing but sophistry and illusion.[2]

In the " Advertisement " to the *Treatise*, Hume had announced his intention to turn to the problems of history, as history is the practical extension of " politics ", that is, of what today would be called political science. The story of man throughout the ages is certainly an essential part of the " science of man ". It is my speculation without factual evidence, that Hume's first trials in the writing of history were made during the unhappy Annandale period.[3]

[1] HL, I, 158. [2] *Phil. Wks.*, IV, 135.
[3] The MS " proofs " that such was the case have been faulted by the fact that the covering dated notations, supposedly in Hume's own hand, have recently been proved to be forgeries. See above, " Preface 1979 ", the close, for a fuller explanation.

My surmise is that Hume's frequent visits to London on "business," 1745–1746, which probably caused some part of the friction with Vincent, were made for the purpose of consulting various libraries which would be open to him through the influence of friends. My further surmise is that the project was temporarily abandoned, on the basis of this experience, until such time as he could find the proper combination of freedom and library facilities to enable him to carry on concentrated research and composition. Fired by the continual gibes of the French critics, David Hume was determined to supply the long needed history of Britain.

The unhappy year that Hume spent in attending the mad Marquess of Annandale and in learning from Captain Philip Vincent that some men are honest and sincere and others not was an unhappy year for the entire British nation. It was the 'Forty-five, the last Jacobite Rising, an upheaval that has been the occasion for much romantic writing, but which may be viewed here more dispassionately through the philosophic eye of the unfortunate tutor himself.

CHAPTER 14

SPECTATOR TO A REBELLION

"The present unhappy troubles."

WITH the passing of two centuries the Jacobite Rising of 1745 inevitably tends to rank either as high romance or as *opéra bouffe*, depending on the temperament of the historian. At the time, however, it was deadly serious to all concerned, with the destiny of a great nation hanging in the balance. A year and a half after its collapse David Hume wrote, realistically enough, that "eight Millions of People" might "have been subdued and reduced to Slavery by five Thousand, the bravest, but still the most worthless amongst them." Hume himself, however, generally favoured the *opéra bouffe* interpretation of the exploits of the brave but, in his opinion, otherwise "worthless" Highlanders. Thus he boasted :

> I wish his Majesty would be pleased to honour me with the Command of either of the *Highland* Battalions, and that I had some honest *Jesuitical* Clergyman to lay my Scruples ; I should think it a very easy Exploit to march them from *Dover* to *Inverness*, rob the Bank of *England* in my way, and carry my Spoils, without Interruption, thro' the whole Nation ; provided the Army were disposed to continue mere Spectators of my Prowess.[1]

The bare factual narrative of the Rebellion is both farcical and romantic, emphasise which you will. In February 1744 France had been ready to invade England and to restore the Stuart dynasty. Britain was saved by the combined action of its home fleet and a providential storm in the Channel. The ardour of France cooled noticeably thereafter, but not that of the Young Pretender. Landing, almost unattended, in the West Highlands of Scotland on 25 July 1745, Prince Charles Edward Stuart set up his standard at Glenfinnan twenty-five days later. Although the clans began to rally to the support of "the yellow-haired laddie," his troops never numbered much more than 5,000. Yet this small band of men, poorly disciplined, poorly armed, and poorly supplied, took Edinburgh on 17 September without shedding a drop of blood, and four days later chased Sir John Cope and the King's army off the field at Prestonpans, or Gladsmuir as the Jacobites preferred to call it. Hamilton of

---

[1] Hume, *Account of Stewart*, pp. 11, 13.

Bangour's *Ode on the Battle of Gladsmuir* was long able to move the heart of the sentimental Scot :

> As over Gladsmuir's bloodstain'd field,
> Scotia, imperial goddess, flew,
> Her lifted spear and radiant shield
> Conspicuous blazing to the view :
> Her visage, lately clouded with despair,
> Now reassum'd its first majestic air.

Yet, sentimental Scot that he was, Robert Burns was to remain unmoved, and many years later is said to have commented, " I dinna like it ava, man, it's far ower sublime."

Royal Court was set up at Edinburgh, and those who had opposed the entry of the Jacobites were required to submit. Professor Colin Maclaurin, who had been responsible for some last-moment fortifications, escaped to England ; physical exertions incurred in the frantic attempts to organise the defence of the city resulted in his early death the following year. Among those who rallied to the Jacobite cause at Edinburgh was Robert Strange, the engraver and later friend of David Hume. After some weeks the Young Pretender led the Highland host across the Border into England on the 9th of November. On the 17th the city of Carlisle surrendered to him, and on the 29th Manchester. By 4 December the rebels had reached Derby ; and London, together with all of South Britain, was thrown into a panic. A camp was set up at Finchley-Common, a few miles south of Weldehall, and the King was resolved to take the field in person in defence of the capital. Prince Charles was not able, however, to risk an engagement, since few or no disaffected English had come to his support. The rebel army, therefore, was soon compelled to retreat into Scotland, entering Glasgow on Christmas Day. Derby, within 125 miles of London, was to remain the high-water mark of rebellion.

But all was not yet over for the Jacobite cause. The rebels took Stirling on 7 January 1746, and won the Battle of Falkirk over the forces of General Hawley ten days later. Every victory, however, had the effect of defeat, for, unaccustomed to discipline and to camp routine, many of the clansmen went home. The Prince was compelled, therefore, to accept the advice of the Chiefs and to retire into the Highlands. Inverness surrendered to him on 20 February, but the dispirited rebels were finally routed at Culloden on 16 April by the vastly superior forces of the King under the Duke of Cumberland. Heartbroken and hopeless, the

Young Pretender bid a sad farewell to his followers and took to the hills.

The next six months of desperate hide-and-seek with the King's men who were scouring the mainland and the islands for him lend the deepest tincture of romance to the mythology of Bonnie Prince Charlie. Once disguised as a woman, and travelling for a few days in the company of the dauntless Flora MacDonald, the Prince finally escaped, landing in France on 29 September. Two years later he was officially expelled from that country under pressure from England, losing thereby any last shred of hope that may have survived the disaster of Culloden. In custody at Fontainebleau in December 1748, and on his way to the borders of France for exile in Italy under terms of the Treaty of Aix-la-Chapelle, the Young Pretender was to be seen by David Hume in person.[1] But not to anticipate so far, it is now fitting to investigate that philosopher's immediate reactions to the Rising of 1745.

During the period in question Hume's letters provide little information, referring only to " the present unhappy troubles " and " this miserable war," and, even more vaguely, to the fact that " unhappily all intercourse with her [the Dowager Marchioness of Annandale at Moffat in Scotland] is cut off at present." The lack of expression of any sentiment beyond such guarded references is fully explained in a letter to Sir James Johnstone :

> You seem uneasy that all my letters have been open'd, and so am I too ; but, as I think I have in all of them us'd the precaution to name no-body, and to date from no place, and even not to subscribe the letters, it can be of no consequence, and can only proceed from the universal practice of opening all letters at present ; though none of mine ever came to me in that manner. A clerk in the post-office opens a letter, runs it over, and, finding it concerns only private business, forwards it presently, and thinks no farther of the matter : so that, what one writes of that kind, seems to me as safe as what one says. However, as you appear to think otherwise, I shall be more cautious for the future.

In short, during the Rebellion, when everyone was suspect, and most of all Scotsmen, David Hume was wisely playing it safe.

That is not to suppose, however, that he did not have strong convictions. His published essays had made it clear that he was a " Revolution Whig," though not of the dogmatic variety. If my supposition concerning the *Three Essays, Moral and Political,* is correct, they were written during the period of the Rebellion,

---

[1] See below, pp. 218 ff.

and, in some measure, constitute his basic thoughts upon it. In February 1748, shortly before publication, he described these essays in detail : " One is against the original Contract, the System of the Whigs, another against passive Obedience, the System of the Tories : A third upon the Protestant Succession, where I suppose a Man to deliberate, before the Establishment of that Succession, which Family he shou'd adhere to, & to weigh the Advantages & Disadvantages of each." Hume might have gone on to say that this third essay was directed against the Jacobites. Though Hume was willing to publish it in 1748, his friend, Charles Erskine, Lord Tinwald, to whose discretion he left the essay, decided to suppress it temporarily ; and " Of the Protestant Succession " did not appear until 1752. Its place in the 1748 volume was taken by " Of National Characters." [1] It is interesting to observe that Hume's good friend and brother-philosopher, Henry Home, retired to the quiet of the Merse during the disturbances at Edinburgh and calmly composed *Essays upon Several Subjects concerning British Antiquities*, a work which signalises the abjuration of his youthful Jacobitism. After the appearance of this book at Edinburgh in 1747, Hume commented slyly to its author : " You do me the Honour to borrow some Principles from a certain Book. I wish they be not esteem'd too subtile & abstruse." [2]

Despite the pressure of his many Jacobite friends, Hume's Whiggish principles remained intact. He could, for instance, sympathise with Sir James Johnstone over the plight of his daughter but none the less point out to him the political necessities of the situation. Sir James's daughter Margaret was the wife of Lord Ogilvy, who had joined the Young Pretender at Edinburgh. After Culloden, Lord Ogilvy escaped to France ; but his lady was taken prisoner and confined in Edinburgh Castle, whence she, too, ultimately escaped. (Is it not an integral part of the *opéra bouffe* situation that romantic captives escape from prison ?) Hume writes to Johnstone in June 1746 :

I am willing . . . to flatter myself, that your anxiety must now be in a great measure over, and that a more happy conclusion of so calamitous an affair, cou'd not be expected, either for private individuals, or for the public. Some little time ago, we had here a conversation with regard to L—— and other persons in her condition, when General St Clair say'd that he heard from some of the ministers, that the intentions of the menaces, or even of the intended prosecutions (if they went so far), were not to proceed to execution ;

[1] See Textual Supplement for further discussion and Hume's letter to Lord Elibank (Hume–Elibank), 437.   [2] NHL, p. 27.

but only to teach our country-women (many of whom had gone beyond all bounds), that their sex was no absolute protection to them, and that they were equally expos'd to the law with the other sex.

Finally in 1749 Hume was to instruct Montesquieu, for purposes of a possible revision of his *Esprit des Loix*, that the abolition by Parliament of the Hereditary Jurisdictions in the Highlands, which had inclined the inhabitants too strongly towards monarchism, was one of the most beneficent results of the 'Forty-five.

Yet Hume had deep personal sympathy for those of his friends who had been politically misguided, for instance, Hamilton of Bangour. Hume's cousin, Alexander Home of Eccles, was the Solicitor-General for Scotland and was earning a name for severity in his dealings with the erstwhile rebels. Hume goes out of his way to expostulate : " . . . I have been told, that the Zeal of Party has been apt sometimes to carry you too far in your Expressions, & that Fools are afraid of your Violence in your new Office. Seek the Praise, my dear Sandy, of Humanity & Moderation. Tis the most durable, the most agreeable, & in the end the most profitable." Then he adds by way of postscript : " For God's sake, think *of Willy Hamilton*."

One does not have to be a Jacobite or even a Scotsman to be moved by the lines of Hume's friend of later years, Tobias Smollett, whose poem *The Tears of Scotland* was called forth by the report of the bloody suppression of the Rebellion by " The Butcher " Duke of Cumberland :

> Mourn, hapless Caledonia ! mourn
> Thy banished peace, thy laurels torn !
> Thy sons, for valour long renowned,
> Lie slaughtered on their native ground ;
> Thy hospitable roofs no more
> Invite the stranger to the door !
> In smoky ruins sunk they lie,
> The monuments of cruelty.
>
>   *   *   *   *
>
> While the warm blood bedews my veins,
> And unimpaired remembrance reigns,
> Resentment of my country's fate
> Within my filial breast shall beat ;
> And spite of her insulting foe,
> My sympathising verse shall flow.
> Mourn, hapless Caledonia ! mourn
> Thy banished peace, thy laurels torn !

A grim smile may have crossed David Hume's countenance, if he chanced upon the pamphlet describing one of the many executions of Jacobites : *The Genuine last Speech of David Hume, Esq ; who was execute at Penrith, upon the 28th of October 1746.*

One of Hume's worries in 1745–6 was the plight of his good friend and benefactor, Archibald Stewart, the Lord Provost of Edinburgh. When the Young Pretender demanded ˙the city's surrender, Stewart, having no adequate means of defence at his command, temporized in the hope that Sir John Cope's forces might come up; but the gates were rushed and the rebels entered unscathed. First jailed by the Jacobites for resisting them, the unfortunate Stewart was later jailed by the government forces for having " surrendered " the city. " Mr. David Hume wrote anxiously to know the state of that affair," John Coutts told Mure of Caldwell in November 1745, adding " I wrote him, enclosed in my letter to Mr. Oswald, and I desired Mr. Oswald to furnish him with a copy of the facts. In case my letter to Mr. Oswald has miscarried, you'll please to forward to Mr. Hume the enclosed letter, with a copy of the enclosed narration, which you may put, if you please, in some better order or dress." [1] The enclosure is lost ; but Hume certainly came to know all the facts of the so-called " surrender " of Edinburgh.

On 24 March 1747 the trial of Archibald Stewart opened in the High Court of Justiciary in Scotland. The accusation was serious (" neglect of duty, and misbehaviour in the execution of his office, as Lord Provost of Edinburgh, before and at the time the rebels got possession of that city in the month of September 1745 ") and was pressed in twelve specific charges. Stewart was defended by Hume's friend, James Ferguson of Pitfour. After several adjournments, the court finally acquitted Stewart on 2 November 1747 by a unanimous verdict. But before this, Hume was so distressed by the prosecution's apparent determination to get a conviction that he was prepared to print a defence of Stewart : *A True Account of the Behaviour and Conduct of Archibald Stewart, Esq ; late Lord Provost of Edinburgh, In a Letter to a Friend.*[2] The preface complains that it was not possible to print it in Edinburgh as the printers were " terrified with the Severity of a certain Magistrate. . . . Poor City! once insulted by the Rebels, and now reduced to Subjection, even by those who ought

---

[1] *Caldwell Papers*, PT. II, VOL. I, 73.
[2] Reprinted as appendix to John V. Price, *The Ironic Hume* (Austin 1965), pp. 153–72. Hume's presentation copy of this rare pamphlet has been noted by J. V. Price : " Hume's ' Account of Stewart ' : an important presentation copy," in *The Bibliotheck*, 6 (1973), 199–202. The title-page is inscribed in Hume's hand : " By David Hume, Esqr, who was under great Obligations to Provost Stewart."

to protect her." The letter is dated " October 20, 1747 " ; but a postscript was added " Novem. 4, 1747," when Hume learned of the acquittal òf two days previous.

Though of no practical avail to Stewart at that late date, the *True Account* was published early in 1748 as a pious act of friendship. On the title-page Ovid is quoted with good effect :

> *Non potuit mea mens, quin esset grata, teneri.*
> *Sit, precor, officio non gravis ira pio.*[1]

The anonymous writer had declared that, " I had just Obligations to Mr. *Stewart*, as well as a great personal Regard for him," and it would hardly have cost Stewart any great effort to infer that his defender was David Hume. Stewart, in turn, reciprocated with the present of " a batch of uncommonly good Burgundy. ' The gift,' said David, in his good-humoured way, ' ruined me ; I was obliged to give so many dinners in honour of the wine.' " [2]

The fifty-one page pamphlet, no matter how neglected today, is an example of Hume at his best in historical narrative. Straight-forward, urbane, and witty, it is also accurate, learned, and philosophical, and displays a solid understanding of the law. The case for Stewart, as presented by Hume, rests upon two factual articles, " the Force of the Garrison, which the Provost commanded " and " the Strength of the Place he was to defend." In regard to the first article, the Edinburgh forces consisted of five units : the Town Guards, the Trained-Bands, the Edinburgh Regiment, the Volunteers, and the Auxiliaries—in all, estimates Hume, " a list of Heroes equal to those of which *Homer* has given us a Catalogue, if not in his *Illiad*, at least in his *Batrachomyomachia*, or Battle of the Frogs and the Mice." The 126 Town Guards were " rather elderly Men, but pretty well disciplined ; and indeed, the only real Force the Provost was Master of. The rest were, in a Word, undisciplined *Britons*, which implies just as formidable an Idea as undisciplined *Romans*, or undisciplined *Indians*. They were nominally divided into the Trained-Bands, the *Edinburgh* Regiment, and the Volunteers. But this Division was really what the Schoolmen call a Distinction without a Difference. For with regard to military Prowess they were much the same." The Trained-Bands were chiefly valuable as ornaments in Birthday parades. " His Majesty's Warrant to raise the *Edinburgh* Regiment was not delivered to the Provost, till the 9th of *September*, seven Days before the Rebels entered the Town.

---

[1] Ovid, *Epistulae ex Ponto*, iv.i, 7–8.
[2] Henry Mackenzie, *Anecdotes and Egotisms*, ed. H. W. Thompson (London 1927), p. 172.

The oldest enlisted, therefore, were now Veteran Troops of seven days standing : The youngest not less than a Quarter of an Hour. Their Number might amount to about 300. I am told, that their Appearance resembled very much that of *Falstaff's* Tatterdemallion Company, which his Friend supposed he had levied by unloading the Gibbets and pressing the dead Bodies."

" The Volunteers, who come next, to the Number of 400, and close the Rear, the Post of Honour in all Retreats, will, perhaps, expect to be treated with greater Gravity and Respect : And no doubt they deserve it, were it only for their well meant Endeavours in Defence of their King and Country. As to their Discipline and Experience, it was much the same with that of the others. I need not add their Courage : For these are Points almost inseparable. Religious Zeal makes a mighty Addition to Discipline ; but is of no Moment when alone. . . . A Friend of mine, who has a poetical Genius, has made a Description of their March from the *Lawn-Market*, to the *West-Port*, when they went out to meet the Rebels ; and has invented a very magnificent Simile to illustrate it. He compares it to the Course of the *Rhine*, which rolling pompously its Waves through fertile Fields, instead of augmenting in its Course, is continually drawn off by a thousand Canals, and, at last, becomes a small Rivulet, which loses itself in the Sand before it reaches the Ocean." This poetical friend, it may be remarked parenthetically, was John Home, the young clergyman and man of letters, who, along with William Robertson and William Wilkie, also clergymen and men of letters, joined the first or College Company of Volunteers. John, later, was caught in the rout at Falkirk and imprisoned in Doune Castle, from which he escaped by knotting blankets into ropes.

The Provost's Auxiliaries were two Regiments of Dragoons which were not under his command at all, but under that of Brigadier-General Fowke. The exploits of the Dragoons and of their commander drew the remorseless gibes of Hume : " I have seen an *Italian* Opera called *Caesare in Egitto*, or *Caesar in Egypt* ; wherein the first Scene *Caesar* is introduced in a great Hurry, giving Orders to his Soldiers, *Fugge, fugge : a'llo scampo*. Fly, fly : to your Heels. This is a Proof, that the Commander at the *Colt-Bridge* is not the first Hero that gave such Orders to his Troops. . . . 'Twas in Consideration of such great Example, I suppose," comments Hume acidly, " that he has been so honourably acquitted, and since promoted ; while Mr. *Stewart* has been imprisoned for fourteen Months, forced to give a Recognizance of

15000 £ for his Appearance, and three times, in a manner, brought upon his Trial. So true the old Proverb, *That it is safer for one Man to steal a Horse, than for another to look over a Hedge*."

Another type of Auxiliary to Provost Stewart's forces is taken up by Hume in due course : " I remember," he points out, " *Cardinal de Retz* says, that a great Prince made very merry with the new levied Troops of *Paris*, during the Civil Wars ; and when he mentioned the Defence that might be expected from the City against the King's Troops, usually called it, *La guerre des pots de chambre*, The War of the Chamber-pots. As it is well known, that a Chamber-pot is a very formidable Machine in *Edinburgh*, I wonder it has not been comprized amongst Provost Stewart's Forces ; at least, amongst his Auxiliaries, in Conjunction with the rest above mentioned."

" The Strength of the Place he was to defend," the second article in Hume's case for Stewart, is thus presented :

You know, that the City of *Edinburgh* is surrounded for the greatest part, by a plain Wall about twenty Foot high, where highest, and about two and a half or three Foot thick, where thickest. It is not, in many Places, flanked by any Bastions : It has not Strength or Thickness enough to bear Cannon. The Besieged would not even have room to handle or charge their Pieces ; but must be set up aloft as Marks to the Enemy, who can annoy them infinitely more, and receive less Harm from them, than if both stood in an open Field.

You know, that this Wall, tho' near two Miles in Length, surrounds not the whole Town, but is supplied on the North by a Lake, which is fordable in many Places.

You know, that this Wall, for a very considerable Space, is overlooked by Houses, which stand within five or six Paces of it, and which it was impossible to destroy because of their Number and Value.

The Town is supplied with Water entirely by Pipes. Its Bread is even, strictly speaking, its daily Bread. For the Bakers never have by them more Flower than serves them a Day, but bring it continually from their Milns on the Water of *Leith*, as Occasion requires.

Besides, as happens in all Civil Wars, there were so many disaffected Persons in Town, that had it been held out but three Hours (which indeed was impossible) it was justly feared, that it would have been set on fire from within, in order to facilitate the Entry of the Rebels ; nay, it was easily possible for the Rebels themselves to set fire to it from without, and force it, by that means, to a speedy Surrender.

In short, Stewart had no alternative but to try to meet the enemy outside the city gates with what forces he could muster. The manoeuvre of General Fowke so to do at Colt-Bridge, in which his two Regiments of Dragoons ended up at North Berwick, twenty miles east of Edinburgh, at the very moment that the rebels were approaching from the west, has already been alluded to.

> In all the trade of War, no feat
> Is nobler than a brave retreat.
> For those that run away and fly,
> Take Place at least of th' enemy.

This was, indeed, *opéra bouffe* at its most farcical! " I shall only say," concludes Hume, after listing the other farcical " defences " of cities as well as routs in battles, " If all these Enormities pass unpunished, and Mr *Stewart* alone the Victim, there are some People, to make Use of the Allusion of a witty Author, that resemble very much the Monster in *Rabelais*, that could swallow a Wind-mill every Morning to Breakfast, and was at last choaked with a Pound of Fresh-Butter hot from an Oven."

The Postscript to the *True Account*, added after Stewart's acquittal, draws the serious distinction between the political Whigs, who were pleased to see justice done and to have an innocent man declared innocent, and the religious Whigs, who were angered at losing a scapegoat. " The Idea I form of a political *Whig*," explains Hume, " is, that of a Man of Sense and Moderation, a Lover of Laws and Liberty, whose chief Regard to particular Princes and Families, is founded on a Regard to the publick Good." On the other hand, " The religious Whigs are a very different Set of Mortals, and in my Opinion, are much worse than the religious *Tories*; as the political *Tories* are inferior to the political *Whigs*. I know not how it happens, but it seems to me, that a Zeal for Bishops, and for the Book of Common-Prayer, tho' equally groundless, has never been able, when mixt up with Party Notions, to form so virulent and exalted a Poison in human Breasts, as the opposite Principles. Dissimulation, Hypocrisy, Violence, Calumny, Selfishness are, generally speaking, the true and legitimate Offspring of this kind of Zeal." It was doubtless this kind of zeal that Hume had felt personally in the affair of the Edinburgh professorship, the mere remembrance of which now served to barb his pen. The distinction here drawn between *Political Whigs* and *Religious Whigs* is to be remembered in connexion with the later controversies over his *History of England*. Hume's part in the Rising of 1745 was entirely on the side-lines of action; but no one could possibly have the slightest doubt that he was the bitter opponent of Jacobitism.

Chapter 15

A MILITARY CAMPAIGN

" The Ministry . . . sent us to seek Adventures on the Coast of France."

After leaving Weldehall on 16 April 1746, David Hume retired to London. Eventful as that day was for Hume personally, it was even more eventful for the nation, for it was the day of Culloden. When the news finally reached the city nine days later Hume must have been deeply thankful. His rejoicing, as befitted a cautious Scot, however, would necessarily have been restrained because a Scottish accent might have proved dangerously provocative. " John Bull," observes Smollett, who was in London on the occasion, " is as haughty and valiant to-night as he was abject and cowardly on the Black Wednesday when the Highlanders were at Derby." [1]   Nevertheless, no matter how restrained, Hume's rejoicing would have been perfectly sincere.

During the succeeding five weeks in London, Hume faced yet again the problem of his career. Even discounting the £75 still owed him by the Marquess of Annandale, he had in little more than a year earned over £400 and was clearly justified in the comment in *My Own Life* that, " My Appointments during that time made a considerable Accession to my small Fortune." But what to do now ? The previous year he had discussed the alternatives with Henry Home : whether to " retire to the South of France or home with such a Competency as may satisfy my Wants, & which consequently ought to satisfy my Ambition." To retire to France at the age of thirty-five, however, would certainly be regarded by his friends as an admission of defeat, and might, furthermore, be difficult to manage at a time when Britain and France were actually at war. No defeatist, Hume was carefully nursing plans for future literary productions. Yet he was reluctant to return home so soon after having been turned out of his tutorship. It was humiliating to have to admit that he had been peremptorily dismissed from the only two positions he had ever held (the Bristol clerkship and the Annandale tutorship), and that he had failed to win the only position he had ever really wanted and fought for (the Edinburgh pro-

---

[1] Quoted in Carlyle, p. 199.

fessorship). Nevertheless, he could live much more cheaply in Scotland than in London. So to Scotland he must go.

On Sunday morning, 18 May, everything was ready, and the heavy baggage had already been dispatched to the ship for Berwick. On Sunday evening, in the midst of farewells to friends, a totally unexpected invitation induced Hume at once, and gladly, to change his mind, and, instead of returning to Scotland, to set off on a projected military expedition to America. " Such a Romantic Adventure," he gayly wrote, " & such a Hurry, I have not heard of before." Having followed the course of the Rebellion of 1745 from the side lines, he was now to be actively engaged in the War of the Austrian Succession and in an important campaign, the projected conquest of Canada. Above all, from a personal point of view, he would be well off. " I doubt not but you will be glad to hear," he informed Sir James Johnstone with obvious satisfaction, " that I have not chang'd my situation for the worse. The office is genteel : I have 10 sh. a-day, besides perquisites, which may be considerable ; and can be put to little expense because I live with the General. The invitation I receiv'd, was as unexpected as that which your friend [the Marquess] gave me."

Lieut.-General James St Clair was a distant relation of Hume's and, when they chanced to meet in London, took an immediate fancy to him. It was the offer to act as secretary to the General and to accompany him on the Canadian expedition that Hume jumped at on that memorable Sunday evening. St Clair had risen from Colonel in 1722, to Major-General in 1741, to Lieut.-General in 1745, and was finally to become General in 1761, the year before his death. St Clair was also a Scottish M.P. from 1722 on. The friendship with the General was to prove a decisive factor in Hume's career, ultimately enabling him to achieve financial independence and to devote himself exclusively to writing.

In order to safeguard Nova Scotia, Newfoundland, and the seaports of New England, the Colonists, under Colonel William Pepperrell, had captured the French fortress of Louisburg on Cape Breton Island in 1745, and were now clamouring for assistance from the home country in order to drive the French completely out of Canada. The plan proposed by them and adopted by the Ministry was to march on Montreal by land and to approach Quebec by way of the St Lawrence. St Clair was to be Commander-in-Chief and his expedition was scheduled to reach the mouth of the St Lawrence River not later than the beginning of August, so as to allow ample time for the campaign before the closing in of winter. This is precisely the plan that was to be carried out successfully by Wolfe and Amherst in 1759, but in 1746 the order of the day might have been : *Haste without forethought*. The General's commission, for instance, was dated 14 May so that officially he had had only four days more preparation than his secretary. The commission itself is remarkable, so far as David Hume is concerned, only for a single clause :

> And Whereas We shall appoint a Judge Advocate, to attend the same Courts Martial, for the more orderly Proceedings of the same, We do hereby, give you Power, in Case of Death, Sickness, or necessary Absence of the said Judge Advocate, to depute another Person, such as in your Discretion, You shall think fit, to execute the said Office. . . .[1]

The two days following the surprise invitation were busy days of preparation. On Wednesday, 21 May, General St Clair and his secretary left London by carriage, arriving the following day at Portsmouth. Eager to set out for America at once in full knowledge that delay meant disaster, St Clair was uneasy from the outset and frustrated in the end. The General's secretary kept a manuscript " Journal," of which three fragments have survived and of which the opening section of the first [2] may be given here in order to spell out the reasons for this frustration :

JOURNAL

May 21. General St. clair departed from London.

May 22. He arriv'd at Portsmouth, where he found nine of the Transport Ships still wanting, & the Wind contrary to their coming to the Downs.

May 23, 24, 25. He embarkt all the forces, except the Royals, on board of the Transports in the Road.

May 26 or 27. The Wind became westerly, which was favourable to their falling to the Downs : Yet they came not for some time ; because they were not all ready.

May 30. The Lords of the Admiralty order'd Commodore Coates to sail as soon as the *Surprize* shoud arrive with the Transports, even tho some of them shou'd be wanting. This Order recall'd.

[1] PRO, SP 41/17 [War Office Papers 1746] ; see also Newhailes, St Clair MSS, bound vols. 2–8. The chief published sources of the expedition are : (1) P. Diverrés, *L'Attaque de Lorient par les Anglais, 1746* (Rennes 1931). (2) Sir John Fortescue, " A Side-Show of the Eighteenth Century," in *Blackwoods Magazine*, ccxxxiii (1933), 330–45. This is the final say by a great historian, written after the publication of much new material by Diverrés. (3) H. W. Richmond, *The Navy in The War of 1739–48* (Cambridge 1920), iii, 20–50. Hume's contributions will be credited separately.

[2] Hume, MS "Journal" (1746) in Pierpont Morgan Library, New York City ; other fragments are in BL and Newhailes.

June 9. The Wind became favourable.

June 12. The Transports arriv'd, after Noon ; & before next day at 7 in the morning all the Forces were embarkt. The rest of the time was employ'd in compleating the Provisions of the transports to six Months.

June 14. General St Clair went on board the *Superbe.*

  15. Set sail from Spithead, & fell down to St Helens. The Wind in the Evening became contrary ; so that we were oblig'd to drop Anchor.

June 24. Weigh'd Anchor upon the Winds becoming fair ; but it chang'd : Upon which we tackt about to return. But in an hour, it became fair again ; & then became contrary. Upon which we were oblig'd to return, in the Morning of June 25, to St Helens.

June 27. At noon the General receiv'd a Letter from the Duke of Newcastle, (by the hands of the Admiralty) telling him that he was order'd back to Spithead, there to wait farther Orders, which shoud be sent him forthwith.

Do. About two hours after the General receiv'd a Letter from the Secretary at War ordering him to disembark all the Troops under his Command, except . . . three Regiments. . . .

Need any more be given ? In short, as Hume elsewhere put it, the General was plagued by " contrary winds and contrary orders."

The Ministry, popularly known as the " Broad Bottomed," were divided in policy and hopelessly inefficient. The Duke of Newcastle notoriously did not know what mind he had from one hour to another, and several others were only lukewarm about the whole idea of the Canadian campaign. Lord Chesterfield was definitely cool. Lord Sandwich and the Duke of Bedford were split over basic naval strategy. To add to the confusion, word was received that a French squadron under the Duc d'Anville, far superior to that of Cotes, had slipped past the British home fleet and was at sea, possibly headed for Louisburg. Hence the orders to St Clair to disembark his troops. The expedition was now laid aside and the provisions for the troops disposed of. Three weeks later the expedition was resumed, four ships being added to the convoy, the whole squadron placed under the command of Admiral Lestock with orders to sail as soon as possible. New provisions had to be bought on the spot.

On 24 July, while still at Portsmouth, David Hume analysed the situation for the benefit of his friend Henry Home :

We are still dependent on Winds & Ministers of State, & consequently in a very uncertain Condition. The Probability seems now to be against our sailing ; & every day we remain here, increases it. The Wind is at present a violent South-west, & the General is ill ; tho we hope, that his Distemper will prove only a fit of the Gout & be no way dangerous. The Season, in which we can safely sail is declard to be limited to 10 days or a fortnight ; & the Admirals Ship is still in the Harbour, & tis a great Chance if she can get out to the Road in that time. This join'd to the declard Aversion of the greatest Part of the Ministry of this Project, renders our Condition very uncertain, not to say worse ; tho how our Governors will justify their Conduct to the Nation or the Nation save itself from the Ridicule of Foreigners, on account of such ill-concerted & vain Attempts I am at a Loss to determine. The revolutions, that have occur'd in this Affair, & the Disappointments we have met with & forsee, prepare us to bear indifferently any Accident ; tho' they no way relax the Diligence of the General in the Execution of what depends on him.

. . . Tho rigorous in exacting Obedience from those he commands, he has Insinuation & Address to gain the Sea Officers & Colonies. All our Captains were exceedingly taken with his Civilities ; & Mr Lestock has publickly declar'd, that the World shall see in one Instance, that tis possible for a Land & Sea Commander to agree.

(Lestock and St Clair were quite properly sensitive over the 1741 disaster at Carthagena, which was universally blamed upon lack of co-operation between the sea and land commanders.)

The General's loyal secretary and friend proceeds to appraise his personal situation. " As to myself, my way of Life is agreeable ; & tho' it may not be so profitable as I am told, yet so large an Army, as will be under the General's Command in America, must certainly render my Perquisites very considerable." Asked whether he was inclined to enter the Service, Hume's answer was, " that at my Years, I cou'd not decently accept of a Commission in the Army, except I got a Company. The only Prospect of working this Point, wou'd be to procure at first a Company in an American Regiment, by the Choice of the Colonies : But this I build not on, nor indeed am I very fond of it."

The day after Hume wrote this letter, all forces re-embarked, but were again prevented from sailing by contrary winds. The joint Commanders were now agreed that nothing could be undertaken against Canada this season, but that they would winter at Boston and prepare for an early campaign in the spring. On 3 August, when the chances of the expedition's ever getting under way seemed hopeless, General St Clair took a step to ensure that his kinsman-secretary would profit, at least, by a government half-pay pension of a crown a day. He created Hume Judge-Advocate. In order to do so, he first made Captain Grant, who had held that office, his aide-de-camp. The commission [1] was preserved by David Hume all his life and is especially

[1] RSE, ix, 6.

interesting in that it is counter-signed by Hume himself as secretary to the General :

To David Hume Esq.

By Virtue of the Power and Authority to me given by His Majesty under his Royal Sign Manual ; I do hereby constitute and appoint you (in room of James Grant Esq resign'd) to be Judge Advocate of all the Forces under my Command. You are therefore carefully & diligently to discharge the Duty of Judge Advocate of the said Forces, by doing & performing all & all manner of things thereunto belonging ; And you are to observe & follow such Orders and Directions from time to time as you shall receive from Myself, or any other your superior Officer, according the Rules and Discipline of War. GIVEN on board His Majesty's Ship Superbe, off St Helens the third of August 1746 in the twentieth Year of His Majesty's Reign.

Jas. St clair

By the General's Command
    David Hume Secretary.

Entered with the Secretary at War.

On 5 August the fleet sailed again, only to be beaten back by contrary winds. Finally, on the 23rd, they actually sailed down the Channel—not to America, but to Plymouth. The embarrassed Ministry, acting on the warworn adage of *Go somewhere and do something*, had belatedly reached a new decision. The troops could be more profitably employed than in wintering in New England : they could make an immediate incursion upon the coast of France. So was a new expedition " spawned out of the abortion of the other." [1] The orders were to proceed first to Plymouth, in the hope of deceiving the enemy that they were actually going on to America, and there to await further orders. Now it was General St Clair's turn to be embarrassed, for it had been he who had originally thrown out the suggestion of a possible thrust at the French coast. Writing with considerable agitation to the Duke of Newcastle on the day of sailing, St Clair explained what he had meant :

It was [in June] when your Grace and some other of the King's servants began to see that things would not be got ready in time to carry the Quebec plan into execution, and then your Grace said that it was hard that after hiring transports and putting the nation to an infinite expense that no benefit would be got to the Public from it. I then at random and as the first thing that came into my head said, why may we not frighten the French and alarm them as they have done us, by sending this squadron with the troops now ordered to some part of the coast of France, and as all their regular troops are on their Flanders and German frontiers it's not impossible but that such an alarm may make them recall some of them. [2]

[1] *Scots Mag.*, x (1748), 176.
[2] Quoted by Richmond, *The Navy in The War of 1739–48*, III, 26.

St Clair and Lestock remonstrated that they had no charts of the French coast, no information as to coastal fortifications, no maps of the land ; and that having none of these things they could make no intelligent decision. But they added that they would obey orders.

In Plymouth on 29 August the joint Commanders received Newcastle's orders : proceed at once to Lorient, or Rochefort, or Rochelle, or Bordeaux, or any other place on the western coast of France, and employ all possible means to procure a diversion from the campaign in Flanders. Amazed at such wide discretionary powers, the Commanders were happily unaware of the frivolous view that Newcastle personally took of the whole undertaking, as it is revealed in a letter of 3 September : "However, it is determined to try it ; and if no good comes of it, I think no hurt can ; for the Admiral will certainly not risk the fleet unnecessarily in hazardous navigation." [1]

Detained at Plymouth by contrary winds, Lestock and St Clair had time to remonstrate further with the Secretary that they had no maps of France, no military information, no horses for the artillery, too few troops, and, finally, no money except a few chests of Mexican dollars. Admiral Anson, who also put in at Plymouth because of foul winds, observed that he had once heard Mr Hume, M.P. for Southwark, remark that he had visited Lorient, and that, while the city was strong by sea, it was weak by land. Under direct orders to move, the joint Commanders seized upon this piece of hearsay (attributed to a merchant and not a soldier) and determined upon Lorient ; they so informed Newcastle on 2 September. Commodore Cotes was at once detached with a small squadron to reconnoitre the coastal approaches to Brittany.

Apprised of the decision to invade the Coast of Brittany, the mercurial Newcastle sent to Plymouth a certain Major MacDonald with plans for the invasion of Normandy, together with some pilots. Upon questioning, MacDonald proved to be a braggart soldier who knew nothing whatsoever about the Norman coast or its defences. The pilots proved equally ignorant. But disturbed by this contrary plan of the Ministry, the Commanders informed Newcastle that they would not budge from Plymouth without express orders. A messenger was immediately dispatched by Newcastle to tell them they might go wheresoever they wished in terms of the original order. They, therefore, reverted to the

[1] *The Navy in The War of 1739-48*, III, p. 27.

Lorient plan. Yet when the expedition finally got under sail on 15 September, the only French map that St Clair had in his possession was a small-scale one of the entire kingdom, which his aide-de-camp, Captain Grant, had been able to pick up in a shop at Plymouth. David Hume was not exaggerating when he wrote that St Clair " lay under positive orders to sail with the first fair wind, to approach the unknown coast, march through the unknown country, and attack the unknown cities of the most potent nation of the universe." [1] The expedition sailed with both the Admiral and the General convinced that nothing could possibly be achieved but failure and that they were under orders to achieve that.   Little wonder if they succeeded !

The British fleet consisted of fifty to sixty ships of which seventeen were men-of-war, and carried five battalions of troops numbering about 4,500—hardly a formidable expeditionary force, even for 1746. Lorient had been chosen for attack because it was the home base of the French East-India Company, the destruction of whose installations and stores would be a severe blow to French trade. But the primary reason for any incursion against the French Atlantic coast was to draw off troops from the campaign in Flanders, where the British were being severely pressed. During the Jacobite Rebellion of 1745 most of the British forces had been withdrawn from the Continent for protection of the homeland, and the bloody Battle of Fontenoy had consequently been lost in May 1746. Since then French progress had gone unarrested, and Brussels and Antwerp had been taken. The idea of a diversion in Brittany, therefore, was fundamentally sound. The only trouble was that it was put into execution so late in the season that it could not possibly have had any great effect. In the event, Namur had surrendered before Lestock sailed, and the decisive action of Roucoux was lost before the Brittany incursion was completed. With Roucoux, the French had completed the conquest of the Austrian Netherlands and had retired into winter quarters ; any detachment they might send thereafter to drive the British out of Brittany could have no effect whatsoever on the Flanders campaign.

Off the Isle de Groix on the south coast of Brittany at eight in the evening of 18 September and under a full moon, the British fleet kept its rendezvous with Commodore Cotes's reconnoitring squadron. A flat but exposed beach at the mouth of the Quimperlé River, ten miles from Lorient, had been selected for the landing.

[1] Hill Burton, i, 444.

Yet instead of making an immediate landing with the temerity and dash requisite to a commando expedition, the aged and over-cautious Admiral Lestock decided to wait for daylight. The decision was fatal, as offshore winds caused a further delay of two days during which time the French took alarm and prepared for the attack. Signal guns fired all day, and signal fires burned all night. When, under cover of the fleet's cannon, the British were finally ready to land in the afternoon of the 20th, they found themselves opposed by a force of upwards of 3,000 militia together with a troop of cavalry. Feinting a landing at one point, the first detachment of 600 redcoats veered sharply to another, divided from the first by a small hill, and hit the beach unopposed. Forming rapidly, they soon chased the French into the hinterland. The General at once published the usual proclamation promising good treatment to the inhabitants if they abstained from hostilities and full payment for provisions and horses. The document is particularly notable because it is countersigned by " David," whose " Hume " somehow got omitted in the excitement.

The first military success lay with General St Clair, but now began his real troubles. Without a local map of the approaches to Lorient, he was confused by several country roads and guessed wrong. The next morning he divided his forces into two columns. His own met with little opposition except random shots in a village ; by way of reprisal the village was sacked. The column under Brigadier-General O'Farrel was ambushed by peasants, and in the ensuing confusion, fired on their own men, killing several. Some of the British soldiers threw down their arms and ran away. Though the two columns joined that evening before Lorient, the panic of the one was somewhat communicated to the other. In truth, the troops were fatigued by the arduous march, weakened from the months of confinement on the transports, smitten with scurvy from poor diet, and shortly to be inundated with rains. Morale was low. By the time preparations for the siege were completed, the fighting men were reduced to little more than 3,000.

Lorient lies, Hume noted, " at the bottom of a fine Bay two Leagues long, the Mouth of which is commanded by the Town & Cittadel of Port-Louis or Blavet, a Place of great Strength & situated on a Peninsula. The Town of l'Orient itself has no great Strength, tho surrounded by a new wall of about 30 Foot high, fortify'd with half Moons, & guarded with some Cannon." [1] At a

[1] HL, i, 95.

council of war aboard the flagship on the 23rd, the Engineers of the British army gave positive assurances that they could either breach the walls or destroy the town by fire within twenty-four hours. St Clair accepted their proposal, and, because the original proclamation had produced no horses from the fiery peasants, Lestock assigned the drudgery of dragging the cannon ten miles over bad roads to a third part of the sailors of the entire fleet.

Returning to camp, St Clair found that his demand to Lorient for surrender at discretion, a large money payment, and four hours' plunder of the town had been rejected by the Governor, the Marquis de l'Hôpital. The French negotiators offered counter-proposals : namely, withdrawal of their troops with all honours of war and absolute security of the town and its goods, including the magazine and storehouses of the East-India Company. Such terms, of course, were preposterous, in view of the fact that a major reason St Clair had to take the town at all was to strike a blow at the French East-India trade. They were, therefore, rejected, and St Clair awaited the arrival of his artillery to force entry.

When the cannon, four twelve-pounders and a mortar, finally arrived, St Clair discovered to his dismay that the Engineers upon whom he relied to take the town were both ignorant and stupid. The cannon had been sent without sufficient ammunition, and the mortar without a furnace in which to heat the shot. When these were brought up, it was found that the bellows for the furnace was still on board the store-ship. The British bombardment opened on the 25th, but as the cannon were set up at a distance of over 600 yards from the walls, far beyond their effective range, they inflicted little or no damage. An immediate council of war, followed by two more on the 26th, produced only further evidence of the incompetence of the Engineers and of their total incapacity to carry out their promises. A second fragment of Hume's " Journal " notes under 25 September : " The Troops seem to be under a great panic. The Appearance of a dozen of French drew out our whole Line : And in the Evening a Party of Bragg's & another of Framptons fired upon each other in a Flurry. Every Body much discourag'd, especially on account of the Rain which fell all day as well as Yesterday, & the day before. The Roads from the Fleet to the Camp render'd quite impracticable. . . ."

During all this time the forces within Lorient had been setting

¹ BL, Add. MS 36638.

up their own batteries and were daily increasing in number by means of the open water-route from Port-Louis, until they out-matched the British, five to one. The comment of David Hume in this connexion is not without its point : "Above fifteen thousand men, completely armed by the East India Company, and brave while protected by cannon and ramparts, still stood in opposition to three thousand, discouraged with fatigue, with sickness, and with despair of ever succeeding in so unequal a contest." [1] To make matters worse, three deserters from the British informed the French that they were being attacked, not by 20,000 as rumour had painted it, but by a mere 3,000.

Under the circumstances, there was nothing for St Clair to do but to admit failure and to raise the siege : to withdraw his troops to safety, and to re-embark them before counter-attack by a vastly superior force and before the approaching equinoctial storms rendered it impossible. After dark on 26 September, therefore, the British army decamped from before Lorient. By two in the morning they reached the beaches unmolested, after a tortuous march through knee-deep mud, and, under cover of the fleet, began to board ship. Delayed by the roughness of the sea, it was not until the 28th, according to Hume's "Journal," that "The General embarkt the last, as he had dis-embarkt amongst the first."

What General St Clair and his secretary did not know— probably well enough for their peace of mind—was that at nine in the evening of the 26th, several hours after the departure of the British from before Lorient, the Marquis de l'Hôpital and his staff had decided to capitulate, and an emissary was sent under cover of a white flag to treat for final terms. When the French appeared, there was no one to surrender to, only four spiked guns and a mortar ! Courageous when surprised, vigorous in strength-ening the fortifications of the town, firm to withstand siege, the French yet determined to surrender at the very moment when they knew that the enemy had no cannon heavy enough to breach their walls, when they knew that their own forces had a five to one superiority in numbers, when they knew that reinforcements of regular troops from Flanders were on the march to relieve the siege ! If there is anything more preposterous than the decision of the British Ministry to order a descent on the coast of France at the worst season of the year, it can only be the decision of the Governor of Lorient to capitulate. A word must be said in passing,

---

[1] Hill Burton, I, 454.

however, for the bravery of the Breton peasants, who were ever eager for a fight to the finish. The Bretons, we are told,[1] still sing of their victory over the English :

> Les Anglais, remplis d'arrogance,
> Sont venus attaquer Lorient,
> Mais les Bas-Bretons,
> A coups de bâtons,
> Les ont renvoyés hors de ces cantons !

Unaware of the success that had just eluded him, the unfortunate General St Clair was grim in determination to carry out his orders to the letter and to seek further occasion to create a diversion of French forces from Flanders. Admiral Lestock was in agreement with him against the majority of their combined staffs. On 1 October, therefore, the fleet weighed anchor and moved south to Quiberon Bay. A violent storm from the southwest arose during this manoeuvre and five transports carrying 900 troops were dispersed ; lacking specific instructions as to a rendezvous, these transports decided to return to England. On 4 October St Clair's troops took a small fort and pillaged several villages on Quiberon Peninsula ; and Lestock's fleet destroyed the *Ardent*, a French man-of-war of 64 guns, and reduced two small forts on the islands of Houat and Hoedic. A promised reinforcement of three battalions from England failed to materialise ; and the joint Commanders received the double intelligence of the approaching French detachment of regulars from Flanders and of the British defeat at Roucoux. There being no reason left to remain in France, the expedition got under sail on 19 October for the return to home ports. In a gale at sea the fleet got dispersed, some of the men-of-war proceeding to Spithead and others with the transports to Ireland. Hume and the General arrived at the Cove near Cork on 29 October.

The question of who was to blame always follows failure, especially failure in affairs public and military. And already from Quiberon Bay, 4 October, Hume addressed a letter to his brother, putting the finger of blame infallibly on the Ministry and the Engineers. " Our first warlike Attempt has been unsuccessful, tho without any Loss or Dishonour. The public Rumour must certainly have inform'd you, that being detain'd in the Channel, till it was too late to go to America, the Ministry, who were willing to make some Advantage of so considerable a sea and land Armament, sent us to seek Adventures on the Coast of France."

[1] *Bulletin archéologique de l'Association Bretonne*, Ser. 3, v, 144.

Hume's scorn for the Engineers was exceeding. "It has long been the Misfortune of English Armies to be very ill serv'd in Enginiers ; & surely there never was on any occasion such an Assemblage of ignorant Blockheads as those which at this time attended us."

Upon his return to England, Admiral Lestock was ordered to strike his flag ; and a month later he died. To the Admiral's credit it must be said that he had worked in perfect harmony with the General ; and it is difficult to see what more he could have done, granting always that he did not have the temperament for dash and daring. Yet the breath of scandal somehow hovers over the aged Lestock. An anonymous letter from Cork, claiming to be written by a participant in the expedition, was published in the *Gentleman's Magazine* for December 1746. The writer says that it was well known that Lestock "had *Boca Chica* on board . . . [who] during this expedition, always acted as president in the councils of war, as being esteem'd the best genius on board." And Nicholas Tindal in his *Continuation of Mr. Rapin's History of England*, says bluntly that Lestock "was under the shameful direction of a woman he carried along with him. . . ." [1]

No insinuations were brought against St Clair, other than of a possible lack of determination. David Hume's warm opinion of the General is evident everywhere. As early as January 1747 he had told Henry Home, "I shall be able, when we meet, to give you the just Cause of our Failure, which proceded very little, if at all, from the General." [2] Some years later, Hume was much disturbed over an account, in the name of Voltaire, which held the 1746 expedition up to ridicule. [3] In January 1756 Hume was driven to seek the advice of Sir Harry Erskine, who had been with him under the General : "I have been set upon by several to write something, though it were only to be inserted in the Magazines, in opposition to this account which Voltaire has given of our expedition. But my answer still is, that it is not worth while, and that he is so totally mistaken in every circumstance of that affair, and indeed of every affair, that I presume nobody will pay attention to him. I hope you are of the same opinion." Erskine, I should conjecture, joined others of Hume's friends in insisting that he should make a public answer.

Under pressure, then, Hume now composed the manuscript

[1] Tindal, *op. cit.*, XXI (1763), 271.   [2] NHL. p. 23.
[3] P. H. Meyer, "Voltaire and Hume's 'Descent on the Coast of Brittany,'" in *Modern Language Notes*, LXVI (1951), 429–35.

generally known as the " Descent on the Coast of Brittany," which
contains a full and accurate account of the expedition, together
with a reasoned defence of St Clair himself :

> Was the attempt altogether impracticable from the beginning? The
> general neither proposed it, nor planned it, nor approved it, nor answered
> for its success. Did the disappointment proceed from want of expedition?
> He had no pilots, guides, nor intelligence, afforded him ; and could not
> possibly provide himself in any of these advantages, so necessary to all military
> operations. Were the engineers blamable? This has always been considered
> as a branch of military knowledge, distinct from that of a commander, and
> which is altogether intrusted to those to whose profession it peculiarly belongs.
> By his vigour in combating the vain terrors spread amongst the troops, and
> by his prudence in timely desisting from a fruitless enterprise, the misfortune
> was confined merely to a disappointment, without any loss or any dishonour
> to the British arms. Commanders, from the situation of affairs, have had
> opportunities of acquiring more honour ; yet there is no one whose conduct
> in every circumstance, could be more free from reproach.[1]

Voltaire is cursorily dismissed by Hume : " A certain foreign
writer, more anxious to tell his stories in an entertaining manner
than to assure himself of their reality, has endeavoured to put this
expedition in a ridiculous light ; but as there is not one circumstance of his narration, which has truth in it, or even the least
appearance of truth, it would be needless to lose time in refuting it." Nevertheless, it was certainly Voltaire's direct attack on
St Clair that prompted Hume's defence.

The work of Voltaire alluded to by Hume in the letter to
Erskine and again in the " Descent on the Coast of Brittany "
is the *History of the War of 1741*, which had been translated into
English late in 1755. The manuscript of this book had been
completed by Voltaire several years previously but had not been
published ; indeed, he himself never brought it out, only utilising
some of the chapters in later historical works. Somehow, however,
the work did get into print, and French editions appeared in 1755
and 1756.[2] The English translation was noticed in the *Monthly
Review* for February 1756, the penultimate paragraph illuminating
the point at issue :

> To this History, our Author has added a short supplement, containing the
> transactions of 1746, and 1747, of which the affairs of Genoa are the chief.

---

[1] Printed in Hill Burton, I, 441–56, from RSE, IX, 12. A crossed-out fragment
of Hume's manuscript (not printed by Hill Burton) reads as follows : " having been
an Eye witness of the Undertaking, & having had Opportunity of knowing the secret
Springs & Causes of the whole, I shall endeavour, for my own Amusement chiefly,
to collect." Sir John Fortescue, it is to be remarked, defends St Clair in much the
same manner as Hume did : *op. cit.*, pp. 344–5.

[2] G. Bengesco, *Voltaire : Bibliographie* (Paris 1882–5), I, 363–6.

He first mentions General Sinclair's memorable descent upon the French coast (the particulars of which are but too well known) concluding the account of it with these words—" In short this great armament produced nothing but blunders and laughter ; whereas every other part of the war was but too serious and terrible."

In the April issue of the *Monthly Review* appeared an answer to Voltaire's ridicule under a brief introduction by the editor. " We are desired to insert the following Paper, and we the more readily comply with the request, as we are assured it comes from unquestionable authority." That " unquestionable authority," the author of the three-page account of the 1746 expedition, was, I believe, David Hume. That the account bears internal evidence of his authorship, may perhaps be sufficiently apparent from the opening paragraph :

> With what facility are we misled by great writers ? how readily do we imbibe their notions without examination ? Most readers believed that Mr. Voltaire's history was composed from undoubted facts ; but we find, that in his relations he is more singular than authentic, more credulous than well informed, and that he cannot quite lose the poet in the historian ; we admire his talents, but we should not overlook his errors, which are many and notorious. His column at the battle of Fontenoy is a chimera, tho' a chimera generally received as a reality among his countrymen.—But of all the misrepresentations, with which his history is filled, there are none so gross, so ridiculous, or so injurious to the English nation, as those which are contained in his account of the descent on the coast of Brittany : He is unacquainted with the destination of the expedition, the number of the troops, the manner of the descent, the causes of the want of success, the reasons for the retreat, and the conduct observed in it.

Hume is certainly correct in his general estimate of Voltaire's narrative—with but one exception. Voltaire knew that the French garrison at Lorient had sought to surrender after the secret departure of the British. To Hume, unaware of the fact, this story must have seemed such fantastic fabrication as not to merit refutation !

If the attribution of the account [1] in the *Monthly Review* to Hume seems reasonable, the circumstances of the composition are not difficult to fill in by way of conjecture. Already engaged upon the longer manuscript defence of St Clair, Hume was called upon by his friends to provide an immediate antidote to the publicity given Voltaire's narrative in the February issue of the *Monthly Review*. His three pages were then dashed off in time to appear in the April number. Having thus reluctantly and against

---

[1] Translated verbatim by the *Journal britannique*, xx (1756), 171–81, and reprinted in *Scots Mag.*, xix (1757), 397–8.

his own better judgment published something on the controversy, Hume willingly stopped work on the " Descent on the Coast of Brittany " altogether. The manuscript, though incomplete and unready for publication, remains the fullest and most authentic contemporary account, comparable to Smollett's better known narrative of the 1741 Carthagena disaster.

David Hume always maintained a sensitive yet dignified aloofness concerning his " Adventures on the Coast of France," choosing not to recall his own prophetic words of 1746 : " . . . how our Governors will justify their Conduct to the Nation or the Nation save itself from the Ridicule of Foreigners, on account of such ill-concerted & vain Attempts I am at a Loss to determine." In *My Own Life* the incident draws the briefest comment : " I then [1746] received an Invitation from General St clair to attend him as Secretary to his Expedition, which was at first meant against Canada, but ended in an Incursion on the Coast of France." But the affair, biographically regarded, deserves better than such terse dismissal. What, it may properly be inquired, had the philosopher-scholar gained by his experiences ?

Much valuable information and insight. The future historian of Britain had observed at first hand the conduct of war, civil and military. He had seen a Ministry bungle plans for the invasion of Canada by hopeless inefficiency and then, to cover their confusion, send a badly equipped expedition off on a reckless mission at the worst season of the year and at the callous risk of thousands of lives. He had seen military commanders hesitate from caution when safety and success lay in acting with precipitation. He had seen a full campaign, even if only a tiny one. He had seen soldiers killed by enemy fire and by friendly fire, and sailors drowned by tumultuous seas. All of these experiences were to be invaluable to the historian. He had seen brave men and timorous men and panic-stricken men. He had also seen a man kill himself, an experience which made a lasting impression upon the philosopher.

Nervous and physical exhaustion had induced Major Forbes, an officer of parts and some learning who had become Hume's friend, to believe that he had violated the military code of honour by dereliction of duty. Hume comforted him and put him to bed. On returning to see his friend in the morning, Hume relates in the letter to his brother, " I found him with small Remains of Life, wallowing in his own Blood, with the Arteries of his Arm cut asunder." Despite surgical assistance, it was clear he would not live. "Never," avers Hume, "a man exprest a more steady Contempt of Life nor more determind philosophical Principles, suitable to his Exit. He beg'd of me to unloosen his Bandage & hasten his Death, as the last Act of Friendship I coud show him : But alas ! we live not in Greek or Roman times."

As man of the world Hume had also made valuable acquisitions during the eight months with General St Clair. The shy, countrified scholar had lived in the General's mess and on a brotherly footing with high-ranking staff officers. With little opportunity for serious study or writing but with plenty of necessity for passing the time, Hume developed the ability to make small-talk and discovered his genuine talent for whist. "Idleness and a gay, pleasurable Life, which steals away hour after hour, & day after day ; & leaves no time for such Occupations as one's sober Reason may approve most of. This is our Case, while on Shore ; & even while on board, as far as one can have much Enjoyment in that Situation." So he wrote to Henry Home from Cork the end of January 1747. He also mentions " an elegant Table " and " Gaiety." The subject of whist, for the first time, begins to intrude into his letters. Though always a little uneasy at the thought of the time lost from serious literary projects, Hume was becoming urbane and able to hold his own on any level of society.

The friendships made on the 1746 expedition were to prove enduring. All of the new friends were Scots. There were James Abercromby and John Clephane and James Edmonstoune ; and other names will appear subsequently. Abercromby was a Colonel who later rose to the rank of General. As a soldier he is remembered—if at all—as the loser of the Battle of Ticonderoga. At various times he was a Scottish M.P. and, as such, in a position to advise and to assist David Hume. Clephane was a physician of urbane wit and sparkling personality, a fine classical scholar, and a connoisseur of art and music. Until his early death in 1758 he drew from Hume some of his most witty and human letters, but unfortunately his own have not survived. As a captain in Brittany James Edmonstoune of Newton had distinguished himself for bravery and military skill in holding a rearward post under severe attack. He spent a long and undistinguished career in the Army, and, though a cousin of Lord Bute's, never rose higher than Lieutenant Colonel. Yet he was the lifelong friend of Hume ; and to his constant moves from post to post in the army, we owe the many charming letters from David to his " Guidelianus."

Edmonstoune was to be one of those devoted friends who have left accounts of the deathbed scene.

As for the half-pay owing to him as Judge-Advocate, Hume did not get it for many years. It was another Annandale case, and Hume fought it with the same vigour and sense of justice— but it was no easier, he discovered, to battle the red tape of a government office than that of an estate in litigation. As late as 1763 he was still seeking his due.[1] " It is the only thing in my life," he told James Oswald, " I ever asked [from the government] : It is the only thing I ever shall ask, and consequently it is the only thing I ever shall obtain." The fact that this reference to the half-pay in 1763 is the last in Hume's letters is perhaps indication that justice was finally done—otherwise he would never have given up the fight.

One final acquisition. Long since a man of large stature, about six feet, David Hume was now a fat man as well. The good table of the General and the prolonged inactive life had done their work. As a man of tremendous bulk, he was often the butt of jokes. He learned to take these good-humouredly as long as they were meant good-humouredly. Like many fat men, too, he learned to laugh at himself. On occasion, however, he could deplore that " my Belly has swelld so enormously. Alas ! that is not an Infirmity, like gre[y hair] to be disguis'd with Powder & Pomaton."[2] In short, Hume had developed into that huge figure—sometimes viewed as comic, sometimes as bizarre, perhaps more often as merely portly—that during the succeeding twenty-five years, was to become so conspicuous in British and Continental literary and social circles. If the Descent on the Coast of Brittany of 1746 had brought something less than glory to British arms, it proved grist to the mill for Hume as historian and as philosopher—and also as *le bon David*.

[1] HL, I, 384.
[2] J. C. Hilson and John V. Price, " Hume and Friends, 1756 and 1766 : Two New Letters," in *The Yearbook of English Studies*, ed. G. K. Hunter and C. J. Rawson, 7 (1977), 121–7.

CHAPTER 16

A MILITARY EMBASSY

"I . . . wore the Uniform of an Officer."

THE problem of his career faced David Hume yet again upon the decision of the Ministry, 12 January 1747, to give up St Clair's expedition to Canada. The Dukes of Newcastle and Bedford pressed for a resumption of the attempt; but Admiral Warren, just back from Louisburg, warned them that success was impossible without further preparation on both sides of the Atlantic.[1] " Our Expedition to North America is now at an End. We are recalld to England : The Convoy is arriv'd, & we re-imbark in a few days," wrote Hume to Henry Home from Cork at the end of January.[2] The voyage to England, however, proved long and tedious. The fleet remained in the Cove near Cork for the first two weeks of February, then made its way to Crook-Haven nearby. On 10 March it left Ireland, sighting Land's End three days later only to be compelled by a violent storm to " turn backward " to the Road of St Mary's in the Scilly Islands. On the 23rd the fleet lay off Plymouth and finally reached Spithead on the 27th.[3]

While still in Ireland General St Clair had not forgotten the welfare of his kinsman. " I have an Invitation," continued Hume in the above letter, " to go over to Flanders with the General, & an Offer of Table, Tent, Horses &c ; I must own, I shou'd have a great Curiosity to see a real Campaign ; but I am deterr'd with the View of the Expence, & am afraid, that living in a Camp, without any Character & without any thing to do, wou'd appear ridiculous. Had I any Fortune, which cou'd give me a Prospect of Leizure & Opportunitys to prosecute my historical Projects, nothing cou'd be more useful to me ; and I shou'd pick up more military Knowledge, in one Campaign, by living in the General's Family & being introduc'd frequently to the Dukes, than most Officers cou'd do after many Years Service. But to what can all this Serve ? I am a Philosopher, & so, I suppose, must continue." Then he added quizzically, " I believe, if I wou'd have begun the World again, I might have return'd an

---

[1] Richmond, *The Navy in The War of 1739–48*, III, 49.
[2] NHL, p. 23.　　　　　[3] Newhailes, 536–7.

Officer gratis ; and am certain, might have been made Chaplain to a Regiment Gratis : But——. I need say no more."

So Hume was in London early in April, looking round, as he had told Home, " to see, if any thing new will present itself. If not, I shall return very cheerfully to Books, Leizure, & Solitude in the Country. . . . And frequent Dissappointments," he admitted, " have taught me that nothing need be despard of, as well as that nothing can be depended on." Already in Ireland he had foreseen that difficulties would arise over the half-pay. In London he joined forces with four others in the same predicament and brought all possible pressure to bear against the Secretary-at-War. The argument of that Minister was, of course, that the expedition to Canada had never taken place and that, therefore, no money should be paid. The affair kept Hume in London all the spring, together with the Micawber-like hope that something might turn up.

Nothing did turn up that met with his complete satisfaction. Sir James Johnstone of Westerhall wanted him back as companion to the Marquess of Annandale, and Hume was not entirely un-willing now that the ogre, Captain Vincent, was dead ; but the Marchioness, it turned out, had " Views somewhere else." By the end of June Hume was forced to confess to Henry Home that, " I have intended every day to write to you, since I came to London, but delay'd it ; in expectation every day of being able to tell you, that I was fixt in some way of Life, that wou'd have been an easy Settlement to me." [1] The crown a day, added to his own little fortune, would have made a frugal man independent for life. The problem of what to do at the age of thirty-six, he dis-cussed with his friend at considerable length : " whether to remain in London, & endeavour to push my Fortune some other way, or return to my Studies at Ninewells."

On the one hand, I consider, that I am at a critical Season in Life ; & that if I retire into a Solitude at present I am in danger of being left there, & of continuing a poor Philosopher for ever. On the other hand, I am not able to form any distinct Project of pushing myself in any particular Profession ; the Law & Army is too late, the Church is my Aversion. A travelling Tutor, some better, but not agreeable. Any Office uncertain, & precarious. Mean-while I lose my time, spend my Money ; fall into necessity, perhaps, & Dependance, which I have sought all my Life to avoid. I am not a good Courtier, nor very capable of pushing my Fortune by Intrigue or Insinuation : Whereas if I wait till I shall be able to make my Name more generally known ; something may offer of itself, & even seek me in my Solitude ; as every thing that has yet presented itself has done. I believe if I wait in London, I shall not for some time spend much, being well provided of good Cloaths, & I am in other Respects a good Oeconomist.   Oswald is very much for my staying in London, & so are many others of my Friends ;   but the Ballance of my Inclinations lies the other way :   Tho I confess, that I felt the Solitude in the Country rather too great, especially as I was so indifferently provided of a Library to employ me.   You'll easily see, that I give you this long Detail in expectation of your Advice and Opinion.

Within a few days, however, Hume was quite ready to return to Scotland.   " All our projects have failed, and, I believe, for ever," he mournfully informed Dr Clephane, who had already been ordered to an Army appointment in Flanders.   " The Secretary-at-War persists in his scruples and delays ;   and Mr Robarts, Pelham's Secretary, says our applications will not succeed.   I suppose he speaks in this the sense of his master. . . . I set out [for Scotland] next week, as fully convinced as Seneca of the vanity of the world, and of the insufficiency of riches to render us happy."   The balance of his inclinations having prevailed, Hume was all set for Scotland.   No Berwick ship offering, he was compelled to take one for Newcastle.   " Our Ship was dirty : Our Accommodation bad :   Our Company sick :   There were four Spies, two Informers, & three Evidences who saild in the same Ship with us :   Yet notwithstanding all these Circumstances we were very well pleas'd with our Voyage, chiefly on Account of its shortness ;   which indeed is almost the only agreeable Circumstance that can be in a Voyage."

At Ninewells in July, Hume, who had by no means given up the half-pay fight even though the War Office had turned down his petition, began a campaign against the Treasury.   He was otherwise busy with several literary ventures which have already been touched upon.   The most important of these was the final revision of the manuscript of the *Philosophical Essays concerning Human Understanding*, preparatory to publishing them.   " Our friend, Harry," Hume wrote to Oswald in October, " is against this, as indiscreet.   But in the first place, I think I am too deep engaged to think of a retreat.   In the second place, I see not what bad consequences follow, in the present age, from the character of an infidel ;   especially if a man's conduct be in other respects irreproachable.   What is your opinion ? "   Whatever Oswald's opinion, the work was in press by February 1748, and Hume could then apologise to his friend Harry :   " I won't justify the prudence of this step, any other way than by expressing my indifference about all the consequences that may follow."   The key point in the debate was that the volume was to include " Of Miracles," which had been suppressed for nearly ten years on the advice of Home. Other literary ventures of 1747 included the printing of the *True Account of . . . Archibald Stewart* and the preparation of the *Three Essays, Moral and Political,* and the third edition of *Essays Moral and Political* for publication. Hume was hardly idle during his solitude in the country.

In November 1747 Hume had begged off going to London to wage the campaign against the Treasury, yet before the end of the following January there he was. General St Clair had sought him out in his solitude, inviting him to be his secretary once more, this time on a secret military embassy to Vienna and Turin. In the midst of important literary activities, Hume was far from enthusiastic, but permitted friends to persuade him to accept. From London, 29 January, he wrote to Oswald :

> I shall have an opportunity of seeing Courts & Camps ; & if I can afterwards, be so happy as to attain leizure and other opportunities, this knowledge may even turn to account to me, as a man of letters, which I confess has always been the sole object of my ambition. I have long had an intention, in my riper years, of composing some History ; & I question not but some greater experience of the Operations of the Field, & the Intrigues of the Cabinet, will be requisite, in order to enable me to speak with judgement upon these subjects. But notwithstanding of these flattering ideas of futurity, as well as the present charms of variety, I must confess, that I left home with infinite regret, where I had treasured up stores of study & plans of thinking for many years. I am sure I shall not be so happy as I should have been had I prosecuted these. But, in certain situations, a man dares not follow his own judgement or refuse such offers as these.

Definitely lukewarm this was—but committed. The same tone is evident in a letter of 9 February to Henry Home : " The doubt and ambiguity " under which he went to London, was soon lifted. " General St Clair positively refused to accept of a Secretary from the Ministry ; and I go along with him in the same station as before. Every body congratulates me upon the pleasure I am to reap from this jaunt : and really I have little to oppose to this prepossession, except an inward reluctance to leave my books, and leisure and retreat. However, I am glad to find this passion still so fresh and entire ; and am sure, by its means, to pass my latter days happily and cheerfully, whatever fortune may attend me."

The man of letters was becoming a little bored with the active life of a man of affairs, a fact which is emphasised indirectly by the final commentary in *My Own Life.*

> Next Year, to wit 1747, I received an Invitation from the General to attend him in the same Station in his military Embassy to the Courts of Vienna and Turin. I there wore the Uniform of an Officer ; and was introduced at

these courts as Aide-de-camp to the General, along with Sir Harry Erskine and Capt Grant, now General Grant. These two Years [1746-1748] were almost the only Interruptions which my Studies have received in the Course of my Life : I passed them agreeably and in good Company.

Lieut.-Col. Erskine, St Clair's nephew, had been Deputy Quartermaster-General of the Lorient expedition and had been badly wounded at the first landing ; Grant will be remembered as having been appointed St Clair's aide-de-camp in order to make room for Hume as Judge-Advocate.

During 1747 the War of the Austrian Succession had not been going well for Britain and her allies. Although Admirals Anson and Hawke had won sweeping victories at sea, the French were everywhere victorious on land. The Ministry suspected that Britain was pouring out subsidies to allies who were not putting the promised number of troops in the field. Austria and Sardinia had failed to invade southern France, as agreed, during the last campaign ; these two courts of Vienna and Turin, moreover, were barely on speaking terms.

General St Clair's commission [1] directed his attention to this deplorable state of affairs and instructed him to proceed at once to Vienna and to impress upon the Queen Empress the absolute necessity of living up to her agreements with Britain, and then to proceed to Turin to do likewise with the King of Sardinia. He was then to attach himself to the Combined Armies and to attend the King of Sardinia during the ensuing campaign. Meanwhile, however, the Ministry was beginning to respond to diplomatic feelers from France, and had appointed Lord Sandwich as British plenipotentiary to negotiate for a peace at Aix-la-Chapelle.

St Clair's party sailed from Harwich on 16 February and landed at Helvoetsluys in Holland the next day, which Hume, adopting the New Style calendar in conformity to Continental practice, designates as 1 March, N.S., in a letter to his brother John Home of Ninewells. " I had the misfortune to be excessively sick," David comments on the voyage, " But the Consolation to see an Admiral as sick as myself." His letter continues in instalments as " a sort of Journal of our Travels " designed to provide " an Account of the Appearances of things, more than of our Adventures," and provides the running commentary of a shrewd observer upon St Clair's mission and upon the countries traversed. [2]

Holland proved a disappointment to the traveller, blanketed

---

[1] Dated 8 Feb. 1748, in PRO, SP 92/57.
[2] HL, I, 114-33. This "Journal" is the source of all otherwise unidentified quotations in the present chapter.

as it was at first in heavy snow, then discovered by the thaw " in all its native Deformity. Nothing can be more disagreeable than that heap of Dirt & Mud & Ditches & Reeds, which they here call a Country, except the silly Collection of Shells, & clipt Ever Greens which they call a Garden." [1] The Prince of Orange, a hard worker who was doing good for the country, posed a nice problem for the political thinker. " Holland was undoubtedly ruin'd by its Liberty ; & has now a Chance of being sav'd by its Prince : Let Republicans make the best of this Example they can." At Breda Hume observed a procession of French prisoners-of-war and was struck by their pitiful condition. " We all said, when they past along Are these the People, that have beat us so often ? I stood behind Lord Albemarle, who was looking over a low Window to see them. One of the ragged Scarecrows, seeing his Lordship's Star & Ribbon, turn'd about to him, & said very briskly Aujourd'hui pour vous, Monsieur, Demain pour le Roi. If they have all this Spirit, no wonder they beat us."

Despite the urgency of the terms of his commission, General St Clair travelled slowly, going out of his way to visit towns and palaces and battlefields. The route ran from Breda to Nimeguen, to Cologne, to Frankfort, to Ratisbon, where the party changed over to a boat, and proceeded down the Danube, a pleasant voyage " with good Weather, sitting at our Ease, & having a Variety of Scenes continually presented to us, & immediately shifted, as it were in an Opera." Vienna was reached on 7 April, the 860 miles from The Hague having been covered in twenty-seven days.

" Germany," wrote Hume in summation and with no little acumen, " is undoubtedly a very fine Country, full of industrious honest People, & were it united it would be the greatest Power that ever was in the World. The common People are here, almost every where, much better treated & more at their Ease, than in France ; and not very much inferior to the English, notwithstanding all the Airs the latter give themselves. There are great Advantages, in travelling, & nothing serves more to remove Prejudices : For I confess I had entertain'd no such advantageous Idea of Germany : And it gives a Man of Humanity Pleasure to see that so considerable a Part of Mankind as the Germans are in so tolerable a Condition." The philosopher was never far removed from the apprentice diplomat.

[1] See Textual Supplement for Hume's excursion to Delft and his description of an iceboat on the Maas River.

Sir Thomas Robinson, the English Ambassador at Vienna, had been awaiting the arrival of the special embassy with ill-disguised impatience. When General St Clair finally arrived on the afternoon of 7 April, he immediately plunged into diplomatic negotiations, although somewhat hampered by the fact that the Imperial Court was at its Easter devotions. The Emperor, however, granted him audience on the 10th ; but the Empress not until Easter Sunday. In the meanwhile St Clair had several talks with the Sardinian representatives. On the 14th the General's staff were presented to the sovereigns and the royal families. Even the Empress Dowager, who had not seen anyone for two months, condescended to see the English travellers. The story is one of the best in Hume's " Journal " :

> You must know, that you neither bow nor kneel to Emperors and Empresses; but Curtsy : So that after we had had a little Conversation with her Imperial Majesty, we were to walk backwards, thro a very long Room, curtsying all the way : And there was very great Danger of our falling foul of each other, as well as of tumbling topsy-turvy. She saw the Difficulty we were in : And immediatly calld to us : Allez, Allez, Messieurs, sans ceremonie : Vous n'etes pas accoutumés a ce mouvement et le plancher est glissant. We esteemd ourselves very much oblig'd to her for this Attention, especially my Companions, who were desperately afraid of my falling on them & crushing them.

The city of Vienna struck Hume as small for a capital but " excessively populous." Moreover, it was " compos'd entirely of Nobility, and of Lackeys, of Soldiers & of Priests." Yet, in such an unpromising atmosphere the pious Maria Theresa had set up a Court of Chastity and banished all debauchees ; loose women were sent " to the Frontiers of Hungary, where they can only debauch Turks & Infidels : All Whore-masters are punishd as they deserve, that is, very severely. . . . I hope you will not pay your Taxes with greater Grudges," archly observed Hume to his brother, " because you hear, that her Imperial Majesty, in whose Service they are to be spent, is so great a Prude." As for that great lady herself, " I think for a Sovereign," he judiciously granted, " she is none of the worst in Europe ; & one cannot forbear liking her, for the Spirit with which she looks, & speaks & acts. But tis a Pity, her Ministers have so little Sense." Hume also confessed that she was not the beauty that romance and subsidies had painted her and that her court was no palace of pleasure. " I have been pretty busy since I came here," he continued more soberly : " & have regretted it the less, that there is no very great Amusement in this Place. No Italian Opera : No French Comedy : No Dancing. I have however heard Monticelli, who is the next Wonder of the World to Farinelli." So writes the man of the world.

Having assured the Empress Queen of Britain's undying friendship, St Clair left Vienna on 26 April for Turin—not by way of Venice, as his official family had fondly hoped, but more directly, by way of Milan. In Styria, ". . . as much as the Country is agreeable in its Wildness ; as much are the Inhabitants savage & deform'd & monstrous in their Appearance. Very many of them have ugly swelld Throats : Idiots, & Deaf People swarm in every Village ; & the general Aspect of the People is the most shocking I ever saw. One wou'd think, that as this was the great Road, thro which all the barbarous Nations made their Irruptions into the Roman Empire, they always left here the Refuse of their Armies before they enterd into the Enemies Country ; and that from thence the present Inhabitants are descended. Their Dress is scarce European as their Figure is scarce human." So comments the philosopher-historian. Higher in the mountains he found the Carinthians as ugly as the Styrians ; but higher yet, the Tyrolians " as remarkably beautiful as the Stirians are ugly."

Then began the descent of the Alps into the plains of Lombardy : ". . . every hours travelling show'd us a new Aspect of Spring. So that in one day, we past thro' all the Gradations of that Beautiful Season, as we descended lower into the Vallies, from its first faint Dawn till its full Bloom & Glory. We are here in Italy . . . [at Trent]," yet " This Town is not remarkable, neither for Size nor Beauty. Tis only famous for that wise Assembly of Philosophers & Divines, who establishd such rational Tenets for the Belief of Mankind." So writes the philosopher.

At Mantua on 11 May Hume managed to produce momentary ecstasy : " We are now in Classic Ground ; & I have kist the Earth, that produc'd Virgil, & have admir'd those fertile Plains, that he has so finely celebrated. *Perdidit aut quales felices Mantua campos.*" [1] The effort was seemingly too great to be sustained, and Hume fast relapsed : " You are tir'd, & so am I, with the Descriptions of Countries : And therefore shall only say, that nothing can be more singularly beautiful than the Plains of Lombardy, nor more beggarly & miserable than this Town." From Cremona, the economist exclaimed, " Alas poor Italy ! . . . The poor Inhabitant Starves in the midst of Nature's Plenty curst : And in the loaded Vineyard dyes for thirst. [2] The Taxes are here exhorbitant beyond all Bounds." Milan goes entirely unmentioned,

[1] Virgil, *Georgics*, ii, 198.   [2] Addison, " A Letter from Italy," ll. 117–18.

although a day was spent there. Turin was finally reached on
8 May. The trip had been, St Clair informed the Duke of Bedford,
vastly delayed " by breaking of Wheels & bad Roads. . . ." [1]

General St Clair's audience with the King of Sardinia produced.
little more than the expected confirmation of the fact that the
Combined Armies had been putting too few troops in the field.
Within a few weeks came the unexpected news that the preliminary peace had been signed at Aix-la-Chapelle. Although
all the powers engaged in the war were totally unsatisfied with the
peace and recognised that it would amount to little more than a
breathing-spell, with Aix-la-Chapelle the Military Embassy to
which Hume was attached as secretary and cypher-officer had
lost its *raison d'être*. St Clair wrote immediately to London asking
for further instructions, and requesting permission to break the
trip home by some sightseeing in Italy.[2] On 16 June David Hume
completed the " Journal " to his brother with the remark : " We
know nothing as yet of the time of our Return. But I believe
we shall make the Tour of Italy & France before we come
home."

Permission for the proposed Grand Tour was not forthcoming.
The Embassy remained at Turin, however, until the end of
November, at the request of the King of Sardinia, as General
St Clair informed London. A picture of Hume at Turin during
this period, friendly but inexact and · distorted, is presented by
James Caulfeild, later Lord Charlemont,[3] and then a young student
of seventeen at the Academy :

Nature, I believe, never yet formed any Man more unlike his real
Character than David Hume. What added greatly to the natural Awkwardness of Hume was his wearing an Uniform, which He wore like a Grocer of
the Trained Bands. Sinclair was a Lieutenant General and was sent to the
Courts of Vienna and Turin as a military Envoy to see that their Quota of
Troops was furnished by the Austrians and Piedmontoise. It was therefore
thought necessary that his Secretary should appear to be an Officer, and
poor Hume was accordingly disguised in Scarlet, while his broad Face was
rendered still broader by a smart Wig a la militaire. . . . The Powers of
Physiognomy were baffled by his Countenance, neither cou'd the most skilful
in that Science pretend to discover the smallest Trace of the Faculties of his
Mind in the unmeaning Features of his Visage. His Face was broad and fat,
his Mouth wide, and without any other Expression than that of Imbecility.
His eyes vacant and spiritless, and the Corpulence of his whole Person was far

---

[1] St Clair to Bedford, 11 May 1748, in PRO, SP 80/180.
[2] St Clair to Bedford, 9 June 1748, in PRO, SP 92/57.
[3] The following paragraphs are based upon Lord Charlemont's " Anecdotes of
Hume," in RIA, MS—12/R/7, ff. 497–531. Printed accounts by Francis Hardy,
Memoirs of . . . Earl of Charlemont (London 1810), pp. 8–9, and M. J. Craig, *The
Volunteer Earl* (London 1948), pp. 42–4, are far from complete and highly censored.

better fitted to communicate the Idea of a Turtle-eating Alderman than of a refined Philosopher. His Speech in English was rendered rediculous by the broadest and most vulgar Scottish Accent, and his French was, if possible, still more laughable. So that Wisdom, most certainly, never before issued from such a Mouth, or disguised herself in so uncouth a Garb. Thus, as We read, the Oracles of old were often delivered by a Stock or Stone. Tho' now near fifty years old He was however strong and healthy, but his Health and Strength, far from being advantageous to his Figure, instead of manly Comeliness, had only the Appearance of heavy Clumsiness and course Rusticity.

The discrepancies between this description and the actual facts are obvious and easily accounted for by the youth and snobbishness of the reporter. In short, Hume was thirty-seven, not Caulfeild's " near fifty "—to a lad of seventeen, there is not much difference !—he was a Scot and spoke like a Scot ; he was born in the country and still had a rustic air about him ; he was big of stature, muscular, and fat, and therefore, if you please, laughable ; and he exhibited that preoccupied stare of the thoughtful scholar that so commonly impresses the undiscerning as imbecile. More philosophic observers, however, than this Academy student were to be thrown into confusion by the phenomenon of David Hume's vacant stare.

James Caulfeild, as he then was, proceeds to sketch a highly complimentary character of Hume. Divested of rhetoric, of superfluous attacks upon Hume's philosophy, and of mis-statements of fact, it would read somewhat as follows : Hume was endowed with " real Benevolence. . . . His Love to Mankind was universal and vehement ; and there was no Service He wou'd not cheerfully have done to his Fellow Creatures. . . . He was tender hearted, friendly, and charitable in the extreme. . . ." This character, it must be realised, was the correction of the brief impressions of 1748 by the composite memories of many meetings in later years, as the young student changed into a peer of the realm, and became an old man inditing his *Memoirs*.

In Turin Caulfeild had sung the praises to his new friend Hume of the Countess of [Duvernan ?], " a Lady of great Beauty, Sense, and Spriteliness," who was as learned as she was attractive. At the age of twenty-four, the Countess "had been married for some years, tho' hitherto childless, her Husband being an old decrepid Man, whom Family Convenience had compelled her to espouse. Her Complexion was that of the most lovely Brunette and her Features, tho' sufficiently regular, were rather beautiful from their extreme Expression and Animation than from their Regularity. Her Mind shone thro' her Countenance with endless Variety,

and was a perpetual Source of Grace and Beauty." Obviously
impressed and eager to make new friends in a strange city, Hume
asked to be introduced to the lady. Caulfeild complied, admitting
that, " I had no more ardent Wish than that the Choice of my
Heart shou'd be admired by a Man whom I so highly esteemed."
Received by the Countess, " not only with Politeness, but with
Pleasure," Hume was " enchanted " with her charms and accomplishments, visiting her daily during the following month. Finally,
somewhat embarrassed by the turn of events, the Countess confessed to Caulfeild that she had " made a compleat Conquest of
this great Philosopher."

" Of all Men, Madam, I have no Reason to doubt the power
of your Eyes," replied the young man gallantly though incredu-
lously, " but in the present Instance, you will give me leave to
suppose, what indeed I have not often found in you, a little female
Vanity. If my Friend were only armed by his Philosophy, I
shou'd think that perhaps a weak Shield against your Charms ;
But Age is usually an Armour of Proof, and, however You may
resemble Venus, I am sure that neither his Figure nor his Manner
are those of Adonis."

The Countess vehemently denied the charge and was soon
able to convince Caulfeild of the fact, going so far as to suggest
that he see it for himself. " At his next Visit, which will probably
be this Evening," she proposed, " only Take the Trouble to hide
yourself behind the Curtain, and you shall be Witness to a Scene,
which, if it does not make you angry, as indeed it ought not, will
at least make you laugh ; and when the Comedy is over and your
Doubts removed, You must then give me leave finally to discharge my troublesome admirer. Give me however your Word
that you will on no account discover yourself, as that might not
be to my advantage."

Hidden behind the curtain that same evening, the youthful
intriguer witnessed a scene from a Restoration comedy. He saw
his " old fat Philosopher " enter the room, plump down on his
knees before the Countess, and protest his passion. Panting,
sighing, groaning, Hume managed to bring forth after considerable
effort, " Ah, Madame, J'etouffe avec l'amour. Chère, Chère
Dame, je suis désolé—abimé—anéanti ! "

" Oh ! pour Anéanti," replied the lady with more wit than
charity, " ce n'est en effet qu'une Operation très naturelle de
vôtre Système." She then ordered him to rise to his feet.

In his hiding place Caulfeild, with " too much Vanity to be

jealous," was vastly entertained with Hume's endeavours to embrace the knees of the Countess. "The picture of old, ugly, blubbering, fat, ungainly Passion" well nigh forced him into open laughter. "Silenus on his Knees to one of the Graces," he mused, "or a Bear making Love to an Italian Greyhound wou'd be Objects rediculous enough. But neither Silenus nor the Bear are Philosophers."

After toying with her unwanted lover for a few moments more, the Countess assumed "the most serious Air of Resentment" and curtly dismissed him. He left the room "in a Burst of blubbering Affliction, Tears trickling down his flabby Cheeks."

The young people were now "at Liberty to laugh at the Comedy" to which they had been spectators. "We are seldom angry with an unsuccessful Rival," commented Caulfeild philosophically. It was, nevertheless, decided that Hume was to be sentenced to "perpetual Exile" at his next visit to the Countess. And so he was.

On the eve of the philosopher's departure from Turin, however, the Countess insisted that Caulfeild should make a clean breast of the affair. The young man did so, assuring Hume that, "far from being offended, I loved him the better for his aimiable Weakness, which by bringing him more upon a level with me, rendered him a fitter Object for my Friendship."

"Ah, the Jade," replied Hume in some agitation, "And did she serve me so? I cannot however be angry. It was indeed but strict Justice. Yet in Revenge I will give you a Piece of Advice, which, if you follow it, will make my Vengeance more compleat perhaps even than I wou'd wish." He then proceeded to lecture his friend with sound and manly advice. "You are young," said he. "You are aimiable. You are beloved. All that is precisely as it ought to be. Yet let me make one short Observation—in French also, tho' that you well know is not my Talent—*Cueillez, Milord, les Fleurs. Cueillez les Fleurs. Mais ne vous faites pas Jardinier.*"

The philosopher in love had not gone unnoticed by his Scottish colleagues on St Clair's staff. Rear-Admiral John Forbes, who was stationed with the British Mediterranean fleet at Vado Bay, wrote to the General on 26 May 1748:

I am extremely glad that Sir Harry is come up to you and hope by that he has got the better of his Indisposition, but as to the one Mr Hume is troubled with I do not know how to account for it considering how pretty the Woemen [sic] are at Turin, but since they cannot keep his Eyes open, I know of nothing that remains but to advise him to get acquainted with a Jesuit and convince

him that faith is superstition, Religion Priestcraft, and that St. Ignatius was
an Impostor and Loilus a fool, and when he has performed this let him come
to the Fleet.

Yet by 8 July Forbes was better informed, writing that, " I am
sorry that Sir Harry and Capt. Grant cannot get the better of
their Agues, for I fear it must deprive them of the disposition and
abilitys that are requisite for the service of the Ladys and consequently must throw all that duty on the shoulders of the Sleeping
Philosopher ; I congratulate him on the attachment he has for
the Countess. . . ." The " new Created Beaw Mr Hume "
formed a topic for jesting, and with the arrival of the philosopher's
trunks on board ship, the Admiral warned that, " if they contain
Lace locks the air of the Ship, and particularly that of the Bread
Room where they are keeped for want of room anywhere else will
infallibly tarnish them." [1]

Forbes makes it clear that Hume was suffering, not only from
love, but also from a physical ailment, the nature of which is
hinted in the first letter above and in the nickname bestowed upon
him of " the Sleeping Philosopher." From Caulfeild we learn the
details. " He was affected by a most violent Fever, attended with
it's natural Symptoms, Delirium and Ravings. In the Paroxisms
of his Disorder He often talked, with much seeming Perturbation,
of the Devil, of Hell, and of Damnation, and one night, while his
Nursetender happened to be asleep, He rose from his Bed, and
made towards a deep Well, which was in the Court-yard, with a
Design, as was supposed, to drown himself, but, finding the Back
Door locked, He rushed into a Room where, upon a Couch, the
Gentlemen of the Family were, He well knew, used to deposite
their Swords, and here He was found by the Servants who had been
awakened by the noise He had made at the Door in endeavouring
to open it, and was by them forcibly brought back to his Bed.
This whimsical Adventure was," adds Caulfeild, " as may well
be supposed, after his Recovery, a Subject of Merriment among
his Friends, and We all agreed in laughing at the Philosopher's
Fears and Desperation."

The philosopher, however, was not to be chastened by the
raillery of his friends, protesting—" and perhaps reasonably
enough," Caulfeild admits—" Why You Boobies, what wou'd you
have of a Madman ? Do you suppose Philosophy to be proof
against Madness ? The Organization of my Brain was impaired,
and I was as mad as any Man in Bedlam."

[1] " Italian Negotiation, 1747," in Newhailes, 548.

The fact of this illness of Hume's lends some credence to another anecdote of the Italian visit, that " he received Extreme unction " from Roman Catholic priests " in a dangerous illness. . . ." George Norvell,[1] the teller of this tale after the death of Hume, is said to have been " cousin german to our David," and his original name to have been Hume. A second version, which was actually published by Norvell, seems more plausible.[2] Upon Norvell's taxing Hume with the fact of his conversion, " He answered in a huff, ' I was in a high fever then, and did not know what I said, or they did to me.' " That Hume's Scottish Presbyterian friends would have protected him from any and all priests is hardly to be doubted ; but that these same friends were above playing a practical joke on a delirious philosopher, I am not so sure. We have Caulfeild's express testimony of how they delighted in teasing him.

One further fact is known about Hume's activities in Turin. For despite his disclaimer in *My Own Life* of having pursued any studies during the two years with General St Clair, he did read at least one important work during the autumn of 1748. This was Montesquieu's *Esprit des Loix*, which had just been published at Geneva. Hume read with interest and attention and prepared a list of reflections which he was later to forward to the author. General St Clair and his three aides-de-camp left Turin on 29 November, taking the direct road over the Alps to Lyons in France. It was a two-week trip and, after a couple of days of rest, the General was scheduled to proceed to Paris, " from whence he proposed to be in England about Christmas Old Stile." Though David Hume apparently kept no journal of this last leg of the journey for the edification of his brother and of posterity, some information can be culled from official State Papers, containing St Clair's dispatches, many of them in the hand of his kinsman-secretary. One letter,[3] dated " Paris, 18th of December 1748 N.S.," though terse concerning the details of the trip from Turin, to Lyons, to Paris, is detailed concerning an incident at Fountainebleau, 15 December. In the post-house inn at Fountainebleau, General St Clair and his party saw the Young Pretender, under guard, and on his way to Pont-beau-voisin, the Italian border,

[1] George Norvell, MS letter, 1 Mar. 1788, to [Alexander Stenhouse], in Keynes Library, King's College, Cambridge ; Alexander Stenhouse, MS letter, 22 Mar. 1788, to George Chalmers, in EU, Laing MSS, II, 451/2.
[2] Hill Burton, II, 8n, from the account, signed " G.N." in *The Edinburgh Magazine* for 1802 ; this account erroneously places the incident at Nice.
[3] St Clair to Bedford, in PRO, SP 92/58.

and exile at Rome. " His Attendants said he was a Prince, but did not name him ; and as he wore a Star & Garter, he was soon known to every body." In Paris the full story of his arrest on 10 December while on the way to the opera and of his temporary imprisonment at the Château de Vincennes was learnt. When it came to drawing the moral, was it the General or the secretary who phrased it as follows ?

Thus by his rash Attempt in Britain, many of his Friends & Followers lost their Lives & Fortunes ; and those, who had been so lucky as to escape to France, & to get into the Service of that Crown, he has now ruin'd their Fortunes, by his unaccountable Behaviour, which seems equally void of Temper & Common Sense. This I hope, will open the Eyes, even of the most blinded, and let them see their Folly, in engaging themselves in such desperate and criminal Enterprizes.

" I shall spend a few days in this place," the General concluded his letter, " in order to recover the Fatigues of my Journey : After which, I propose soon to have the Honour of paying my Respects to your Grace at London." So David Hume had perhaps a week in Paris, and it seems probable that it was at this time, rather than in 1734 when he was not very likely to have been staying at first-class hotels with ambassadors, that the incident occurred which he relates in the " Natural History of Religion " (1757) :

I lodged once at Paris in the same *hotel* with an ambassador from Tunis, who, having passed some years at London, was returning home that way. One day I observed his Moorish excellency diverting himself under the porch, with surveying the splendid equipages that drove along ; when there chanced to pass that way some *Capucin* friars, who had never seen a Turk ; as he, on his part, though accustomed to the European dresses, had never seen the grotesque figure of a *Capucin* : And there is no expressing the mutual admiration, with which they inspired each other. Had the chaplain of the embassy entered into a dispute with these Franciscans, their reciprocal surprize had been of the same nature. Thus all mankind stand staring at one another ; and there is no beating it into their heads, that the turban of the African is not just as good or as bad a fashion as the cowl of the European. *He is a very honest man*, said the prince of Sallee, speaking of de Ruyter. *It is a pity he were a Christian*.[1]

Presumably General St. Clair held to his schedule of being in London by Christmas 1748, Old Style. The embassy was at an end, and David Hume was financially independent for the first time, as appears from the comment in *My Own Life* : " . . . my Appointments, with my Frugality, had made me reach a Fortune, which I called independent, though most of my Friends were inclined to smile when I said so : In short I was now Master of near a thousand Pound." The long sought-for goal of being able to devote himself entirely to literature became possible in 1749.

PART III

DISTINGUISHED MAN OF LETTERS

1749–1763

CHAPTER 17

ACHIEVEMENT OF AMBITION

"These Symptoms of a rising Reputation gave me Encouragement."

AT London early in 1749 David Hume found himself still little known in the world of letters. "On my return from Italy," he laments in *My Own Life*, "I had the Mortification to find all England in a Ferment on account of Dr. Middletons Free Enquiry [into the Miraculous Powers which are supposed to have subsisted in the Christian Church from the Earliest Ages through several successive Centuries] ; while my Performance [the *Philosophical Essays concerning Human Understanding*] was entirely overlooked and neglected. A new Edition, which had been published at London of my Essays, moral and political, met not with a much better reception." Yet within eight years, that is by 1757, Hume was generally acknowledged to be the leading man of letters, not only of North Britain, but of South Britain as well ; and, on the Continent, the unrivalled inheritor of the mantle of Montesquieu. The young Boswell in 1762 had no hesitation in naming Hume as " the greatest Writer in Brittain." [1]

This sudden acclaim was not, however, without its negative side, for in certain quarters Hume was considered rather as the inheritor of the mantle of notoriety worn in the seventeenth century by Hobbes, and more recently by Mandeville. Nevertheless, in 1763, when he crossed the Channel to receive the homage of France, the name of David Hume, whether as *bête noire* or as *bel esprit*, was known to everyone in the republic of letters. In consequence of this publicity, as well as of a great stream of publications, the present period in Hume's career, 1749–63, is so full and so complex as to require a preliminary over-all sketch before the painting in of the details. On the surface, it is a period of brilliant literary activity, of extensive controversy, and of final and enduring public recognition. Beneath the surface, it is also a period of personal storm and stress, of continued frustration and even humiliation.

The publications of 1748 had effected an innovation in that Hume was finally prepared to name himself as their author.

Philosophical Essays was announced in April as " By the author of the *Essays Moral and Political* " ; and the *Three Essays* and the third edition of the *Essays Moral and Political* appearing in November bore the name of " David Hume, Esq." Henceforth Hume was to acknowledge all of his major publications. Yet only in *My Own Life*, drafted in April 1776, and in the Advertisement to the last edition of his collected *Essays and Treatises*, published posthumously in 1777, did he openly declare himself to have been the anonymous author of the *Treatise* ; and in the Advertisement to *Essays and Treatises* he mentions it only to repudiate it.

After 1748 new works appeared in rapid succession. In 1751 appeared the new version of Book III of the *Treatise*, entitled the *Enquiry concerning the Principles of Morals* ; but although esteemed by Hume, " of all my writings, historical, philosophical, or literary, incomparably the best : It came unnoticed and unobserved into the World." The following year appeared the *Political Discourses*, " the only work of mine, that was successful on the first Publication : It was well received abroad and at home." In 1754 the *History of England* began to be published, the set of six volumes being completed in 1762. Though the first volume (on the House of Stuart) was poorly received, the finished *History* soon became the most popular one ever written in Britain. In France from the beginning, Hume was the " English Tacitus ". Meanwhile, in 1757, *Four Dissertations* completed Hume's major publications of this period ; and, indeed, of his lifetime. It was these works, then, from 1748 to 1762 that brought him into the literary limelight and secured for him a permanent high reputation.

A mere list of books does not prove a writer's popularity without a record of sales. Within three years of publication, the *Philosophical Essays* had reached a third edition ; within two years, so had the *Political Discourses*. Meanwhile, in 1753, Hume had begun to bring out collected editions of his non-historical works, excluding the *Treatise*. The first edition of *Essays and Treatises on Several Subjects* came out in four volumes, 1753–56, and by 1764 had reached a fourth edition. The same process was repeated with the *History*. Before the first collected edition of 1762, both the Stuart and the Tudor volumes had reached two editions ; and a second edition of the entire *History of England* appeared in 1763. If in 1748 Hume considered himself " independent . . . Master of near a thousand Pound," within less than fifteen years, he had become "not only independent, but opulent ", and by 1769 " Very opulent (for I possessed a Revenue of 1000 pounds a year)."

The controversies over Hume's publications, philosophical and religious, historical and literary, will be treated in due course. At the moment, it will suffice to say that however spirited and acrimonious they were, they drew no direct reply from Hume, because, as he has explained in *My Own Life*, " I had fixed a Resolution, which I inflexibly maintained, never to reply to any body ; and not being very irascible in my Temper, I have easily kept myself clear of all literary Squabbles "—a statement which, if not strictly true in fact, is certainly true in spirit. The replies to Hume proved so numerous as to justify his further remark that " Answers, by Reverends and Right Reverends, came out two or three in a Year. . . . These Symptoms of a rising Reputation gave me Encouragement as I was ever more disposed to see the favourable than the unfavourable Side of things ; a turn of Mind, which it is more happy to possess than be born to an Estate of ten thousand a Year."

The rise and progress of Hume's reputation may be delineated through the opinions of certain influential periodicals, British and Continental, and of certain important individuals. The commonly accepted account of Hume's vogue in the 1750s is that it began in France with the publication of the *Political Discourses* and ultimately redounded to Britain. The facts, however, do not support this thesis, but tend to show, on the contrary, that his fame burst out spontaneously on both sides of the Channel in 1752, that the fires were fed by the later publications, 1754–62, and by the increasing tempo of the several controversies. Articles of 1752 in two leading periodicals, one English and one Continental, may be cited in this connexion.

The January 1752 number of the *Monthly Review* is virtually a Hume number, the first article dealing with the *Enquiry concerning the Principles of Morals*, and the second with the *Political Discourses*. The first article is nineteen pages in length, while the second is twenty-five and is continued in the February issue for another ten. That these reviews prove that Hume's reputation was already at the beginning of 1752 firmly established in Britain may be seen by an excerpt from each. The review of the *Enquiry* opens :

The reputation this ingenious author has acquir'd as a fine and elegant writer, renders it unnecessary for us to say any thing in his praise. We shall only observe in general, that clearness and precision of ideas on abstracted

and metaphysical subjects, and at the same time propriety, elegance and
spirit, are seldom found united in any writings in a more eminent degree than
in those of Mr. *Hume.* The work now before us will, as far as we are able
to judge, considerably raise his reputation ; and, being free from that sceptical
turn which appears in his other pieces, will be more agreeable to the generality
of Readers. . . .

The review of the *Political Discourses* opens :

Few writers are better qualified, either to instruct or entertain their readers,
than Mr. *Hume.* On whatever subject he employs his pen, he presents us with
something new ; nor is this his only merit, his writings (as we observed in the
preceeding article) receive a farther recommendation from that elegance
and spirit which appears in them, and that clearness of reasoning, which
distinguishes them from most others. The discourses now before us, are upon
curious and interesting subjects ; abound with solid reflections ; and shew
the author's great knowledge of ancient and modern history, and his comprehensive views of things. . . .

These honeyed words, though unsigned, are from the same hand,
that of William Rose,[1] Scot and co-founder with Ralph Griffith
in 1749 of the *Monthly Review.* Dr Rose was the learned translator
of Sallust and one of the reviewers for the *Monthly* until his death
in 1786 ; he also ran a boarding-school for boys in Chiswick. In
1760 David Hume was to acknowledge his " great Regard " for
Rose, but declined to accept an invitation to join forces with him
and William Strahan in an unspecified periodical venture.

Though by no means accepting the Humean philosophy, the
Monthly, through Rose and other reviewers, was always firm in
respecting Hume as the leading literary genius of the period and
in deprecating acrimonious attacks on him. One such attack of
March 1754 provoked the reviewer to remark : " It were greatly
to be wished, that all who employ their pens in defence of natural
and revealed religion, would write like gentlemen, and treat their
adversaries with decency and good manners ; then might they
justly expect to meet with a favourable reception from the public,
and if they could not always be admired, would seldom fail of being
respected."

The first volume of Hume's *History* was roundly castigated in
the *Monthly* of March 1755 by Roger Flaxman, a Scottish Presbyterian minister, but with extenuating praise of his genius : " It
will be unnecessary for us to repeat here, what we have already
more than once had occasion to say, with respect to the abilities
of this very ingenious writer ; that we shall always with pleasure

---

[1] B. C. Nangle, *The Monthly Review, First Series 1749–1789. Indexes of contributors
and articles* (Oxford 1934), under " Hume."

see him employing on subjects to which they are adequate : among which we are sorry to say (convinced by the work now before us) the history of his own country is the last he ought to have attempted." In February 1757 the *Monthly* bestowed its praise on Hume in Rose's comment on *Four Dissertations* : " There are but few of our modern Writers, whose works are so generally read, as those of Mr. Hume. And, indeed, if we consider them in one view, as sprightly and ingenious compositions, this is not at all to be wondered at : there is a delicacy of sentiment, an original turn of thought, a perspicuity, and often an elegance, of language, that cannot but recommend his writings to every Reader of taste."

The *Bibliothèque raisonnée* devoted a five-page article in the third quarter of 1752 to Hume's three recently published works. The *Enquiry concerning the Principles of Morals* is said to expound its theses " with much clarity, precision, and force " ; the *Political Discourses* are acknowledged to be already " greatly esteemed " ; but the *Philosophical Essays*, written " in imitation of the celebrated Bayle, attempts to spread a universal doubt concerning human understanding and to make religion itself appear to be the fruit of stupidity and imposture." " Of Miracles," in particular, is declared to be specious in reasoning ; yet its author is acknowledged as one of " the most subtle advocates of unbelief." Here, then, in 1752 are Hume's most important works, except the *Treatise*, presented to the Continental reading public.

That it was not the *Political Discourses* alone that brought Hume into the public eye is further attested by one Scottish and two German periodicals. The 1754 *Scots Magazine* opens : " For a preface to this volume we have chose one of the many ingenious essays writ by our learned contryman, David Hume, Esq." The essay chosen was " Of the Liberty of the Press," which had been published first in 1741. The *Gelehrte Erlanger Zeitungen* reviewed the *Philosophical Essays* in June, and the *Political Discourses* in September 1753. The *Göttingische Zeitungen von Gelehrten Sachen* took up the *Philosophical Essays* in May 1753, the *Political Discourses* in August, and the *Enquiry concerning the Principles of Morals* in March 1754. By the time that the *History of England* began to appear, the name of Hume was already well known to most learned circles in Europe.

The frequent refutations of his works kept his name before the English public and the frequent translations of both the works and the refutations kept it before the Continental public. The *Political*

Discourses appeared in French in 1752 in two different editions, and the collected works, always excepting the *Treatise*, in 1758–60. In German, the collected works appeared in 1754–56, and the *Four Dissertations* in 1759. There were other reprints in periodicals, such as the *Mercure de France*, which between 1756 and 1760 reprinted no fewer than six of the essays, some of which drew replies from correspondents. When J. A. Trinius's *Freydenker Lexicon* was published at Leipzig in 1759, five pages were devoted to the bibliography of David Hume and the replies to him.

All this evidence is not meant to imply, to be sure, that the *Political Discourses* did not ultimately become the most famous of Hume's books abroad. It did, as he was assured by his chief early translator, the Abbé Le Blanc. The translation, wrote Le Blanc from Paris, 25 August 1754, " thanks to the excellence of the original, is selling here like a novel." On 1 October he added : " Even our ministers [of state] are no less pleased than the public. M. le Comte d'Argenson, M. le Maréchal de Noailles, in a word all those who have any part in the government here, have spoken of your work as one of the best that were ever written on these matters." On Christmas Day Le Blanc wrote that he was constantly engaged in spreading Hume's fame throughout Europe. Yet the following February he was compelled to acknowledge that Maupertuis had inquired from Berlin : " How is it possible that such a man is not better known here and is not the admiration of Europe ? " [1]

In Italy Hume's reputation made progress early. At Rome on 15 November 1755 Robert Adam observed that, " David Humes Essays & his History are in great repute. The last I am not much surprizd at. . . . But the first I own I did not imagine till I found on inquiring, the Misbelievers about Rome are not few in number, which soon removed all my Doubts. . . ." [2] In 1756 Hume was surprised and pleased to receive a letter and the copy of a new book " from the Count Algarotti, a famous Virtuoso of Venice." By 1761 Hume's reputation had spread sufficiently to earn a place for all his works on the index of prohibited books of the Roman Catholic Church. [3] Yet two years later, undeterred by this prohibition, Professor Carlo Denina of the Royal School of Turin could ask the following questions which carried their own answers :

[1] RSE, VI, 3–7.   [2] MS in Adam Box, SRO.
[3] *Index Librorum Prohibitorum* (Rome 1911), p. 160 : " Hume, David. *Opera omnia.* Decr. 19 ian. 1761 ; 10 Sept. 1827."

" Amongst the learned in Europe, who does not know the celebrated works of David Hume ? Who has not read, and who has
not admired his History ? " [1] Already in 1757, however, after
the death of Montesquieu, Le Blanc had categorically announced
to Hume : " You are the only one in Europe who can replace
M. le Président de Montesquieu."

To the great Montesquieu belongs the credit for having been
the first distinguished thinker to recognize the genius of Hume.
Upon   reading   the   *Essays   Moral   and   Political*   of   1748,
Montesquieu's   attention   centered   upon   " Of   National
Characters," which, in a letter to Hume the next year, he termed
" a fine dissertation in which you accord a much greater influence
to moral causes than to physical causes. It seemed to me, as far
as I am capable of judging, that you had gone to the root of the
matter, difficult as that was to do, that your manner of writing
showed the hand of a master, and that the work was filled with
very new ideas and reflections." [2] (In upholding the moral as
against the physical causes as paramount in the moulding of
national characters, Hume was opposing, not only Montesquieu
among the moderns, but also Bodin, Charron, Dubos and
Arbuthnot ; and among the ancients, Hippocrates, Plato and
Aristotle.) Montesquieu also sent Hume (as he learned from
his friend John Stewart, the wine merchant) a copy of *Esprit des
Loix* which he had already read in Turin.

For his part, Hume sent the *philosophe* a copy of the *Philosophical
Essays* together with a long letter of appreciation, taking the
occasion to offer detailed criticism of *Esprit des Loix* of the kind
that he himself was forever begging from friends. (Montesquieu
found Hume's remarks " full of light and good sense ".) Written
in French, Hume's letter concludes with the avowal : " I have
consecrated my life to philosophy and to fine letters, and this
pacific ambition, exempted from every species of envy, will
procure me, I hope, your favourable indulgence." It did, and
the older man accepted the invitation to a correspondence which
was carried on until his death in 1755. Later in 1749, in some
unknown manner, Hume helped to put through the press at
Edinburgh a translation of two chapters of the *Esprit des Loix*, for
which Montesquieu had supplied his final corrections. For his
part, the *philosophe* made unsuccessful efforts to get Hume's
Political Discourses translated.

At London one of the finest tributes paid to Hume—though

[1] Quoted in *Scots Mag.*, xxvi (1764), 467.   [2] RSE, vi, 46.

unknown to him at the time—came from the young Edward Gibbon, who informed his father in December 1758, " I am . . . to meet . . . the great David Hume." In 1773 Gibbon chided a friend visiting Edinburgh : " You tell me of a long list of Dukes, Lairds, and Chieftains of Renown to whom you are recommended ; were I with you, I should prefer one David to them all." This devotion to Hume was to be rewarded with a letter of 1776 in congratulation upon the *Decline and Fall*, a letter which Gibbon acknowledged, " overpaid the labor of ten years." [1] A Scottish compliment, recorded by Ramsay of Ochtertyre, is also to be placed on the record : " For a number of years Lord Elibank, Lord Kames, and Mr. David Hume were considered as a literary triumvirate, from whose judgment, in matters of taste and composition, there lay no appeal." [2] And Hume's efforts as literary patron to bring about a renaissance of Scottish letters were to form no inconsiderable part of his activities during the present period.

On the surface, then, the " Symptoms of a rising Reputation " point to extraordinary public success and to a fruitful and happy private life. For recognition as a successful man of letters also brought with it other varieties of success. At Edinburgh in 1751 Hume was elected secretary of the Philosophical Society, and, in 1752, Keeper of the Advocates' Library ; in 1754 he was one of the founders of the Select Society, an important instrument in the intellectual and cultural developments of the capital city ; and throughout the remainder of his life, he was the good friend of most of the leading men of letters, clerical as well as lay. In Scotland he was, in Gibbon's phrase, " the great David Hume." In England, Andrew Millar, the publisher, took pride in informing a group of clergymen in 1764 that he no longer numbered the editions of Hume's works because he considered them " as Classicks."

Beneath the surface, however, the current of Hume's life ran far from smooth. Its course was troubled by a series of bitter disappointments and frustrations : the failure in 1752 to achieve appointment to the Chair of Logic at Glasgow University ; the insult offered him in 1754 over the purchase of books for the Advocates' Library ; the debacle of the first Stuart volume, 1754–55 ; the attempted excommunication from the Church of Scotland, 1755–57 ; the suppression in London of a projected volume of " Five Dissertations " in 1756 under pressure from civil

---

[1] Gibbon, *Private Letters, 1753–1792*, ed. R. E. Prothero (London 1896), I, 21–2, 190 ; *Memoirs*, ed. O. F. Emerson (Boston 1898), p. 167.   [2] Ramsay, I, 319.

and ecclesiastical authorities ; the outcry against the Tudor volumes in 1759. Added to the earlier failures of the *Treatise* and the Edinburgh professorship, these new indignities proved almost too much for a man of genius to endure, despite his " being naturally of a cheerful and sanguine Temper." The only hint in *My Own Life* of the new frustrations appears in connexion with the *History of England*; but that it applies to the entire series is beyond doubt. " I was, however," writes Hume, " discouraged ; and had not the War been at that time breaking out between France and England, I had certainly retired to some provincial Town of the former Kingdom, have changed my Name, and never more have returned to my native Country."

" It is not so easy to put right what has once been set wrong," he consoled himself; " but Time does Justice to every body ; at least to every Book. For a man frequently lives and dies under Calumny and Obliquy ; but a Book is in a hundred Places at once to defend itself, & is not so easily susceptible of Misrepresentation." Hume was to be proved correct in this long-term view. Yet he never could fully understand how mistaken he was in the opinion definitively expressed in the posthumous *Dialogues concerning Natural Religion* that " none but fools ever repose less trust in a man, because they hear, that, from study and philosophy, he has entertained some speculative doubts with regard to theological subjects." [1]

Success and failure, side-by-side, characterise the years 1749–63. The more literary success Hume achieved, the more insufferable he found the hostility of certain sections of society. The sense of resignation to the fact that intellectually he was more than a century ahead of his contemporaries was hard to achieve. Attempting to new-model the basic thinking of his age, Hume met with but limited success and was irked by repeated failures and by repeated efforts to coerce him. His ultimate resignation to the hard facts of history was gained only through the adulation of France in later years. That success partially repaid for failure at home but also, in some measure, galled it, for no man likes to feel alien in his native land. Therein lies the deepening pathos of the last period of Hume's life.

[1] Hume–Poland, 135 ; *Dialogues*, p. 221.

Chapter 18

LEISURE AND LAUGHTER

" I am in the Humour of displaying my Wit."

THROUGHOUT the spring of 1749 David Hume remained in London widening his literary contacts. The *Philosophical Essays*, which Andrew Millar had published the previous 22 April, had gone unanswered and seemingly unnoticed despite the presence of the inflammatory essay " Of Miracles." Oddly enough it was Hume himself, acting as temporary reader for Millar, who was instrumental in the bringing out of the first refutation in *Ophiomaches ; or Deism Revealed*, an anonymous work in two volumes by an Irish clergyman, the Reverend Philip Skelton. Breaking his journey at Oxford on his way to London to seek a publisher, Skelton was introduced to Dr John Conybeare, the Dean of Christ Church. Conybeare handed him a copy of *Philosophical Essays*, suggesting that he should introduce into his manuscript some comments on the section " Of Miracles " ; and Skelton acquiesced.

The sequel as told by Skelton's biographer seems authentic :

> Upon Mr. Skelton's arrival in London, he brought his manuscript to Andrew Millar the Bookseller, to know if he would purchase it, and have it printed at his own expense. The Bookseller desired him, as is usual, to leave it with him for a day or two, until he would get a certain gentleman of great abilities to examine it, who could judge, if the sale would quit the cost of printing. These gentlemen who examine manuscripts, in the Bookseller's cant, are called " triers." " Can you guess (he [Skelton] said to me) who this gentleman was, that tried my Deism Revealed." " No, I cannot." " Hume the infidel." He came it seems to Andrew Millar's, took the manuscript to a room adjoining the shop, examined it here and there for about an hour, and then said to Andrew, print.[1]

The incident points to the growing intimacy between Hume and Millar. According to the notice in the *Daily Advertiser*, Millar brought out Skelton's book on 2 June.

By early summer 1749 Hume had left London for Scotland, where he settled down at Ninewells for two years of intensive literary activity. In some unknown manner he was instrumental in the publication at Edinburgh in April 1750 of a translation of two chapters of Montesquieu's *Esprit des Loix*. His main interests

---

[1] Samuel Burdy, *Life of the late Rev. Philip Skelton* (London 1816), II, 351.

lay, however, in writing the *Enquiry concerning the Principles of Morals* (with the appended " A Dialogue "), the *Political Discourses*, and the earliest draft of his posthumously published *Dialogues concerning Natural Religion*, and also in reading and taking notes for his long projected *History of England*. But before looking into these serious and important enterprises of some of the most productive years of his life, it might be well to glance at some less serious with which he was amusing himself and his friends from time to time.

Deep in the nature of David Hume ran a streak of frivolity. Like many another earnest intellectual, he found relaxation in banter and sometimes even in a practical joke. " Dr. Robertson used frequently to say," remarks Dugald Stewart, " that in Mr. Hume's gaiety there was something which approached the *infantine* ; and that he had found the same thing so often exemplified in the circle of his other friends, that he was almost disposed to consider it as characteristical of genius." [1]

The printing of the second edition of the *Philosophical Essays* in 1750, for instance, called forth the following comment from Hume in a letter to Dr Clephane at London :

> You'll scarcely believe what I am going to tell you ; but it is literally true. Millar had printed off some Months ago a new Edition of certain philosophical Essays ; but he tells me very gravely, that he has delay'd publishing because of the Earthquakes. I wish you may not also be a Loser by the same common Calamity. For I am told the Ladies were so frightened that they took the Rattling of every Coach for an Earthquake, & therefore wou'd employ no Physicians but from amongst the Infantry : Insomuch that some of you Charioteers had not gain'd enough to pay the Expenses of your Vehicle. But this may only be Waggery & Banter, which I abhor.

Hume's jests with intimate friends are legion and his letters are replete with wit and with witticisms. The topic of his own obesity, as has already been noted, became a perennial favourite ; and perhaps nowhere did he do better with it than in a letter of 1751 to the vivacious Mrs Dysart of Eccles :

> My Compliments to his Sollicitorship [Alexander Home, Solicitor-General for Scotland]. Unfortunately, I have not a horse at present to carry my fat carcass to pay its respects to his superior Obesity. . . .
> Pray tell the Sollicitor, that I have been reading lately in an old Author called *Strabo*, that in some cities of ancient Gaul, there was a fixt legal standard establish'd for corpulency, & that the Senate kept a measure, beyond which, if any Belly presum'd to encrease, the Proprietor of that Belly was oblig'd to pay a fine to the Public, proportionable to its rotundity. Ill wou'd it fare with his Worship & I, if such a law shou'd pass our Parliament. For I am afraid we are already got beyond the statute.

[1] Dugald Stewart, *Biographical Memoirs of Smith, Robertson, and Reid* (Edinburgh 1811), p. 211.

I wonder, indeed, no Harpy of the Treasury has ever thought of this method of raising money. Taxes on Luxury are always most approv'd of : and no one will say, that the carrying about a portly Belly is of any use or Necessity. Tis a mere superfluous ornament and is a proof too, that its Proprietor enjoys a greater plenty than he puts to a good use : and therefore, 'tis fit to reduce him to a level with his fellow-subjects by Taxes & impositions. As the lean people are the most active, unquiet, & ambitious, they every where govern the world, & may certainly oppress their antagonists whenever they please. Heaven forbid that Whig & Tory shou'd ever be abolish'd : For then the Nation might be split into Fat and Lean & our Faction, I am afraid, wou'd be in piteous taking. The only comfort is, if they opprest us very much, we shou'd at last change sides with them.

Besides, who knows, if a tax were impos'd on Fatness, but some jealous Divine might pretend, that the Church was in danger.

I cannot but bless the memory of Julius Caesar, for the great esteem he exprest for Fat men, and his aversion to lean ones. All the World allows, That that Emperor was the greatest Genius that ever was ; and the greatest Judge of mankind.

But I shou'd ask your Pardon, Dear Madam, for this long dissertation on Fatness & Leanness, in which you are no way concern'd. For you are neither Fat nor lean ; and may indeed be denominated an arrant Trimmer.

As a literary wit, outside his intimate letters, Hume fancied himself as following in the tradition of Dean Swift. " I have frequently had it in my Intentions," he admitted to Gilbert Elliot in 1751, "to write a Supplement to *Gulliver*, containing the Ridicule of Priests. Twas certainly a Pity that Swift was a Parson. Had he been a Lawyer or Physician, we had nevertheless been entertain'd at the Expense of these Professions. But Priests are so jealous, that they cannot bear to be touch'd on that Head ; and for a plain Reason : Because they are conscious they are really ridiculous. That Part of the Doctor's Subject is so fertile, that a much inferior Genius, I am confident, might succeed in it."

Years ago Hume had announced that " the Church is my aversion," and its priests he always considered fit subject for ridicule. His character of a clergyman, appended as a note to the essay " Of National Characters " of 1748 was, in the course of time, to attract considerable attention and to draw heavy sacerdotal fire.[1] A French officer visiting Edinburgh in 1763, almost certainly General La Rochette, was told by Hume that Scotland was the " Land of Bibles." Hume went on to say that he knew a certain minister who thanked God every day that there were so many more Bibles in that country than in those of warmer clime. Hume estimated the inhabitants of Scotland at one and a half millions and the Bibles at three millions. When asked by Lord Hailes if he knew how the Articles of the Church of England came to be

[1] See below, pp. 260 ff.

Thirty-nine, Hume replied, " Had there been fewer, there would have been something wanting ; and had there been more, there would have been something redundant." [1]

Early in 1751 Hume had actually attempted to get published, as he informed Elliot, " a little Endeavour at Drollery against some People who care not much to be jok'd upon." The printers at Edinburgh refused to bring it out, he further confessed to Clephane, " a good sign, you'll say, of *my* prudence and discretion." Hume wanted " to be thought a good Droll," however, and finally secured the desired publication in London.

The occasion of Hume's *Petition of the Grave and Venerable Bellmen, or Sextons, of the Church of Scotland, To the Honourable House of Commons*—for such is the title of the skit—was the decision of the General Assembly of the Church of Scotland to seek redress from parliament for their small stipends. The schoolmasters followed suit. So great, however, was the clamour raised by the gentlemen heritors of the Church (including John Home of Ninewells), who would have had to pay the increase out of their own pockets, that it was finally deemed prudent to abandon the attempt. The heritors, it would seem, were followers of the maxim of Lord Auchinleck, the father of Boswell, that " a poor clergy was ever a pure clergy." [2]

Hume's broadside is part of a considerable controversy of 1748–51 on the clerical issue.[3] Apart from the obvious fact that the clergy really did need an augmentation of stipend, his skit is good fun and makes some shrewd thrusts ; it is also a document to be considered when evaluating Hume's basic position on religion and the church. The *Petition* is accompanied by " A Letter to a Member of Parliament," dated 27 January 1751 and signed by " Zerobabel MacGilchrist,[4] Bellman of Buckhaven." " Zerobabel MacGilchrist " closed his letter with the easy promise : " Now, worthy and honourable Sir, if you will be the instrument of the *Lord* in this holy undertaking, I do hereby promise you in my own name, and in that of all my brethren, that he amongst us, whom the *Lord* will bless with the comfortable task of doing you the last service in our power, shall do it so carefully, that you never shall find reason to complain of." [5]

---

[1] NLS, MS 3803, f. 57 ; HMC, Fourth Report (London 1874), p. 532. [2] Ramsay, II, 556. [3] W. L. Mathieson, *The Awakening of Scotland : A History from 1747 to 1797* (Glasgow 1910), pp. 148–52. [4] In Gaelic " *Mac 'ille Chriosda*," i.e. " Son of Christ's gillie or servant." [5] The only extant copy is in the Bodleian. The *Petition* was reprinted without indication of authorship in *The Scotch Haggis* (Edinburgh 1822), pp. 187–91, itself a rare collection ; also as Appendix B to John V. Price, *The Ironic Hume* (Austin 1965), 173–5.

The bellman's petition is supported by the following reasons :

That it can be proved demonstrably from Scripture and reason, that the cause of religion is as intimately and inseparably connected with the temporal interests and world grandeur of your Petitioners as with any of these ecclesiastics whatsoever.

That your Petitioners serve in the quality of grave-diggers, the great use and necessity of their order, in every well regulated commonwealth, has never been called in question by any just reasoner ; an advantage they possess above their brethren, the Reverend Clergy.

That their usefulness is as extensive as it is great ; for even those who neglect religion, or despise learning, must yet, sometime or other, stand in need of the good offices of this grave and venerable order.

That it seems impossible the landed gentry can oppose the interests of your Petitioners ; since by securing so perfectly as they have hitherto done, the persons of their fathers and elder brothers of the aforesaid gentry, your Petitioners next, after the physicians, are the persons in the world to whom the present proprietors of land are the most beholden.

That as your Petitioners are but half ecclesiastics, it may be expected they will not be altogether unreasonable nor exorbitant in their demands.

That the present poverty of your Petitioners in this kingdom is a scandal to all religion, it being easy to prove, that a modern Bellman is not more richly endowed than a primitive apostle, and consequently possesseth not the twentieth part of the revenues belonging to a Presbyterian Clergyman.

That whatever freedom the profane scoffers and free-thinkers of the age may use with our Reverend Brethren the Clergy, the boldest of them trembles when he thinks of us ; and that a simple reflection on us has reformed more lives than all the sermons in the world.

That the instrumental music alloted to your Petitioners being the only music of that kind left in our truly reformed churches, is a necessary prelude to the vocal music of the Schoolmaster and Minister, and is by many esteemed equally significant and melodious.

That your Petitioners trust the Honourable House will not despise them on account of the present meanness of their condition ; for having heard a learned man say, that the Cardinals who are now Princes, were once nothing but parish curates of Rome, your Petitioners observing the same laudable measures to be now prosecuted, despair not of being one day on a level with the nobility and gentry of these realms.

Besides personal and religious topics, Hume's drollery was frequently exercised on politics, particularly on the " most terrible *ism* of them all, that of Jacobitism." His general attitude has already been seen in *A True Account of . . . Archibald Stewart*, but in his letters the chief butt is James Fraser, another medical friend of the Lorient expedition. A hot-headed Highlander and a rabid Jacobite, Fraser is a passing target in letters to various common friends : " I hope Fraser is converted " ; " My Compliments to . . . Mr. Fraser ; that is, if you converse with him ; that is, if he is at all conversible " ; " Fraser . . . is an honest, good-humoured, friendly, pleasant fellow (though, it must be confessed, a little turbulent and impetuous), and I should be sorry to disoblige him." In both 1750 and 1751 Hume wrote skits against Fraser, of which only the second has survived. The first was described by its fond author as " very witty. I contriv'd it one Night, that I coud not sleep for the Tortures of Rheumatisms : And you have heard of a great Lady, who always put on Blisters, when she wanted to be witty."

The 1751 jest was an elaborate hoax designed to cure Fraser " of his politics and patriotism," though Hume, to be sure, had no real expectation of working such a miracle. " Is it likely," he inquires of Clephane, " that reason will prevail against nature, habit, company, education and prejudice ? I leave you to judge." The hoax itself was to be perpetrated through the agency of Colonel Abercromby and was explained to him in a covering letter. The Colonel was to read to Fraser an ostensible letter from Hume vigorously denouncing his Jacobite politics and calling attention to an enclosed manuscript which Hume was supposedly seeking to get printed. It was left to Abercromby to decide whether he should insert in the newspapers the following advertisement concerning this manuscript : " Speedily will be publish'd. Price 1 sh. A Letter to a certain turbulent Patriot in Westminster, from a Friend in the Country." Abercromby was also given the discretion to say to Fraser, " that you suspect too much Study has made me [Hume] crazy ; otherwise I had never thought of so foolish a thing."

The manuscript[1] itself, addressed " To THE RIGHT HON^ble the LORD-CHIEF-JUSTICE REASON, and the HON^ble the JUDGES, DISCRETION, PRUDENCE, RESERVE, and DELIBERATION, THE PETITION of THE PATIENTS OF WESTMINSTER against JAMES FRASER, apothecary," treats Fraser as an apothecary who by his good cheer had cured many of the sick and by his practice of medicine had killed no more than he should :

That in all hypocondriacal Cases he was Sovereign, insomuch that his very Presence dispell'd the malady, cheering the Sight, exciting a gentle Agitation of the Muscles of the Lungs & Thorax, & thereby promoting Expectoration, Exhileration, Circulation, and Digestion.

That your Petitioners verily believe, that not many more have dy'd from amongst them, under the Administration of the said James Fraser, than actually dye, by the Course of Nature, in Places where Physic is not at all known or practic'd : Which will scarcely be credited in this sceptical & unbelieving Age.

---

[1] Reprinted in HL, II, 340–2.

But having come under the influence of certain Jacobite politicians, Fraser " had given himself entirely up to the Care of Dame PUBLIC, and had utterly neglected your Petitioners." That lady " was of a most admirable CONSTITUTION," however, and needed little medical attention.

That, notwithstanding this, the said James Fraser uses all Diligence & Art to perswade the said Lady, that she is in the most desperate Case imaginable, & that nothing will recover her but a Medicine he has prepard, being a Composition of *Pulvis pyrius*, along with a Decoction of northern Steel, and an Infusion of southern *Aqua sacra* or holy Water.

That this Medicine or rather Poyson was at first wrapt up under a Wafer, markt Patriotism ; but had since been attempted to be administrated without any Cover or Disguise.

That a Doze of it had secretly been pour'd down the Throat of the said Dame Public, while she was asleep, & had been attended with the most dismal Symptoms, visibly heightening her Vapours, & encreasing her Flux, & even producing some Symptoms of the bloody kind. And had she not thrown it up with great Violence, it had certainly prov'd fatal to her.

" May it therefore please your Worships," the Petition concludes, " to discharge the said James Fraser from any farther Attendance on the said Dame Public, & to order him to return to the Care & Inspection of your Petitioners & their Families."

" The Humour of displaying my Wit " led Hume to produce yet another political skit as late as 1761, this time directed against Pitt, the " Great Commoner." The only known information about this effort, which apparently saw the light of publication, is contained in a letter of 3 March 1761 from Rear-Admiral George Murray at London to his brother, General James Murray, both of whom were good friends of the philosopher. The Admiral was clearly no professional author :

David Hume values him selfe on prognosticating your greatness. I wanted him to write to you but he thought it might appear for ward, tho I assur'd him had you conquerd the old world as well as the new his correspondence woud a been acceptable. He has wrote a houmorous thing I here by send you which has done no good to your friend Pitt. Still as he is exprest by no name but Gowler [i.e., Howler].

I had forgot to tell you that My Wife launch a little guirl tother day but that tells nothing with us.[1]

If David's fling in the name of *Gowler*, that is, of Pitt himself, was actually as humorous as the Admiral's letter was unintentionally, it might be well worth a search in the voluminous pamphlet literature of the day. That it was not is perhaps sufficiently evident from the skits already looked at. For sustained satire in

[1] EU, Laing MSS, ii, 601.

the manner of Swift was clearly not Hume's forte. His recognition of this fact and his sensitivity concerning it are expressed in the letter to Elliot in connexion with the *Bellman's Petition* :

> I do not pay Compliments, because I do not desire them. For this Reason, I am very well pleas'd you speak so coldly of my Petition. I had, however, given Orders to have it printed, which perhaps may be executed : Tho' I believe I had better have left it alone. Not because it will give Offence, but because it will not give Entertainment : Not because it may be call'd profane ; but because it may perhaps be deservedly call'd dull. To tell the Truth, I was always so indifferent about Fortune, & especially now, that I am more advanc'd in Life, & am a little more at my Ease, suited to my extreme Frugality, that I neither fear nor hope any thing from any man, and am very indifferent either about Offence or Favour. Not only, I woud not sacrifice Truth & Reason to political Views, but scarce even a Jest. You may tell me that I ought to have revers'd the Order of these Points, & have put the Jest first : As it is usual for People to be the fondest of their Performances on Subjects on which they are least made to excel. And that, consequently, I woud give more to be thought a good Droll, than to have the Praises of Erudition, & Subtility, & Invention.—This malicious Insinuation, I will give no Answer to. . . .

If every clown wishes to be a Hamlet, why may not an occasional Hamlet wish to be a clown ? Yet Hume was discerning in recognising his own shortcomings. Kindly wit and the gentle thrust were, however, well within his powers, and they serve to render his serious works more humane and to place his letters amongst the most entertaining and lively, as well as informative, of a great century of letter-writing.

CHAPTER 19

CITIZEN OF EDINBURGH

" I removed from the Countrey to the Town ; the true Scene
for a man of Letters."

IN March 1751 John Home of Ninewells married Agnes Carre of
Cavers in Roxburghshire. His brother recounts the story to Mrs
Dysart of Eccles :

> Our Friend, at last, pluckt up a resolution, & has ventur'd on that dangerous
> encounter. He went off on Monday morning ; and this is the first action
> of his life, wherein he has engag'd himself without being able to compute
> exactly the consequences. But what Arithmetic will serve to fix the proportion
> betwixt good & bad Wives, & rate the different classes of each ? Sir Isaac
> Newton himself, who cou'd measure the courses of the Planets, and weigh the
> Earth as in a pair of scales, even he had not Algebra enough to reduce that
> amiable Part of our species to a just equation : and they are the only heavenly
> bodies, whose orbits are as yet uncertain.

With a new Lady Ninewells coming to the house, David and
Katherine (who had been living with John all along), held council
and decided that they had better not intrude upon the new family
circle. The decision was reached reluctantly, as David later made
clear : " I lived several years happy with my brother at Ninewells,
and had not his marriage changed a little the state of the family,
I believe I should have lived and died there."

> Since my Brother's departure [continued Hume to Mrs Dysart], Katty
> & I have been computing in our turn ; and the result of our deliberation is,
> that we are to take up house in Berwick, where if Arithmetic & Frugality dont
> deceive us (& they are pretty certain Arts) we shall be able, after providing
> for Hunger, Warmth, & cleanliness, to keep a stock in reserve, which we may
> afterwards turn either to the purpose of hoarding, Luxury or charity. But I
> have declar'd beforehand, against the first. I can easily guess which of the
> other two, you and Mr Dysart will be most favourable to. But we reject your
> Judgement. For nothing blinds one so much as inveterate Habits.

But Berwick was too provincial a town to hold any real attraction
for Hume. Dr Clephane offered a room in his house at London,
and that was decidedly better. " A man of letters ought always
to live in a capital, says Bayle," Hume acknowledged to Clephane.
Yet, as a Scotsman, Hume never felt quite at ease in London.
There was, to be sure, the capital of Scotland ; and two
unnamed friends offered him rooms. Katherine, however,

rendered acceptance impracticable, even if David had been willing to forgo some of his cherished independence. By the end of June he was able to tell Michael Ramsay that " Our Sister in law behaves well and seems very desirous we should both stay," but that " After some Deliberation, I am resolved to settle in Edinburgh. . . . Besides other Reasons, which determine me to this Resolution ; I would not go too far away from my Sister, who thinks she will soon follow me. . . ." So to Edinburgh went David, to stay at " Mrs Freebairn's till Katty come to a Resolution." During the late summer he took " a Jaunt to the West Country," visiting Mure at Glanderston near Glasgow.

" While Interest remains as at present," Hume had informed Ramsay, " I have £50 a year, £100 worth of Books, a great Store of Linnens and fine Cloaths, & near £100 in my Pocket, along with Order, Frugality, a strong Spirit of Independency, good health, a contented Humour, & an unabating love of Study. In these circumstances, I must esteem myself one of the happy & fortunate : And so far from being willing to draw my Ticket over again in the Lottery of Life, there are very few prizes with which I would make an Exchange." Katherine, he goes on to say, " can join £30 a year to my Stock, & brings an equal love of Order & Frugality, [and] we doubt not to make our Revenues answer." It was not, however, until the following Whitsunday that Hume had his own " house " in Riddle's Land, Lawnmarket, in the neighbourhood in which he had been born.

" In 1751," wrote Hume in *My Own Life* with obvious recollection of Bayle, " I removed from the Countrey to the Town ; the true Scene for a man of Letters." And despite temporary residence in London and Paris, he was to remain a citizen of Edinburgh for the rest of his life. The Edinburgh into which he now thrust his roots deeply was little changed physically since his student days. Britain's third city in size, after London and Bristol, Edinburgh at mid-century had a population slightly over 50,000. Then just beginning to grow fast, it was to reach the 80,000 mark in 1775.[1]

Reputed as one of the most cosmopolitan towns of Britain, one of the most Continental, Edinburgh was also reputed as one of the filthiest. " That most picturesque (at a distance) and nastiest (when near) of all capital cities," noted Thomas Gray.[2] An unnamed English soldier passing through with the Duke of Cumberland's army in 1746 provides a racy description :

[1] Wm. Maitland, *History of Edinburgh* (Edinburgh 1753), pp. 220–1 ; Arnot, *History of Edinburgh* (Edinburgh 1788), pp. 339–40.
[2] Gray, *Works*, ed. Edmund Gosse (New York 1885), II, 209.

Edinburgh is certainly a fine City, and, I believe, can boast of the highest Houses in *Europe* ; notwithstanding, it has its Faults, and those very great, meaning its Nastiness, which is composed of Excrements in all Parts of the Town ; and in a Morning, about seven o'clock, before the Excrements are swept away from the Doors, it stinks intolerably, for which, I believe, it exceeds all parts of the World : For after ten o'clock in the Evening, it is Fortune favors you if a Chamberpot, with Excrements, &c. is not thrown on your Head, if you are walking the Streets ; it is then not a little Diversion to a Stranger, to hear all Passers-by, cry out with a loud Voice, sufficient to reach the Tops of the Houses (which are generally six or seven Stories high, in the Front of the High-Street,) *Hoad yare Hoand, i.e.* hold your Hand, and means, do not throw till I am past.[1]

With due poetic licence, the poets of Edinburgh of the eighteenth century took a certain civic pride in its very stenches, Henry Erskine, for instance, devoting an entire poem to *The Cloaciniad.* A far better poet than Erskine, Robert Fergusson, provides a far better defence of the " flowers " of *Auld Reekie* through the philosophical principle of polarity :

> On stair wi' *tub*, or *pat* in hand,
> The barefoot *housemaids* loe to stand,
> That antrin fock may ken how *snell*
> Auld Reekie will at *morning smell* :
> Then, with an *inundation big* as
> The *burn* that 'neath the *Nor' Loch brig* is,
> They kindly shower Edina's roses,
> To *quicken* and *regale* our *noses.*
> Now some for this, wi' satire's leesh,
> Ha'e gi'en auld Edinburgh a creesh ;
> But without souring nocht is sweet ;
> The morning smells that hail our street,
> Prepare, and gently lead the way
> To simmer canty, braw and gay :
> Edina's sons mair eithly share
> Her spices and her dainties rare,
> Then he that's never yet been call'd
> Aff frae his pladie or his fauld.

City magistrates might rule that at the sound of the trumpet at ten o'clock in the evening the contents of privies should be carried down to the gutters and emptied ; simple housemaids, however, found it easier to open the windows and dump. Reformers[2] followed reformers, but few reforms were made. While the word *water-closet* appeared in the language about 1755, that simple utilitarian device did not appear at Edinburgh during the

---

[1] *A Journey through part of England and Scotland along with the Army under the Command of His Royal Highness the Duke of Cumberland,* 3rd edn. (London 1747), pp. 93–4.
[2] See, e.g. [Anon.], *The City Cleaned, and Country Improven* (Edinburgh 1760).

eighteenth century. Walking up the High Street in 1773, Dr Johnson grumbled in Boswell's ear, " I smell you in the dark ! "

The unknown English soldier already mentioned did not take long to discover one of the secrets of the Canongate : " there is vast Numbers of Bawdy-Houses in this Street ; which amongst the Frequenters of, it is a common Question to ask, If they have got a Pair of Canon-Gate *Breeches*, meaning the Venereal Distemper, which rages here. . . ." But he does have the grace to conclude his description of the city with a compliment to the women, backhanded though it may be : " The Women here use the *Scots* Plaids about their Heads and Shoulders . . . ; these are very good Cover-sheets, and serve to hide the Nastiness of their Undress. Great numbers of the Ladies of *Edinburgh* are very handsome, light-haired, and fair Complexions, with Freckles : along the Streets, they have a noble Walk and erect Deportment." The fashion of plaids shortly changed, however, for Ramsay of Ochtertyre expressly testifies " that when I returned to Edinburgh in 1752, one could scarcely see a lady in that piece of dress. For a while they were retained by matrons attached to old modes, and by the lower classes of people ; but in the course of seven or eight years the very servant-maids were ashamed of being seen in that ugly antiquated garb." [1]

If at mid-century Edinburgh was a city suffering from physical growing pains, it was rapidly maturing in intellect. It was, in brief, beginning to reap the golden harvest that had begun to be sown several generations earlier in the lecture-rooms of the university. For if David Hume was among the first to produce masterpieces of literary expression and thought, he was not long alone. The 1750s brought a resurgence of Scottish literature that for more than a quarter of a century was to maintain that poor country on a higher level than her rich sister to the south. It was into this stimulating atmosphere that Hume moved in 1751, and his career thereafter was inseparably bound up with the developments of the Scottish Enlightenment.

The story of Hume's arrival, " being turned of forty," " at the dignity of being a householder " is related to Clephane in January 1753 :

About seven months ago, I got a house of my own, and completed a regular family ; consisting of a head, viz myself, and two inferior members, a maid and a cat. My sister has since joined me, and keeps me company. With frugality I can reach, I find, cleanliness, warmth, light, plenty, and contentment.

[1] Ramsay, ii, 88.

What would you have more? Independence? I have it in a supreme degree. Honour? that is not altogether wanting. Grace? that will come in time. A wife? that is none of the indispensable requisites of life. Books? that *is* one of them ; and I have more than I can use. In short, I cannot find any blessing of consequence which I am not possessed of, in a greater or less degree ; and without any great effort of philosophy, I may be easy and satisfied.

Hume's " house " at Riddle's Land, on the south side of Lawn-market and near the head of the West Bow, survives to this day, although somewhat altered in the passage of time. It is in a typical six-story, smoke-blackened, stone building with a narrow staircase approached through a tunnel of a " close." Sanitary conditions in the eighteenth century would have been as good here, and as bad, as anywhere else in the city. The Humes, brother and sister, remained at Riddle's Land but a year, removing at Whitsunday 1753 to Jack's Land, beyond the Netherbow in the Canongate and in the vicinity of the Tolbooth prison. This building no longer stands, more's the pity since Hume remained there nine years, during which time he wrote and published almost all of the *History of England*.

Intimate glimpses of Hume's life in his " very small " house in Jack's Land are provided by his good friend, the Reverend Alexander Carlyle of Inveresk,[1] one of the Moderate clergy. " . . . When he [Hume] lived in the Cannongate," reveals Carlyle, " during the time he wrote his History, he was an early riser, and being very laborious in his studies, he had little time for exercise, and therefore, his custom was, early in the morning to walk round Salisbury Craigs and return to breakfast & his Studies." His economy was strict and he " kept only one maid Servant whom he never parted with all her life & such was the sweetness of his temper that even when he became opulent & his manner of living rose in proportion to his circumstances, he never put a Housekeeper over her for fear of affronting her." Peggy Irvine, for such was her name, is further described by Carlyle as " much more like a man than a woman " ; she was, moreover, something of a domestic tyrant. " I remember one night," Carlyle recounts, " that David Hume, who, having dined abroad, came rather late to us [that is, a group of the Moderate clergy just in town from the country], and directly pulled a large key from his pocket, which he laid on the table. This he said was given him by his maid Peggy . . . that she might not sit up for him,

---

[1] The following paragraphs are pieced together from Carlyle : (1) MS letter to Mr Eben. Marshall, 26 Sept. 1801, in EU, MS Do. 4.41/96, and (2) *Autobiography*, pp. 285-91.

for she said when the honest fellows came in from the country, he never returned home till after one o'clock."

In his necessary frugality Hume " was much abroad at dinner, which in those days was at 2 o'clock—and what was singular at that time he gave no veils [gratuities] to Servants, tho' he was invited 4 or 5 times a week, and what was more singular still tho' he was a great eater, but drank very moderately he returned to his Studies in the Evening with clearness and assiduity. With respect to his not giving veils," continues Carlyle, " the truth is that in those days he could not afford it, for he had not £50 p ann : tho' he wore fine cloaths. The Servants too finding that he was facetious & good company, and made their Masters & mistresses very happy, were always as glad to see him as if he had paid them for every dinner." It took the great good nature of Hume to help to break down the objectionable practice of handing out gratuities to servants in private homes after every visit.

The great good nature of David Hume also sufficiently atoned for his reputation as " the Atheist," according to another of Carlyle's anecdotes :

. . . When Mr. Robert Adam, the celebrated architect, and his brother, lived in Edinburgh with their mother, an aunt of Dr. Robertson's, and a very respectable woman, she said to her son, " I shall be glad to see any of your companions to dinner, but I hope you will never bring the Atheist here to disturb my peace." But Robert soon fell on a method to reconcile her to him, for he introduced him under another name, or concealed it carefully from her. When the company parted she said to her son, " I must confess that you bring very agreeable companions about you, but the large jolly man who sat next me is the most agreeable of them all." " This was the very Atheist," said he, " mother, that you was so much afraid of." " Well," says she, " you may bring him here as much as you please, for he's the most innocent, agreeable, facetious man I ever met with."

And Carlyle goes on, " This was truly the case with him ; for though he had much learning and a fine taste, and was professedly a sceptic, though by no means an atheist, he had the greatest simplicity of mind and manners with the utmost facility and bene-volence of temper of any man I ever knew. His conversation was truly irresistible, for while it was enlightened, it was naive almost to puerility."

Despite his frugality, Hume was able to give " little suppers now & then to a few select friends," simple meals consisting of " roasted hen and minced collops, and a bottle of punch . . . and . . . best of all, he furnished the entertainment with the most instructive and pleasing conversation, for he assembled whosoever were most knowing and agreeable among either the laity or clergy. This he always did, but still more unsparingly when he became what he called rich. For innocent mirth and agreeable raillery I never knew his match. Jardine [another of the Moderate clergy], who sometimes bore hard upon him—for he had much drollery and wit, though but little learning—never could overturn his temper."

The philosopher's good-natured pleasantry sometimes touched upon religion, and even that the doting Carlyle could take with equanimity. Witness the following :

Being at Gilmerton, where David Hume was on a visit, Sir David Kinloch made him go to Athlestaneford Church, where I preached for John Home. When we met before Dinner, " What did you mean," says he to me, " by treating John's congregation to-day with one of Cicero's academics ? I did not think that such heathen morality would have passed in East Lothian." On Monday, when we were assembling to breakfast, David retired to the end of the dining-room, when Sir David entered : " What are you doing there, Davy ? come to your breakfast." " Take away the enemy first," says David. The baronet, thinking it was the warm fire that kept David in the lower end of the room, rung the bell for a servant to carry some of it off. It was not the fire that scared David, but a large Bible that was left on a stand at the upper end of the room. . . .

In June 1751 Hume had informed Michael Ramsay that he owned a mere " £100 worth of Books," yet in January 1753 he boasted to Clephane of having " more than I can use." This rapid progression provides yet another instance of how Hume's career was repeatedly determined by unforeseen events. Actually, two incidents are involved, both fortuitous, one a defeat and the other a victory.

The defeat, the second in the academic realm, occurred at Glasgow University. The manuscript " Minutes of the University Meetings " [1] report the bare facts : that on 27 November 1751 the Professor of Moral Philosophy, Thomas Craigie, who had succeeded Hutcheson in 1746, died at Lisbon, whither he had gone for the sake of his health ; that he was succeeded, 22 April 1752, by Adam Smith, who transferred from the Chair of Logic he had held since 9 January 1751 ; and finally, that on 6 May 1752 " Mr. James Clow, Tutor to the Earl of Galloway's children was elected unanimously " to be Professor of Logic in Smith's place. Such is the official record of the Senatus, providing no indication of

[1] In Glasgow University Library.

" fechtin and fasherie." Some details can be supplied, but the complete story is still unavailable.

When the serious state of Professor Craigie's health became apparent to his colleagues in the autumn of 1751, preliminary jockeying for position began in case of his death. The great influence behind the scenes was that of the third Duke of Argyll, formerly the Earl of Islay, who was popularly known as " the King of Scotland." In 1748 Hume had instructed his friend Lord Tinwald to present a copy of the new edition of *Essays Moral and Political* to the Duke.

> His Grace is oblig'd to me [wrote Hume with a touch of asperity], that I have not dedicated them to him, & put him out of Countenance, by the usual Fawning & Flattery of Authors. He is also oblig'd to me, that having once had the Honour of being introducd to him, I have not incumber'd his Levees, but have left him the free Disposal of all his Favours to Voters, & Cabballers, & Declaimers, & Spies, & such other useful People. I have a Regard for his Grace, & desire this Trifle may be considerd as a Present, not to the Duke of Argyle, but to Archbald Campbell, who is undoubtedly a Man of Sense & Learning.

Officially invested with the royal patronage of Scotland, the Duke was customarily consulted about all patronage. Adam Smith, for instance, attended his levee at Edinburgh and evidently received the nod of approval to apply for the transfer from the Logic Chair to that of Moral Philosophy. But the question of Smith's successor remained open, and David Hume had many friends and well-wishers at Glasgow, both in and out of the University, who pressed his candidacy.[1]

William Mure of Caldwell, Hume's intimate friend, wielded considerable influence through Sir John Maxwell of Pollock, Rector of the University in 1751, and William Ruat, the Professor of Church History, his first cousin. Mure himself became Rector in 1752. Gilbert Elliot of Minto, another intimate of Hume's, was also influential and, although opposed to Hume's religious principles, supported his candidacy. Hercules Lindesay, Professor of Civil Law, was for Hume ; but no personal relations between the two are known. William Cullen, Professor of Anatomy, was a strenuous partisan and later became Hume's physician and close friend. Adam Smith, the young scholar who at the age of twenty-eight had already made a distinguished name for himself,

---

[1] John Rae, *Life of Adam Smith* (London 1895), pp. 44-7. Rae seemingly has had the last word in discrediting the possible candidacy of Edmund Burke for the chair of logic.

approved highly of David Hume but was wary of possible public reactions.

Hume and Smith had certainly become acquainted by this time. During the years 1748–51, under the patronage of Henry Home, Smith had delivered two series of lectures at Edinburgh on literature and criticism and a third on jurisprudence ; Smith was also the friend of Oswald of Dunnikier. It is, therefore, a reasonable supposition that on some of Hume's visits to Edinburgh during the winters of 1749–1750 and 1750–1751, he met Smith through Home or Oswald. He may also have attended some of the lectures, particularly if they were actually delivered before the Philosophical Society, of which he was a member.[1] In the autumn of 1751, Hume took a jaunt to the west of Scotland, where he visited Mure and other friends in the vicinity of Glasgow. It was probably on this trip that the idea of his candidacy was conceived ; and it is likely enough, too, that on this trip he saw Smith once more.

Hume had enemies, however, as well as friends at Glasgow. Leechman, Professor of Divinity, had used his influence earlier against Hume's appointment at Edinburgh, and it is hardly to be supposed that he would now favour him as a colleague. Other members of the Senatus would also take the lukewarm attitude which Adam Smith had expressed to Cullen :

> I should prefer David Hume to any man for a colleague ; but I am afraid the public would not be of my opinion ; and the interest of the society will oblige me to have some regard to the opinion of the public. If the event, however, we are afraid of should happen [that is, the death of Craigie], we can see how the public receives it. From the particular knowledge I have of Mr Elliot's sentiments, I am pretty certain Mr Lindsay must have proposed it to him, not he to Lindsay.[2]

Public opinion, it turned out, at least the opinion of the clergy, was in violent opposition to Hume. In short, his appointment was possible only if the Duke of Argyll would support it—but he would not.[3]

The affair is summarised by Hume for the benefit of Clephane : " You have probably heard that my friends in Glasgow, contrary to my opinion and advice, undertook to get me elected into that College ; and they had succeeded, in spite of the violent and solemn remonstrances of the clergy, if the Duke of Argyle had had

---

[1] The conjecture is made by W. R. Scott in *Adam Smith as Student and Professor* (Glasgow 1937), pp. 49–50.
[2] John Thomson, *Life, Lectures and Writings of William Cullen* (Edinburgh 1832), 1, 606.   [3] See Textual Supplement.

courage to give me the least countenance." On 21 January 1752 Hume penned a letter of thanks to Cullen for " your zeal for my interests." The letter concludes : " Whatever the reverend gentlemen may say of my religion, I hope I have as much morality as to retain a grateful sentiment of your favours, and as much sense as to know whose friendship will give greatest honour and advantage to me." Certain it is, therefore, that the clergy of Glasgow, like their brethren of Edinburgh, had given formal advice against the election of David Hume as Professor of Logic. So the academic infatuation with respectable mediocrity once more triumphed ; and, while Professor Clow of Glasgow remains as insignificant as Professor Cleghorn of Edinburgh,[1] Scotland's most distinguished philosopher never held a philosophy chair.

The Glasgow appointment would, of course, have provided Hume with a considerable library for his historical studies. That may be why he allowed his friends to promote his candidacy. But his disappointment was brief. After defeat at Glasgow came victory at Edinburgh, his first victory in a public contest. Pent up with exultation, he wrote to Clephane :

I have been ready to burst with vanity and self-conceit this week past ; and being obliged from decorum to keep a strict watch over myself, and check all eruptions of that kind, I really begin to find my health impaired by it, and perceive that there is an absolute necessity for breathing a vein, and giving a loose to my inclination. You shall therefore be my physician. . . . You must sustain the overflowings of my pride ; and I expect, too, that by a little flattery you are to help Nature in her discharge, and draw forth a still greater flux of the peccant matter. 'Tis not on my account alone you are to take part in this great event ; philosophy, letters, science, virtue, triumph along with me, and have now in this one singular instance, brought over even the people from the side of bigotry and superstition.

All of this was " a very pompous exordium," Hume granted, to the prosaic announcement that on 28 January 1752 he had been elected Librarian to the Faculty of Advocates, " a genteel office, though of small revenue."

The manuscript " Minutes of the Faculty " indicate that,

some members proposing, that a dignified Member of their own body, vizt. Mr. Kenneth Mackenzie, Advocate, Professor of the Civil Law in the University of Edinburgh should be named to that office, and others inclining that Mr David Home should be elected. It was agreed that the matter should be put

---

[1] See Douglas Nobbs, " The Political Ideas of William Cleghorn, Hume's Academic Rival," in *Journal of the History of Ideas*, xxvi, 575–86 ; also Mossner, " Adam Ferguson's ' Dialogue on a Highland Jaunt with Robert Adam, William Cleghorn, David Hume, and William Wilkie '," in *Restoration and Eighteenth-Century Literature* (Chicago 1963), 297–308. Cleghorn died at 35 without publishing.

to a vote : And the Rolls being call'd and votes distinctly mark'd and taken down, & number'd it was found that the Majority had declared for the latter : Upon which the Dean and Faculty declared the said Mr David Home duly elected Keeper of their Library, and appointed that the Annual Salary of forty pounds Sterling should be paid to him yearly on that Account, and in regard that he was to have their Minutes, Acts and records under his Custody, they appointed him also Clerk to the Faculty which office had been lately resign'd by Mr David Falconer with power to the said Mr Home to officiate therein by a Depute.[1]

At the following meeting, 6 February, according to the minutes : " Mr David Home was received as Keeper of the Advocates Library and Clerk to the Faculty and had thereupon the Oath *de fideli* administrated to him."

Now let Hume himself continue with a behind-the-scenes account. As soon as the resignation of Thomas Ruddiman from the Keepership was announced, Hume's friends proposed his name without even consulting him. An opposition, headed by Robert Dundas, Lord President, and his son, the Dean of Faculty, formed and settled upon Professor Mackenzie as candidate. " The violent cry of Deism, atheism, and scepticism," explains Hume, " was raised against me ; and 'twas represented that my election would be giving the sanction of the greatest and most learned body of men in this country to my profane and irreligious principles." The opposition became so vigorous a week before the election that Hume's partisans held a secret caucus to recruit their forces : " they raised the cry of indignation against the opposite party ; and the public joined them so heartily, that our antagonists durst show their heads in no companies nor assemblies : expresses were despatched to the country, assistance flocked to us from all quarters, and I carried the election by a considerable majority, to the great joy of all bystanders." The " smiles of a hundred fair ones " had exerted no mean influence on his behalf, notes Hume with evident self-satisfaction ; and " One has broken off all commerce with her lover, because he voted against me ! and Mr Lockhart, in a speech to the Faculty, said there was no walking the streets, nor even enjoying one's own fireside, on account of their importunate zeal. The town says, that even his bed was not safe for him, though his wife was cousin-german to my antagonist." The town, indeed, was almost as aroused as it had been over the trial in 1747 of Provost Stewart. " 'Twas vulgarly given out," exults the victor, " that the contest was betwixt Deists and Christians ; and when the news of my success came to the playhouse, the whisper ran that the Christians were defeated." " Are you not surprised," Hume slyly asks Clephane, " that we could keep our popularity notwithstanding this imputation, which my friends could not deny to be well founded ? " Public demonstrations ensued, and a torchlight parade was put on by the famous corporation of Edinburgh porters and messengers. " The whole body of cadies brought flambeaux, and made illuminations to mark their pleasure at my success ; and next morning I had the drums and town music at my door, to express their joy, as they said, of my being made a great man."

So David Hume at long last became " a great man " in his own city. He was now " master of 30,000 volumes " and free to turn professional historian. In *My Own Life* he relates how " in 1752, the Faculty of Advocates chose me their Librarian, an Office from which I received little or no Emolument, but which gave me the Command of a large Library." That £40 is " little " emolument is true enough, but what he meant by " no " emolument becomes evident only in the sequel.

Walter Goodall was Hume's assistant at the library, an inheritance from the Ruddiman regime. Watty, as he was known to everyone, had two loves, Mary Queen of Scots, and liquor. Both loves, it would appear, were involved in the following anecdote. Entering the library one day, Hume found Watty snoring— drunkenly ?—over the manuscript of his treatise. Hume gleefully tiptoed up to the fiery Jacobite and, " laying his mouth to Watty's ear, roared out with the voice of a Stentor, that queen Mary was a whore and had murdered her husband." Watty stumbled to his feet, " and before he was awake, or his eyes well opened, he sprung upon Mr Hume, and seizing him by the throat, pushed him to the farther end of the library, exclaiming all the while that he was some d——n'd Presbyterian parson, who was come to murder the character of queen Mary, as his predecessors had contributed to murder her person." [1] His fancy tickled at being called a Presbyterian minister, David frequently repeated the anecdote to his friends among the Moderate clergy. Watty, also, took it in good part.

The serenity at the Advocates' Library did not last long, for there were those who were chagrined at Hume's appointment and eager to find some pretext to discredit him. On 4 April 1754 Hume,

[1] First told in *The Weekly Magazine, or Edinburgh Amusement*, xxxiv (1776⁴), 48, and repeated in Chalmers, *Eminent Scotsmen*, art. " Goodall." Somewhat different versions are to be found in Mackenzie, *Anecdotes and Egotisms*, p. 171, and Joseph Grant, in NLS, MS 3005, f. 212.

as Keeper of the Library, ordered from a list of offerings of Thomas Osborne, bookseller in London, seventy-four items. When the Curators met on 27 June, after long deliberation, they ordained that three of these items " be struck out of the Catalogue of the Library, and removd from the Shelves as indecent Books & unworthy of a place in a learned Library." The books in question were all French : the *Contes* of La Fontaine, *L'Ecumoire* of Crébillon *fils*, and *L'Histoire amoureuse des Gaules* of Bussy-Rabutin. " And to prevent the like abuses in time to come," the Curators " appoint that after this no Books shall be bought for the Library without the Authority of a meeting of the Curators in time of Session, and of two of them in time of Vacation." So concludes the memorandum written in Hume's own hand.[1] The Curators were James Burnet (later Lord Monboddo), Sir David Dalrymple of Newhailes (later Lord Hailes), Thomas Miller of Glenlee, and Peter Wedderburn (father of Alexander Wedderburn).

The manuscript " Register of the proceedings of the Curators & Keeper of the Library in relation to their Office Beginning Anno 1725 "[2] reflects this difference of opinion between the Curators and the Keeper. In it the names of the books are crossed out and the following note is entered by Hume : " Expung'd by positive Orders of four curators after long Deliberation." But this note, in turn, is altered to read, also in Hume's hand : " Expung'd by Order of the curators after mature Deliberation." Does this change indicate a softening of Hume's attitude or direct orders of the irate Curators ? Probably the latter, because Hume continued to be vastly disturbed by the affair.

The Keeper was between the horns of a dilemma : to stand on his rights and risk dismissal or to submit and lose self-respect ? Or to put it another way : should he, for the sake of honour, risk losing the 30,000 volumes that he so desperately needed for the writing of the *History of England*? There was, in any event, nothing to be done until the end of vacation and the opening of the Session in the autumn. However silly the whole affair was— and the censoring of alleged indecent books nearly always turns out to be silly—it still had to be resolved. Hume was of many minds and at the end of November remained undecided. Having met Robert Dundas of Arniston, younger, who had recently become Lord Advocate, and having told him that the restoration of the three books to the library was a matter of indifference, he yet wrote to Arniston the following day that he had changed his

[1] RSE, ix, 16.   [2] NLS, MS F.R. 118.

mind and that, " The expelling these books I could conceive in no other light than as an insult on me, which nothing can repair but the re-instating them."

Hume reasons thus : " There is a particular kind of insolence which is more provoking as it is meaner than any other, 'tis the *Insolence of Office*, which our great poet mentions as sufficient to make those who are so unhappy as to suffer by it, seek even a voluntary death rather than submit to it." The letter continues :

As to the three books themselves, your Lordship has little leizure from more grave and important occupations to read them ; but this I will venture to justify before any literary society in Europe, that if every book not superior in merit to *La Fontaine* be expelled the Library, I shall engage to carry away all the remains in my pocket. I know not indeed if any will remain except our fifty pound Bible, which is too bulky for me to carry away. If all worse than *Bussi Rabutin*, or *Crebillon*, be expelled, I shall engage that a couple of porters will do the office. By the bye, *Bussi Rabutin* contains no bawdy at all, though if it did, I see not that it would be a whit the worse. For I know not a more agreeable subject both for books and conversation, if executed with decency and ingenuity. I can presume, without intending the least offence, that as the glass circulates at your Lordship's table, this topic of conversation will sometimes steal in, provided always there be no ministers present. And even some of these reverend gentlemen I have seen not to dislike the subject.

Thomas Gray, the sage and serious poet of *An Elegy Wrote in a Country Church Yard*, who once expressed the wish to read in paradise " eternal new romances of Marivaux and Crébillon," might possibly have understood Hume's levity ; but the Lord Advocate of Scotland could not or would not. Arniston, indeed, went so far as to persuade two of the Curators who had previously been ready to redress Hume to remain intractable.

Hume now made his final decision, which, needless to say, was not suicide but a brilliant stroke of policy. He explained it to Adam Smith on 17 December : " I saw it then impossible to succeed, & accordingly retracted my Application : But being equally unwilling to lose the Use of the Books & to bear an Indignity ; I retain the Office, but have given Blacklock, our blind Poet, a Bond of Annuity for the Sallary. I have now," he advised, " put it out of these malicious Fellows power to offer me any Indignity ; while my Motives for remaining in this Office are so apparent. I shou'd be glad that you approve of my Conduct : I own I am satisfy'd with myself." By this stroke Hume at once retained his library post, fostered Scottish letters, performed an act of charity—and maintained his honour.

Little more than two years later, however, on 4 January 1757, Alexander Wedderburn informed the Faculty of Advocates that his friend David Hume, Esq., wished to resign his office of Librarian, " and to assure them that he had and would always retain a due sense of the honour done him by the Faculty in conferring that Office upon him. . . ." The Faculty asked Wedderburn if he had the signed commission of Hume and, when it appeared that he had not, instructed him to get it. Hume's letter of 8 January to Charles Binning, Vice-Dean of the Faculty, is curt :

Sir
A few days ago I sent the Faculty a verbal Resignation ; but as I am told, that it is expected I shou'd give a Resignation under my hand, and as I am very desirous to deliver over the Charge of the Library as soon as possible, I have been induc'd to write you at present, and beg of you to inform the Faculty, that they may choose me a Successor, whenever they think proper.

The resignation was accepted, and at the same meeting of the Faculty Adam Ferguson was elected Hume's successor.

On the face of it, there is no good reason for Hume's precipitate resignation from the Keepership of the Library in January 1757. No hint appears in any of his letters nor in those of his friends. His second Stuart volume, to be sure, had recently been sent to the press ; but, as yet, he was undetermined whether to proceed on to King William or to go back to the Tudors. If the former, he felt that he would be better off at London, although he did not relish making the change and he lamented the lack of public libraries in that city. If he decided on the Tudors—as he actually did within a few months—he would be well enough, or even better off, at the Advocates' Library. The liberty of that library, indeed, remained his even after the resignation ; and in June 1757 he escorted the Reverend George Ridpath to see " the collection of Medals Ancient and Modern, and the Mummy in the Advocates' Library." [1] The resignation, it may be conceded, was not prompted by any reason connected with historical research.

Hume's salary would be unaffected by the resignation because, since the quarrel with the Curators, he had given a bond of annuity for it to his protégé the blind poet, Thomas Blacklock. But then Blacklock would be the loser, a fact that Hume would deplore, even though in 1757 he was well enough off to give Blacklock something out of his own pocket. It would, therefore, seem that there must have been a good and sufficient reason for the resignation, though a reason unconnected with Hume's own literary projects. Without information, therefore, conjecture is

---

[1] Ridpath, p. 143.

again in order ; and my conjecture is that Hume resigned as the result of a deal to secure the office for his friend Adam Ferguson.

Son of a Highland clergyman, Ferguson had been bred to the church and had served as chaplain to the Black Watch (The Royal Highland Regiment), seeing active service during the 'Forty-five and subsequently in Flanders. Sir Walter Scott tells the story— which need not perhaps be investigated too closely—that at the Battle of Fontenoy, Ferguson led the column with a broadsword in his hand. The commanding officer ordered him to the rear, but without effect. He then reminded Ferguson that his commission did not entitle him to the post he had assumed. " D——n my commission," retorted the chaplain heatedly, tossing it towards the Colonel.[1]

A clergyman by profession, a soldier by inclination, and a gentleman by instinct, Ferguson was always a layman at heart. In 1754 he resigned from the ministry in a fit of disgust over the failure of the Duke of Atholl to give him a living. During the next two years he acted as tutor to a young Scot studying law at Leipzig University, returning to Edinburgh before the close of 1756. There he immediately entered into the society of the men of letters, lay and clerical, and soon became their boon companion. As early as 1757 David Hume called Ferguson " a Man of Sense, Knowledge, Taste, Elegance, & Morals." But Ferguson was without means of livelihood. In later years his friends were assiduous in forwarding his career, and it seems likely that that is what they did regarding the Keepership of the Advocates' Library. At a preliminary caucus, they might have decided, once Hume had approved the scheme, that they could secure Ferguson's election if the opposition had no opportunity to form. The most significant fact of all is that Ferguson was proposed and elected at the very meeting that Hume's letter of resignation was received.

So ended David Hume's first—and last—public post at Edinburgh, a post which he had held conscientiously for five years.[2] When he resigned in 1757 Hume owed the Curators seven pounds, ten shillings, nine pence, and three farthings. The manuscript " Treasurer's Accounts 1738–1792 " indicate that this debt remained unpaid until 1770.

---

[1] Scott, review of *Works of John Home*, ed. Henry Mackenzie (Edinburgh 1824), in *Quarterly Review*, xxxvi (1827), 196.
[2] See the estimate by W. K. Dickson, one of Hume's successors in the twentieth century, " David Hume and The Advocates' Library," in *Juridical Review*, xliv (1932), 1–14.

CHAPTER 20

POLITICAL DISCOURSES

" It was well received abroad and at home."

SOON after his removal to Edinburgh, David Hume began to assume his rightful role in the intellectual and cultural developments of the city. Late in 1751 he was elected joint secretary of the Philosophical Society of Edinburgh.[1] This society had been instituted in 1731 to collect and to publish essays on medicine and surgery ; and under the editorship of its secretary, Dr Alexander Monro the Elder, Professor of Anatomy at the University, five volumes of *Medical Essays and Observations* had appeared and had been well received in Britain and on the Continent. In 1737, at the suggestion of Professor Colin Maclaurin, the scope of the organisation was enlarged to include philosophy and literature and a wider membership basis was provided. This new-modelled Society for Improving Arts and Sciences was more generally known as the Philosophical Society of Edinburgh. The Earl of Morton was elected president, and Maclaurin one of two secretaries. Henry Home was an original member and so was the Reverend Robert Wallace. When David Hume entered is unknown, but his secretaryship apparently dates from the election held the first Thursday of December 1751.

The meetings of the society had been interrupted by the Rising of 1745, and before they could be resumed the following year, Maclaurin had died. The loss of this leading spirit was almost a death-blow, but reorganisation was finally effected in 1751. Lord Morton retained the title of president and Professor Alexander Monro the Younger and David Hume became the joint secretaries. Under their editorship a volume of *Essays and Observations, Physical and Literary, Read before a Society in Edinburgh and Published by Them* appeared in 1754. That the preface bears the indelible stamp of Hume's hand may be observed from the following short passage :

The sciences of theology, morals, and politics, the society are resolved entirely to exclude from their plan. However difficult the inferences in these

---

[1] " History of the Society " in *Transactions of the Royal Society of Edinburgh* (Edinburgh 1788), I, 3–100 ; Maitland's *Edinburgh*, p. 355 ; *Scots Mag.*, LXVI (1804), 421–3.

sciences, the facts on which they are founded, are extremely obvious ; and we could not hope, by our collections, to be in this respect of any service to the public. The great delicacy of the subject, the imperfections of human understanding, the various attachments and inclinations of mankind, will for ever propagate disputes with regard to these parts of erudition. And it is the peculiar happiness of geometry and physics that as they interest less the passions of men, they admit of more calm disquisition and inquiry.[1]

A second volume appeared in 1756 ; but prior to the appearance of the third volume in 1771, Hume had resigned his office. The resignation was probably made at the time of his departure for France in 1763, for in 1760 Benjamin Franklin acknowledged Hume's printed circular letter to the members of the society, and as late as 1762 sent him a paper on the use of the lightning-rod. This paper was published in the 1771 volume. In 1769 Henry Home was president ; and in 1783, through the influence of William Robertson, the organisation was chartered as the Royal Society of Edinburgh, and as such still functions.

As co-editor of the 1754 *Essays and Observations,* David Hume seized the opportunity of acting as peacemaker on behalf of Henry Home. The first article in the volume, " Of the Laws of Motion," was by Home, who now publicly maintained the same anti-Newtonian position that he had previously maintained in the correspondence with Andrew Baxter. The article was answered by John Stewart, Professor of Natural Philosophy at Edinburgh, in " Some Remarks on the Laws of Motion, and the Inertia of Matter." Besides handling Kames roughly, Stewart goes out of his way to belittle Hume :

> That something may begin to exist, or start into being without a cause, hath indeed been advanced in a very ingenious and profound system of the sceptical philosophy ; but hath not yet been adopted by any of the societies for the improvement of knowledge. Such sublime conceptions are far above the reach of an ordinary genius ; and could not have entered into the head of the greatest physiologist on earth. The man who believes that a perception may subsist without a percipient mind or a perceiver, may well comprehend, that an action may be performed without an agent, or a thing produced without any Cause of the production. And the author of this new and wonderful doctrine informs the world, that, when he looked into his own mind, he could discover nothing but a series of fleeting perceptions ; and that from thence he concluded, that he himself was nothing but a bundle of such perceptions.

A footnote refers to the " Treatise on Human Nature, 3 vols. octavo. This is the system at large, a work suited only to the comprehension of Adepts. An excellent compend or sum whereof,

[1] Reprinted in *Scots Mag.*, xvi (1754), 184–5.

for the benefit of vulgar capacities, we of this nation enjoy in the Philosophical Essays, and the Essays Moral and Political."

The affront goes deeper, however, than appears on the printed page. For what really happened was that Stewart's paper as originally read before the Philosophical Society contained no personal abuse, that being inserted only in the copy prepared for the printer. As secretary, therefore, Hume might have had the last word in the preface to the volume. But he refused to do so, as he informed Stewart in a pacific yet strong letter :

> I am so great a Lover of Peace, that I am resolv'd to drop this Matter altogether, & not to insert a Syllable in the Preface, which can have a Reference to your Essay. The Truth is, I cou'd take no Revenge, but such a one as wou'd have been a great deal too cruel, & much exceeding the Offence. For tho' most Authors think, that a contemptuous manner of treating their Writings, is but slightly reveng'd by hurting the personal Character & the Honour of their Antagonists, I am very far from that Opinion. Besides, I am as certain as I can be of any thing (and I am not such a Sceptic, as you may, perhaps, imagine) that your inserting such remarkable Alterations in the printed copy proceeded entirely from Precipitancy & Passion, not from any form'd Intention of deceiving the Society. I wou'd not take Advantage of such an Incident to throw a Slur on a man of Merit, whom I esteem, tho' I might have reason to complain of him.

Hume then proceeds to a consideration of the ethics of controversy. " When I am abus'd," he writes, " by such a Fellow as Warburton, whom I neither know nor care for, I can laugh at him : But if Dr Stewart approaches any way towards the same Style of writing, I own it vexes me : Because I conclude, that some unguarded Circumstance of my Conduct, tho' contrary to my Intention, had given Occasion to it. . . . All Raillery ought to be avoided in philosophical Argument ; both because it is unphilosophical, and because it cannot but be offensive, let it be ever so gentle." As for Henry Home, Hume admits that he thinks his argument mistaken but protests against " so many Insinuations of Irreligion, to which . . . [his] Paper gave not the least Occasion." Stewart is sharply rebuked : " This Spirit of the Inquisitor is in you the Effect of Passion, & what a cool Moment wou'd easily correct. But where it predominates in the Character, what Ravages has it committed on Reason, Virtue, Truth, Liberty, & every thing, that is valuable among Mankind ? "

Regarding himself, Hume protests further :

> . . . allow me to tell you, that I never asserted so absurd a Proposition as *that any thing might arise without a Cause* : I only maintain'd, that our Certainty of the Falshood of that Proposition proceeded neither from Intuition nor Demonstration ; but from another Source. *That Caesar existed, that there is*

such an Island as Sicily ; for these Propositions, I affirm, we have no demonstrative nor intuitive Proof. Woud you infer that I deny their Truth, or even their Certainty? There are many different kinds of Certainty ; and some of them as satisfactory to the Mind, tho' perhaps not so regular, as the demonstrative kind.

The crux of the matter to the man of letters is the problem of the communication of ideas : " Where a man of Sense mistakes my Meaning, I own I am angry : But it is only at myself : For having exprest my Meaning so ill as to have given Occasion to the Mistake." As peacemaker, Hume further engaged to persuade Henry Home not to bring up the controversy at the next meeting of the Philosophical Society and, if it was brought up by others, to prepare Stewart " to mollify the matter." There was moreover no further comment on the controversy. The volume appeared on 2 May 1754 and Hume kept his pledge of silence in the preface.

As a member of the Philosophical Society, Hume had already shown how controversy ought to be conducted. Robert Wallace, his opponent, had defended Hume's candidacy for the Edinburgh chair and had continued to take an interest in his career. On reading the essay " Of National Characters," which appeared simultaneously in 1748 in the *Three Essays* and in the third edition of *Essays Moral and Political*,[1] Wallace was greatly offended by the long footnote on the character of clergymen, an excoriating analysis purporting to show how their peculiar vices are caused by the nature of their profession. Hume charges the clergy with the vices of hyprocisy, over-zealousness, exaggerated ambition, overweening conceit, theological hatred and revenge. (As early as 1749, Montesquieu, in a letter to Hume, reacted humourously to the " character " of clergymen : " . . . you maltreat the ecclesiastical order a little. You will readily believe that while Mr. Stuart [John Stewart] and I could not entirely agree with you, we contented ourselves with admiring you. We did not believe that these gentlemen were as you stated, but we found you giving very good reasons why they must have been."[52]) Though a liberal in theology and ecclesiastical polity, Wallace wrote a refutation, when none had appeared a year or so after the essay's publication. This took the form of " A Letter from a Moderate Freethinker to David Hume Esquire concerning the Profession of the Clergy. In Which It is shewed That Their Vices Whatever They Are Are Owing to Their Disposition and Not to

---

[1] Reprinted in *Phil. Wks.*, III, 246–7.   [2] RSE, VI, 46.

the Bad Influence of Their Profession." [1] Willing enough to condemn certain of the clergy in certain times and certain places, Wallace rises to the defence of the modern enlightened Protestant clergy :

Have not we seen a great number of the Protestants take a great deal of trouble to promote knowledge and an impartiall examination of all Doctrines & opinions, even the most sacred, and to banish implicit faith and pious frauds ? In truth, we who are freethinkers have been generally obliged to them. 'Tis pity that we should not be more gratefull. Who were the Persons who had the cheif hand in raising an extraordinary spirit for inquiring into naturall Philosophy as well as into the Foundations of Divinity & Morality, towards the end of Oliver Cromwell's life & immediately after the Restoration of Charles IId ? Were they not the Latitudinarian Divines, as they were called att that time ? Who have been cherishing this spirit ever since, and called loudly upon mankind to search and examine all Doctrines and opinions of whatsoever nature & whatsoever importance, to prove all things, to hold fast on to that which is good, not to believe every spirit, but to prove the spirit ? Have they not been the Protestant Clergy ? Have they not been taking every thing to pieces in Religion & morality, & calling upon the Laity to admitt nothing but what was either self evident or could be deduced from self evident propositions by a clear inference ? . . . Has not the examining spirit taken its use or derived its cheif Credit from the Protestant Clergy themselves & been in a manner forced upon the people, who were not calling in Question the Principles of Religion & morality & had no doubts about their truth ? That the spirit of inquiring might be encouraged & promoted, have not the Clergy found out a multitude of Objections to their own Doctrines, which had never entered into any heads but their own ? . . . It is certain that ever since the Restoration there is a high spirit in Brittain for inquiring into all Doctrines & opinions whatsoever, & that this spirit has been much promoted by the Clergy. Sceptics have been much obliged to them. Without their assistance the freethinkers had never been able to do the mighty feats they have done, and were the Clergy intirely to abandone our Interests, we would perhaps find it Difficult to preserve our Conquests & might be in a fair way to be totally routed. When I consider this I cannot att all justify your severity against the Clergy in this article.

Expressing the philosophy of Scottish Moderatism, Wallace was hurt at Hume's strictures against the clergy in general : " Thus I have made some remarks on your Performance and cannot help thinking that on this occasion you have come short of your usual accuracy. I cannot Discover such a depth of Genius as I have often admired in you even in cases in which I imagined you was mistaken. I cannot but observe that there are few Subjects in which One would less choose to be Dogmaticall, never the less you appear to be more of a Dogmatist & less inclined to Scepticism than usual." And the " Letter from a Moderate Free- thinker " concludes in a tone of conciliation behind the façade of

[1] This and the subsequent Wallace MSS are in EU, Laing MSS, II, 96.

irony : " How unaccountable is it that wise and good men who are well acquainted with life & have seen the world should so often go out of their way to fall upon the inoffensive Clergy, a body of men who have appeared in all nations in all ages and in all Religions. . . . I protest such a Conduct would allmost look like bigottry in any other sett of Gentlemen than freethinkers : But I hope that our order will Correct their mistakes and I dare say no man will be more ready than your self to give them a good example."

Wallace's manuscript was probably completed in 1751, shortly before the time that he and Hume began to be thrown together at the meetings of the Philosophical Society. It is a commentary on the honourable character of that clergyman that the " Letter " was never published. Other Scottish clergymen, however, did refute Hume publicly. In 1755 the Reverend Robert Traill, Minister of Banff, published *The Qualifications and Decorum of a Teacher of Christianity Considered* ; and in 1760 Professor Alexander Gerard of Aberdeen University published *The Influence of the Pastoral Office on the Character Examined*. Both of these sermons had been preached before the Synod of Aberdeen, which city and university had become a centre of anti-Humean activities. Some years later Wallace read over his own manuscript and penned on the envelope :

I can read the pamphlet easily enough. It is a good pamphlet & in a manner is quite finished.

It was written soon after Mr Hume's piece was published, att least before I had seen any Sermon or refutation of Mr Hume's observations.

I have never compared it with Mr Gerard's Sermon on the same Subject ; & do not think it needfull to publish it.

This is written, Wednesday, September 5. 1764.

The incident had actually been closed, so far as Wallace was concerned, thirteen years previously.

During the summer of 1751 Hume had come to entertain so high an opinion of Wallace as to permit him to read in manuscript one of the papers that he was to publish the following year as *Political Discourses*. This was apparently by way of reciprocation for the courtesy Wallace had shown in asking Hume's opinion of a composition upon which he had been working for at least five or six years and which was to appear in 1753 under the title of *A Dissertation on the Numbers of Mankind in Antient and Modern Times*. Wallace's paper has an interesting history. It had been presented at a meeting of the Philosophical Society prior to the disruption of the 'Forty-five, and the manuscript was carried by Lord Morton over to France on a visit of 1746. Morton, indeed, was actually in the town of Lorient when it was besieged by General St Clair (and David Hume). As a result of that expedition, all British citizens without proper credentials were ordered to be imprisoned ; and Lord Morton, whose passport had expired, spent three months in the Bastille.[1] There all his papers were confiscated, including Wallace's, which still bears the mark of identification. Released late in 1746, Morton received his papers back and returned to England in May 1747. Wallace's note on the original manuscript concludes : " My Lord gave me back the paper when he returned from France."

The paper which Wallace had read before the Philosophical Society and which subsequently underwent such romantic adventures was an elementary study of the thesis that the ancient world was much more populated than the modern ; it concluded with seven suggestions for the increase of modern population. After the paper had been returned to him, Wallace began to expand it into a learned dissertation, and it was this enlarged version that was read by Hume in the summer of 1751. The subject had already attracted the interest of Hume and, as early as April of the previous year, he had written to Dr Clephane : " The last thing I took my hand from was a very learned, elaborate discourse, concerning the populousness of antiquity not altogether in opposition to *Vossius* and *Montesquieu*, who exaggerate that affair infinitely ; but, starting some doubts, and scruples, and difficulties, sufficient to make us suspend our judgment on that head." The following February Hume elaborated on the subject to Elliot, writing from Ninewells : " I have amus'd myself lately with an Essay or Dissertation on the Populousness of Antiquity, which led me into many Disquisitions concerning both the public & domestic Life of the Antients. Having read over almost all the Classics both Greek and Latin, since I form'd that Plan, I have extracted what serv'd most to my Purpose : But I have not a Strabo, & know not where to get one in this Neighbourhood." And he proposes that Elliot procure him a copy from the Advocates' Library. It is thus probable that Hume had entered upon the subject independently of Wallace.

In the long history of speculation on the question, David Hume was the first to maintain, however sceptically, the superior populousness of the modern world over the ancient world. The whole

[1] *Mémoires du Marquis d'Argenson* (Paris 1857–8), iii, 74.

matter may seem academic to the twentieth century but it was integral to the Age of Enlightenment ; it was, indeed, a development of the Ancient-Modern controversy which had been waged throughout the seventeenth century and extended into the eighteenth. Hume regarded it as " the most curious & important of all Questions of Erudition." In his treatment, he was to reject the idea of decline which had held complete sway over the mind of man until the middle of the seventeenth century ; he was also to reject the " modernist " idea of progress, which was becoming dominant in the eighteenth century. Matters of fact, in the Humean philosophy, are not to be explained in terms of any *a priori* dogma. Hume's essay " Of the Populousness of Antient Nations " is further remarkable for an incidental discussion of slavery, a discussion that has been said to express " the largest and most philosophical views on slavery generally." [1]

Writing on 22 September 1751 " To The Reverd Mr Robert Wallace Minister of the Gospel at Edinburgh," from Caldwell, the estate of Mure, at Glanderston near Glasgow, Hume clarifies the issues of their controversy :

Sir

After I had the Pleasure of seeing you, I took a Resolution of printing the Papers you was so good as to peruse, along with some others, under the general Title of *Political Discourses*. . . .

Before that on the Populousness of antient Nations I intend to prefix a Note to the following Purpose. ' An eminent Clergyman in Edinburgh having wrote, some Years ago, a Discourse on the same Question with this of the Populousness of antient Nations, was pleas'd lately to communicate it to the Author. It maintaind the opposite Side of the Argument to what is here insisted on, & contain'd much Erudition & good Reasoning. The Author acknowledges to have borrow'd, with some Variations, from that Discourse two Computations *viz* that with regard to the Number of Inhabitants in *Epirus*, and that with regard to those in *Belgium*. If this learned Gentleman be prevail'd on to publish his Dissertation, it will serve to give great Light into the present Question, the most curious & important of all Questions of Erudition.'

This Note, however unexceptionable it may seem to me, I woud not venture to print without your Consent ; as not knowing how you might relish it. I hope it will give Offence to no Body, that you & I have a Correspondence together on literary Subjects.

There has been printed at London, but not yet publish'd an *Enquiry concerning the Principles of Morals* of which I have order'd a Copy to be sent you ; I hope you will not find my Ethics liable to much Exception, on the Side of Orthodoxy, whatever they may on the Side of Argument & Philosophy. [2]

[1] *Enc. Brit.*, 11th edn., art. " Slavery." For a fuller treatment of the whole population problem, see Mossner, " Hume and the Ancient-Modern Controversy, 1725–1752 : A Study in Creative Scepticism," in University of Texas *Studies in English*, xxviii (1949), 139–53. See Textual Supplement.

[2] NHL, pp. 28–9.

Wallace responded with equal courtesy, and if he had not already given up the idea of publishing his " Letter from a Moderate Freethinker," he certainly did so now. His reply is dated 26 September :

Sir

What you write from Glanderston of your resolution to print your twelve Political Discourses gives me a great deal of pleasure. The sight you was pleased to allow me of one of them makes me long for the rest and I am perswaded they will be very ingenious & full of fine observation.

I thank you for the present you have ordered me of a Copy of your " Inquiry concerning the Principles of Moralls." Whether Orthodox or Heterodox I cannot answer but I dare say it will be curious and give me a usefull instruction : and I can be finely entertained with an ingenious vain of Thinking tho very different from my own & much out of the common road (the more uncommon perhaps the greater entertainment, if one is not a bigott & can make proper allowances to a philosophicall genius). If ever I publish any thing I shall make you some small requitall, for I cannot hope to repay you in full value.

As for your intended Note relating to my Discourse on the numbers of mankind I have very great reason to be much pleased with it. If ever my little work shall be published such an encomium cannot fail to be an usefull introduction to it & create a mighty prepossession in my favour. It is more to be sure than I deserve & I could never have had the assurance to have proposed it but it might be interpreted rather whim & conceit than real modesty should I refuse such a handsome recommendation & a favourable testimony from such a fair & ingenious antagonist. I wish only it be not too favourable, & when the Discourse appear, it may answer expectation & you may not be thought rather to have been partial than just & to have been misled by an excess of generosity.

I will only add that I am not afraid our Correspondence will give any offence, nor do I believe that any with whom I have any great Connexion have such narrow souls. But if they have it would be too great a sacrifice to refuse what is so agreeable, the compliment of such an ingenious & learned Gentleman as Mr Hume & I hope I shall allways have the boldness to do justice to Gentlemen of your Character. P.S. I shall be glad to know by the shortest note when your Discourses will be published.

Three days later Hume answered this " very obliging Letter " and inquired, " Why cannot all the World entertain different Opinions about any Subject, as amicably as we do ? "

The prestige gained through the favourable notice in Hume's *Political Discourses* induced Wallace to bring out his own work. In making final revisions and in adding a long " Appendix Containing Additional Observations concerning the Numbers of Mankind in Antient and Modern Ages ; with Some Remarks on Mr. Hume's Political Discourse, Intituled, *Of the Populousness of Antient Nations*," Wallace had the assistance of two members of the Edinburgh faculty, Kenneth Mackenzie, Professor of Civil Law, and Charles Mackie, Professor of History, as well as of David Hume himself. The two professors were solidly on the side of Wallace, holding no high opinion of Hume's scholarship. Mackenzie, who had been defeated by Hume for the Keepership of the Advocates' Library, went so far as to remark : " For all the Puffs that Gentleman [Hume] makes by numerous Quotations from the Antients I suspect his Knowledge of the Roman Story is got much at Second Hand from the Modern Compilers or at Best from a very light and cursory View of the Antients themselves or that he writes what comes first into his Head when it has the least Appearance of favouring his present Purpose." Be that as it may, there are, to the contrary, Hume's own statement that he had " read over almost all the Classics both Greek and Latin," and more to the point, evidence in his early manuscript notes that the reading of the classics in 1750 was, at the very least, a second reading. Modern students of demography agree with Hume, rather than with Wallace, though rejecting some of his details.

Hume was of assistance to Wallace as to both style and matter. He passed on a corroborative passage from " Matchiavel " with the remark : " I very fairly lend it you. You know I am in your Debt." Again, " I was told by Captain Rutherford, that in New york, they seldom raise black Children in their Cities (which deserve only the Names of Villages). They give them away for nothing to the People in the Country, who raise them." Yet, in general, Hume was most useful in regard to style : " I have endeavour'd to correct a few Expressions with regard to the Language." He was finical about Scotticisms, as always, warning, " The word ' expiscate ' which you use Page 170 is Scotch ; and I suspect ' Prestations ' which is us'd in Page 176." Typical stylistic alterations include : Wallace's *As therefore is not the least appearance, so neither seems there to be the smallest chance, that there shall be any sudden increase of mankind* . . . to Hume's, *Nay not only is there not the least appearance, but there seems not to be even the smallest chance* . . . ; Wallace's . . . *the superiour populousness of the antient to that of the modern world, is not so certain as the passionate admirers of antiquity believe it to be* to Hume's, . . . *as is believ'd by the passionate admirers of antiquity* ; Wallace's *for tho' they did not neglect trade, yet among them it was more confined to agriculture, being their chief employment* to Hume's, *among them fewer hands were employed in Trade ; trade was more confined ; agriculture was more encouraged, & was indeed their principall occupation.*

In the nature of things, however, the assistance that Hume

and Wallace rendered one another could hardly amount to very much. " It is not for Want of Care & Attention in me," apologised Hume, " that you do not see more Alterations on your Margin ; but from your own Care & Attention." The important fact was that the controversy was being conducted on the very highest level, totally unlike, for example, Stewart's treatment of the two Humes. The controversialists themselves were well aware of their unusual conduct, as is apparent in Hume's remark to Wallace : " I have great Reason to thank you for your Civilities, which are so far beyond what I have any Pretensions to. But Authors have so often faild in this particular, even in Controversies, the least interesting, that you are resolv'd, I see, to strain the Point on the other Side, and to set a new Example of Politeness." And " a new Example of Politeness " the Hume-Wallace controversy appeared to the Age of Enlightenment.

The Earl of Morton sent copies of the two works to Montesquieu, who sought to find translators for them and in July 1753 wrote to Hume : " The public, which will admire the two works, will equally admire the two friends who have so nobly relinquished the petty interests of the intellect for those of friendship ; as for myself, I shall be most pleased if I can hope for some place in that friendship." Somehow word got abroad that both parties had appealed to the Frenchman to settle the issue. So the following year Montesquieu wrote in answer to an inquiry from the Abbé Le Blanc, Hume's translator : " It is true, Sir, that I have received two letters, one from Mr Wallace and one from Mr Hume, in which those two illustrious men who think so differently on the same question both speak in such a noble, disinterested manner and so modestly concerning themselves that I could scarcely admire their candour sufficiently and was inclined to have their letters printed, had they consented, and had certain complimentary passages concerning me permitted it. They did not write to me in order to settle their dispute, as you were informed ; I am not capable of that and, if I were arbiter, I should decide just as he did who judged the contest between the two shepherds in Virgil." [1]

Fame of the amicable controversy redounded largely to the credit of Hume, the more distinguished figure, Wallace's share being generally overlooked. In 1764, at the time of Hume's triumphal residence in Paris, Wallace became disturbed over the

[1] Montesquieu, *Correspondance* (Bordeaux 1914), II, 460-1, 537-8 ; see Virgil, *Eclogues*, III, *ad fin.*

current garbled versions of the affair. Sorting out the papers concerned, he bundled them together and penned a note on the outside to justify himself, at least to posterity, for he published nothing further on the subject. The note reads in part :

> This bundle contains many manuscripts relating to Mr Wallace's Dissertation on the numbers of Mankind which he afterwards published. . . . And because some were pleased to say that Mr David Hume author afterwards of the history of England had made Mr Wallaces bad language good by his corrections of the press Mr Wallace has kept many of the proof sheets which he corrected (and they are in this bundle). These Corrections made by Mr Hume are corrected by his own hand : these Corrections were both few & of little consequence as may be seen here by inspecting the Corrections themselves & by letters inclosed here in which he acknowledges that they were but very few ; Mr Wallace hearing this calumny kept all he could find but some were lost before he heard that such a thing had been said.

Wallace was right, and it is regrettable that due credit was not given him by his contemporaries. Had they known of Wallace's defence of Hume in an ecclesiastical controversy of 1756,[1] as well as in an academic controversy of 1745, he would surely have been thought the perfect exemplar of a divine in an enlightened age.

Wallace's work did not end the population debate. Mirabeau, in *L'Ami des Hommes* (1756), upheld Wallace's views, while the Marquis de Chastellux, in *De la félicité publique* (1772), upheld Hume's. Mirabeau (Hume was told) had " learned the English language on purpose to read your works in the Original " and later became a friend. In Germany, Hume was backed by the two theologians, Johann Peter Süssmilch and Hermann Samuel Reimarus. Finally, Thomas Malthus synthesized the arguments of Hume and Wallace in the *Essay on the Principle of Population* (1798).[2]

Some six years after the celebrated controversy with Wallace, Hume found himself guardian of the peace in an incipient controversy about economics between Wallace and Lord Elibank.[3]

Hume's *Political Discourses* of 1752 were not, of course, restricted to the essay " Of the Populousness of Antient Nations," nor was it that historical study, indeed, that established him at the summit of British economists and political scientists. Of the original twelve *Political Discourses*, seven would today be classified as in the field of economics. Of the other five, the dissertation

---

[1] See Ch. 25, below.   [2] Malthus in his preface actually cites " Hume, Wallace, Dr. Adam Smith and Dr. Price."   [3] See Textual Supplement.

on population has already been examined. The remaining four are more strictly speaking political in nature. " Of the Protestant Succession " had been available for publication in 1748 in *Three Essays, Moral and Political,* but had been withheld at the last moment on the advice of friends who feared that Hume's position as a " very sceptical " Whig might prove embarrassing to his patron, General St Clair, whose brother had been attainted as a Jacobite after the rising of 1715. In 1752 Jacobitism was so completely on the decline that the essay created no appreciable stir.

" Of the Balance of Power " argues that that modern British policy, if not the phrase, had been employed by the ancient Greeks ; and Hume lauds Britain for maintaining " her station, as guardian of the general liberties of Europe, and patron of mankind." " Of Some Remarkable Customs " is an historical development of the proposition, " that all general maxims in politics ought to be established with great caution." The final non-economic essay, " Idea of a Perfect Commonwealth," proposes a republican form of government so restricted as to be impracticable ; though, written with Holland's constitutional system in mind, it is free of the romance of political utopias (and later influenced the Federalists, especially James Madison, in formulating the guiding philosophy of the American constitution).

The seven discourses on economics are : " Of Commerce," " Of Luxury," " Of Money," " Of Interest," " Of the Balance of Trade," " Of Taxes," and " Of Public Credit." Written in essay form in a pellucid style, these discourses turned the searchlight of rational and historical inquiry upon problems of vast interest to an age that was slowly sloughing itself out of the moribund skin of mercantilism. If these discourses have the virtues of the essay form, they likewise have its vices and lack the connexion and the system of the treatise. Consequently they do not provide the rationale of capitalism that was later to be achieved by Hume's good friend Adam Smith in the *Wealth of Nations.* The most important features of the new " free-trade " capitalistic thinking, however, are present, as Smith himself would have been the first to acknowledge.

Hume's broad philosophical approach to the problems of economics is stated in the introductory paragraphs to the first essay, that " Of Commerce " :

The greater part of mankind may be divided into two classes ; that of *shallow* thinkers, who fall short of the truth, and that of *abstruse* thinkers, who go beyond it. The latter class are by far the most rare ; and I may add, by far the most useful and valuable. They suggest hints, at least, and start difficulties, which they want, perhaps, skill to pursue ; but which may produce fine discoveries, when handled by men who have a more just way of thinking. At worst, what they say is uncommon ; and if it should cost some pains to comprehend it, one, has however, the pleasure of hearing something that is new. An author is little to be valued, who tells us nothing but what we can learn from every coffee-house conversation. . . .

I thought this introduction necessary before the following discourses on *commerce, luxury, money, interest,* &c. where, perhaps, there will occur some principles which are uncommon, and which may seem too refined and subtile for such vulgar subjects. If false, let them be rejected : But no one ought to entertain a prejudice against them, merely because they are out of the common road.[1]

Let us, by way of sample, review a few of the principles of the new science of economics—the word itself was unknown in 1752 —to see how fully they demolish the basic tenets of mercantilism or State regulation of commerce and industry for the prime purpose of increasing the quantity of money in national circulation. Conversely, let us see how they foreshadow the systematic presentation of " free-trade " capitalism by Adam Smith. The list may be limited to the four topics of labour, consumers' goods, money, and commerce.

I. LABOUR : Every thing in the world is purchased by labour ; and our passions [i.e., our wants] are the only causes of labour. . . . Every person, if possible, ought to enjoy the fruits of his labour, in a full possession of the necessaries, and many of the conveniences of life. No one can doubt, but such an equality is most suitable to human nature, and diminishes much less from the happiness of the rich, than it adds to that of the poor.

II. CONSUMERS' GOODS [Luxury, in eighteenth-century terminology] : Luxury is a word of uncertain signification, and may be taken in a good as well as in a bad sense. In general, it means great refinement in the gratification of the senses ; and any degree of it may be innocent or blameable, according to the age, or country, or condition of the person. . . . These indulgences are only vices, when they are pursued at the expense of some virtue, as liberality or charity ; in like manner as they are follies, when for them a man reduces himself to want and beggary.

III. MONEY : Money is not, properly speaking, one of the subjects of commerce ; but only the instrument which men have agreed upon to facilitate the exchange of one commodity for another. It is none of the wheels of trade : It is the oil which renders the motion of the wheels more smooth and easy. . . . Money is nothing but the representation of labour and commodities, and serves only as a method of rating or estimating them.

IV. COMMERCE : From these principles we may learn what judgment we ought to form of those numberless bars, obstructions, and imposts, which all nations of Europe, and none more than England, have put upon trade ;

[1] See Textual Supplement.

from an exorbitant desire of amassing money, which never will heap up beyond its level, while it circulates ; or from an ill-grounded apprehension of losing their specie, which never will sink below it. Could any thing scatter our riches, it would be such impolitic contrivances. But this general ill effect, however, results from them, that they deprive neighbouring nations of that free communication and exchange which the Author of the world has intended, by giving them soils, climates, and geniuses, so different from each other.

A shrewd anticipator of Adam Smith, David Hume was also his shrewd critic. A few months before his death in 1776 he read the first volume of the *Wealth of Nations* and wrote his friend: " Euge ! Belle ! Dear Mr Smith : I am much pleas'd with your Performance ; and the Perusal of it has taken me from a State of great Anxiety. . . . If you were here at my Fireside, I shoud dispute some of your Principles. I cannot think, that the Rent of Farms makes any part of the Price of the Produce, but that the Price is determined altogether by the Quantity and the Demand. It appears to me impossible that the King of France can take a Seigniorage of 8 per cent upon the Coinage. No body would bring Bullion to the mint : It woud be all sent to Holland or England, where it might be coined and sent back to France for less than two per cent. . . . But these and a hundred other Points are fit only to be discussed in Conversation. . . ." In anticipating Ricardo and in detecting an error of fact, the dying Hume still remained a good critic of economic theory.

The Age of the Enlightenment found Hume's economic and political observations subtle but discerning. As usual, his thought was seminal and provoked much appreciation and much publication.[1] In short, after 1752 David Hume was read by a wider circle than could ever possibly have read his metaphysical works. That circle he was soon vastly to extend with the *History of England*.

[1] Lord Elibank's *Inquiry into the Original and Consequences of the Public Debt* (1753), e.g., was directly inspired by the *Political Discourses*. The most complete modern study of Hume as economist is Eugene Rotwein's *David Hume : Writings on Economics* (Edinburgh 1955).

CHAPTER 21

PAX ECCLESIASTICA

" There is here a very good society of men of letters."

Mr Amyat, King's Chymist, a most sensible and agreeable English gentleman, resided in Edinburgh for a year or two. He one day surprised me [that is, William Smellie, printer, antiquarian, and biographer] with a curious remark. There is not a city in Europe, said he, that enjoys such a singular and such a noble privilege. I asked, What is that privilege? He replied, Here I stand at what is called the *Cross of Edinburgh*, and can, in a few minutes, take fifty men of genius and learning by the hand. The fact is well known ; but to a native of that city, who has all his days been familiarized with it, and who has not travelled in other countries, that circumstance, though very remarkable, passes unnoticed : Upon strangers, however, it makes a deep impression. In London, in Paris, and other large cities of Europe, though they contain many literary men, the access to them is difficult ; and, even after that is obtained, the conversation is, for some time, shy and constrained. In Edinburgh, the access of men of parts is not only easy, but their conversation and the communication of their knowledge are at once imparted to intelligent strangers with the utmost liberality. The philosophers of Scotland have no nostrums. They tell what they know, and deliver their sentiments without disguise or reserve. This generous feature was conspicuous in the character of Mr Hume. He insulted no man, but, when the conversation turned upon particular subjects whether moral or religious, he expressed his genuine sentiments with freedom, with force, and with a dignity which did honour to human nature.[1]

Besides the complimentary reference to Hume from a candid opponent of his views, the above passage is important in that it stresses the " clubbability " of the Edinburgh men of letters of the eighteenth century. Two essential features of the club were present : accessibility of the members to one another (in this case, through the smallness and compactness of the city) and their freedom of discussion. In the first half of the century, the intellectual and cultural influences of the Rankenian Club have already been noted ; in the second half of the century, other organisations continued the tradition.

The Philosophical Society of Edinburgh, though indulging occasionally in philosophy, generally restricted itself to science. The Select Society had the broadest interests and the most extensive cultural influences. The Poker Club was restricted to politics.

[1] Wm. Smellie, *Literary and Characteristical Lives of Gregory, Kames, Hume, and Smith* (Edinburgh 1800), pp. 161–2.

Hume was a member of all three groups and played a leading role in their activities.

Outside Edinburgh, the Literary Society of Glasgow was founded early in 1752 ; and at the meeting of 23 January, Adam Smith, a charter member, read an " Account of some of Mr. David Hume's Essays on Commerce," from the recently published *Political Discourses*.[1] The following year Hume was elected a member. As an absentee, he was expected to send in a paper once a year. His letter of 9 January 1755 to Smith explains a misconception in this regard :

> I beg you to make my Compliments to the Society, & to take the Fault on Yourself, If I have not executed my Duty, & sent them this time my Anniversary Paper. Had I got a Week's warning, I shou'd have been able to have supply'd them ; I shou'd willingly have sent some Sheets of the History of the Commonwealth or Protectorship ; but they are all of them out of my hand at present, & I have not been able to recall them.

At Aberdeen, the Philosophical Society, popularly known as the " Wise Club," was not founded until 1758. Though never a member of this distinguished organisation, Hume was yet an integral part of its functioning. Professor Thomas Reid explains this paradox to Hume :

> Your Friendly adversaries Drs Campbell & Gerard as well as Dr Gregory return their compliments to you respectfully. A little Philosophical Society here of which all the three are members, is much indebted to you for its entertainment. Your company would, although we are all good Christians, be more acceptable than that of Saint Athanasius. And since we cannot have you upon the bench, you are brought oftener than any other man to the bar, accused and defended with great zeal but without bitterness. If you write no more in morals politicks or metaphysicks, I am afraid we shall be at a loss for subjects.[2]

The truth of Reid's assertion is attested by a glance at the minutes of the club.[3]

David Hume's capacity for friendship combined with his sense of gregariousness as man of letters to make him eminently clubbable. But Hume was never quite happy in large groups in which he was apt to become tongue-tied. What Hume preferred was a society which was select in number and in membership. " I must confess," he wrote in one of his early essays, " That my own particular choice . . . leads me to prefer the company of a few

---

[1] *Notices and Documents illustrative of the Literary History of Glasgow* (Glasgow 1831), pp. 132-3.   [2] RSE, VII, 3.
[3] " Minutes of the Philosophical Society in Aberdeen, 1758-1771," in Aberdeen University Library, MS 539.

select companions, with whom I can, calmly and peaceably, enjoy the feast of reason, and try the justness of every reflection, whether gay or serious, that may occur to me. But as such a delightful society is not every day to be met with, I must think, that mixt companies, without the fair-sex, are the most insipid entertainment in the world, and destitute of gaiety and politeness, as much as of sense and reason. Nothing can keep them from excessive dulness but hard drinking ; a remedy worse than the disease." [1] In his youth Hume had been able to indulge in the feast of reason with such friends as Patrick Elibank, Gilbert Elliot, Henry Home, William Mure, James Oswald, and Michael Ramsay. In the middle and late 1740s he had added the witty group of soldiers and physicians in General St Clair's circle : James Abercromby, John Clephane, James Edmonstoune, and Harry Erskine. And, after moving to Edinburgh in the 1750s, he found solace among the Moderate group of Presbyterian clergymen: Hugh Blair, Alexander Carlyle, John Home, John Jardine and William Robertson. Had he been intimately associated with this group earlier, his famous note on the character of the clergy would surely not have appeared in the form that it did.

The friendship of Hume with liberal-minded clergy has given rise to much misapprehension, but it is readily explained by Carlyle :

He [Hume] took much to the company of the younger clergy, not from a wish to bring them over to his opinions, for he never attempted to overturn any man's principles, but they best understood his notions, and could furnish him with literary conversation. Robertson and John Home and Bannatine and I lived all in the country [Carlyle was writing of 1753], and came only periodically to the town. Blair and Jardine both lived in it, and suppers being the only fashionable meal at that time, we dined where we best could, and by cadies assembled our friends to meet us in a tavern by nine o'clock : and a fine time it was when we could collect David Hume, Adam Smith, Adam Ferguson, Lord Elibank, and Drs. Blair and Jardine, on an hour's warning. . . . This intimacy of the young clergy with David Hume enraged the zealots on the opposite side, who little knew how impossible it was for him, had he been willing, to shake their principles.[2]

Amongst the Moderates, Robert Wallace was an independent spirit surviving from an older generation and, if not always included in the fold by the politically-minded younger Moderates themselves, normally voted on their side at the General Assembly. He was always ranked as a Moderate by the High-Flying faction. Ramsay of Ochtertyre reports that Wallace " was considered as

---

[1] *Phil. Wks.*, iii, 194*n*, and see p. 187 on arts of conversation.   [2] Carlyle, pp. 288–9.

a man who wished to keep aloof from ecclesiastical politics " ; but, at the same time, " No man had a greater number of friends, and perhaps the happiest part of his life was spent in conversation." [1] The mutual esteem of Hume and Wallace, however, seemingly never deepened into intimacy.

Alexander Carlyle was described by Sir Walter Scott as " the grandest demigod I ever saw," and he was commonly known as *Jupiter* Carlyle because of his godlike features and imperious air. A great leader of men, " Jupiter " was one of the dominant figures among the Moderates, a good politician and a worldly man out of the pulpit. When asked by Lord Elibank to explain " the reason that the young clergymen of that period so far surpassed their predecessors of his early days in useful accomplishments and liberality of mind," Carlyle responded, " That the Professor of Theology at Edinburgh was dull, and Dutch, and prolix "—" that he could form no school, and the students were left entirely to themselves, and naturally formed opinions far more liberal than those they got from the Professor." [2] Such is Carlyle's classical account of the rise and success of the new Moderatism.

Hugh Blair shone in the pulpit and on the lecture platform alike. He was vain, fussy, and pompous, but " he was the least envious I ever knew," admits Carlyle. " He had truly a pure mind, in which there was not the least malignity ; for though he was of a quick and lively temper, and apt to be warm and impatient about trifles, his wife, who was a superior woman, only laughed, and his friends joined her." [3] In the pulpit he was a spellbinder. Boswell, in his own inimitable way, remarks that, " Blair would stop hounds by his eloquence." [4] Blair was not, however, able to stop David Hume, who took advantage of their intimacy on one occasion to remonstrate :

. . . permit me . . . the freedom of saying a word to yourself. Whenever I have had the pleasure to be in your company, if the discourse turned upon any common subject of literature or reasoning, I always parted from you both entertained and instructed. But when the conversation was diverted by you from this channel towards the subject of your profession ; tho I doubt not but your intentions were very friendly towards me, I own I never received the same satisfaction : I was apt to be tired, and you to be angry. I would therefore wish for the future, wherever my good fortune throws me in your way, that these topics should be forborne between us. I have, long since, done with all inquiries on such subjects, and am become incapable of instruction ; tho I own no one is more capable of conveying it than yourself.

[1] Ramsay, 1, 245. [2] Carlyle, pp. 64, 63.
[3] *Ibid.*, p. 307. [4] *Boswell Papers*, XIII, 109.

This letter was written in 1761, and the intimacy, if anything, deepened thereafter. During the period of Hume's residence in Paris, he kept in touch with " my Protestant Pastors " at Edinburgh by writing common letters addressed to Blair.

If Blair had possibly harboured the secret ambition of being the instrument of converting the " Great Infidel," it is not likely that John Home ever did. After the collapse of the Rebellion, John was ordained minister of Athelstaneford, a parish recently vacated by the death of the Reverend Robert Blair, famous as a forerunner of the " Graveyard School " of poetry. But John harboured quite different poetical ambitions, which were later to be the cause of a furore in Scottish ecclesiastical circles.[1] Carlyle, as usual, has been able to sketch a brilliant portrait :

> John Home was an admirable companion, and most acceptable to all strangers who were not offended with the levities of a young clergyman, for he was very handsome and had a fine person, about 5 feet 10½ inches, and an agreeable catching address ; he had not much wit, and still less humour, but he had so much sprightliness and vivacity, and such an expression of benevolence in his manner, and such an unceasing flattery of those he liked (and he never kept company with anybody else)—the kind commendations of a lover, not the adulation of a sycophant—that he was truly irresistible, and his entry to a company was like opening a window and letting the sun into a dark room.[2]

As cousins, the two Humes disputed the spelling of their surname. David once proposed that they should determine the controversy by casting lots. " Nay," says John, " that is a most extraordinary proposal indeed, Mr Philosopher—for if you lose, you take your own name, and if I lose, I take another man's name." A second source of friendly difference, the only other on temporal matters, lay in the means of conviviality. John, uncompromisingly Scottish, refused to give up his country's agelong alliance with France and would drink nothing but claret. Port, the cheaper wine since the Union because of England's preferential tariffs with Portugal, he eschewed. His epigram became famous :

> Firm and erect the Caledonian stood,
> Old was his mutton, and his claret good ;
> " Let him drink port," an English statesman cried—
> He drank the poison, and his spirit died.

David, being a philosopher with a sceptical bent and a man of the world with a keen palate, kept a cellar well stocked with both vintages.[3]

---

[1] See Ch. 26, below.   [2] Carlyle, p. 310.   [3] Home-Mackenzie, I, 164.

Greatly beloved by David Hume was John Jardine, six feet two of a man with large bones and a huge zest for life. " David Hume and Dr. John Jardine were . . . both admirable," observes Carlyle, " and had the peculiar talent of rallying their companions on their good qualities." Carlyle adds that Jardine " played delightfully on the unbounded curiosity and dupish simplicity of David Hume. . . ." The fact is substantiated by Henry Mackenzie : Jardine's " playful vivacity often amused itself in a sort of mock contest with the infantile (if I may use such a phrase when speaking of such a man) simplicity of David Hume, who himself enjoyed the discovery of the joke which had before excited the laugh of his companions around him." One night after a visit with Jardine, David politely declined to be lighted down the stairs and tumbled in the dark. Rushing forward with a candle, Jardine lifted the heavy bulk of his friend, slyly remarking, " Davie, I have often tellt ye that ' natural licht ' is no sufficient." Carlyle further attests that Jardine was a politician and " a great support to Robertson and our friends in the management of ecclesiastical affairs, as he was the son-in-law of Provost Drummond, and kept him steady, who had been bred in the bosom of the highflyers. . . . In politics he was artful, in other affairs quite trusty." Politician that he was, Jardine collapsed in action during the General Assembly of 1766 but at the moment of a decisive victory by his party. Carlyle pushed his way through the crowd to the prostrate man and asked in a whisper, was it not a faint ? " No, no," replied he, " it is all over." [1]

The undisputed leader of the party of young Moderates was William Robertson, who was equally distinguished as a minister, as Principal of Edinburgh University, and as a historian. After the Rebellion, during which he had shared martial adventures with Carlyle and Home, Robertson turned his talents to ecclesiastical polity. Uniting together with some of the younger lawyers who were elders in the church, Robertson and his group won their first victory in the General Assembly of 1752, their " Reasons of Dissent from the Judgment and Resolution of the Commission " being generally regarded as the " Manifesto of the Moderate Party." During the following ten years his power grew at the expense of Patrick Cumming, leader of the old Moderates, until in 1762 after his appointment as Principal to the university, he and the younger group were in complete control. His rule lasted until his resignation in 1780. Under Robertson, the Moderates

---

[1] Carlyle, pp. 278–9, 285, 490–2 ; Home-Mackenzie, I, 14.

espoused the cause of Church authority and discipline, standing solidly behind the doctrine of patronage in behalf of which David Hume had written his *Bellman's Petition* in 1751.

In personality Robertson was a little more cool and perhaps a little less likable than the others in the circle around Hume. Carlyle hints at this defect in remarking, " that though he was truly a very great master of conversation, and in general perfectly agreeable, yet he appeared sometimes so very fond of talking, even when showing-off was out of the question, and so much addicted to the translation of other people's thoughts, that he sometimes appeared tedious to his best friends. . . . Robertson's translations and paraphrases on other people's thoughts were so beautiful and so harmless that I never saw anybody lay claim to their own ; but it was not so when he forgot himself so far as to think he had been present where he had not been, and done what he had not the least hand in. . . ." [1] Elevated to a pedestal next to Hume as historian, Robertson perhaps took the honour with a little less modesty and charm. His love of letters, however, was no less deep than that of Hume, as is attested by his motto : *Vita sine litteris mors.* In a wider sense, this emphasis upon humanity and the humanities may be taken as the basic principle of Moderatism and, indeed, of the Enlightenment.

Such was the inner circle of liberal divines who became the good friends of David Hume early in the 1750s and remained his good friends throughout life. They helped to fight his battles when he was attacked by the bigots ; and he, when in government office, gave them his official patronage and, always, the weight of his prestige and influence. It was, to a considerable extent, their camaraderie that rendered Edinburgh agreeable to Hume during the latter part of his life, when alien forces were seeking to render it uncomfortable for him or even to drive him out.

Hume's cronies at Edinburgh were not, to be sure, limited to clergymen. Among the friends of his youth who still resided there were Henry Home and Lord Elibank ; and the three, according to Ramsay of Ochtertyre, formed a critical triumvirate from whose judgement in matters of taste there lay no appeal. In 1752 Home had become a Lord of Session in Scotland's supreme civil court under the title of Lord Kames, and in 1763 was to become a Lord of Justiciary in Scotland's supreme criminal court. Elibank, retired from the army, was a man of fashion and a dilettante in letters. Unlike Home, who had renounced his youthful Jacobitism,

---

[1] Carlyle, pp. 299–301.

Elibank remained zealous to the lost cause throughout life. Both were great patrons of the young in the arts ; and Kames—if it really was he who provided David Hume with a room in James's Court—was still patronising the not-so-young, for Hume was now well into his forties.

Among Hume's new friends outside the clergy, the leaders were Adam Smith and Alexander Wedderburn. Though Smith, after removing to Glasgow University in 1751, was not often in Edinburgh, the friendship with Hume ripened and was evidently based upon a complete meeting of minds as well as sympathy of temperaments. Hume's letters abound with appeals to Smith to spend vacation periods in Edinburgh, to transfer university posts —anything so as to get together with him. In later years Hume always kept a room available for Smith.

Wedderburn was of a very different stamp, brilliant and volatile, impetuous in speech and in action. Both Smith and Hume took a great fancy to the ambitious and talented young man and laid down a programme of study for him to pursue. In 1753 Hume provided Wedderburn with an enthusiastic letter of introduction to Dr Clephane at London :

> This is delivered to you by my friend Mr Wedderburn, who makes a jaunt to London, partly with a view to study, partly to entertainment. I thought I could not do him a better office, nor more suitable to both these purposes, than to recommend him to the friendship and acquaintance of a man of learning and conversation. . . . But I will say no more of him, lest my letter fall into the same fault which may be remarked in his behaviour and conduct in life ; the only fault which has been remarked in them, that of promising so much that it will be difficult for him to support it. You will allow that he must have been guilty of some error of this kind, when I tell you that the man, with whose friendship and company I have thought myself very much favoured, and whom I recommend to you as a friend and companion, is just twenty.

At London, Wedderburn entered his name in the books at the Inner Temple in order to establish himself as a student of the law. His ambition was to be called to the English bar as affording greater scope for his talents, but he was under family persuasion to try the Scottish bar first.

Admitted an advocate in Scotland in 1754, Wedderburn's promising career was precipitately ended three years later when he insulted the opposing counsel, refused to apologise to the court, stripped off his gown and laid it on the bar with the dramatic exit lines : " My Lords, I neither *retract* nor *apologise*, but I will save you the trouble of *deprivation* ; there is my gown, and I will never wear it more ;—*virtute me involvo.*"[1] Passing on to London, Wedderburn took chambers in the Temple and was speedily called to the English bar, where he had a spectacular career, ultimately becoming the first Scotsman to reach the Woolsack. He was successively created Lord Loughborough and Earl of Rosslyn. His enterprises and escapades during his stay in Edinburgh from 1754 to 1757 were deeply to involve the circle of David Hume.[2]

Allan Ramsay the Younger, painter and man of letters and the earlier friend of Hume, was now temporarily back in Scotland between expeditions to London and Rome. As in the case of Smith, the two could not have been together very much, but their later exchange of letters is proof that they were kindred spirits. In 1756 Ramsay writes delightfully from Rome : " The Pope himself is short and fat, the Pretender is long and lean ; which is all I am able to inform with regard to either. As to the Devil, I have not yet seen him, and am too diffident of reports, especially when they concern heads of parties, to send you any description of his person by hearsay." He also transcribes a pretended inscription in Greek, which, he asserts, he found in a lumber-room of the palace Farnese. " I must own it gave me great pleasure to meet with this ancient monument chiefly upon your account, who I know are very backward in believing miracles. . . . It is true the beliefs of the miracles here contained is not in itself conducive to salvation ; but if I can bring you to believe in any miracle, I flatter myself it will serve as an easy introduction to the belief of others, that are more profitable, tho not so regularly attested." [3]

In 1754 Ramsay painted a much neglected but highly revealing portrait of his friend Hume. Wearing a scholar's cap of rich but well-worn crimson velvet, and dressed in a well-tailored brown coat and a handsome flowered white waistcoat, the somewhat dandified philosopher of forty-three is eminently human. The face is not unhandsome : a high forehead, long straight nose, heavy dark brown eyebrows, grey-blue eyes, generous but sensitive and essentially diffident mouth. The musing and courageous regard of the eyes is evident, but the face is enlivened with the suspicion of a smile. Ramsay's perception that Hume's clothes expressed a desire to be looked at admiringly is an accurate reflection of Hume's own views on the " natural virtues "— definitely not to be confused with the " monkish virtues."

---

[1] Lord Campbell, *Lives of the Lord Chancellors* (London 1868), VII, Chs. 162–3.
[2] Besides the present chapter, see Chs. 25 and 26, below.
[3] RSE, VI, 103.   [4] See the frontispiece.

Later Ramsay settled in London and in 1761 [1] was appointed portrait-painter to George III, a post at which he laboured so diligently as to provoke the witticism of Laurence Sterne : " Mr. Ramsay, you paint only Court Cards, the King, Queen, and Knave." In 1766 Ramsay painted the well-known portrait of Hume in the formal dress of an Embassy Secretary.[2] At about the same time, he painted Hume's " pupil," Jean-Jacques Rousseau.

At Edinburgh in 1754 Ramsay was the leading spirit in bringing together the men of letters into a new organisation which was to prove the most fruitful of the Scottish Enlightenment. The members of the Select Society included most of the important figures from the law, the university, and the church, with a few choice selections from the social world. David Hume, Lord Kames, and Adam Smith were the chief representatives of letters and philosophy. The foundation meeting, attended by fifteen, was held on 22 May, with Ramsay presiding and Adam Smith presenting the proposals. According to good authority, this inaugural speech of Smith's was also his last. The " Rules and Orders " adopted that day were calculated to keep the Society select in membership and free in discussion.

It was provided " That every Member may propose any subject of debate, except such as regard Revealed Religion, or which may give occasion to vent any Principles of Jacobitism." Meetings were to be held at the Advocates' Library on Wednesday evenings at six o'clock between the middle of November and the middle of August. The first regular meeting was presided over by Wedderburn, with Walter Goodall acting as clerk ; at the second meeting, Adam Smith was in the chair. At the third meeting, 26 June, David Hume was elected treasurer and a member of the standing committee on orders, laws, and regulations. He was several times re-elected.[3]

On 4 December, his turn having finally been reached in rotation, Hume presided ; the topic for debate was *Whether ought we to prefer ancient or modern manners, with regard to the Condition and treatment of Women ?* And the president named as his choice of topic for the following meeting : *Whether the Difference of national Characters be chiefly owing to the Nature of different Climates, or to moral and political Causes ?* So fruitful did this subject prove that the Society took it up again the following February and again as late

[1] For this date, see Alastair Smart, *The Life and Art of Allan Ramsay* (London 1952), pp. 119–20.   [2] See *Boswelliana*, ed. Charles Rogers (London 1874), p. 255.
[3] NLS, MS entitled " Rules and Orders of the Select Society " and " Minutes of the Procedure of the Select Society ", Adv. 23.1.1.

as 1757. Like most of the topics debated by the Select Society, this one had already been treated by Hume in an essay. The irrepressible Wedderburn, however, proposed a non-Humean topic : *Whether the law of Queen Joan of Naples, allowing licensed stews would be advantageous to a nation?* But the Committee for Questions would have none of it, although it clearly dealt neither with Revealed Religion nor with Jacobitism. When Wedderburn took the issue directly to the Society, he was politely put off by having his appeal ordered to lie on the table. The minutes of the meetings provide no account of the debates, the names of the debaters, or the final vote taken ; but tradition has it that David Hume, like Adam Smith, made no public speech. It is to be remarked that from the very moment of foundation the Society was too large to suit Hume's view of " the company of a few select companions, with whom I can, calmly and peaceably, enjoy the feast of reason. . . ."

The founders had passed a rule, " That the Society shall consist of fifty Persons," but with the proviso that, " the Number . . . be afterwards augmented, as the Society shall see cause." A year after the founding, David Hume explained to Allan Ramsay, then at Rome, how this proviso was working :

It [the Society] has grown to be a national concern. Young and old, noble and ignoble, witty and dull, laity and clergy, all the world are ambitious of a place amongst us, and on each occasion we are as much solicited by candidates as if we were to choose a Member of Parliament. . . . Our friend young Wedderburn has acquired a great character by the appearance he has made. Wilkie the minister has turned up from obscurity, and become a very fashionable man, as he is indeed a very singular one. Monboddo's oddities divert ; Sir David's [Sir David Dalrymple of Newhailes] zeal entertains ; Jack Dalrymple's rhetoric interests. The long drawling speakers have found out their want of talents, and rise seldomer. In short, the House of Commons was less the object of general curiosity at London than the Select Society at Edinburgh. The Robinhood, the Devil, and all other speaking societies, are ignoble in comparison. Such felicity has attended the seed which you planted.

Alexander Carlyle offers further information about the " long drawling speakers " and how their efforts unexpectedly led to felicitous results :

Mr. Robert Alexander, wine merchant, a very worthy man, but a bad speaker, entertained us all with warm suppers and excellent claret, as a recompense for the patient hearing of his ineffectual attempts, when I thought he would have beat out his brains on account of their constipation. The conversation at those convivial meetings frequently improved the members more by free conversation than the speeches in the Society. It was those meetings in particular that rubbed off all corners, as we call it, by collision, and made the *literati* of Edinburgh less captious and pedantic than they were elsewhere.[1]

Carlyle's parting shot was, of course, directed against the rival literati of London.

Hume's letter to Ramsay also announces " a project of engrafting on the Society a scheme for the encouragement of arts and sciences and manufactures in Scotland, by premiums partly honorary, partly lucrative. A box is opened for donations, and about one hundred guineas have been given in. We hear of considerable sums intended by Lord Hopetoun, Morton, Marchmont, &c., who desire to be members." Hume further explains that this new organisation, the Edinburgh Society for Encouraging Arts, Sciences, Manufactures, and Agriculture in Scotland, was to be kept apart from the parent Select Society. " A premium, I remember," his account concludes, " is promised to the best discourse on Taste, and on the Principles of Vegetation. These regard the belles lettres and the sciences ; but we have not neglected porter, strong ale, and wrought ruffles, even down to linen rags. . . ." Hume and Adam Smith were appointed to Committee III, " For Belles Lettres & Criticism," along with the ministers, Hugh Blair, William Wilkie, and George Wishart. The first prize of a gold medal was won by Alexander Gerard, Professor of Moral Philosophy and one of Hume's " friendly adversaries " at Aberdeen, for his *Essay on Taste*.

Replying to Hume from Rome, Ramsay was not entirely happy about the new turn of events.

> Can a Man, O Philosopher [he inquired], be both sorry and glad at the same time ? If the thing is possible, I am in these circumstances. For I am glad to hear that there is any society of men amongst you who give a particular attention to the improvement of the art of our dear country ; but I am afraid at the same time that this scheme, by bringing in a new set of members of another Species, will destroy that which we had set on foot ; and I could have wished that some other ways had been fallen upon, by which porter might have been made thick, brick thin, and the nation rich, without our understanding being at all the poorer for it. Is not Truth more than meat, and Wisdom than raiment ?[2]

Intellectual snobbery apart, Ramsay had put his finger upon one of the causes of disintegration of the Select Society, namely, its inevitable tendency to become less and less select. By 1759 the membership numbered 135. The immediate cause of its demise, apparently in 1763, was the issue of teaching Scotsmen to speak

---

[1] Carlyle, p. 312.   [2] RSE, vi 103.

English as well as to write English.[1]   After 1763 the remnants of
the Select Society met in the rooms of a Masonic Club in St Giles
and hence are sometimes referred to as the St Giles's Society.

For nearly ten years, however, the Select Society of Edinburgh
exerted a great influence on the national life of Scotland, culturally,
intellectually, socially.   In October 1762, shortly before its demise,
a letter was printed in the *Scots Magazine* on the " Advantages of
societies formed for improvement in literature."   This letter,
although not so intended, may be taken as the funeral bell of the
Select Society.   It reads in part :

> In a word, an institution of this kind, when properly conducted, enlarges
> our views, improves our reasoning, and forces the mind from every narrow
> notion.   An ingenious author observes, that nothing is prefereable to a select
> company, where one has an opportunity of trying the justness of every reflection
> that may occur.   I doubt, whether the admirable productions of that gentleman,
> or those of his friends, would have reflected so great honour of late upon
> Scotland as they have done, had they not mutually enjoyed the happiness of
> a Select Society.

The unintentional irony of this passage lies in the capitalisation
of the last two words !

One of the direct results of the Select Society has been noted
by Carlyle :

> From the Revolution, (when the Church had been chiefly filled with
> incumbents that were ill-educated,) down to this period, the Clergy of the
> Established Church had always been considered in a subordinate light, and
> as far inferior to the Members of the other Learned Professions, in knowledge
> and in liberal views.   But now, when compared together, on this theatre for
> the exhibition of talents, they were found to be entitled to at least an equal
> share of praise ; and having been long depressed, they were, in compensation,
> as usual, raised full as high as they deserved.[2]

Put in a broader view, the cultural success of the Select Society
in no small measure marks the success of the philosophy of Moderatism in the Church, which itself was part-and-parcel of the
philosophy of the Scottish Enlightenment.

Political activities of the group of Moderates in alliance with
Hume and similar-minded laymen can be observed in the Poker
Club, instituted at the beginning of 1762 for the purpose of
fostering the Scottish militia, which had been suppressed by
Parliament after the Rebellion of 1745.   At first limited to fifteen
choice spirits, chiefly from the Select Society, the club expanded
to include many more.   The meetings were informal and the dis-
cussions forthright.   Adam Ferguson proposed the name " Poker "

---

[1] See Ch. 27, below.   [2] Quoted in Stewart, *Smith, Robertson, and Reid*, p. 314.

as suggestive of the aim of the group to stir up the militia question, and the name was approved because it was deemed to be sufficiently obscure to the general public. Meeting at Thomas Nicholson's tavern, the members paid a modest shilling a head for dinner and confined their drinking to sherry and claret. Carlyle describes how, " In a laughing humour, Andrew Crosbie was chosen Assassin, in case any officer of that sort should be needed ; but David Hume was added as his Assessor, without whose assent nothing should be done, so that between *plus* and *minus* there was likely to be no bloodshed." [1]

The militia issue was dealt with by Ferguson in an anonymous pamphlet of 1761 entitled *The Proceedings in the Case of Margaret, called Peg, only Sister of John Bull.* David Hume, however, because of his good nature and artlessness, was not let into the secret of the authorship. Determined to find out, he accused Jardine and Carlyle in turn. Upon their repeated denials he then brazenly took the authorship to himself and so forced the hand of the conspirators.

Hume's eulogy of the Poker Club comes in a letter of 1763 to Ferguson from France : " I really wish often for the plain roughness of the *Poker,* and particularly the sharpness of Dr Jardine, to correct and qualify so much lusciousness " in Paris. And again, after telling of meeting the Dauphin, Hume remarks, " That Prince seems a reasonable Man, but woud be the better of being *roasted* sometimes in the *Poker.*" That Hume himself was *roasted* sometimes in the Poker is made certain by Carlyle : " . . . when everybody wondered what could have made a clerk of Sir William Forbes run away with £900—I know that very well, says John Home to David ; for when he was taken, there was found in his pocket your *Philosophical Works* and Boston's *Fourfold State of Man.*" The deliberate linking of the sceptic with the evangelist was indeed a *roasting* ! [2]

---

[1] Carlyle, p. 441.   [2] *Ibid.*, p. 291.

CHAPTER 22

THE OPPOSITION GATHERS

" I meet with many Answerers in this Countrey."

REFUTATIONS of Hume's publications began to pile up during the 1750s. In 1757 he informed the Abbé Le Blanc : " I meet with many Answerers in this Countrey ; some of whom treat me with Civility, others in the usual Style of Controversy." And in 1766 he told Turgot : " I cou'd cover the Floor of a large Room with Books and Pamphlets wrote against me, to none of which I ever made the least Reply, not from Disdain (for the Authors of some of them, I respect) but from my Desire of Ease and Tranquility." Of this period he further remarked in *My Own Life* :

> Mean-while, my Bookseller, A. Millar, informed me, that my former publications (all but the unfortunate Treatise) were beginning to be the Subject of Conversation, that the Sale of them was gradually encreasing, and that new Editions were demanded. Answers, by Reverends and Right Reverends, came out two or three in a Year : And I found by Dr Warburtons Railing that the Books were beginning to be esteemed in good Company.

The remark is well within the bounds of truth since answers to the two *Enquiries* (including " Of Miracles ") alone totalled two in 1751 ; four in 1752 ; five in 1753 ; three in 1754 ; and two in 1755.

" Of Miracles," perhaps naturally enough considering the temper of the age, was chiefly responsible for the sudden interest taken in Hume. It had appeared in 1748 as Section X of *Philosophical Essays concerning Human Understanding*, where it was followed by Section XI, " Of the Practical Consequences of Natural Religion " (later called " Of a Particular Providence and of a Future State "). The two sections are related in argument and designed to be considered together, although that has seldom been done by controversialists. They constitute an important practical application of the central features of Hume's philosophical thinking (particularly his analysis of cause and effect) ; they undermine the evidential value of miracles as the foundation of religious systems and establish limits to the argument from design.

The purpose of the essay " Of Miracles," despite a few linguistic lapses on the part of the author, is to determine, not the philosophical issue of the possibility of miracles, but the evidential issue " that no human testimony can have such a force as to prove a miracle, and make it a just foundation for any . . . system of religion." [1] In so delimiting the issue to history and to religion, Hume was following in a well-established pattern. Samuel Clarke in his popular Boyle Lecture, for instance, had explained that a miracle

is a work effected in a manner unusual or different from the common and regular method of Providence by the interposition either of God Himself, or some intelligent agent superior to man, in the proof or evidence of some particular doctrine or in attestation to the authority of some particular person. And if a miracle so worked be not opposed by some plainly superior power nor be brought to attest to a doctrine either contradictory in itself or vicious in its consequences—a doctrine of which kind no miracles in the world can be sufficient to prove—then the doctrine so attested must necessarily be looked upon as Divine, and the worker of the miracle entertained as having infallibly a commission from God. [2]

Citing an argument against the *real presence* found in the writings of Dr Tillotson, Hume opens " Of Miracles " : " I flatter myself, that I have discovered an argument of a like nature, which, if just, will, with the wise and learned, be an everlasting check to all kinds of superstitious delusion, and consequently, will be useful as long as the world endures." This argument he summarises as follows :

A miracle is a violation of the laws of nature ; and as a firm and unalterable experience has established these laws, the proof against a miracle, from the very nature of the fact, is as entire as any argument from experience can possibly be imagined. Why is it more than probable, that all men must die ; that lead cannot, of itself, remain suspended in the air ; that fire consumes wood, and is extinguished by water ; unless it be, that these events are found agreeable to the laws of nature, and there is required a violation of these laws, or in other words, a miracle to prevent them ? Nothing is esteemed a miracle, if it ever happen in the common course of nature. It is no miracle that a man, seemingly in good health, should die on a sudden : because such a kind of death, though more unusual than any other, has yet been frequently observed to happen. But it is a miracle, that a dead man should come to life ; because that has never been observed, in any age or country. There must, therefore, be a uniform experience against every miraculous event, otherwise the event would not merit that appellation. And as an uniform experience amounts to a proof, there is here a direct and full *proof*, from the nature of the fact, against the existence of any miracle ; nor can such a proof be destroyed, or the miracle rendered credible, but by an opposite proof, which is superior. [3]

The plain consequence is (and it is a general maxim worthy of our attention), " That no testimony is sufficient to establish a miracle, unless the testimony be

[1] *Phil. Wks.*, IV, 105.

[2] *A Defence of Natural and Revealed Religion*, edd. Letsome and Nicholl (London 1739), II, 165.

[3] In a footnote Hume adds : " A miracle may be accurately defined, *a transgression of a law of nature by a particular volition of the Deity, or by the interposition of some invisible agent.*"

of such a kind, that its falsehood would be more miraculous, than the fact, which it endeavours to establish : And even in that case there is a mutual destruction of arguments, and the superior only gives us an assurance suitable to that degree of force, which remains, after deducting the inferior." When any one tells me, that he saw a dead man restored to life, I immediately consider with myself, whether it be more probable, that this person should either deceive or be deceived, or that the fact, which he relates, should really have happened. I weigh the one miracle against the other ; and according to the superiority, which I discover, I pronounce my decision, and always reject the greater miracle. If the falsehood of his testimony would be more miraculous, than the event which he relates ; then, and not till then, can he pretend to command my belief or opinion.[1]

The second part of this essay enumerates several difficulties in the proof of miracles : the appraisal of testimony ; the credulity of man, especially when ignorant ; the opposing claims for miracles in the different religions. The Jansenist miracles " wrought in France upon the tomb of the Abbé Paris," which Hume had personally investigated in 1734, are named as among the best attested in modern times, and yet are totally rejected by both Jesuits and Protestants alike.[2] After a brief sketch of the miraculous history presented in the Pentateuch, Hume inquires :

I desire any one to lay his hand upon his heart, and after a serious consideration declare, whether he thinks that the falsehood of such a book, supported by such a testimony, would be more extraordinary and miraculous than all the miracles it relates ; which is, however, necessary to make it be received, according to the measures of probability above established.

And the essay concludes on an ironical note :

So that, upon the whole, we may conclude, that the *Christian Religion* not only was at first attended with miracles, but even at this day cannot be believed by any reasonable person without one. Mere reason is insufficient to convince us of its veracity : And whoever is moved by *Faith* to assent to it, is conscious of a continued miracle in his own person, which subverts all the principles of his understanding, and gives him a determination to believe what is most contrary to custom and experience.[3]

" Of a Particular Providence and of a Future State " takes the prudential form of a dialogue between the author and " a friend who loves sceptical paradoxes." This " sceptic " (who is surely Hume himself) argues that limitations be placed upon the argument from design and upon customary inferences as to the moral attributes of the Deity. " When we infer any particular cause from an effect, we must proportion the one to the other, and can

---

[1] *Phil. Wks.*, IV, 93–4.
[2] Hume's friend, the Reverend Robert Wallace, for instance, had composed MS " Observations on the Account of the Miracles of the Abbe Paris " (in EU, Laing MSS, II, 620/21).   [3] *Phil. Wks.*, IV, 108.

never be allowed to ascribe to the cause any qualities, but what are exactly sufficient to produce the effect. . . . Allowing, therefore, the gods to be the authors of the existence or order of the universe ; it follows, that they possess that precise degree of power, intelligence, and benevolence, which appears in their workmanship. . . ."

The argument is pressed home against suppositions concerning the moral qualities of the Deity :

Are there any marks of a distributive justice in the world ? If you answer in the affirmative, I conclude, that, since justice here exerts itself, it is satisfied. If you reply in the negative, I conclude, that you have then no reason to ascribe justice, in our sense of it, to the gods. If you hold a medium between affirmation and negation, by saying, that the justice of the gods, at present, exerts itself in part, but not in its full extent ; I answer, that you have no reason to give it any particular extent, but only as far as you see it, *at present*, exert itself.

Furthermore, the inference from a unique effect (the world) to a unique cause (the Deity) is branded as unphilosophical. In practice, consequently, historical religion loses utility for those who are capable of thinking for themselves :

All the philosophy, therefore, in the world, and all the religion, which is nothing but a species of philosophy, will never be able to carry us beyond the usual course of experience, or give us measures of conduct and behaviour different from those which are furnished by reflections on common life. No new fact can ever be inferred from the religious hypothesis ; no event foreseen or foretold ; no reward or punishment expected or dreaded, beyond what is already known by practice and observation.[1]

Christian apologists and theologians took the alarm immediately at this bold frontal attack upon the religious bastion but, with the exception of Skelton, who has already been noticed, did not rush into print. Typical of one segment of the clergy—though by no means of the majority—was William Warburton, who could conceive of no terms but abuse. When *A Familiar Epistle to the Most Impudent Man Living* (an anonymous pamphlet by Lord Bolingbroke) was published in 1749, few in the world of letters had any doubt concerning the addressee. That same year, Warburton, in the last stages of completion of his *Julian*, inquired of his friend Hurd :

I am strongly tempted too to have a stroke at Hume in parting. He is the author of a little book called " Philosophical Essays," in one part of which he argues against the being of a God, and in another, (very needlessly you will say,) against the possibility of miracles. He has crowned the liberty of the press. And yet he has a considerable post under the Government. I

---

[1] *Phil. Wks.*, IV, 116–17, 120–1.

have a great mind to do justice on his arguments against miracles, which I think might be done in few words. But does he deserve notice? Is he known amongst you? Pray answer me these questions. For if his own weight keeps him down, I should be sorry to contribute to his advancement to any place but the pillory.[1]

The following year Warburton informed another friend, Doddridge, that, " some people of consideration " had urged him " to take to task at the end of the second volume of Julian a chapter of one Hume on Miracles in a rank atheistical book called *Philosophical Essays*." [2] But for some reason Warburton, who was seldom shy of controversy on any subject, held back on Hume and never published the attack on " Of Miracles " that he had actually composed.

He did, however, in 1751, get in a thrust that must have irritated Hume greatly. In annotating Pope's *Dunciad*, III, 224 :

> But, " Learn, ye DUNCES ! not to scorn your God,"

Warburton commented : " The hardest lesson a *Dunce* can learn. For being bred to *scorn* what he does not understand, that which he understands least he will be apt to *scorn* most. Of which, to the disgrace of all Government, and (in the Poet's opinion) even of that of DULLNESS herself, we have had a late example in a book entitled, *Philosophical Essays concerning Human Understanding*." (Warburton does not make it clear how Pope, who had died in 1744, disapproved of Hume's book of 1748.) Warburton continued to rail in personal letters and brought his influence to bear against Hume's later works, both before and after publiction.[3] Curiously he does not seem to have connected the Hume of the *Enquiries* and later works with the anonymous author of the *Treatise*, a work which, as we have seen, he may actually have reviewed.

Among the first to answer Hume were representatives of the two English universities, the Reverends Thomas Rutherforth, of Cambridge, and William Adams, of Oxford. Both Rutherforth's *Credibility of Miracles defended against the Author of Philosophical Essays* and Adams's *Essay on Mr. Hume's Essay on Miracles* appeared in 1751.[4] Both writers, in general, treat Hume as a serious philosopher and a formidable antagonist. Their arguments, however, are vitiated by the fact that they ignore his doctrine of causality,

---

[1] Warburton, *Letters from a late eminent Prelate to one of his Friends* (New York 1809), p. 10.
[2] *Letters to and from Philip Doddridge*, ed. T. Stedman (Shrewsbury 1790), p. 207.
[3] See, especially, Ch. 24, below.
[4] Adams's *Essay* came out in Dec. 1751, although it is dated 1752 on the title-page.

as well as Section XI of the *Philosophical Essays*, and ascribe to the Deity powers that Hume would not allow as fair inferences from the facts of nature. In so doing, they are typical of many other replies to Hume that need not concern us here.

Rutherforth makes much of the newness of Hume's argument : " But the state of this question [of miracles] hath been lately much altered. Instead of being called upon to clear up the testimony, which supports the miracles of Christ and his apostles ; we are now challenged to shew, that any testimony whatsoever can be sufficient to prove the truth of these, or of any other miracles." [1] Adams injects the personal issue into his opening and closing. He opens with the admission that " Mr. Hume hath many of the talents of a fine writer, and hath justly obtained that character by the agreeable *Essays Moral and Political*, with which he has obliged the world. What he hath wrote well will create a prejudice in favour of his errors ; and these will have all their bad influence ; when recommended by so able an advocate." But he closes with the question :   " And I here ask my reader, whether he has anywhere met with either a more sceptical, disputatious turn of mind, or a more imperious, dogmatical style, than in the writings of this author ? " [2]   This personal note of Adams's was not, however, strong enough to suit some of the more ardent critics, nor was it to prevent Hume from forming a friendly acquaintance with him some years later.

In the Reverend John Leland's *View of the Principal Deistical Writers* of 1754 no mention was made of Hume. The omission was made good, however, in a second volume of the following year, the Irish Noncomformist minister explaining that, " I was put in mind of a considerable omission I had been guilty of in not taking notice of Mr. *Hume*, who was looked upon as one of the most subtil writers that had of late appeared against Christianity." Leland dealt with Hume in some 135 pages and returned to the attack in a third volume of 1756. He was chiefly interested in " Of Miracles " and expressed agreement with an unnamed correspondent that Hume " with all his art . . . has plainly discovered a bad heart. . . ."   Writing to Colonel Edmonstoune at Dublin in 1757, Hume commented tersely, " My Compliments to Dr Leland, & tell him, that he has certainly mistaken my Character." [3]

Two other critics of Hume on miracles require mention :

---

[1] Rutherforth, *Credibility of Miracles*, p. 2.   [2] Adams, *Essay*, pp. 1, 127–9.
[3] Leland, *Deistical Writers* (2nd edn.), II, Preface, 80 ; NHL, p. 43.

John Douglas, later Bishop of Salisbury, and George Campbell, Principal of Marischal College, Aberdeen. In *The Criterion : or, Miracles Examined* (1752) Douglas describes Hume as a "very ingenious, but very whimsical Author." (Douglas himself rejects all Roman Catholic miracles while, at the same time, refusing to question Biblical miracles.) Campbell's *Dissertation on Miracles : Containing an Examination of the Principles advanced by David Hume, Esq ; in an Essay on Miracles* (1762) is the most elaborate of the eighteenth century and is further remarkable in that it drew comment from Hume himself.

A member of the group at Aberdeen that devoted so much energy to the study of Hume, Campbell made sincere efforts to treat his antagonist strictly as a philosopher, but did not wholly succeed. One of his efforts at fairness, however, did secure, through the Reverend Hugh Blair as intermediary, Hume's criticisms of his as yet unpublished work. Hume's letter to Blair deals with both the tone and the matter of Campbell. Those parts dealing with the tone are also self-revelatory :

Sir,

I have perused the ingenious performance, which you was so obliging as to put into my hands, with all the attention possible ; tho not perhaps with all the seriousness and gravity which you have so frequently recommended to me. But the fault lies not in the piece, which is certainly very acute ; but in the subject. I know you will say, it lies in neither, but in myself alone. If that be so, I am sorry to say that I believe it is incurable.

I could wish that your friend had not chosen to appear as a controversial writer, but had endeavoured to establish his principles in general, without any reference to a particular book or person ; tho I own he does me a great deal of honour, in thinking that any thing I have wrote deserves his attention. For besides many inconveniences, which attend that kind of writing, I see it is almost impossible to preserve decency and good manners in it. This author, for instance, says sometimes obliging things of me much beyond what I can presume to deserve ; and I thence conclude that in general he did not mean to insult me : yet I meet with some other passages more worthy of Warburton and his followers than of so ingenious an author. . . .

I could wish your friend had not denominated me an infidel writer, on account of ten or twelve pages which seem to him to have that tendency : while I have wrote so many volumes on history, literature, politics, trade, morals, which, in that particular at least, are entirely inoffensive. Is a man to be called a drunkard, because he has been seen fuddled once in his lifetime ?

. . . Your friend . . . is certainly a very ingenious man, tho a little too zealous for a philosopher. . . .

Other parts of the letter to Blair criticise passages in Campbell and develop a few of Hume's own ideas :

Sect. I. I would desire the author to consider, whether the medium by which we reason concerning human testimony be different from that which

leads us to draw any inferences concerning other human actions ; that is, our knowledge of human nature from experience ? Or why is it different ? . . .
Sect. II. No man can have any other experience but his own. The experience of others becomes his only by the credit which he gives to their testimony ; which proceeds from his own experience of human nature.
Sect. III. . . . I find no difficulty to explain my meaning, and yet shall not probably do it in any future edition. The proof against a miracle, as it is founded on invariable experience, is of that *species* or *kind* of proof, which is full and certain when taken alone, because it implies no doubt, as is the case with all probabilities ; but there are degrees of this species, and when a weaker proof is opposed to a stronger, it is overcome. . . .
Sect. IV. Does a man of sense run after every silly tale of witches or hobgoblins or fairies, and canvass particularly the evidence ? I never knew any one, that examined and deliberated about nonsense who did not believe it before the end of his inquiries.

After the appearance of Campbell's *Dissertation,* Hume wrote to him on 7 June 1762 in a friendly spirit :

It has so seldom happened that controversies in philosophy, much more in theology, have been carried on without producing a personal quarrel between the parties, that I must regard my present situation as somewhat extraordinary, who have reason to give you thanks for the civil and obliging manner in which you have conducted the dispute against me, on so interesting a subject as that of miracles. Any little symptoms of vehemence, of which I formerly used the freedom to complain, when you favoured me with a sight of the manuscript, are either removed or explained away, or atoned for by civilities, which are far beyond what I have any title to pretend to. It will be natural for you to imagine, that I will fall upon some shift to evade the force of your arguments, and to retain my former opinion in the point controverted between us ; but it is impossible for me not to see the ingenuity of your performance, and the great learning which you have displayed against me.

Hume then proceeds to explain his resolution " always to leave the public to judge between my adversaries and me, without making any reply." And after relating how the essay " Of Miracles " had been born at the Jesuit College of La Flèche, he concludes slyly, " I believe you will allow, that the freedom at least of this reasoning makes it somewhat extraordinary to have been the produce of a convent of Jesuits, tho perhaps you may think the sophistry of it savours plainly of the place of its birth."

Principal Campbell responded entirely in the Moderate spirit of Robert Wallace, and the first paragraph of his letter warrants quotation :

Sir,
    The very obliging letter you favour'd me with of the 7th instant I received, but not till several days after it came to Aberdeen, as I happened to be in the country at the time. The testimony you are pleas'd to give in favour of my performance, is an honour of which I should be entirely unworthy, were I not

sensible of the uncommon generosity you have shown in giving it. Ever since I was acquainted with your works, your talents as a writer, have, notwithstanding some difference in abstract principles, extorted from me the highest venerations but I could scarce have thought, that, in spite of differences of a more interesting nature, even such as regard morals and religion, you could ever force me to love and honour you as a man. Yet no religious prejudices (as you would probably term them) can hinder me from doing justice to that goodness and candour, which appear in every line of your letter.[1]

The miracles controversy did not end with the amicable exchange with Campbell. In some measure, it is still not over, Hume almost annually having his attackers and defenders in the pages of the philosophical and theological journals. Yet the drift of his influence is clear enough and may—perhaps not unfairly—be put in the words of the amateur theologian Soame Jenyns, who, as early as 1776, noted that miracles and prophecies " must now depend for much of their credibility on the truth of that religion, whose credibility they were at first intended to support." [2] No small share of the alteration in the fundamental assumptions of the theology of the nineteenth and twentieth centuries may rightfully be ascribed to Hume's luminous scepticism and fearless criticism.

Although " Of Miracles " excited keen interest in the 1750s and 1760s, the other philosophical works of Hume were also attracting attention—even the long neglected *Treatise of Human Nature.* Oddly enough, the first book-length refutation of Hume's *Treatise* came from the pen of his friend, adviser, and patron of long standing, Henry Home. It was published anonymously at Edinburgh in March 1751 as *Essays on the Principles of Morality and Natural Religion.* Twelve years previously, it will be recalled, David had tried in vain to beat his book into Henry's head, and Henry had finally come to understand it—or so he said—through his own efforts. His first reaction had been to write down some objections, objections that probably led eventually to the publication of the *Essays.*

Henry Home was always an individualist in his thinking : in religion, more a Deist than a Christian ; in politics, a Jacobite latterly turned Whig ; in philosophy, an Aristotelian rather than a Newtonian, and one, moreover, who had been " crucified," as he told Boswell, by Locke's chapter on " Power." In regard to Home's philosophy, it will only be necessary to observe here

---

[1] RSE, iv, 11.

[2] Jenyns, *View of the Internal Evidence of the Christian Religion* in *Works* (London 1790), iv, 5.

that the *Essays* provide such a curiously inconsistent amalgam of old and new ideas, metaphysical, physical, and theological, as could never have found favour with most contemporary thinkers in any one of those fields. The spirit of the work, however, if not the reasoning, appealed to David Hume. " The author's manner of thinking," the Advertisement explains, " may, in some points, be esteemed bold and new. But freedom of thought, will not displease those who are led, in their inquiry, by the love of truth. To such only he writes : and with such, he will, at least, have the merit of a good aim ; of having searched for truth, and endeavoured to promote the cause of virtue and natural religion." David Hume also relished, doubtless, the respectful tone in which he was referred to by his old friend : " The figure which this author deservedly makes in the learned world, is too considerable, to admit of his being past over in silence." [1]

In 1751 Hume inquired of Michael Ramsay in London, " Have you seen our Friend Harrys Essays ? " and proceeded to observe with perhaps more politeness than truth that, " They are well wrote ; and are an unusual instance of an obliging method of answering a Book." That Hume considered the *Essays* no real answer to his own philosophy is certain ; his attitude is revealed in the defence of Home's character, but not of his philosophy, in the 1754 controversy with Professor Stewart. Hume was also no little amused by the sequel, in which the author of the *Essays* was attacked by the Scottish Highflyers for being as poor a Christian as himself.[2]

The appearance at Edinburgh in 1753 of the anonymous *Delineation of the Nature and Obligation of Morality. With Reflexions upon Mr. Hume's Book, intitled, An Inquiry concerning the Principles of Morals* led to another exchange of letters between Hume and one of his antagonists. The following letter, of which the opening is quoted, is said to have been left by Hume at the shop of the publishers, Hamilton, Balfour, and Neill, with instructions to forward to the unknown author :

To *the* Author of ' *The Delineation of the Nature and Obligation of Morality* '

Sir,
        When I write you, I know not to whom I am addressing myself ; I only know he is one who has done me a great deal of honour, and to whose civilities I am obliged. If we be strangers, I beg we may be acquainted as soon as you think proper to discover yourself ; if we be acquainted already, I beg we may

[1] [Home], *Essays*, p. 103.   [2] See Ch. 25, below.

be friends ; if friends, I beg we may be more so. Our connection with each other, as men of letters, is greater than our difference as adhering to different sects or systems. Let us revive the happy times, when Atticus and Cassius the Epicureans, Cicero the Academic, and Brutus the Stoic, could, all of them, live in unreserved friendship together, and were insensible to all those distinctions, except so far as they furnished agreeable matter to discourse and conversation. Perhaps you are a young man, and being full of those sublime ideas, which you have so well expresst, think there can be no virtue upon a more confined system. I am not an old one ; but being of a cool temperament, have always found, that more simple views were sufficient to make me act in a reasonable manner ; νηθε, χαι μέμνηδο απιστειν ; in this faith have I lived, and hope to die.[1]

James Balfour of Pilrig, advocate, and the following year Professor of Moral Philosophy at Edinburgh University, replied in kind, though still preserving his anonymity.[2] But Balfour never entertained Hume's proffer of friendship, and in 1768 continued the attack upon him in anonymous *Philosophical Essays*. Inquiring about this work from Gilbert Elliot, Hume commented :

It has no manner of Sense in it ; but is wrote with tolerable Neatness of Style : Whence I conjecture it to be our Friend, Sir David's [Dalrymple]. I am obligd to him for the Treatment which he destines me, to be lock'd up for five Years in a Dungeon, then to be hangd, and my Carcass to be thrown out of Scotland. He supports himself, indeed, by the Authority of Plato, whom I own to be truly divine. Pray, have you seen the Book ? Is it Sir David's ? I think it has not so many Attempts at Humour, as that pious Gentleman would employ.[3]

After hearing from Elliot, Hume replied : " I did not think of Balfour : It is very true : He woud fain, I see, be candid, and civil, as in his other Book ; if his Zeal for the House of the Lord woud permit him."

Other refutations of Hume's ethics and metaphysics included, in 1753, the anonymous *Some Late Opinions concerning the Foundation of Morality, Examined,* and Bishop Robert Clayton's *Some Thoughts on Self Love, Innate-Ideas, Free-Will, Taste, Sentiment, Liberty ; and Necessity, etc. occasioned by reading Mr. Hume's Works* ; and, in 1754, *Admonitions from the Dead, in Epistles to the Living* and *An Inquiry into the Grounds and Nature of the several Species of Ratiocination.* In

---

[1] Epicharmus, 119 (Ahrens). Hume's letter was set up in print separately as *Letter from David Hume, Esq., to the Author of the Delineation of the Nature and Obligation of Morality,* but with no indication of date and place of publication. That the publication was late is proved by the watermarked date of 1794 on the paper. See p. 25 in Catalogue 34 (March 1950) of Peter Murray Hill Ltd. The MS is now in the NLS. HL, I, 172–4 copies the printed form.
[2] B. Balfour-Melville, *The Balfours of Pilrig* (Edinburgh 1907), pp. 113–16.
[3] For the reference in Balfour, see *op. cit.,* pp. 49–51.

which, the Argument made use of in the Philosophical Essays of D. Hume, Esq ; is occasionally taken notice of. The first two epistles of the *Admonitions from the Dead* purport to be from Lord Bolingbroke to David Hume. The once " pompous, proud, ambitious " Bolingbroke, who had died in 1751, is thoroughly chastened and informs the " great Metaphysician " that, " What you have said is frivolous ; all that I wrote, extended as it was, and amplified by every Circumstance which could be urged in Favour ; and cloathed in all the empty Pomp of Words, was Sound instead of Meaning, and in the Place of Argument was Ostentation." However he might have demurred at the first part of this verdict, Hume heartily concurred with the second, writing :

> Lord Bolingbroke's posthumous Productions have at last convinc'd the whole World, that he ow'd his Character chiefly to his being a man of Quality, & to the Prevalence of Faction. Never were seen so many Volumes, containing so little Variety & Instruction : so much Arrogance & Declamation. The Clergy are all enrag'd against him ; but they have no Reason. Were they never attack'd by more forcible Weapons than his, they might for ever keep Possession of their Authority.

The author of the *Inquiry into the Grounds and Nature of the Several Species of Ratiocination* is remarkable for his attempt to understand Hume's analysis of cause and effect and Hume's discrimination into the degrees and kinds of evidence—even as applied to miracles. " This gentleman indeed," he charitably concedes, " for ought I know, may be as great an unbeliever as his adversaries have endeavoured to represent him : But it is to God and himself only, for any thing that can be inferred from the arguments he has hitherto made public. His own reasonings must have operated upon his mind in a very extraordinary manner indeed, if, in *mere* consequence of *them*, he is either an *infidel* or an *enthusiast*." [1]

It was not until 1764 that a far greater *Inquiry* than that just cited marked the first full-scale investigation into the Humean philosophy by a thinker of distinction. Thomas Reid's *Inquiry into the Human Mind, on the Principles of Common Sense*, appeared exactly twenty-five years after the *Treatise of Human Nature.* Apart from its value as philosophy in its own right laying the foundation for the Scottish school of Common Sense, the work is important in that it inaugurated that radical misunderstanding of Hume which was to dominate modern thinking for well over a century. The Reverend Thomas Reid had been Professor of Philosophy at King's College, Aberdeen, since 1751 and in 1764

[1] *Inquiry*, p. 27 ; the author gives his name on the title-page as A.G.O.T.V.O.C.

became Professor of Moral Philosophy at Glasgow University in succession to Adam Smith.

Like Campbell before him, Reid solicited Hugh Blair to induce Hume to look over his manuscript. A little nettled by all this sudden attention, Hume told Blair sharply, " I wish that the Parsons would confine themselves to their old occupation of worrying one another, and leave Philosophers to argue with temper, moderation, and good manners " ; but he relented upon being assured that Reid was a philosopher as well as a parson.[1] In due course, some sections of Reid's manuscript were passed on to him ; and he wrote directly to Reid :

> By Dr Blair's means I have been favoured with the perusal of your performance, which I have read with great pleasure and attention. It is certainly very rare, that a piece so deeply philosophical is wrote with so much spirit, and affords so much entertainment to the reader ; tho I must still regret the disadvantages under which I read it, as I never had the whole performance at once before me, and could not be able fully to compare one part with another. To this reason, chiefly, I ascribed some obscurities, which, in spite of your short analysis or abstract, still seem to hang over your system. For I must do you the justice to own, that when I enter into your ideas, no man appears to express himself with greater perspicuity than you do ; a talent which, above all others, is requisite in that species of literature which you have cultivated. There are some objections, which I would willingly propose, to the chapter ' Of Sight,' did I not suspect that they proceed from my not sufficiently understanding it ; and I am the more confirmed in this suspicion, as Dr Blair tells me, that the former objections I made, had been derived chiefly from that cause. I shall therefore forbear till the whole can be before me, and shall not at present propose any farther difficulties to your reasonings. I shall only say, that if you have been able to clear up these abstruse and important subjects, instead of being mortified, I shall be so vain as to pretend to a share of the praise ; and shall think that my errors, by having at least some coherence, had led you to make a more strict review of my principles which were the common ones, and to perceive their futility.
>
> As I was desirous to be of some use to you, I kept a watchful eye all along over your style ; but it is really so correct, and so good English, that I found not any thing worth the remarking. There is only one passage in this chapter, where you make use of the phrase, *hinder to do*, instead of *hinder from doing*, which is the English one ; but I could not find the passage when I sought for it. You may judge how unexceptionable the whole appeared to me, when I could remark so small a blemish. I beg my compliments to my friendly adversaries, Dr Campbell and Dr Gerard, and also to Dr Gregory, whom I suspect to be of the same disposition, tho he has not openly declared himself such.

Reid's reply may be quoted in part :

> . . . I thought my self very happy in having the means of obtaining at second hand, through the friendship of Dr Blair, your opinion of my

---

[1] Quoted in Stewart, *Smith, Robertson, and Reid*, p. 417 ; the letter itself is not extant.

performance ; and you have been pleased to communicate it directly, in so polite & friendly a manner as merits great acknowledgements on my part.

Your keeping a watchfull Eye, over my Style with a view to be of use to me, is an Instance of Candor and Generosity to an Antagonist, which would affect me very sensibly although I had no personal concern in it. And I shall always be proud to follow so amiable an Example. . . .

In attempting to throw some new light upon these abstruse Subjects, I wish to preserve the due mean betwixt Confidence and Despair. But whether I have any Success in this Attempt or not, I shall always avow my self your Disciple in Metaphysicks. I have learned more from your writings in this kind than from all others put together. Your System appears to me not only coherent in all its parts, but likeways justly deduced from principles commonly received among Philosophers : Principles, which I never thought of calling in Question, untill the conclusions you draw from them in the treatise of human Nature made me suspect them. If these principles are Solid your System must stand ; and whether they are or not, can better be judged after you have brought to Light the whole System that grows out of them, than when the greater part of it was wrapped up in clouds and darkness. I agree with you therefore that if this System shall ever be demolished, you have a just claim to a great share of the Praise, both because you have made it a distinct and determinate mark to be aimed at, and have furnished proper artillery for the purpose.[1]

The remainder of Reid's letter describing the activities of the Philosophical Society at Aberdeen has already been presented.

What Reid completely failed to notice in Hume's letter is the pervasive irony : Reid had so thoroughly misconceived him that Hume contented himself with the correction of a Scotticism ! The ironical statement that Hume's only contribution to philosophy lay in the reducing to absurdity of the whole modern system, Reid took perfectly seriously both in his letter and in the *Inquiry* itself. In the " Dedication to James Earl of Findlater and Seafield, Chancellor of the University of Old Aberdeen," Reid wrote :

I acknowledge, my Lord, that I never thought of calling in question the principles commonly received with regard to the human understanding, until the *Treatise of human nature* was published, in the year 1739. The ingenious author of that treatise, upon the principles of Locke, who was no sceptic, hath built a system of scepticism, which leaves no ground to believe any one thing rather than its contrary. His reasoning appeared to me to be just : there was therefore a necessity to call in question the principles upon which it was founded, or to admit the conclusion.

In the introduction, the point is turned into sheer farce :

It seems to be a peculiar strain of humour in this author, to set out in his introduction, by promising, with a grave face, no less than a complete system of the sciences, upon a foundation entirely new, to wit, that of human nature ;

[1] RSE, VII, 3.

when the intention of the whole work is to shew, that there is neither human nature nor science in the world. It may perhaps be unreasonable to complain of this conduct in an author, who neither believes his own existence, nor that of his reader ; and therefore could not mean to disappoint him, or to laugh at his credulity.

And in the conclusion, the *Treatise of Human Nature* is branded the " monster " of modern scepticism born in the year 1739.

Thomas Reid was the sole philosopher worthy of the name who dealt at any length with the *Treatise of Human Nature* during the lifetime of its author, and, prior to Kant, he remained the most thorough.[1] Little wonder that Hume was ready to renounce publicly that *Treatise* which, after a quarter of a century, could still engender in its readers so little understanding of its basic ideas !

[1] James Beattie will be treated in Ch. 38, below.

CHAPTER 23

THE HISTORY OF ENGLAND

" Every body writes me & tells me, that the Conspiracy of the
Booksellers contributed very much to retard the Sale."

" HUMAN Nature is the only science of man," Hume had written
in the *Treatise of Human Nature*, and the pronouncement forms the
basis for his concern with both philosophy and history. The two
are closely akin because the development of the human mind,
which it is the historian's task to trace, provides the materials from
which the philosopher derives the very principles of thinking and
conduct. A passage in the *Enquiry concerning Human Understanding*
emphasises these interconnexions of philosophy and history :

> Its [i.e. history's] chief use is only to discover the constant and universal
> principles of human nature, by shewing men in all varieties of circumstances
> and situations, and furnishing us with materials, from which we may form
> our observations, and become acquainted with the regular springs of human
> action and behaviour. These records of wars, intrigues, factions, and revolu-
> tions, are so many collections of experiments, by which the politician or moral
> philosopher fixes the principles of his science ; in the same manner as the
> physician or natural philosopher becomes acquainted with the nature of
> plants, minerals, and other external objects, by the experiments, which he
> forms concerning them.[1]

The recognition of this essential affinity of history and philosophy
is what makes Hume's *History of England* " philosophical."

Hume's intention to compose a national history arose out of
his pervasive study of the " science of man ". The first trials in
the actual composition of history were possibly made during the
unhappy Annandale period, 1744–5, but could hardly have
amounted to much. After Hume's return from Turin in 1749,
a second trial was presumably made. But even London had no
public libraries before the opening of the British Museum in 1759
and Hume was always diffident of being rebuffed by the noble
Whig families where the private historical collections were to be
found. The happy circumstance of his being elected Keeper of
the Advocates' Library in Edinburgh in January 1752, " a
genteel office, though of small revenue ", provided him with a
library of some 30,000 volumes and the long-sought-for opportunity of turning historian in earnest. The transition from
philosopher proper to philosopher-historian was easily made.

[1] *Phil. Wks.*, IV, 68.

The six-volume *History of England*, which appeared between 1754 and 1762, became a popular classic within the lifetime of its author. It remained standard throughout the nineteenth century until finally superseded by the more " scientific " research histories of the twentieth century. It was largely this work that made Hume's name familiar to all who could read, and provided him with ultimate financial wellbeing. The story of its composition and publication, early vicissitudes and later successes, forms an important part of the biography of the man of letters.

Originally planning to commence with the reign of Henry VII and to continue down to the accession of the House of Hanover, Hume actually commenced with the Union of the Crowns and ended with the Revolution. That completed, he turned back to the Tudors, and, finally, to the early periods from the invasion of Julius Caesar, thus producing six quarto volumes of the *History of England, from the Invasion of Julius Caesar to the Revolution in 1688*. An early critic spitefully commented on this order of composition : " For having undertaken to conjure up the spirit of absolute power, he [Hume] judged it necessary to the charm, to reverse the order of things, and to evoke this frightful spectre by writing (as witches use to say their prayers) *backwards*." [1]

In January 1754, after two years of concentrated effort, the first Stuart volume was nearing completion and Hume was prepared to consider means of publication. Why he did not go directly to Andrew Millar, who was by now his major publisher, remains uncertain—but probably it was because of a truly amazing offer from the Edinburgh firm of Hamilton, Balfour, and Neill.

Hume had had no previous dealings with Gavin Hamilton as a publisher, nor had that gentleman in his capacity of Baillie in the Edinburgh Town Council in 1744–45 backed Hume's candidacy for the professorship. But by 1754 Hamilton was convinced that in Hume's still uncompleted history he had found the answer to a publisher's prayer for a best-seller. Hamilton's letter of 29 January to William Strahan in London is nothing if not enthusiastic :

My Dear Willie,
     in any important step I make, in bussiness, I should rekon my self very much out of my duty to you as on of my sincerest freinds if I did not un bosome my self, lett this serve for preamble to what I am going to say.

  [1] Richard Hurd, " Post-script " to *Moral and Political Dialogues* (edn. of London 1761).

I have within these ten days concluded a bargain that is rekoned very bold by every body that hears of it, and some think it rash, because they never heard of the like pass here ; tho' at the same time I remain very well content with my bargain.

John Balfour and I have agreed to pay 1200 £ sterling of coppy money, for a single impression of a book, 'tis the history of great britain composed by David Hume our scots authour. I print 2000 and have right to print no more, the calcul will stand thus, to print 3 quarto volls which it will make, will cost with advertisements and incidents about 320 per voll ; the book will sell at 15/ bound or ten shillings to Bk. Sellers in sheets, but lett us rekon the London coppies only producing 9 shillings, then 2000 coppies will yeald about 920 £ sterling per voll after deducing 320 £ for printing and 400 £ to the authour which is not payable very soon, there remains of proffit for our selves about 200 £ per voll, which we are content to putt up with as we are perswaded that this first impression will be short while in hands, and this is the next question, how do you know that ? all I can say to you in the bounds of a very short letter is that we have been at due pains to inform our selves of the merit of the work and are well satisfyed on that head that it is the prittyest thing ever was attempted in the English History, the three volls contians three grand periods, the first from the union of the Crowns to the death of the king, the 2d voll from the death of the king to the Revolution, and the last till the treaty of Utrecht, the facts are well vouched and thrown together into a light as to give the treu character of the times, it is neither whig nor tory but truely imparshal.

I am with sincerity, yours

Gavin Hamilton.[1]

This letter bespeaks the openness and honesty of Hamilton's character and his zeal for Hume's historical undertaking. It also bespeaks his immoderate notions of how to conduct a publishing house and an innocence not very common among booksellers of that day or, indeed, of any day. Hume, on the contrary, was shrewder in business affairs and quick to see the impossibility of the arrangements. Despite Hamilton's statement, therefore, Hume did not in fact conclude the bargain on the terms alleged. The contract actually signed is not extant, but the following features are vouched for in Hume's letters. First, he would not contract in advance for more than one volume or for more than one edition at a time. Second, he agreed to accept £400 for a first edition of 2,000 copies of the first volume alone. Third, if that first edition proved acceptable, he was willing to consider Hamilton's proposal of a further £600 for a second.[2]

The sheets of Volume I were through the Edinburgh press by the beginning of September 1754, and Hume was presenting advance bound copies to friends early the next month. So elated was Gavin Hamilton over his future prospects that he forwarded

[1] Quoted in *Letters of David Hume to William Strahan*, ed. G. Birkbeck Hill (Oxford 1888), p. 3, *n*2.   [2] HL, I, 234-5, 193.

a stock of sheets and books to London, where he proposed to set up shop and to sell his Hume. The historian, on 16 October, provided him with a letter of introduction to John Wilkes, because, as he explained, " Mr Hamilton is of Opinion, that your Countenance & Protection wou'd be of Use to him in London. He is a very honest Man ; and I dare venture to recommend him to your good Offices."

At London Hamilton at once leased a shop and sought the co-operation of the local booksellers in distributing the *History*. The following notices in the *Daily Advertiser* speak for themselves :

[November 9] On Wednesday, Nov. 20, will be publish'd in Quarto: (Price in Boards Fourteen Shillings)
THE HISTORY OF GREAT BRITAIN, Vol. I. Containing the Reigns of JAMES I and CHARLES I. By DAVID HUME, Esq.

[November 18] On Wednesday next will be publish'd,
THE FIRST Volume of Mr. HUME's History of GREAT BRITAIN.
To be had of Mr. Hamilton, the Publisher, at the Golden Head, next Pinchbeck's Toyshop, facing the Hay-market ; also of Mess. Longman, Knaptons, Hitch and Hawes, Millar, Dodsleys, Rivingtons, Payne, Wilson, and Durham, Booksellers.

On 17 December Hume informed Adam Smith that " The Sale indeed has been very great in Edinburgh ; but how it goes on at London, we have not been precisely inform'd," and on the same day he specified to the Earl of Balcarres that the Edinburgh sale had amounted to " about four hundred and fifty in five weeks." The notice in the *Daily Advertiser* was repeated eighteen times between 21 November 1754 and 21 January 1755. After that— silence. Sometime before the middle of April 1755 Gavin Hamilton was back in Edinburgh, having relinquished his shop in London. He was especially nettled by an offer from Andrew Millar to buy out his rights in the *History*, an offer which he had peremptorily rejected.

In *My Own Life* Hume recounts the initial failure of the *History* in poignant language :

I was, I own, sanguine in my Expectations of the Success of this work. I thought, that, I was the only Historian, that had at once neglected present Power, Interest, and Authority, and the Cry of popular Prejudices ; and as the Subject was suited to every Capacity, I expected proportional Applause : But miserable was my Disappointment : I was assailed by one Cry of Reproach, Disapprobation, and even Detestation : English, Scotch, and Irish ; Whig and Tory ; Churchman and Sectary, Free-thinker and Religionist ; Patriot and Courtier united in their Rage against the Man, who had presumed to shed a generous Tear for the Fate of Charles I, and the Earl of Strafford :

And after the first Ebullitions of this Fury were over, what was still more mortifying, the Book seemed to sink into Oblivion. Mr Millar told me, that in a twelve-month he sold only forty five Copies of it. I scarcely indeed heard of one Man in the three Kingdoms, considerable for Rank or Letters, that cou'd endure the Book. I must only except the Primate of England, Dr Herring, and the Primate of Ireland, Dr Stone ; which seem two odd Exceptions. These dignifyed Prelates separately sent me Messages not to be discouraged.

The stunning miscarriage for both author and publisher seems the more unaccountable in view of the fact that, within ten years, the completed *History of England* was to become the most popular and best-selling history published in Britain before Gibbon. A further complication is inherent in the fact that, while the work sold moderately well in Scotland, it sold almost not at all in England. In attempting to analyse the failure, Hume gave consideration to three possible causes : the spirit of irreligion in the work, the attempt of the Whig ministers to discredit it, and the conspiracy of the London booksellers.

That the strokes at religion in the first Stuart volume had any appreciable influence in stopping the sale was never accepted by Hume. Priding himself on his impartiality, he had informed a friend prior to publication that, " A few Christians only (and but a few) think I speak like a Libertine in religion ; be assured I am tolerably reserved on this head. . . . I composed it *ad populum*, as well as *ad clerum*, and thought, that scepticism was not in its place in an historical production." He was, therefore, taken completely by surprise when Baillie Hamilton wrote from London that the " Cry of the Clergy " had been raised against him. To Millar, Hume commented that that " Cause . . . coud never have produced that Effect, that it was rather likely to encrease the Sale, according to all past Experience ; that you had offered (as I heard) a large Sum for Bolingbroke's Works, trusting to this Consequence. . . ."[1] He further argued that irreligious strokes ought to have given more offence in Scotland than in England, but had not.

The fact remains, however, that some critics did seize upon two short passages dealing with the early Protestant Reformation and the Roman Catholic Church, the first of which Hume characterised as exhibiting " enthusiasm," and the second " superstition." On the basis of these passages, the critics stigmatised the entire work as irreligious or even atheistical. The two passages in question were commented upon briefly by William Rose in the March 1755 issue of the *Monthly Review*, and at

[1] HL, I, 189, 249–50.

considerable length by the Reverend Daniel MacQueen in his *Letters on Mr Hume's History of Great Britain* (Edinburgh 1756). MacQueen was not, to be sure, disturbed by the charge of Catholic superstition—that being no more than the truth from his point of view—but he was alarmed by the charge of Presbyterian enthusiasm.

Taking all things into consideration, Hume concluded that he had, at worst, been needlessly impolitic. " I am convinced that whatever I have said of religion should have received some more softenings," he acknowledged. " There is no passage in the History which strikes in the least at revelation. But as I run over all the sects successively, and speak of each of them with some mark of disregard, the reader, putting the whole together, concludes that I am of no sect ; which to him will appear the same thing as the being of no religion." So, when preparing the second edition of Volume I for the press in 1759, Hume deleted the two controversial passages.

He had not, however, altered his views concerning the rights and duties of a historian. In 1756, prior to putting Volume II to press, he had drafted a spirited preface in defence of his position. The preface was not printed as such but was reduced to a footnote in a shortened and toned-down version.[1] The manuscript of the suppressed preface has survived and is of such general value in the understanding of Hume on both history and religion as to warrant reproduction in full :

It ought to be no matter of Offence, that in this Volume, as well as in the foregoing, the Mischiefs which arise from the Abuses of Religion, are so often mentioned, while so little in comparison is said of the salutary Consequences which result from true & genuine Piety. The proper Office of Religion[2] is to reform Men's Lives, to purify their Hearts, to inforce all moral Duties, & to secure Obedience to the Laws & civil Magistrate. While it pursues these useful Purposes, its Operations, tho' infinitely valuable, are secret & silent ; and seldom come under the Cognizance of History. That adulterate Species of it alone, which inflames Faction, animates Sedition, & prompts Rebellion, distinguishes itself on the open Theatre of the World. Those therefore who attempt to draw Inferences disadvantageous to Religion from the Abuses of it mentiond by Historians, proceed upon a very gross & a very obvious Fallacy. For besides, that every thing is liable to Abuse, & the best things the most so ; the beneficent Influence of Religion is not to be sought for in History : That Principle is always the more pure & genuine, the less figure it makes in those Annals of Wars, & Politics, Intrigues, & Revolutions, Quarrels & Convulsions, which it is the Business of an Historian to record & transmit to Posterity.

[1] Hume, *Hist.*, VOL. II (1756), 449.   [2] The most memorable statement of this thesis appears in the *Dialogues concerning Natural Religion* (1779), p. 220.

It ought as little to be matter of Offence, that no religious Sect is mentioned in this Work without being expos'd sometimes to some Note of Blame and Dissapprobation. The Frailties of our Nature mingle themselves with every thing, in which we are employ'd ; and no human Institution will ever reach Perfection. The Idea of an Infinite Mind, the Author of the Universe seems at first Sight to require a Worship absolutely pure, simple, unadorned ; without Rites, Institutions, Ceremonies ; even without Temples, Priests, or verbal Prayer & Supplication ; Yet has this Species of Devotion been often found to degenerate into the most dangerous Fanaticism. When we have recourse to the aid of the Senses & Imagination, in order to adapt our Religion, in some degree to human Infirmity ; it is very difficult, & almost impossible, to prevent altogether the Intrusion of Superstition, or keep Men from laying too great Stress on the ceremonial & ornamental Parts of their Worship. Of all the Sects, into which Christians have been divided, the Church of England seems to have chosen the most happy Medium ; yet will it undoubtedly be allowd, that during the Age, of which these Volumes treat, there was a Tincture of Superstition in the Partizans of the Hierarchy ; as well as a strong Mixture of Enthusiasm in their Antagonists. But it is the Nature of the latter Principle soon to evaporate and decay ; A Spirit of Moderation usually succeeds, in a little time, to the Fervors of Zeal : And it must be acknowledg'd, to the Honor of the present Presbyterians, Independants, & other Sectaries of this Island, that they resemble in little more but in Name their Predecessors, who flourished during the civil Wars ; & who were the Authors of such Disorder. It woud appear ridiculous in the Eyes of the judicious Part of Mankind to pretend that even the first Reformers in most Countries of Europe, did not carry Matters to a most violent Extreme, & were not, on many Occasions, liable to the Imputation of Fanaticism. Not to mention, that uncharitable Spirit, which Accompanied Zealots of all kind, & which led the early Reformers, almost universally, to inflict upon the Catholics, & on all who differed from them, the same Rigors, of which they themselves so loudly complaind.[1]

These Hints, however obvious, the Author thought proper to suggest, with regard to the free & impartial Manner, in which he has treated religious Controversy : He is content to submit to any Censure, if there be found a single Passage objected against, to which these Considerations do not afford a compleat Answer. As to the civil & political Part of his Performance, he scorns to suggest any Apology, where he thinks himself intitled to Approbation. To be above the Temptations of Interest is a Species of Virtue, which we do not find by Experience to be very common : But to neglect at the same time all popular & vulgar Applause, is an Enterprize much more rare & arduous. Whoever in a factious Nation pays Court to neither Party, must expect that Justice will be done him by Time only, perhaps only by a distant Posterity.[2]

The appearance of Volume II in 1756, where Hume was somewhat more cautious in his comments on religion, gave rise

---

[1] In a first version this last sentence reads : ". . . which led the early Reformers, almost universally, to send the Catholics to Hell, as fast as they were themselves sent thither by their Antagonists."

[2] MS in Keynes Library, King's College, Cambridge. The MS is endorsed : " Draft of Preface to a volume of D Hume's History—in David Hume's own hand found among my father's papers," that is, the collection of Gilbert Elliot of Minto. It was printed by Hill Burton (II, 11–13) with numerous mistakes and some omissions.

to an unpleasant incident. The Reverend John Brown brought out in 1757 a jeremiad entitled *An Estimate of the Manners and Principles of the Times* in which he accused " A certain Writer of our Times, bent upon *Popularity* and *Gain*," of having introduced irreligious sentiments into his work solely for the purpose of stimulating sales. In a second volume of the following year, Brown returned to the attack :

When this Gentleman found that his History, though larded with Irreligion, did not sell among the *licentious* ; and that the *serious* were shocked at his Treatment of Religion, and on that Account were not Purchasers ; he ordered his Agent (but too late) to expunge the exceptionable Passages ; assigning for the Reason of his avoiding every Thing of this Kind in his second Volume, " that he would not *offend the Godly*." Now this very Man, in Defiance of all Decency, hath for several Years carried on a Trade of Essaywriting ; in the Course of which he hath not only misrepresented, abused, and insulted the most essential Principles of *Christianity*, but, to the utmost of his Power, shaken the Foundations of all Religion. In these sorry Essays, he had no fear of offending the *Godly*, because he knew the *Godly* were not to be his *Buyers* : But when he finds that his History must *sell* among the *Godly*, or *not sell* at all ; *then* comes the Panic upon him ; *then*, forsooth, he will not *offend the Godly*. Here, therefore, a *Character* is clearly developed. With St. Paul, *Godliness* was Gain ; But with *this* Man, *Gain* produceth *Godliness*.[1]

Brown's malevolent accusations were apparently based upon several of Hume's letters to Millar. Outraged by this misuse of personal correspondence, Hume wrote in rebuke to Millar : " What Sort of Behaviour this is to make use of a private Letter, without the Permission of the Person to whom it was addressd, is easily conceivd ; but how he came to see any of my Letters I cannot imagine ; nor what I wrote that coud give him any handle for his Calumny." As for Dr Brown himself, Hume held him beneath contempt :

I doubt not but I coud easily refute Dr Brown ; but as I had taken a Resolution never to have the least Altercation with these Fellows, I shall not readily be brought to pay any Attention to him : And I cannot but be displeas'd, that your Inadvertance or Indiscretion (for I cannot give it a better Name) shoud have brought me to this Dilemma. I fancy Brown will find it a difficult Matter to perswade the Public that I do not speak my Sentiments in every Subject I handle, & that I have any View to any Interest whatsoever. I leave that to him and his Gang : For he is a Flatterer, as I am told, of that low Fellow, Warburton. And any thing so low as Warburton, or his Flatterers, I shoud certainly be ashamd to engage with.[2]

The Reverend Josiah Tucker was in complete agreement, protesting to Lord Kames, " I was extremely hurt in observing with what Arrogance & Indecence Mr. H[ume] was treated by that

[1] Brown, *Estimate*, I, 57–8 ; II, 86–7.   [2] HL, I, 249–50.

superficial Creature, ye Author of ye Estimate. He is himself below Mr. H's Notice." [1]

As for Warburton, it is perhaps worth remarking in passing, that he had already expressed his private judgment of the historian: " He is an atheistical Jacobite, a monster as rare with us as a hippogriff." [2]

From Scotland came a piquant suggestion, at once economic, literary, and religious, concerning Hume's *History*. In a tract of 1757 entitled *The Moderator* (No. II), the Reverend John Witherspoon ironically proposed that the Edinburgh booksellers, who seemed likely to lose £400 over a work " wherein great honour is done to the church of Scotland," should petition that they be " indemnified to that extent out of his Majesty's bounty of £1,000, or that the whole impression be bought up by the society for propagating Christian knowledge, to be dispersed in the highlands and islands, where it may be very useful in preventing the growth of Popery, and, by the fine style in which it is written, serve to introduce the *English* language."

The spirit of irreligion in Hume's *History* had not been sufficiently strong to prevent all of the *Godly* from admiring the book, in particular, those " two odd Exceptions," the primates of England and Ireland. Boswell, recording an interview with Hume in 1775, provides further details :

> He told me that Herring, Archbishop of Canterbury, sent a message to him by Ruat that if ever he came to London he should have an apartment in his Palace at Lambeth. David was diverted with the thought of his being there among the Chaplains. It was his History that pleased the Arch Bishop, and his Grace sent him a present of ten guineas. He never knew of it till after the Archbishop's death, when, on settling an Account with Andrew Millar, he found stated, " ten guineas sent to you by the ArchBp. of Canty." He said he never was in London during the Bishop's life after the invitation. I said, " Perhaps the Arch Bishop did not know that you had written any bad book. You would have done very well at Lambeth ; you would have given them good Politicks, and they would have given you good Religion." [3]

It is perhaps needless to speculate as to exactly what had attracted the primates to Hume's *History*, but it is easy to believe that it was less his religious than his political position.

The influence of politics and politicians as a cause of the initial failure of Volume I was taken more seriously by Hume. Shortly before his death, he was still complaining about it,

---

[1] Tucker, MS letter of 6 July 1758, in SRO, Abercairny Papers, GD 24.
[2] *A Selection from Unpublished Papers of the Right Reverend William Warburton*, ed. Francis Kilvert (London 1841), p. 257. [3] *Boswell Papers*, XI, 41–2.

and some of his remarks on the subject were copied down by John Home : " he recurred to a subject not unfrequent with him—that is, the design to ruin him as an author, by the people that were ministers, at the first publication of his history : and called themselves Whigs, who, he said, were determined not to suffer truth to be told in Britain." [1] One instance of what Hume had in mind is recorded by the Earl of Charlemont :

> Nothing ever gave Hume more real Vexation than the Strictures made upon his History in the House of Lords by the great Lord Chatham. They were indeed carried to an extraordinary length when Mrs. McCauly, as an Historian was preferred to him, and her constitutional Writings, were declared to be the only Antidote to his Poison. . . . Soon after that Speech I met with Hume, and ironically wished him Joy of the high Honour that had been done him. " Zounds, Man," said He, with more Peevishness than I had ever seen him express, " He's a Goth—He's a Vandal ! " [2]

The instance is not entirely pat, however, because Pitt became the Earl of Chatham only in 1766, by which time Hume's *History* was successful. Yet Pitt's antagonism dated from the first publication and in 1757 he permitted Smollett, by arrangement with the booksellers, to dedicate to him the *Complete History of England, Deduced from the Descent of Julius Caesar to the Treaty of Aix La Chapelle, 1748.*

That the first volume of Hume's *History of the Stuarts* was detested by the Whigs is indisputable. Many, like Warburton, even went so far as to brand it " Jacobite." The epithet, of course, was nonsense, as was immediately perceived by Horace Walpole, nephew of the great Whig statesman. Four months after publication Walpole wrote about Hume's " book, which, though more decried than ever book was, and certainly with faults, I cannot help liking much. It is called Jacobite, but in my opinion is only not *George-abite* ; where others abuse the Stuarts, he laughs at them ; I am sure he does not spare their ministers." [3] Others, too, denied that Hume was a Jacobite ; but the age of Whig supremacy insisted that he was, at least, a Tory, and the appellation is still customarily employed.

" I have the impudence to pretend that I am of no party, and have no bias," Hume had written before publication. Afterwards he shrewdly explained the Tory label which had been pinned

---

[1] Quoted in Home-Mackenzie, I, 175.
[2] Lord Charlemont's " Anecdotes of Hume," in RIA, MS—12/R/7, f.523.
[3] *Walpole Letters*, III, 294. Thomas Comber wrote : " Mr. *Hume* . . . appears to me not a *Jacobite*, but a Republican. . . ." See his *Vindication of the Great Revolution in England* (London 1758), p. 131n.

upon him : " With regard to politics and the character of princes and great men, I think I am very moderate. My views of *things* are more conformable to Whig principles ; my representations of *persons* to Tory prejudices. Nothing can so much prove that men commonly regard more persons than things, as to find that I am commonly numbered among the Tories." Hume's sympathy for the persons of the Scottish dynasty of Stuarts was inevitably interpreted by a Whiggish age as a Tory bias. But Hume continued his efforts at impartiality, and pointed out that if Volume I was somewhat on the Tory side, Volume II would be somewhat on the Whig side. " I wish," he added, " the two Volumes had been publishd together. Neither one Party nor the other, wou'd, in that case, have had the least Pretext of reproaching me with Partiality." [1]

A passage in *My Own Life*, however, would seem to paint a picture of rancorous partisanship. Referring there to later revisions of the Stuart volumes, he writes with some asperity :

> But though I had been taught by Experience, that the Whig Party were in possession of bestowing all places, both in the State and in Literature, I was so little inclined to yield to their senseless Clamour, that in above a hundred Alterations, which farther Study, Reading, or Reflection engaged me to make in the Reigns of the two first Stuarts, I have made all of them invariably to the Tory Side.

The explanation of this tirade lies in the increasing bitterness against England and its ruling party that Hume developed, beginning in the late 1750s and culminating during the violent anti-Scottish campaigns of the 1760s and 1770s, a bitterness that will be traced in due course. The high rhetorical colouring of the passage obscures the fact that he was actually far more impartial than he would seem to imply.[2]

The hue-and-cry against Hume died down considerably with the appearance of Volume II in 1756—but whether this was mainly due to political or religious considerations remains doubtful ; there is good reason to believe that trade motivations were paramount. George Dempster, a friend of Hume's, provides a broad hint in his observation that " David Hume's second volume is come out printed at London and favourably received—more so than the first from that circumstance." [3]

---

[1] HL, I, 185, 237, 218.   [2] For a study of this point, see Mossner, " Was Hume a Tory Historian ? Facts and Reconsiderations," in *Journal of the History of Ideas*, II (1941), 225–36 ; for a more general study of Hume's Toryism and of his *History*, see the same, " An Apology for David Hume, Historian," in *PMLA*, LXVI (1941), 657–80. See also *David Hume : Philosophical Historian* with introductory essays by David F. Norton and Richard H. Popkin (Indianapolis 1965).   [3] Dempster, *Letters to Sir Adam Fergusson, 1756–1813*, ed. Sir James Fergusson (London 1934), p. 14.

As early as 12 April 1755 Hume harboured some vague misgivings concerning the influence of the London booksellers in retarding sales. Writing to Millar, he still placed the major blame, however, on Hamilton's unbusinesslike procedures. " He [Hamilton] is a very honest Man, & far from being interested : But he is passionate & even wrong headed to a great Degree. He has made it sufficiently appear in his Conduct of this whole Affair. I think the London Booksellers have had a sufficient Triumph over him ; when a Book, which was much expected & was calculated to be popular, had had so small a Sale [in] his hands." By 3 May Hume began to think somewhat differently, expressing himself to Strahan :

> Every body writes me & tells me, that the Conspiracy of the Booksellers contributed very much to retard the Sale. . . . You are better acquainted with these Matters than me : But if the Booksellers had not a great Influence, whence coud proceed the great Difference of the Sale in Scotland & England ? The Freedoms with Religion ought here to have given more Displeasure ; & the Cry of Jacobitism as much, notwithstanding what may be imagin'd.

The thesis of the " Conspiracy of the Booksellers " was further extended by Hume in a letter of September 1757 to Colonel Edmonstoune at Dublin. Hume is inquiring about the *Epigoniad* of his friend William Wilkie :

> Has it had any Success in Ireland ? I fancy not : For the Criticklingys in Dublin depend on the Criticklings in London, who depend on the Booksellers, who depend on their Interest, which depends on their printing a Book themselves. This is the Cause, why Wilkies Book is at present neglected, or damn'd as they call it : But I am much mistaken, if it end so. Pray, what says the Primate of it ? I hear he has the Generosity to support damnd Books, till their Resurrection ; and that he is one of the Saints who pray them out of Purgatory. I hope he is an honest Fellow, and one of [us.] [1]

The fullest eighteenth-century statement of the " Conspiracy of the Booksellers " in connexion with the *History of England* appeared in 1777, some months after the death of Hume and in comment on *My Own Life* :

> He [Hume] has observed in the nineteenth page of his Life, that his History of Great Britain met at first with an indifferent reception. But with respect to this, Mr. Hume himself was mistaken. The first edition of the History of Great Britain, for the reigns of James the First and Charles the First, was printed at Edinburgh, A.D. 1754, for *Hamilton, Balfour, and Neil*. Hamilton, upon his expectations from this book, took a shop, and settled in London. He applied to the London booksellers to take copies of the History from him, but none of them would deal with an *interloper*. Hamilton, sadly distressed, has recourse to *his friend*, Mr. Millar : Millar *obliges* him by taking

---

[1] NHL, p. 42.

fifty copies : but when gentlemen, in his well-frequented shop, asked for the book, " Pho (says Millar generously) " it is incomplete, another volume is coming out soon. You are welcome to the use of this in the mean time." Thus did Millar circulate the fifty copies among some hundred readers without selling one. And by this ingenious device attained his favourite purpose, of getting Hamilton to sell him his right in the copy for a trifle, as being an insignificant performance.[1]

These allegations of a " Conspiracy of the Booksellers " are substantially supported by the known facts. During most of the eighteenth century the talents of London booksellers for organisation were highly developed. They included both skill in co-operative publishing and remarkable ability to protect leading members of the trade against competition. Because the powers of the Stationers' Company were at a low ebb, independent organisation for promotion and protection of literary property was inevitable. The first such organisation to have a name and a clearly defined programme was the Printing Conger of 1719. This combination was followed in 1736—a year of great copyright controversy—by the Second Conger, which in turn was succeeded by the Chapter Coffee House group. In the period of Hume's historical writing a Third Conger was formed, principally to offset incursions being made by printers and booksellers in Ireland and Scotland.[2]

The Third Conger was inspired by a setback in the courts, where Andrew Millar had led a London group of seventeen against twenty booksellers at Edinburgh and Glasgow. On the surface, victory of the independents crushed the pretensions of the London group ; in actuality, it provoked them into one of the most successful propaganda campaigns in the history of restraint of trade. Using every means at hand to reduce the success of books which they did not own, they developed a highly efficient communication system. It extended to provincial booksellers, to whom riders brought news of books—which to push, which to pass by. It often included direct threat of trade retaliation. It sometimes involved an offer to buy entire stocks (for which " correct editions " would be substituted). It nearly always relied upon a determined and damaging criticism of the books to be

[1] [S. J. Pratt], *Supplement to the Life of David Hume, Esq.* (London 1777), pp. 15–17. The same account appears in the *Caledonian Mercury* for 26 May 1777 and also in Pratt's *Curious Particulars and Genuine Anecdotes respecting the late Lord Chesterfield and David Hume, Esq.* (London 1788), pp. 4–5.

[2] For further details of the conger system, as well as of other features of the present chapter, see Mossner and Ransom, " Hume and the ' Conspiracy of the Booksellers ' : The Publication and Early Fortunes of the *History of England*," in University of Texas *Studies in English*, xxix (1950), 162–82.

curtailed. There is no question that the Third Conger worked. In his *Case of Authors*, which is much more than an indictment of booksellers, James Ralph concludes that in this period, " the Booksellers were Masters of the Avenues to every Market and by the Practice of one Night's Postage could make any Work resemble Jonah's Gourd after the Worm had smote it." [1]

It was this booksellers' gourd-blight which smote the prospects of the innocent Gavin Hamilton and forced him out of London in less than five months. By that time David Hume had recognised and repented his blunder in not having dealt with Millar originally. So Hume, after congratulating Millar on the triumph of the London booksellers over Hamilton, added :

> To make the Triumph more compleat, I wish you wou'd take what remains into your hands, & dispose of it in a few Months. I beg of you to think again seriously [of] that Matter. If you will return to your former Offer, I will engage to make it effectual, or if the Baillie refuses to comply, I wou'd rather make out the Difference from my own Pocket : So much do I desire to have the Affair under your Management. You need have no Correspondence with him. Write to me, & I shall manage the Matter.

By 3 May Hume was " glad that Mr Millar has renewed his Offer, which I find Baillie Hamilton is resolv'd to accept of," but it was not easy to bring Hamilton to terms. He had extravagantly bound up " a considerable Number of Copies of the first Volume," which made negotiations for the sheets the more difficult. By the end of November a settlement had apparently been reached, and Hume commented with satisfaction : " It is easy for me to see, that Mr Millar has certainly offerd to take from Baillie Hamilton 900 copies at nine Shillings. He never woud have offerd seven at the beginning. It was a strange Infatuation in the Baillie to refuse it." In the meanwhile Hume, well advanced in the composition of Volume II, had refused even to consider an offer of £800 for a first edition from Hamilton, but was willing to accept £750 from Millar for an edition of 1750 copies. So was the firm of Hamilton, Balfour, and Neill completely read out of any further connexion with the *History of England*, and so did Andrew Millar take it over.

In February 1757 Hume opened negotiations with Millar for the final sale of all author's rights in Volumes I and II for the sum of 800 guineas. His principal motive in so doing was to rid himself of the burden of business details. For the two Tudor volumes of 1759 Hume asked £700 and for the two volumes of 1762 (Julius

---

[1] Ralph, *The Case of Authors by Profession* (ed. of London 1762), p. 60.

Caesar to the Accession of Henry VII), £1,400. In all these transactions, Hume was certainly not the financial loser. Nor in selling his rights did he by any means lose interest in the work as literature. He remained acutely concerned with maintaining the integrity of the text and was much distressed by the corruptions which had entered into the collected octavo edition of 1763. Ironically, it was this "abominable Octavo Edition of my History" that was the ultimate means of establishing his popularity.

The activity—or rather the studied inactivity—of the Third Conger in regard to Hume's *History* is indicative of no hostility to Hume personally or to his work. The opposition of the London booksellers was directed solely against printed matter from Edinburgh. Before Millar took over the literary property, the London booksellers associated with him in the defeat of Hamilton had employed Tobias Smollett to write a "complete" history of England in competition with Hume's. Smollett's contract was severe : he was required to finish the manuscript by the end of 1756, that is within fourteen months. This prodigious feat of writing was completed on schedule ; the first three quarto volumes appeared early in 1757 and the fourth a year later. In April 1758 Hume remarked to Millar, "I am afraid, this extraordinary Run upon Dr Smollett has a little hurt your Sales : But these Things are only temporary." With great understanding, Hume recognised that the new *History* was only journalism and, with great good humour, he maintained an acquaintance with its author. How he would have reacted had he lived to know that his own *History* was frequently to be joined with Smollett's in the nineteenth century to form a single set, cannot, of course, be determined. Probably he would have realised that the union was a booksellers' device to avoid unprofitable rivalry and to promote "completeness."

From all this welter of activity over the *History of England* arises a new picture of Hume as a man of literary business as distinct from an author. Despite his temporary disappointment at the world's coldness towards his first volume, he moved through business affairs concerning the venture with reason and with quick decision. When the transplanting of Scottish print to London did not thrive, he came to terms—very profitable terms— with opponents of that plan. Although sometimes displeased with the editorial results, Hume managed to relieve himself of most of the burdens of mere publication—still on very profitable terms. Through all this time, he maintained a dispassionate and, on the whole, a courteous attitude towards all participants : towards Hamilton, in his unprofitable management ; towards Millar, in his money-making ; towards other bookselling friends like Strahan, whose advice never quite solved any problem for him ; towards the later " proprietors " of his book ; and particularly towards Smollett, his successful although not victorious competitor in the increasingly competitive field of historical authorship.

What Hume had given the world in his *History of England* was a broad, sweeping narrative of the national developments, philosophically coherent, artistically ordered, and pre-eminently readable. He made no pretence of " research " scholarship but anticipated the modern synthetic historian in uniting and enlivening the sometimes ponderous research of others. " I have inserted,' he candidly explains, " no original Papers, and enter'd into no Detail of minute, uninteresting Facts. The philosophical Spirit which I have so much indulg'd in all my Writings, finds here ample Materials to work upon." Causes, motivations, characters, are more his concern than the mere recording of the facts. His acknowledged criteria for writing history are " style, judgement, impartiality, care." It was the magic of style that made him popular and assured him a permanent place in literature.

After shedding " a generous Tear for the Fate of Charles I," for example, Hume proceeds to analyse the historical lessons to be learned from the event :

The tragical death of Charles begat a question, whether the people, in any case, were entitled to judge and to punish their sovereign ; and most men, regarding chiefly the atrocious usurpation of the pretended judges, and the merit of the virtuous prince who suffered, were inclined to condemn the republican principle, as highly seditious and extravagant : But there still were a few, who, abstracting from the particular circumstances of this case, were able to consider the question in general, and were inclined to moderate, not contradict, the prevailing sentiment. Such might have been their reasoning : If ever, on any occasion, it were laudable to conceal truth from the populace, it must be confessed, that the doctrine of resistance affords such an example ; and that all speculative reasoners ought to observe, with regard to this principle, the same cautious silence which the laws, in every species of government, have ever prescribed to themselves. Government is instituted in order to restrain the fury and injustice of the people ; and being always founded on opinion, not on force, it is dangerous to weaken, by these speculations, the reverence which the multitude owe to authority, and to instruct them beforehand, that the case can ever happen when they may be freed from their duty of allegiance. Or, should it be found impossible to restrain the license of human disquisitions, it must be acknowledged, that the doctrine of obedience ought alone to be *inculcated*, and that the exceptions, which are rare, ought seldom or never to be mentioned in popular reasonings and discourses. Nor is there any danger that mankind, by this prudent reserve, should universally degenerate into a state of abject servitude. When the exception really occurs, even though it be not previously expected and descanted on, it must, from its very nature, be so obvious and undisputed, as to remove all doubt, and overpower the restraint, however great, imposed by teaching the general doctrine of obedience. But, between resisting a prince and dethroning him, there is a wide interval ; and the abuses of power which can warrant the latter violence, are greater and more enormous than those which will justify the former. History, however, supplies us with examples even of this kind ; and the reality of the supposition, though for the future it ought ever to be little looked for, must, by all candid enquirers, be acknowledged in the past. But, between dethroning a prince and punishing him, there is another very wide interval ; and it were not strange, if even men of the most enlarged thought should question, whether human nature could ever, in any monarch, reach that height of depravity, as to warrant, in revolted subjects, this last act of extraordinary jurisdiction. That illusion, if it be an illusion, which teaches us to pay a sacred regard to the persons of princes, is so salutary, that to dissipate it by the formal trial and punishment of a sovereign, will have more pernicious effects upon the people, than the example of justice can be supposed to have a beneficial influence upon princes, by checking their career of tyranny. It is dangerous also, by these examples, to reduce princes to despair, or bring matters to such extremities against persons endowed with great power, as to leave them no resource, but in the most violent and most sanguinary counsels. This general position being established, it must, however, be observed, that no reader, almost of any party or principle, was ever shocked, when he read, in ancient history, that the Roman Senate voted Nero, their absolute sovereign, to be a public enemy, and, even without trial, condemned him to the severest and most ignominious punishment, a punishment from which the meanest Roman citizen was by the laws exempted. The crimes of that bloody tyrant are so enormous, that they break through all rules, and extort a confession, that such a dethroned prince is no longer superior to his people, and can no longer plead, in his own defence, laws which were established for conducting the ordinary course of administration. But, when we pass from the case of Nero to that of Charles, the great disproportion, or rather total contrariety of character immediately strikes us ; and we stand astonished, that, among a civilized people, so much virtue could ever meet with so fatal a catastrophe. History, the great mistress of wisdom, furnishes examples of all kinds ; and every prudential, as well as moral precept, may be authorised by those events which her enlarged mirror is able to present to us. From the memorable revolutions which passed in England during this period, we may naturally deduce the same useful lesson, which Charles himself in his later years inferred, That it is dangerous for princes, even from the appearance of necessity, to assume more authority than the laws have allowed them. But, it must be confessed, that these events furnish us with another instruction, no less natural, and no less useful, concerning the madness of the people, the furies of fanaticism, and the danger of mercenary armies.[1]

" The writing of history is itself an historical event," we are reminded by a modern philosopher,[2] which is but another way of

---

[1] Hume, *Hist.* (Edinburgh 1792), VII, 148–50.
[2] John Dewey, *Logic, the Theory of Inquiry* (New York 1938), p. 237.

saying that history is the past interpreted for the present. Every age, consequently, requires its own interpretation of the past and no other will quite do. Although Hume's *History* is not for our times, it is proper to turn to it for either of two reasons : to enjoy it as literature, or to learn from it how the greatest mind of the Enlightenment interpreted the past for his age. Certainly the *History of England* could never be mistaken for the product of any age other than that in which it was written. Its merits and its limitations are the merits and limitations of the Enlightenment. The merits, at any rate, were recognised as such by Hume's brother historian and crusader for Enlightenment, Voltaire, who in 1764 wrote :

> Nothing can be added to the fame of this *History*, perhaps the best ever written in any language. . . . Mr Hume, in his *History*, is neither parliamentarian, nor royalist, nor Anglican, nor Presbyterian—he is simply judicial. . . . The fury of parties has for a long time deprived England of a good historian as well as of a good government. What a Tory wrote was disowned by the Whigs, who, in their turn, were given the lie by the Tories. Rapin Thoiras, a foreigner, alone seemed to have written an impartial history ; yet prejudice sometimes stains the truths that Thoiras relates. Whereas in the new historian we find a mind superior to his materials ; he speaks of weaknesses, blunders, cruelties as a physician speaks of epidemic diseases.[1]

Despite the initial failure due to the " Conspiracy of the Booksellers " and, to a less degree, to political and religious controversies, the Age of Enlightenment ultimately agreed with Gavin Hamilton that Hume's was " the prittyest thing ever attempted in the English History." Or as the Earl Marishal of Scotland, George Keith, was to put it : " To the highflyers you are therefor a sad Whig, to the Whigs an hidden Jacobite, and to reasonable men, *le bon David*, a Lover of truth." [2] With his success, history began to be cultivated in earnest. By 1770 Hume could afford to be somewhat complacent over his share in that exploitation. " I believe," he remarked, " this is the historical Age and this the historical Nation."

---

[1] Voltaire, review of *L'Histoire complète de l'Angleterre* in *La Gazette Littéraire* (2 mai 1764) in *Œuvres complètes* (Paris 1883–7), xxv, 169–73.

[2] RSE, v, 116.

CHAPTER 24

FOUR DISSERTATIONS

" Two Essays of mine . . . which from my abundant
Prudence I suppress'd."

HAVING taken the decisive step of publishing " Of Miracles "
and " Of a Particular Providence and of a Future State," in
1748, Hume continued to apply his philosophical tenets to
religion in the 1750s. Apart from historical observations on
religion in the first Stuart volume, he was primarily concerned
with philosophical and psychological investigations into the
theory of religion. The *Dialogues concerning Natural Religion* and
" The Natural History of Religion " are his most comprehensive
and important contributions to the philosophy and psychology
of religion respectively. But the first remained unpublished until
1779, three years after his death, and the second underwent
ordeal by fire before appearing in 1757. Hume's notion of the
function of creative scepticism is stated in a letter of March 1751
to Gilbert Elliot of Minto :

> If in order to answer the Doubts started, new Principles of Philosophy
> must be laid ; are not these Doubts themselves very useful ? Are they not
> preferable to blind, & Ignorant Assent ? I hope I can answer my own Doubts :
> But if I coud not, is it to be wonder'd at ? To give myself Airs, & speak
> magnificently, might I not observe, that Columbus did not conquer Empires
> & plant Colonies ?

Hume was already composing the *Dialogues* when he consulted
Elliot. The three speakers in that work are Cleanthes, a theist
adhering to the modern empirical philosophy; Demea, a
fideistic divine yet alternatively a rationalist; and Philo, a
sceptic. Cleanthes may be taken historically as Bishop Butler of
the *Analogy of Religion*; Demea as Samuel Clarke; and Philo,
as a letter to Elliot makes positive (" . . . I shou'd have taken
on me the Character of Philo, in the Dialogue, which you'll own
I coud have supported naturally enough ") as Hume himself.[1]

In order to avoid " that Vulgar Error . . . of putting
nothing but Nonsense into the Mouth of the Adversary," Hume

---

[1] On these historical identifications, see Mossner, " The Enigma of Hume," in
Mind, xiv (1936), 334–49. See Textual Supplement for further discussion of the
Dialogues.

asked for Elliot's assistance " in supporting Cleanthes." . His friend's argument, published many years later by Dugald Stewart in the eighth edition of the *Encyclopaedia Britannica*, may not have been of much value to Hume. Of more importance was Elliot's success in dissuading Hume from publishing the *Dialogues*.

As late as March 1763 Hume, playfully rebelling against this injunction, inquired of his friend : " Is it not hard & tyrannical in you, more tyrannical than any Act of the Stuarts, not to allow me to publish my Dialogues ? Pray, do you not think that a proper Dedication may atone for what is exceptional in them ? I am become much of my friend Corbyn Morrice's Mind, who says, that he writes all his Books for the sake of the Dedications." That Hume's threat of publishing under cover of a dedication was not entirely in jest may perhaps appear from an exchange of letters later in the same year with Hugh Blair. From Edinburgh in September Blair wrote to Hume, who was then at London on the way to France, to congratulate him on " going to a Country where you will want nothing of being worshipped, except bowing the knee to you. . . ." In religion alone, banters Blair, the *philosophes* may consider you " as being somewhat bigotted. . . . For this indeed they make an excuse that the hypocrisy of the Country may have somewhat infected even you, as a native." Then he comes to the point at issue : " But had you but gone one Step farther—I am well informed, in several Poker Clubs in Paris your Statue would have been erected. If you will show them the MSS of certain Dialogues perhaps this honour may still be done you. But for Gods sake let that be a posthumous work, if ever it shall see the light : tho' I really think it had better not." [1] So it is certain that the *Dialogues* had circulated in manuscript among the friendly Moderate divines in Edinburgh and that it was on their advice, as well as Elliot's and undoubtedly Adam Smith's, that it remained unpublished. Hume replied to Blair : " I have no present thoughts of publishing the work you mention ; but when I do, I hope you have no objection of my dedicating it to you." [2] Had Blair had the temerity to permit Hume to carry out this threat, the *Dialogues* might well have appeared during his lifetime. But that was not to be, and Hume apparently left the manuscript alone, except for some minor revisions in about 1761, until shortly before his death.[3]

---

[1] RSE, iii, 51.   [2] NHL, p. 72.   [3] For my new interpretation of the *Dialogues*, see " Hume and the Legacy of the *Dialogues*," in *David Hume : Bicentenary Papers*, ed. George Morice (Edinburgh 1977), pp. 1–22. See Textual Supplement.

To return to " The Natural History of Religion " and the curious story of the " Four ", " Three ", " Five ", " Three " and yet again, " Four " " Dissertations." [1] The story opens in June 1755, when Hume wrote to Andrew Millar :

> There are four short Dissertations, which I have kept some Years by me, in order to polish them as much as possible. One of them is that which Allan Ramsay mentiond to you. Another of the Passions ; a third of Tragedy ; a fourth, some Considerations previous, to Geometry & Natural Philosophy. The whole, I think, wou'd make a Volume a fourth less than my Enquiry [concerning the Principles of Morals] ; as nearly as I can calculate : But it wou'd be proper to print it in a larger Type, in order to bring it to the same Size & Price. I wou'd have it publish'd about the new Year ; I offer you the Property for fifty Guineas, payable at the Publication. You may judge, by my being so moderate in my Demands, that I do not propose to make any Words about the Bargain. It wou'd be more convenient for me to print here ; especially one of the Dissertations, where there is a good deal of Literature, but as the Manuscript is distinct & accurate, it wou'd not be impossible for me to correct it, tho' printed at London. I leave it to your Choice : tho' I believe, that it might be as cheaply & conveniently & safely executed here. However, the Matter is pretty near indifferent to me.

These four dissertations which Millar accepted for publication had probably been composed 1749–51, after Hume's return from Turin and before he plunged into active composition of the *History* in the spring of 1752. The first, so coyly alluded to as " that which Allan Ramsay mentiond to you," and again, as containing " a good deal of Literature," is " The Natural History of Religion." " Of the Passions " is a brief reworking of Book II of the *Treatise*. " Of Tragedy " is a short essay on the aesthetic problem of why grief in art is enjoyable. The fourth dissertation, " some Considerations previous to Geometry & Natural Philosophy " was presumably a reworking of Book I, Part II, of the *Treatise*.

This fourth item was never actually set up in type. Its history is summed up by Hume in a letter of 25 January 1772 to William Strahan, who had in the meanwhile succeeded Millar in the publishing business. It is there referred to as " on the metaphisical Principles of Geometry." The passage reads : " I sent them [the four dissertations] up to Mr Millar ; but before the last was printed, I happend to meet with Lord Stanhope, who was in this Country, and he convincd me, that either there was some Defect in the Argument or in its perspicuity ; I forget which ; and I wrote to Mr Miller, that I woud not print that Essay. . . ."

Of Philip, second Lord Stanhope, it has been said that, " He

---

[1] For a fuller discussion, see Mossner, " Hume's *Four Dissertations* : An Essay in Biography and Bibliography," in *Modern Philology*, XLVIII (1950), 37–57.

had great talents, but fitter for speculation than for practical objects of action. He made himself one of the best—Lalande used to say the best—mathematicians in England of his day, and likewise deeply skilled in other branches of science and philosophy." [1]

Stanhope had married in 1745 the Hon. Grizel Baillie, a distant cousin of David Hume's, and the two cousins exchanged sprightly letters over the course of years. Apropos of the quarrel with Rousseau in 1766, the Countess wrote to Hume : " If there is a Hell, that man will fry ; bad as you are, I think you'll not go to the same place." [2] Beyond Hume's ambiguous and incomplete explanation to Strahan of the conference with Lord Stanhope, nothing whatsoever is known of the suppressed dissertation, the manuscript itself having disappeared.

The three remaining essays, however, Millar remonstrated, " woud not make a Volume," continued Hume in the 1772 letter to Strahan, and " I sent him up these two, which I had never intended to have publishd." In addition to the original three remaining, the proposed volume was now to include " Of Suicide " and " Of the Immortality of the Soul," the incendiary nature of both which was granted by Hume himself. For better or for worse, however, they were printed by Millar as numbers IV and V of what was re-entitled, " Five Dissertations, to wit, The Natural History of Religion. Of the Passions. Of Tragedy. Of Suicide. Of the Immortality of the Soul." This title, apparently in Hume's hand, was inscribed on a bound copy of proof sheets that was in the possession of the Advocates' Library (now the National Library of Scotland) in 1875. It has since been lost, which is regrettable, because " Five Dissertations " was never published.[3]

Hume's 1772 letter to Strahan is neither clear nor full on why " Five Dissertations " was not published. All he says in reference to " Of Suicide " and " Of the Immortality of the Soul " is, first, that they " were printed by Andrew Millar about seventeen Years ago, and . . . from my abundant Prudence I suppress'd [them] "; and, second, that, " They were printed ; but it was no sooner done than I repented ; and Mr Millar and I agreed to suppress them at common Charges. . . ." While there is no reason to doubt the truth of these statements, it is plain that Hume was not telling the whole truth. His " abundant Prudence " is evident in his

---

[1] P. H. Stanhope, *History of England* (London 1836–54), III, 242.
[2] RSE, VII, 45.
[3] All that is known about this lost copy is contained in T. H. Grose's account in the " History of the Editions," prefixed to *Phil. Wks.*, III, 71.

original disinclination to publish these " two obnoxious Dissertations " at all ; yet the question arises, why, once he had allowed them to be printed, did he again change his mind ? The lost bound copy of proof sheets referred to above provides some evidence. On it was attached a note initialled " A.R.," presumably standing for Allan Ramsay. The note opened : " This book contains a piece of Mr. D. Hume's, of which there is, I believe, but another copy existing. Having printed the volume as it here stands, Mr. Hume was advised by a friend, to suppress the Dissertation upon Suicide ; which he accordingly did." The combined testimony of Hume and Ramsay, therefore, is to the effect that the suppression took place in two stages, " Of Suicide " preceding " Of the Immortality of the Soul," and that it was effected by Hume himself voluntarily in the name of prudence after friendly persuasion. The persuasion, there is some reason to believe, came from Adam Smith.

Yet even Hume and Ramsay combined do not tell the complete story of the suppression, for they fail to mention pressure, if not intimidation, from official sources. The basic facts of this new phase are provided in an unprinted letter by William Warburton, who had been dogging Hume ever since 1749—if not since 1739. Warburton's letter of 14 February 1756 to the Reverend Thomas Balguy of St John's College, Cambridge, is the earliest known reference to the suppression :

> Hume has printed a small Vol : which is suppressed, & perhaps forever,— on the *origin of Religion,* on *the Passions, on suicide,* & on the *immortality.* The Vol. was put into my hands & I found it as abandoned of all virtuous principle, as of all philosophic force.—I believe he was afraid of a prosecution, & I believe he would have found one : For the Attorney is now in a disposition to support the religious principles of Society, and with vigour.—He finds a generous connivance, infamously abused—and the other day he told me, he was going *to support & defend us.*—I said *it was high time.* The person marked out for prosecution is one Annet, a Schoolmaster on Tower hill, the most abandoned of all two legged creatures.[1]

Here, then, is a different version of the suppression and one which is supported by further testimony.

Dr William Rose, as one of the editors of the *Monthly Review,* kept a close check on the literary pulse, and, as a friend of Hume's, was in a position to know the inside story of the 1756 suppression.

---

[1] This letter [II, No. 32] appears in a collection of three MS volumes of Warburton's letters transcribed in 1863 by James Crossley. A fourth volume is an " Abstract " of the letters to Balguy. The four Crossley volumes are now in the University of Texas Library, the legacy of Dr R. H. Griffith.

His statement, though appearing as late as 1784, provides valuable substantiation of Warburton's :

> The Writer of this article knows that the essays here mentioned [" Of Suicide " and " Of the Immortality of the Soul "] were written by Mr. Hume. That almost thirty years ago they made a part of a volume, which was publicly advertised to be sold by Mr. Millar ; that, before the day fixed for publication, several copies were delivered to some of the Author's friends, who were impatient to see whatever came from his pen ; that a noble Lord, still living, threatened to prosecute Mr. Millar, if he published the essays now before us ; that the Author, like a bold veteran in the cause of infidelity, was not in the least intimidated by this menace, but that the poor bookseller was terribly frightened, to such a degree, indeed, that he called in all the copies he had delivered, cancelled the two essays, and with some difficulty, prevailed upon Mr. Hume to substitute some other pieces in the room of those objected to by the noble Lord ; that, by some means or other, however, a few copies got abroad, and have been clandestinely circulated. . . . [1]

How is this testimony of Warburton and Rose to be reconciled with that of Hume and Ramsay? To begin with, there is the connexion between Warburton and Millar. Late in 1755 Warburton had announced to Balguy that Millar was to be his publisher for the future. And undoubtedly Millar, in accordance with well-established publicity practice of the eighteenth-century booksellers, had distributed copies of " Five Dissertations " in advance of publication to people influential in the world of letters. A copy, therefore, was put into Warburton's hands. Exactly what happened then is conjectural ; but it seems likely that Warburton brought it to the attention of several officials, governmental and ecclesiastical, and demanded action. One of these officials was the Attorney General, William Murray, whose acquaintance with Hume over the Annandale tutorship has previously been noted. A second official was the Lord Chancellor, Philip Yorke, Earl of Hardwicke, who earlier in his career, when Attorney General, had prosecuted several deistic writers. A third official was Thomas Sherlock, Bishop of London, and Warburton's ecclesiastical superior. I should further conjecture that after these interviews Warburton informed Millar that the Church of England would demand, and that the government would agree to, a prosecution if the book was published. No trace has been found of the alleged threatening letter from Hardwicke.

Later hearsay accounts of the 1756 suppression actually refer to an official prosecution ; but of that there is no evidence whatsoever and it is probably a fabrication. The reactions of Hume and

[1] *Monthly Review*, LXXX (1784[1]), 427. For the attribution to Rose, see Nangle *The Monthly Review . . . Indexes*, p. 99, No. 1400.

Millar to Warburton's intimidation are problematical, but the result is clear. Millar must have been a man of some strength of character as he had boldly brought out the *Works* of Lord Bolingbroke in 1754, yet two years later he apparently exerted his influence over Hume to suppress the " two obnoxious Dissertations " and to tone down some passages in the " Natural History of Religion." For his part, Hume had already yielded to friendly persuasion to suppress one of the dissertations, and although a great exponent of the freedom of the press, desired neither controversy, notoriety, nor martyrdom. He had, in addition, good reason to believe that at the coming General Assembly of the Church of Scotland in May 1756 he would be investigated as an infidel writer ; and a publicly ordered suppression at London would play into the hands of the Scottish Highflyers and make it difficult for his friends in the Moderate Party to defend him.[1] For these reasons Hume might reluctantly have been inclined to give in ; his hand, moreover, may have been forced bv an ultimatum from Millar. At all events, " Five Dissertations " was suppressed in part voluntarily and in part under pressure. " The liberty of the press is not so secured in any country, scarce even in this," Hume acknowledged a few years later, " as not to render . . . an open attack of popular prejudices somewhat dangerous."

With the excision of the two essays of suicide and immortality, however, " Five Dissertations " was again reduced to three ; " and I wrote," therefore, Hume goes on to say in the 1772 letter to Strahan, " a new Essay on the Standard of Taste, to supply their place." This essay was finished in the spring or summer of 1756. The completed work, now entitled *Four Dissertations*, was published on schedule, Monday, 7 February 1757—but not without further action on the part of Warburton and further problems of composition and of suppression on the part of Hume.

Once again, prior to publication, a copy of the book was put into Warburton's hands. Not satisfied with the omission of the two essays and with the revision of some passages of the " Natural History of Religion," the truculent Warburton wrote to Millar on 7 February. This time he did not threaten a public prosecution, but he bullied for a voluntary suppression and hinted his intention of bringing out a devastating reply :

Sir, I supposed you would be glad to know what sort of book it is which you are about to publish with Hume's name and yours to it. The design of the first essay [that on natural religion] is the very same with all Lord Bolingbroke's, to establish *naturalism*, a species of atheism, instead of religion :

[1] See Ch. 25, below.

and he employs one of Bolingbroke's capital arguments for it. All the difference is, it is without Bolingbroke's abusive language.

All the good his mutilation and fitting it up for the public has done, is only to add to its other follies, that of contradiction. He is establishing atheism ; and in one single line of a long essay professes to believe Christianity. All this I shall show in a very few words in a proper occasion.

In the meantime, if you think you have not money enough, and can satisfy your conscience, you will do well to publish it ; for there is no doubt of the sale among a people so feverish, that to-day they burn with super-stition, and to-morrow freeze with atheism. But the day of the publication and the *fast day* will be in admirable contrast to one another.

I dare say you knew nothing of the contents ; but the caution of poor Mr. K[incaid ?] was admirable on a like occasion with this very man, Hume. He wrote to Mr. K. to offer him a copy, that had nothing to do with religion, as he said. Mr. K. replied, that might be ; but as he had given great offence, and he (Mr. K.) was himself no judge of these matters, he desired to be excused.

You have often told me of this man's moral virtues. He may have many, for aught I know ; but let me observe to you, there are vices of the *mind* as well as of the *body* ; and I think a wickeder mind, and more obstinately bent on public mischief, I never knew.[1]

The " mutilation " of the " Natural History of Religion " noticed by Warburton, is a clear reference to two short passages prudentially changed by Hume. They do not amount to much, merely altering phraseology that might conceivably have led to the charge of blasphemy.[2] In February or March 1757 Hume laconically remarked to Adam Smith : " You have read all the Dissertations in Manuscript ; but you will find that on the natural History of Religion somewhat emended in point of Prudence. I do not apprehend, that it will much encrease the clamour against me."

In May Warburton made good his threat to Millar by bringing out anonymous *Remarks on Mr. David Hume's Essay on the Natural History of Religion : Addressed to the Rev. Dr. Warburton.* The dissimulation lay in the fact that the remarks, originally made by Warburton on the margin of Hume's book, were pieced together with an introduction by the Reverend Richard Hurd. Although boasting to Hurd that, " I will trim the rogue's jacket, at least sit upon his skirts," Warburton's answer to Hume is limited to abuse —" a puny Dialectician from the North . . . who came to the attack with a beggarly troop of routed sophisms." Hume, on hints from Millar, soon saw through the hoax and linked together the names of Hurd and Warburton. The latter, Hume assured Millar, was a " low Fellow. . . . And any thing so low as Warburton, or his Flatterers, I shoud certainly be ashamd to

---

[1] *Warburton's Unpublished Papers,* pp. 309–10. [2] See below, Appendix E, p. 618.

engage with." When writing his own life in 1776, however, Hume permitted himself to describe the *Remarks* as having been written " with all the illiberal Petulance, Arrogance, and Scurrility, which distinguishes the Warburtonian School. This Pamphlet," he added, " gave me some Consolation for the otherwise indifferent Reception of my Performance." Warburton's pamphlet is remembered today solely through Hume's outburst.

' One other feature of the publication of *Four Dissertations* remains to be mentioned, the dedication " To the Reverend Mr. Hume, Author of *Douglas*, a Tragedy." It will suffice to say here that this dedication involved David Hume in a controversy raging in Scotland over the propriety of a minister's writing a play and of ministers' attending the performances.[1] The chief consequence of the affair so far as *Four Dissertations* is concerned was that that work received wide publicity with the scandalmongers spreading rumours concerning the suppression of 1756. Yet the suppression, involving so eminent a figure as Hume, could hardly have been kept quiet under any circumstances.

Among the ephemeral addresses, admonitions, ballads, letters, plays, and songs dealing with the controversy over *Douglas* during the first half of 1757, many mention Hume by name and no fewer than six allude to the suppressed dissertations. *The Usefulness of the Edinburgh Theatre Seriously Considered* is heavily ironical :

> Another advantage peculiar to the *North-British* stage is not so well known, but no less true. To this we owe the cure of that dark and desperate wound given through David's sides to the liberty of the press. The public need not now lament the suppression of his celebrated essay on the *lawfulness of suicide* : This is more beautifully represented in the character of *Lady Barnet*, who throws herself over a rock with more than *Roman* courage. Nor need we mourn the loss of his incomparable treatise on the *mortality of the soul*, while viewing Glenalvon nobly *risking eternal fire*. It is hoped the next Production of our Reverend author will solace us too for the want of the 'Squire's third and last essay, on the *advantages of adultery*, that we may have a complete triumph over the impotent malice of the late Ch[ancello]r [Hardwicke] and the B[isho]p of L[ondo]n [Sherlock], who murdered these real essays in cold blood.

The mysterious reference to a suppositious essay of Hume's on adultery is repeated in another of the *Douglas* squibs and in several of the notices appearing after the death of Hume. It may merely have been based upon scattered passages in his printed works ; or it may be the truth that, among the essays he had written without ever intending to publish, there was one on the subject of adultery. Hume's intriguing remark of 1757 may just be meant seriously : " I believe I shall write no more History ; but proceed directly to attack the Lord's Prayer & the ten Commandments & the single Cat ; and to recommend Suicide & Adultery : And so persist, till it shall please the Lord to take me to himself." [1]

Even before the publicity ensuing from the *Douglas* affair of 1757, news of the suppression had already leaked out. In Scotland, the Reverend George Ridpath heard about it and made the following entry in his diary, 4 June 1756 : " Robert [Turnbull] . . . confirmed what Brown had before been telling me, that David Hume had got printed at London a Collection of Atheism which his bookseller Andrew Millar dares not sell." [2] Notoriety of the suppressed " Collection of Atheism," it would seem, was also being used to promote the sale of the *Treatise* in London, for John Noon and M. and T. Longman, the original publishers, advertised that work in the *Daily Advertiser* of 26 January 1756 and the *London Evening Post* of 10 February. [3]

The " two obnoxious Dissertations " themselves, the primary cause of the suppression and of most of the ensuing notoriety, remained to plague Hume throughout the rest of his life. For the suppression, it turned out, was not complete. Andrew Millar, despite his promise to Hume to cut out the two essays and to burn the sheets, succumbed to importunity from the eminent in the world of letters and allowed an indeterminate number of copies to get into circulation. As early as 27 May 1756 Hume responded to a request from Millar : " I have no Objection to Mr Mitchels having a Copy of the Dissertations." Mitchell, it will be remembered, had been a classmate of Hume's at Edinburgh University, and the two had always maintained cordial relations. Moreover, what made Mitchell particularly safe at the moment was that he had just been appointed British Ambassador to the court of Frederick the Great and had left London on 17 April. Mitchell's copy, then, was the only copy authorised by Hume beyond one or two that he kept for himself.

Yet during the course of years the existence of several other copies came to his attention. From Paris he wrote to Millar in May 1764 in regard to one of these :

---

[1] NHL, p. 43. The " single Cat " is presumably the single Catechism of the Anglican Church (1549–1604) as distinct from the two of the Presbyterian, the Shorter and Larger Catechisms (Westminster Assembly, 1647).   [2] Ridpath, p. 73.
[3] Noon had previously advertised the *Treatise*, 7 and 9 Dec. 1754 in the *Daily Advertiser*, identifying it as " By the Author of The History of Great Britain, now published in Quarto."

I never see Mr Wilkes here but at Chapel, where he is a most regular, & devout, and edifying, and pious Attendant. I take him to be entirely regenerate. He told me last Sunday, that you had given him a Copy of my Dissertations, with the two which I had suppressd ; and that he forseeing Danger from the Sale of his Library, had wrote to you to find out that Copy and to tear out the two obnoxious Dissertations. Pray how stands that Fact ? It was imprudent in you to intrust him with that Copy : It was very prudent in him to use that Precaution : Yet I do not naturally suspect you of Imprudence, nor him of Prudence. I must hear a little farther before I pronounce.

Millar's reply tells a different story and one unmistakably closer to the truth :

I take Mr Wilkes to be the same man he was acting a part. He has forgot the story of the Dissertations. The fact is upon importunity I lent to him the only copy I preserved and for years never could recollect he had it till his Books came to be sold. Upon this I went immediately to the Gentleman that directed the sale, told him the fact & reclaimed the two Dissertations which were my Property. Mr Coates who was the person imediatly delivered me the volume and so soon as I got home I tore them out and burnt them that I might not lend them to any for the future. Two days after Mr Coats sent me a note for the volume as Mr Wilkes had desired it should be sent to him to Paris. I returned the volume but told him the two Dissertations I had tore out of the volume and burnt being my Property. This is the Truth of the matter and nothing but the truth. It was certainly imprudent for me to lend them to him.[1]

Living in Paris temporarily as a political outlaw from Britain, John Wilkes thus had returned to him a copy of " Five Dissertations " from which the two essays had been torn out.

Two years later the existence of two other copies came to light. Allan Ramsay's note on the bound copy of proof sheets, which has already been quoted in part, proceeds : " A copy, however, had somehow got into the hands of Mr. Muirhead, a man of letters, who had made a very valuable collection of books. Mr. Hume, after the death of Mr. Muirhead,[2] employed me to beg that copy from the nephew, who very politely delivered it up." This copy, then, was returned to Hume, but what he did with it is unknown. Ramsay's note concludes : " Upon this Mr. Hume gave me leave to keep the present copy, which he had lent me ; I promising not to show it to any body." Ramsay's copy has disappeared ; but its place in the National Library of Scotland has been taken by a copy of *Four Dissertations* in which are bound printed sheets of the original edition of the two

[1] RSE, vi, 31. Humphrey Cotes was Wilkes's friend and agent.
[2] Muirhead died on 12 June 1766.

suppressed dissertations with final corrections in the hand of Hume.[1] Pasted on the flyleaf is Hume's own note : " This Book is to be considerd as a Manuscript and to be deliverd to Mr Strahan according to my will." Strahan, however, acting on the advice of several of Hume's friends after his death, refused to publish, and so no authorised edition of the two essays has ever appeared.

The two essays, however, were published surreptitiously from some of the copies that Millar had let slip through his fingers. The story of one of these and of a transcript made from it illustrates how such publication may have been effected. In a letter [2] of 17 December 1776, James Beattie, Professor of Moral Philosophy at Aberdeen University, and one of Hume's bitterest opponents, informed Mrs Elizabeth Montagu that " These Essays were printed ; but suppressed by the Bookseller, in consequence of a threatening message from the Lord Chancellor Hardwicke." He then proceeds : " A few copies, however, got abroad ; one of which is in the hands of a Gentleman in England, who gave me this account, and promised to let me have a copy in manuscript, as he could not part with the printed one." One or another of such loose copies was responsible for the first publication of the two essays in a French translation of 1770.

Items X and XI of a miscellany entitled *Recueil Philosophique ou Mélange de Pièces sur la Religion & la Morale* are " Dissertation sur l'immortalité de l'âme " and " Dissertation sur le suicide," respectively, and are described as " Traduite de l'Anglois." Modern scholars attribute the editorship to Jacques André Naigeon, and the translation of the Hume essays to Baron d'Holbach. How Holbach got a copy seems unascertainable ; but this much can be said with certainty, that he did not use the copy that had been forwarded to Wilkes at Paris, because from that copy the two items had been cut out. Hume, it is also clear, knew nothing about this French translation, as it remains unmentioned in his 1772 letter to Strahan, where he lists all the copies that he knew about and where he is up in arms about the report of an unsanctioned English edition. About this last Hume comments : " I am not extremely alarmd at this Event, but if threatening him [" some rascally Bookseller "], woud prevent it, I woud willingly employ that means. I am afraid all will be in vain ; but if you know him, be as good as [to] try what can be done ; and also learn from what hand he had the Copy. I believe an Injunction in Chancery might be got against him ; but then I must acknowledge

[1] NLS, MS 509.   [2] In Aberdeen University Library, Beattie MSS.

myself the Author and this Expedient woud make a Noise and render the Affair more public. In a post or two, I may perhaps get you more particular Intelligence of the Booksellers Name."

Report of the publication, however, proved groundless. Richardson and Urquhart had advertised in the *London Chronicle* of 4 January 1772 a collection entitled *Beauties of the Magazines*, which contained, among many other items, "some Essays by D. Hume, Esq. not inserted in the late Edition of his Works." But the essays in question prove to be the innocuous "Of Impudence and Modesty" and "Of Love and Marriage," which Hume had withdrawn from his collected works in 1764, and "Of Avarice," which he had withdrawn in 1770.

Although Hume's deathbed efforts to induce Strahan to bring out an authorised posthumous edition were not successful, an unauthorised version appeared at London in 1777, entitled simply *Two Essays* and with no indication of either author or publisher. The outrageously high price of five shillings for a mere forty-one pages is convincing proof that some unscrupulous person was seeking to profit by the notoriety of the suppressed work of the recently deceased Hume. The name of David Hume was first put to the suppressed essays in 1783 in *Essays on Suicide, and The Immortality of the Soul, Ascribed to the late David Hume, Esq. Never before published. With Remarks, intended as an Antidote to the Poison contained in these Performances. By the Editor*, a work as disingenuous as the former. Several other editions and attacks in English, French, and German appeared before the close of the century.

In view of the tumult occasioned by *Four Dissertations*, it is not easy to interpret the remark of Hume in his autobiography concerning the "indifferent Reception of my Performance." Certainly he could not have meant that it went unnoticed, for the *Critical Review* of February 1757 observes that "The ingenious Mr. Hume, already so well known to the learned world by his four volumes of essays, and the history of Great Britain, hath once more excited the attention of the public by the dissertations now before us. . . ."

The "Natural History of Religion" inevitably received most attention. In addition to the Warburton-Hurd scurrility, the work was respectfully handled in two anonymous pamphlets by the Reverends Caleb Fleming and Thomas Stona. Fleming's *Three Questions Resolved. . . . With a Postscript on Mr. Hume's Natural History of Religion* appeared in 1757 and Stona's *Remarks upon the Natural History of Religion*, the following year. Stona finds no conviction in Hume's arguments, while Fleming, to the contrary, concludes that Hume " has finely exposed superstition and popery : professeth himself an advocate of pure theism, and so far as he is a theist, he cannot be an enemy to pure Christianity." More judicious than either is the review by William Rose in the *Monthly* for February 1757. Hume's first dissertation, concludes Rose, " abounds with shrewd reflections, and just observations, upon human nature ; mixed with a considerable portion of that sceptical spirit, which is so apparent in all his works ; and with some insinuations, artfully couched, against the Christian religion." In Scotland, Ridpath, who had first heard Hume's dissertations described as a " Collection of Atheism," after reading the work himself, commented, " The *Natural History of Religion* is entertaining, and has curious things in it, but its tendency is bad."

What is the teaching of David Hume in the three controversial works on religion ? The two suppressed essays need not delay us long, because, however cogent in argument, they are but popular renditions of principles implicit in all his thinking on the subject. " Of the Immortality of the Soul " opens with a statement of its thesis :

> By the mere light of reason it seems difficult to prove the Immortality of the Soul. The arguments for it are commonly derived either from *metaphysical* topics, or *moral*, or *physical*. But in reality, it is the gospel, and the gospel alone, that has brought life and immortality to light.

" Of Suicide," purporting to accept philosophical theism, argues the incapacity of man to commit any act against the divine will :

> 'Tis impious, says the old Roman superstition, to divert rivers from their course, or invade the prerogatives of nature. 'Tis impious, says the French superstition, to inoculate for the small-pox, or usurp the business of providence by voluntarily producing distempers and maladies. 'Tis impious, says the modern *European* superstition, to put a period to our own life, and thereby rebel against our creator ; and why not impious, say I, to build houses, cultivate the ground, or sail upon the ocean ? In all these actions we employ our powers of mind and body, to produce some innovation in the course of nature ; and in none of them do we any more. They are all of them therefore equally innocent, or equally criminal. . . .
> 'Tis a kind of blasphemy to imagine that any created being can disturb the order of the world or invade the business of providence ! It supposes, that that Being possesses powers and faculties, which it received not from its creator, and which are not subordinate to his government and authority. A man may disturb society no doubt, and thereby incur the displeasure of the Almighty : But the government of the world is placed far beyond his reach and violence.

This is eloquence, no doubt—but is it philosophy ?   The debate continues to this day and competent authorities still disagree.

The " Natural History of Religion " is quite another matter. Alone of all the so-called dissertations it is truly a work of scholarship.   The problem presented is essentially modern, and to 'Hume should go the credit for being the first great modern to treat of it systematically.   From it arises much modern thinking on the subject.   Again blandly assuming the validity of philosophical theism in the form of the argument from design, Hume restricts himself to the " origin of religion in human nature," that is, to the psychological bases of religion.   The limitations that he actually placed upon the argument from design had already been stated in Section XI of the *Enquiry concerning Human Understanding* and were to be further developed in the posthumous *Dialogues concerning Natural Religion.*[1]

The thesis of the " Natural History of Religion " is the paramount one in all of Hume's philosophical productions, the essential a-rationality of human nature, here applied specifically to religion, which is treated as a natural product of the human mind.   Sentiment, emotions, affections precede reason and philosophy in human nature and always remain dominant.   The monotheistic deity of Christianity is, therefore, an advanced concept far beyond the primitive or popular mind in early or in late ages.   The popular mind is ruled by hopes and fears, and out of these hopes and fears creates a religion of multifarious outside controlling forces ;   in short, polytheism.   Polytheism thus antedates monotheism, and even after the general acceptance of philosophy still survives in the popular mentality.

The doctrine of one supreme deity, the author of nature, is very ancient, has spread itself over great and populous nations, and among them has been embraced by all ranks and conditions of men : But whoever thinks that it has owed its success to the prevalent force of those invincible reasons, on which it is undoubtedly founded, would show himself little acquainted with the ignorance and stupidity of the people, and their incurable prejudices in favour of their particular superstitions.   Even at this day, and in *Europe*, ask any of the vulgar, why he believes in an omnipotent creator of the world ; he will never mention the beauty of final causes of which he is wholly ignorant : He will not hold out his hand, and bid you contemplate the suppleness and variety of joints in his fingers, their bending all one way, the counterpoise which they receive from the thumb, the softness and fleshy parts of the inside of his hand, with all the other circumstances, which render that member fit for the use, to which it was destined.   To these he has been long accustomed ; and he beholds them with listlessness and unconcern.   He will tell you of the

[1] See Ch. 40, below.

sudden and unexpected death of such a one : The fall and bruise of such another : The excessive drought of this season : The cold and rains of another. These he ascribes to the immediate operation of providence : And such events, as, with good reasoners, are the chief difficulties in admitting a supreme intelligence, are with him the sole argument for it.

The historical comparison of polytheism with monotheism yields some unexpected results. If the former is bad philosophy and the latter is good philosophy, their actual influences upon human conduct have not been entirely so adjusted. Polytheism breeds superstition : " full scope is given, for knavery to impose on our credulity, till morals and humanity be expelled the religious systems of mankind." At the same time, polytheism naturally requires toleration and " renders all the various deities, as well as rites, ceremonies, or traditions, compatible with each other." Monotheism works conversely : high moral standards are held up, but intolerance sets in, for " the worship of other deities is regarded as absurd and impious." This intolerant spirit breeds controversy and war. Furthermore, all popular religions, as distinct from philosophical religions, have a bad influence on morality. " It is certain, that, in every religion, however sublime the verbal definition which it gives of its divinity, many of the votaries, perhaps the greatest number, will still seek the divine favour, not by virtue and good morals, which alone can be acceptable to a perfect being, but either by frivolous observances, by intemperate zeal, by rapturous exstacies, or by the belief of mysterious and absurd opinions." It is, therefore, the duty of the philosopher to combat all influences which so degrade human nature and to seek for himself the " calm sunshine of the mind." But such is the general infirmity of human nature that that seems possible only for the few and is precariously maintained even by them.

What a noble privilege is it of human reason to attain the knowledge of the supreme Being ; and, from the visible works of nature, be enabled to infer so sublime a principle as its supreme Creator ? But turn the reverse of the medal. Survey most nations and most ages. Examine the religious principles, which have, in fact, prevailed in the world. You will scarcely be persuaded, that they are any thing but sick men's dreams : Or perhaps will regard them more as the playsome whimsies of monkies in human shape, than the serious, positive, dogmatical asseverations of a being, who dignifies himself with the name of rational.

Yet if the historical and psychological perspectives prove so devastating, what is the philosopher to do ? What conclusions can he come to ? Can he remain satisfied with those conclusions ?

The whole is a riddle, an aenigma, an inexplicable mystery. Doubt, uncertainty, suspence of judgment appear the only result of our most accurate scrutiny, concerning this subject. But such is the frailty of human reason and such the irresistible contagion of opinion, that even this deliberate doubt could scarcely be upheld ; did we not enlarge our view, and opposing one species of superstition to another, set them a quarrelling ; while we ourselves, during their fury and contention, happily make our escape into the calm, though obscure, regions of philosophy.

CHAPTER 25

DRUM ECCLESIASTIC

*" They intend to give me over to Satan, which they think
they have the power of doing."*

" PHILOSOPHERS must judge of the question ; but the Clergy have
already decided it, & say he is as bad as me. Nay some affirm him
to be worse, as much as a treacherous friend is worse than an open
Enemy." So wrote David Hume in June 1751 to Michael Ramsay
in reference to Henry Home's recent *Essays on the Principles of
Morality and Natural Religion.* Thus early began the campaign of
the religiously zealous against the two Humes, a campaign that
was to come to a head in 1755 and again in 1756. The irony of
linking together the " Great Infidel " with his professed refuter was
lost, we may be sure, upon neither of them, particularly since
Home was an elder of the church and, after 1752, a judge of the
supreme civil court of Scotland. He had, moreover, piously concluded his *Essays* with a prayer, which, although common talk had
it that it had been dictated by the Reverend Hugh Blair, was not
deemed sufficiently Christian by the Evangelical Party. David and
Henry were linked together in yet another way, as the friends and
political helpmeets of the Moderate Party. It was thus up to the
Moderates to defend both of them against untoward attacks of the
rival faction out of friendship, ecclesiastical polity, and their own
philosophy of humanity.

One such attack is of particular interest :

Maxim XII. As to the world in general, a moderate man is to have great
charity for Atheists and Deists in principle, and for persons that are loose
and vicious in their practice ; but none at all for those that have a high
profession of religion and a great pretence to strictness in their walk and
conversation.

Maxim XIII. All moderate men are joined together in the strictest bond
of union, and do never fail to support and defend one another to the utmost,
be the cause they are engaged in what it will.

So was solemnised the union of the two Humes with the Moderates
by one of the shrewdest and wittiest of the opposition, the Reverend
John Witherspoon, who later became President of the College of
New Jersey (now Princeton) and the only clerical signatory of the
Declaration of Independence. Witherspoon's satire on the

Moderates, entitled *Ecclesiastical Characteristics : Or, The Arcana of Church Policy*, " Being an Humble Attempt to open up the Mystery of Moderation. Wherein is shewn a plain and easy way of attaining to the *Character* of a *Moderate Man*, as at present in repute in the *Church* of *Scotland*," ran through five editions between 1753 and 1763. Such excellent caricature is it that the originals remain easily discernible.

Several others of the list of thirteen alleged Moderate maxims run :

Maxim I. All ecclesiastical persons, of whatever rank . . . that are suspected of heresy, are to be esteemed of great genius, vast learning, and uncommon worth ; and are, by all means, to be supported and protected.

Maxim II. When any man is charged with loose practices, or tendencies to immorality, he is to be screened and protected as much as possible. . . .

Maxim III. It is a necessary part of the character of a moderate man, never to speak of the Confession of Faith but with a sneer ; to give sly hints, that he does not thoroughly believe it ; and to make the word orthodoxy a term of contempt and reproach.

Maxim IV. A good preacher must not only have all the above and subsequent principles of moderation in him, as the source of every thing that is good ; but must, over and above, have the following special marks and signs of a talent for preaching. 1. His subjects must be confined to social duties. 2. He must recommend them only from rational considerations, viz. the beauty and comely proportions of virtue, and its advantages in the present life, without any regard to a future state of more extended self-interest. 3. His authorities must be drawn from heathen writers, *none*, or as few as possible, from Scripture. 4. He must be very unacceptable to the common people.

Maxim V. A minister must endeavor to acquire as great a degree of politeness, in his carriage and behaviour, and to catch as much of the air of a fine gentleman, as possibly he can.

Maxim VI. It is not only unnecessary for a moderate man to have much learning, but he ought to be filled with a contempt of all kinds of learning but one ; which is to understand Leibnitz's scheme well ; the chief parts of which are so beautifully painted, and so harmoniously sung by Lord Shaftsbury, and which has been so well licked into form and method by the late immortal Mr. H[utcheso]n.[1]

The affair of the Church of Scotland *versus* the two Humes was part of the internal struggle for supremacy within that church, which led, with the ultimate triumph of the Moderates, to what is known as " The Awakening of Scotland." The liberal or Moderate Party was wresting the leadership away from the Evangelical Party, commonly known as the Popular or Highflying Party. Repressive methods and stern discipline in church rule (as, for example, in the backing of lay patronage rather than of popular

[1] Witherspoon, *Works*, 2nd edn., rev. and corr. (Philadelphia 1802), III, 211–56.

election) and liberal ideas in intellectual matters characterised the Moderates. Their programme included the steering of the ministry away from the rigid bibliolatry of seventeenth-century Presbyterianism in the direction of enlightened thinking and preaching. The educational scheme of the Moderates included the ill-fated *Edinburgh Review*, of which only two numbers appeared, January–July 1755 and July 1755–January 1756. The founders of this periodical were the ministers Blair, Jardine, and Robertson, together with Adam Smith and Alexander Wedderburn, the last of whom was apparently the prime mover and all of whom were the good friends of David Hume. Yet, for fear of untowardly offending the pious, and despite Witherspoon's Maxims XII and XIII, the greatest name in British letters was excluded from the list of sponsors and his recent *History of the Stuarts* passed unnoticed in its reviews.

At first Hume did not even share the secret of the identities of the anonymous editors. Henry Mackenzie tells how he learned :

> The merits of the work strongly attracted his [Hume's] attention, and he expressed his surprise, to some of the gentlemen concerned in it, with whom he was daily in the habit of meeting, at the excellence of a performance written, as he presumed, from his ignorance on the subject, by some persons out of their own literary circle. It was agreed to communicate the secret to him at a dinner, which was shortly after given by one of their number. At that dinner he repeated his wonder on the subject of the Edinburgh Review. One of the company said he knew the authors, and would tell them to Mr Hume upon his giving an oath of secrecy. " How is the oath to be taken," said David, with his usual pleasantry, " of a man accused of so much scepticism as I am ? You would not trust my Bible Oath ; but I will swear by the το καλον and the το πρεπον never to reveal your secret." He was then told the names of the authors and the plan of the work, but it was not continued long enough to allow of his contributing any articles.[1]

Jardine and Blair reviewed the books on religion. True to the principles of Moderatism, they praised those works which were well reasoned and well written and damned those which were effusions of enthusiasm and centos of Biblical quotations. The discourses of Thomas Sherlock, Bishop of London, for instance, are praised because of the " order, perspicuity, and simplicity " of the style and because " They rouse the virtue of Christians by proper motives, and put to silence the doubts and cavils of Infidels by most convincing arguments." A sermon by Robertson, himself one of the editors, gives rise to the following approbation :   " We are likewise persuaded that to every reader

---

[1] Home-Mackenzie, I, 25.

of taste and judgment, this discourse will appear to be a very proper specimen of the great improvement that has been made in the art of preaching in this part of the united kingdoms." To Francis Hutcheson, author of *A System of Moral Philosophy*, posthumously published, is rendered the " praise of having removed a great deal of rubbish from the science of morals, and of having treated his subject in a very distinct and masterly manner."

The Evangelical school of divines is roughly handled, together with Seceders and Hutchinsonians, the latter, in opposition to the prevailing Newtonianism, having sought to derive natural philosophy from Scripture alone. Thomas Boston the Younger and the late Ebenezer Erskine are singled out for special attack. *A Collection of Sermons* of the latter provoked the following :

> Such are the sentiments, such the stile and manner of these discourses, which, however acceptable they may be to such readers as are more apt to be catched with sound than sense ; are in our opinion but little calculated to promote that reformation of manners, which ought to be one great object of every preacher's attention : On the contrary, they are so full of childish conceits and fancies ; the sublime doctrines of christianity are treated of, in such a low and ludicrous manner, and are so disfigured with obscure and sometimes indecent allegories ; there is so little morality, and such a peevish and illnatured spirit to be found in them ; that we are sorry to say, they seem to be rather calculated to do harm than good ; to expose religion to contempt and ridicule, instead of recommending the love and practice of it.

Boston's " vulgarisms " of style are branded as " indecent in conversation, but much more so in a solemn discourse from the pulpit. . . ."

The educational campaign of the Moderates conducted through the pages of the *Edinburgh Review* was not, to be sure, ignored by the Highflyers. They responded with letters to the newspapers, a sixpenny *View of the Edinburgh Review, pointing out the Spirit and Tendency of that Paper,* and, for those who could not afford the sixpence, a cheap redaction of the *View*, entitled *A New Groat's Worth of Wit for a Penny.* Boston's letter printed in the *Edinburgh Evening Courant* of 27 April 1756 is a fair sample of the tone of the counter-attack. It ends : " Tho' I am not so much *Shaftsburian,* as to think Ridicule the Criterion of Truth, yet it is my Opinion, that when a certain Set of Men presume to palm themselves as *Censors and Critics* upon the World, the Way to make them blaze is to oppose them : But if Nobody condescends to take any Notice of them, they quickly go out like the Snuff of a Candle, leaving a Stench behind them." The editors of the *Edinburgh Review* had already come to the same conclusion regarding the

Highflyers and had suspended publication in the hope of preventing Boston and company from blazing into white heat. But the *Review*, as will shortly be seen, had already struck several moderate blows in the pending affair of the two Humes.

That affair had really got under way in 1753 with the publication of *An Estimate of the Profit and Loss of Religion, Personally and publicly stated : Illustrated with References to Essays on Morality and Natural Religion.* This 392-page quarto was chiefly aimed, as is evident from the title, at Lord Kames under the pseudonym of " Sopho," but has also much to say about " his assistant *David Hume* Esq." The purpose is stated in the conclusion : " If religionists can do atheists no good, it is a duty incumbent upon all who believe in God the Father Almighty, to hinder these demented men from doing harm to others." And three questions are proposed for the serious consideration of ministers and ruling elders of the Church of Scotland :

I. Whether public teachers of atheism and infidelity are to be continued and acknowledged members of their church, or to be excommunicated ?

II. Supposing that it is their opinion that such ought to be excommunicated; whether the sentence ought to be pronounced by an inferior, or by the supreme church-judicature ? The reason of this question is, that infidelity is offensive to all christians, and atheism to all that believe a God and a providence.

III. Which is best and most expedient, to take the case of such doctors and teachers, residing within their ecclesiastical jurisdiction, immediately into judicial consideration ; or to delay for some time, (and how long ?) in hopes of their *coming to themselves,* and of their spontaneous repenting and retracting their errors ? [1]

This anonymous and abusive seeker of infidel blood was the Reverend George Anderson, a retired Army chaplain and at the moment chaplain to Watson's Hospital in Edinburgh. In 1755 David Hume described him to Allan Ramsay as " the godly, spiteful, pious, splenetic, charitable, unrelenting, meek, persecuting, Christian, inhuman, peace-making, furious Anderson, [who] is at present very hot in pursuit of Lord Kames. He has lately wrote a letter to his son, which they say is a curiosity. He mentions his own great age, which leaves him no hopes of being able long to survive the condemnation of that atheistical, however just, judge [Kames]. He therefore leaves me as a legacy to his son, and conjures him, as he expects his blessing, or the blessing of Heaven, never to cease his pursuit of me till he bring me to condign punishment. Is not this," suggests Hume, " something like Hamilcar,

---

[1] [George Anderson], *Estimate of the Profit and Loss of Religion* (Edinburgh 1753), pp. 389–91.

who swore Hannibal on the altar to be an eternal enemy to the Roman people ? "

The significance of Anderson's beating of the " drum ecclesiastic " in 1753 did not pass unnoticed, for it was probably no coincidence that the 1754 *Scots Magazine* opened with a reprint of Hume's essay " Of the Liberty of the Press." The comment of the editor is pointed :

> The subject will appear of great importance to every one who sets a just value on a privilege by which the people of this island are happily distinguished, and on which depends the preservation of their liberties, civil and religious. It is by the exercise of this privilege that such works as this subsist ; and by such works as this the privilege is preserved and strengthened : for a brave people will always acknowledge the justness of the maxim which is elegantly expressed in our motto, and will encourage and support everyone of their fellow subjects whose behaviour is strictly conformable to it :
>
> *Ne quid falsi audeat, ne quid veri non audeat.*[1]

Professor John Stewart's attack on the two Humes in 1754, previously described, was probably only isolated and not part of the concerted effort of the persecuting cabal, who despite the warning of the *Scots Magazine* were fully prepared in 1755 to institute proceedings against the Humes, judge and librarian.

On 23 May, the day following the opening of the General Assembly, there appeared *An Analysis of the Moral and Religious Sentiments contained in the Writings of Sopho, and David Hume, Esq ; Addressed to the consideration of the Reverend and Honourable Members of the General Assembly of the Church of Scotland.* Though sometimes attributed to Anderson, the pamphlet was the work of the Reverend John Bonar of Cockpen, a member of the High-Flying Party.[2] Bonar brings up for the consideration of the Assembly, " the public attack which in this country has of late been made on the great principles and duties of natural and revealed religion, in the works of DAVID HUME, Esq ; and in the essays of an author who has been distinguished by the name of SOPHO. It is true," he acknowledges, " one of these gentlemen has some how got the character of a fine writer, and subtle disputant ; and the latter, it is said, holds a place of great importance in this country, and even bears an office in your church. But as I am well assured, that neither the art of the one, nor the power of the other, will avail to overthrow those principles they so boldly attack ; so I am persuaded, that by neither will ye be diverted from doing your duty ; and your duty unquestionably it is, to give warning of the

---

[1] Cicero.
[2] Henry Higgs, *Bibliography of Economics, 1751–1775* (Cambridge 1935), No. 1131.

poison contained in these volumes, and to testify to the whole Christian world your abhorrence of such principles." [1]

The stated method of the book is " to analyse the works of these celebrated authors, giving their own expressions under the different heads to which they seem to belong." Kames is disposed of in eleven propositions and Hume in six. Hume is alleged to have maintained :

(1) All distinction betwixt virtue and vice is merely imaginary. (2) Justice has no foundation further than it contributes to public advantage. (3) Adultery is very lawful, but sometimes not expedient. (4) Religion and its ministers are prejudicial to mankind, and will always be found either to run into the heights of superstition or enthusiasm. (5) Christianity has no evidence of its being a divine revelation. (6) Of all the modes of Christianity Popery is the best, and the reformation from thence was only the work of madmen and enthusiasts.

There is little need to comment on these propositions except to remark that Hume might perhaps have acknowledged half of them as plausible inferences from his publications.

Bonar's charges remained unanswered until 6 June, four days after the rising of the Assembly, when there appeared *Observations upon a Pamphlet, intitled An Analysis of the Moral and Religious Sentiments contained in the Writings of Sopho, and David Hume, Esq ; &c*, which was from the pen of the Reverend Hugh Blair, although Wedderburn, Wallace, and Kames may have had a hand in it. Two principles of Moderatism are laid down as indisputable : first, " The freedom of inquiry and debate, tho' it may have published some errors to the world, has undoubtedly been the source from whence many blessings have flowed upon mankind . . ." ; second, " The proper objects of censure and reproof are not freedom of thought, but licentiousness of action ; not erroneous speculations, but crimes pernicious to society. . . ." Blair's comment on the treatment afforded Hume is apposite :

Were the author of the *Analysis* to meet with no greater degree of candour than he has shewn to others ; it were not unnatural to conclude, from his extracts from Mr. *Hume*, that his zeal for religion was more affected than real. Every fair reader must admit, and regret, that there are to be found in the writings of this elegant Author some principles by no means consistent with sound doctrine : There was therefore no necessity for ascribing to him positions which he does not advance, in order to support the charge of irreligion against him. This conduct of the author of the *Analysis* can scarcely be accounted for ; as it manifestly leads to do harm rather than good to the cause he pretends to support.[2]

[1] [Bonar], *Analysis*, p. 2.　　　[2] [Blair], *Observations*, pp. 1–2, 22.

Both of these pamphlets were, of course, remarked upon in the *Edinburgh Review,* as were also two others. One of these was a clearly demented attack on Hume under the grim and suggestive title of *The Deist Stretched Upon a Death-Bed ; Or a Lively Portraiture of a dying Infidel.* The author is identified by the reviewer as Andrew Moir, a former student of divinity, who had been expelled from the university and excommunicated from the church. The second was the Reverend Robert Traill's *Qualifications and Decorum of a Teacher of Christianity* on which the reviewer comments, in passing, that the writer " takes occasion to animadvert pretty smartly on the author of a late Essay concerning miracles."

To return to the 1755 General Assembly, where the question of the infidelity of the two Humes had been referred to the Committee of Overtures. On 28 May that body presented a resolution which was passed unanimously by the Assembly :

> The General Assembly of the Church of Scotland being filled with the deepest concern on account of the prevalence of Infidelity and Immorality, the principles whereof have been to the Disgrace of our Age and Nation, so openly avowed in several Books published of late in the Country and which are but too well known amongst us do therefore judge it proper and necessary for them to express the utmost abhorrence of those impious and infidel principles which are subversive of all Religion Natural and Revealed and have such pernicious Influence on life and morals, and they do earnestly recommend it to all the Ministers of this Church to exercise the Vigilance and to exert the Zeale which becomes their Character, to preserve those under their Charge from the Contagion of these abominable Tenets, and to Stir up in them a Solicitous concern, to guard against them, and against the Influence of these who are Infected with them.[1]

This pious declaration against sin is proof that the Moderates under the capable guidance of William Robertson had won an important victory. Personalities had been by-passed, and the witch hunt was not up immediately.

Hume announced the victory in a letter to Allan Ramsay : " The last Assembly sat on me. They did not propose to burn me, because they cannot. But they intend to give me over to Satan, which they think they have the power of doing. My friends, however, prevailed, and my damnation is postponed for a twelvemonth. But next Assembly will surely be upon me." Hume's nonchalance over the matter is indicated in the further remark : " Meanwhile I am preparing for the Day of Wrath, and have already bespoken a number of discreet families, who have promised to admit me after I shall be excommunicated." The

---

[1] " Act against Infidels and Immorality," in " Assembly Register, 1755." Glasgow University Library.

question of Lord Kames had not been settled either. " They will not at once," continued Hume to Ramsay, " go to extremities with him, and deliver him over to Satan, without any preparation or precaution. They intend to make him be prayed for in all the churches of Scotland during six months, after which, if he do not give signs of repentance he is to be held as *anathema maranatha*."

Behind the façade of humour, however, the situation was sufficiently serious. It was evident that the campaign of persecution against the two Humes was not over, that the bigots would soon be at it again. The young Wedderburn, attending his first General Assembly as a ruling elder, is said to have remarked about the general censure that, while the names of his two friends were not included, they would consider it *brutum fulmen*.[1] The discreet families that would admit David Hume after excommunication would be legion but the atmosphere might still be uncomfortable. David was, indeed, beginning to revive thoughts once more of retiring into sunny and sociable France ; and no man can be happy at the thought of being driven out of his native country. His friend Harry would be harder hit and would undoubtedly be compelled to resign his judgeship. While no direct action had been taken against him at the Assembly, he had been slighted by the pointed omission of his name from its customary place on the list of the Commission.[2] Little wonder that he was preparing to pull in his metaphysical horns somewhat if the situation got too hot. David, for his part, made no such preparations.

The new campaign got under way early. Discounting the rattle of small-arms fire in the newspapers and periodicals throughout the summer and autumn of 1755, the first siege gun boomed in January 1756 with the publication of the anonymous *Letters on Mr Hume's History of Great Britain*. The announcement in the *Scots Magazine* was careful to explain that, " In these letters two passages relative to the reformation are particularly considered." The historical problem involved has already been looked into. The point of interest here is that Hume was represented by the Reverend Daniel MacQueen of the Old Kirk in Edinburgh as a Scot who held Protestantism in contempt and who thought that not all features of Catholicism were completely repugnant.

The pivotal date of the 1756 campaign was the opening of the General Assembly at Edinburgh on 20 May. Five days previously

---

[1] Campbell, *Chancellors*, VI, 19n.
[2] N. Morren, *Annals of the General Assembly of the Church of Scotland* (Edinburgh 1840), II, 60.

the furious Anderson finally made good the promise of 1753 to write a " dissertation upon excommunication " by bringing out anonymously at Glasgow *Infidelity a Proper Object of Censure*. The sub-title states the thesis : " Wherein is shewn, The indispensible Obligation that lies upon Church-rulers to exercise the Discipline instituted by Christ, upon such *avowed Infidels* as have been solemnly initiated Members of the Christian Church by Baptism ; and, if irreclaimable, to cast them out of the Christian Society." The advertisement in the *Edinburgh Evening Courant* points out that, " The above is particularly recommended to the Perusal of the Members of the ensuing General Assembly, as it is possible the Question which was before the last Assembly may be this Year resumed.—Whether the Infidel Writers of our own Country shall be censured or not ? " In the pamphlet Anderson reviews the case of the two Humes and strenuously attacks the Moderate principles laid down in Blair's *Observations upon the Analysis*. Though by no means relinquishing Lord Kames, Anderson presses the charge against David Hume as an " avowed Infidel " because he had been honest enough to put his name to some of his publications.

On 20 May, with the opening of the General Assembly, Anderson continued the assault upon the Humes under cover of *A Remonstrance against Lord Viscount Bolingbroke's Philosophical Religion. Addressed to David Mallet, Esq ; the Publisher*, a work which he saw fit to acknowledge, possibly because the Viscount was dead and his publisher was in London. The *Monthly Review* concludes comment on this work with the exclamation : " What a happiness is it, that the spirit and zeal of this northern Divine can only manifest themselves in print ! " [1] The very same day appeared *A View of the Edinburgh Review*, which has already been presented as a frontal attack upon the Moderate Party. On 25 May, while the Assembly was still seated, Traill's refutation of Hume's character of the clergy was advertised once again in the papers, and on the 27th, MacQueen's letters on Hume's *History*.

While the Highflyers were laying down this barrage of publications, the Moderates were entrenching themselves and planning defensive strategy against the expected all-out assault. The Reverend Alexander Carlyle tells of their plans for " Assembly parties " to be held at the Carriers' Inn in the lower end of the West Bow, a most unlikely place for distinguished ecclesiastics. The landlord had been ordered to lay in twelve dozen of claret at 18s. a dozen, and an attempt was made to insure strict privacy.

---

[1] *Monthly Review*, xvi (1757[1]), 242.

" But we could not be concealed," Carlyle admits with a certain complacency ; " for, as it happens in such cases, the out-of-the-way place and 'mean house, and the attempt to be private, made it the more frequented—and no wonder, when the company consisted of Robertson, Home, Ferguson, Jardine, and Wilkie, with the addition of David Hume and Lord Elibank, the Master of Ross, and Sir Gilbert Elliot." [1] For the duration of the 1756 Assembly, the Carriers' Inn was known as the *Diversorium*.

New techniques were introduced by the Highflyers. First, the question of prosecuting infidels was not brought up directly on the floor, but at a meeting of the Committee of Overtures on 27 May. After a general discussion of modern infidelity, it was recommended that the inquiry be confined to one David Hume, Esq., who had been bold enough to acknowledge some of his infidel writings publicly. Here was a second departure : to concentrate on Hume because he could be charged with infidelity, whereas Kames could be charged with perhaps no more than heterodoxy ; the decorum of charging a judge of the supreme court with anything seems also to have been given due consideration. Accordingly the following day at the meeting of the committee, a written overture was presented :

> The General Assembly, judging it their duty to do all in their power to check the growth and progress of infidelity ; and considering, that as infidel writings have begun of late years to be published in this nation, against which they have hitherto only testified in general, so there is one person, styling himself *David Hume, Esq.*, who hath arrived at such a degree of boldness as publicly to avow himself the author of books containing the most rude and open attacks upon the glorious Gospel of Christ, and principles evidently subversive even of natural religion and the foundations of morality, if not establishing direct Atheism ; therefore the Assembly appoint the following persons, ——, as a committee to inquire into the writings of this author, to call him before them, and prepare the matter for the next General Assembly.[2]

The speech of the reverend mover of the overture being well received, young Wedderburn, impetuous as always, rose to his feet to move the dropping of the name of David Hume. Good sense, bitter irony, and sharp sarcasm characterise Wedderburn's maiden speech [3] before the Assembly. He opened :

> I trust, Moderator, it is wholly unnecessary that I should follow the example of the reverend divine who has preceded me, by making any profession of zeal for the pure Presbyterian church established in this country. I say with him, " peace be within her walls ! prosperity within her bulwarks ! " Our object is the same, and we can only differ as to the means by which that object

---

[1] Carlyle, p. 324.   [2] Morren, *Annals of the General Assembly*, II, 86–7.
[3] Campbell, *Chancellors*, VI, 21–5

is, under Providence, to be attained. Now, notwithstanding the headlong fervour I see prevailing in some quarters, and the impatient eagerness to crush Mr. Hume with the censures of the Church, I would humbly advise the venerable Assembly to dismiss the overture, and to trust to reason and scripture for the refutation of his errors.

Have all who are now disposed to concur in this vote, inquired the orator, read the writings to be condemned ? By how many have they been understood ? Will all agree upon the interpretation of them ?

I would, with all possible respect, request you to recollect the procedure in another meeting of intelligences, with which I would venture to compare this venerable Assembly only for eloquence, and a deep theoretical knowledge of divine truth. When these casuists, though of more than mortal grasp of thought

> . . . reason'd high
> Of providence, fore-knowledge, will and fate,
> Fixed fate, free will, fore-knowledge absolute,
> They found no end, in wandering mazes lost.

The opinions complained of, however erroneous, are of an abstract and metaphysical nature—not exciting the attention of the multitude—not influencing life or conduct. . . . What advantage do you really expect from the course which is proposed ? Is there any chance of your convincing Mr. Hume, and of making him cry *peccavi*? Alas ! I am afraid he has withstood the reasonings of the subtlest philosophers who have attempted to refute him ; and you can hardly expect that a miracle should again be performed—one of your number being specially empowered to speak to him.

Suppose you pass the sentence of the Greater Excommunication upon him ? " But this is a sentence which the civil power now refuses to recognize, and which will be attended with no temporal consequences. You may wish for the good of his soul to burn him as Calvin did Servetus ; but you must be aware that, however desirable such a power may appear to the Church, you cannot touch a hair of his head, or even compel him against his will to do penance on the stool of repentance." What if he laughs at your anathemas ? What if he is grave and sarcastic ? Finally, are you sure of your jurisdiction in this case ? You assert that Mr Hume is not even a Christian. " Why are you to summon him before you more than any Jew or Mahometan who may happen to be travelling within your bounds ? Your *liber*, as we lawyers call it, is *ex facie* inept, irrelevant, and null, for it begins by alleging that the defender denies and disbelieves Christianity, and then it seeks to proceed against him and to punish him as a Christian. . . . For these reasons I move ' That while all the members of the General Assembly have a just abhorrence of any doctrines or principles tending to infidelity or to the prejudice of our holy religion, that they drop the overture anent Mr. David Hume, because it would not, in their judgment, minister to edification.' "

Wedderburn, so the account goes, was " rather roughly handled by several clerical speakers who followed " ; and one can well believe it. This young upstart of an elder with his technical legal jargon insolently presuming to instruct the grey-haired clergy in matters of ecclesiastical polity ! Yet when reports of the speech reached David Hume back at the *Diversorium*, his heart must have warmed over the good intentions of the orator, while at the same time he must have winced over the impolicy of the management. Wiser heads than Wedderburn's, however, were prepared to continue the battle before the committee. The astute William Robertson manoeuvered things so skilfully as to be able to close the debate himself after two days of discussion. At the last, many of the clergy left the meeting in order to avoid casting their vote on one side or the other. The question was finally put : *Transmit the overture to the Assembly or not ?* The negative carried, 50 to 17 ; and Wedderburn's resolution was then passed.

Perhaps one of the coolest and wisest of the Moderates who sat on the sidelines and did not enter into the debate but who voted on the right side, was the Reverend Robert Wallace. Exercised over the prejudiced account of the debates in the Committee of Overtures which had been given to the public in the June number of the *Scots Magazine*, Wallace composed his own account, " for I will confess I was clearly of the opinion that those who contended against the churches meddling in this matter had by far the better in the Debate."

Although prepared for publication, Wallace's pamphlet was ultimately suppressed. The legend on the manuscript title-page, " Printed Edinburgh 1756," is sufficient evidence of the author's intention, however, and of how nearly he carried it out. The title reads : " The necessity or expediency of the churches inquiring into the writings of David Hume Esquire and calling the Author to answer before the spiritual Courts " ; and it was provided with an explanatory subtitle : " Considered with some reflections on Christians being occasionally in company with scepticall or Infidel Writers ; In which there are some animadversions on the account in the Scotch Magazine for June, 1756, of the Debates in the Committee of Overtures of the Generall

Assembly 1756 concerning these subjects." Little known as it is, Wallace's manuscript [1] provides inside information about a crucial incident in the life of David Hume as well as about the state of Enlightenment in Scotland in 1756.

Wallace argues that the defeat of the overture must not be construed as a victory of laymen over clergymen. Quite the contrary! "I can only remember one or two of the Ruling Elders who spoke upon it (I think few of them were present.) And of the ministers not only a great majority opposed the overture but ministers of all sorts & complexions, young and old ministers, ministers who scarce agreed in any other Vote during the whole Assembly and such as think very differently in many other matters of Ecclesiasticall Polity & Which is in a particular manner remarkable many opposed it from contrary views & upon Contradictory principles." But lest he give the wrong impression, Wallace continues : "Att the same time it was evident to all that were present that not one of the members of the committee justified any of Mr Humes errors, not one of them asserted the innocence of error, or that errors as well as vices were not the proper object of church Censure. The whole debate turned on the necessity or expediency of inquiring into the writings of Mr Hume or calling the author before the church Courts."

The problem, then, becomes simply one of expediency : whether the said David Hume is capable of edification and whether proceedings should be instigated against him? Given the character of the man and of the age, a church censure, argued the Moderates, is not the best way of convincing him of his errors. "Is it not more probable," Wallace inquires, "that he might be convinced of his errors by the private Conversation of such of the Clergy as chance to be of his acquaintance or by a treatise written cooly with soft words & strong arguments than by authoritative censures and condemnations? " A miracle may be wrought upon Hume, he is willing to concede, "but shall we act contrary to all probability upon the presumption that a miracle will be wrought or will it be said that Mr Hume has been such a sincere and impartiall enquirer after truth that a miracle ought to be wrought for his sake ? "

After all, why is Mr Hume, in particular, singled out for investigation? If the doctrine of church censure is valid, "why do not the Gentlemen who insist on this argument act impartially and carry it the full length it ought to go ? Is he the only man

---

[1] EU, Laing MSS, ii, 97.

who deserves such correction ? . . . Are there not many criminalls in higher & lower life, vitious, immoral, and abandoned in their lives, Drunkards, revellers, whore-mongers, adulterers, contemners of Christian worship, despisers of Christian Piety, open supporters of impious, lewd, and immoral Principles in companies ? . . . Why will they not therefore exercise Discipline impartially against all who in the abstract deserve high Censures according to the Christian law, or will they stop short att David Hume and a few calm, contemplative, wronghead writers ? "

So far as Mr Hume's writings are concerned, they are less well known than is his name. Trial in a church court could only have the effect of making them better known, read, and discussed by everyone. The conduct of such a trial, again, would in itself be difficult. " Mr Hume is a very subtile man himself and believed to be allowed the help of lawyers. Whenever a trial is made the supporters of the overture will perhaps find more than they imagine att present how much such subtile men can puzzle & perplex. They will have a particular advantage in having Mr Hume's writings for their text for this Gentleman, having so much of the sceptick in him, rarely admitts any thing on any one side of a Question but he finds out something to plead for the other. This humour appears in his Philosophy, Divinity, History, & every thing else."

Technically, it must be acknowledged that Mr Hume, having never formally renounced his baptism, is still within the church ; yet practically, he has done so in his writings, and " there can be no necessity nor advantage in ejecting such persons by a formall judgement." The modern world, avers Wallace, is no longer the small Christian society that it once was and conditions have vastly changed. Let us, therefore, he urges, " exercise this Discipline in as far as it is practicable in our times, which must be confessed to be greatly corrupted. But let us not exercise a Discipline that will do more harm than good. . . . Let us allways remember that if the Doctrine & worship & essentiall parts of the Government of a church are kept pure, Discipline may be greatly relaxed att the same time that the Church may continue a happy instrument in the hands of Providence of comforting & confirming the pious, reclaiming the wicked, & may serve as a mighty bulwark against vice, errors, & impiety."

Most of all was Wallace disturbed by the " impotent & ridiculous attack " upon the good character of certain clergy-men " that they had been seen accidentally standing in the streets with Mr Hume or had been known to have been in companies where he was present, especially as this Gentleman, with all his errors, is confessed to be a very honest and benevolent man in common life & entertaining in Conversation." Is there, then, no difference " between being in company with Drunkards or other kinds of debauched persons and with such as are ingenious, well bred, decent in conversation, respectfull to the company where they are, & ready & able to enter upon any usefull or proper Disquisition ? One can scarce be in company with Debauched men in their debauchries without partaking with them, att least without seeing & hearing what is abominable ; even in their sober hours little can be expected from them but what is gross & sensual." On the contrary, " Ingenious Gentlemen who have a turn for reading & study are much more agreeable & usefull companions. A good man may often both be entertained and instructed by them and whatever may be the character in other respects of Gentlemen who are well bred & of a sober & honest character in common life, pious & good men will seldom be in any danger from their conversation."

Furthermore, " the Clergy need not be affraid to encounter Gentlemen of this sort be they ever so scepticall or heterodox. If we suppose that they are rather wrongheaded than wronghearted, that in their enquiries into nature & Philosophy they have been led into mistakes by some unlucky train of thinking, that they are far from rejoicing in such mistakes, that they secretly lament (which I know well is the case with some) ; if we suppose that they look upon themselves as unfortunate on this very account & are sorry they cannot have the same comfortable view of nature and providence with other Gentlemen ; if they are disposed to converse on these subjects with learned & ingenious men, 'twere pity to debarr them from the company of any of the Clergy with whom they would wish to converse." This passage, it is to be remarked, is a fine tribute to Hume and provides insight into his character and thinking on the subject of religion.

Wallace also argues, conversely, that the clergy ought not to set themselves completely apart from the rest of human society. To society they belong because it is society they are trying to influence. And, like other decent members of society, it is the prerogative of the clergy, if they choose, to drink, to dance, to go to the theatre and other places of entertainment, to talk to intellectuals even including infidels.

The pamphlet ends with the plea for all to be charitable,

tolerant, and broad-minded, in a word, enlightened. The arguments here developed by Wallace, the practical applications of the philosophy of the Moderates, are probably much the same as those that he had touched upon in 1745 in his memorable defence of Hume before the Ministers of Edinburgh and the Town Council in connexion with the university professorship. If Hume knew of the present effort, he might well have echoed his remark of eleven years previous : " Mr Wallace's Conduct has been very noble & generous ; & I am much oblig'd to him." Why Wallace's pamphlet was not published is not known, yet it is likely that the Robertson junto urged him to let well enough alone and not to risk stirring up the bigots any further.

Undoubtedly Robertson was steering the politic course, for the bigots were still at it, hammer and tongs. The indefatigable and unrelenting Anderson, with another change in tactics, suddenly turned on Lord Kames once more, lodging a complaint against the printers and publishers of the *Essays on the Principles of Morality and Natural Religion* before the Presbytery of Edinburgh. While the process was still before that body, however, the aged chaplain died. Fleming, Kincaid, and Donaldson, the printers and publishers of Kames's book, judiciously insisted that the action should not be dropped for lack of prosecutor. As a result, the case was dismissed in January 1757 with the usual pious generalisations engineered by the Moderates.

By that time the rigidly righteous were off on another tack and content to let the affair of the two philosophical Humes lag. They had something more immediately important at hand, the case of a Moderate clergyman who had actually treated with the devil by writing a play and of Moderate clergymen who had compromised themselves by attending the public performances. Such unchristian outrages demanded their full attention. The new campaign involved David Hume and Lord Kames indirectly ; the prime object of attack was the Reverend John Home. The affair of the two Humes consequently became in 1757 the affair of the three Humes.[1]

Lord Kames, in the meanwhile, had been re-examining his philosophical tenets. Astonishingly unlearned in metaphysics, Kames was being instructed by Wallace that his doctrine. of necessity, which had caused so much commotion, had been promulgated by many unquestionable Calvinistic authorities, including the great Jonathan Edwards in New England. Acting

[1] See Ch. 26, below.

on this new information, Kames—probably again with the aid of Blair—brought out anonymously in December 1756 *Objections against the Essays on Morality and Natural Religion Examined.* Strangely enough, however, Jonathan Edwards was not happy about this use of his name and authority. In 1758 he authorised the publication at Edinburgh of *Remarks on the Essays, on the Principles of Morality, and Natural Religion,* in which he repudiated all connexion with Kames. By 1758 Kames had really begun to see the error of his ways, and in a second edition of the *Essays* partially retrenched. With the third edition in 1778, the most obnoxious of his philosophical positions were recanted. So ended the unfortunate excursion of an amateur into the bog of metaphysics and theology.

No amateur in philosophy, David Hume sat tight and made no retrenchments and no recantations. In the spring of 1757 he advised Adam Smith that " For my Part, I expect that the next Assembly will very solemnly pronounce the Sentence of Excommunication against me : But I do not apprehend it to be a Matter of any Consequence. What do you think ? " Unfortunately we do not know what Smith thought, but probably it was much the same as Allan Ramsay, who had written to Hume from Rome before the 1756 affair broke : " . . . I have heard nothing about the farce that was to have been acted in the General Assembly. . . . Whether the farce was clapt or hiss'd, I beg you to make offer of my best services to Lord Kames and his Lady." [1]

In regard to the 1756 affair, it is meet to make two inquiries : first, what was the final result of the attempt at excommunication ? and, second, what would have been the consequence had David Hume actually been excommunicated ? The first question has been answered by Ramsay of Ochtertyre, and there is little reason to dissent materially from his judgement :

> Like most other processes against heresy, this attempt did no good to the cause of religion. On the contrary, the two culprits were more caressed and admired than ever, and by none more than by the moderate clergy, who took care to disclaim the principles of the one, and to apologise for those of the other. It was even pretended that Lord Kames was chiefly reprehensible for pushing the doctrine of Calvin too far. In a word, this rash and feeble attempt to check the progress of freethinking, convinced the philosophers of Edinburgh that they had no longer anything to dread from the Church courts.[2]

Though essentially sound, Ramsay does perhaps exaggerate the effects. For David Hume in 1757 still expected further attention from the Church courts, and for years complained of the restrictive climate of opinion of his native country. His classic statement was made to Adam Smith in 1759 : " Scotland suits my Fortune best, & is the Seat of my principal Friendships ; but it is too narrow a Place for me, and it mortifies me that I sometimes hurt my Friends." Here is no exulting, but rather a sober evaluation of the facts.

The second question, what would have been the consequences had David Hume actually been excommunicated in 1756, is not idle speculation because consideration of it in the broad view, rather than in the personal as hitherto, leads to the realisation of the fundamental reasons why the sentence was not pronounced. Re-examination of the history of the affair will also serve as reminder that the leading clergy of the Moderate Party were fully aware of its high seriousness, and that in their endeavour to muffle the " drum ecclesiastic " they were fighting, not merely for their friends, but for the future of Scottish civilisation.

Charges of heterodoxy hurled against clerics by brother clerics are not the present concern, but rather the question of free speech and free publication by laymen. Scotland had been reasonably free in this regard since the shameful hanging at Edinburgh in 1697 of Thomas Aikenhead, a youth still in his teens, for having orally ridiculed some passages in the Old Testament. In England, the quaint custom of getting a grand jury to condemn infidel or blasphemous books to be publicly burnt at the hands of the common hangman still survived and was occasionally resorted to. In England also, as late as 1762, the elderly schoolmaster, Peter Annet, was sentenced to stand in the pillory and to suffer a year's hard labour for his *Free Enquirer*. But these are isolated cases and offer no just parallel to the case of Hume.

For David Hume was no unknown schoolboy and no elderly schoolmaster. He was a man whose intellect had already made a terrific impact upon thinking men throughout Europe, who was recognised as a great genius, and who was generally admitted to be Britain's leading man of letters. The initial personal discomfort that he might have suffered as the result of excommunication, therefore, is of little import. The ensuing reactions of the outside world, it is certain, would have worked less against him than against the church and the country that had attempted to stifle his thinking and his publishing. Scotland would have become the laughing-stock of England, and Britain would have become the laughing-stock of Europe. Hume himself would have become the martyred hero of both Britain and Europe.

To speculate further is perhaps less rewarding—whether the witch hunt would have been up for good in Scotland and civilisation set back a century?—or whether public reaction would have swept the Moderates back into control of the Church? Suffice it to say that the leaders of the Moderates were cognisant of the implications of the situation and realised that they were not dealing solely with the issue of their friend David Hume. As enlightened clergymen they knew the dangers of a martyr of the Enlightenment within their Church or even within Scotland. For martyr of the Enlightenment is certainly what David Hume would have been and his every word, consequently, would have been incendiary. The Moderates knew that their infidel friend might possibly be provoked into becoming a Scottish Voltaire dedicated to a war of extermination, *écraser l'infâme*. They knew also that he could be lulled into inaction.

CHAPTER 26

THE BARD AND THE CHURCH

" Did you ever hear of such Madness & Folly as our
Clergy have lately fallen into ? "

IF 1755 and 1756 had brought out-and-out victories for the
Moderate Party, 1757 brought but Pyrrhic victory. In this fracas,
as in the others, David Hume was involved, and with him also,
Henry and John. It was an affair of the three Humes, as the
witty Witherspoon scathingly pointed out :

*On a little name, which has produced three great heroes to support the
declining glory of Britain.*

An impious j[udge], a wicked sceptic sage,
A stage-playing priest ; O glorious NAME and AGE !

Witherspoon's comment on the epigram blasts at Moderatism
and its union with the name of Hume :

What is the glory and honour of any state or church ? Is it not politeness
in the one, and mildness and moderatism in the other ? Do not then these
three gentlemen promote the glory of this church and nation ? Is it not our
honour to tolerate the two first ? Is it not both our honour and happiness to
have produced, nourished, and to possess the last ?

In reference to Hume's " character " of the clergy Witherspoon inquires, " Now, who are the clergy with whom D[avid]
H[ume] corresponds, and from whom he must form a judgment
of the rest ? Are they overburdened with apparent sanctity ?
Their enemies themselves will not so much as pretend it. I hope
therefore, that in the next edition he will either wholly leave out
this passage, or at least make an honourable exception in favour
of the *moderate* clergy of his own dear country, where all things are
at present going on so very wondrous well." The writings of
Hume, Witherspoon alleges,[1] have transformed Scotland into " a
land of players " and opened the door " for the admission of the
clergy to that improving amusement "—which brings us back to
the Reverend John Home and his *Douglas ; a Tragedy*, for which,
it seems, David was held responsible.

---

[1] [Witherspoon], *The Moderator*, No. II [Edinburgh 1757].

Soon after his adventures in helping to suppress the Rebellion, John Home had composed a poetical drama taken from a subject in Plutarch and entitled *Agis*. But the great David Garrick in London refused to bring it on the stage. Back in Scotland the disappointed poet turned to a native theme, that of *Douglas*. In October 1754 David Hume was able to announce that, " I have seen John Humes new unbaptized Play ; and it is a very fine thing. He now discovers a great Genius for the Theatre." A few days later Hume exulted over Scotland's new dramatic genius in a letter to Professor Joseph Spence of Oxford University :

> As you are a lover of letters, I shall inform you of a piece of news, which will be agreeable to you : we may hope to see good tragedies in the English language. A young man called Hume, a clergyman of this country, discovers a very fine genius for that species of composition. Some years ago, he wrote a tragedy called *Agis*, which some of the best judges, such as the Duke of Argyle, Sir George Lyttleton, Mr Pitt, very much approved of. I own, though I could perceive fine strokes in that tragedy, I never could in general bring myself to like it : the author, I thought, had corrupted his taste by the imitation of Shakespeare, whom he ought only to have admired. But the same author has composed a new tragedy on a subject of invention ; and here he appears a true disciple of Sophocles and Racine. I hope in time he will vindicate the English stage from the reproach of barbarism.

In February 1755 John once again mounted his good horse Piercy for London and presented the completed *Douglas* to Garrick. Once again the Englishman—" the best Actor, but the worst critic in the World " pronounced David Hume—rejected the offering as unsuited to the stage. As late as June, observed Elliot to Clephane, John's horse " has not yet recovered from his London journey. Poets always ride hard." [1] In Edinburgh the Moderate clergy rallied patriotically around their brother poet. The literary triumvirate of the Select Society, Lord Elibank, Lord Kames, and Mr David Hume, offered suggestions ; and revisions were effected. It was David Hume who in April 1756 voiced the determination of the Edinburgh men of letters that " our friend Hume's ' Douglas ' is altered and finished, and will be brought out on the stage next winter, and is a singular, as well as fine performance, steering clear of the spirit of the English Theatre, not devoid of Attic and French elegance." The decision to bring the tragedy on at Edinburgh was unprecedented, and marks the increasing growth of Scottish independence. In their fever over the literary aspects of *Douglas*, however, the Moderates neglected the possible ecclesiastical consequences,

---

[1] *A Genealogical Deduction of the Family of Rose of Kilravock* (Edinburgh 1848), p. 459.

for the Church of Scotland held a long record of opposition to stage-plays.

The *Edinburgh Evening Courant* of 4 December 1756 announced that,

> A new Tragedy called *Douglas*, written by an ingenious gentleman of this country, is now in rehearsal at the Theatre, and will be performed as speedily as possible. The expectations of the public from the performance are in proportion to the known talent and ability of the author, whose modest merit would have suppressed a Dramatick work which we think by the concurrent testimony of many gentlemen of taste and literature will be an honour to the country.

This advertisement is especially interesting in that it publicly injects the spirit of nationalism and suppresses the clerical character of the playwright. The company bringing out the play at the Theatre in the Canongate was English, and the leading actor and manager was West Digges. According to a well-known but not well-authenticated tradition, " the first rehearsal took place in the lodgings in the Canongate, occupied by Mrs Sarah Warde, one of Digges's company ; and that it was rehearsed by, and in presence of the most distinguished literary characters Scotland ever could boast of." The parts were taken by the cronies Hugh Blair, Alexander Carlyle, Adam Ferguson, John Home, David Hume, and William Robertson ; and the audience included Lord Elibank, Lord Kames, Lord Milton, Lord Monboddo, and the Reverends William Home and John Steele. " The company, all but Mrs Warde, dined afterwards in the Erskine Club, in the Abbey." [1]

The story of the distinguished amateur rehearsal sounds almost too pat to be true ; yet it is likely enough that, on one occasion or another, the coterie did get together to run over the play in order to prove that it was fitted for the stage. It is pleasant to think of the stout and awkward David Hume in the part of the young hero, Glenalvon, even if only as reader. Be that as it may, it was not long before the town was fully aware of the authorship of *Douglas* and of the notable group sponsoring its production. The humour of the situation was not neglected by the opposition.

A broadside, entitled simply *Theatre*, appeared shortly before the first performance on Tuesday, 14 December 1756, and is remarkable for naming David Hume as sole ticket-seller :

> As the Manager has been informed, That a Report prevails, that no Persons will be admitted into the Theatre on *Tuesday* the 14th instant, but

---

[1] Hill Burton, I, 420n.

Clergymen, at which Rumour many other Persons are offended ; He thinks it his Duty to acquaint the Public, That the Pit alone is particularly kept by order for the Fraternity. The boxes are already let to Ladies, (except the Box prepared for the Moderator) ; and there will be several vacant Places in them, which will no doubt be filled by Gentlemen who do not belong to that ancient and venerable society.

As the Novelty of the Sight, and Grandeur of the Preparations for their Reception in the Theatre, may reasonably be presumed to excite an extraordinary Curiosity ; to prevent the least Offence at any Distinction or Preference, the whole House is laid at one Price ; and the two Galleries will be elegantly illuminated with Sconces, &c. and hung with black. It is to accommodate the Public, and particularly such Brothers as may in case of a great Throng, not find Admittance below Stairs, or in the First Gallery, that the Upper Gallery is new benched, and ornamented in an elegant Manner, and is perfectly cleared from every Disorder and Indecorum it was formerly subject to ; and is rendered as warm, as decent, and as commodious as any Part of the House, no Expence being spared for the Mournful Occasion. . . .

No Person whatever (The Author Excepted) can be admitted behind the Scenes.

The whole to be concluded with a Solemn Farce, called the Address, never before acted ; where the Five principal Characters will be exhibited in their true Colours.

Tickets printed for the Occasion to be had at the Lodgings of D[avid] H[ume], Esq ; and no other Tickets will be received at the Door, nor will any Money be taken there.

Guards will be placed about the House, and a sufficient Number of Beadles with Flambeaus will attend the Avenues, for the Conveniency of the Brethren.

The performance, in accordance with the customary subterfuge employed since the Licensing Act of 1737, was advertised as " A concert of Music. After which will be presented (gratis) The New Tragedy Douglas. Taken from an Ancient Scots Story and Writ by a Gentleman of Scotland." On the morning of the 14th, a broadside Prologue to the long expected Tragedy of Douglas, As it is to be acted this evening in the theatre in the head of the Canongate damned Garrick :

> Now shall the English curse their Garrick's name,
> Who banish'd Douglas far from Drury-Lane,
> Nor would thy humble earnest pray'r regard,
> But void of merit the great work declar'd.

The immediate success of the " great work " was overwhelming, " and it is believed "—so runs the account in the Scots Magazine—" there never was so great a run on a play in this country. Persons of all ranks and professions crouded to it : and many had the mortification to find the house so full when they came to the door that they could not get in." A more intimate account reveals that " The applause was enthusiastic, but a better criterion of its merits was the tears of the audience, which the tender part of the drama drew forth unsparingly." Another is even more specific : " There was not, I believe, one dry eye in the whole house." Sad to relate, however, this last spectator may have been a little myopic, because George Wallace reports that " I was desired to bring a white handkerchief and yet I walked off dry-eyed. . . ." [1]

The Highflyers, as was to be expected, took a very different view of the matter, representing all drama, be it never so moral in tone, as a delusion of Satan. An official *Admonition and Exhortation* of the Edinburgh Presbytery was published on 5 January 1757 : " The opinion which the Christian church has always entertained of stage plays and players, as prejudicial to the interest of religion and morality, is well known ; and the fatal influence which they commonly have on the far greater part of mankind, particularly the younger sort, is too obvious to be called into question." On 2 February the Glasgow Wild Party gratuitously endorsed the action of their Edinburgh confreres : " The presbytery, deeply affected with this new and strange appearance, do think it their duty to declare, as they hereby do, that they agree with the Reverend presbytery of Edinburgh, in the sentiments published by them, with respect to stage-plays." [2] *Libels* or formal accusations were instituted at Edinburgh, not only against John Home, but also against Alexander Carlyle and others for merely having attended performances.

So the battle was on between Highflyers and Moderates. On reading the report from Glasgow, the Reverend George Ridpath caustically remarked, " it appears that these people continue the same fools they have been for a long, long period." The Presbytery of Duns, too, protested against the Edinburgh-Glasgow manifestoes, commenting : " We cannot allow ourselves to think that a thing, really criminal in itself, can be innocent or indifferent on the other side of the Tweed."

Here was a broil, which David Hume stirred up even more by rushing publicly to the defence of his namesake. *Four Dissertations* being nearly ready for publication by Millar in London, David, with the consent of John, determined upon a dedication " To the Reverend Mr. Hume, Author of *Douglas*, a Tragedy." This dedication—" the only one I ever wrote or

[1] *Scots Mag.*, XVIII (1756), 624 ; Home-Mackenzie, I, 38 ; *Letters of George Dempster*, pp. 25, 28.   [2] *Scots Mag.*, XIX (1757), 18, 48.

probably shall ever write, during the course of my Life "—was
an indictment of intolerance :

> It was the practice of the antients to address their compositions only to
> friends and equals, and to render their dedications monuments of regard and
> affection, not of servility and flattery. In those days of ingenuous and candid
> liberty, a dedication did honour to the person to whom it was addressed,
> without degrading the author. If any partiality appeared towards the patron,
> it was at least the partiality of friendship and affection.
>
> Another instance of true liberty, of which antient times can alone afford
> us an example, is the liberty of thought, which engaged men of letters, however
> different in their abstract opinions, to maintain a mutual friendship and
> regard ; and never to quarrel about principles, while they agreed in inclina-
> tions and manners. Science was often the subject of disputation, never of
> animosity. . . .
>
> I have been seized with a strong desire of renewing these laudable practices
> of antiquity, by addressing the following dissertations to you, my good friend :
> For such I will ever call and esteem you, notwithstanding the opposition,
> which prevails between us, with regard to many of our speculative tenets.
> These differences of opinion I have only found to enliven our conversation ;
> while our common passion for science and letters served as a cement to our
> friendship. I still admired your genius, even when I imagined, that you lay
> under the influence of prejudice ; and you sometimes told me, that you
> excused my errors, on account of the candor and sincerity, which, you thought,
> accompanied them.
>
> But to tell truth, it is less my admiration of your fine genius, which has
> engaged me to make this address to you, than my esteem of your character
> and my affection to your person. . . .

With all due respect to the good intentions of the two Humes,
it must be admitted that the dedication was inexpedient and
could only result in further inflaming the bigots. Hume himself
recognised " the Singularity of the undertaking," and his
Moderate friends the inexpediency. So on 20 January Hume
was forced to inform Millar :

> The Dedication of my Dissertations to Mr Hume was shown to some of his
> Friends here, Men of very good Sense, who were seiz'd with an Apprehension,
> that it wou'd hurt that Party in the Church, with which he had always been
> connected, and wou'd involve him, and them of Consequence, in the Suspicion
> of Infidelity. Neither he nor I were in the least affected with their Panic ;
> but to satisfy them we agreed to stand by the Arbitration of one Person, of
> great Rank & of known Prudence ; and I promis'd them to write to you
> to suspend the Publication for one Post, in case you shou'd have resolv'd to
> publish it presently.

On 1 February Hume could tell Strahan that, " You will probably
see it [the dedication] published in a few days " ; but, after the
appearance of *Four Dissertations* on the 7th, he had to explain
further to Mure of Caldwell :

Pray, whether do you pity or blame me most, with regard to this Dedication of my Dissertations to my Friend, the Poet ? I am sure I never executed any thing, which was either more elegant in the Composition, or more generous in the Intention : Yet such an Alarm seiz'd some Fools here (Men of very good Sense, but Fools in that Particular) that they assaild both him & me with the utmost Violence ; and engag'd us to change our Intention. I wrote to Millar to suppress that Dedication : Two Posts after I retracted that Order. Can any thing be more unlucky, than that in the interval of these four days, he shoud have opend his Sale, & dispos'd of 800 Copies ; without that Dedication, whence, I imagin'd, my Friend wou'd reap some Advantage, & myself so much Honor. I have not been so heartily vexd at any Accident of a long time. However, I have insisted that the Dedication shall still be publish'd.

Republication of the dedication in several of the weeklies and monthlies at both London and Edinburgh must have circulated it far beyond the sphere of those purchasing copies of *Four Dissertations*. During the following six months, David Hume could hardly have complained of lack of publicity, for the " paper bullets " of controversy, as George Dempster put it, were " flying with great vehemence."

Carlyle had entered the lists enthusiastically, first with *A full and true History of the Bloody Tragedy of Douglas, as it is now to be seen acting at the Theatre in the Canongate*, which was designed to raise the curiosity of the lower orders of society, and had the good effect of filling the house for an additional two nights, and secondly with *An Argument to prove that the Tragedy of Douglas ought to be publicly burnt by the Hands of the Hangman*, " which, in the ironical manner of Swift, contained a severe satire on all our opponents." [1] Ferguson, the new Keeper of the Advocates' Library, produced *The Morality of Stage-Plays Seriously Considered*, justifying the lawfulness of dramatic writings from the example of Scripture. Wedderburn is credited with having written several of the numerous ballads, broadsides, and skits ridiculing personalities among the fanatics. The leader of that party, the Reverend Alexander Webster, was the most vulnerable of all. Sandy's weakness for the bottle—Carlyle says he was " a five-bottle man "—led to the nickname of *Dr Bonum Magnum*. The pity of it, according to the wits in 1757, was that the doctor had made so many enemies by his opposition to *Douglas* that no one would drink with him during the ensuing Assembly. In the background of all this controversy, hovered Wallace, as usual, full of good council. As usual, also, Wallace penned the most discerning tract, which, as usual, he ultimately suppressed.

Wallace's manuscript is entitled " An Address to the Reverend

---

[1] Carlyle, p. 328.

the Clergy of the Church of Scotland By a Layman of their Communion on occasion of composing acting & publishing the Tragedy called Douglass." He remarks at the opening : " Some of you of late have appeared extremely zealous against Theatricall representations. . . . But I begin to suspect they intend to make a national Business of this matter & would have The General Assembly of the Church to interpose their Authority in a manner that will not be agreeable. I imagine this is a very wrong measure. I hope there shall be found a sufficient number of wise men who shall be able to prevent it. . . ." The consequences of such an action are carefully weighed :

If indeed the Generall Assembly could procure a totall suppression of the play house att Edinburgh, this would effectually answer their purpose. But before they attempt this they will find a very strong interest working against them. It will be the stronger that this noise about the playhouse will be considered as arising from the Clergy & such as are under their speciall influence. The British nation in generall are not very fond of the power of the Church. The Nobility & gentry will not incline to be totally Deprived of the entertainments of the theatre which they consider not only as innocent but improving. Whatever regard the Laity in Generall have for the pious and morall instructions of the Clergy, they do not choose to be Dictated to in their amusements & Diversions which they do not believe to be unlawfull. I think the season seems to be past for the Clergy to interpose by their Acts and Declarations. The calm and wiser part of them are certainly of this opinion. It is believed the wiser and more powerfull part of the Ruling Elders will be of the same mind and it is hoped notwithstanding the press or the policy which has given rise to much zeal all things will be managed with a just temper & moderation.[1]

All things were not, however, managed " with a just temper & moderation." The case against Carlyle was pressed hard by the bigots : he had been seen with players, had dined with them, had been present at a performance of the play. *The Lybell V. Mr. Carlyle. 1757* makes these accusations and cites a long inventory of witnesses to prove them. Amongst the laity named are Lord Elibank, Adam Ferguson, and " David Hume Esquire late Keeper of the Advocats Library in Edinburgh." Amongst the clergymen named are Blair, Home, and Robertson. Carlyle fought the action to the finish and won, first before the Synod, and finally, after an appeal by the prosecution, before the General Assembly. The Assembly, however, proceeded to debate the question " Whether there should be an overture anent the stage ? " which, despite an impassioned speech for the negative by Wedderburn, was carried by a large majority. An act was then proposed by the fanatics subjecting to ecclesiastical censure all Church

---

[1] EU, Laing MSS, ii, 620¹.

members, lay as well as clerical, who attended *any* theatrical exhibition.   Strongly opposed by the Moderates and, of course, by Wedderburn, this repressive measure was rejected.   At this moment, however, the Robertson junto played politics by joining in the passage of an act entitled " Recommendation to Presbyteries to take care that none of the ministers of this Church attend the Theatre." [1]

The strategy behind this unexpected move was that " manners are stronger than laws," and the sequel proved that the act was totally neglected.   Carlyle exults in the fact that, " now that the subject had been solemnly discussed, and all men were convinced that the violent proceedings they had witnessed were the effects of bigotry or jealousy, mixed with party-spirit and cabal, the more distant clergy returned to their usual amusement in the theatre when occasionally in town.   It is remarkable," he concludes, " that in the year 1784, when the great actress Mrs Siddons first appeared in Edinburgh, during the sitting of the General Assembly, that court was obliged to fix all its important business for the alternate days when she did not act, as all the younger members, clergy as well as laity, took their stations in the theatre on those days by three in the afternoon." [2]

On 2 April 1757 the Reverend George Ridpath wrote in his *Diary* :   " Read *Douglas* again, and am on the whole very well pleased with it. . . .   I am pretty confident it is a work that will last, and as, with all its other qualities, it is strictly pure and innocent in point of its morals, those sons of dulness, faction, or malignity, who have shown so much bitterness against it, must appear to a succeeding age in a very wretched light."   Curiously enough, these sentiments were approved by the Reverend John Wesley, who would scarcely have classed himself as a son of the Enlightenment.   For on 9 June Wesley wrote in his *Journal* :   " I was astonished to find, it [*Douglas*] is one of the finest Tragedies I ever read.   What pity, that a few lines were not left out, and that it was ever acted at Edinburgh."

But what was happening all this time to the Reverend John Home, the more or less innocent cause of the disturbance ?   Actually very little, for John, as early as the issue over David's dedication, had apparently determined to give up his clerical career for that of a man of letters.   After the successs of *Douglas* at Edinburgh, John had gone up to London, where he met with a very different reception from his two earlier visits.   Garrick was

---

[1] Campbell, *Chancellors*, VI, 27-9.   [2] Carlyle, pp. 338-9.

most cordial but did not feel that he could back down to the extent of bringing on the play at his own Drury-Lane Theatre. *Douglas*, therefore, was brought on at Rich's Covent Garden Theatre on 14 March with the famous Peg Woffington as Lady Randolph. Hume's dedication had prepared the English literary world for this event, and it was not disappointed—or not very much. The success was high but lacked the flowing tears of Edinburgh.[1] The blame for this lack of effusion was placed, in varying degrees, on the broad shoulders of David Hume for having puffed the play too extravagantly. But the two Humes could well afford to smile.

As a professional man of letters, John was starting off under favourable auspices. The critics, on the whole, had been kind to his *Douglas*. Thomas Sheridan, manager of the Theatre-Royal at Dublin, had sent him the present of a gold medal of the value of two guineas with an inscription honouring him for having " enriched the English stage with such an excellent tragedy." [2] The medal also symbolises the perils incident to the professional career, because it had been struck by Sheridan as a cheap means of compensation for an unsuccessful author's third night. But John's future seemed assured, as he had already been taken under the patronage of Lord Bute, Scotland's political patron saint, who procured for him a handsome pension from His Royal Highness the Prince of Wales. David rejoiced over the good fortune of his friend, exclaiming " Il est le mieux renté de tous les beaux esprits." [3]

Back in Scotland late in the spring, John preached a farewell sermon to his congregation at Athelstaneford on Sunday, 5 June, which drew tears from many of the people. He took a house for the summer near Braid and invited David to come and live with him. But the philosopher was too circumspect to accept, recognising, no doubt, that he had already brought enough embarrassment upon his friends, the Moderates.

Of that fact, there is no doubt. As early as 16 February Ridpath had called Hume's dedication " a very strange phenomenon, and, if there be any sense in it, it is so much in the sublime as to be above the reach of ordinary capacities," and the controversialists of the opposing camp took full advantage of Hume's relations with the Moderates. Some features of this attack by association have been seen earlier in connexion with the suppressed " Five Dissertations " and again with Witherspoon's

---

[1] Thackeray, in *The Virginians*, Ch. 59, has given a classic description of a London performance of " Mr. Home's dreary tragic masterpiece."
[2] *Scots Mag.*, xix (1757), 662.   [3] Boileau, *Sat.* ix.

Moderator ; but the point was reiterated by many another broad-side and pamphlet both farcical and serious. Henry Home also comes in for his share of abuse. *A Letter to the Reverend the Moderator, and Members of the Presbytery of Haddingtoun*, denounces Henry's " atheistical book " and " David Home [who] is not afraid nor ashamed to own his Infidelity," and calls for the continuation of Anderson's crusade against both. John is castigated for setting forth, " not for caution, but for example, the cursed principles and doctrine of his intimate acquaintance and beloved friend, David Home the Infidel, concerning the warrantableness of self-murder. . . . We see, by the growth of Infidelity, the fatal effects of thus permitting David and John Homes to go on after the manner they do without being censured."

Chief among those who seized the occasion to give vent to their prejudices was the youthful John Maclaurin (son of Professor Colin Maclaurin), later Lord Dreghorn on the Scottish bench. Maclaurin, who was certainly no sympathiser with the Old Party in the Church, exerted his pique against the Select Society, which had not opened its doors to him. Ramsay of Ochtertyre remarks on Maclaurin's lack of worldly wisdom : " The friends of the three Homes, whom he had lashed severely with great indiscretion, were a mighty body at that time in this country, whom no wise man would have provoked." [1] David and John, as the leading lights of the Select Society, get their due share of ridicule from Maclaurin. Witness the *Apology for the Writers against the Tragedy of Douglas* :

> Some years ago, a few gentlemen in this town assumed the character of being the only judges in all points of literature ; they were and still are styled the *geniuses*, and lately erected what they called a *select society*, which usurps a kind of aristocratical government over all men and matters of learning. The first and fundamental maxim of this dictatorial club is, That a punctilious correctness of style is the *summum bonum* of all composition : though the greatest genius should shine throughout a work, yet if in it is found an unguarded expression, a slip in syntax, or a peccadillo in grammar, *ad piper et farras* with it. Hence *Shakespear* of late is so much decried, that a noted historian, the Coryphaeus of this society, when disapproving of a wretched sentiment, adds, " What could Shakespear have said worse ? " *Addison*, till those gentlemen appeared, was universally esteemed as the finest writer *England* produced ; but they
>
> > *Cast him like an useless weed away.*
>
> If you believe them, there are ten errors in every page of his *Spectators* : and the above-mentioned author has a copy of them, in which this decalogue of errors in every page is marked with his own hand. . . . Let the reader compare *Voltaire* and *Hume,* with *Shakespear* and *Addison*, and give the preference to the former, if he can.

[1] Ramsay, i, 445.

The Reverend author of *Douglas* was a worthy member of this society, and his tragedy, long before it appeared in public, was by this society, extolled with all the noise of declamation ; and the little merit it has, exaggerated with all the amplifications of bombast. A famous author whom I have mentioned more than once, said, in private, that " he would give the *English* 200 years past, and 200 years to come, and they would not be able to produce such another tragedy ; " and the same gentleman has publicly told his namesake, that " he possesses the true theatrical genius of *Shakespeare* and *Otway*, refined from the unhappy barbarism of the one, and licentiousness of the other." This author must be forgiven for these rhodomontades ; for he frankly owns, that " it is less my admiration of your fine genius, which has engaged me to make this address to you, than my esteem of your character, and my affection to your person." Love, we all know, is blind ; and it would be unpolite to blame *Corydon* for running out extravagantly in the praises of *Alexis*.

In a second blast, a three-act farce of some wit, Maclaurin pursued the philosopher, the dramatist, and the Select Society, the title of *The Philosopher's Opera* revealing his chief game. In this piece figure Satan ; Mr Genius as David Hume ; Mrs Sarah Presbytery, the relict of Mr John Calvin ; and her son Jacky as John Home. The plot concerns Mr Genius's wooing of the elderly lady and his puffing of Jacky's play into success. Satan attempts to flatter Genius by observing that he has read his books. " Why, then, Sir," replies that not very bashful author, " You are convinced, I suppose, that there is no God, no devil, no future state ; —that there is no connection betwixt cause and effect ;—that suicide is a duty we owe ourselves ;—adultery a duty we owe to our neighbour ;—that the tragedy of *Douglas* is the best play ever was written ; and that *Shakespear* and *Otway* were a couple of dunces.—This, I think, is the sum and substance of my writings." After the departure of Genius, Satan admits his sad perplexity : " 'Faith, I don't know well what to think of him. Are you sure he is true blue on our side ? I confess, I have some suspicion, that he is a shrewd fellow, endeavouring to convert men to Christianity, by writing nonsense against it."

The Usefulness of the Edinburgh Theatre Seriously Considered, previously mentioned in connexion with " Five Dissertations," includes a swinging attack on the three Humes and the Moderates : " When the inhabitants have an opportunity, three times a-week at least, to hear and *gratis* too, the pure gospel of *Shakespear*, of *Sopho*, and *St David*, is it not ridiculous, and contrary to every rule of good policy, to squander away some thousand pounds, in maintaining above a score of pragmatical fellows, merely to retail the antiquated gospel of *St Matthew* or *St John*, to speak evil of dignitaries, and bring a railing accusation against their worthy reforming brethren ? " The Select Society and its prize-giving off-shoot also come in for the usual ridicule. Witherspoon, in addition to his farcical performances, continued the assault with the *Serious Enquiry into the Nature and Effects of the Stage*, " Being an Attempt to show, That contributing to the Support of a Public Theatre, is inconsistent with the Character of a Christian."

But by far the strangest anti-Moderate effort is that attributed to John Haldane, an upholsterer and a staunch Cameronian : *The Players Scourge : Or a Detection of the ranting prophanity and regnant impiety of stage plays, and their wicked encouragers and frequenters : and especially against the nine prophane Pagan Priests who countenanced the thrice cursed tragedy called Douglas.* After urging that the players ought to have their tongues cut out of their heads and their faces marked with a burning iron and be " sent back to their native lands of England and Ireland, whence the most of our wickedness proceeds," the fiendish upholsterer proceeds to curse the Moderate ministers, individually and collectively.

Some intimations of the *Douglas* affair reached France in due course of time. In 1760 Voltaire published a comedy, *Le Caffé, ou L'Ecossaise*, translated—so he brazenly avers in the preface—from the English of " Mr Hume, Minister of the Church at Edinburgh," who is further described as " brother of the celebrated philosopher Mr Hume, who has plumbed with so much fortitude and wisdom the depths of metaphysics and morals : these two philosophers equally lend honour to their native country, Scotland." And in 1764 the story came to the attention of Rousseau through Julie Bondeli : " The Scots, it is said, are about to begin the Republic of Plato. Already they have chased out one of their ecclesiastics because he had the misfortune to write three good tragedies. The English have sheltered the author and his talents ; and the moralists are now debating whether they were driven to acclaim Mr Hume [Home] with so much urbanity from a taste for the beautiful or from a desire to vex the Scots." [1]

The issues of the *Douglas* controversy were both ecclesiastical and cultural. In the first realm, the Moderates had incurred great losses and were ultimately saved from defeat only by Robertson's masterly strategy. That victory, however, was Pyrrhic, for John Home was driven out of the Church, becoming in the words of David, " the late Rev. Mr. John Home." Another feature of this victory-in-defeat was the discrediting of the

---

[1] Quoted in Rousseau, X, 327.

Reverend Patrick Cumming, who had been nominal leader of the Moderates. Because of his pusillanimous conduct, the inner circle around Robertson dubbed Cumming *Dr Turnstile*. The way was now clear for Robertson to assume full authority, which he did by 1762.

In the second realm, the cultural, the Moderates and their allies won a complete victory. As early in the campaign as 11 January 1757 there had appeared a broadside ironically treating of this issue, entitled the *Votes of the P[resbyter]y of E[dinburg]h* :

> *Resolved,* That Learning, Genius, and Merit are the Bane of Society, and ought to be discouraged.
> *Resolved,* That Ignorance, Dulness, and Demerit are the Glory of this *covenanted* Church, and ought, therefore, to be encouraged.
> *Resolved,* That every Proposition, which silly people alone maintain, is true. . . .
> *Resolved,* That Improvements of all Sorts are hurtful to Society.
> *Ordered,* That no Alteration be ever attempted to be made of the Principles, the Customs, and the Manners of Men.
> *Resolved,* That the Poets are publick Nuisances, and ought, like noxious Weeds, to be extirpated. . . .
> *Resolved,* That the present Time is the same with that of the *Covenant.*
> *Ordered,* That the People of *Scotland* remain forever in Barbarity.

The tone sounds very much like Wedderburn's, but that admittedly is a guess. In any event, Scottish literature was saved. The reactionary forces had come out into the open, and public opinion would henceforth prevent them from any attempted return to the seventeenth century. The enlightened forces would remain free to foster national letters, and that was one of the foremost ambitions of David Hume.

Chapter 27

SCOTLAND'S AUGUSTANS

" The People most distinguish'd for Literature in Europe."

In 1757 David Hume was fired with pride over the literary achievements of Scotland :

> Really it is admirable how many Men of Genius this Country produces at present. Is it not strange that, at a time when we have lost our Princes, our Parliaments, our independent Government, even the Presence of our chief Nobility, are unhappy, in our Accent & Pronunciation, speak a very corrupt Dialect of the Tongue which we make use of ; is it not strange, I say, that, in these Circumstances, we shou'd really be the People most distinguish'd for Literature in Europe ? [1]

The implications of this statement as to the cultural ideals of Hume and the Edinburgh men of letters, in general, require elucidation, forming, as they do, a national programme of Enlightenment.

Basic to the programme was the distinction between the spoken and the written language. " Notwithstanding all the Pains, which I have taken in the Study of the English Language," wrote Hume to John Wilkes in 1754, " I am still jealous of my Pen. As to my Tongue, you have seen that I regard it as totally desperate and Irreclaimable." It is certainly true that Hume spoke with a Lowland pronunciation all his life. A description of it and a sample of it are spelled out by a relative who knew him for many years :

> Notwithstanding his opportunitys, his conversations in Britain, and his mastery of several languages ; being so much abroad and in the best of Company, nay his propriety in penning the English language and idiom, yet in Common conversation, he retained the accent, expression and vulgarity of his paternal stile on the Banks of the White Water & Tweed, in such a degree that you would have imagined he had never conversed with any person but the commonest farmer in the Merse or ever sett foot out of the parish of Chirnside, had not the matter contain'd in his Discourse discovered the man of Letters. . . . Often when I have been walking &ca with him—he fell into reveries was silent for a time, was I suppose forming of a Syllogism, turning a period, or investigating a problem—then would fall a talking loud to himself. —If I ask'd what he was saying " Lord canna ye let a Body amuse them

[1] HL, i, 255.

selves without always clattering, I did nae ken ye was there and nae matter ye had nae bus'ness to meddle wi me." [1]

Why, it may be asked, was David Hume so ashamed of his provincial speech? Why did he devote so much effort to the writing of standard English? Since the Union of the Parliaments, Scotland had sent her representatives to London; and the spoken language, which had not hitherto been an issue, became one immediately. As Henry Home reports [2] of Lord Dun before the House of Lords in 1737, " Deil *ae* word, from beginning to end, did the English understand of his speech." William Adam tells [3] similarly of the predicament of Lord Pitfour when in the company of some English lawyers at Lincoln's Inn Fields: " Pitfour . . . was at the head of the table, where he told one of his Scotch stories, which, from not being understood, did not produce a smile ; when he called out to me (being at the further end of the table,) in despair, ' My story is not understood, Adam ; for God's sake translate for me, as I can utter no sound like an Englishman but sneezing.' " Not limited to sneezing, however, the intercourse between the two kingdoms obliged the Scots to learn to make themselves understood in southern English.

The gradual infiltration of English into Edinburgh University, both as language and as literature, has already been made evident. In 1760 the Reverend Hugh Blair was elected Professor of Rhetoric without a salary, and two years later was appointed Regius Professor of Rhetoric and Belles-Lettres. Edinburgh thus established the first chair of English in the British Isles—perhaps for the very reason that English was still, in Scottish ears, almost a foreign language. Before that, and outside the University, Adam Smith had delivered two courses of lectures on literature and literary criticism 1748–51 ; and these courses were repeated several times by Robert Watson before 1756. Three years later Blair took them over within the University.[4] When in 1761, therefore, the Edinburgh Select Society sponsored the lectures of Thomas Sheridan on the English tongue, the city was well prepared to sit attentive.

Sheridan, son of the friend of Dean Swift and father of the great dramatist, was an Irish actor from Dublin and thereby admirably

---

[1] George Norvell, MS letter of 1 Mar. 1788, in Keynes Library, King's College, Cambridge.   [2] Ramsay, II, 543, *n*2.
[3] Wm. Adam, *Sequel to the Gift of a Grandfather* (priv. ptd. 1836), p. 30.
[4] H. W. Meikle, " The Chair of Rhetoric and Belles-Lettres in the University of Edinburgh," in *University of Edinburgh Journal* (1945), 89–92.

qualified to teach the Scots of Edinburgh how to speak the English of London correctly. The Scots of Edinburgh were peculiarly gullible, however, because of their sensitivity to the charge of being provincial. In 1756 Sheridan had published *British Education ; or, The Source of the Disorders of Great Britain*, the sub-title of which explains his purpose : " Being an essay towards proving, that the immorality, ignorance, and false taste, which so generally prevail, are the natural and necessary consequences of the present defective system of education. With an attempt to shew, that a revival of the art of Speaking, and the study of our own language, might contribute in a great measure, to the cure of those evils." The book itself argues further that by developing rules and fixing the standard of English, that language will become a third classical, and the only modern, universal language.

Sheridan gave two series of lectures on Elocution and the English Tongue at St Paul's Chapel, Edinburgh, where for four weeks he held three hundred gentlemen enthralled at a guinea apiece. He then gave a shortened two weeks' series for ladies and for those gentlemen who had had the misfortune of missing the first series. At his last lecture Sheridan announced that the Select Society of Edinburgh was promulgating a plan for pro-moting the reading and speaking of the English language in Scotland.[1]

Elaborate " Regulations " were shortly published by the Select Society. The document opens :

As the intercourse between this part of Great Britain and the capital daily increases, both on account of business and amusement, and must still go on increasing, gentlemen educated in Scotland have long been sensible of the disadvantages under which they labour, from their imperfect knowledge of the ENGLISH TONGUE, and the impropriety with which they speak it.

Experience hath convinced Scotsmen, that it is not impossible for persons born and educated in this country, to acquire such knowledge of the English Tongue, as to write it with some tolerable purity.

But with regard to the other point, that of speaking with propriety as little has been hitherto attempted, it has generally been taken for granted, that there was no prospect of attempting any thing with a probability of success ; though, at the same time, it is allowed to be an accomplishment, more important, and more universally useful, than the former.

In view of these circumstances the Select Society proposes :

That it would be of great advantage to this country if a proper number of persons from England, duly qualified to instruct gentlemen in the knowledge of the English Tongue, the manner of pronouncing it with purity, and the

[1] *Scots Mag.*, XXIII (1761), 389–90.

art of public speaking, were settled in Edinburgh ; and if, at the same time, a proper number of masters from the same country, duly qualified for teaching children the reading of English, should open schools in Edinburgh for that purpose.

A voluntary subscription was, therefore, enlisted and a group named as Ordinary Directors and Extraordinary Directors to put the scheme into practice. Included were many of Hume's best friends : Lords Alemoor, Elibank, and Kames ; Johnstone and Dempster, advocates ; and Blair, Ferguson, Jardine, and Robertson from clergy and university. Shortly thereafter a Mr Leigh was engaged as master ; and with that feeble—and perhaps misguided—effort the strength of the Select Society came to an end.

The name of David Hume was not associated with this last effort of the Select Society. That may have been because, at the moment, he was in London ; or it may have been because he was not swept away by the hysteria over the claims of Sheridan. In the following year, when the lectures had been published, Hume expressed his disapproval to Boswell : " Mr. Sheridan's Lectures are vastly too enthusiastic. He is to do every thing by Oratory. It is like the verse in the Song extolling Drunkeness.

> Alexander hated thinking,
> Drank about at Council-board,
> He subdued the world by drinking
> More than by his conq'ring sword." [1]

Hume's distaste for the pretensions of Sheridan does not mean that he was not interested in the promotion of pure English. One feature of his campaign for pure English was the drawing up of a list of " Scotticisms " that were rigidly to be excluded from all written works. This six-page list appeared in some copies of the *Political Discourses* of 1752 and was later reprinted in the *Scots Magazine*, where it aroused considerable comment.[2] The list includes examples of the latinised and gallicised vocabulary of the Scottish university man of the eighteenth century and some more homely words and idioms of Lowland Scots ; it does not, of course, include any Gaelic, a language known only to a few educated Edinburgh people.

Hume's later bitter antagonist, James Beattie, published in 1779 another list of Scotticisms. In writing elsewhere about the early education of his son, Beattie typifies the attitude of the Scottish intellectual class :

[1] *Boswell Papers*, I, 129.   [2] *Scots Mag.*, XXII (1760), 686–7 ; XXVI (1764), 187–9.

At home, from his Mother and me, he learned to read and write. His pronunciation was not correct, as may well be supposed : but it was deliberate and significant, free from provincial peculiarities, and such as an Englishman would have understood ; and afterwards, when he had passed a few summers in England, it became more elegant than what is commonly heard in North Britain. He was early warned against the use of Scotch words and other similar improprieties ; and his dislike to them was such, that he soon learned to avoid them ; and, after he grew up, could never endure to read what was written in any of the vulgar dialects of Scotland. He looked at Mr. Allan Ramsay's poems, but did not relish them.[1]

In a letter to an Englishman Beattie discusses the difficulties of a Scot's writing standard English :

The greatest difficulty in acquiring the art of *writing* English, is one which I have seldom heard our countrymen complain of, and which I was never sensible of till I had spent some years in labouring to acquire that art. It is, to give a *vernacular* cast to the English we write. I must explain myself. We who live in Scotland are obliged to study English from books, like a dead language. Accordingly, when we write, we write it like a dead language, which we understand, but cannot speak ; avoiding, perhaps, all ungrammatical expressions, and even the barbarisms of our country, but at the same time without communicating that neatness, ease, and softness of phrase, which appears so conspicuously in Addison, Lord Lyttleton, and other elegant English authors. Our style is stately and unwieldy, and clogs the tongue in pronunciation, and smells of the lamp. We are slaves to the language we write, and are continually afraid of committing *gross* blunders ; and, when an easy, familiar, idiomatical phrase occurs, dare not adopt it, if we recollect no authority, for fear of Scotticisms. In a word, *we* handle English as a person who cannot fence handles a sword ; continually afraid of hurting ourselves with it, or letting it fall, or making some awkward motion that shall betray our ignorance. An English author of learning is the master, not the slave of his language, and wields it gracefully, because he wields it with ease, and with full assurance that he has the command of it.

In order to get over this difficulty, which I fear is in some respects insuperable after all, I have been continually poring upon Addison, the best parts of Swift, Lord Lyttleton, &c. The ear is of great service in these matters ; and I am convinced the greater part of Scottish authors hurt their style by admiring and imitating one another. At Edinburgh it is currently said by your critical people, that Hume, Robertson, &c write English better than the English themselves ; than which, in my judgment, there cannot be a greater absurdity. I would as soon believe that Thuanus wrote better Latin than Cicero or Caesar, and that Buchanan was a more elegant poet than Virgil or Horace. In my rhetorical lectures, and whenever I have occasion to speak on this subject to those who pay any regard to my opinion, I always maintain a contrary doctrine, and advise those to study English authors, who would acquire a good English style.[2]

---

[1] *Essays and Fragments in Prose and Verse*, by James Hay Beattie (priv. ptd. 1794), pp. 13–14. In a London edn. of 1799, included (II, 5) in an edn. of James Beattie's *Minstrel*, the last sentence is omitted.

[2] Wm. Forbes, *An Account of the Life and Writings of James Beattie, LL.D.* (Edinburgh 1806), II, 16–19. It is perhaps worthy of note that the term " barbarism " in respect to language derives from Johnson's *Dictionary* of 1755.

This often-quoted passage, though perceptive to a degree, is somewhat misleading. It sets up a valid distinction between the spoken and the written language, a distinction which exists in fact, whether it is between the colloquial and the formal, on the one hand, or between the vernacular and the standard, on the other. Beattie tends, however, to exaggerate the differences between standard and vernacular, for the English tradition in Scotland was stronger than he seems to imply. The main strength of the English tradition lay in the fact that in the seventeenth century the Scots had accepted the English, rather than a Scottish, translation of the Bible. Brought up on the reading of the Bible from infancy, every Scot was deeply imbued with English. Added to this is the further fact that there simply did not exist in Beattie's time any large body of Scottish vernacular literature outside the realm of poetry, and even in that realm there were the influential examples of William Drummond of Hawthornden in the seventeenth century and James Thomson in the earlier eighteenth century, who had written exclusively in English. The elder Allan Ramsay recognized both English and the vernacular as part of the native Scottish tradition and wrote in both.

The eighteenth century Scottish men of letters adhered to that European, particularly French, outlook which had been the cultural heritage of educated Scotland. Their outlook was cosmopolitan and enlightened; and their medium of expression was standard English. They rejected two other quite distinct levels of Scottish culture. They rejected the Gaelic tradition, their very ignorance of which was to render them the easy dupes of a Macpherson; they overlooked the Gaelic revival of the mid-century, heralded by such poets as Dugald Buchanan, Rob Donn, Duncan Ban McIntyre, and Alexander MacDonald; and they remained oblivious of the Gaelic New Testament, which concerned both Dugald Buchanan and the Reverend J. Stuart of Killin, Duncan McIntyre's editor, and which received support from so unlikely a source as Dr Johnson.[1] In trying to purge themselves of all provincialism, the *literati* also rejected the native Lowland tradition and so neglected the earlier vernacular poetry of James Watson and Allan Ramsay, and were oblivious in the 1770s of Robert Fergusson and David Herd, and, to some extent, condescended even to the genius of Robert Burns.

[1] In Edinburgh in 1767, Hume challenged Buchanan to quote anything so impressive and sublime as Shakespeare's *Tempest* Act IV, Scene 1, lines 148–58, and Buchanan replied by quoting from Revelation XX, 11–13. David Daiches, *The Paradox of Scottish Culture : The Eighteenth-Century Experience* (London 1964), p. 97.

What might have happened to Scottish poetry had David Hume and his group recognised the vernacular, instead of the English, tradition is anyone's guess. In the event, however, and even with the enduring world-success achieved by Burns, the native tradition slowly languished despite repeated attempts to revitalise it.[1] To this extent, the programme of the eighteenth-century men of letters proved to be discerning, and the literary future of Scotland lay in standard English. The immediate failure of their programme in the third quarter of the eighteenth century lay in the fact that the English-writing poets whom they actually backed were without genuine talent. The Blacklocks, Homes, and Wilkies are today among the great unread.

David Hume's patronage of the English-writing poets of Scotland was dictated by literary and personal considerations : his standards of criticism, his greatness of heart, his loyalty to friends, and his love of country. The combination, however human and however excusable, was unable to guarantee excellence of art. As a critic, Hume is not all of a piece. His stated theory is of a broad Classicism ; his implicit theory is of a broad Romanticism ; while his applied criticism is of a narrow Classicism intolerantly interpreted.[2]

To reconcile these divergences in the work of an otherwise consistent and systematic thinker is not simple, yet some explanation is in order. Classicism is a theory of aesthetics having a rationalistic basis ; it postulates an ideal of uniformity and of conformity to standards while it minimises individual differences. Romanticism is one having an empirical basis ; it is primarily concerned with the individual, and demands no ideals of universalism or of conformity. As an empirical philosopher of the " Science of Human Nature," Hume might have been expected to produce a Romantic aesthetics. Yet the problem is further complicated by the fact that in the history of European art up to his time—and Hume was frankly concerned with no other—almost all the masterpieces had been conceived on Classical principles. The history of art, in other words, provided empirical evidence over the course of many centuries of the practice of a Classical aesthetics. So in remaining Classical and neglecting the Romantic implications of his thinking on aesthetics, Hume was preferring one type

---

[1] I am implying no evaluation of the latest revival of the native tradition.
[2] Numerous studies of Hume's aesthetics have appeared recently. See the bibliography of Oliver Brunet in *Philosophie et Esthetique chez David Hume* (Paris 1965), 897–908. See also the bibliography below under Cohen and Mossner.

of empirical evidence to another. In this he was perhaps being more conservative than usual. He gave short shrift, however, to poets' claims to supernatural inspiration : " Their fire is not kindled from heaven. Its runs along the earth ; is caught from one breast to another ; and burns brightest, where the materials are best prepared, and most happily disposed." [1]

The crucial test for all aesthetic theories of the eighteenth century was the treatment of Shakespeare. Acknowledged as one of the great geniuses of all time, Shakespeare was the outstanding exception to the notion of Classical dominance. Hume's handling of the Shakespearian issue, therefore, is revealing. " For God's sake read Shakespeare," he admonished John Home, " but get Racine and Sophocles by heart. It is reserved to you and you alone, to redeem our stage from the reproach of barbarism." In the *History of England* Hume subjected Shakespeare to the strict canons of Classical criticism :

If Shakespeare be considered as a Man, born in a rude age, and educated in the lowest manner, without any instruction either from the world or from books, he may be regarded as a prodigy ; If represented as a Poet, capable of furnishing a proper entertainment to a refined or intelligent audience, we must abate much of this eulogy. In his compositions, we regret, that many irregularities, and even absurdities, should so frequently disfigure the animated and passionate scenes intermixed with them ; and at the same time, we perhaps admire the more those beauties, on account of their being surrounded with such deformities. A striking peculiarity of sentiment, adapted to a singular character, he frequently hits, as it were by inspiration ; but a reasonable propriety of thought he cannot for any time uphold. Nervous and picturesque expressions, as well as descriptions, abound in him ; but it is in vain we look either for purity or simplicity of diction. His total ignorance of all theatrical art and conduct, however material a defect ; yet, as it affects the spectator rather than the reader, we can more easily excuse, than that want of taste which often prevails in his productions, and which gives way only by intervals to the irradiations of genius. A great and fertile genius he certainly possessed, and one enriched equally with a tragic and comic vein ; but he ought to be cited as a proof, how dangerous it is to rely on these advantages alone for attaining an excellence in the finer arts. And there may even remain a suspicion, that we over-rate, if possible, the greatness of his genius ; in the same manner, as bodies often appear more gigantic on account of their being disproportioned and mishapen. [2]

This passage would have pleased a Voltaire, who would yet have insisted on reinforcing it ; but it would not have pleased many Englishmen or even many Scots. Henry Home had some share in getting the original version toned down, as did also Allan

---

[1] *Phil. Wks.*, III, 177.   [2] Hume, *Hist.* (Edinburgh 1792), VI, 191–2.

Ramsay.[1] Milton, the great classical poet, naturally fares better with Hume :

> It is certain that this author, when in a happy mood, and employed on a noble subject, is the most wonderfully sublime of any poet in any language ; Homer and Lucretius and Tasso not excepted. More concise than Homer, more simple than Tasso, more nervous than Lucretius ; had he lived in a later age, and learned to polish some rudeness in his verses ; had he enjoyed better fortune, and possessed leisure to watch the return of genius in himself, he had attained the pinnacle of perfection, and borne away the palm of epic poetry.[2]

The " characters " of the British authors inserted in the *History*, it is to be remarked, constitute the first attempt in English to introduce literary and cultural history into what had previously been strictly political history. If brought together they would, in a sense, constitute the first " History of English Literature " ever printed, fragmentary though it would be.

In considering Hume's critical views on poetry and his patronage of several poets, it is well to bear in mind that he himself was no poet. We have his express word to Boswell in 1775 : " He said he had never written any verses." To John Armstrong, who " set a very high value on Poetry," Hume rejoined—as he told Boswell—" Ay, ay, Doctor, you do not consider that we prose writers think ourselves the strength of the army, the Infantry, and you Poets the horse, only for scowring the Country." [3] The remark implies a utilitarian standard of literature in addition to the aesthetic. The manuscript verses in Hume's own hand which survive among his papers are not of his own composition and, upon examination, prove to be copies from several different poets, including his old friend, Hamilton of Bangour.[4] Others of Hume's friends, it is perhaps worthy of note, were also poets and song writers, including Sir Gilbert Elliot of Minto and his sister Miss Jean Elliot, Mrs Alison Cockburn, Lady Anne Lindsay.

David Hume's patronage of John Home has been observed in passing. A copy of *Douglas* was sent by David to the Abbé Le Blanc in Paris with the explanation :

> Tis *Douglas*, a new Tragedy, wrote by Mr John Hume, a very ingenious, young Gentleman, a Friend & Relation of mine. The Fate of this Gentleman's Performance was very extraordinary. It was refus'd by the Manager of

---

[1] For Home, see Sir James Prior, *Life of Edmond Malone* (London 1860), pp. 374–5; for Ramsay, RSE, vi, 103. [2] Hume, *Hist.* (Edinburgh 1792), vii, 343–4.
[3] *Boswell Papers*, xi, 4.
[4] RSE, ix, 7–11. Hill Burton (i. 227–35) and Greig (p. 84) accepted some of these verses as Hume's own. See below, Appendix I, pp. 621–3, for a posthumous attempt to palm off other verses on Hume.

Drury-Lane Theatre ; and for that Reason was oblig'd to be brought on in our Theatre in this City. In order to raise it from obscurity, I wrote to the Author the Dedication, prefix'd to the Four Dissertations, which had so good an Effect, that the Tragedy was brought on in Covent Garden, and extremely well receivd by the Public. I am perswaded, that there is not any Tragedy in the Language so well adapted to your Theatre, by reason of the Elegance, Simplicity, & Decorum, which run thro' the whole of it. I wou'd be much pleas'd to see it translated into French, and to find it successful with those good Critics who so much abound in Paris.[1]

But even the French, sad to say, recognised that " Elegance, Simplicity, & Decorum " are not sufficient in themselves to make good drama. A good many Englishmen, indeed, rebuked Hume for the extravagance of his praise in the dedication to *Four Dissertations*. And apparently few in London were impressed with the exultation of that Aberdeen man in the front row of the shilling gallery at Covent Garden Theatre, who called down the first night : " Ou fie, lads ! fat think ye o yir Willy Shakespeare noo ? "[2]

Out of charity, friendship, and literary patriotism, David Hume attempted to raise still other works from obscurity. His efforts on behalf of Blacklock are in point. Born poor, and blinded by smallpox in infancy, Thomas Blacklock was a perennial object of literary wonder. In a letter of 1754 Hume describes his first meeting with this prodigy :

The first time I had ever seen or heard of Mr Blacklock was about twelve years ago, when I met him in a visit to two young ladies. They informed me of his case, as far as they could in a conversation carried on in his presence. I soon found him to possess a very delicate taste, along with a passionate love of learning. Dr Stevenson[3] had, at that time, taken him under his protection ; and he was perfecting himself in the Latin tongue. I repeated to him Mr Pope's Elegy to the Memory of an unfortunate Lady, which I happened to have by heart : and though I be a very bad reciter, I saw it affected him extremely. His eyes, indeed, the great index of the mind, could express no passion : but his whole body was thrown into agitation. That poem was equally qualified to touch the delicacy of his taste, and the tenderness of his feelings. I left the town a few days after ; and being long absent from Scotland, I neither saw nor heard of him for several years. At last an acquaintance of mine told me of him, and said that he would have waited on me, if his excessive modesty had not prevented him. He soon appeared what I have ever since found him, a very elegant genius, of a most affectionate grateful disposition, a modest backward temper, accompanied with that delicate pride, which so naturally attends virtue in distress.

Hume proceeds with a discussion of how Blacklock could employ description so well in his poetry :

[1] HL, I, 260.   [2] Campbell, *Chancellors*, VII, 355. *nf.*
[3] The physician, not the professor.

I have asked him whether he retained any idea of light or colours. He assured me that there remained not the least traces of them. I found, however, that all the poets, even the most descriptive ones, such as Milton and Thomson, were read by him with pleasure. Thomson is one of his favorites. I remembered a story in Locke of a blind man, who said that he knew very well what scarlet was : it was like the sound of a trumpet. I therefore asked him, whether he had not formed associations of that kind, and whether he did not connect colour and sound together. He answered, that as he met so often, both in books and conversation, with the terms expressing colours, he had formed some false associations, which supported him when he read, wrote, or talked of colours : but that the associations were of the intellectual kind. The illumination of the sun, for instance, he supposed to resemble the presence of a friend ; the cheerful colour of green, to be like an amiable sympathy, &c. It was not altogether easy for me to understand him : though I believe, in much of our own thinking, there will be found some species of association. 'Tis certain we always think in some language, viz. in that which is most familiar to us ; and 'tis but too frequent to substitute words instead of ideas.

Yet concerning love, Blacklock could experience more than a mere idea :

Apropos to this passion, I once said to my friend, Mr Blacklock, that I was sure he did not treat love as he did colours ; he did not speak of it without feeling it. There appeared too much reality in all his expressions to allow that to be suspected. " Alas ! " said he, with a sigh, " I could never bring my heart to a proper tranquillity on that head." Your passion, replied I, will always be better founded than ours, who have sight : we are so foolish as to allow ourselves to be captivated by exterior beauty : nothing but the beauty of the mind can affect you. " Not altogether neither," said he : " the sweetness of the voice has a mighty effect upon me : the symptoms of youth too, which the touch discovers, have great influence. And though such familiar approaches would be ill-bred in others, the girls of my acquaintance indulge me, on account of my blindness, with the liberty of running over them with my hand. And I can by that means judge entirely of their shape. However, no doubt, humour, and temper, and sense, and other beauties of the mind, have an influence upon me as upon others."

"You may see from this conversation," concludes Hume judiciously, " how difficult it is even for a blind man to be a perfect Platonic." [1]

A volume of Blacklock's poems had been privately printed at Glasgow in 1746 ; but, in the confusion over the late Rebellion, it attracted little attention. Another edition was brought out at Edinburgh in 1754, and David Hume entered upon a vigorous sales campaign, dunning his friends with letters. He wrote to Adam Smith, for instance, 27 February :

Dear Sir,
    I am writing kind of circular Letters, recommending Mr Blacklock's Poems [to] all my Acquaintance, but especially to those, whose Approbation wou'd contribute most to recommend them [to] the World. They are, indeed,

[1] HL, i, 200–202.

many of them very elegant, and wou'd have deserv'd much Esteem had [t]hey come from a Man plac'd in the most favorable Circumstances. What a Prodigy are they, when considerd as the Production of a man so cruelly dealt with, both by Nature [and] Fortune? When you add to this, that the Author is a Man of the best Dispositions, that I have ever known, and tho' of great Frugality, is plac'd in the most cruel Indigence, you will certainly think his Case more deserving of Pity & Regard than any you have almost met with. Mr Foulis has Copies to dispose of, which I have sent him ; & which he will disperse without expecting any Profit. I must entreat you, not only to take a Copy yourself, but also to take a few more & [dis]pose of among your Acquaintance. I trust at least to have half a dozen disposd of by your [me]ans. I have sold off above fifty in a few days. The Price is three Shillings. That you may [rec]ommend them with a safer Conscience, please read the Ode to a young Gentleman going to the Coast of Guinea, that on Refinement in metaphysical Philosophy, that to a Lady on the Death of her Son ; the Wish, an Elegy ; the Soliloquy. I am much mistaken, if you do not find all these [v]ery laudable Performances ; & such as wou'd be esteem'd an Ornament to Dodesley's Miscellanies [o]r even to better Collections. . . .

My Compliments to Mr & Mrs Betham. If that Lady can be engag'd to have an Esteem of Mr Blacklock's Productions, she wou'd be of great Service in dispersing them. Tho born blin[d,] he is not insensible to that Passion, which we foolish People are apt to receive first by th[e] Eyes ; and unless a man were both blind & deaf, I do not know how he cou'd be altogether secure of Impressions from Mrs Betham.

Another in the series of sales letters, Hume sent to Robert Dodsley, the poetical bookseller in Pall Mall, together with the gift of six copies of Blacklock's poems. Dodsley forwarded the letter and one of the volumes to Joseph Spence, formerly Professor of Poetry and, at the time, Professor of Modern History at Oxford. Spence, in turn, published through Dodsley in November 1754 *An Account of the Life, Character, and Poems of Mr. Blacklock : Student of Philosophy, in the University of Edinburgh*, in which he used materials from Hume's letter to Dodsley, identifying the writer as the " Author of the Moral Essays." The bookseller also opened subscription lists for a quarto edition of Blacklock. Hearing of these benevolent intentions, Hume wrote directly to Professor Spence on 15 October a long letter, some parts of which have already been used in this account. In it Hume tells of further charity :

He [Blacklock] has gained about one hundred guineas by this last [Edinburgh] edition of his poems, and this is the whole stock he has in the world. He has also a bursary, about six pounds a year. I begun a subscription for supporting him during five years ; and I made out twelve guineas a year among my acquaintance. That is a most terrible undertaking ; and some unexpected refusals I met with, damped me, though they have not quite discouraged me from proceeding. We have the prospect of another bursary of ten pounds a year in the gift of the Exchequer ; but to the shame of human nature, we met with difficulties. Noblemen interpose with their valet-de-chambres or nurses' son, who they think would be burdens on themselves. Could we ensure but thirty pounds a year to this fine genius and man of virtue, he would be easy and happy : for his wants are none but those which nature has given him, though she has unhappily loaded him with more than other men.

Within two months, through the chance of his quarrel with the Curators of the Advocates' Library, Hume was personally able to provide Blacklock with a considerable augmentation to his income. " I retain the Office " [of Keeper], he explained to Adam Smith, " but have given Blacklock, our blind Poet, a Bond of Annuity for the Sallary [of £40]."

Spence was so interested in Blacklock as to make a trip to Scotland in order to meet him. And early in 1756 Dodsley brought out the new subscription edition of *Poems by Mr. Blacklock*, " To Which is Prefix'd, an Account of the Life, Character, and Writings, of the Author, by the Reverend Mr. Spence, Late Professor of Poetry at Oxford." In this account all references to Hume are omitted—but let Hume himself tell of Spence's expurgations and bowlderisings :

[I commend] Spence's industry in so good a work, but there is a circumstance of his conduct that will entertain you. In the Edinburgh edition there was a stanza to this effect :

> The wise in every age conclude,
> What Pyrrho taught and Hume renewed,
> That dogmatists are fools.

Mr Spence would not undertake to promote a London subscription, unless my name, as well as Lord Shaftesbury's (who was mentioned in another place) were erased : the author frankly gave up Shaftesbury, but said that he would forfeit all the profit he might expect from a subscription, rather than relinquish the small tribute of praise which he had paid to a man whom he was more indebted to than to all the world beside. I heard by chance of this controversy, and wrote to Mr Spence, that, without farther consulting the author, I, who was chiefly concerned, would take upon me to empower him to alter the stanza where I was mentioned. He did so, and farther, having prefixed the life of the author, he took occasion to mention some people to whom he had been obliged, but is careful not to name me ; judging rightly that such good deeds were only *splendida peccata*, and that till they were sanctified by the grace of God they would be of no benefit to salvation.[1]

Blacklock's reference to Hume had appeared in the ode " On the Refinements in Metaphysical Philosophy " and a note had identified him as " Author of a Treatise on Human Nature." The philosopher swallowed his pride over Spence's rudeness and never broke off relations with him ; he also continued to act as Blacklock's chief patron. In 1757 Hume saved Blacklock from certain disaster by persuading him not to attempt to give lectures on oratory to young men preparing for the bar and the pulpit. Instead, Blacklock entered the church, being licensed in 1759.

Hume's representation that the Scots are " the People most distinguish'd for Literature in Europe " is expressed in a letter of 2 July 1757 to Gilbert Elliot, which was largely given up to an account of William Wilkie, who had just published at Edinburgh an epic poem on an Homeric subject and entitled the *Epigoniad*. Jubilantly Hume requests Elliot to spread the good news throughout London :

I suppose that, by this time, you have undoubtedly read & admir'd the wonderful Production of the Epigoniad, and that you have so much Love for Arts & for your native Country, as to be very industrious in propagating the Fame of it. It is certainly a most singular Production, full of Sublimity & Genius, adorn'd by a noble, harmonious, forcible, & even correct versification. We generally think the Story deficient & uninteresting ; but perhaps the new Fancy of crossing the Invention of all modern Romance Writers may make some Atonement, and even bestow an Air of Novelty on the Imitation of Homer. As I cannot but hope that this Work will soon become a Subject of Conversation in London, I shall take this Opportunity of supplying you with some Anecdotes with regard to the Author, besides such as you already know, of his being a very worthy & a very entertaining man, adorn'd with all that Simplicity of Manners, so common to great Men, & even with some of that Rusticity & Negligence which serve to abate that Envy to which they are so much expos'd.

You know he is a Farmer's Son, in the Neighbourhood of this Town, where there are a great Number of Pigeon Houses. The Farmers are very much infested with the Pigeons, and Wilkie's Father planted him often as a Scarecrow (an Office for which he is well qualify'd) in the Midst of his Fields of Wheat. It was in this Situation that he confesses he first conceiv'd the Design of his Epic Poem, and even executed Part of it. He carry'd out his Homer with him, together with a Table & Pen & Ink, & a great rusty Gun. He compos'd & wrote two or three Lines, till a Flock of Pigeons settled in the Field, then rose up, ran towards them, & fir'd at them ; return'd again to his former Station, & added a Rhyme or two more, till he met with a fresh Interruption.

Two or three Years ago, Jemmy Russel put a very pleasant Trick on an English Physician, one Dr Roebuck, who was travelling in this Country. Russel carry'd him out one day on horseback to see the Outlets of the Town, and purposely led him by Wilkie's Farm. He saw the Bard at a small Distance sowing his Corn, with a Sheet about his Shoulders, all besmear'd with Dirt & Sweat, with a Coat & Visage entirely proportion'd to his Occupation. Russel says to his Companion, *Here is a Fellow, a Peasant, with whom I have some Business : Let us call him.* He made a Sign, & Wilkie came to them. Some Questions were ask'd him with regard to the Season, to his Farm & Husbandry, which he readily answer'd ; but soon took an Opportunity of making a

Digression to the Greek Poets, and enlarging on that Branch of Literature. Dr. Roebuck, who had scarce understood his rustic English, or rather his broad Scotch, immediatly comprehended him, for his Greek was admirable : And on leaving him, he coud not forbear expressing the highest Admiration to Russell, that a Clown, a Rustic, a mere Hind, such as he saw this Fellow was, shou'd be possest of so much Erudition. *Is it usual*, says he, *for your Peasants in Scotland to read the Greek poets ? O yes*, replies Russel, very coolly, *we have long Winter Evenings ; and in what can they then employ themselves better, than in reading the Greek Poets ?* Roebuck left the Country in a full Perswasion that there are at least a dozen Farmers in every Parish who read Homer, Hesiod, & Sophocles, every Winter Evening, to their Families ; and, if ever he writes an Account of his Travels, it is likely he will not omit so curious a Circumstance.

Wilkie is now a settled Minister at Ratho, within four Miles of the Town ; He possesses about 80 or 90 £ a year, which he esteems exorbitant Riches. Formerly, when he had only 20 £, as Helper, he said that he could not conceive what Article, either of human Convenience, or Pleasure, he was deficient in : Nor what any man could mean by desiring more Money. He possesses several Branches of Erudition, besides the Greek Poets ; and, particularly, is a very profound Geometrician, a Science commonly very incompatible with the lively Imagination of a Poet. He has even made some new Discoveries in that Science ; and he told me, that, when a young Man, he threw Cross & Pile, whether he wou'd devote himself chiefly to Mathematics or to Poetry, & fears that he rather crost the Bent of his Genius in taking to the latter. Yet this man, who has compos'd the second Epic Poem in our Language understands so little of Orthography, that, regularly thro' the whole Poem, he always spelt the Word *yield* in this manner, *ealde* ; and I had great Difficulty to convince him of his Mistake.

Loyal Scot that he was, Elliot found it impossible to go along with David Hume's rating of Wilkie in the same class with Homer and Milton. " I find the Public, with you," Hume reluctantly conceded some weeks later, " have rejected the Epigoniad, for the present. They may do so if they please : But it has a great deal of Merit, much more than any one of them is capable of throwing into a Work." In London both the *Critical* and the *Monthly* damned the *Epigoniad*. Oliver Goldsmith wrote in the *Monthly* : " The Epigoniad seems to be one of these *new old* performances ; a work that would no more have pleased a peripatetic of the academic grove, than it will captivate the unlettered subscriber to one of our circulating libraries." Yet David Hume remained loyal to his critical principles, to his friend, and to his native country. He spluttered once more over the " conspiracy " of the London book-sellers to hinder the sales of all provincial publications and he proposed that Andrew Millar bring out a second edition : " As the Author is my very good Friend & Acquaintance, I shoud be much pleasd to bring you to an understanding together ; If the bad success on the first Edition has not discouragd you, I wou'd engage him to make you Proposals for that Purpose. He will correct all the Blemishes remark'd."

Millar was persuaded and early in 1759 brought out "The Second Edition, Carefully Corrected and Improved. To Which is Added, a Dream. In the Manner of Spenser." In April Hume wrote somewhat coyly to Adam Smith : " The Epigoniad, I hope, will do ; but it is somewhat up-hill Work. As I doubt not but you consult the Reviews sometimes at present, you will see in the critical Review a Letter upon that Poem ; and I desire you to employ your Conjectures in finding out the Author. Let me see a Sample of your Skill in knowing hands by your guessing at the Person." With William Robertson, however, Hume was forthright :

> The Epigoniad I cannot . . . promise for [its success] ; tho' I have done all in my Power to forward it, particularly by writing a Letter to the critical Review, which you may peruse. I find, however, some good Judges profess a great Esteem for it ; but *habent et sua fata libelli* : [1] However, if you want a little Flattery for the Author (which I own is very refreshing to an Author) you may tell him that Lord Chesterfield said to me he was a great Poet. I imagine that Wilkie will be very much elevated by Praise from an English Earl, and a Knight of the Garter, & an Ambassador, and a Secretary of State, and a Man of so great Reputation. For I observe that the greatest Rustics are commonly most affected with such Circumstances.

Since much of the castigation of the *Epigoniad* in the reviews of 1757 had been on the basis of diction, Hume's letter in the April 1759 issue of the *Critical Review* stresses the corrections and the improvements to the second edition.

> The public has done so much justice to the gentlemen engaged in the Critical Review, as to acknowledge that no literary journal was ever carried on in this country with equal spirit and impartiality : yet, I must confess that an article published in your Review of 1757, gave me great surprize, and not a little uneasiness. It regarded a book called the Epigoniad, a poem of the Epic kind, which was at that time published with great applause at Edinburgh, and of which a few copies had been sent up to London. The author of that article had surely been lying under strong prepossessions, when he spoke so negligently of a work which abounds in such sublime beauties, and could endeavour to discredit a poem, consisting of near six thousand lines, on account of a few mistakes in expression and prosody, proceeding entirely from the author's being a Scotchman, who had never been out of his own country. As there is a new edition published of this poem, wherein all or most of these trivial mistakes are corrected, I flatter myself that you will gladly lay hold of this opportunity of retracting your oversight, and doing justice to a performance, which may, perhaps, be regarded as one of the ornaments of our language. I appeal from your sentence, as an old woman did from a

---

[1] Terentianus Maurus, *Carmen heroicum de litteris, syllabis et metris*, 258.

sentence pronounced by Philip of Macedon : —I appeal from Philip, ill-counselled and in a hurry, to Philip, well-advised, and judging with delibera-tion. The authority which you possess with the public makes your censure fall with weight ; and I question not but you will be the more ready, on that account to redress any injury, into which either negligence, prejudice, or mistake, may have betrayed you.

The letter was unsigned ; but an editorial preface, probably by Smollett, accepted the rebuke in good faith : " By perusing the following article, the reader will perceive, that how subject soever we, the Reviewers, may be to oversights and errors, we are not so hardened in critical pride, and insolence, but that, upon conviction, we can retract our censures, and provided we be candidly rebuked, kiss the rod of correction with great humility." It would be futile, however, to attempt to follow Hume's further argument that " The author, inspired with the true genius of Greece, and smit with the most profound veneration for Homer, disdains all frivolous ornaments ; and relying entirely on his sublime imagination, and his nervous and harmonious expression, has ventured to present to his reader the naked beauties of nature, and challenges for his partizans all the admirers of genuine antiquity." It is difficult to believe that Smollett could have read this sentence without an indulgent, patriotic smile, although there is evidence that many another Scot took it seriously. Certainly few English did.

Any literary revival which is not perfectly spontaneous in nature inevitably smells of the lamp. The patriotic impulses of David Hume and his associates to foster such a revival among the English-writing poets of Scotland definitely smacks of artificiality. The Scottish intellect produced undoubted masterpieces in the productions of Hume, Robertson, and Smith, but it produced none on the imaginative level because then, as at no other time, could mere patronage and well-wishing produce genius. Patriot-ism also has a fixed tendency to degenerate into provincialism, as is well illustrated in the case of the ill-fated *Edinburgh Review* of 1755.

The preface to the first issue of the *Edinburgh Review*, drawn up by Alexander Wedderburn, is a manifesto of the Scottish Enlighten-ment : " The design of this work is, to lay before the Public, from time to time, a view of the progressive state of learning in this country." It proceeds with a historical sketch of those political and religious factors in the seventeenth century which had retarded literary development. Two obstructions to the progress of knowledge were now at mid-eighteenth-century in the process of being removed : " the difficulty of a proper expression in a country where there is either no standard of language, or at least one very remote " and " the slow advance that the country had made in the art of printing."

The essential provincialism of this plan is made evident in " A Letter to the Authors of the *Edinburgh Review*," which was printed at the close of the second and final issue. The writer was Adam Smith, himself one of the editors. The letter opens :

Gentlemen,

It gives me pleasure to see a work so generally useful, as that which you have undertaken, likely to be so well executed in this country. I am afraid, however, you will find it impossible to support it with any degree of spirit, while you confine yourselves almost entirely to an account of the books published in Scotland. This country, which is but just beginning to attempt figuring in the learned world, produces as yet so few works of reputation, that it is scarce possible a paper which criticises upon them chiefly, should interest the public for any considerable time. The singular absurdity of some performances which you have so well represented in your first number, might divert your readers for once ; But no eloquence could support a paper which consisted chiefly of accounts of such performances.

The charge, then, is provincialism and the cure is cosmopolitanism : " that you should enlarge your plan ; that you should still continue to take notice, with the same humanity and candour, of every Scotch production that is tolerably decent. But that you should observe with regard to Europe in general the same plan which you followed with regard to England. . . ." Smith points out that " this task [will not] be so very laborious as at first one might be apt to imagine. For tho' learning is cultivated in some degree in almost every part of Europe, it is in France and England only that it is cultivated with such success or reputation as to excite the attention of foreign nations." He compares the literature of these two nations and particularly cites the *Encyclopédie* and the recent publications of Rousseau as the type of foreign literature that might advantageously be brought to the attention of Scottish readers. It is instructive to note in passing that Smith's own list of British philosophers stops short with Hutcheson and fails to mention his friend Hume.

Adam Smith's letter was the last word of the *Edinburgh Review*. The provinciality of the *Review*, however, was deeper than he had imagined. It was really twofold : the lack of sufficient genius in Scotland to provide materials for comment and the lack of courage of its editors. " Edinburgh is a hot-bed of genius. I have had the good fortune to be made acquainted with many authors of the first distinction ; such as the two Humes, Robertson, Smith,

Wallace, Blair, Ferguson, Wilkie, etc." exclaims Matthew Bramble ; but then Bramble is the mouthpiece of that loyal Scotsman, Tobias Smollett. Though Edinburgh *was* a hot-bed of genius, it was still unable to produce enough good literature to fill the pages of an *Edinburgh Review*. But that deficiency was partly due to the pusillanimity of the editors, who had excluded both the person and the works of Scotland's greatest man of letters. Without Hume and besides Smith himself, who was there of sufficient breadth of intellect to carry out the newly proposed plan ? Furthermore, if every last cookery book was deemed worthy of a review solely because it was printed in Scotland, why was not the *History of England*? Finally, what is to be made of Smith's deliberate exclusion of Hume from his list of philosophers ? The fact that the *Edinburgh Review* failed within a year despite its self-denying policy is but further proof of an inherent narrowness of vision. Any periodical that was afraid to deal with the nation's leading man of letters, whether in approval or in disapproval, was doomed to failure from the start. The *Edinburgh Review* was never truly national, but only provincial.

The thesis of David Hume that the Scots were " the People most distinguish'd for Literature in Europe " received welcome if unexpected support in 1764 from the Professor of Eloquence and Belles-Lettres in the Royal School of Turin, Carlo Giovanni Maria Denina. The professor is certainly unequivocal : in literature, the English are going downhill while the Scots are going uphill. " The good writers in our days bear no proportion to those who adorned England thirty years ago. But this deficiency in England is amply compensated, by the many eminent authors who at present make such a distinguished figure in Scotland. The Scotch, as they form but one nation with the English, and write the same language, conceal . . . from the observation of the neighbouring nations that sensible decline in the genius and literature of England, which would otherwise be conspicuous to all Europe. . . . It is now an incontestable fact, that the principal authors who have adorned the British literature in these latter times, or do honour to it in the present days, have received their birth and education in Scotland."

Among the poets, Denina singles out Blacklock, Home, Mallet, Thomson, and Wilkie for tribute ; but he concedes that, " Poetry, however, is not the species of literature by which the Scotch have acquired their unrivalled glory." Rather it is history. " England, though it abounds in almost every species of fine

writing, has scarce produced one good historian. It was reserved
to the Scotch to give the finishing stroke to such an essential branch
of the English literature." "The celebrated works of David
Hume," of course, head the list. "Had Mr Smollett preferred,
as a great genius ought, lasting glory to present gain, and a celebrated name to the money of the bookseller, he would have had
great merit as an historian." To "the ingenious Mr Robertson,"
is due "immortal praise." A final stroke of Denina's must have
warmed the hearts of all those Scots who found themselves
in difficulty when writing standard English : "Some people,
infatuated with the pride and vanity of being born in the metropolis of a nation, persuade themselves that they alone are capable
of writing their own language ; and of course will scarcely believe
that the Scotch bid fair to carry off the prize of language even
from the English themselves." [1]

Hume and Denina were certainly overstating the case for Scottish literature. Nevertheless, the third quarter of the eighteenth
century, with all its deficiencies, *was* an Augustan Age for Scotland,
and the prophetic lines [2] of the English poet Aaron Hill proved truer
than much prophecy :

> Once more, O North ! I view thy winding shores,
> Climb thy bleak hills and cross thy dusky moors.
> Impartial view thee with an heedful eye,
> Yet still by nature, not by censure try.
> England thy sister is a gay coquet,
> Whom art enlivens, and temptations whet :
> Rich, proud, and wanton, she her beauty knows,
> And in a conscious warmth of beauty glows :
> Scotland comes after, like an unripe fair,
> Who sighs with anguish at her sister's air ;
> Unconscious, that she'll quickly have her day,
> And be the toast when Albion's charms decay.

---

[1] Quoted in *Scots Mag.*, xxvi (1764), 465–7. Denina's *Essay on the Revolutions
of Literature* had appeared at Glasgow in 1763.
[2] "Written on a Window in North Britain."

CHAPTER 28

THE INDIFFERENCE OF ENGLAND

" The Barbarians who inhabit the Banks of the Thames."

LONDON was frequently in the thoughts of David Hume in the later 1750s, alternately attracting and repelling him. This attraction and repulsion was, in some measure, controlled by his changing attitudes towards the other two major cities in his orbit, Edinburgh and Paris. The call of Paris was becoming stronger and stronger. That cosmopolitan centre began to symbolise the perfect haven for the man of letters, where he would be welcomed for the power of his intellect and the productions of his pen without nationalistic or religious bias. Yet Hume remained apprehensive of Paris because of its very perfection : " I believe it will be safer for me not to go thither, for I might probably settle there for life." Loyal Scot that he was, Hume was averse to leaving his native land ; but he was, nevertheless, distressed by persecution and hurt by the embarrassment that his very presence brought upon his friends. So he reluctantly came to the conclusion that if he ever gave up Edinburgh, it had better be for London.

In 1757 Hume was progressing well with the *History of the Tudors* and was beginning to debate whether to proceed forward to William and Mary or backward to the early periods. The former would prove more popular but would require residence in London for the accumulation of materials, and he complained that there were no public libraries in London. This lack meant that Hume would be dependent upon gaining admission to the private collections of the great English families ; and he did not relish the thought of possibly being rebuffed by Whig ministers. With a vacillation which was to characterise his later life, he postponed decision on the future course of the *History* as long as possible, but in 1758 was compelled to go to London to put the *Tudors* through the press.

Foreseeing this eventuality, Hume had written to Dr Clephane the previous September :

I shall certainly be in London next summer ; and probably to remain there during life ; at least, if I can settle myself to my mind, which I beg you to have an eye to. A room in a sober, discreet family, who would not be averse to admit a sober, discreet, virtuous, frugal, regular, quiet, good-natured man of a bad character; such a room, I say, would suit me extremely, especially if I could take most of my meals in the family ; and more especially still, if it was not far distant from Dr Clephane's. I shall then be able, dear Doctor, to spend £150 a year, which is the sum upon which, I remember, you formerly undertook me.

But Hume was never to be re-united with his beloved Doctor. Clephane had been induced to take an appointment in the fatal expedition of 1758 against St Malo, was taken ill, and died at sea. On 15 August 1758 Hume placed the manuscript of the *Tudors* in " two white Iron Boxes," to be forwarded to Strahan by stagecoach, because, he explained, " I go up on Horseback " within a few weeks.

Rumour of Hume's possibly permanent removal from Scotland brought expressions of grief from friends and of glee from enemies. Among the friends was George Dempster, who, as early as December 1756, had lamented that David Hume,

at length weary with the spirit of persecution which he meets with in the clergy and even in people of a more liberal way of thinking, proposes to go up to London in the spring, and abandoning an ungrateful country shelter himself under the wing of liberty and enjoy the society of men who know how to estimate his merit. I am really sorry for the loss we shall sustain. I have always considered him as the Socrates of Edinburgh and I have seldom differed from his opinions without discovering soon after that education and prejudice had blinded my eyes while his were opened by speculation and philosophy.[1]

Dempster's tribute is all the more touching in that it came from a man who had just written : " It seems difficult for me (for me who dotes upon David) to believe that he can have a great regard for even the best mode of religion and the least extravagant if we consider how destitute he is of that only support of it, Faith."

Before Hume's departure for London in the summer of 1758, an unknown enemy printed a broadside *Advertisement* :

Whereas I D[avi]d H[u]me, Esq ; of *North-Britain, Philo-Scot,* have by great Travel, and much Study, for the benefit of Mankind, discovered and brought to Perfection my Opiatismos, or Universal Soporific, Antiophthalmic, Cacodemoniac, Medicine, which stills, deadens, and infallibly cures, all vapourish Terrors or Perturbations of the Mind, whether occasioned by Fraud, Fornication, Murder, or Adultery, Whimsies of a Future State, or Fear of a Judgment to come, as can be attested by the N[o]b[ili]ty, Gen[tr]y, and Cl[erg]y of that Kingdom, in the Metropolis of which I have peaceably practised for above these twenty Years with astonishing Success :

---

[1] Dempster, *Letters to Fergusson*, p. 22.

And now, prompted by the Love I also bear my Fellow Subjects of *South-Britain*, and embracing the Opportunity of that Favourable Disposition I have long observed there to receive my wonderful Medicine, and before it shall be abated, by the Visitations and Calamities of War which it does not yet appear to be :*

I hereby give Notice to the N[o]b[ili]ty, Gen[tr]y, my L[ord]s the Bis[ho]ps, the Cl[erg]y, and others whom it may concern, that upon the first Day of *July*, and third Year of this present War, I set out Post from my bibliopolic Mansion, with my Retinue, called *Legion*. . . .

After my Arrival in the great City, I hereby promise to exhibit this my powerful Soporific, in modern monthly Dozes, at the small Price of Sixpence, with good Allowance to such as shall take a Quantity for Sea Service, and the Benefit of the Navy, where it is taken with great Success, except in an Engagement and a Storm, unless the Ad[mira]l shall happen to think otherways.

N.B. To prevent Counterfeits, my Packets are sealed with my Coat of Arms, *viz.* A Lion Rampant ; the Supporters, a Judge and Vulture : Motto, *Devorare appetens.*[1]

At London in September, David Hume took up lodgings with the sisters Anne and Peggy Elliot, poor relations of the Minto family, who ran a boarding house for Scottish gentlemen at Lisle Street, Leicester Fields. With these ladies David soon became a great favourite, and he always stayed with them when in London for years to come. After the absence of a full decade and particularly after the constraining atmosphere that he had meanwhile endured at Edinburgh, London seemed good to Hume. He felt free from bigotry and respected in his own right as man of letters. The following January he acknowledged to Robertson that " I used every expedient to evade this journey to London, yet it is now uncertain whether I shall ever leave it."

Of the Scots that Hume had associated with in London twenty years previous, James Thomson had died and Sir Andrew Mitchell had gone to Berlin as ambassador to Frederick the Great ; but John Armstrong, David Mallet, and James Oswald of Dunnikier, the last now Commissioner of Trade, were still about. So were the newer friends of the military expeditions, General St Clair and Sir Harry Erskine—but, alas, not Clephane. " The late Rev. Mr John Home," as David irreverently called him, was private secretary to Scotland's leading statesman, Lord Bute. " The still Rev. Adam Ferguson " was tutor to the sons of the same lord, while David and other friends played at politics to secure a professorship for him at Edinburgh University.

---

[1] The Seven Years' War having broken out in July 1756, " the first Day of *July*, and third Year of the present War " sets the date of Hume's supposed departure as 1 July 1758. In the coat of arms, the " Lion Rampant " is Hume ; the " Judge " is Lord Kames ; and the " Vulture " may be taken as Robertson.

Sir Gilbert Elliot had become a Lord of the Admiralty. Allan Ramsay was winning fame as a portrait painter. Robert and James Adam were prominent architects. Alexander Wedderburn, observed Hume with satisfaction, " is advancing with great Strides in his Profession " of the law. " He only stops now & then to take up an Apple ; & sometimes a Cockleshell. But no body entertains at present any doubt of his Success." [1]   With Andrew Millar and his associates, Thomas Cadell and William Strahan, Hume maintained social, as well as business, relations.

Welcomed by all these old friends, Hume made many new friends during his London visits of 1758–59 and 1761. One interesting group consisted of those clerical answerers to his writings who had treated him, as befits the philosopher, with courtesy and respect. At Hume's desire, Drs William Adams, John Douglas, and Richard Price were invited to a dinner at Cadell's house in the Strand. The learned clerics, we are assured, " were all delighted with David," who long remained on good terms with them, exchanging visits and letters. " You have treated me much better than I deserve," Hume admitted to Adams, and, presumably, to the others as well. [2]

When Boswell and Johnson visited Adams at Oxford in 1776, Adams then being Master of Pembroke College, Boswell discovered on his bookshelves a copy of the quarto edition of Hume's *Essays and Treatises* handsomely bound in morocco. Much annoyed by the friendliness of Adams to Hume, Boswell took " the liberty to object to treating an infidel writer with smooth civility. . . . Where the controversy is concerning the truth of religion," he urged, " it is of such vast importance to him who maintains it, to obtain the victory, that the person of an opponent ought not to be spared." Johnson took up the cudgels in Boswell's behalf : " If my antagonist writes bad language, though that may not be essential to the question, I will attack him for his bad language." Adams's polite demurrer, " You would not jostle a chimney-sweeper," brought Johnson's famous retort, " Yes, Sir, if it were necessary to jostle him *down*." Johnson was a man who tried to live up to his principles and, on the occasion of his first meeting with Hume, presumably at London during one of the present visits, snubbed him publicly. In November 1762 Boswell's *Journal* records Hume on the subject of Johnson :

[1] NHL, p. 47.
[2] *Reminiscences and Table Talk of Samuel Rogers*, ed. G. H. Powell (London 1903), p. 67.

" He holds Mr. Hume in abhorrence and left a company one night upon his coming in." [1]

Happily, some few controversialists took a different view, Richard Price, for example, who in 1758 had joined the ranks of the writers against Hume with his *Review of the Principal Questions and Difficulties in Morals*. Some years afterward, Price told Hume, " I am not, I hope, inclin'd to dislike any person merely for a difference in opinion however great ; or to connect worth of character and God's favour with any particular Set of Sentiments," [2] Dr Douglas, later Bishop of Salisbury, who, like Adams, had refuted Hume on miracles, also corresponded with him on historical subjects. From Edinburgh in 1760 Hume warmly remembered " our Acquaintance & Correspondence, which gave me so much Entertainment when I was in London." Mrs Anderson, the sister of Douglas, kept the British Coffee-house near Charing Cross, where Scots in London were wont to meet for refreshment, social, political, and artistic, as well as of the table.

Other new literary acquaintances included Edmund Burke, from Ireland, who brought out in 1759 the second edition of his *Philosophical Inquiry into the Origin of Our Ideas of the Sublime and Beautiful*. Professing to admire this " very pretty treatise," Hume was pleased to meet the young Irishman at the table of David Garrick. Burke disputed Hume's authorities for his account of the Irish massacre of 1641, while Hume stoutly maintained their validity. Though tolerant of Hume for some years to come, Burke subsequently became an outspoken critic of his philosophical and religious principles, informing Boswell that he spoke to him only because the present liberal state of society required it. [3]

A more congenial spirit to Hume was Benjamin Franklin, over from America as Deputy-Postmaster-General for the Colonies. The two probably met at Strahan's, where Franklin had business to transact, and they met again at Edinburgh in the autumn of 1759. Three years later Franklin contributed, at Hume's request, a paper to the Edinburgh Philosophical Society on the use of the lightning-rod. In thanks Hume paid him a generous compliment :

I am very sorry, that you intend soon to leave our hemisphere. America has sent us many good things, gold, silver, sugar, tobacco, indigo, etc. ; but you are the first philosopher, and indeed the first great man of letters, for whom we are beholden to her. It is our own fault, that we have not kept him ; whence it appears, that we do not agree with Solomon, that wisdom is above

[1] *Johnson*, II, 442–3 ; *Boswell Papers*, I, 128.   [2] RSE, VI, 85.   [3] Robert Bisset, *Life of Edmund Burke* (London 1798), II, 425–8 ; *Boswell Papers*, XI, 268.

gold ; for we take care never to send back an ounce of the latter, which we once lay our fingers upon.[1]

With the opening of the British Museum on 15 January 1759 Hume could no longer grumble over the lack of public libraries in London. As early as 2 November 1758 he had applied for a ticket of admission to consult manuscripts of England under the Tudors. On 3 March 1759 he was also granted leave to study in the Reading Room for six months, leave that was renewed twice, on 31 July and 6 November 1761.[2] On 30 December 1758, the young Gibbon had written his father that " I am also to meet at Mrs. Cilesia's the great David Hume. I shall seek his acquaintance without being discouraged by Maty." [3] Matthew Maty, formerly editor of the *Journal Britannique*, was one of the Under-Librarians at the British Museum and was already acquainted with Hume ; but his warning to Gibbon is puzzling. Other men of letters that Hume met include Dr Thomas Birch, secretary of the Royal Society and author of the *General Dictionary*, and Robert Wood, classical scholar and Under-Secretary of State.

In high society, where Hume was sometimes induced to make an appearance, he became acquainted with Lord Chesterfield, Lord Shelburne, and Lord Temple, and also George Grenville and Charles Townshend. With the last two, he did not get along very well. In Colonel Isaac Barré, Lord Shelburne's chief political henchman, however, he found kindred feelings, and the two exchanged pleasant, witty letters. And Hume was charmed by such personalities as Lady Mary Coke, Lady Harvey, and Mrs Elizabeth Montagu, the famous Bluestocking.

One lady, however, Hume could not endure. Lord Charlemont relates [4] that, " I never saw him so much displeased, or so much disconcerted as by the Petulance of Mrs. Mallet, the pert and conceited Wife of Bolingbroke's Editor. This lady, who was not acquainted with Hume, meeting him one night at an Assembly, boldly accosted him in these Words—' Mr. Hume, Give me leave to introduce myself to you. We Deists ought to know each other.' —' Madam,' replied He, ' I am no Deist. I do na style myself so, neither do I desire to be known by that Appellation.' " With David Mallet, himself, Hume was on more friendly terms and happy to secure his services in helping him to excise Scotticisms

[1] HL, i, 357–8.   [2] Arthur Sherbo, " Some Early Readers in the British Museum," in *Transactions of the Cambridge Bibliographical Society*, vi (1972), 56–64.
[3] Gibbon, *Private Letters*, i, 21–2. Mrs Cilesia was the eldest daughter of David Mallet by his first wife.   [4] Lord Charlemont, " Anecdotes of Hume," in RIA, MS –12/R/7, f.523.

from the *History of England.* Of Mallet's literary talents, however, he held no high opinion.

Yet David Hume was not on a mere social jaunt to London to enlarge his circle of friends—much as he enjoyed doing so. Primarily there to put his Tudor volumes through the press, he was happy to take the occasion to assist in the printing of books by William Robertson and Alexander Gerard. Professor of Moral Philosophy and Logic at Marischal College, Aberdeen, Gerard had been awarded a gold medal by the Select Society of Edinburgh for an *Essay on Taste* in the contest opened in 1757. One of the committee of award, Hume felt himself obliged to help Millar in the correction of this work, which was published in May 1759.[1] It could hardly have been by way of returning the favour that Gerard brought out the following year *The Influence of the Pastoral Office on the Character Examined ; with a View, especially, to Mr. Hume's Representation of the Spirit of that Office.*

Robertson had been at work on the *History of Scotland* since 1753 and, on Hume's advice, had rejected a handsome offer from Gavin Hamilton in Edinburgh of £500 for one edition of 2,000 copies. Early in 1758 Robertson had gone up to London, where he offered the work to Millar. In some perplexity, that most scrupulous publisher consulted Hume as to whether Robertson would not be in competition with him. Hume replied in the negative : " Some part of his Subject is common with mine ; but as his Work is a History of Scotland, mine of England, we do not interfere ; and it will rather be an Amusement to the Reader to compare our Method of treating the same Subject. I give you Thanks, however, for your Attention in asking my Opinion." Hume further clarified the situation for Millar : " I am very glad that Mr Robertson is entering on Terms with you. It was indeed my Advice to him, when he set out for London, that he shoud think of no other Body ; and I ventur'd to assure him, that he woud find your way of dealing frank & generous." Such initial generosity on the part of Hume characterises all his relations with Robertson.

While the *History of Scotland* was going through the press, Hume read the corrected sheets, made comparisons with his own treatment of crucial issues (notably that of Mary Queen of Scots), and on several occasions, sent his rival new information which required revisions and cancels in the printed text. The *History of Scotland* appeared on 29 January 1759, but even before that date Hume was joyously forwarding to the author enthusiastic reports

---

[1] Nichols, *Literary Anecdotes,* II, 326.

from advance readers. " Dr [John] Blair tells me, that Prince Edward is reading you, and is charmed. I hear the same of the Princess and Prince of Wales. But what will really give you pleasure, I lent my copy to Elliot during the holidays, who thinks it one of the finest performances he ever read ; and tho he expected much, he finds more."

Robertson, for his part, was seemingly incapable of the generosity and open-mindedness of Hume. To begin with, he had actually gone so far as to request Hume not to write on the same period as himself and, when Hume had not seen fit to alter his plans, had refused to exchange ideas with him over the controversial Marian issue. " It would have been much better," deplored Hume from London, " had we communicated before printing, which was always my desire, and was most suitable to the friendship which always did, and, I hope always will, subsist between us." Immediately after Robertson's public appearance, Hume reverted to the same topic : " You are at present the best Critic in Britain of my Performance ; as I am perhaps of Yours ; and if Entreaties can prevail on you to make you be particular in your Remarks on me, I woud not spare them ; If the Promise of a reciprocal Censure will do, I make you the same Promise. This is the best Way in which we can now supply the Place of a previous Communication."

Disquieted though he was by Robertson's jealous suspicions, Hume exulted in his good reception. " You have very good Reason to be satisfy'd with the Success of your History. . . . I have not heard of one who does not praise it warmly. . . . The Town will have it, that you was educated at Oxford ; thinking it impossible for a mere untraveld Scotsman to produce such Language." Brushing aside all personal feelings, Hume proceeded :

I am diverting myself with the Notion how much you will profit by the Applauses of my Enemies in Scotland. Had you & I been such Fools as to have given way to Jealousy, to have entertaind Animosity & Malignity against each other, and have rent all our Acquaintance into Parties ; what a noble Amusement shoud we have exhibited to the Blockheads, which now they are likely to be disappointed of ? All the people whose Friendship or Judgement either of us value, are Friends to both, & will be pleas'd with the Success of both ; as we will be with that of each other. I declare to you, I have not, of a long time, had a more sensible Pleasure than the good Reception of your History has given me within this Fortnight.

Hume's intimation that Robertson's *History* would meet with a better reception than his own proved to be well grounded. With the appearance of the *History of the Tudors* on 12 March, Hume had to suffer unfavourable comparison with Robertson. Disappointed as he was and no little mortified, he managed to conceal his feelings under playful banter. " A plague take you ! " he remonstrated. " Here I sat near the historical summit of Parnassus, immediately under Dr Smollett ; and you have the impudence to squeeze yourself by me, and place yourself directly under his feet. Do you imagine that this can be agreeable to me ? " So popular did Robertson prove that Millar rushed through a second edition before the end of April. Concerning his own *Tudors*, Hume sadly remarked in *My Own Life* that, " The Clamour against this Performance was almost equal to that against the History of the two first Stuarts." From the start, nevertheless, Hume sang the praises of Robertson to his French correspondents and promoted a French translation.

Just as Hume's friendship with Wallace was celebrated in France, so his friendship with Robertson was celebrated in Italy. In 1765 Peter Crocchi translated the first book of the *History of Scotland* into Italian, and in the preface informed the world how the two great rivals lived in perfect harmony. Crocchi had had the story from Colonel Edmonstoune and forwarded a copy of his translation to Hume, together with a covering letter, by the hands of Boswell, who was then at Siena. " Happy, if I can prevail upon the literati of this age to follow your noble example," exclaimed Crocchi.[1]

Hume continued to advise Robertson concerning his literary career, for now that the *History of Scotland* was in print, Robertson was casting about for a fresh subject to turn his attention to. Hume advised against the " Age of Leo the Tenth " on the ground of the wide range of scholarship involved, and suggested instead " the antient History, particularly that of Greece." The " Age of Charles the V," which Robertson was seriously considering, did not appeal to Hume, who countered with " an Idea, which has sometimes pleas'd me, & which I had once entertaind Thoughts of attempting," that is, short lives in the manner of Plutarch. " If one Volume were successful you might compose another at your Leizure ; & the Field is unexhaustible." Finally Hume passed on a suggestion, originating with Lord Mansfield and repeated by General St Clair, that Robertson would be well provided for in England if he were willing to leave the Church of Scotland. " Only the Matter must be kept a Secret," Hume cautioned ; " & you

[1] RSE, iv, 48.

must step at once from the one Church into the other." Robertson, however, did not follow Hume in this suggestion, probably to Hume's ultimate satisfaction. Nor did Robertson follow Hume's literary advice, for in 1769 he published the *History of the Reign of Charles V* in three volumes. Running over the first sheets as they fell from the press in London, Hume acknowledged to Robertson that " They even excel, and, I think, in a sensible degree, your *History of Scotland*. I propose to myself great pleasure in being the only man in England, during some months, who will be in a situation of doing you justice, after which you may certainly expect that my voice will be drowned in that of the public."

In April 1759 Andrew Millar brought out Adam Smith's *Theory of Moral Sentiments*.[1] Whether Hume had been proof-reader or not, the publication gave rise to one of his most charming letters to an intimate friend. This letter is perhaps all the more charming because it cannot totally conceal Hume's mortification in his own lack of literary success.

Lisle Street Leicester Fields
12 April. 1759

Dear Smith

I give you thanks for the agreeable Present of your Theory. Wedderburn & I made Presents of our Copies to such of our Acquaintance as we thought good Judges, & proper to spread the Reputation of the Book. I sent one to the Duke of Argyle, to Lord Lyttleton, Horace Walpole, Soames Jennyns, & Burke, an Irish Gentleman, who wrote lately a very pretty Treatise on the Sublime. Millar desird my Permission to send one in your Name to Dr Warburton. I have delayd writing to you till I cou'd tell you something of the Success of the Book, and coud prognosticate with some Probability whether it shoud be finally damnd to Oblivion, or shoud be registerd in the Temple of Immortality. Tho' it has been publishd only a few Weeks, I think there appear already such strong Symptoms, that I can almost venture to fortell its Fate. It is in short this— But I have been interrupted in my Letter by a foolish impertinent Visit . . . [about which Hume goes on inexorably for a full page]. But what is all this to my Book ? say you—My Dear Mr Smith, have Patience: Compose yourself to Tranquillity : Show yourself a Philosopher in Practice as well as Profession : Think on the Emptiness, & Rashness, and Futility of the common Judgements of Men : How little they are regulatd by Reason in any Subject, much more in philosophical Subjects, which so far exceed the Comprehension of the Vulgar. *Non si quid improba Roma, Elevet, accedas examenque improbum in illa, Perpendas trutina, nec te quaesiveris extra.*[2] A wise man's Kingdom is his own Breast : Or, if he ever looks farther, it will only be to the Judgement of a select few, who are free from Prejudices, & capable of examining his Work. Nothing indeed can be a stronger Presumption of Falshood than the Approbation of the Multitude ; and Phocion, you know, always suspected himself of some Blunder, when he was attended with the Applauses of the Populace.

---

[1] See Textual Supplement for Smith's praise of Hume.   [2] Persius, *Satires*, i, 5–7.

Supposing, therefore, that you have duely prepard yourself for the worst by all these Reflections ; I proceed to tell you the melancholy News, that your Book has been very unfortunate : For the Public seem disposd to applaud it extremely. It was lookd for by the foolish People with some Impatience ; and the Mob of Literati are beginning already to be very loud in its Praises. Three Bishops calld yesterday at Millar's Shop in order to buy Copies, and to ask Questions about the Author : The Bishop of Peterborough said he had passd the Evening in a Company, where he heard it extolld above all Books in the World. You may conclude what Opinion true Philosophers will entertain of it, when these Retainers to Superstition praise it so highly. The Duke of Argyle is more decisive than he uses to be in its Favour : I suppose he either considers it as an Exotic, or thinks the Author will be serviceable to him in the Glasgow Elections. Lord Lyttleton says, that Robertson & Smith and Bower [a mere journalist !] are the Glories of English Literature. Oswald protests he does not know whether he has reapd more Instruction or Entertainment from it : But you may easily judge what Reliance can be put on his Judgement, who has been engagd all his Life in public Business & who never sees any Faults in his Friends. Millar exults & brags that two thirds of the Edition are already sold, & that he is now sure of Success. You see what a Son of the Earth that is, to value Books only by the Profit they bring him. In that View, I believe it may prove a very good Book.

Charles Towns[h]end, who passes for the cleverest Fellow in England, is so taken with the Performance, that he said to Oswald he wou'd put the Duke of Buccleugh under the Authors Care, & woud endeavour to make it worth his while to accept of that Charge. As soon as I heard this, I calld on him twice with a View of talking with him about the Matter, & of convincing him of the Propriety of sending that young Nobleman to Glasgow : For I coud not hope, that he coud offer you any Terms, which woud tempt you to renounce your Professorship : But I missd him. Mr Towns[h]end passes for being a little uncertain in his Resolutions ; so perhaps you need not build much on this Sally.

In recompense for so many mortifying things, which nothing but Truth coud have extorted from me, & which I coud easily have mutiply'd to a greater Number ; I doubt not but you are so good a Christian as to return good for evil and to flatter my Vanity, by telling me, that all the Godly in Scotland abuse me for my Account of John Knox & the Reformation &c. I suppose you are glad to see my Paper end, & that I am obligd to conclude with

Your humble Servant

David Hume. [1]

Strange to say, the irresolute Townshend did not forget his offhand proposal, and Smith was not loath to accept the offer of £300 a year and a similar pension for life. In January 1764 he resigned his Glasgow professorship and, shortly thereafter, set out for France as travelling tutor to the young duke. Smith, to be sure, had an eye on the future opportunities afforded to compose the *Wealth of Nations*. In the summer of 1759, when David Hume learned that a new edition of Smith's *Theory* of

[1] NHL, pp. 51–5.

Moral Sentiments was being projected, he immediately sent his friend several cogent arguments to be taken into consideration.

Andrew Millar's remarkable championing of Scottish letters in the year 1759 includes, in summary, besides Hume's *Tudors*, Gerard's *Essay on Taste*, Robertson's *History of Scotland*, Smith's *Theory of Moral Sentiments*, and the second edition of Wilkie's *Epigoniad*. David Hume had some influence on all of these transactions, whether in steering the authors to Millar or in helping to put the works through the press. In the case of the *Epigoniad* he also wrote the " Letter to the Authors of the Critical Review." One other minor literary interest of Hume's London visits was his proposal to Millar, " that it was worthy of so eminent a Bookseller, as he, to make a compleat elegant Set of the Classics, which might set up his Name equal to the Alduses, Stevens, or Elzivirs. . . ." Millar never acted on this suggestion, however, and the Foulis brothers at Glasgow came as close to carrying it out as did any British publisher of the eighteenth century.

With the publication of the *History of the Tudors* David Hume had to decide whether to remain in London permanently or to return to Edinburgh. This decision was certainly influenced by the fact that on 27 July 1759 he signed a contract with Millar to write the history of England from the Roman invasion to the accession of Henry VII, for which he was to receive £1400—a sure sign that the astute Millar now considered the *History of England* a success. " This is the first previous agreement ever I made with a Bookseller," Hume wrote Adam Smith. " I am in doubt whether I shall stay here & execute the Work ; or return to Scotland, & only come up here to consult the Manuscripts." But Hume's doubt could not have lasted very long, for by 10 October 1759 [1] he was back at Ninewells, and a week later at Edinburgh.

Home once more, his first " very laborious, but not unentertaining Occupation " was " in adding the Authorities to the Volumes of the Stuarts," for the omission of which he had been chidden by Horace Walpole. His second and principal occupation was the writing of the early English history. " I find the Advocates Library," he told Millar, " very well provided of Books on this Period ; but before I finish I shall pass a considerable time in London, to peruse the Manuscripts in the Musaeum." Despite this optimism concerning the resources of the Advocates'

[1] On that date he signed, as witness, a " Tack of John Home of Ninewells to Peter Johnson " (NLS, MS 582, f.77).

Library, Hume was compelled to borrow many books from friends and to buy, through Millar, many more. Shrewdly, he engaged with the Curators of the library, however, " to take from me such as they want at the Price."

Writing at a furious pace, " some days fourteen hours," [1] Hume had completed his manuscript within nineteen months, but by no means equalling the record of Smollett. Unlike Smollett, too, Hume had the advantage of his earlier attempt at composition on this period of history.[2] The drudgery of poring over a great many dull books he took in good spirits, comparing himself to a sportsman seeking hares, who does not mind the difficulty of the terrain if only he can find enough hares. He also recognised the scholar's need for rest and relaxation and remarked to friends that the power that he particularly wished to possess was that of sleeping whenever he pleased.[3]

After a brief respite at Ninewells in June 1761, Hume hastened back to London to complete his research and to see the work through the press. " You may expect to have a very troublesome Dun upon you," he had warned Strahan, " in making Demands of a regular Visit of your Devil : and I shall be able to cure you of some Indolence . . . which is growing upon you. If this Indolence comes from Riches, I hope also to cure it another way, by gaining your Money at Whist. . . ." At London Dr Birch noted that David Hume had come through his herculean labours of the past two years remarkably well and " without the least apparent diminution of his former bulk." [4] A very troublesome dun Hume must indeed have proved to Strahan, for the two volumes of the *History of England from the Invasion of Julius Caesar to the Accession of Henry VII* were published on 11 November.[5] Little more than a month later Hume set out on the return journey to Scotland.

Without the vacillations of his previous visit of 1758–59, Hume in 1761 harboured not the least intention of remaining permanently in London. His mind was now firmly made up that his future happiness lay in Edinburgh. Gone were the hopes, formerly expressed to Ridpath, that at London he might " shelter himself under the wing of liberty and enjoy the society

---

[1] Thomas Birch as quoted in George Harris, *Life of Lord Chancellor Hardwicke* (London 1847), III, 409.   [2] See above, Ch. 13, the close. A comparison of the *History* with the memoranda of 1745 shows that in the printed work Hume followed his early outline and sometimes the very phrasing.   [3] For Allan Ramsay's comment on Hume's circle in Edinburgh, September 1760, see Textual Supplement.
[4] Birch, as above.   [5] The date on the title-page is 1762.

of men who know how to estimate his merit." The " Socrates of
Edinburgh " was determined to remain henceforth at Edinburgh.
In view of the facts that Hume had vastly widened his circle of
friends at London and had been courteously received even by
several of his leading antagonists, how is this change of mind
to be accounted for ?

David Hume's reversal of attitude towards England coincided
with changing political and social conditions. The Seven Years'
War had broken out in July 1756, and England, under the
brilliant leadership of William Pitt, soon found that she was indeed,
not only a European, but a world power. Clive was winning
India, and Wolfe in 1759 won Canada. The French navy was
virtually destroyed, and French commerce was swept off the
seas. English self-confidence, which had long been at an ebb,
underwent a swift resurgence. At the crest of this tide George III
acceded to the throne in 1760. With Pitt's pronouncement that
hereafter the government would seek the best talent wherever to
be found, the auguries seemed good for Scotland. Lord Bute was
the power behind the throne, and, for the first time since the
Union, Scotland appeared to be in a favourable position politically.
English nationalists, however, immediately began the cry of
favouritism, instituting a violent and prolonged anti-Scottish
campaign. London was no longer a peaceful haven for a Scotsman.

With the accession of George III, Hume remarked cynically :
" I was glad to observe what our King says, that Faction is at an
End and Party Distinctions abolish'd." Experience had taught
him better. He had only recently seen how little the English
really trusted the Scots by their refusal to reinstate a Scottish
militia. He was continually being disgruntled by the irresponsible
branding of his *History* as Jacobite. He was becoming frightened
by the rise of the London mob and " the general Rage against
the Scots." He deplored the wave of nationalism under the
leadership of Pitt. Dismayed and humiliated by the lack of
respect shown to men of letters by those who guided the destiny
of the country, he allowed his deep-set aversion to soliciting
favours from the great to become almost a mania. " I am inclined
to throw up altogether, and to turn my back on those barbarians
(your great men, I mean) with disdain . . .," he exploded
indignantly in 1763. The previous year he had bemoaned that,
" It is strange, that Great Men in England should slight &
neglect Men of Letters when they pay court to them ; & rail at

them when they do not." The complaint had been occasioned by the inconstancies of Charles Townshend. Hume then went on to pronounce : " But I attach myself to no great Man, and visit none of them but such as happen to be my Friends, and particular Acquaintance. I wish they woud consider me as equally independent with themselves or more so."

The love of independence, the increasing distrust of the English, the sense of the dignity of being a man of letters, the aversion to becoming attached to a Great Man—all of these principles had been put to the test during Hume's visit to London in the summer and autumn of 1761, when a brilliant young English Earl had unexpectedly proffered friendship and patronage. In 1761, at the age of twenty-four, William Petty, Lord Fitzmaurice, had inherited the title of Earl of Shelburne and entered the House of Lords. He also entered upon a turbulent political career marked, first, by bitter opposition to Pitt and, after 1763, by prolonged alliance with him. At his town house in Hill Street, Shelburne had already given evidence of his two supreme interests in life, politics and the arts and sciences. There he gathered about him what Horace Walpole called " the little knot of young orators " and there, too, he welcomed men of letters and of science. To Hill Street David Hume was inevitably led by some of his Scottish friends already in the Shelburne coterie.

The following letter from Hume to Lord Shelburne, written the day before leaving London, tells its own poignant story :

December 12, 1761.

My Lord,

An accident, a little unexpected, has hastened my journey to Scotland a little sooner than I intended. I was offered a chaise that sets out to-morrow morning, where I could sit alone and loiter and read and muse for the length of four hundred miles. Your lordship may judge, by this specimen of my character, how unfit I am to mingle in such an active and sprightly society as that of which your Lordship invited me to partake, and that in reality a book and a fireside, are the only scenes for which I am now qualified. But I should be unfit to live among human creatures could I ever forget the obligations which I owe to your Lordship's goodness, or could ever lose the firm resolution of expressing my sense of them on all occasions. I beg your Lordship to believe that, though age and philosophy have mortified all ambition in me, yet there are other sentiments which I find more inherent in me, which I shall always cherish, and which no time can efface. And when I shall see your Lordship making a figure in the active scenes of life, I shall always consider your progress with a peculiar pleasure, though perhaps accompanied with the regret that I partake of it at so great a distance. I remember to have seen a picture in your Lordship's house of a Hottentot who fled from a cultivated life to his companions in the woods and left behind him all his fine accoutrements and attire. I compare not my case to his ; for I return to very sociable, civilized people. I only mean to express the force of habit which renders a man accustomed to retreat and study unfit for the commerce of the great world, and makes it a necessary piece of wisdom for him to shun it after age has rendered that habit entirely inveterate. This is the only excuse I can give to your Lordship for being so much wanting to my own interest as to leave London when you had contrived to make it so agreeable a habitation to me.

I did not hear of this vehicle till to-day, and to tell the truth, I rather chose to express my sentiments to your Lordship in writing, than to wait upon you in person, because however imperfectly I may have executed my purpose of discovering my sense of the obligations I owe your Lordship, I still could do it better by writing than by speech.

I am, with the greatest sincerity, My Lord,

Your Lordship's most obedient and most humble servant

David Hume.

That Hume was to all intents and purposes deliberately fleeing from the " cultivated life " of London is confirmed by a letter that he wrote the same day to General Robert Clerk, a Scotsman close to the Earl. " As I always kept the Purpose of returning " to Edinburgh, Hume apologises, "I could not resist this Temptation" of accepting the chaise ; " tho you & perhaps Lord Shelburn[e] may think my Departure a little abrupt." He requests Clerk to attempt to supply the defects in the letter to Shelburne. " Surely nothing could be more amiable, more free, more easy, than my Lord's Commerce and Society : Nothing could open better Prospects than the cultivating his Friendship : But," he regretfully notes, " these Considerations lose their Influence on a Recluse and an Ascetic, who retains no Ambition, who has lost his Relish for Pleasure, and who is becoming every day unqualify'd for any Pursuit but Sauntering & Study & Indolence." [1]

By the close of 1761 David Hume wanted no place among " the Barbarians who inhabit the Banks of the Thames " and was relieved at the prospect of retiring permanently to Edinburgh. His bitterness against the English received full expression three years later, when he wrote to Gilbert Elliot : " I do not believe there is one Englishman in fifty, who, if he heard that I had broke my Neck to night, woud not be rejoic'd with it. Some hate me because I am not a Tory, some because I am not a Whig, some because I am not a Christian, and all because I am a Scotsman. Can you seriously talk of my continuing an Englishman ? Am I, or are you, an Englishman ? Will they allow us to be so ? Do

[1] NHL, pp. 64-5.

they not treat with Derision our Pretensions to that Name, and with Hatred our just Pretensions to surpass & to govern them ? " [1] How Edinburgh would fare in direct competition with Paris still remained a question. For the time being, nevertheless, Hume was sure of himself.

[1] HL, I, 436, 470.

PART IV

CITIZEN OF THE WORLD

1763-1769

CHAPTER 29

SCOTLAND FOR EVER?

" A man of letters in a remote country."

" I HAVE hitherto been a wanderer on the face of the earth, without any abiding city ; but I have now at last purchased a house, which I am repairing, tho I cannot say that I have yet fixed any property in the earth, but only in the air ; for it is the third story of James's Court, and it cost me five hundred pounds. It is somewhat dear, but I shall be exceedingly well lodged." So David Hume announced his re-attachment to Edinburgh on Whitsunday 1762. This " very pretty little House, which I . . . repair'd and furnish'd to my Fancy," he was proud of. Around the living room he hung the set of classical line-engravings which had been presented to him by his friend Robert Strange, the Jacobite artist. The setting impressed Boswell when he paid a visit in November 1762 and found Hume " sitting at his ease reading Homer." [1]

James's Court, on the north side of the Lawnmarket, represented to Hume the acme of cosmopolitan living afforded by Edinburgh. Completed in 1727, this vast building was inhabited throughout the century by people of dignity and rank, who constituted a parliament or corporation regulating all public measures of the court. They held private receptions and balls and employed a scavenger of their own. Hume's " house," presumably the third story facing south and the sixth facing north (for the court was built on the north side of the steep ridge of the Castle Hill), commanded a magnificent prospect of Edinburgh, the Canongate, and the seaport of Leith ; across the Firth of Forth rose the hills of Fife. In later years Hume, having " a View of Kirkaldy from my Windows," liked to remind Adam Smith of their proximity. Katherine Home and Peggy Irvine, needless to say, joined the new domestic establishment. Only one item was lacking for complete elegance—a chaise, and that was purchased in May 1763.

The years of necessary frugality were over, and Hume was now able to afford any luxury which his modest way of living could possibly suggest. While in London in 1761 he had invested in the public funds, Andrew Millar advancing him £1,000 ; for

---

[1] HL, I, 405 ; *Boswell Papers*, I, 126, and see also XI, 91, 99.

several years Millar continued to advise him on financial matters. Having long declaimed against the stocks, Hume was now exposed to the many jokes of his friends. His rebuttal was that he had bought real stock and was not a jobber.[1] In *My Own Life* Hume writes of this period with quiet satisfaction : " the Copy Money, given me by the Booksellers, much exceeded any thing formerly known in England : I was become not only independent, but opulent. I retired to my native Country of Scotland, determined never more to set my Foot out of it ; and retaining the Satisfaction of never having preferred a Request to one great Man or even making Advances of Friendship to any of them. As I was now turned of fifty, I thought of passing all the rest of my Life in this philosophical manner. . . ."

The " philosophical manner " of living that Hume laid down for himself at Edinburgh did not prove to be so uneventful as he may have anticipated. Three episodes, in particular, caused him some perturbation. Two were literary controversies, the Marian and the Ossianic ; the third was personal and involved the loss of intimacy with one of his oldest friends, Henry Home. This last will be treated first, as it was certainly first in importance to the tranquillity of Hume.

Though sometimes called a quarrel, there is no evidence that requires it to be called more than loss of intimacy. The two men always remained on speaking terms and were not infrequently seen together at social affairs. For the last six or seven years of Hume's life, their relations must have mended somewhat, since on several occasions they were one another's guests. Be that as it may, the complete understanding and deep intimacy of the early years had given way to a certain coldness and perhaps even bitterness. The occasion of the estrangement is unknown—probably there was no single occasion but a series of incidents and attitudes over the course of time.

Henry Home was a man whose character seems perfectly reflected in the admirable portrait by David Martin. A Scottish Voltaire is Lord Kames in appearance, thin of face, hawk-beaked, bright of eye, a man, moreover, of strong mind and imperious will, sharp of tongue, and abounding in broad raillery. " An iron mind in an iron body," David is said to have remarked. The hardness is well illustrated in his brutal joke [2] as he sentenced to death

[1] HL, I, 356, 371 ; T. E. Ritchie, *Account of the Life and Writings of David Hume* (London 1807), p. 143.

[2] Henry Cockburn, *Memorials of His Time* (Edinburgh 1909), p. 108n. Variants of the anecdote appear in *Caldwell Papers*, PT. II, VOL. II, 129n.

Matthew Hay, an old acquaintance and opponent at chess—
" That's checkmate to you, Matthew ! " Perhaps Harry's otherwise pervasive wit did not include himself as subject, and certainly
one of David's practical jokes backfired in an unforeseen manner.
Having received a letter addressed to " Mr. Hume, the Atheist,"
David mischievously re-directed it to Harry, who was affronted
and not prone to forgive for a considerable time.[1]

The cooling-off of the friendship, however, is hardly to be
attributed to a practical joke. It arose, rather, from fundamental
differences in character, the independence of mind of the younger
man and the domineering temperament of the older. These traits
can be discerned in the " character " of Kames that Hume
provided for Boswell : " He is a man very apt to change his
favourites. He is positive in opinion. He is fond of young people,
of instructing them and dictating to them ; but whenever they
come up and have a mind of their own, he quarrels with them." [2]
Probably the speaker was thinking of his own relations with Kames
after he had rejected the advice of 1748 to continue the suppression
of the essay " Of Miracles." That was perhaps the first overt
act of self-assertion on the part of David and may possibly
have provided Harry with the occasion to refute him publicly
in the *Essays on the Principles of Morality and Natural Religion* of
1751.

Yet no real quarrel and no real enmity can be conjured up
from the evidence on either side. In 1754 Hume had written
during the controversy with Professor Stewart, " I wou'd sooner
give up my own Cause than my Friend's." In 1759 he confessed
to Adam Smith : " I am afraid of Kames' *Law Tracts*. A man
might as well think of making a fine sauce by a mixture of worm-
wood and aloes, as an agreeable composition by joining metaphysics and Scottish law. However, the book, I believe, has merit ;
though few people will take the pains of enquiring into it." In
1762 he recommended Millar to bring out Kames's *Elements of
Criticism*, but granted the difficult problem of personality. " As
to the advice you desire me to give him [Kames]," Hume informed
Millar, " it is certainly very salutary ; but I fancy neither I nor
any other of his Friends will ever venture to mention it." Writing
to Hugh Blair from Paris two years later, Hume went as far as
he ever did on the subject of Kames, but even that is tempered by
a friendly act :

---

[1] MS notes of George Chalmers in EU, Laing MSS II, 451/2.
[2] *Boswell Papers*, I, 129.

Our Friend, I mean, your Friend, Lord Kaims had much provokd Voltaire who never forgives, & never thinks any Enemy below his Notice. He has accordingly sent to the Gazette Literaire an Article with regard to the Elements of Criticism, which turns that Book extremely into Ridicule, with a good deal of Wit. I tryd to have it suppress'd before it was printed ; but the Authors of that Gazette told me, that they durst neither suppress nor alter any thing that came from Voltaire. I suppose his Lordship holds that satiric Wit as cheap as he does all the rest of the human Race, and will not be in the least mortify'd by his Censure.

A final remark of Hume on Kames was retailed to Boswell by Adam Smith as late as 1781 : " When one says of another man he is the most arrogant Man in the world, it is meant only to say that he is very arrogant. But when one says it of Lord Kames, it is an absolute truth." [1]

The Kames story shows no signs of an open quarrel or of real enmity. In 1749 he directed Hume to open a lawsuit against the Annandale estate. In 1757 he helped Hume interpret a statute of Henry VII's reign. In 1758 he sent him Josiah Tucker's papers on economics and politics and continued to give advice on proposed new essays. In 1762 he was willing to accept Hume's recommendation to Millar. In 1773 he named Hume his surrogate for eliminating Scotticisms from the fifth edition of *Elements of Criticism.*[2] A final remark to Boswell in 1778 suggests Kames's interpretation of the estrangement. Boswell, in describing as a mental stupor Hume's ease when dying in the belief of annihilation, noted that Kames agreed, adding " A Man who thinks in that manner must have no warmth of friendship." [3]

Kames evidently thought Hume somewhat ungrateful; Hume increasingly minded Kames's well-meant but highhanded attempts to rule his life. Ramsay of Ochertyre, who knew Kames well after 1752, corroborates this interpretation :

From the time I knew him, he [Kames] had a succession of clever *élèves* who afterwards attained to eminence. Although he assuredly meant them exceedingly well, and did them material service, yet, strange to tell, sooner or later most of them dropped the connection. It would be indelicate to inquire whether this was their fault or his. Possibly he expected more court from them than they were disposed to pay ; and with him there was no medium, his fondness and dislike being equally ardent and undisguised.[4]

The so-called Marian controversy had been opened in 1754 with the publication of Walter Goodall's two-volume *Examination of the Letters said to have been written by Mary Queen of Scots to James,*

---

[1] *Boswell Papers*, xv, 12.
[2] Ian S. Ross, *Lord Kames and the Scotland of his Day* (Oxford 1972), p. 350.
[3] *Boswell Papers*, xv, 276.   [4] Ramsay, i, 205.

Earl of Bothwell. An ardent Jacobite, Goodall hotly defends the innocence of the romantic Queen in the murder of her husband, Lord Darnley, at the Kirk o' Field. Hume, in his *Tudors*, critically reviews the evidence and concludes that Mary was probably guilty. Robertson, in " A Critical Dissertation concerning the Murder of King Henry, and the Genuineness of the Queen's Letters to Bothwell," appended to the second volume of his *History of Scotland*, leaves the issue more open.

The controversy flared up again with the publication at Edinburgh in February 1760 of *An Historical and Critical Inquiry into the Evidence produced by the Earls of Murray and Morton against Mary Queen of Scots. With an Examination of the Rev. Dr Robertson's Dissertation, and Mr Hume's History with respect to that Evidence.* Published anonymously, this work was generally attributed to William Tytler of Woodhouselee, a W.S., and member of the Select Society. Both Hume and Robertson were disturbed at the examiner's belligerency and unfairness. Neither answered directly, although Hume later added a note to his published account. In a letter to Lord Elibank, who was also of strong Jacobite sympathies, Hume expressed his attitude :

> I hope your Lordship, as my Friend, will congratulate me on the Resolution I took in the beginning of my Life, that is, of my literary Life, never to reply to any body. Otherwise, this Gentleman, I mean, this Author might have insulted me on my Silence. I am sure your Lordship wou'd have disowned me for ever as a Friend, if I had enterd the Lists with such an Antagonist. Mr Goodal is no very calm or indifferent Advocate in this Cause ; yet he disowns him as an Associate ; and confesses to me & all the World that I am here right in my Facts, and am only wrong in my Inferences.

Concerning this last point, Hume elsewhere is emphatic that " a Man is not Rogue and Rascal and Lyar because he draws a false Inference." [1] In the note referred to above, Hume dismisses the whole question curtly : " There are, indeed, three events in our history, which may be regarded as touchstones of partymen. An English Whig, who asserts the reality of the popish plot ; an Irish Catholic, who denies the massacre in 1641 ; and a Scots Jacobite, who maintains the innocence of Queen Mary, must be considered as men beyond the reach of argument or reason, and must be left to their prejudices." [2]

The Marian controversy was—and is—a touchy business among the Scots. It placed the friendship of both Hume and Robertson with such advocates of the unfortunate Queen as

[1] HL, 1, 320-1 ; NHL, p. 61.
[2] Note " N " to Ch. 39 of *Hist.* in collected edns.

Sir Alexander Dick and Lord Elibank on a somewhat precarious basis. Hume's own normal equanimity was deeply disturbed, as is evidenced by his tirade in the letter to Lord Elibank : " It is an old Proverb, *Love me, love my Dog* : But certainly it admits of many Exceptions : I am sure, at least, that I have a great Respect for your Lordship ; yet have none at all for this Dog of Yours [that is, presumably Tytler]. On the contrary, I declare him to be a very mangey Cur : Entreat your Lordship to rid your hands of him as soon as possible : And think a sound beating or even a Rope too good for him." Yet Hume's temper must have subsided quickly since two thick lines are drawn through the passage ; the extant manuscript, by the way, is no more than a draft and the letter may never have been posted.[1]

The Ossianic affair opened in 1759 and soon involved David Hume, along with the other men of letters of Scotland, England, and, eventually, of all Europe. It began with a conversation between John Home and James Macpherson, teacher and poet of the Highlands. The English poet, William Collins, had presented John with the manuscript of " An Ode on the Popular Superstitions of the Highlands of Scotland, Considered as the Subject of Poetry," and John discussed with Macpherson the problems of translating from Gaelic into English. Encouraged by Home and other friends, Macpherson published anonymously at Edinburgh early in 1760 *Fragments of Ancient Poetry, Collected in the Highlands of Scotland, and Translated from the Galic or Erse Language.* An anonymous preface to this unpretentious little volume, actually written by the Reverend Hugh Blair, states that " The Public may depend on the following Fragments as genuine Remains of ancient Scottish Poetry " and that " there is Reason to hope that one Work of considerable Length, and which deserves to be styled an heroic Poem might be recovered and translated, if Encouragement were given to such an Undertaking."

Scotland at once accepted the *Fragments* as " national works," and David Hume wrote in August 1760 that " we have endeavoured to put Mr Macpherson on a way of procuring more of these wild flowers," in particular, the epic alluded to in the preface. Subsidised by the Edinburgh circle, Macpherson brought back from the Highlands, not one, but two complete epics, which were published as *Fingal : an Ancient Epic Poem, in Six Books* (1761) and *Temora : an Ancient Epic Poem, in Eight Books* (1763). Both poems are further described on their title-pages as " Composed by

[1] See Textual Supplement for Hume's later contretemps over Queen Mary with Elibank.

Ossian, the Son of Fingal," and "Translated from the Galic Language, by James Macpherson." In 1763, also, Blair brought out a *Critical Dissertation on the Poems of Ossian, the Son of Fingal.* " Aristotle," argues the professor with simple logic, " studied nature in Homer. Homer and Ossian both wrote from nature. No wonder that among all the three, there should be such agreement and conformity."

With this series of publications, the Ossianic controversy was on in earnest. The major issue during the eighteenth century was always historical and moral, rather than literary, for Macpherson vehemently insisted that he was a translator of ancient documents, and with equal vehemence refused to produce the documents. When his character was, therefore, impugned by English critics, the Scottish national character tended to be impugned along with his. National politics had entered the controversy the moment that Lord Bute had helped to subsidise the publication of the two epics.

From the outset David Hume was torn between nationalistic prepossessions and critical suspicions : the former inclined him emotionally to accept this " Homer of Scotland," while the latter led him to doubt intellectually that two such long works had come down by word of mouth over the course of so many centuries in such perfectly regular and polished form. Though there is little doubt that scepticism dominated his thinking concerning Ossian, Hume did provide Macpherson in February 1761 with a letter of introduction to Strahan. " You may readily believe," he wrote, " that I advis'd him to think of nobody but our Friend, Mr Millar, in disposing of the Copy " of *Fingal.* Macpherson is described as " a sensible, modest young Fellow, a very good Scholar, and of unexceptionable Morals." But Millar and Macpherson, for reasons unknown, did not come to terms.

By 1762, however, Hume had changed his mind about the character of the translator, telling Boswell that he was a " most curious fellow. He is full of highland Prejudices. He hates a Republic and he does not like Kings. He would have all the Nation divided into Clans, and these clans to be allways fighting. . . . Lord Bute does not know what to do with him. . . . As he is a Scotchman, Lord Bute does not chuse to put him upon the list of Pensioners, and therefore generously gives him two hundred a year out of his own pocket." [1] That situation could not long endure, and in the following year Bute found a means of disposing

---

[1] *Boswell Papers,* I, 127–8.

of the truculent translator. " He will probably depart for Florida with Governor [George] Johnstone," Hume told Blair, " and I would advise him to travel among the Chickisaws or Cherokees, in order to tame him and civilize him."

Hume was also becoming more and more concerned over the nationalistic reasoning displayed in Blair's impending *Dissertation*. " It is a fine piece of criticism," he averred ; " but it were to be wished that he had kept it a little lower than Homer. For it might be a very excellent Poem and yet fall short of *the Iliad*." [1] To offset the effects of nationalistic prejudice and to determine the authenticity of Ossian, once and for all, Hume directed Blair's attention to the necessity of careful factual investigation :

> My present purpose . . . is, to apply to you in the name of all the men of letters of this, and I may say of all other centuries, to establish this capital point, and to give us proof that these poems are, I do not say so ancient as the age of Severus, but that they were not forged within these five years by James Macpherson. These proofs must not be arguments, but testimonies. . . . Now the testimonies may, in my opinion, be of two kinds. Macpherson pretends that there is an ancient manuscript of part of Fingal in the family, I think, of Clanronald. Get that fact ascertained by more than one person of credit ; let these persons be acquainted with the Galic ; let them compare the original and the translation ; and let them testify the fidelity of the latter. But the chief point in which it will be necessary for you to exert yourself, will be to get positive testimony from many different hands, that such poems are vulgarly recited in the Highlands, and have there been long the entertainment of the people. This testimony must be as particular as it is positive. . . . [2]

Yet Blair did not prove equal to the task. His researches ended in the very generalities that Hume had warned him against ; and the Scottish men of letters and the Scottish nation were left vulnerable to much subsequent ridicule. Although Blair's testimonial " Appendix " of 1765 expressly certified that, " Ossian has been always reputed the Homer of the Highlands," [3] Hume, at least, remained unconvinced. " My scepticism," he informed Blair, " extends no farther, nor ever did, than with regard to the extreme Antiquity of those Poems, and it is no more than Scepticism." He continued to rally the professor : " No body ever heard you express any Remorse for having put Ossian on the same footing with Homer."

James Macpherson's literary career went on in its own perverse way. His *Introduction to the History of Great Britain and Ireland* of 1771 drew Hume's caustic remark to Adam Smith that, " of all men of Parts," Macpherson " has the most antihistorical Head in the

---

[1] *Boswell Papers*, i, 128.   [2] HL, i, 399–400.
[3] Appendix to *Critical Dissertation* in the *Works of Ossian* (London 1765), ii, 450.

Universe." His translation of the *Iliad* into English blank verse of two years later drew further fire from Hume to the same correspondent : " Have you seen Macpherson's Homer ? It is hard to tell whether the Attempt or the Execution be worse."

The main Ossianic controversy, which had been dying down, flared up anew in 1774–75. Ten years previous, the misguided Blair had boasted to Hume that " I have converted even that Barbarian Sam. Johnston . . . who as L. Elibank tells me owns himself now convinced." [1] Johnson was far from being convinced, however, and his original doubts were strengthened by personal investigations when in 1773 he made the tour of Scotland with Boswell. By the close of the following year it was generally reported in literary circles that Johnson's forthcoming *Journey to the Western Islands of Scotland* would attack the character of Macpherson. Incensed by these reports, that worthy attempted to intimidate the aging man of letters, but succeeded only in inspiring the famous letter of 20 January 1775.

There is something heroic in the moral ring of Johnson's sentences :

Mr James Macpherson—I received your foolish and impudent note. Whatever insult is offered me I will do my best to repel, and what I cannot do for myself the law will do for me. I will not desist from detecting what I think a cheat, from any fear of the menaces of a Ruffian.

You want me to retract. What shall I retract ? I thought your book an imposture from the beginning, I think it upon yet surer reasons an imposture still. For this opinion I give the publick my reasons which I here dare you to refute.

But however I may despise you, I reverence truth and if you can prove the genuineness of the work I will confess it. Your rage I defy, your abilities since your Homer are not so formidable, and what I have heard of your morals disposes me to pay regard not to what you shall say, but to what you can prove.

You may print this if you will.

Jan. 20. 1775   Sam: Johnson.[2]

Yet is there anything heroic in Johnson's severe criticism of the Scottish national character in his book ? Was it worthy of the respected literary critic and the venerated moralist to write : " The Scots have something to plead for their easy reception of an improbable fiction : they are seduced by their fondness for their supposed ancestors. *A Scotchman must be a very sturdy moralist, who does not love Scotland better than truth : he will always love it better*

[1] RSE, iii, 53.   [2] *Johnson*, ii, 297, n2.

*than inquiry ; and if falsehood flatters his vanity, will not be very diligent
to detect it " ?* [1]

There was, however, one " very sturdy moralist " who, though
a Scot, loved truth and inquiry better than Scotland, and that was
David Hume. On 6 March 1775, some weeks after the appearance
of Johnson's *Journey*, Boswell took tea with Hume at James's Court
and found him seething with indignation :

> He spoke of Mr. Johnson's *Journey* in terms so slighting that it could have
> no effect but to shew his resentment. He however agreed with him perfectly
> as to Ossian. But then he disbelieved not so much for want of testimony, as
> from the nature of the thing according to his apprehension. He said if fifty
> barea—d highlanders should say that *Fingal* was an ancient Poem, he would
> not believe them. He said it was not to be believed that a people who were
> continually concerned to keep themselves from starving or from being hanged,
> should preserve in their memories a Poem in six books. He said that Homer
> had once been written, which made a great difference. He said that the late
> Mr. Wood had written a very ingenious dissertation to prove that the use of
> letters was not known in Homer's time. But that he was wrong ; for we
> find in Homer a letter is brought from the King of ——. He said that the
> extensive fame of Ossian was owing to the notion that the poems were so
> ancient ; that if McPherson had given them as his own, nobody would have
> read them to an end. He acknowledged that there were some good passages
> in them, and perhaps there might be some small parts ancient. He said the
> highlanders, who had been famed as a warlike people, were so much flattered
> to have it thought that they had a great Poet among them that they all tried
> to support the fact, and their wish to have it so made them even ready to
> persuade themselves into it. I told him Mr. Johnson's saying that he could
> undertake to write an epick poem on the story of Robinhood which the half
> of the people of England should say they had heard in their youth. Mr. Hume
> said the people of England would not be so ready to support such a story.
> They had not the same temptation with the highlanders, there being many
> excellent english Poets.[2]

The contrast between Hume's position and Johnson's is
illuminating. Johnson calls for evidence and yet more evidence ;
Hume, following the argument developed in " Of Miracles,"
rejects one whole class of evidence. Johnson brands national
prejudice as immoral ; Hume insists that the Scottish " will to
believe," in this instance, is but a perfectly natural psychological
phenomenon and in no wise to be confused with deliberate falsehood. At the same time, Hume's failure ever to conceive the
possibility that great poets might exist among the warlike Highlanders illustrates the limitations of his scepticism as a historical
method : for even in his own lifetime Scotland's Gaelic tradition

---

[1] *Johnson's Journey to the Western Islands of Scotland*, ed. R. W. Chapman (London
1934), p. 108. My italics.   [2] *Boswell Papers*, x, 109–11.

produced at least seven great poets—John MacCodrum, Alexander MacDonald (*Alasdair mac Mhaighstir Alasdair*), Dugald Buchanan, John Roy Stewart, Rob Donn, Duncan McIntyre (*Donnachadh Bàn nan Oran*), and William Ross—of whom MacDonald, McIntyre, and Ross are thought by some competent Scottish critics today to be at least the equals of the Lowland poets Fergusson and Burns, if not actually their superiors.

Hume's indignation at Macpherson for his frauds and at Johnson for his aspersions on the Scottish national character enlisted his pen as well as his tongue. For it was at this time that he wrote " Of the Poems of Ossian." This critique was almost certainly completed before the middle of June, by which time Hume had become acquainted with Macpherson's newly published *History of Great Britain, from the Restoration, to the Accession of the House of Hannover* with its two companion volumes of *Original Papers*. Since neither work is mentioned in Hume's catalogue in the critique of all of Macpherson's publications, the inference is plain that the critique had already been completed and was not thereafter revised.[1]

" Of the Poems of Ossian " is a careful development of the general arguments laid down to Boswell at the tea table. Hume's case for the total rejection of the evidence for the authenticity of Macpherson's Ossian brings on a comparison with the miracles at the tomb of the Abbé Pâris. " On such occasions," declares Hume, " the greatest cloud of witnesses makes no manner of evidence. What Jansenist was there in Paris, which contains several thousands, that would not have given evidence for the miracles of Abbé Paris ? The miracle is greater, but not the evidence, with regard to the authenticity of Ossian." Finally, Hume's logic relentlessly leads him to the conclusion that " The only real wonder in the whole affair is, that a person of so fine a taste as Dr. Blair, should be so great an admirer of these poems ; and one of so clear and cool a judgment collect evidence of their authenticity."

Having arrived at this conclusion, a man of good faith and of deep friendship had no alternative but to suppress the essay. After all, it had been Hume himself who in the early stages of the controversy had encouraged and even, in a manner, forced Blair to look for evidence. This evidence convinced Blair of the authenticity of the Ossianic epics ; it convinced Hume only of its own

[1] RSE, ix, 17 ; printed with minor errors and omissions in Hill Burton, i, 471–80, and *Phil. Wks.*, iv, 415–24.

futility. While he might deplore Blair's judgment, Hume was not the man to ridicule a friend in public. Although " Of the Poems of Ossian " remained in manuscript out of consideration for a friend, its defence of the moral integrity of Scotland must have warmed the philosopher's aging heart.

The belated literary and financial success that Hume began to enjoy in the early 1760s did not entirely compensate for the still remaining uncongenialities of Edinburgh. With the completion of the *History of England from the Invasion of Julius Caesar to the Revolution in 1688*, Hume was relieved from the constant pressure of composition and dubious about committing himself to a new undertaking. Millar, to be sure, was always pressing for a continuation ; but Hume refused to be drawn in. " I may perhaps," he wrote to the publisher in March 1763, " very soon gather silently together the Books which will enable me to sketch out the Reigns of K. William and Q. Anne ; and shall finish them afterwards, together with that of George I, in London. But "—and there is now always a " but " when London is mentioned—" to tell you the Truth, I have an Aversion to appear in that Capital till I see that more Justice is done me with regard to the preceding Volumes. . . . The general Rage against the Scots is an additional Discouragement. I think the Scotch Minister [Lord Bute] is obligd to make me some Compensation for this." The hint here dropped that the government owed him a pension or a place is not without its later significance.

A year earlier Hume had discussed with Millar another possible historical venture. " I give you full Authority," he advised, " to contradict the Report, that I am writing or intend to write an ecclesiastical History : I have no such Intention ; & I believe never shall. I am beginning to love Peace very much, and resolve to be more cautious than formerly in creating myself Enemies." Despite this denial, the report circulated for many years, and there is little doubt that Hume was sometimes tempted. For once a man of letters, always a man of letters ; and Hume was not fond of indolence, although he professed to joke about it. " The Truth is, I am entirely indolent at present," he admitted near the close of 1762 ; " and I am very happy in that indolent State. My Friends tell me, that I will not continue long so, and that I will tire of having nothing to do but read and converse ; but I am resolvd to resist, as a Temptation of the Devil, any Impulse towards writing, and I am really so much ashamd of myself when I see my Bulk on a Shelf, as well as when I see it in a Glass, that I would fain prevent my growing more corpulent either way. To keep my Mind at rest & my Body in motion seems to be the best Recipe for both Maladies."

The real truth of the matter, however, seems to have been quite different. Hume had come to feel frustrated, restless, and unhappy. He was beginning to lose all ambition and all relish for pleasure and to develop " a total indifference towards every thing in human life." London he dreaded more than ever, what with the violent anti-Scottish campaign of John Wilkes in *The North Briton*,[1] during 1762 and 1763, and the fanatical hatred of Charles Churchill in *The Prophecy of Famine : A Scots Pastoral*, of January 1763. Even in Edinburgh, his presence was unwelcome to many. " The Scotch Minister " did not recognise the obligation to do something for him and, as a matter of fact, was not even thinking about him.

Lord Bute, on the contrary, was thinking about Hume's friendly rival in history. So it was that on 25 July 1763 William Robertson was appointed Historiographer Royal for Scotland, " a place disused ever since the Union, and heretofore of £40 but now, on account of the great abilities of this Gentleman, increased to £200 per annum." [2] Alexander Carlyle observed on this occasion that " Honest David Home, with the heart of all others that rejoices most at the prospect of his friends, was certainly a little hurt with this last honour conferred upon Robertson." [3] There is no doubt that the appointment, made on the understanding that Robertson would later write a history of England, was a blow to Hume. Mortified by his own repeated failures and touched to the quick by Robertson's easy success, Hume had yet managed outwardly to conceal his true feelings. He was bound, nevertheless, to interpret Lord Bute's preference of Robertson over himself as a rebuff, as final evidence that he, David Hume, never would receive due recognition of his genius in either Scotland or England. The thought of France as the promised land for the man of letters must instantly have recurred to him with renewed intensity. At that very moment of wounded pride, chance intervened once more in

---

[1] No. 12 (12 Aug. 1762) of the *North Briton* commented on the recent pension given to John Home : " There is one *Scottish pension* I have been told of, which afforded me real pleasure. It is Mr. *Hume's* ; for I am satisfied that it must be given to Mr. *David Hume*, whose writings have been so justly admired abroad and at home, and not to Mr. *John Hume*, who has endeavoured to bring the name into contempt by putting it to two insipid tragedies, and other trash in the *Scottish miscellanies*."

[2] Notice in *Lloyd's Evening Post* of that date.

[3] Quoted in *Thorpe's Autograph Catalogue* (1833), PT. II, Item 267 ; Hill Burton, II, 164.

his career, offering him the opportunity to go to Paris in a position of dignity—" A lucky accident has given him relief," added Carlyle to his statement above. From Paris in March 1764, Hume wrote with accumulated bitterness : " I have been accustom'd to meet with nothing but Insults & Indignities from my native Country : But if it continue so, *ingrata patria, ne ossa quidem habebis*."

CHAPTER 30

THE CALL OF FRANCE

" My Situation was . . . the most wonderful Event in the World :
I was now a Person clean & white as the driven Snow."

On his way to London in August 1763, David Hume may well
have taken the opportunity to review in his mind the incessant call
of France, which, having opened with Montesquieu fourteen years
previous, had finally become irresistible. The several translations
of his works had brought him many readers and nearly as many
admirers at Paris, of whom the Abbé Le Blanc and the governmental ministers, the Comte d'Argenson and Maréchal de
Noailles, have been mentioned in passing. Other older statesmen
include President de Brosses and President Hénault ; and, among
the younger group, Trudaine de Montigny and Turgot. Charles
Pinot Duclos, perpetual Secretary of the French Academy and a
distinguished man of letters, was one of Hume's most outspoken
partisans. Victor, Marquis de Mirabeau, and Jean, Marquis de
Chastellux, were interested in Hume's speculations on luxury and
population. That famous novelist and Anglophile the Abbé
Prévost translated the *History of the Stuarts* ; and another novelist,
Crébillon the Younger, was an early admirer of Hume and later
dedicated a novel to him.

De l'Esprit (1758) of the *philosophe* Claude-Adrien Helvétius
had met with great opposition in France and had been condemned
by the Parlement of Paris. Early the following year the author
wrote to Hume proposing that they should translate one another's
publications. Hume, who did not value Helvétius's work highly
as philosophy, found sufficient excuse for not complying in the
fact that an English translation had already been advertised.
The buoyant *philosophe* then let it be known that he desired to
become a member of the Royal Society of London and solicited
Hume's aid. The Scot replied evasively that the undertaking
was difficult and success not likely. Accepting this broad hint
and dropping the project, Helvétius expressed himself as highly
gratified at the honour done him. David Hume, who would do
anything for a friend, did not relish being imposed upon by a
shallow and ambitious outsider.

From friends travelling on the Continent came flattering accounts of Hume's prestige at Paris. John Stewart, the wine merchant, for instance, reported in 1759 that " The principal motive I have for troubling.you with an epistle is to express my gratitude for the obligations I owe to your friendship, for under the title of your friend I have been more caressed here than ever stranger was by people of distinguished merit and a high rank in life." Casual mention that Hume was contemplating a visit to Paris " gave a most general & unfeigned satisfaction to a great number of People you would like to live with and who, as far as my penetration goes, would be very happy to have you amongst them." And again, they " would go to the Indies to serve you . . . you're the man of the world they hold in highest esteem." Andrew Stuart of Torrance told William Johnstone, in December 1762, that " our friend David Hume . . . is so much worshipped here that he must be void of all passions if he does not immediately take post for Paris. In most houses where I am acquainted here one of the first questions is, Do you know M. Hume whom we all admire so much ? " In the following spring Lord Elibank was even more forthright : " no author ever yet attained to that degree of Reputation in his own lifetime that you are now in possession of at Paris. . . ."[1]

The Parisian admirers of Hume were not limited to men of letters, *philosophes*, and statesmen. Acting on a suggestion from Le Blanc, Hume sent a copy of his *History of the Stuarts* to Mme Dupré de St Maur, wife of the translator of *Paradise Lost*. Her letter of thanks, dated 15 December 1757, is the first homage he received from a French lady and must have been highly palatable : " Little versed as I am in the English language, you have made it easy for me by the clarity and beauty both of your style and of your ideas. I found your history a treatise of philosophy applied to the most interesting facts. Never has any book held my attention so completely, and never have I had so good an opinion of myself as when I was reading you."[2] The letter closes with the hope that, with the coming of peace, Hume will go to Paris to gather the fruits of the reputation that he has acquired there.

Refreshing as the correspondence with Mme Dupré de St Maur must have been, it paled into insignificance beside another that began some three years later. Alexander Murray, the exiled Jacobite brother of Lord Elibank, forwarded to Hume a letter from his cousin, " the most amiable and accomplished Lady in this

[1] RSE, vii, 49–50 ; iv, 167 ; v, 8.   [2] RSE, iv, 85.

kingdom, or indeed any other." This same lady inspired Louis Dutens, the British diplomatist, to exclaim, " I never saw so much wit, grace, and beauty united in one person. Mme de Boufflers, at the age of thirty, had all the bloom of twenty : she was justly esteemed the most amiable woman of her time ; and the more she was known, the more she was admired.—I was delighted with her grace, her figure, and her understanding." [1] It was this great lady of France, Marie-Charlotte-Hippolyte de Campet de Saujeon, Comtesse de Boufflers-Rouverel, who on 13 March 1761 sought out David Hume in his philosophical retreat at Edinburgh and offered him her protection and friendship.

This first letter from the woman who was to become the most important in Hume's later life is so revealing of character as to require presentation in its entirety.

For a long time, Sir, I have struggled with conflicting sentiments. The admiration which your sublime work has awakened in me and the esteem with which it has inspired me for your person, your talents, and your virtue, have frequently aroused the desire of writing to you, that I might express those sentiments with which I am so deeply smitten. Considering, however, that I am unknown to you, that my approbation will seem pointless to you, and that reserve and even privacy are more suitable to my sex, I am timid of being accused of presumption and of allowing myself to be known to my own disadvantage by a man whose good opinion I shall always regard as the most flattering and the most precious of blessings. Nevertheless, although the reflections I have made on this subject appeared to have much force, an irresistible inclination rendered them unavailing ; and I can only add one further instance to a thousand others to justify the truth of that remark which I read in your *History of the Stuarts* : " Men's views of things are the result of their understanding alone : their conduct is regulated by their understanding, their temper, and their passions."

Thus, when my reason tells me I ought to remain silent, my enthusiasm prevents me from following its authority.

Though a woman and of no advanced age, and despite the dissipated life one leads in this country, I have always loved reading ; and there are few good books in any language or of any kind that I have not read, either in the original or in translation. And I can assure you, Sir, with unquestionable sincerity, that I have found none which, in my judgment, unites so many perfections as yours. I know no words to express how I felt while reading that work. I was moved, transported, and the emotion which it engendered is, in some manner, painful in its continuance. It elevates the soul and fills the heart with sentiments of humanity and benevolence. It enlightens the mind by showing that true happiness is closely united with virtue and discovers, by the same light, what is the end, the sole end, of every reasonable being. In the midst of the calamities which, on all sides surrounded Charles I, we see peace and security shining brightly and accompanying him to the scaffold ; whereas trouble and remorse, the inseparable attendants of crime, follow the

---

[1] RSE, vi, 70 ; Louis Dutens, *Memoirs of a Traveller, Now in Retirement* (London 1806), ii, 8.

steps of Cromwell, even to the throne. Your book also teaches how the best
of things are liable to abuse, and the reflections made on this subject ought to
increase our vigilance and diffidence in ourselves. It animates the reader
with a noble emulation ; it inspires love of liberty ; and it teaches, at the same
time, submission to the government under which we are obliged to live. In a
word, it is a rich mine of morality and of instruction, presented in colours so
bright, that we believe we see them for the first time.

The clearness, the majesty, the touching simplicity of your style delight
me. Its beauties are so striking that, despite my ignorance of the English
language, they cannot escape me. You are, Sir, a wonderful painter. Your
pictures have a grace, a naturalness, an energy surpassing the reaches of the
imagination.

But how can I express the effect produced upon me by your divine
impartiality ? I would that I had, on this occasion, your own eloquence with
which to express my thought ! In truth, I believed that I had before my eyes
the work of some celestial being, free from human passions, who, for the sake
of mankind, has deigned to write the history of these latter times.

I dare only add that in all the products of your pen, you show yourself
a perfect philosopher, a statesman, an historian of genius, an enlightened
political scientist, a true patriot.

All these sublime qualities are so far above the understanding of a woman,
that it is fitting I should say little about them ; and I have already great need
of your indulgence for my heresies against prudence and propriety, by the
excess of my veneration for your attainments. This I pray you, Sir, and, at the
same time, the most profound secrecy. The step I have taken is perhaps
extraordinary. I fear that I shall be reproached for it ; and I would be grieved
if the sentiment which prompted it should not be recognised. I have the
honour to be, Sir, Your most humble and most obedient servant,

Hyppolyte De Saujon, Comtesse De Boufflers.

They tell me, Sir, that you have a mind to come to France with the peace.
I earnestly wish that you will carry out this resolution, and that I may be able
to help make your sojourn agreeable.

Paris, 13 March 1761.[1]

To this amazing protestation, at once so formal, so effusive,
and so sincere, David Hume replied with real pleasure and with
simple dignity. Dismissing any rhetorical effort at false modesty,
he assumes that the praise of his *History* must be founded on his
impartiality, which, whatever the scholarly merit of the work, is
genuine. He recommends to Madame's reading his friend
Robertson's *History of Scotland*. He craves her indulgence for his
own uncourtliness because, since youthful residence in France,
" I have rusted amid books and study ; have been little engaged
in the active, and not much in the pleasurable scenes of life ;
and am more accustomed to a select society than to general companies." The letter closes on a formal note : " But all these

---

[1] RSE, iii, 65 ; the entire series of letters to Hume is iii, 65–103. See Textual
Supplement for Hume's inquiry to Elibank.

disadvantages, and much greater, will be abundantly compensated by the honour of your Ladyship's protection ; and I hope that my profound sense of your obliging favours will render me not altogether unworthy of it." [1]

In a subsequent exchange of letters of the same year, the Comtesse subtly endeavoured to render their relations more personal than that of a lady-protector and a man of letters. She protested that her expressions of admiration were sincere and that, should Hume come to Paris, she would be happy to provide lodgings. " In a word, I shall try to make your stay in France agreeable and induce you to prolong it." Hume, however, fought shy of committing himself to so intimate an arrangement, replying somewhat stiffly, " as I am sensible, that I shall, in many respects, stand in need of your indulgence, you must excuse me, if I be solicitous to avoid giving you any superfluous trouble, and decline, though with all imaginable sense of gratitude, the obliging offer, with which you have been pleased to honour me."

The following May, writing in English for the first time, the Comtesse acknowledged the gift of Hume's early history, which had arrived without indication of the donor. " Some little perhaps, of the pride so common in my sex, but much more the desire to contract an obligation with a man of your merit, and to obtain from him so valuable a favour, have persuaded me, I was indebted to you for it." Not having sent the gift, Hume was naturally somewhat embarrassed in explaining that, while he had made efforts to have a copy conveyed to her, he had been unsuccessful. The embarrassment is thrown off, however, in his first display of gallantry :

But, Madam, what new wonder is this which your letter presents to me ? I not only find a Lady, who, in the bloom of beauty and height of reputation, can withdraw herself from the pleasures of a gay Court, and find leisure to cultivate the sciences ; but deigns to support a correspondence with a man of letters in a remote country, and to reward his labours by a suffrage the most agreeable of all others, to a man who has any spark of generous sentiments or taste for true glory. Besides these unusual circumstances, I find a Lady, who, without any other advantages than her own talents, has made herself mistress of a language commonly esteemed very difficult to strangers, and possesses it to such a degree as might give jealousy to us who have made it the business of our lives to acquire and cultivate it.

Long the patron of Jean-Jacques Rousseau, the Comtesse turned to her new-found friend for help when on 11 June 1762 Rousseau was forced to flee the country because of the condemnation of his *Emile* by the Parlement of Paris. Three days later she wrote Hume that she was advising Rousseau to seek refuge in England since " I could not, in my opinion, choose for him in all Europe a protector more respectable for his genius and more commendable for his humanity." She then proceeds with an analysis of the character of Jean-Jacques :

> M. Rousseau passes with most people in this country for a singular man. That epithet, in its true meaning, is justly applied to him because he differs widely from accepted ways of behaviour and of thought. He is sincere, noble-minded, and disinterested. He dreads every form of dependence and, consequently, has preferred being in France earning his living by copying music to receiving favours from his best friends who are eager to mend his ill fortune. This delicacy may seem excessive but is not blamable, and it attests high ideals. He shuns contact with the world and is happy only in solitude. This predilection for retirement has made him enemies ; the pride of those who sought him out has been wounded by his rebuffs. But despite his apparent misanthropy, I do not believe that the man exists who is more gentle, more humane, more compassionate of the afflictions of others and more patient in his own. In a word, his virtue is so pure, so constant, so uniform, that those who hate him have been able to find only in their own hearts reasons for suspecting him. As for me, I would rather be deceived by these favourable appearances than doubt his sincerity.

Touched to the quick, Hume replied immediately, " Good God ! Madam, how much I regret my being absent from London on this occasion, which deprives me of an opportunity of showing in person my regard for your recommendation, and my esteem, I had almost said veneration, for the virtue and genius of M. Rousseau. I assure your Ladyship there is no man in Europe of whom I have entertained a higher idea, and whom I would be prouder to serve ; and as I find his reputation very high in England, I hope every one will endeavour to make him sensible of it by civilities, and by services, as far as he will accept of them."

Under the impression that Rousseau was already at London, Hume dispatched letters to Gilbert Elliot, John Home, and Robert Wood, requesting them to wait on the exile and to do everything in their power to get him settled there or to send him on to Edinburgh. To Elliot he laid bare a proposal : " Our present King and present Minister are desirous of being thought encouragers of learning : can they have a more proper opportunity of showing to the whole world that they are in earnest ? Monsieur Rousseau is now thrown out of his ordinary course of livelihood ; and tho he rejects presents from private persons, he may not think himself degraded by a pension from a great monarch." To Rousseau himself Hume wrote that " I will use the Freedom of telling you bluntly, without affecting the Finesse of a well-turnd Compliment, that, of all men of Letters in Europe, since the Death of President Montesquieu, you are the Person whom I most revere, both for the Force of your Genius and the Greatness of your Mind." Rousseau actually was nowhere near London. He had sought sanctuary at Môtiers-Travers in Neuchâtel, an independent principality in the Jura under the protection of the King of Prussia. Hume was so informed by his old friend George Keith, Hereditary Earl Marischal of Scotland and Governor of Neuchâtel. With the approval of Frederick the Great, the genial Keith welcomed his " honest savage."

Attainted as a rebel after the Jacobite rising of 1715, Keith had long been an exile from Britain and was sympathetic to all exiles and to all sufferers from oppression. " A sort of Guebre by religion," who had " never been opprest with religious Prejudices," Keith relished the company of David Hume, one of his standing jokes being to address him as " Defender of the Faith." [1] Affectionately he took Jean-Jacques to his bosom and endeavoured to foster a friendship between him and Hume. To the refugee he presented an engraving of Hume and incessantly praised his virtues, instancing the amicable controversy with Wallace and the attempt of the Scottish clergy to excommunicate " this Antichrist (for such he is in Scotland just as you are in Switzerland)." Elaborating on an already good story, Keith went on : " David sat down among the lamas and listened with admirable *sang-froid* to all the abuse directed against him, taking his snuff and keeping his silence. His *sang-froid* disconcerted the lamas ; they left without excommunicating him." [2]

Lord Marischal's fondest dream was that all three friends (David, Jean-Jacques, and himself) should live the philosophical life together at Keith Hall, near Aberdeen. To Rousseau he wrote :

I shall give you a couple of rooms in my house, and as many to *le bon David*. Neither of you will enter the rooms of the other ; there will be a parlour for the exchange of visits. We shall have *placidam sub libertate quietem*, which is my motto. Each of us will contribute to the upkeep of the little republic according to his income, and each will tax himself. Food will be no great item, inasmuch as trout, salmon, seafood, and vegetables cost me nothing. David will pay for the roast-beef because he eats it. We shall need two carriages when we feel the urge for a drive. There will be no need for other rules or laws in our republic ; each will make his own spiritual and temporal regulations. Such is my castle ; the foundations are already laid.[3]

[1] RSE, v, 99–100 ; *Boswell Papers*, iii, 12.
[2] Rousseau, viii, 97.   [3] *Ibid.*, viii, 170.

In pursuit of this acknowledged " castle in Spain," Keith, who had recently bought his peace with the Hanoverian dynasty, returned to Scotland in the autumn of 1763 to look over the situation in person and to report back to his two friends.

Hume had concluded his letter to Mme de Boufflers concerning Rousseau with the admission : " I will not allow myself to think that I shall always be condemned to admire you at a distance, and that I shall never have an opportunity of enjoying that conversation of whose charms I have heard such frequent accounts." The lady seized upon this passage to strengthen their personal ties, writing again in English. Charmingly feminine, she acknowledges that she does not perfectly fulfil the idea that Hume has seemingly formulated of her. " Perhaps, Sir, I confess it with ingenuity, had I been doom'd to be never personally acquaint'd with you, I should not have generosity enough, to correct your judgement of me." But as she is supremely confident that they will meet, " What a Shame indeed for me, and disappointment for you : in place of the object, your imagination has adorn'd with such shining qualifications, to find a person, to whom nature has granted but indifferent ones. A great part of my youth is over. Some delicacy in features, mildness and decency in countenance, are the only exterior advantages, I can boast of. And as for interior, common sense, improved a little, by early good reading, are all I possess." Her English, she avows, is " confined," yet she adds winningly, " if I am intitled to some elegancy I owe it to the repeated readings of your admirable works." The persecution of Rousseau is treated as it may affect Hume's future actions. " Is it possible, Sir, that this late unhappy event could deprive of the honour of your presence, a country filled with your fervent admirers, and where every one will endeavour to out do each other in expressing the veneration and regard you so justly deserve ? " [1]

Andrew Stuart of Torrance, just returned from Paris, provided his friend with a detailed account of the Comtesse and of her " partiality " for him ; but Hume was still reluctant to bind himself in any manner. With the signing of the Treaty of Paris in February 1763, however, war between the two nations could no longer serve as a pretext for not going to Paris. And with the Peace, the impetuous Comtesse took matters into her own hands : if Hume would not come to France, she would go to England. The decision once reached, arrangements were easy to make, as

[1] RSE, III, 69.

she had many English friends of rank and much influence with both French and English diplomatists. Everyone was charmed with the notion of a distinguished French lady visiting England for pleasure and thereby strengthening amity between the two countries. She left Paris on 17 April 1763 accompanied by Lord Elibank, her cousin and Hume's close friend. In the party, also, were Lord Tavistock, eldest son of the Duke of Bedford, and Topham Beauclerk.[1]

Prior to leaving Paris, Mme de Boufflers had taken Lord Elibank into her confidence : " her only errand to England " was " the hopes of meeting " David Hume at London. Elibank at once began to compose a letter to his friend apprising him of the facts of the case, but, hating inordinately the use of his pen, he put the " half finished Scrol " in his pocket. After depositing his fair charge in London, he travelled down to Edinburgh, where he learned that Hume was at Ninewells. The incomplete Paris letter he now enclosed in another short one dated 11 May and forwarded both to Hume. " You cannot in Decency," pleaded Elibank, " neglect the opportunity of gratifying this flattering Curiosity, perhaps Passion, of the most Amiable of gods Creation." [2]

At London before the end of April, " Madame Blewflower," as she was affectionately called by the mob on the streets,[3] met with a reception unparalleled for a private lady from foreign parts. Everyone in the court circle vied for the privilege of entertaining the visitor. On 17 May Horace Walpole gave a breakfast in her honour at his " toy castle " at Strawberry Hill. Among the guests were Lady Mary Coke, the Duke and Duchess of Grafton, Lord Hertford, Lord and Lady Holdernesse, and Lord Villiers. The guest of honour was less taken with the extravagancies of the pseudo-Gothic castle than with the continuous fanfare of French horns and clarinets during the serving of breakfast. She was perfectly enchanted when her host showed her his private printing-press, which just happened to be set up with a poem addressed to her.

Parties followed parties in London and in the country. Lord Tavistock escorted her to Woburn to visit his parents, the Duke and Duchess of Bedford, and subsequently to Wakefield Lodge in Northamptonshire to visit the Duke of Grafton. In her honour Lord Shelburne gave a dinner and a play. The various visits of the Comtesse assumed almost the proportions of a royal progress. She found it all very exciting—and very fatiguing.

[1] Rousseau, IX, 240. [2] RSE, v, 8.
[3] J. H. Jesse, *George Selwyn and His Contemporaries* (London 1882), I, 242-3.

One call was made at her express desire, for she insisted that Topham Beauclerk should take her to meet England's great man of letters. Accordingly the two drove in a coach to the unpretentious chambers of Dr Johnson in the Temple, where they were entertained with his conversation. Hardly had they left, relates Beauclerk, when a noise like thunder sounded after them.

This was occasioned by Johnson, who it seems, upon a little recollection, had taken it into his head that he ought to have done the honours of his literary residence to a foreign lady of quality, and eager to show himself a man of gallantry, was hurrying down the stair-case in violent agitation. He overtook us before we reached the Temple-gate, and brushing in between me and Madame de Boufflers, seized her hand, and conducted her to her coach. His dress was a rusty brown morning suit, a pair of old shoes by way of slippers, a little shrivelled wig sticking on the top of his head, and the sleeves of his shirt and the knees of his breeches hanging loose. A considerable crowd of people gathered round, and were not a little struck by this singular appearance.[1]

Mme de Boufflers had intended to remain in England only two months, yet she lingered on—waiting. The aristocracy of London would have been mightily astonished had they had any intimation that the grand lady from France was waiting for the arrival of so uncourtly a figure as David Hume, another mere man of letters, and, in addition, " Great Infidel " and Scot ! She had, to be sure, spoken highly of his abilities to anyone who would listen, but of her " passion " she gave no hint beyond the confidence to her cousin, except possibly to another Scottish friend of Hume's, Dr John Pringle. On the back of a letter of 21 April that Hume had addressed to Andrew Millar, Pringle wrote cryptically : " Dr P. presents his compts. to Mr H. and *acquaints him that* Madame Boufflers arrivd in town within these few days, & he hears would be happy to see Mr H." [2]

While Mme de Boufflers was waiting for him at London with growing impatience, where was David Hume ? Lord Elibank, it will be recalled, had not found him at Edinburgh and had supposed he was at Ninewells. Before Elibank's letter of 11 May reached Ninewells, however, Hume had gone off on a pleasure jaunt to Knaresborough and Harrogate with Sir Gilbert Elliot and Sir Harry and Lady Erskine.[3] It was not, therefore, until 3 July that Hume sat down at Edinburgh to write to Mme de Boufflers. She could hardly have felt requited for her efforts with

---

[1] *Johnson*, II, 405–6.
[2] HL, I, 387, *n*I. The words italicised were added by Millar.
[3] G. F. S. Elliot, *The Border Elliots* (Edinburgh 1897), p. 382. According to *The Jenkinson Papers 1760–1766* (ed. N. S. Jucker, London 1949, pp. 153–4), Hume arrived at Knaresborough on 15 May.

his opening : " Being engaged in a party to a remote corner of
the country, I was informed very late of the visit, with which your
Ladyship has been pleased to favour this island. . . . I delayed
for some time paying my respects to your Ladyship by letter, in
hopes that I might possibly be able to do it in person, and thereby
to gratify that desire by which I have long been possessed, of making
myself known to a Lady so universally valued, and who had done
me so much honour, by giving me marks of her attention." Mme
de Boufflers may also have found Hume's apology strangely feeble :
" But the reasons which detain me in this country are so powerful,
that I find I must lay aside for the present so flattering a project,
and must reserve that happiness to a time, which I shall always
keep in my eye, when I may be able to pay my respects to your
Ladyship at Paris." Most of the remainder of this long letter is
impersonally devoted to a discussion of the affairs of Rousseau.

After receiving this somewhat evasive letter, Mme de Boufflers
carried through her most recent intention of leaving for Paris on
23 July with Topham Beauclerk as her escort. Her well-laid plans
had apparently produced nothing.

Why had David Hume acted so seemingly ungraciously ? At
the time when the English nobility, and even the crusty English
lexicographer, were outdoing themselves in courtesies to the lady
from France, why was the Scottish philosopher so cold and so
distant ? Without sufficient evidence, these questions can only
be speculated about, yet they demand consideration.

David Hume was a Scot who had come to detest London and
the Great Men of England ; he was a Scot who spoke like a Scot,
a countryman still uncomfortable in high society, a man of letters
who deemed himself the equal of any man of any rank—for all
these reasons Hume would not have relished meeting the Comtesse
in the drawing-rooms of London. In his letter of 3 July, indeed,
he had intimated as much. " I am only afraid," said he acidly,
" that, to a person acquainted with the sociable and conversible
parties of France, the showy and dazzling crowds of London
assemblies would afford but an indifferent entertainment, and
that the love of retreat and solitude, with which the English are
reproached, never appears more conspicuously, than when they
draw together a multitude of five hundred persons."

Well and good, Hume was unwilling to meet the Comtesse
at London—but would he meet her elsewhere ? A man of fifty-
two, though still attractive to women and attracted by them,
Hume was somewhat frightened of the " passion " that common

friends insisted she held for him, and desirous only of a philo-sophical retirement. Mme de Boufflers, moreover, was quite unaccustomed to English or Scottish standards of living. Wife of the Comte de Boufflers, she was the principal mistress of the Prince de Conti, the third man of the realm. That she also indulged herself, like other French ladies of quality, with *chevaliers servants* was common gossip. For an aging man of letters to permit himself to become involved in the tangled life-patterns of such a woman—however flattering the thought might possibly be to his vanity—was not a matter for precipitation. In London, it was simply unthinkable. In Paris, however, it was just conceivable. For these and kindred reasons, presumably, Hume refused to go to London but indulged himself in vaguely pleasurable thoughts about life in Paris in the indefinite future.

It seems unlikely, however, that Hume would ever visit Paris on his own initiative. What was needed was increased resentment against Scotland, as well as against England, to drive him out of his inertia—the course of this resentment has already been traced—and, furthermore, opportunity to go to Paris in a position of honour. That opportunity was afforded him in the early summer of 1763 by Lord Hertford and is described in *My Own Life*:

I received in 1763 an Invitation from Lord Hertford, with whom I was not in the least acquainted, to attend him on his Embassy to Paris, with a near Prospect of being appointed Secretary to the Embassy, and in the mean while, of performing the functions of that office. This Offer, however inviting, I at first declined ; both because I was reluctant to begin Connexions with the Great, and because I was afraid that the Civilities and gay Company of Paris woud prove disagreeable to a Person of my Age and Humour : But on his Lordship's repeating the Invitation, I accepted of it.

Francis Seymour Conway, Earl of Hertford, had the reputation of being highly respectable, deeply pious, moderately dull, and somewhat parsimonious. He was a good family man, whose domestic circle was enlarged in 1763 by the addition of a thirteenth child. Though first cousin to Horace Walpole, Hertford had little in common with that sparkling, witty, cynical, worldly, and confirmed bachelor. On first meeting Hertford, David Hume described him as " the most amiable nobleman of the Court of England," an opinion that he never gave up.

It was His Majesty's pleasure on 12 April 1763 to appoint the respectable but undistinguished Earl of Hertford to the most important of his ambassadorial posts, the Court of France. At the same time His Majesty appointed as Secretary to the Embassy, at a salary of £1,000 a year, Charles Bunbury, Esq., a young man whose sole claim to fame was that he had married a sister of the fabulously wealthy Duke of Richmond, Lady Sarah Lennox, whose hand had been sought by the King himself. Before the end of May Lord Hertford dispatched part of his retinue to Paris to prepare the ambassadorial quarters for residence. Protocol required, however, that he himself should remain in England until such time as his counterpart in France, the Comte de Guerchy, was ready to leave that country. The Comte was not ready until October.

The pious Hertford was offended by the naming of a well-known rake as Secretary to the Embassy, but was unable to get the appointment rescinded. Nevertheless, he " was resolved," as he told David Hume, " never to see, or do business with his Secretary," and to name a personal assistant of his own choice, who would inherit the official post when, and if, Bunbury was forced out. He first considered Louis Dutens, but Dutens preferred to return to his former station at Turin.[1] In June, or possibly earlier, Hertford directed Robert Wood, one of the Under-Secretaries of State, to make a similar offer to David Hume.

It is not difficult to understand why Lord Hertford turned his back on the young rake, but it is not easy to understand why he turned to the " Great Infidel." David Hume was led to believe that " the Idea first came into my Patron's Head without the Suggestion of any one Mortal." In consideration of the general opinion of Hertford's political ineptitude, as well as of his piety, however, it seems strange that he recognised so clearly and without any prompting that the appointment of David Hume was the most brilliant that Britain, in her new effort to win the friendship of France, could possibly have made. Is there, therefore, any reason to believe that Hertford, wittingly or unwittingly, was subject to outside pressure ?

Horace Walpole, who ought to have been in a position to know something about the extraordinary decision of his cousin, explains that " The decorum and piety of Lord Hertford occasioned men to wonder, when, in the room of Bunbury, he chose for his secretary the celebrated freethinker, David Hume, totally unknown to him ; but this was the effect of recommendations from other Scots, who had much weight with Lord and Lady Hertford." [2] Walpole

---

[1] Dutens, *Memoirs of a Traveller*, ii, 38.
[2] Walpole, *Memoirs of the Reign of King George III* (London 1894), i, 209.

names no names, but he may easily have been correct, because Hume did have many influential Scottish friends in London. He also had many influential English friends, one of whom was Robert Wood.

On Hume's return from the vacation jaunt, probably about the middle of June, he had found awaiting him, not only the letters from Lord Elibank and Dr Pringle informing him of the visit of Mme de Boufflers, but also that which Robert Wood had written at Lord Hertford's behest. To the last Hume responded with inquiries, which Wood answered, on 28 July, in the only extant letter of the series. Wood makes it clear that Hertford still wanted Hume as his personal secretary and would do everything in his power to get him appointed as Embassy Secretary, but could make no promise as to when that would occur. " In short," Wood urges, " as I advise Lord Hertford to invite you so I advise you to accept the invitation because I really think you'll be of use to one another & I don't doubt but you'll find it answer." He concludes, " But we shall talk over this matter when you come to town which I would advise you to do soon that I may initiate you in our Mystery's." Is the last word to be taken as a hint of some sort of secret understanding ? Or does it merely refer to the inner workings of the office of Secretary of State ? The indications would seem to be, at any rate, that Wood had, indeed, brought pressure to bear upon Hertford to extend the invitation to Hume but that there were circumstances involved that he did not wish to commit to paper.[1]

Some slight clue to the nature of these circumstances is disclosed in a letter of 11 September from Mme de Boufflers to Hume.[2]

Although I charged M. D'Eon to tell you, Sir, the regret that I had for not having the honour of seeing you in England, I can yet rely only upon myself to explain to you what it was. I remained a whole month longer than I had intended, hoping always that you would come to London ; and without your letter which did not set any precise time, and which flattered me that you would make a journey to France, I should not have left yet.

The reception which was given me in England is so flattering that I dare not speak of it, for fear that what I would say would be attributed to vanity rather than to gratitude ; and if I had had the pleasure of seeing you, nothing would have been lacking to my trip to make it the most satisfactory possible in all respects.

Since you will shortly be in Paris, I delay until that time to speak to you, Sir, on the subject of M. Rousseau for whom I shall never cease to have all the friendship and all the esteem that I believe he merits. Unfortunately, with him it is necessary to rest content in simple appearances, since he refused

[1] RSE, vii, 101.   [2] RSE, iii, 70.

to accept more effectual tokens of support. He has talked of dying, but he is now recovered.

I have the honour to be, Sir, with all the sentiments that you know I hold for you,

Your most humble and most obedient servant,

H. De Saujeon Ctesse. De Boufflers.

11 September 1763

Is there not an intimation in several sentences of this letter that Mme de Boufflers, before leaving England, had been in the secret of Lord Hertford's invitation? If so, it may not be un-reasonable to conjecture that she had had some part in the original suggestion of Hume's name or, at least, in heartily seconding it.[1]

There is in this letter, in all events, a new sureness of tone. Mme de Boufflers confirms, in so many words, what Elibank had previously told Hume, that the purpose of her visit to England was to see him, and she is fully aware that Hume has been informed of her true sentiments for him. She knows for certain that Hume is going to Paris as secretary to Lord Hertford. She implies that she would have preferred to remain in London until Hume's arrival, and then to have had the pleasure of returning to France in his company and of presenting him to his admirers in Paris. As a woman of understanding and tact, however, she is prepared to go on ahead in order to save him from any possible embarrass-ment. Her complete knowledge of the situation and her consum-mate diplomacy are evident throughout. In short, she had triumphed and, for the moment, was quite willing to retire into the background : David Hume was to be hers. How much of all this strategy the philosopher himself recognised is not determin-able—perhaps rather little.

David Hume accepted Lord Hertford's offer as a result of Wood's last letter and left Edinburgh 10 August. At London his last misgivings vanished and he was eminently pleased with Lord and Lady Hertford. " Even that Circumstance of Lord Hertford's Character, his great Piety, ought to make my Connexions with him more agreeable," he noted, " both because it is not attended with any thing sour & rigid, and because I draw the more Honour from his Choice, while he overlookd so many seeming Objections which lay against me on that head." All of Hume's friends were

---

[1] Greig's brilliant conjecture (p. 282) that Mme de Boufflers had put the name of Hume into Hertford's mind " in such a way that he supposed that he had first thought of it himself " is thus given some substantiation by the above documents. The case is still by no means, however, open-and-shut.

similarly pleased, and Hume reports Elliot as saying that " my Situation was, taking all its Circumstances, the most wonderful Event in the World : I was now a Person clean & white as the driven Snow, and that, were I to be proposd for the See of Lambeth, no Objections could henceforth be made to me." [1]

As " a Person clean & white as the driven Snow " Hume was not actually offered a bishopric but on 20 August he was invited to dinner at the Royal Chaplain's table at St James's. There he found himself in the company, among others, of Thomas Birch, David Mallet, Robert Wood—and Samuel Johnson. Birch reports the incident [2] in a letter to Philip Yorke, Lord Royston and later Earl of Hardwicke : " . . . I met at the Chaplain's Table at St James David Hume, the Historian, who has just come to town at the Invitation of the Earl of Hertford, who I find, has an intention of taking him with him to France, if he can make it worth Mr. Hume's while. His Lordship is to set out for Paris about a month hence. Your Lordship will smile," continued Birch, " when I tell you, that another of our Company at dinner to day was Sam. Johnson. . . ." On this occasion, the Great Moralist obviously did not walk out on the Great Infidel.

" Lord Hertford's choice of secretary has occasioned much laughing here," observed George Macartney. " Questions are ask'd whether Mr. Hume as part of the family will be obliged to attend prayers twice a day, and whether his Lordship has got a good clever Chaplain to keep him steddy, &c. and a thousand Jokes of that kind, Nay some people go so far as to suppose, that either he is now become a convert to infidelity, or that his former Devotion was all Collusion and Hypocrisy." [3] Taking the joking in good part, Lord Hertford obtained from the King a pension for Hume of £200 a year for life. He also informed Hume that he would be expected to be useful to Lord Beauchamp, his eldest son, in his studies ; and Hume cautiously inquired of Adam Smith what he knew of the character of the young man. Hertford's efforts to oust Bunbury still proved unavailing, and that man-about-town remained in England enjoying his salary without doing any work.

A sorrowful meeting took place at London between Hume and Earl Marischal Keith, who had just arrived in England after an

[1] HL, I, 392–3.

[2] Birch in Hardwicke Papers, BM, Add. MS 35400, ff. 110v., 111r. ; Birch's journal, Add. MS 4478c, f. 417r.

[3] *Letters to Henry Fox, Lord Holland* (London 1915), p. 186.

absence of forty-eight years. Still dreaming of his " castle in Spain " with David Hume and Jean-Jacques Rousseau, Keith was distressed to find David on the eve of departure for France. David himself was heartbroken over the turn of events and "bawled like a calf," wrote Keith to Jean-Jacques. The unhappy Keith proceeded to Scotland where, despite Macpherson's poetical effusion on " The Earl Marischal's Welcome to his Native Country," he found bigotry and hypocrisy rampant. " I see that our *bon David*," he sadly informed Jean-Jacques, " is regarded by many people as a monster. I imagine that's what determined him to go to France." [1] Finding the Scottish weather as insufferable as the Scottish temper, the aged Marischal sold his estates and returned to warmer climes.

As the time for departure approached, Hume's spirits began to soar. " I go," he exulted, " to a Place of the World which I have always admird the most." Yet in his exuberance he did not forget old friends. To Alexander Carlyle he wrote of " the Case of poor Blacklocke [which] gives me great Distress. . . ." To Hugh Blair he outlined careful procedure for investigation into the authenticity of Macpherson's Ossian. On a personal note he explained to Blair that,

I carried only four books along with me ; a Virgil, a Horace, a Tasso, and a Tacitus : I could have wished also to carry my Homer, but I found him too bulky. I own that in common decency, I ought to have left my *Horace* behind me, and that I ought to be ashamed to look him in the face. For I am sensible that at my years no temptation would have seduced *him* from his retreat ; nor would he ever have been induced to enter so late into the path of ambition. But I deny that I enter into the path of ambition : I only walk into the green fields of amusement, and I affirm, that external amusement becomes more and more necessary as one advances in years, and can find less supplies from his own passions or imagination.

To Mme de Boufflers he wrote : " I now give you warning, Madam, that your declarations in my favour have been so frequent and public, both in France and England, that you are bound in honour to maintain them, and that you cannot with a good grace retract upon a personal acquaintance the advantageous terms in which you have so often been pleased to speak of me." The letter concludes, " I wish your Ladyship could persuade M. de Guerchy to come to his station here in London, that I might the sooner have an opportunity of throwing myself at your feet. . . ."

The Comte de Guerchy finally left Paris on 9 October. On Thursday, 13 October, Lord and Lady Hertford and their official

---

[1] Rousseau, x, 102 ; i, 126.

entourage left London, embarking at Dover the following morning. Late that afternoon they were forced to land at Boulogne, instead of at Calais, because of a strong SE. wind. Lord Hertford consequently failed to receive the honours due to an ambassador.[1] On the afternoon of the 15th, they set out for Paris, arriving there on the 18th.

In his pocket Hume carried letters to several of the friends of Lady Hervey. "Do not think, Sir," said that most charming lady,[2] the former Molly Lepel celebrated by Pope and Gay, "I mean them as recommendations : you can want none,—the name of *David Hume* is the best and greatest recommendation you can have, in a country where merit and talents meet with more admirers than they find enviers and maligners in this. I look upon the letters I enclose to you as directions to find the most amiable people, and the most worthy of being acquainted with you, of any I know. That to Mme de Boufflers is rather a congratulation to her on your arrival. . . ."

[1] Hertford to Halifax, 15 Oct. 1763, from Boulogne, in PRO, SP 78/258.
[2] RSE, v, 68.

CHAPTER 31

THE ADULATION OF FRANCE

" They consider me as one of the greatest geniuses in the world."

THE arrival in France of the first peacetime British Ambassador since the outbreak of the Seven Years' War was overshadowed by that of his private secretary. Though David Hume during the previous two decades had occasionally thought of taking refuge in France from the persecution of Scotland and the intolerance of England, he entered that country in 1763 with dignity and was afforded the reception of a hero. No sooner had he set foot in the British Embassy in Paris than young Lord Beauchamp informed him that they must instantly go to the Duchesse de la Vallière's. Protesting that he had had no time to recover from the effects of the journey, Hume was told that he must go, though it were in boots. " I accordingly went with him in a travelling Frock," relates Hume, " where I saw a very fine Lady reclining on a Sopha, who made me Speeches & Compliments without Bounds." A fat gentleman standing nearby and wearing a star of the richest diamonds took up the " Style of Panegyric " ; he was the Duc d' Orléans, a Prince of the Blood. The evening ended with supper at President Hénault's, who received the distinguished visitor with open arms and voiced compliments in the name of the Dauphin. So was the tone set for the triumphal stay in France of a Scottish man of letters.

But how was it possible that Mme de Boufflers had permitted another lady—even a duchess—to have the honour of introducing this lion of lions to French society ? Alas ! the best-laid plans had miscarried, and under the most humiliating of circumstances. The Comtesse had the measles ! From L'Isle Adam, a château of the Prince de Conti's, she had sent a letter of explanation : " Scarce recover'd from the measles I cannot Sir write myself, am oblig'd to use another hand, the same reason prevents my being at Paris on your arrival as was my intention, it gives me great concern to be hinder'd from giving you that proof of my esteem and regard, & doing myself the honour of being the first in the Kingdom who pays what is due to so illustrious a man. . . ." [1] The

[1] RSE, III, 71.

letter is in the hand of her English secretary, Lydia Becquet, but is signed by the Comtesse herself. In reply Hume regretted her illness and acknowledged that " Your Ladyship was the first person to whom I had proposed to pay my respects at Paris. . . ." Pending her recovery, however, he did not lack the caresses of other great ladies.

At Fontainebleau, where the ambassadorial party went after three days in Paris, the courtiers vied with one another in adulation of Hume—dukes and marshals and foreign ambassadors. After a dinner at the Duc de Praslin's, the Secretary of State, Hume retired to a corner to converse with somebody when a tall and elegantly dressed gentleman entered and immediately called out to the Duchesse de Praslin, " I say, Madame Duchesse, how happy I am ! I saw M. Hume at the Court today ! " With complacent humour, the great man observed, " I retain a Relish for no kind of Flattery but that which comes from the Ladies." The greatest and professedly the sincerest of flatterers were Mme de Pompadour, mistress of Louis XV, and the Duchesse de Choiseul, " Wife of the Favourite and prime Minister." " All the Courtiers, who stood around when I was introduc'd to Mme de Pompadour," continued Hume, " assurd me she was never heard to say so much to any Man." From " the Royal Family downwards," he wrote to friends at Edinburgh, the French " seem to have it much at heart to persuade me, by every expression of esteem, that they consider me as one of the greatest geniuses in the world."

By way of illustration, he recounts his presentation to the children of the Dauphin at Versailles :

> The Duc de Berry, the eldest, a boy of ten Years old, stept forth, and told me, how many Friends & Admirers I had in this Country, and that he reckond himself in the Number, from the Pleasure he had receivd by the reading of many Passages in my Works. When he had finish'd, his Brother, the Count de Provence, who is two Years younger, began his Discourse, and informd me, that I had been long & impatiently expected in France ; and that he himself expected soon to have great Satisfaction from the reading of my fine History. But what is more curious ; when I was carry'd thence to the Count d'Artois, who is but five Years of Age, I heard him mumble something, which, tho he had forgot it in the way, I conjectur'd, from some scatterd Words, to have been also a Panegyric dictated to him. . . . It is conjecturd that this Honour was pay'd me by express Orders from the Dauphin, who indeed is not, on any Occasion, sparing in my Praise.[1]

The sudden impact of this French adulation brought up the inevitable comparison that had been for so long tormenting Hume.

[1] NHL, pp. 75–6.

" But can I ever forget," he inquired of Adam Smith, " that it is the very same Species, that wou'd scarce show me common Civilities a very few Years ago at Edinburgh, who now receive me with such Applauses at Paris ? "

Yet the first three crowded and exciting weeks at Paris and at Fontainebleau proved almost too much for the philosopher to endure. " I am convinced," he wrote, " that Louis XIV never, in any three weeks of his life, suffered so much flattery : I say suffered, for it really confounds and embarrasses me, and makes me look sheepish. . . . I really wish often for the plain roughness of the *Poker* . . . to correct and qualify so much lusciousness. . . . I am sensible that I set out too late, and that I am misplaced ; and I wish, twice or thrice a day, for my easy chair and my retreat in James's Court." Indiscriminate flattery from everyone who saw him—and everyone insisted on seeing him—became an intolerable burden for a man who had never liked large social gatherings. In yearning for the Poker and for James's Court, Hume was yearning for the select circle of intimate friends. " I suppose," wrote he in an early letter to Blair, " this, like all other violent Modes, will pass ; and in the mean while, the Hurry & Dissipation, attending it, gives me more pain than Pleasure. . . . I am determin'd to retrench, and to abandon the fine Folks before they abandon me."

During those first three weeks Hume discovered that his use of French, unpractised for many years, was not sufficient to carry him along. In desperation, he thought of resigning his post and went so far as to discuss with Alexander Wedderburn, who was in Paris at the moment, the possible means of inducing Lord Hertford to substitute Andrew Stuart of Torrance. Imperceptibly, however, Hume recovered the facility of speaking French and, with command of the language, soon gained command of the situation. The crisis eased.

Gradually he contracted the circle of his acquaintance, dropping mere courtiers and mere beautiful ladies. The jesting advice of Lord Marischal proved unneeded when he wrote : " I wish they [" the beautiful and great ladies "] don't seduce, and send you back a *petit-maître* ; *et très adroit à faire la tapisserie*. A coquette taught Hercules himself to spin." [1] After six weeks Hume could tell Robertson that " I . . . am falling into Friendships, which are very agreeable ; much more so than silly, distant Admiration. They now begin to banter me, and tell droll Stories

[1] RSE, v, 102.

of me ; which they have either observd themselves or have heard of from others ; so that you see I am beginning to be at home."

One droll story of Hume playing at charades is related by Mme d'Epinay and may be taken in either a kindly or a satirical spirit :

The celebrated David Hume, the great historian of England, who is known and esteemed for his writings, has not so much talent for [parlour games] as all our pretty women had settled that he had. . . . He had been cast for the part of a sultan sitting between two slaves, and employing all his eloquence to win their love. Finding them inexorable, he had to try to find out the reason of their resistance. He was placed upon a sofa between the two prettiest women in Paris ; he looked at them fixedly, smote the pit of his stomach and his knees several times, and could find nothing to say but, " Well, young ladies ; well, there you are, then ! Well, there you are ! There you are, then ? " He kept on saying this for a quarter of an hour, without being able to think of anything else. At last one of the young ladies got up and said impatiently : " Ah ! I suspected as much ; this man is good for nothing except to eat veal ! " Since then he has been banished to the role of spectator, but is none the less feted and flattered. . . . All the pretty women have taken possession of him ; he goes to all the smart suppers, and no feast is complete without him. . . .[1]

With the advent of kindly, personal banter, the " silly, distant admiration " was no longer oppressive, and Hume could remark indulgently that " I eat nothing but Ambrosia, drink nothing but Nectar, breathe nothing but Incense, and tread on nothing but Flowers." Life was settling down to a new and pleasing pattern.

If flattery was difficult for Hume to bear, affection was not. He revelled in affection and only half-ashamedly told Hugh Blair of an incident, " which may appear silly, but which gave more Pleasure than perhaps any other I had ever met with " :

I was carry'd . . . to a Masquerade by Lord Hertford : We went both unmaskd ; and we had scarce enterd the room, when a Lady in mask, came up to me and exclaimd, ' Ah ! M. Hume, you've done well in coming here without a mask. You will be loaded tonight with courtesies and civilities ! And you will see by unmistakable proofs in what affection you are held in France." This Prologue was not a little encouraging ; but as we advanc'd thro' the Hall, it is difficult to imagine the Caresses, Civilities and Panegyrics which pourd on me from all Sides : You wou'd have thought, that every one had taken Advantage of his Mask to speak his mind with Impunity. I cou'd observe, that the Ladies were rather the most liberal on this Occasion ; but what gave me chief Pleasure was to find, that most of the Elogiums bestowd on me, turnd on my personal Character ; my Naivety & Simplicity of Manners, the Candour & Mildness of my Disposition &c.
Non sunt mihi cornea fibra. I shall not deny, that my Heart felt a sensible

---

[1] *Mémoires et Correspondance de Mme d'Epinay* (Paris 1818), III, 284.

Satisfaction from this general Effusion of good will ; and Lord Hertford was much pleas'd and even surpriz'd ; tho', he said, he thought that he had known before upon what Footing I stood with the good Company of Paris.

A later anecdote illustrative of the affectionate esteem in which he was held was forwarded by Hume to " my Protestant Pastors " in Edinburgh. " Not long ago," he relates, " as I came into a Company, I heard D'Alembert exclaim, *Et verbum caro factum est*. And the Word was made Flesh. This was thought a very good Jest on my past & present Life ; and was much repeated. A Lady in telling the Story, said, *Et verbum carum factum est* [And the Word was made beloved]. When told of her Mistake, she wou'd not allow it to be one." [1]

The most amazing feature of Hume's vogue in Paris is that it was not a passing fad but lasted throughout the entire twenty-six months of his stay. " The more I recoiled from their excessive Civilities," he acknowledges in his autobiography, " the more I was loaded with them." The typical travelling English aristocrats, however, never could understand the situation and continued to condescend to him, or to despise him, or to ridicule him just as they were accustomed to do in London.

Arriving at Paris in the autumn of 1765, Horace Walpole was perfectly amazed to find the tall, stout, and ungainly Scottish man of letters not the laughing-stock of Parisian society. " Mme du Deffand says I have *le feu moqueur*," wrote Walpole, " and I have not hurt myself a little by laughing at whisk and Richardson, though I have steered clear of the chapter of Mr. Hume ; the only Trinity now in fashion here." In private letters, however, Walpole explored the " chapter of Mr. Hume " quite thoroughly : he " is fashion itself, although his French is almost as unintelligible as his English " ; he is " treated here with perfect veneration " ; he is " the only thing in the world that they believe implicitly ; which they must do, for I defy them to understand any language that he speaks." " It is incredible the homage they pay him," commented Walpole after repeating another anecdote about Hume : " M. de Guerchy told me that a French lady asking him who Mr Hume was, and being told, begged him not to mention it, as it would give her *bien mauvais air* not to know *him*." As to the *salons*, Walpole proceeds, " the style of conversation is solemn, pedantic, and seldom animated, but by a dispute. I was expressing my aversion to disputes : Mr Hume, who very gratefully admires the tone of Paris, having never known any other tone, said with

[1] HL, I, 437–8 ; 496.

great surprise, ' Why, what do you like, if you hate both disputes and whisk ? ' " [1]

Another snob, although no dilettante, Lord Charlemont, found Hume's fashion at Paris " truely rediculous." How could the French, and particularly the French women, think his conversation delightful ? " And yet no Lady's Toilet was compleat without Hume's Attendance. An Acquaintance with our Philosopher was necessary to the *bel Air*. At the Opera his broad unmeaning Face was usually seen *entre deux jolis Minois*, and his Philosophy, which had formerly been detrimental to his Views of Gallantry, might here have insured his Success. . . . How my Friend Hume was able to indure the Encounter of these french Female Titans, I know not." [2]

George Selwyn, wit and politician, was in perfect agreement with Walpole and Charlemont. He wrote to Lord Holland concerning Hume : " . . . in common Society he seems a man of the most clumsy capacity I ever saw, and to speak the truth, the fuss which the people of this Country have made with a man on account of perfections of which I am confident they are no judge, and whose manners are so unlike their own, has lessened them not a little in my opinion." [3]

Hume's vogue in Paris was undoubtedly born out of the prevailing Anglomania, together with the interest in abstract speculation and in history, and the further fact that for nearly a decade he had been recognised as Britain's greatest man of letters. The further facts that he held a position at the British Embassy and that he was Scottish, not English, also worked to his advantage. But all these reasons combined hardly make clear why the vogue lasted without diminution. The true explanation lies rather in Hume's charm of personality.

Andrew Stuart of Torrance, who was in Paris in the spring of 1764, informed Baron Mure of the lionising of Hume and of how he yet managed to remain his old self : " All ranks of people—courtiers, ladys, old and young, wits, and *scavans*, vie with one another in the incense they offer up to the celebre Mousr. Hume. Amidst all this intoxicating worship, he preserves his own natural style and simplicity of manners ; and deigns to be cheerful and jolly, as if no such things had happened to him. His manner, though differing in some respects from the French, does not fail,

[1] *Walpole Letters*, vi, 298, 301, 309, 332, 370.
[2] Lord Charlemont, " Anecdotes of Hume," RIA, MS—12/R/7, ff. 522-3.
[3] *Letters to Lord Holland*, p. 200.

however, to succeed with them." [1] From Scotland the delightfully effervescent Mrs Alison Cockburn accurately sensed the hold that this charm of her old friend held over the French, a people she despised or pretended to despise :

From the flint Hills of the north—from the uncultured Daughter of Caledon —Will the World Sage of France deign to receive a few lines—they come from the heart of a friend, and will be Deliverd by the Hand of an enemy. Which " O Man of Mode " is most indifferent to thee ! Insensible thou art alike to gratitude or resentment, fit for the Country that worships thee. Thou art equaly insensible to Love or hate. A momentary applause, ill begot & worse brought up—an abortion, a fame not founded on truth, has bewitched Thee and thou has forgot those who overlooking thy errors, loved thy Worth. Idol of Gaul I worship thee not. The very cloven foot, for which thou art worshipd, I despise—yet I remember Thee with affection. I remember that in spite of vain philosophy, of dark Doubts, of toilsome learning, God had stampd his Image of Benignity so strong upon *thy Heart* that not all the Labours of Thy Head, coud efface it. Idol of a foolish people be not puffed up—it is easy to overturn the faith of a multitude that is ready to do evil. An apostle of Less Sense might bring to that Giddy Nation, Libertinism ; Liberty they are not born to. This will be sent to you by your good friend Mr Burnet, who goes much such an errand as you have given yourself thro Life. Viz : in Search of truth—& I believe both are equaly impartial in the Search, tho indeed he has more visible interests for Darkning it than ever you had.[2]

Like Alison Cockburn, the French found Hume to be truly *le bon David* ; and their original admiration for his intellect was consequently augmented by affection for his person. Viewed with affection, a tall, stout, and ungainly foreigner, speaking ill the language, could never be truly ridiculous. On the contrary, his every awkwardness, his every *gaucherie* seemed to be lovable—even his later affectation that he could speak French like a native, an affectation which was neatly taken off by a linkboy at the *Comédie Française*, who, having heard him speak, addressed him by the title of *Milor*.

Of all this, Charlemont saw perhaps some faint glimmer, but Selwyn and Walpole were totally blind. To Walpole, Hume was ridiculous, not only because he was so obviously a Scotsman, but also because he was a serious writer, and anyone who took a serious writer seriously was himself ridiculous. By such a short and simple method did Walpole airily dismiss " Jesuits, Methodists, philosophers, politicians, the hypocrite Rousseau, the scoffer Voltaire, the Encyclopedists, the Humes, the Lyttletons, the Grenvilles, the atheist-tyrant of Prussia, and the mountebank of history,

---

[1] *Caldwell Papers*, PT. II, VOL. I, 256.

[2] RSE, IV, 28. The carrier of the letter, Hume's " enemy " and " good friend," was James Burnet, later Lord Monboddo.

Mr. Pitt. . . ." [1] The method was susceptible of refinement : imagine, for example, the exquisite pleasure to be derived from tormenting so serious and so sensitive a creature as " the hypocrite Rousseau " ! The Walpolian mentality was soon to turn to that pleasure.

After his first panic over the excessive adulation of the court at Fontainebleau, David Hume began to discover the *salons* of Paris —and, with the discovery, his panic subsided once and for all. For in the *salons* Hume recognised the prototype of the select society. The Gallic original, however, was more highly select than any that Hume had encountered at either Edinburgh or London, more carefully organised, more aristocratic, and, paradoxically, more democratic. In the *salon* all were expected to learn gracefully and unobtrusively ; all were accepted as artistic, intellectual, or social equals. The artificial aristocracy of birth bowed to the natural aristocracy of talent ; to patronise talent was the privilege of birth and wealth. The seriousness of this ideal of service inevitably drew a gibe from the frivolous Walpole : " Nay, I don't pay homage to their authors. Every woman has one or two planted in her house, and God knows how they water them."

A kind of intellectual clearing-house, the *salon* was presided over by a Great Lady—one whose greatness lay, however, less in social position, than in beauty, charm, intellect, wit, and genuine desire to serve others and to foster enlightenment. Although she might, on occasion, countenance cards, games, music, and even dancing, the main entertainment was always conversation. She might be a *femme savante* or not, but she must have the talent to draw the best out of others. Depending on her interests and capacities, the conversation might be artistic, literary, or philosophical. In the decadent age of Louis XV, conversation of serious people frequently dealt with those ideas which, before the close of the century, were to tear down the whole structure of the *ancien régime* : in this respect, the *salon* was one of the last refuges of freedom of thought and freedom of expression. Out of this spirit of intimacy, freedom, and cosmopolitanism, stimulated perhaps by the sheer beauty of the drawing-room itself and by the sheer grace of all the activities going on, evolved those friendships between man and man and between man and woman that it was a supreme function of the *salon* to foster.

The ladies of the *salons* Hume carefully differentiated from the

---

[1] *Walpole Corr.* (Yale), x, 184.

" Young and Brilliant " and giddy of the Court. The ladies of the *salons* were more mature, " past thirty," and they were " Women of Sense and Taste and Knowledge." In company they were characterised by the decency of their behaviour. " Scarce a double Entendre ever to be heard ; scarce a free Joke." But Hume shrewdly observes, " What lies below this Veil is not commonly supposed to be so pure."

On the relations that he maintained with the leading hostesses of the *salons* largely depended Hume's happiness in Paris—Mme Geoffrin, Mme du Deffand, Mlle de Lespinasse, and above all, Mme de Boufflers. It was the illness of the last that induced Hume to seek consolation and diversion elsewhere ; and it was his being a foreigner and *le bon David* that permitted him—up to a point— to do what few of the French were permitted to do, to circulate from one *salon* to another as he pleased. The exclusiveness of "the good Company of Paris " and other features of the *salons* are emphasised by Hume in a letter of 26 April 1764 to Hugh Blair. The unusual testiness expressed derives from the fact that his friend had ventured to recommend a certain travelling Scotsman, who had formerly snubbed him at Edinburgh. Robert Wallace also wrote to introduce the same man, adding, " I dare say you will introduce him to the good company where you are, and will be ready to put him on the best methods of enjoying and improving himself at Paris."

" Your Recommendations have great Weight with me," acknowledged Hume to Blair ; " but if I be not mistaken, I have often seen Coll. Lesly's Face in Edinburgh ; It is a little late, he has bethought himself of being *ambitious*, as you say, of being introducd to my Acquaintance : The only Favour I can do him is, to advise him, as soon as he has seen Paris, to go to a Provincial Town, where People are less shy of admitting new Acquaintance, and are less delicate Judges of Behaviour." In reality, the Secretary had been studiously polite, had introduced Lesly to the Ambassador, who asked him to dinner with seven or eight other Britishers.

What Hume wanted to make perfectly clear to Blair was that " the ridiculous Idea . . . that I might introduce him to the good Company of Paris, nothing can be more impracticable : I know not one Family to which I coud present such a man, silent, grave, awkward, speaking ill the Language, not distinguishd by any Exploit or Science or Art. . . . No people are more scrupu- lous of receiving Persons unknown ; and I shoud soon lose all

Credit with them, were I to prostitute my Recommendations of this Nature." The Paris of "Plays, Operas, & Bawdy-houses" alone was open to the travelling "Lords, Earls, Marquesses and Dukes" from Britain—"No body minded them; they kept Company with one Another; and it wou'd have been ridiculous to think of bringing them into French Company." When the disagreeable Mrs Mallet turned up in France, Hume reacted similarly. "I fancy she is angry with me," he admitted, "and thought herself neglected by me while in Paris. I heard of her thrusting herself everywhere into Companies, who endeavoured to avoid her; and I was afraid she woud have laid hold of me to enlarge her Acquaintance among the French."

To return to the *salonnières*—Lady Hervey had provided Hume with a letter of introduction to Mme Geoffrin, and it is likely enough that she was the first that he visited. Of all the leading hostesses, Marie-Thérèse Rodet Geoffrin was the only *bourgeoise*; the death of her husband in 1749 had left her command of a tremendous fortune. In the endeavour to foster a friendship, Lady Hervey painted Hume a picture of Mme Geoffrin in January 1764. By that time, Hume had probably limned it out for himself:

There are few heads naturally better than hers; there is no heart that can surpass the friendly warmth of hers; unimproved by books, of which she has read but few, her strong natural sense and uncommon sagacity owes all its experience to her knowledge of the world. I never knew any one seize every part of a character so soon, or paint it so strongly. She has a great deal of wit, and particularly excels in the narrative, which is always short and lively. The vain, the affected, and the worthless, may fear her; but the foibles of her friends, and even of those acquaintances who frequent her, are safe; nothing escapes her observation, but nothing transpires from her tongue to their prejudice: if once she loves any one, (and when she says she does, she may be believed,) she never gives them time to apply to her to be of any use to them.[1]

Even the irritable Horace Walpole was captivated by Mme Geoffrin: "I . . . think she has one of the best understandings I ever met, and more knowledge of the world."

Twelve years older than Hume, Mme Geoffrin took an almost motherly interest in him, yet tempered with affectionate familiarity and charming coquetry. He was always her "fat wag" or her "fat rascal." He loved the endearments and remained devoted throughout life. With the appearance of a new French translation of his complete *History* in 1765, he sent her a sumptuously bound set. In reply she jestingly chided him with having gone too far

[1] RSE, v, 69.

in his capacity of *fat and lovable Wag* : he has ruined her library !
" The state of humiliation that my poor books are in next to the
magnificence of yours pierces my heart. . . . No—I shall not
forgive you for the revolution that you have brought about in my
library. Alas ! I preferred it as it was. Now it is a calamity to me,
and it will be my ruin if the devil of pride surges through my head
and makes me want to be as magnificent as your fatal present.
Vanity of vanities ! says the sage. I shall repeat this maxim all
day to keep me from the folly of wanting to imitate you." [1] It is
impossible in translation to reproduce the flavour of any letter of
Mme Geoffrin's for she pretended to take pride in her inability
to spell correctly ; she also purposely propagated stories of her
own ignorance. After Hume had left France and it became clear
that he would not return, Mme Geoffrin wrote pathetically : " I
wish that I could forget you, but I cannot."

The good and kindly Mme Geoffrin opened the doors of her
salon on the rue Saint-Honoré to foreigners of parts as well as to
Parisian artists and men of letters. On Mondays she gave dinners
to artists, and on Wednesdays to men of letters. David Hume
is numbered among those who visited the Wednesday soirées most
often. And undoubtedly he profited by her expertness in drawing
out the best conversational talents of the socially timid. After
such an experience, the ordinarily boring Abbé de Saint-Pierre
exclaimed, " Madame, I am only an instrument on which you
have skilfully played." [2] But love and admire her as he did, Hume
could not always have been perfectly satisfied with her *salon* for,
in the attempt to avoid contention, the guiding hand of Mme
Geoffrin was ubiquitous and sometimes heavy. To a philosopher,
the deliberate avoidance of the controversial issue may become as
irksome as ill-tempered discussion of it ; and there may well have
been times when Hume would have been inclined to accept Grimm's
humorous gibe :

Mother Geoffrin could so manage things that the conversation in her *salon*
never touched upon domestic news or foreign news ; news of the Court or
news of the city ; news of the North or news of the South ; news of the East
and the West ; topics of politics or of finance ; of peace or of war ; of religion
or of government ; of theology or of metaphysics ; of grammar or of music,
or, in general, any topic whatsoever. . . .[3]

If David Hume ever found the safety of Mme Geoffrin tedious,
he could have found immediate relief in the spice of the Marquise

[1] RSE, v, 36.   [2] Morellet, *Eloges de Mme Geoffrin* (Paris 1812), pp. 11-12.
[3] Grimm, *Correspondance littéraire*, ed. M. Tourneaux (Paris 1885), viii, 438.

du Deffand, that " old blind *débauchée* of wit," as Horace Walpole cruelly described her after their first meeting. Walpole lived to do penance for his maliciousness, however, for Mme du Deffand, though aged sixty-eight and twenty years his senior, developed an infatuation for him that, despite frantic efforts on his side, he came partially to return. Walpole's early portrait of her remains one of the best :

> She goes to operas, plays, suppers, Versailles ; gives suppers twice a week ; has everything new read to her ; makes new songs and epigrams, ay, admirably, and remembers every one that has been made these fourscore years. She corresponds with Voltaire, dictates charming letters to him, contradicts him, is no bigot to him or anybody, and laughs both at the clergy and the philosophers. In a dispute, into which she easily falls, she is very warm, and yet scarce ever in the wrong ; her judgement on every subject is as just as possible ; on every point of conduct as wrong as possible ; for she is all love and hatred, passionate for her friends to enthusiasm, still anxious to be loved, I don't mean by lovers, and a vehement enemy, but openly.[1]

Mme du Deffand, in brief, was almost the perfect reverse of Mme Geoffrin, whom she cordially detested. Like Mme Geoffrin, however, she took an immediate liking for David Hume, and during his first half year in Paris, he was a frequent guest at her suite in the Convent of St Joseph, rue St Dominique. For once her caustic wit was silenced, and her characterisation of Hume to Voltaire is plain and unvarnished : " He is gay, simple, and good." [2] It is not likely that Hume was greatly attracted by the personality of Mme du Deffand, who was always professing boredom but whose interests were pervasive. Yet he would have liked the freedom of conversation that she permitted—unquestionably also he was drawn to her young companion, a woman of illegitimate but noble birth, Julie de Lespinasse.

The charm, brilliance, and passionate nature of Mlle de Lespinasse attracted many others besides Hume, as Mme du Deffand came to learn. Madame was accustomed to sleep during most of the day and to arise refreshed at about seven in the evening in time to receive her guests. One day towards the end of April 1764 she arose earlier than usual to find that a select few of the guests had already arrived, were gathered in the chamber of Mademoiselle, and were paying her court. Amazed and angered, the Marquise learned that this early visitation was no accident but a custom of long standing. Mme du Deffand could bear no sister near the throne—Julie de Lespinasse, who had been her

---

[1] *Walpole Letters*, vi, 312, 404–5.
[2] Mme du Deffand, *Correspondance complète*, ed. Lescure (Paris 1865), i, 305.

companion for ten years, left the house, never to return and always to be hated. On her death twelve years later, Mme du Deffand wrote coldly to Horace Walpole : " Mlle de Lespinasse died tonight, two hours after midnight ; once this would have been a crisis for me, today it is nothing at all." [1]

At the time of the rupture in 1764 Julie de Lespinasse was a woman of thirty-two and at the height of her powers. Well versed in literature, philosophy, and science, she could speak, in addition to her native tongue, English, Italian, and Spanish. With the generous assistance of Mme Geoffrin and other friends, she was able to set up her own establishment on the rue St Dominique—and to the new *salon* swarmed many of the former frequenters of the nearby Convent of St Joseph. These deserters Mme du Deffand immediately struck from her list of friends, making a single exception for the aged President Hénault, whose mistress she had formerly been.

When David Hume, as a diplomatic foreigner, sought to remain on good terms with both ladies, he was compelled by the elder to make a choice. " How many times have I told you," he implored, " that I was ready to espouse the loves of my friend, but that I find it repugnant to embrace her hatreds ? " In reluctantly following his heart and his inclination to the new *salon*, Hume came into sharp disfavour—though no open break—with Mme du Deffand. No longer was he " gay, simple, and good." Henceforth, he was the " Peasant " or the " Peasant of the Danube "—it is significant that these expressions appear chiefly in letters to Walpole. Hume was also jeered at as the " grand priest of the Idol of the Temple "—proof that Lespinasse or no Lespinasse, Walpole or no Walpole, David Hume would not long have remained welcome at the Convent of St Joseph. For the " Temple " was the palace of the Prince de Conti and its " Idol " was the Comtesse de Boufflers. No " grand priest " of that hated rival was to be tolerated.

Even after his return to England Hume tried in vain to renew the original warm relation with Mme du Deffand. A letter complaining that while she had been the first to receive him enthusiastically he had abandoned her, drew pathetic denials from Hume. Her response was a cool rebuff. " I desired most sincerely to be your friend. I flattered myself that I had succeeded, and it is with great chagrin that I find out I was mistaken." [2]

---

[1] Mme du Deffand, *Correspondance complète*, ed. Lescure (Paris 1865), II, 551.
[2] RSE, IV, 72.

To Horace Walpole she confided her fears that Hume might return to France and she was jubilant when he did not. " He has displeased me," she added venomously. " Hating idols, I detest their priests and their adorers." Though relenting momentarily at the time of Hume's death, her final comment on him two years later was still tinged with malice : " M. Hume, with his great mind and all his philosophy, never succeeded in gaining happiness by all his reasonings." [1] No more complete misunderstanding of Hume's life and philosophy is possible.

With Julie de Lespinasse, Hume was tender and fatherly. " I went to see Mademoiselle L'Espinasse, D'Alembert's Mistress, who is really one of the most sensible Women in Paris," he informed Gilbert Elliot in September 1764. A year later, when she was dangerously ill of the smallpox, he commented to Mme de Boufflers, " I am glad that D'Alembert forgets his philosophy on that occasion."

The precise nature of the liaison between D'Alembert and Mlle de Lespinasse remains mysterious. Julie had nursed the *philosophe* through illness some months previous and thereafter he took up permanent residence in her house. His undoubted love for her was apparently returned only with affection and devotion. Unsuspected by many of her contemporaries, Julie was the victim of two passions of the rarest intensity, the first for the respectable Marquis de Mara, the second for the worthless Comte de Guibert. Her two posthumous volumes of letters form one of the richest treasure-troves in the world's literature of passion. Though Hume and the other frequenters of her *salon* may have had no more than an intimation of her secret life, they must have sensed something of the turmoil within. Her *salon*, through the force of her personality and the eclecticism of her taste, became the most popular in Paris, and thanks to the presence of D'Alembert the most intellectual. There, David Hume found the " feast of reason " in the company of women of charm and power and there, too, he found the quiet appreciation of his own talents that afforded real satisfaction and pleasure.

Hume's intimacy with D'Alembert and Julie de Lespinasse continued throughout the years. In 1767 Julie charmingly asked Hume for a complete set of his works because she wished to perfect her English and needed to read books interesting for depth of matter and conciseness of style. Hume obligingly sent over the

---

[1] Mme du Deffand, *Correspondance complète,* ed. Sainte-Aulaire (Paris 1867), III, 346.

six volumes of his *History*. Writing for Julie, whose eyesight was failing, D'Alembert replied, " Mlle de L'Espinasse prays you to remember that you have promised the new edition of your philosophical works. She already has your *History,* but, as the proverb goes, *You can't have too much of a good thing.*" On another occasion, D'Alembert urged Hume's return to Paris in a somewhat metaphysical manner : " Farewell, my dear friend. I love you as God is loved, that is to say, as we do not see Him, and as we do not delude ourselves that we do see Him. I believe, however, or rather I feel that *visibility* does no harm to friendship ; and I am somewhat *anthropomorphic,* Be that as it may, absent or present, *vale et me ama.*" [1] A letter of 1773 observes simply, " We often speak of you to one another." [2] In his will, Hume left a legacy of £200 to D'Alembert.

[1] I, BOZ 147, Biblioteka Narododowa, Warsaw, Poland. [2] RSE, III, 14, 21.

CHAPTER 32

THE COMTESSE DE BOUFFLERS

"You have saved me from a total indifference towards
every thing in human life."

WHETHER called " Divine Comtesse " in affection, or " Idol of the
Temple " in derision, Mme de Boufflers was something of an
enigma to everyone. That she was exceedingly attractive—if not
beautiful—is attested by all who met her and is borne out in her
portraits. She has all the charm of Dresden china : a figure
dainty and slight, delicate features crowned with dark hair in a
simple coiffure, eyes that burn brightly. That she was a distinguished—if not the most distinguished—*salonnière* of the
eighteenth century was universally acknowledged, as was also her
social charm and poise, and her interest in the arts and learning.
She also attempted to write plays and some say that she actually
published books. The enigma of Mme de Boufflers lies not in such
externals, but in character ; and while the readings of her character vary, they yet agree on essentials.

The combined comments of two discerning men who knew
her may be taken as representative of the masculine point of view.
Horace Walpole, after describing her as a *savante*, proceeds : " She
is two women, the upper and the lower. I need not tell you that
the lower is gallant, and still has pretensions. The upper is very
sensible, too, and has a measured eloquence that is just and pleasing
—but all is spoiled by an unrelaxed attention to applause. You
would think she was always sitting for her picture to her biographer." Jean-Jacques Rousseau remarked to one of her intimate
friends : " As to Mme de Boufflers, one must adore her " ; but
in his *Confessions* he was to accuse her of having made improper
advances to him under guise of patroness, and in a private letter
was even more outspoken.[1]

The feminine point of view, much the subtler, is best represented by Mme du Deffand, who, though a rival and enemy for
many years, resumed friendship late in life. Her judgment of
Mme de Boufflers is carefully weighed and the resulting enigma is
skilfully pointed :

[1] *Walpole Letters*, vi, 407 ; Greig, p. 313.

Her mind, though not eminent . . . is highly capable of consistency and application. . . . She knows a good deal and knows it well, confidently, and flawlessly. You can say that she has all the mind it is possible to acquire ; but what she has, and there is no gainsaying that she has much, she owes more to art than to nature.

Her conversation, without being cold or tedious, is neither very brilliant, nor very piquant, nor very animated ; she says nothing ill, nothing flat, but she essays few witticisms. . . .

Her heart . . . is as artificial as her mind. You cannot say of her that she has neither vices, nor virtues, nor even shortcomings and failings ; but you do not find in her sentiments, or passions, or prudences, or preferences, or hate.

Her good qualities, for she has several, result from the emptiness of her character and from the slight impression that everything around her makes on her ; she is not envious, or scandal-mongering, or dangerous, or interfering, because she is occupied solely with herself and not with others. . . .

Her ethics are most austere, always mounted on high principles, which she announces in a firm and decided tone and in the sweetest voice ; she seems like a flute which is pronouncing laws and delivering oracles. What is amusing, though a little annoying, is that this lofty morality is not perfectly in accord with her conduct ; what is even more amusing is that the contrast does not startle her. She will tell you coldly that it is against good order for a woman to live apart from her husband, that the mistress of a Prince of the Blood is a woman in disgrace ; but she says all that so ingenuously, so persuasively, with a voice so pretty and a manner so sweet, that you are not even tempted to find it ridiculous ; she is only *drôle*—the word seems made expressly for her. . . .[1]

Drôle, then, may be taken as the epithet for Mme de Boufflers. It is true that she was a moralist and had drawn up her own " Rules of Conduct." These read, in part :

In conduct, simplicity and reason.
In appearance, propriety and decency.
In dealings with others, justice and generosity.
In the use of wealth, economy and liberality.
In discourse, clarity, truth, and precision.
In adversity, courage and pride.
In prosperity, modesty and moderation.
In society, charm, ease, courteousness.
In domestic life, integrity and kindness without familiarity. . . .
To sacrifice everything for tranquillity of soul.
To combat misfortunes and afflictions by temperance.
To permit one's self only innocent railleries, which cannot wound. . . .[2]

It is likewise true that Mme de Boufflers was living apart from her husband and that she was a mistress of a Prince of the Blood. It is no less true that she was naïve in her mixture of the theory and practice of ethics.

One day, for instance, she upbraided the Maréchale de

[1] Quoted in *Walpole Corr.* (Yale), VIII, 84ff.
[2] Paul Emile Schazmann, *La Comtesse de Boufflers* (Lausanne 1933), p. 145.

Mirepoix, her intimate friend, for associating with Mme de Pompadour, saying, " She is, after all, merely the first prostitute of the Kingdom." A little vexed, Mme de Mirepoix returned, " Don't ask me to count up to three." [1]

This repartee was widely circulated and disturbed Mme de Boufflers no little. Just why she was so disturbed is what perplexed all who knew her. Such liaisons did not disturb her close friends, the Maréchale de Mirepoix and the Maréchale de Luxembourg, nor the Duchesse de Chartres, nor Mlle de Lespinasse, nor a dozen others of her acquaintance. Only Mme de Boufflers herself knew the answer, but she seemingly found it incapable of expression, except once when she observed that, " I wish to give back to virtue by my words what I take away from it by my actions."

Less than a year after her marriage in 1746 to Edouard de Boufflers, the Comtesse gave birth to a son. Shortly thereafter, her husband passed out of her life, to resume importance, paradoxically, only with his death in 1764. In 1752, at the age of twenty-seven, the Comtesse had begun a liaison with the widowed Prince de Conti, aged thirty-four ; and they were to remain friends until his death in 1776—the greatest possible tribute to her beauty, grace, and understanding. Her devotion to the Prince, she regarded as a " sacred duty " ; but, with her enigmatical ethics, she also found it a " torment." From neither duty nor torment did she ever flinch.

Louis-François de Bourbon, Prince de Conti, was a remarkable man. A brave and skilful generalissimo of the French Army in Italy, he had won the battle of Coni in 1744 and retired from the Army three years later. He held the confidence of Louis XV in maintaining secret diplomatic missions throughout Europe until 1755, when he was ousted by the intrigues of Mme de Pompadour. Immediately he assumed the leadership of the opposition and earned the King's appellation of " my cousin the advocate." The Prince was also well versed in the arts and sciences and was a liberal patron. He protected Rousseau and Beaumarchais, among others, not because he agreed with them, but because he detested censorship. In religion he was a sceptic, but not an atheist, and kept the Abbé Prevost as his chaplain—on condition that he never should say the mass. He was a good talker and of unexampled grace and dignity in society, though he has sometimes been accused of overweening pride and arrogance. A handsome man, the Prince

[1] Sainte-Beuve, *Nouveaux Lundis*, 19 Jan. 1863. According to Sainte-Beuve, Mlle Marquise, mistress of the Duc d'Orléans, rated the second position.

de Conti lived handsomely and lavishly. In an age of many libertines, his reputation as a libertine was almost unapproached ; but he permitted himself only one principal mistress at a time. A violent quarrel with Mme d'Arty in 1751 had made Mme de Boufflers's succession possible.

As Grand Prior of Malta, the Prince de Conti maintained as his Paris residence the Temple, situated north of the Seine in the eastern extremity of the old city. Within the fortified walls of the spacious enclosure, the original thirteenth-century square and turreted edifice of the Knights Templars was surrounded by more modern buildings. One of the smaller of these, facing north on the rue Notre-Dame-de-Nazareth and with a simple garden on the south, was assigned to Mme de Boufflers. An elegant and spacious town-house, elevated somewhat above the others, was reserved for the Prince himself. There he entertained, on a scale rivalling that of the Royal Palace, with theatre-parties, grand assemblies, and intimate soirées. For the Temple had its own theatre, its grand assembly room, and its small salon. All were decorated with white wainscoting, with facings and casings of pressed copper, and with high glass windows offering a vivid contrast to the austerity of the ancient fortress.

On Mondays the Prince de Conti was accustomed to give suppers to fifty or a hundred people. In the centre of the grand assembly room, the Prince and the Comtesse received their guests with formal dignity. The men stood in three ranks, the ladies sat on dainty chairs in a circle. But it was in the small " Salon of the Four Mirrors " that the distinctive reputation of the Temple was made. Mme de Boufflers was the soul of the *salon*, and Anglo-mania its prevailing atmosphere. Tea in the English fashion was served early in the evening as the last rays of the sun, reflected in the mirrors, tinted the walls with living colours. In the tradition inaugurated by the Regent to encourage free conversation, no servants were present. The ladies, wearing dainty aprons, lighted the lamps under the urns, poured the tea, cut the cakes, and passed the plates. For incidental music, there might be a singer or a player upon the lute or the harpsichord. In the painting of " Tea in the English fashion at the Prince de Conti's " made by Michel-Barthelémy Ollivier in 1766, the child prodigy Mozart is seated upon a high chair before an open harpsichord.[1] On Fridays, it

---

[1] Mozart was in Paris in both 1763 and 1766. For evidence that the painting is to be dated 1766, see G. Cafron and R. Yve-Plessis, *Vie privée du Prince de Conty* (Paris 1907), p. 117, *n*1.

was the custom of Mme de Boufflers to gather together a few select friends in her own house.

David Hume was introduced to the Temple in November or December 1763, after his presentation at court and after the recovery of the Comtesse from the measles. The two had already met when Mme de Boufflers wrote to Hume : " I shall not go to the comedy tomorrow. The play bores me. I shall stay at home. If you wish to come here, I shall conduct you to the Temple, that is to say, to M. the Prince de Conti's. Without this explanation you might perhaps think that it is to church." [1] Such was Hume's first invitation to a formal Monday supper. Soon afterwards he began to fall under the spell of the " Divine Comtesse," and within a year was generally reputed to be the most fervent idolater at the Temple. " They say," Mme de Verdelin told Rousseau, " that he is madly in love with Mme de Boufflers." [2]

At the time of their first meeting Mme de Boufflers was aged thirty-eight, Hume fifty-two. Of their early relations during the winter months in Paris, 1763–64, there is no record. That a warm feeling was being engendered, however, may be inferred from Hume's letter of 15 May 1764 to the Comtesse in Holland, where she had gone, in the company of Lord and Lady Holdernesse, to visit her son, who was studying at the University of Leyden. " I am afraid," acknowledges Hume, " that, as I sit down at present to write you without any subject, you will conjecture that I think of you often, and that the pleasure of your society (shall I say, of your friendship ?) is not easily made up by other connexions or conversation." After banter about Court intrigues, well aware that the Comtesse and the Prince pretended to be completely indifferent to such matters, Hume concludes : " Be only assured, dear Madam, and with the greatest seriousness, though at the end of a foolish letter, that were he [Lord Holdernesse] to carry you farther, my wishes for your welfare would still follow you and that nothing can diminish, and scarce augment, my respectful attachment towards you." In reply Mme de Boufflers admits that, "Your letter made me Smile," but news of the death of M. the Maréchal de Luxembourg prevents further pleasantry. " I write only," she charmingly concedes, " that you may not be discontent with me and to assure you of my friendship." [3]

During the two or three weeks after the return to Paris of the Comtesse in the middle of June, their friendship mellowed into something more intimate than friendship. This new phase is

---

[1] RSE, III, 72.   [2] Rousseau, xv, 187.   [3] RSE, III, 74.

revealed in the exchange of letters in July and August when Hume had followed the Court to Compiègne and the Comtesse had gone to the château of the Prince de Conti at L'Isle Adam, only ten leagues away and also on the Oise River. The two had agreed that the lady should be the first to open the correspondence, and on 6 July she had indeed begun a long and severe critique upon John Home's *Douglas*, when she was interrupted by the arrival of a letter of the same day from Hume. Writing from the heart, if a little playfully, Hume admits that he had been desperately endeavouring to keep his promise and not to write first, when a commission from the Maréchale de Mirepoix provided him with a pretext. " And I believe really," he says, " without giving myself too great airs of fortitude, that, were it not for so great a handle, I could have held out two or three days longer at the least. For you must not imagine, but I make advantage of the ten leagues of interval that lie between us, and feel already some progress in the noble resolution I have formed of forgetting you entirely before the end of the summer."

At Compiègne, continues Hume, he lives in a kind of solitude and retirement. " You cannot imagine, Madam, with what pleasure I return as it were to my natural element, and what satisfaction I enjoy in reading and musing, and sauntering amid the agreeable scenes that surround me." But, yes, she can, for she had resolved to take up her studies and literary amusements once more. " If you have been so happy as to execute your purpose, you are almost in the same state as myself, and are at present wandering along the banks of the same beautiful river, perhaps with the same books in your hand, a Racine, I suppose, or a Virgil, and despise all other pleasure and amusement. Alas ! why am I not so near you, that I could see you for half an hour a day, and confer with you on these subjects ? " Recovering himself quickly, however, he adds, " But this ejaculation, methinks, does not lead me directly in my purposed road, of forgetting you." A postscript gives the forgotten commission of the Maréchale, the original pretext for writing.

Mme de Boufflers's letter of 6 July had opened : " You are my *Maître* of philosophy and ethics ; and I have often told you that, if I have ideas a little more just and a little more elevated on these subjects than most people, I am obliged to you for having developed them." On receipt of Hume's highly personal letter, she immediately interrupted the critique of *Douglas* to reply. Like Hume, she wrote from the heart :

If there is any resemblance in our actual occupations, it is not the only one between us since there is even more in our resolutions. You wish to break away from me ; I do not know your motive but, at least, I do know the one that compels me to want to break away from you. It is not ungracious, and I shall not hesitate to tell it to you. It is that you have an uprightness and a goodness of heart that I esteem, a genius that I admire, and a good humour that pleases me ; you are a foreigner and, sooner or later, you will go away ; your coming here only gave me distaste for most of the people I have to live with. If this were the only drawback, I should find a remedy for books take the place of many things ; but the worst of it is that I cannot be contented with simple esteem and cool admiration. As soon as these sentiments are aroused in me, my sensibility is touched and my affections engaged, with the result that I suffer real sorrow when circumstances bring about separation from those who have merited such progress over my heart. . . . I look upon myself as a feeble shrub that has thrown out its roots too far and is thereby exposed to greater damage and risk. As a matter of fact, I am afraid that reflection and prudence are useless to me at present so far as you are concerned. But if you are working so fruitfully on your side, that may give me courage. . . .

Farewell, my dear *Maître*, I am going to make haste to love you no longer so as not to feel ashamed to be the last to end this useful undertaking. But as I have not yet started it, I may be permitted for today to assure you that I love you with all my heart. [1]

The deepening affection of the previous weeks in Paris had aroused Hume to a declaration of love—for sake of caution, phrased negatively—which, in turn, had elicited a declaration on the part of the Comtesse—phrased much more openly. If this was the reply that Hume had sought—whether he would admit it to himself or not—his answering letter of 14 July presents a change of front inspired, doubtless, by stark timidity of the path he was hastening down. He is, in turn, cold, impersonal, passionate, evasive—and yet somehow hopeful. " I shall venture to say, dear Madam," he begins, " that no letter, which even you have ever wrote, conveyed more satisfaction than did that with which you favoured me. What pleasure to receive testimonies and assurances of good-will from a person whom we highly value, and whose sentiments are of such importance to us ! " But he soon approaches the crux of the matter : the Comtesse is not entirely free. " Common sense requires," he explains, " that I should keep at a distance from all attachments that can imply passion. But it must surely be the height of folly, to lay myself at the mercy of a person whose situation seems calculated to inspire doubt, and who, being so little at her own disposal, could not be able, even if willing, to seek such remedies as might appease that tormenting sentiment. And," he adds, " if I sometimes join the chimerical project of relaxing the severities of study, by the society of a person dear to me, and who could have indulgence for me, I consider it a pleasing dream, in which I can repose no confidence. My only comfort is, that I am myself a person free as the air we breathe, and that, wherever such a blessing might present itself, I could there fix my habitation."

The cold reception of John Home's *Douglas* by Mme de Boufflers produces a statement of curious intensity : " I can even kiss the hand, with pleasure and passion, which signs the verdict against me : I could only have kissed it with more pleasure, had it acquitted my friend." The letter ends with the inquiry whether the Comtesse would not " come to Paris about the middle of August, and stay there for some time " ? Timid of the suggested intimacy of an assignation, however, Hume immediately recoils into the coolly formal : " My question proceeds not merely from curiosity. I could wish to enjoy your company, before the return of winter recalls us to our former dissipations."

Perplexed by this two-directional letter, the Comtesse patiently wrote eight pages of self-analysis and of explanation of her relations with the Prince de Conti. She begins rhetorically : " I am going to ask you a question. . . . Do you think that I have a heart that is tender, charitable, and susceptible of friendship ? I give you a few moments to think about it." After an indicated pause, she assumes that Hume has answered in the affirmative and proceeds with her analysis. She is grieved, she says, that she has caused him pain but is hurt that he has had any doubt about the sincerity of her friendship. Painstakingly and circuitously she approaches the central issue of her liaison with the Prince. Her unselfish devotion to him is " the most pleasing of sentiments, the founda-tion and the support of all the others," and this devotion, she chides, Hume has dared to profane. As a result of her unselfish devotion, she has little affection left for others and, she emphasises, " You will make me still more miserly of it in the future."

Turning directly to Hume, she inquires :

But why do you always appear to repent your attachment to me, when I evince one for you so true and so firmly established ? I acknowledge that it will sometimes be hindered by absence and by duties which another and older attachment has imposed upon my gratitude. These duties are sacred. They would exact the sacrifice of myself if the occasion arose. My inclination, too, impels me to fulfil them, and they would give me nothing but satisfaction, if the religion, the devotion, with which I discharge them were always recognised. For all that, such as they are, and such as I consider them, they do not absorb me wholly ; they leave a place in my heart for other sentiments, and I am able to command the greater part of my time and to give it to you. Scrutinize yourself, however, for, whatever it may cost me, and whatever price I set upon your friendship, I should prefer it to be cut short rather than confirmed, if you must suffer or if I must foresee the end.

She closes by saying that she will probably be in Paris when Hume is there and will keep him informed of her plans. " Farewell ! I flatter myself that you will not be less pleased with this letter than with the other. I would have to have little art, indeed, to have ill-expressed a friendship that my heart feels so warmly." [1]

This candid declaration on the part of the Comtesse drew from Hume a candid, though unexpected, answer. Impersonally, but certainly not coldly, he exclaims, " What amiable, what unaffected, what natural expressions of good-will and friendship ! " Yet as to their allowing themselves to proceed with the course of their affection—that is out of the question. The decision is entirely in the spirit of Antony's exclamation—" I must from this enchanting queen break off ! " " I am uneasy," explains Hume, " that, notwithstanding all you can say, I should not have the prospect of passing much of my time with you. Our connexions and course of life led us into very different roads : but my comfort is, that these may alter : my regard for you is unalterable : I shall firmly believe the same of your indulgence towards me." In brief, Hume is reluctant to hold a second place in the affections of the Comtesse.

Softening at the close of the letter, however, Hume writes a moving farewell to the love that might have been : " I kiss your hands, my dear, my amiable friend, with the greatest devotion and most sincere affection. Among other obligations, which I owe you, without number, you have saved me from a total indifference towards every thing in human life. I was falling very fast into that state of mind, and it is perhaps worse than even the inquietudes of the most unfortunate passion "—but the poignancy of the farewell is lost in the insipidity of the following phrase—" how much, then, is it inferior to the sweetness of your commerce and friendship ! "

Mme de Boufflers was angry with the anger of a woman scorned. She answered immediately, exclaiming, " You reply in two pages, when I wrote you eight ! " The letter continues with a sharp rebuke and a scarcely concealed warning :

Do you want to confirm me in the idea which I hold, that your sex like to be handled roughly, that they requite harshness with eagerness and kindness with neglect ? for to confess to you my opinion of men, the majority seem to me to have by nature servile souls. One can be seduced by them, but one can scarcely, it seems to me, esteem them. Their homage is accepted but cannot flatter. Sometimes it is discernment that they lack, sometimes delicacy, and almost always generosity. . . . For you towards whom love bore me only as a consequence of esteem, you, I separate from this crowd of slaves, and I attribute to you an entirely different character. If I was mistaken, my affection and the foundation upon which it chiefly rests would soon be destroyed. . . . I am by nature as proud as I am sensitive, as much borne to disdain as to tenderness, and whoever does not respond to my friendship soon seems to me unworthy of it. I want to flatter myself, my dear *Maître*, that I shall have to make use of only the more agreeable of these two sentiments towards you and that you will not force me to use that painful prudence, which often obliges us to constrain and to lock up those affections which are the most agreeable and the most innocent in the fear of creating ingrates. Nevertheless, I cannot keep from saying : I waited a long time for your letter, I waited impatiently for it, and I am not satisfied with it. We shall see what excuse you will give me !

This stern letter of 30 July had opened with a schedule of the Comtesse's activities for the following month and with an invitation to Hume to accompany her, together with the Prince de Conti and his daughter, on a ten-day visit to the Prince's magnificent palace at Saint-Martin de Pontoise.

The letter brought Hume to his knees with the most passionate declaration to date, but still with a residue of independence. After denying the charge of indifference, he protests :

I will never, but with my life, be persuaded to part with the hold which you have been pleased to afford me ; · you may cut me to pieces, limb by limb ; but like those pertinacious animals of my country, I shall expire still attached to you, and you will in vain attempt to get free. For this reason, Madam, I set at defiance all those menaces, which you obliquely throw out against me. Do you seriously think, that it is at present in your power to determine whether J shall be your friend or not ? In every thing else your authority over me is without control. But with all your ingenuity, you will scarce contrive to use me so ill, that I shall not still better bear it : and after all, you will find yourself obliged, from pity, or generosity, or friendship, to take me back into your service. At least, this will probably be the case, till you find one who loves you more sincerely and values you more highly ; which with all your merit, I fancy it will not be easy for you to do. I know, that I am here furnishing you with arms against myself : you may be tempted to tyrannize over me, in order to try how far I will practise my doctrine of passive obedience : but I hope also that you will hold this soliloquy to yourself : This poor fellow, I see, is resolved never to leave me : let me take compassion on him ; and endeavour to render our intercourse as agreeable to him and as little burdensome to myself as possible. If you fall, Madam, into this way of thinking, as you must at last, I ask no farther ; and all your menaces will vanish into smoke.

Good God ! how much am I fallen from the airs which I at first gave myself ! You may remember, that a little after our *personal* acquaintance, I told you, that you was obliged *à soutenir la gageure*, and could not in decency find fault with me, however I should think proper to behave myself. Now, I throw myself at your feet, and give you nothing but marks of patience and long-suffering and submission. But I own, that matters are at present upon a more proper and more natural footing ; and long may they remain so.

Directly Hume admits that he is the Comtesse's slave and glories in the fact. " And can you treat me with contempt because I am willing to be that person's slave ? For, let me tell you, that there is an expression in your letter against slavery, which I take a little to myself, as said against me ; but I still maintain

> Nunquam libertas gratior extat
> Quam sub rege pio. [1]

Pray, go to your Latin dictionary," admonishes the *Maître*, " to interpret this passage : You will find that *regina*, if it would agree with the measure, would suit much better with the sense."

Perhaps it is not unreasonable to imagine that the " *Maître* of philosophy and ethics " in writing this account of his submissiveness to a woman may vaguely have recalled his schoolboy " An Historical Essay on Chivalry and modern Honour." If he did, the irony was inescapable. " As a Cavalier is compos'd," the schoolboy had observed, " of the greatest Warmth of Love, temperd with the most humble submission & Respect, his Mistresses Behavior is in every point, the Reverse of this, & what is conspicuous in her Temper is the utmost Coldness along with the greatest Haughtyness & Disdain ; untill at last Gratitude . . . reduces her tho unwilling to the Necessity of commencing a Bride." Now at the age of fifty-three and more than a quarter of a century after having written so disdainfully of modern honour, Hume was compelled to recant.

At this critical juncture, Hume's somewhat mysterious quarrel with the Hon. Alexander Murray intervenes at once to becloud and to clarify his relations with Mme de Boufflers. Brother of Lord Elibank and cousin of the Comtesse, Murray was a political exile in Paris and associated there with exiled Jacobites. Along with his brother, he is also suspected of having had a hand in the mysterious Jacobite " Elibank Plot " of 1752-53.[2] In 1761 he had forwarded to Hume the first letter from the Comtesse. Upon Hume's arrival in Paris, Murray had sought his support in the effort to obtain a Parliamentary pardon ; but Hume, circumspect of embarrassing Lord Hertford by treating with a Jacobite, had

---

[1] Claudian, *De Consulatu Stilichonis*, III, 114-15.
[2] Sir Charles Petrie, " The Elibank Plot, 1752-3," in *Transactions of the Royal Historical Society*, Fourth Series, XIV (1931), 175-96.

done little. By that time, also, Murray was involved in a lawsuit brought by a certain Mrs Blake for reasons unknown. Hume again, despite solicitations, did not bestir himself officially on Murray's account and privately was of the opinion that he was in the wrong. The case was finally decided in July 1764, the French judges giving the verdict to Murray. Mme de Boufflers was the sole person appearing in behalf of her cousin. After the judgment, Murray, who was a man of violent temper and who acknowledged only friends or enemies, sent Hume an abusive letter, threatening him, oddly enough, with retaliation by his brother, who, he averred, was ready to prove in print that Hume was wrong in his interpretation of the character of Mary Queen of Scots.[1]

Upon receipt of Murray's letter, Hume enclosed it, together with the draft of a letter of his own to Lord Elibank, in a packet, which he dispatched to the Comtesse. She replied on 15 August, commenting indignantly on Murray's outrageous conduct. In a postscript, she admitted that she did not approve of several expressions in Hume's proposed letter to Elibank.[2] She also wrote in reproof to Murray.

The impact of this fatuous quarrel was not yet spent. For as Hume informed Mme de Boufflers on 18 August :

> About an hour after I had sent off my last pacquet, a friend of mine enterd my room, who informed me, with a certainty which admitted of no doubt, that you, dear Madam, you (this word cannot be too frequently repeated, in order to give emphasis to the sentence and augment surprise), that you, I say, had occasioned all the quarrel between Mr Murray and me, by telling him of the bad opinion I had of him and his lawsuit, &c. &c. . . . Thus you, who of all human creatures are the least *tracassière*, are here the author of a fray ; you, who have created me so many new friends, are here robbing me of my ancient ones.

His reactions to the accusations are then detailed :

> Have you ever had any experience of the situation of our mind, when we are very angry with the person whom we passionately love ? You have, surely : can any thing be more tormenting and more absurd ? How many projects of revenge, which we fondly cherish, and then fly from with horror ! How many images of tenderness, which pride and indignation make us instantly regret ! I thought of means, by which I might mortify and punish a person, who had behaved so treacherously towards me ; for this epithet I thought your conduct richly merited : but I then reflected ; is this the person for whose welfare I would sacrifice my existence ; and can I now think of taking pleasure in her pain and uneasiness ?

---

[1] EU, Laing MSS, ii, 503.   [2] RSE, iii, 78.

In such a state of mind, he received the Comtesse's letter of the 15th, which effected a complete reversion of sentiment :

I was in this state of mind when I received yours. The very sight of your handwriting, I own, began the cure : but the persual of those soft and obliging and amicable expressions, which you employ, penetrated me to the soul ; and I saw a new world around me. Those circumstances of conduct, which I had before clothed in so many black colours, and from which I drew so many strange inferences, now appeared only a trivial indiscretion ; which I was glad you could sometimes be guilty of, in order to excuse much greater of my own. Accept all of my penitence, Madam, for sentiments, which, though confined within my own bosom, I regard no less as violations of my duty towards you : accept also my thanks, for taking me so soon from a state of mind, in which my folly might have otherwise long detained me.

In a fit of joy, Hume instantly sat down and wrote a placatory letter to Murray and expunged some harsh expressions from that to Elibank. " I beseech you, dear Madam," he concludes, " continue to like me a little : for otherwise I shall not be able in a little time to endure myself."

The quarrel was over. Murray gallantly admitted that he had been in the wrong, and a friendly exchange of letters forestalled any possible rupture between Hume and Elibank. But what about the Comtesse ? Had she, in reality, deliberately instigated the incident as a warning against further arousing her " sentiment of disdain " ? Infatuated as he was, Hume found it easy to persuade himself to the negative—that she had been guilty of no more than " a trivial indiscretion "—and, indeed, that seems to have been the fact. The Comtesse's reply of 18 August admits no more than just that ; but the burden of the letter is complaisance and affection. " Having once convinced me of the sincerity of your affection, you have," she acknowledges, " acquired complete ascendancy over me, your interests come before mine, and I willingly sacrifice for your gratification the dignity which becomes me. I do not imagine that you can desire stronger proofs of my sentiments, and I flatter myself that you will be content with them and that the agitation which distresses you on my account will at least be stayed." [1] The Murray incident, at all events, had wrung from Hume the most passionate declaration that he was ever to pen. Henceforth Mme de Boufflers could have had no possible doubt of her sway over him. She may also have been justifiably tempted to complacency over her theory that men prefer to be handled roughly.

The invitation to visit Saint-Martin de Pontoise had been

[1] RSE, III, 79.

reluctantly declined by Hume because " there is just now arrived in France a very ancient and very intimate friend of mine, Mr Elliot, who is wholly a stranger there, and whom I cannot totally neglect. . . . Is it not strange," he archly inquires, " that I should think my attention to him an incumbrance on the present occasion ? " Elliot remained some three weeks before departing for Brussels and leaving Hume to complete arrangements about a school in Paris for the two Elliot boys. During his brief visit Elliot was able to size up the emotional state in which he found his old friend and, apparently, thought it too delicate a subject for personal discussion. From Brussels on 15 September, however, he ventured to give advice. " Before I conclude," he wrote, " allow me in friendship also, to tell you, I think I see you at present upon the very brink of a precipiece. One cannot too much clear their mind of all little prejudices, but partiality to ones country is not a prejudice. Love the French as much as you will, many of the Individuals are surely the proper objects of affection, but above all continue still a Englishman." [1]

The very vehemence with which Hume replied to Elliot, together with the careful avoidance of mentioning Mme de Boufflers in this connexion, is token that the shaft had struck home. " I cannot imagine," he explodes, " what you mean by saying that I am on a Precipice." Then he breaks out into a violent tirade against the English nation,[2] instancing his own slim chances of ever being appointed Embassy Secretary. Triumphantly he points out that Mme de Boufflers had drafted a letter to the Duke of Bedford to engage his support ; but " I instantly forbid her to write to England a Line about my Affair. I bear too great a Respect to her, to expose her to ask a Favour, where there was so little Probability of Success." Testily he concludes, " Thus have vanish'd the last hopes of my obtaining Justice in this point : Here is surely a new Ground of Attachment to England."

During September and early October of 1764, Hume saw much of the Comtesse, visiting her at the château on the Oise once and perhaps twice. " I went very contentedly," he informed Elliot, " to L'Isle Adam, where I remain'd for four days." The spirit of this intensified intimacy is reflected in a letter of 12 October. " I shall never, I hope," he tells the Comtesse as if in deliberate defiance of Elliot's warning, " be obliged to leave the place where you dwell. . . . Believe me (and surely you do believe me), that no one can bear you a more tender and more sincere friendship,

[1] RSE, v, 13.   [2] See Textual Supplement.

or desire more earnestly a return of like sentiments on your part. This long absence convinces me more fully than ever before, that no society can make me compensation for the loss of yours, and that my attachment to you is not of a light or common nature." Despite the ambivalence of the diction, in part brought about by writing in English for a French correspondent, the tone of Hume's letter is both serious and dignified, serene and confident, and less suggestive of the devoted friend than of the accepted lover.

Before the end of October, however, the death of Edouard de Boufflers, the Comtesse's long absent and little missed husband, brought an abrupt end to the philosopher's new-found happiness. Immediately on hearing the news Hume became acutely aware that the Comtesse would be determined to become the legal wife of the Prince de Conti and that, consequently, she would have no further use for a lover. Wounded to the quick by his accurate anticipation of the coldblooded and ruthless ambition of the Comtesse, he penned to her a letter of resentful irony :

This late incident, which commonly is of such moment with your sex, seems so little to affect your situation either as to happiness or misery, that I might have spared you the trouble of receiving my compliments upon it : but being glad of taking any opportunity to express my most sincere wishes for your welfare, I would not neglect an occasion which custom had authorised.

Receive, then, with your usual, I cannot say, with your constant, goodness, the prayers of one of your most devoted friends and servants. I hope that every change of situation will turn out to your advantage. In vain would I assume somewhat of the dignity of anger, when you neglect me : I find that this wish still returns upon me with equal ardour.

I hear . . . that you are to be in Paris on Saturday. I shall be there about that day se'nnight : I hope that your etiquette, which allows you to receive relations and particular friends, opens a wide-enough door for my admission.

By writing this letter in advance of any overt act on the part of the Comtesse, Hume was deliberately, and bitterly, reducing himself from the position of lover to that of confidant. The letter is thus at once an assertion of independence and an attempt at face-saving.

All Paris buzzed with rumours of the impending marriage, as the Duchess of Northumberland noted in her diary under 2 November : " . . . the news of Paris was that the Prince of Conti was certainly to marry Mme de Boufflers. . . . People thought it very extraordinary in every way, as the Princes of the Blood very seldom marry women so much their inferiors and still more extraordinary that any man should marry a woman who was once his mistress and who he had quitted as such, for the last seven years. It is true his friendship has always appeared to continue in the strongest manner, but it is seldom people marry for friendship. . . ." [1]

Assuming his self-appointed role of friendly adviser, Hume wrote to the Comtesse on 28 November in general appraisal of the situation and in open warning of its consequences : " On the whole, I am fully persuaded, from what I hear and see, that the matter will end as we wish. But in all cases, I foresee, that, let the event be what it will, you will reap from it much honour and much vexation."

Twelve days later he collected his mature thoughts into a long letter of advice, advice that he must have been reasonably sure would not be followed but which was required by duty both to the Comtesse and to himself :

What advice, then, can I give you, in a situation so interesting ? The measure which I recommend to you requires courage, but I dread, that nothing else will be able to prevent the consequences, so justly apprehended. It is, in a word, that after employing every gentle art to prevent a rupture, you should gradually diminish your connexion with the Prince, should be less assiduous in your visits, should make fewer and shorter journeys to his country seats, and should betake yourself to a private, and sociable, and independent life at Paris. By this change in your plan of living, you cut off at once the expectations of that dignity, to which you aspire ; you are no longer agitated with hopes and fears ; your temper insensibly recovers its former tone ; your health returns ; your relish for a simple and private life gains ground every day, and you become sensible, at last, that you have made a good exchange of tranquillity for grandeur. Even the dignity of your character, in the eyes of the world, recovers its lustre, while men see the just price you set upon your liberty ; and that, however the passions of youth may have seduced you, you will not now sacrifice all your time, where you are not deemed worthy of every honour.

And why should you think with reluctance on a private life at Paris ? It is the situation for which I thought you best fitted, ever since I had the happiness of your acquaintance. The inexpressible and delicate graces of your character and conversation, like the soft notes of a lute, are lost amid the tumult of company, in which I commonly saw you engaged. A more select society would know to set a juster value upon your merit. Men of sense, and taste, and letters, would accustom themselves to frequent your house. Every elegant society would court your company. And tho all great alterations in the habits of living may at first appear disagreeable, the mind is soon reconciled to its new situation, especially if more congenial and natural to it. I should not dare to mention my own resolutions on this occasion, if I did not flatter myself, that your friendship gives them some small importance in your eyes. Being a foreigner, I dare less answer for my plans of life, which may lead me far from this country ; but if I could dispose of my fate, nothing could be so much of my choice as to live where I might cultivate your friendship.

[1] *Extracts from the Diaries of the First Duchess of Northumberland*, ed. J. Greig (London 1926), pp. 60-1.

Your taste for travelling might also afford you a plausible pretence for putting this plan in execution : a journey to Italy would loosen your connexions here and if it were delayed some time, I could, with some probability expect to have the felicity of attending you thither.

This letter bespeaks the philosopher and the moralist, but it, no less, bespeaks the man in the throes of an emotional crisis ; it constitutes Hume's final appeal to the Comtesse. She was blunt in her honesty : " My health is really very good and my mind, on the surface, very calm. There is the truth, since you wish me to tell it to you. I do not speak to you of my friendship because, although it is most sincere, I could talk of it only coldly in my present situation, which absorbs my whole being." [1] The Comtesse, in short, had no intention of taking Hume's advice and of retiring into private life. Burning with ambition, she needed Hume as acutely as ever, no longer as lover, but only as confidant and potential go-between.

The Prince de Conti was unhurried in coming to a decision. The situation was sufficiently complicated for him. Marriage would entail, to begin with, the loss of the Temple with its annual income of 50,000 livres—although, to a man of his immense wealth, that could hardly have been a prime consideration. Perhaps more important to his imperious pride was the fact that the Comtesse de Boufflers simply did not have the rank to marry a Prince of the Blood. Furthermore, it is true that the Prince had, for some time, relinquished her as lover, though remaining a devoted friend. Finally, the Prince was genuinely distressed in March 1765 over the death of Mme d'Arty, his former principal mistress and dear friend, an event that may have been of some weight in his ultimate decision not to marry. Soon afterwards, at any rate, he requested Hume to bring his influence to bear upon Mme de Boufflers to relinquish her ambition of dying a princess. Thus was Hume trapped between the cross-fire of two friends.

Despite her protestations to the contrary, so agitated was Mme de Boufflers that her delicate health began to be affected. She had long suffered from the vapours, or melancholia, and had frequently agonised Hume with dark hints of suicide. Now, at the repeated suggestion of friends who felt that a change of climate and of society might help her recover nervous stability, she left for England at the end of June to visit Lord and Lady Holdernesse. To the Marquise de Barbantane, who was in the secret, Hume commented :

[1] RSE, III, 83.

I am sorry to inform you, that our friend left this place, full of the same sentiments, which she expressed to me in the most lively terms ; and though her journey and a new scene and new company may occasion some dissipation, I foresee that, on her return, she will take up the matter precisely where she left off, and may perhaps feel her disagreeable situation more sensibly on account of the interval. I can hope for no event that will restore her peace of mind, except one, which is not likely to happen ; and she herself is sensible of it.

He continued with an explanation of his own share in the undertaking : " I have wrote in the terms, which the Prince desired ; though I wonder he should expect a great effect from any thing that can be wrote or said by any body on that head. If he does not choose to apply the proper remedy, he need expect no cure." The letter that Hume wrote to Lord Holdernesse on behalf of the Prince is not extant, but in his reply Holdernesse promised to observe " the most inviolable Secresy even to the person concerned unless she brings with her a suspicion of my having been wrote to & should tax me with it in which case I cannot deceive her." [1] After several weeks Hume was in total despair. " I foresee," he confided to Mme de Barbantane, " that all the former disputes and vexations will return never to have an end."

Hume's prediction proved correct. From England Mme de Boufflers informed him that she felt more miserable than ever and that his approaching departure from France, which was being rumoured, was a contributory factor. Just before leaving London at the end of July, she was in tears over the turn of events. The impending loss of a devoted friend at the very moment that she needed him most could only reinforce the steadfast conviction that she was taking the one road open to her, the continuing dedication of her life to the Prince. Throughout the last five months of Hume's stay in France, the Comtesse remained of the same mind. Always patient, always understanding, and always affectionate, Hume became more and more troubled over this unrealistic decision and its consequent strain and unhappiness for her. During these final months, although his affection for the Comtesse was to remain steadfast, his infatuation slowly waned. Slowly, too, he began to waver from his resolution never to leave the place where she dwelt.

David Hume was now restored to his original position as counsellor and friend to Mme de Boufflers, her *Maître* of philosophy and ethics. Together they busily laid plans for the future welfare of their protégé Jean-Jacques Rousseau and, upon his arrival in

[1] RSE, III, 79.

Paris, gave him the protection of the Temple. Hume's intention to spend the Christmas holidays with the Comtesse at L'Isle Adam was thwarted by a great fall of snow ; he could get no farther than Moselle and was forced to return to Paris. On 4 January 1766 Mme de Boufflers bade a fond farewell to her *Maître* and his " pupil." Hume left Paris undecided as to his future course, but actually never again to see the " Divine Comtesse." From London his first letter was addressed to her, as was, from his deathbed in Edinburgh ten years later, one of his last letters.

David Hume left France richer in experience and in happiness. The homage of the people of France had salved the wounded intellectual pride of the philosopher and the love of a great lady of France had brought serenity to the man. Even the " inquietudes of the most unfortunate passion," as he had reminded Mme de Boufflers in the summer of 1764 at the time of his fruitless resolution to forget her, were as nothing compared to the obligations he owed her—" You have saved me from a total indifference towards every thing in human life." That tribute came from the heart and Hume never found reason to repent of it.

CHAPTER 33

THE *PHILOSOPHES*

" The seiks in the Rue Royale."

THE *salons* of Paris were dominated by women ; they set the tone and they directed the conversation. To David Hume this feminine domination was a revelation of social grace affording, at its best, the most exquisite enjoyment. Nevertheless, charming as it is, there are times when a man demands stimulation more virile. Hume was, therefore, not long in France before he could remark, " I naturally sought and obtained Connexions with the learned." And his first comment on them is significant for its implied contrast with the learned that he had encountered elsewhere : " The Men of Letters here are really very agreeable ; all of them Men of the World, living in entire or almost entire Harmony among themselves, and quite irreproachable in their Morals. . . . Those whose Persons & Conversation I like best are d'Alembert, Buffon, Marmontel, Diderot, Duclos, Helvetius ; and old President Henau[l]t. . . ." [1]

The list, somewhat strangely, does not include the leading host of the Parisian men of letters, Baron d'Holbach, with whom Hume had earlier been in correspondence. Prior to Hume's departure from England, Holbach had written of his " strongest desire of getting acquainted with one of the greatest philosophers of any age, and of the best friend to mankind." Shortly after Hume's return to England in 1766, Holbach was still of the same mind. " I am very proud, I must own," he told Hume, " of being remembcred by a great man, whose friendship, at least, I know to value as it deserves." [2] One of the first *philosophes* that Hume met at Paris, the German-born Paul-Henri Thiry, Baron d'Holbach, was devoting all his efforts and his great wealth to the interests of the arts and sciences. Skilled in languages, ancient and modern, and well read in modern literature, philosophy, and science, he had contributed articles on metallurgy to the *Encyclopédie* and was a patron of its general editors, Diderot and D'Alembert.

Holbach's house on the rue Royale, Butte St Roche, was the meeting place—facetiously named the " synagogue"—of the

[1] HL, I, 419-20.   [2] RSE, v, 72, 74.

leading intellectuals at the sumptuous dinners with costly wines served every Sunday and Thursday. In later years Hume was to write to Suard, " I suppose that the Baron's house is on the same footing as formerly, a common receptacle for all men of letters and ingenuity." Mme d'Holbach, always exquisitely gowned, was a sweet, gentle, and somewhat frustrated hostess who heartily detested her husband's philosophy and, indeed, all philosophy. Her mother, Mme d'Aine, on the contrary, was sprightly and delighted in exchanging badinage with all comers. In the château of Grandval, a few miles up the Seine, Holbach entertained more privately and even more lavishly.

Though Hume's private opinion of Holbach's abilities is not available, he did express his " sincere and inviolable attachment to him." Two other Britishers held widely divergent opinions of the Baron. Laurence Sterne thought that " This Baron is one of the most learned noblemen here, the great protector of wits, and the Scavans who are no wits. . . ." Horace Walpole, of course, was cynical : " I sometimes go to Baron d'Olbach's ; but I have left off his dinners, as there was no bearing the authors, and philosophers, and *savants*, of which he has a pigeon-house full. The Baron is persuaded that Pall Mall is paved with lava or deluge stones. In short, nonsense for nonsense, I like the Jesuits better than the philosophers." [1] Walpole did concede, however, that Holbach was " the host of Europe."

D'Alembert was Hume's favourite among the *philosophes*. To a foundling exposed near the church of St Jean le Rond in Paris was given the name of Jean Le Rond, to which the man himself later added the surname of D'Alembert. Educated in philosophy and theology by the Jansenists, he acquired higher mathematics by himself. After trying the law and medicine, he won his first laurels by a series of mathematical treatises, being admitted a member of the Academy of Sciences. Later he extended his researches into the fields of literature, music, and philosophy, became associated with Diderot in the preparation of the *Encyclopédie*, and was admitted to the French Academy. In person, D'Alembert was slight of build, reserved in manner, and, despite a high-pitched voice, a brilliant conversationalist and mimic. Mme Geoffrin was the first to introduce him to Parisian society, but it was at Mme du Deffand's that he met Julie de Lespinasse.

In a letter to Horace Walpole, no friend to a *philosophe*, David Hume provides an estimate of the character and abilities of

[1] *Letters of Laurence Sterne* (Oxford 1935), p. 151 ; *Walpole Letters*, VI, 370.

D'Alembert.   As to character,

. . . D'Alembert is a very agreeable companion, and of irreproachable morals. By refusing great offers from the Czarina and the King of Prussia, he has shown himself above interest and vain ambition.   He lives in an agreeable retreat at Paris, suitable to a man of letters.   He has five pensions : one from the King of Prussia, one from the French King, one as member of the Academy of Sciences, one as member of the French Academy, and one from his own family.   The whole amount of these is not 6000 livres a year ; on the half of which he lives decently, and gives the other half to poor people with whom he is connected.   In a word, I scarce know a man, who, with some few exceptions (for there must always be some exceptions) is a better model of a *virtuous* and *philosophical* character.

Perhaps in his last sentence Hume had in mind Lord Marischal's comment on D'Alembert : " He wants a part of your quiet temper, he is fire and lightning." [1]   As to D'Alembert's abilities, Hume writes in cool appraisal :

I believe I said he was a man of *superior parts,* not a *superior genius* ; which are words, if I mistake not, of a very different import.   He is surely entitled to the former character, from the works which you and I have read : I do not mean his translation of Tacitus, but his other pieces.   But I believe he is more entitled to it from the works which I suppose neither you nor I have read, his Geometry and Algebra.[2]

The greatest proof of Hume's friendship with D'Alembert is that in the strange events of 1766 in regard to Rousseau, Hume made D'Alembert " absolute Master " of the conduct of the controversy in Paris.   Like the Earl of Charlemont and others, D'Alembert had noticed the vacant stare of his friend and had taken the privilege of their intimacy to warn him about it.   " I remember," he was to write to Hume in 1766, " when you were once talking to me and at the same time staring fixedly at me that I advised you in a friendly manner to break off as much as possible that habit because it might play you a nasty trick. . . .   It is not necessary to gaze intently at the people you are speaking to. . . ." [3] But unhappily Hume was unable to eradicate the habit of a lifetime ; and his innocent stare was to reduce to a state of temporary hysteria so high-strung a person as Rousseau.

One of the greatest geniuses of the French Enlightenment and perhaps its most seminal mind, Denis Diderot was strongly attracted to Hume.   Though himself a massive figure of a man, Diderot was amazed at the tremendous bulk of the Scottish philosopher, acknowledging that he would have mistaken him for a fat well-fed Bernardine monk—*un gros Bernardin bien nourri.*[4]

[1] RSE, v, 110.   [2] HL, ii, 110.   [3] RSE, iii, 6.
[4] *Caldwell Papers,* pt. ii, vol. i, 256.

Educated by the Jesuits, Diderot learned early to detest their religion. His literary versatility was almost as remarkable as Voltaire's. Throughout life he poured forth an endless stream of novels, plays, poetry, and essays on aesthetics, philosophy, and religion. His eloquence animates the pages of Holbach's atheistical *Système de Nature*, which appeared in 1770. Fearlessly Diderot suffered imprisonment in 1746 for the *Pensées philosophiques*, one of his earliest works, and then plunged immediately into the vast undertaking of the *Encyclopédie*. Suppression of the licence to print in 1752 frightened off several of his associates and a second suppression in 1759 frightened off even more. Almost single-handed Diderot brought out the seventeenth volume of text in 1765 and the eleventh volume of plates in 1772—a herculean task by a herculean man.

"He who only knows Diderot in his writings," observes Marmontel, " does not know him at all. When he grew animated in talk, and allowed his thoughts to flow in all their abundance, then he became truly admirable." This was the Diderot that Hume associated with at Baron d'Holbach's—he was not a frequenter of the *salons*—and it is not too much to assume that Hume, perhaps for the first time in his life, met in him his master in rational argumentative conversation. No letters from Hume to Diderot have survived, but several from Diderot to Hume bespeak deep intimacy and complete understanding. Diderot writes of his " well-beloved and greatly-honoured David " ; " my dear David, you are of all nations, and you will never demand from a poor wretch his baptismal certificate " ; " Mme Diderot will kiss your two large Bernardine cheeks " ; " your round and smiling face " ; " I salute you—I love you—I revere you." [1]

Diderot's closest friend after his mistress, Sophie Volland, was the German-born man of letters, Friedrich Melchior Grimm, who is not listed among Hume's favourites. In religion and philosophy, Grimm was of the Holbachian school. His confidential *Correspondance littéraire*, subscribed to by numerous German rulers and by Catherine II of Russia, began in 1750 and went on till 1790. The shrewd, cold appraisals of contemporary literature are a mine of information concerning the spread of enlightenment throughout Europe and have seldom been convicted of error in the passage of time.

David Hume first appears in the *Correspondance littéraire* in August 1754 with a French translation of his *Political Discourses*,

[1] RSE, iv, 80, 78, 79.

a work which, observes Grimm, " is highly esteemed in England and deserves to be everywhere." By October Grimm is more cautious in his praise, writing that " In spite of the fame that he [Hume] has acquired in his country, and the reputation that he is beginning to have in France, he does not appear to be a man of the first power." To his credit, it must be said that Grimm was probably led off the track by a poor rendition into French ; he himself cautions as much and frequently damns the translators. By January 1759 Grimm has recovered his perspective, stating categorically that " David Hume is today one of the best intellects of England ; and as philosophers belong less to their native country than to the universe which they enlighten, this man . . . can be included in the small number of those who by their wisdom and by their works have benefited mankind." He proceeds with an appreciative and instructive comparison between Hume and Diderot : Hume " has not the colour, nor perhaps the depth of genius of M. Diderot. The French philosopher has the air of a man inspired. . . . M. Hume is comparable to a brook, clear and limpid, which flows always evenly and serenely, and M. Diderot, to a torrent whose impetuous and rapid force overwhelms whatever opposes passage. . . ." The complete *History of England* drew the unstinted admiration of Grimm in March 1763 : " M. Hume proves by his example that the writing of history belongs by right to the philosophers, exempt from prejudice and from passion." [1]

Shortly before Hume's departure for England in January 1766, and after having known him personally for two years, Grimm's admiration is tempered and is even a little spiteful :

M. Hume ought to love France, where he has received the most distinguished and most flattering reception. . . . What is still more pleasant is that all the pretty women had a great run on him, and that the fat Scottish philosopher was pleased with their society. This David Hume is an excellent man ; he is naturally placid ; he listens attentively, he sometimes speaks with wit, although he speaks little ; but he is clumsy, he has neither warmth, nor grace, nor charm of humour, nor anything that properly appertains to the chirping of those charming little mechanisms known as pretty women. Oh, what a ludicrous people we are ! [2]

Grimm's professed inability to understand why pretty women were attracted to Hume sounds strangely like the opinion of Mme d'Epinay—and it may well have originated with her, for she was his mistress. The absence of Grimm's name from Hume's list of favourites is matched by its absence from all his letters ; the two men, it would seem, failed to attract one another.

[1] Grimm, *Corr. litt.*, II, 178, 415 ; IV, 69–70 ; V, 245. [2] *Ibid.*, VI, 458.

As to the others on Hume's list of favourites, Helvétius proved more agreeable as a man than as a philosopher. Mme Helvétius, however, had some pretensions of being a *salonnière* ; and the men of letters found her husband in the role of host in the rue Sainte-Anne a little trying because, as Marmontel observed, " he was continually composing his book in company." Jean-François Marmontel, poet, dramatist, and critic, was the madcap protégé of Mme Geoffrin and the close friend—" the tool," said the baneful Mme du Deffand—of D'Alembert. Hume advised Hugh Blair that Marmontel's *Poetics* " is worth your Perusal," but Blair found it disappointing.

Charles Pinot Duclos, novelist, historian, and Academician, could not long have been a companion of Hume's because, before the end of 1763, he retired to England and later to Italy, having made himself obnoxious to the French government. Georges-Louis Leclerc, Comte de Buffon, the famous zoologist, was, according to Hume, more the " Man of the World " than any other of the learned : " in his Figure and Air and Deportment he answers your idea of a Mareschal of France rather than of a Philosopher." Hume bought the first two volumes of Buffon's *Natural History*, but returned them to the bookseller when the author presented him with copies. Despite Buffon's aristocratic airs, Hume continued to like him.

Had Hume drawn up a similar list of favourites among the men of letters at the close of his stay in Paris, he might have added new names, including those of his early admirers, Turgot, the economist and statesman, Trudaine de Montigny, the statesman, and Chastellux, the social historian. It was this last who made the statement that the name of David Hume is " as respectable in the republic of letters as that of Jehovah was among the Hebrews." The Abbé Le Blanc, Hume's early translator, and Jean-Baptiste-Antoine Suard, his later translator, might also have been included. In June 1764 Hume wrote to Le Blanc regretting " my Misfortune in meeting with you so seldom. I shall lay hold of every opportunity with Pleasure that may bring us together. . . ." He had earlier written to Suard in similar terms. Le Blanc was an abbé and affords a reminder of Hume's train of abbés—Elizabeth Stuart had written, " I know You have in your train all the Abbies in france, who shall have more vanity in obliging Mousieur Hume, than desire of gaining the kendom of heaven." [1] The train included Le Bon, Colbert (who called cousins with Hume), Galiani,

Georgel, Joly, Morellet, and Raynal—to whom may be added the Bishop of Senlis and the Archbishop of Toulouse.

Two French poets were drawn to Hume, one in friendship, the other in controversy. The controversialist was Pierre-Laurant-Buyrette de Belloy, author of a tragedy entitled *Le Siège de Calais*. The public received the stage production enthusiastically and De Belloy was awarded a gold medal by Louis XV and a gold snuff-box by the mayor of Calais. The issue was patriotic, for, still smarting under the terms of the Treaty of Paris, France was ready to be reassured of the heroism of the French and the barbarism of the English as illustrated in Edward III's conquest of Calais in 1347. The story goes that, having taken the city, the English king demanded that six leading citizens should be delivered over to him for capital punishment. The first citizen to volunteer was Eustace de Saint-Pierre. Upon the pleas of his queen, however, Edward finally relented and pardoned the six courageous burghers. De Belloy, taking advantage of his theatrical success, published the work in 1765, adding historical notes in criticism of Hume's treatment of the subject in the *History of England*.

The controversy—if such it may be termed—Hume chose to ignore, though he did send a copy of the book to Hugh Blair. The incident may be dismissed with the amusing contemporary account of Charles Collé, who writes that De Belloy

has relieved M. Hume (without naming him) as sentinel. This English historian, whom we find so admirable and who is now in Paris in the suite of the ambassador of England, wished to cast some doubts on the authenticity of the deed of Eustace de Saint-Pierre ; and M. de Belloy has proved to him that he was only an Englishman, that is to say a man jealous and envious of the glory of the French, whose superiority in all respects will ever bring despair to the heart of that nation which imitates us and which hates us.[1]

The second poet, Claude-Joseph Dorat, was friendly to that nation which so assiduously imitated the French and especially to its great philosopher, to whom he addressed the third of his poetical *Epîtres*. We French, sings Dorat, love England :

> Nous aimons vos graves chimères
> Et vos jeux tristement sensés.
> Nous ornons ce que vous pensez ;
> Nous savons de nos mains légères
> Polir vos goûts et vos talents.
> Vous avez quelques diamants,
> Mais vous manquez de lapidaires.

---

[1] Charles Collé, *Journal et Mémoires*, ed. Honoré Bonhomme (Paris 1868), III, 23.

> Ce négligé qui nous déplait,
> Nous l'égayons par la parure ;
> Et notre France est le creuset
> Ou l'or de l'Europe s'épure.

As for " England's " philosopher, Dorat begs his indulgence in neglecting the thinker for the man :

> Hume, souris à mes chansons,
> Enfants légers de mon délire :
> Ma main, parcourant tous les tons,
> Aime à s'égarer sur la lyre.
> J'oublois, pour déraissoner,
> Le philosophe respectable,
> Et ne voyois que l'homme aimable
> Qui voudra bien me pardonner.

Hume's triumphal stay in Paris was commemorated by two French artists. One of their portraits is well known, the other is not. Charles-Nicholas Cochin, the Younger, painter, engraver, architect, antiquarian, and Secretary of the Academy of Painting, did a famous profile of Hume, which, as engraved in 1764 by S. C. Miger, was widely circulated. Louis Carogis, called Carmontelle, painter and writer of bagatelles, was a reader, along with Charles Collé, to the Duc d'Orléans. At the request of the Duc, Carmontelle had earlier done that fascinating portrait of Laurence Sterne which makes him look like a younger Voltaire. It was presumably also for the Duc's collection that Carmontelle painted Hume in water-colours. After being " lost " for many years, the portrait is now in the Scottish National Portrait Gallery.[1]

But to return to the " seiks [sheiks] in the Rue Royale," as Hume facetiously called them. Nowhere in the world could he have matched his wits with such an assemblage of genius. The Edinburgh circle of divines and professors was dwarfed in comparison. What would we not give today for a Boswell's account of a typical session ! Some facts are happily available—but only a few, and intimations rather than complete records. One thing that is certain is that the principle of exclusion was rigidly applied —the *philosophes* would not perform for the benefit of the un-initiated. Samuel Rogers relates the reception of Horne Tooke by D'Alembert, to whom he had presented a letter of introduction :

Dressed *à-la-mode*, he presented the letter, and was courteously received by D'Alembert, who talked to him about operas, comedies, and suppers, &c.

---

[1] Carmontelle also did a water-colour portrait of Mme de Boufflers (together with the Duchesse de Lazun).

Tooke had expected conversation on very different topics, and was greatly disappointed. When he took leave, he was followed by a gentleman in a plain suit, and who had perceived his chagrin. " D'Alembert," said the gentleman, " supposed from your gay apparel that you were a petit-maître." The gentleman was David Hume. On his next visit to D'Alembert, Tooke's dress was altogether different ; and so was the conversation.[1]

In the letter naming his favourites among the learned of Paris, a letter addressed to Blair, Hume adds : " It would give you & Jardine & Robertson great Satisfaction to find that there is not a single Deist among them." The irony was hardly to be missed by Hume's " Protestant Pastors." Diderot makes clear how Hume learned the fact :

> The first time that M. Hume found himself at the table of the Baron, he was seated beside him. I don't know for what purpose the English philosopher took it into his head to remark to the Baron that he did not believe in atheists, that he had never seen any. The Baron said to him : " Count how many we are here." We are eighteen. The Baron added : " It isn't too bad a showing to be able to point out to you fifteen at once : the three others haven't made up their minds.[2]

Present at one of the sessions in the rue Royale was Hume's friend, Andrew Stuart of Torrance. Having the temerity to make " a battle in favour of a future state," Stuart only got laughed at for his pains and was derisively dubbed the " Immortal Soul." [3] The Baron's militant atheism earned for him the title of the " Personal Enemy of God," and his club maintained that Christianity would be abolished in Europe by the end of the eighteenth century.

Religion, its superstitions and its evil consequences to society, provided a constant and fertile topic of conversation. On returning from a visit to England in 1765, Holbach expatiated on the craze for suicide in that country. Diderot explained that the vogue for travel among the English was sometimes instigated by the desire to find a convenient place in which to kill themselves. Hume instanced the complications that he had become involved in as Embassy Secretary to see that justice was done to a starving Englishman, who had thrown himself into the Seine but who had been fished out alive. " No political negotiation," he went on, " had been more intriguing than this affair." He had been obliged to go twenty times to see the First President before he could make him understand that there was not in any of the

---

[1] Rogers, *Table-Talk*, ed. A. Dyce (New Southgate 1887), p. 125.
[2] Diderot, *Lettres à Sophie Volland*, ed. André Babelon (Paris 1938), II, 77. Many years later Samuel Romilly heard much the same story from Diderot. Slightly different versions are given by Boswell and Samuel Rogers. [3] Carlyle, p. 292.

treaties between France and England any article that forbade an Englishman from drowning himself in the Seine under penalty of being hanged. He added that if his compatriot had unfortunately been jailed, he would have risked losing his life equally for not having drowned himself as for having drowned himself. Diderot was bitter : "If the English are completely insane, . . . the French are also completely ridiculous." [1]

Hume's account of the English missionary, who, having converted an American Indian, brought him to London for exhibition, provided much merriment. The Indian, after being catechised, was invited to partake of the sacrament. The minister then inquired, "Well, my son, do you not feel more animated with the love of God ! . . . Is not your soul warmed ? "—" Yes," replied the little Huron, "wine does very well ; but if I had been given brandy, I believe that my soul would have fared better yet." The *philosophes* were agreed that Christianity was nearly extinguished in England but deprecated the fact that the English were turning to Deism, rather than to atheism. Diderot summed up the general opinion : "A people who think that it is belief in a God and not good laws which make men honest seem to me but little advanced." [2]

Also applauded was Hume's story of how the Duc de Nivernais had been surprised to find the Dauphin, several months before his death, reading in bed the philosophical works of David Hume. The Duc was even more surprised when the Dauphin explained that "This reading is most consoling in the state that I am in." [3] Here, indeed, were signs of the times, good augury that Christianity was fast waning !

Even before Hume went to Paris, the *philosophes* had got wind of his not too seriously projected ecclesiastical history. Enthusiastically they began to bring pressure to bear. In June 1763 Helvétius wrote to Hume : "I am told that you have abandoned the most wonderful subject in the world, to write the History of the Church. Just think ! the subject is worthy of you just as you are worthy of the subject. It is, therefore, in the name of England, of France, of Germany, of Italy, and of posterity that I beseech you to write this history. Consider that only you are in a position to do it—that many centuries will go by before a Monsieur Hume is born, and that it is a service that you owe to the universe present and future." [4] That the pressure upon Hume was continued is

[1] Diderot, *op. cit.*, ii, 76. [2] *Ibid.*, ii, 76–7.
[3] *Ibid.*, ii, 105. [4] RSE, v, 52.

attested by Grimm's announcement in the *Correspondance littéraire* for April 1766, soon after Hume's departure, that "We frequently begged M. Hume, during his stay in France, to write an *Ecclesiastical History*. This would be, at the present time, one of the most beautiful undertakings of literature, and one of the most important services rendered to philosophy and to humanity." [1] Throughout the years, D'Alembert brought up the subject frequently, writing, as late as 1773, "I shall never be consoled . . . for being deprived of this Ecclesiastical History that I have requested of you so many times and that you, perhaps alone in Europe, are in a position to write, and that would certainly be as interesting as the Greek and Roman history, if you take the trouble to paint in her true colours our mother Holy Church." [2] In view of all this friendly interest in his own project, it seems appropriate to inquire why Hume did not write the ecclesiastical history. Was it mere desire to avoid making new enemies, as he had previously told Millar, or was there some lack of understanding with the *philosophes* that may have induced him to drop the subject? [3]

Champion of the select society for the free and familiar exchange of thought, David Hume ought to have revelled in the philosophical sessions on the rue Royale, and, no doubt, he did so up to a point. Yet there is reason to believe that he was not perfectly content. During his visit to Paris early in 1763, Gibbon had not been able to approve of the "intolerant zeal" of the *philosophes*, who "laughed at the scepticism of Hume, preached the tenets of atheism with the bigotry of dogmatists, and damned all believers with ridicule and contempt." [4] The *philosophes* simply could not understand Hume's sceptical or agnostic position and were inclined to think that he had not entirely thrown off the shackles of bigotry. "So that poor Hume," wrote Sir James Macdonald from Paris to an English correspondent, "who on your side of the water was thought to have too little religion, is here thought to have too much." [5] Many years later Hume himself confessed that Lord Marischal and Helvétius "used to laugh at me for my narrow way of thinking in these particulars."

The Baron's atheistical club did, however, (according to a tradition in the Hume family) present the philosopher with a large gold medal, the inscription on which is unfortunately unrecorded. If Hume could have known that his grand-niece was to atone for

[1] Grimm, *Corr. litt.*, VII, 13.   [2] RSE, III, 21.   [3] See Textual Supplement for Hume's letter of 27 August 1765 to Millar.   [4] Gibbon, *Memoirs*, p. 135.   [5] Macdonald is quoted by George Horne in a letter of 6 June 1764, printed in *Gent.'s Mag.*, LXIII (1793), 644.

his Parisian indiscretions by giving this medal to an Edinburgh church and that the gold was to be melted down and made into a censer by a craftsman of Paris, he might well have approved of the historical cycle.[1] For the genial Scottish sceptic must have been somewhat amused, and perhaps a little shocked, by the dogmatic atheism of the rue Royale, just as formerly in Edinburgh he had occasionally been riled by displays of dogmatic theism. Over the ubiquitous dogmatism on the issue of religion, the philosopher of human nature may well have been inclined to despondency.

There is further reason to believe that Hume experienced some disappointment in his relations with the *philosophes*. Their dogmatism, he found, was not confined to atheism, but extended into metaphysics, economics, and related social subjects. Although Newton and Locke were the great names among them, that of Descartes was by no means dead. Consequently their variety of empiricism was tinged with a metaphysical necessitarianism which was repugnant to Hume's way of thinking. Take the case of the *Economistes* or *Physiocrates*, of whom François Quesnay and the Sieur de Gourmay were the leading theorists, and Hume's friend Turgot the principal practical representative.

With Turgot himself, Hume was always politely firm in rejecting the single tax on land proposed by the *Physiocrates*, as well as their " agreeable and laudable, if not too sanguine hope, that human Society is capable of perpetual Progress towards Perfection. . . ." To the Abbé Morellet, however, Hume was more forthright :

> I see that, in your prospectus [for a *Dictionnaire de Commerce*], you take care not to disoblige your economists, by any declaration of your sentiments ; in which I commend your prudence. But I hope that in your work you will thunder them, and crush them, and pound them, and reduce them to dust and ashes ! They are, indeed, the set of men the most chimerical and most arrogant that now exist, since the annihilation of the Sorbonne. I ask your pardon for saying so, as I know you belong to that venerable body. I wonder what could engage our friend, M. Turgot, to herd among them ; I mean, among the economists ; tho I believe he was also a Sorbonnist.[2]

Hume, himself, never took the trouble to thunder and crush and pound the *Physiocrates* openly, leaving that duty to Adam Smith.

What must have struck Hume about the *a priori* character of the Holbachian atheism, the Helvétian materialism, and the Physiocratic economics, was that it showed a complete indifference to his

---

[1] See newspaper clipping, in the Edinburgh Room of the Edinburgh Public Library, of letter of 6 Sept. 1932 by N. D. Macdonald, a member of the Hume family by marriage.   [2] HL, II, 93-4, 180, 205.

own philosophy of mitigated scepticism. The old Aristotelian dogmatism of the schools was but replaced in France by a new dogmatism of inevitable progress. To some extent, therefore, Hume must have felt intellectually sequestered, intellectually lonely. The early conviction that he might have to wait for a distant posterity for the understanding of his philosophy may have been deepened by his experiences with the intelligentsia of France. There can be little doubt that he left that country, despite its adulation and its veneration, convinced that in his own thinking he was still far in advance of the world. Nor perhaps is it idle to speculate that this intellectual loneliness formed one of the reasons why he never returned to France for permanent residence. If such is the fact, then it is a fact of no little pathos.

David Hume never met the major prophet of the French Enlightenment, for Voltaire had long since retired to the Swiss frontier as " Patriarch of Ferney." In reply to Mme du Deffand's first eulogy of Hume, Voltaire wrote : " You have only to send him to me ; I will speak to him and, above all, listen to him." [1] That attempts actually were made to " send " him to Voltaire is explained by Hume :

> When I arriv'd here, all M Voltaire's Friends told me of the Regard he always express'd for me ; and they perswaded me, that some Advances on my part were due to his Age & woud be well taken. I accordingly wrote him a Letter, in which I expressd the Esteem which are undoubtedly due to his Talents ; and among other things I said, that, if I were not confind to Paris by public Bussiness, I shou'd have a great Ambition to pay him a Visit at Geneva. . . . But I am absolutely confind to Paris & the Court and cannot on any account leave them for so much as three Days.[2]

Voltaire, for his part, always professed the highest regard for Hume. In 1762 he told Boswell that Hume was " *Un vraye Philosophe*," and Dr John Moore, ten years later, that " you mos write him that I am hees great admeerer ; he is a very great onor to Ingland, and abofe all to Ecosse." In 1765, Voltaire was reported by the Swedish Ambassador at Madrid, a friend of Hume's, to be in the habit of calling Hume *my St David*.[3]

Hume, as is perhaps evident in the above letter, was not completely enthusiastic over Voltaire. He held no high opinion of him as a philosopher, and as a historian, the account of the " Descent on the Coast of Brittany " probably still rankled. He

---

[1] Voltaire, *Œuvres*, XLI, 247.
[2] NHL, pp. 78–9. Hume's letter has not yet been found. It is mentioned by Voltaire in a letter of 19 November 1763 to the Comte d'Argental.
[3] *Boswell Papers*, IV, 130 ; *Caldwell Papers*, PT. II, VOL. II, 201 ; RSE, IV, 47.

also had occasional qualms about his satiric wit. In April 1764, as has been seen, he made futile efforts to get Voltaire's ridicule of Lord Kames's *Elements of Criticism* suppressed before publication and in 1766 he was not to relish Voltaire's intervention in the Rousseau *affaire*. Nevertheless, it is posterity's loss, at least so far as anecdotal history is concerned, that the two never came together.

The second great prophet of Enlightenment, a former *philosophe* but now their enemy, arrived in Paris in December 1765 to place himself under the protection of David Hume. The events that followed were to form the *cause célèbre* of the learned world in the eighteenth century and are still the subject of dispute.

CHAPTER 34

EMBASSY SECRETARY

" I am now possess'd of an Office of Credit."

IF David Hume spent much of his time in Paris wining and dining in high society, frequenting the feminine *salons* and the masculine gatherings of the *philosophes*, he was yet able to carry on his duties at the English Embassy and to be, in reality, an " Ambassador of Good Will " eminently qualified to heal the diplomatic wounds occasioned by the recent war. " Mr. Hume is received at Paris as Mr. Hume," it was early reported to Lord Marischal ; " the good fortune of seeing him here is regarded as one of the sweetest fruits of the peace." [1] Lord Hertford was not slow to recognise that the affection of the French for his private secretary was a matter of diplomatic import. " He has got an Opinion, very well founded," noticed Hume in December 1763, " that the more Acquaintance I make, & the greater Intimacies I form with the French, the more I am enabled to be of Service to him : So he exacts no Attendance from me ; and is well pleasd to find me carryd into all kinds of Company. He tells me, that if he did not meet me by Chance in third Places, we should go out of Acquaintance."

Yet with the passage of time, normal routine set in ; and by June 1764 Hume could say " I continue to live here in a manner amusing enough, and which gives me no time to be tir'd of any Scene. What between public Business, the Company of the learned and that of the Great, especially of the Ladies, I find all my time fill'd up. . . ." The original notion that Hume would also act as tutor to the amiable young Lord Beauchamp seems never to have materialised, the duties being assumed by Lord Hertford's chaplain, the Reverend James Trail.

The esteem of Lord Hertford for Hume developed into the warmest attachment. " I can count upon Lord Hertford's friendship," acknowledged Hume to his brother in July 1765, " as much as on any man's in the World. One day, last Spring, he came into my Room ; and told me that he heard of many People, who endeavourd, by their Caresses, to perswade me, that

I ought to remain in France : But he hop'd, that I woud embrace no Scheme of Life, which wou'd ever separate him and me ; He now lovd me as much as ever he esteemd me ; and wishd we might pass our Lives together. He had resolvd several times to have opend his Breast so far to me ; but being a man of few words and no Professions, he had still delayd it ; and he now found himself much reliev'd by this Declaration of his Desires and Intentions."

The declaration bears out the truth of Lord Chesterfield's comment that Hertford was " the honestest and most religious man in the world, and moreover very much a gentleman in his behavior to every body." An incident in France further reveals his character. One night he stopped at an inn on the road to Paris with a retinue of thirty horsemen. In the confusion of receiving so many guests, the innkeeper, an Irishman named Doughterty, was unable to take down all their names, in accordance with the fixed custom, to present them to the Commandant of the town. His apologies were refused and he was clapped in jail, where he languished for eleven days until he could appeal to Lord Hertford, who procured his immediate release.[1]

During the first several months in Paris, Lord Hertford had resided at the Hôtel de Grimberg in the rue St Dominique, but in March 1764 he took the Hôtel de Brancas (formerly known as the Hôtel de Lassay and the Hôtel de Lauraguais) at the junction of the rue de l'Université and the rue de Bourbon. This large mansion near the Louvre—" quite a pallace," remarked Lady Sarah Bunbury—cost him £500 annually. He had some thoughts of relinquishing it after a year but retained it throughout his embassy. In it there was a separate apartment for David Hume, certainly the most luxurious that man of letters had ever had. On occasion, of course, Hume and Lord Hertford followed the court to Fontainebleau and Compiègne.

An intimate picture of Hume in the home life of the Hertford family in the Hôtel de Brancas is provided by young Robert Liston, tutor to the sons of Sir Gilbert Elliot : " We have . . . had the Honour and the pleasure to dine with their Excellencies the Earl and Countess of Hertford.—I never found myself easier & happier any where. They are extremely agreeable people and (which is generally the Case) have infinitely less Ceremony, and behave to you with more attention and familiarity than a poor Country Laird and his Lady. Mr Hume makes a good honest droll good-natured

---

[1] *Gent.'s Mag.*, XLVII (1771), 160 ; *Lloyd's Evening Post*, 5 Oct. 1765.

sort of figure at their Table, and really puts you in mind of the mastiff-Dog at the fire side. I had like to have bursted out two or three Times at the notion of it." [1]

Lord Hertford's appointment of David Hume as his secretary, after refusing to accept Charles Bunbury, had not gone un-criticised. In the *London Evening Post* of 13–15 March 1764 there was printed an anonymous letter castigating the appointment and representing the embassy as totally of Scottish complexion. The letter was reprinted in the *Gazette and London Daily Advertiser* of 16 March. Upon complaint of Lord Marchmont, Hume's Berwickshire neighbour, the House of Lords resolved that these letters were " false, malicious, and scandalous, a gross and wanton Breach of Privilege of this House, and tending to the Dishonour of the Nation " ; and the two printers were sentenced to fines of £100 each and to be imprisoned in Newgate until payment was made. " I was in London," joked Baron Mure to Hume several weeks later, " when a man was fined in £100 for taking your name in vain." [2]

The writer of the letter, according to Horace Walpole,[3] was John Wilkes, who on Christmas Day 1763 had retired to France for fear of Parliamentary discipline. Wilkes, if he really was the writer, coolly called upon the English Ambassador soon after his arrival in Paris. Lord Hertford, to be sure, was " Not at Home " to such a notorious adversary of His Britannic Majesty ; and Wilkes left a card for him and another for David Hume. Some-what to his surprise, both the Ambassador and the secretary returned the visit. Wilkes, however, was never presented at court by Hertford, nor was he ever invited to dinner at the Embassy, most especially not to the dinner of 4 June 1764 honouring the birthday of King George III. To this dinner were invited, according to Hume's announcement in the *London Chronicle* of 13 June, " all the English of Rank and Condition in this Place, to the Number of seventy Persons. . . ." Wilkes, for his part, laughed at the pointed omission and scoffed at the company present, " The *Macs* and *Sawneys* not in the French service." A regular, if enigmatic, attendant of services at Lord Hertford's chapel, Wilkes had to tolerate there both the Scottish secretary and the Scottish chaplain, whom he considered " a dull preacher." Concerning Lord Hertford and Lord Beauchamp, however, Wilkes

---

[1] MS letter of 11 Feb. 1765, in NLS, MS 5517, f. 13.
[2] *Journal of the House of Lords*, 19 Mar. 1764 (xxx, 511) ; *Caldwell Papers*, PT, II, VOL. I, 251. [3] Walpole, *Memoirs of George III*, I, 311.

was willing to concede " their real sterling sense, great intrinsic worth, and (what sets off the whole) their amiable manners." [1]

In March 1764 Lord Hertford opened a concerted campaign to secure Hume's appointment as Embassy Secretary, in the course of which he engaged Hume, somewhat against his inclination, to solicit the aid of those personal friends who had most credit with Lord Bute, namely Elliot, Erskine, Home, and Oswald. " I own," Hume told Elliot, " that notwithstanding all the plausible Appearances, my Hopes of Success are but moderate." The campaign ended in a total defeat, which inspired Hume to cynicism : " The King has promisd it ; all the Ministers have promisd it : Lord Hertford earnestly sollicits it : Yet have I been in this Condition above six Months : and I never trouble my head about the Matter, and have rather laid my Account that there is to be no such thing."

A full year later, nettled by repeated failures and embarrassed by the scarcely hidden insinuations of French statesmen that an ambassador who could not so much as name his own secretary must indeed be impotent at home, Lord Hertford wrote " a very earnest, and very pressing Letter " to the Prime Minister, George Grenville. This time, instead of the customary ambiguities and half-promises, he met with flat refusal, to which was added hostile comment on Hume personally. Nonplussed, Hertford at once promised to make Hume reparation from his private fortune for the breach of faith of the ministry. This generosity came from a man who had the reputation of being parsimonious !

A few weeks later, in June 1765, the recurrent and false rumour that Bunbury was going as Secretary to Ireland gave Hertford a final opportunity on behalf of Hume. " My Lord throws up immediately," wrote Hume, " if this demand is not complied with." Yet Hertford's letter to Lord Halifax, Secretary of State, Southern Department, though written in the strongest terms, makes no such threat directly. The tottering Grenville ministry, however, dared raise no further protest and on 2 July Halifax informed Hertford, " It is with great Pleasure I acquaint your Excellency, that His Majesty has been graciously pleased to comply with your Request, in appointing Mr. Hume Secretary to your Embassy ; and that the usual Instruments are preparing at my office." [2] Hume's commission under the Great Seal is dated 3 July 1765. His appointments included £1200 a year, £300 for equipage, and 300 ounces of plate for the table.

[1] Percy Fitzgerald, *Life and Times of John Wilkes* (London 1888), I, 240–1, 262–4.
[2] PRO, SP 78/267.

" So that in spite of Atheism & Deism, of Whiggism & Toryism, of Scoticism & Philosophy, I am now possess'd of an Office of Credit, and of 1200 Pounds a Year ; without Dedication or Application, from the Favour alone of a Person, whom I can perfectly love & respect," observed Hume dryly. " I find it has cost my Lord," he continued, " a very hard Pull ; and when I consider the Matter alone, without viewing the Steps that led to it, I am sometimes inclined to be surprizd how it has happen'd." [1]

One of the pleasantest features of the final victory was that Mme de Boufflers had taken it upon herself to write to the Duke of Bedford in England " that the time was now come, and the only time that probably woud ever occur, of his showing his Friendship to her," by backing Hume's candidacy. In the country when he received the letter, Bedford hastened to London, only to find the appointment already confirmed. Hume rejoiced vastly in the goodness of the intention and found much pleasure in informing his friends about it ; the previous year he had positively refused to permit Mme de Boufflers to take this step. All of Hume's friends, Scottish, English, and French, rejoiced likewise over his final vindication, President Hénault, for example, writing : " A thousand and a thousand congratulations, Sir, and yet another thousand. Your country has rendered justice to you. What a wonderful miracle ! But in increasing your well-being, it has added nothing to your celebrity." [2]

The " wonderful miracle," however, was not to last. For Lord Hertford, having learned from Grenville that the matter was concluded, had written to Lord Halifax, as early as 4 July, requesting a leave of absence for a short period " in order to settle some of my private affairs which have suffered by my absence. I was apprized of the loss I underwent in this respect, but as I knew that till his Majesty was pleased to appoint Mr Hume to be Secretary to the embassy I would not leave the court of France, I did not importune his Majesty on that head." [3] Hertford's request was granted, and it was intimated to him that upon his arrival in London the new Rockingham ministry (in which his brother, General Conway, succeeded Halifax as Secretary of State, Southern Department) would offer him the Lord Lieutenancy of Ireland. It was also hinted that he would be succeeded in Paris by the Duke of Richmond. Now the Duke of Richmond, it was obvious, could not retain Hume as Secretary without affronting Sir Charles Bunbury, his brother-in-law, who had been rejected by Lord

[1] HL, i, 510.   [2] RSE, v, 55.   [3] PRO, SP 78/267.

Hertford ; " he could appoint none but his Brother," Lord George Lennox. Hume's days of office were consequently numbered from the very start.

Before leaving Paris, therefore, Lord Hertford told Hume that he intended to take him to Ireland as Secretary in conjunction with Lord Beauchamp. In London, Hertford accepted the Irish appointment on 1 August, " not very gladly," observed Horace Walpole, " but to accommodate his brother, and his nephew Grafton." [1] Six days later Richmond accepted the French appointment. But Hertford's proposal to name Hume as conjunct Secretary at Dublin, however, met with the usual violent anti-Scottish clamour, and he was compelled to settle for Lord Beauchamp alone. " I am told," wrote Hume a few weeks later, " that Lord Hertford's Intentions in my Favour made a great Fray in London. The Princess Amelia said, that she thought the Matter might be easily accomodated. Why cannot Lord Hertford says she make him a Bishop ? The Lord Lieutenant has many good Bishoprics to dispose of." When this story reached Edinburgh, the Reverend John Jardine chuckled that David Hume " would have made an admirable Irish Bishop." [2] Still, at Lord Hertford's insistence, the King granted Hume a pension of £400 a year for life, free of all deduction, and to commence the moment he retired from the Secretaryship.

Hume himself was content not to go to Ireland in an official position. " For I never had much Ambition," he told his brother, " I mean, for Power & Dignities ; and I am heartily cur'd of the little I had. I believe a Fireside & a Book, the best things in the World for my Age & Disposition." He owned, in particular, that he had no talent for speaking in public, and he abhorred the thought of having to drink and carouse with the Irish. He added the further point that " It is like Stepping out of Light into Darkness to exchange Paris for Dublin." When Lord Hertford made him the extraordinary offer of Keeper of the Black Rod (Usher to the House of Commons in Ireland) at £900 a session, the duties of which office a proxy would be happy to perform for £300, Hume declined that too. " I would not run into the Ways of the World and catch at Profit from all hands," he commented to Adam Smith. " I am sure you approve of my Philosophy." [3]

Lord Hertford had proceeded directly to Ireland without returning to France to take formal leave of Louis XV. Soon after

[1] *Walpole Letters*, IV, 388.   [2] RSE, III, 55.
[3] See Textual Supplement for Alison Cockburn's advice.

his arrival at Dublin Castle on 18 October, he had fitted up an apartment for Hume and invited him for a social visit. Working to prevent any visit from Hume, however, was the Reverend James Trail, former Embassy chaplain in Paris, whom Hertford had recently made Bishop of Down and Connor. From Dublin before the middle of November, Trail wrote to Hume, imploring him to stay away from Ireland. A few days later he forwarded a copy of this letter to Dr William Hunter, Hume's acquaintance in London, requesting him to use his influence to dissuade Hume, should he already be in that city.

I find every Day, almost every Hour, [explained Trail to Hunter,] new Proofs how necessary it was to make Use of every Method to prevent Mr. Hume's coming into this Country. His Character as a Philosopher is an object of Universal Disgust not to say Detestation in this Country ; & his historical Character, especially where Ireland & the Stewarts are concerned, is excessively disliked. It is therefore become an object of Importance both to himself & to this Family [the Hertfords] that he set not a foot in this Kingdom. If he knows any Thing of the World, & if he reflects but a single moment, I think my Letter must infallibly determine him to remain in England. . . . In short he must not come here ; I am sure my Lord himself sees the insuperable objection ; & therefor I the more chearfully undertake the Task, that my Lord may not, in Contradiction to all his Feelings for Mr. Hume, be at last reduced to the disagreeable Necessity of laying an absolute Embargo upon him and his Philosophy. I am well persuaded that Mr. Hume will not require any sort of argument to be used with him to induce him to serve my Lord ; all I wish is only that he may see Things in their true Light ; it is his Understanding & not his Will that I want to move.

A postscript to the letter makes it clear that the Bishop had consulted Lord Hertford, who had reluctantly and discomfitedly consented to its being posted :

My Lord desires that this Letter may not be shewn to any Person whatsoever ; he thinks that nothing but extream Necessity would justify its being shewn to Mr. Hume. The Copy I inclose had likewise better be destroyed, if Mr. Hume has already received the Original.[1]

Upon receipt of Trail's original letter, Hume at once wrote to Lord Hertford begging to be relieved of his promise to visit Dublin.[2] Hertford's reply of 10 December affords further evidence of the affinity between the two men :

I love my friends, and abhor prejudices of all kinds. I have a difficulty in persuading myself, when they are void of foundation, that they can long resist. You will therefore easily believe that I was unwilling to think you could continue to be unpopular in Ireland. Your apartment was fitted up

[1] V. G. Plarr, " Unpublished Letters to William Hunter," in *Chambers's Journal*, Sixth Series, IX (1906), 56–7.
[2] This letter is not extant, but its existence is to be inferred from Hertford's reply.

in the castle ; it still remains so.   I mentioned it with satisfaction to many people.   Those who pretend to know this country remonstrated against my impatience to see you, and told me I should endanger the popularity of my administration.   I treated it as it deserves, and as I shall always think of it, although I yielded to the entreaties of my friends in permitting the bishop to give you an account of it.   In the light of fatigue and trouble to yourself, I have some consolation.   If you had come to Dublin you must have grown popular . . . in spite of all prejudices.[1]

Finally on 1 January 1766 Hume announced to the Reverend Hugh Blair that, " I shall not go to Ireland. . . . Lord Hertford has been so good as to excuse me.   You have heard of the great Fortune of Trail, who is I believe your Acquaintance and a very honest Fellow."   *Le bon David* had recognised the painful fact that he was truly *persona non grata* in Ireland and had candidly admitted that the Bishop had acted in good faith and was " a very honest Fellow."   An unpleasant incident was closed.

After Lord Hertford's departure from Paris on 21 July and until the Duke of Richmond presented his credentials to the French King on 17 November, David Hume was Chargé d'affaires.   By 1765 Hume was by no means an untried and inexperienced diplomat. He had learned much from the two expeditions with General St Clair, 1746-48, and he had been Lord Hertford's assistant for nearly two years.   With the current diplomatic issues, he was thoroughly familiar ; and he enjoyed the utmost goodwill of Lord Hertford and the new Secretary of State, General Conway, both of whom were eager for him to make a good showing.   " I heartily wish you success," wrote Hertford, " and hope it will be soon obtained, for your own honour, before the arrival of the Duke of Richmond."   Conway wrote in the same tenor :   " I need not I am sure tell you in how much lights both National & personal I am interested in the success of your . . . negociations which my Brother has equally at heart with myself.   & . . . I have great hopes of Your Success.   Which being now in your hands wou'd do you the greatest honour & credit, as well as contribute much to our's." [2]

" As I am the only English Minister here at present," remarked Hume in August 1765, " I live in a great Hurry of Business."   He was scarcely exaggerating, for in addition to routine business there were numerous special problems and three important diplomatic issues in course of negotiation.   The special problems covered a wide range :   assistance to English merchants and to various

Protestants in France ; the attempt of a starving Englishman to drown himself in the Seine ; the internal disruption of France as revealed in the Assembly of the Clergy ; the capture of the nephew of Cardinal de Bernis by the Sallee Rovers ; payment for hospitalised soldiers ; the exchange of prisoners of war.

The three important diplomatic issues were the demolition of the fortifications and the harbour of Dunkirk, the indemnification by the French government for the paper money held by the Canadian merchants who had recently become British citizens, and the recurring violations by French nationals of the Newfoundland fisheries. All were inherited from Lord Hertford and all derived from the Treaty of Paris of 1763 or from earlier treaties. In none of these matters was Hume, during his less than four months as Chargé d'affaires, able to bring about a settlement, any more than Lord Hertford had been during his twenty months. As a matter of fact, the Newfoundland dispute remained unsettled until the Convention of 1904, some 139 years later, and the Dunkirk dispute until the Peace of Versailles in 1783, some eighteen years later ; the " Canada Bills " negotiation was taken out of Hume's hands by the French government and was concluded at London early in 1766 by General Conway himself.

That Hume was an able diplomatist is proved both by the series of sixteen dispatches [1] and the several memorials that he wrote during his brief tenure of office and by the consistent approval of his superiors in London, General Conway and King George III. On 27 August Conway congratulated Hume that, " your Conduct . . . has been very satisfactory to His Majesty and his Servants, from the Speediness of your application, and the Solidity of the Arguments so properly urged by You in that Conference." [2]

The dispatches indicate Hume's awareness of the subtlety and evasiveness of the French ministers, the Duc de Choiseul and the Duc de Praslin. In the dispatch of 28 August, for instance, concerning French irregularities in Newfoundland in defiance of treaty stipulations, Hume reports Praslin as at first denying that it was any concern of the French ministry if their nationals broke the treaty—" What harm was there . . . if a few Frenchmen, disavow'd by the Government, shou'd cut out some oaks in a Country which consisted of one boundless and unmeasurable Forest ? Wou'd we refuse a thirsty Foreigner the Liberty of drinking in the Thames ? "—yet later, in connexion with French men-of-war in

[1] Reprinted in NHL, pp. 89–130 ; see also section II of the introduction to that edition.   PRO, SP 78/267.

the Gulf of St Lawrence, as insisting upon their presence " in order to keep the French Fishermen from transgressing Treaties." The inconsistency of Praslin's arguments is underscored by Hume in a cautionary observation to General Conway : " Your Excellency will please to observe that I deliver the Duke of Praslins answer, as nearly as I can remember it ; That his Majesty may see where it is satisfactory, either by disavowing past Encroachments, or by justifying the French Pretensions."

Several of the dispatches, such as the above, make dramatic reading and reveal the master of historical narrative. All of them show a full comprehension of the implications of the situation. There is no doubt, however, that Hume found himself handicapped throughout his tenure of office by the facts that he was a commoner dealing with great dukes and that his status was purely temporary. As Voltaire had quipped to Boswell, *Un Chargé d'affaires est guères chargé.*[1]

Keeping a sharp eye on the internal affairs of France, the British Embassy was not unaware of the smouldering discontent which was eventually to result in the French Revolution. As early as November 1763 Lord Hertford had observed that an easy indolent Prince, " addicted to Mistresses and Favourites," was playing into the hands of seditious elements ; " Though these Flames break out in every part of the Kingdom the Nation itself does not as yet appear to be in any Combustion. But Things are so much prepared for it, that no Body of Men lie near the Scene of Action without being in some Degree affected by it ;—and what appears the most dangerous Symptom the Army itself are ready to catch the Contagion." [2] In 1765 Hume noted that " the Authority of the Crown is somewhat low in France, [and] all public Bodies are apt to beome troublesome " ; but, he concluded, " it is not likely France, were she disposd, will soon be in a Situation to disturb the Tranquillity of Europe." Hume had actually taken the pains to inquire of Baron d'Holbach if he did not think that there would soon be a revolution in France favourable to liberty. " No," replied the Baron, " for our nobility have all become poltroons." [3]

The Embassy Secretary was not only a man of affairs, but an historian and a man of wit, as is seen in his relations with Father

---

[1] *Boswell Papers*, IV, 130.   [2] PRO, SP 78/259.
[3] NHL, pp. 96, 98 ; Carlyle, p. 292. Carlyle actually says that Hume asked the question of Baron Montesquieu ; but the latter was dead by 1755 and Hume had not met him on earlier visits to France. Holbach's name appears later in the same passage.

Gordon, Principal of the ancient Catholic Scots College of St Andrew. Soon after his arrival in Paris Hume had received the Principal's permission to inspect the thirteen or fourteen manuscript folios of memoirs of James VII and II. " I must own," wrote the historian to the Earl of Hardwicke, " that I see from these Memoirs, that I have in one particular somewhat mistaken K. Charles's Character. I thought that his careless negligent Temper had renderd him incapable of Bigotry ; and that he had floated all his Life between Deism & Popery : But I find, that Lord Halifax better knew his Sentiments, when he says, that the King only affected Irreligion in order to cover his Zeal for the Catholic Religion. . . . I shall probably take soon Advantage of a new Edition of my History to correct my Mistakes in this particular ; and in a few others of no great Moment." The corrections he actually made, however, were few, which is more the pity because the memoirs have disappeared and Hume's several letters concerning them provide the only clues to their contents.

On another occasion, Hume asked Father Gordon if he had any commands to London.

" No," said the Principal, " but a Pope's bull to create a Scots bishop." Hume replied that he would be happy to send it.

" You are not serious," said the Principal.

" Yes," said Hume, " of all things I should like to send the Pope's Bull." And he sent it under cover to the Secretary of State, with great good humour.[1]

One of the duties of the Embassy Secretary was to be of service to the travelling British. " Since the peace," observed Horace Walpole morbidly, the way to Paris had become, " like the description of the grave, . . . the way of all flesh." Hume's first opportunity to be of service occurred in 1763 before he left London. Tobias Smollett, having gone to France for his health, had had a case of books seized and impounded by French customs officials. An appeal to Hume secured their release, and Smollett's gratitude. " I am infinitely obliged to D. H[ume]," he wrote, " for the favourable manner in which he has mentioned me to the earl of H[ertford]. I have at last recovered my books, by virtue of a particular order to the director of the douane, procured by the application of the English resident [Richard Neville Neville] to the French ministry." [2]

In Paris the demands upon Hume increased. Old Scottish

---

[1] EU, Laing MSS, ii, 451/2, MS notes of George Chalmers.
[2] Letter IV in Smollett's *Travels through France and Italy.*

friends were, however, a joy to see again and to introduce to new
French friends : Elliot, Colonel Keith, Robert Strange, Andrew
Stuart of Torrance, and Wedderburn.   Hume arranged for the
schooling of Elliot's two boys at the military academy of the Abbé
Choquart and kept an avuncular eye on them and on their young
tutor, Robert Liston.   To Colonel Keith, Hume confided some of
his adventures with the Parisian ladies, and Keith retailed them
to the Edinburgh circle.   " *Pour ce qui passe dessous la Ceinture, tout
cela va pour rien*—do you remember that ?—What excellent Ladies
you live amongst ! "   So Hugh Blair teased Hume on hearing
Keith's account.[1]   With Stuart and Wedderburn, Hume discussed
the intricacies of the Douglas Cause, the early investigation of
which had brought them to France.   Another more recent
Scottish friend was Sir James Macdonald of Sleat, a direct
descendant of the Lords of the Isles.   This brilliant and accomplished youth passed like a meteor over the Scottish, English, and
French scenes, astonishing and charming everyone with his genius
and sociability—but, like a meteor, he soon burned out, dying of
a consumption at Rome in 1766.   " We . . . lose in him,"
lamented Hume, " a very extraordinary young Man in all
Respects."   Macdonald was one of the few Scottish intellectuals
who, firmly grounded in the Gaelic as well as in the classical
tradition, might—had he lived longer—have been able to get to
the root of the Ossianic mystery.

Among English friends and acquaintances in France in the
years 1763–1765 were Adam Smith,[2] Colonel Barré,[3] General
Clarke, John Crawford, David Garrick, Lord Holdernesse, Lord
Ossory, Josiah Tucker, and Horace Walpole.   The last was, as frequently, tart with Hume, as is evidenced in his "Paris Journals" :

> After dinner went with Mr Hume to Baron d'Holbach, a good-natured
> German settled in France, who keeps a table for strangers, the *beaux esprits*
> of the country etc.   As we went Mr Hume proposed to communicate the
> negotiation to me, which he said grew more difficult from our frequent changes
> and unsettled state.   He said he concluded I had been sent to assist and
> moderate the Duke of Richmond, and owned he wondered I had not talked to
> him on that head.   I desired to be excused from knowing any thing of the
> matter, and assured him, as is true, that I was come to France to avoid politics,
> not to get farther into them.   I supposed he had been jealous of my coming,
> and was glad to satisfy him.

Dr Josiah Tucker, the genial clergyman and economist who had
opened a correspondence with Hume through the good offices of

---

[1] RSE, III, 54.   [2] See Textual Supplement.
[3] Hume's letter to Barré, enquiring about " that Meteor Clarke," NHL, p. 87.

Lord Kames, met Hume at Compiègne and, on returning to Paris, wrote in thanks. " The very friendly & polite Treatment I had the Honour of receiving at Compiègne demands my earliest Acknowledgements : And I do pay them so much & more willingly, as I am ambitious of shewing that the Articles of my Creed do not differ from Yours on the Subject of Humanity & Benevolence, & especially of Gratitude." [1]

Out of the distant past, Michael Ramsay of Mungale remembered David Hume and wrote from London to introduce Charles Burney, the musicologist and father of the later famous Fanny Burney. Ramsay was now tutor to Lord Eglintoune, who had taken a fancy to Burney. In Paris, Hume introduced Burney to Lord Hertford ; and the two, together with Lord Eglintoune, subsequently attempted to secure for him the position of King's musician. Ramsay's letter, after apologising for his negligence as a correspondent, went on : " No friend you have, and you have more real ones than any man I ever knew without including admirers : I say, no one of them enters with a purer satisfaction into every honor and every agreable circumstance of life you enjoy than I do. I hear often of you, & no longer ago than this morning by Tristram Shandy. . . ." [2]

It was in May 1764 that David Hume had a famous exchange with the man called by Voltaire " the Rabelais of England," and by the English " Yorick " or " Tristram Shandy." In 1762 the Reverend Laurence Sterne, on his first visit to Paris, had enjoyed a reception almost equal to Hume's of the following year. Now in 1764 he was forced to play second lion to the philosopher. He himself relates the circumstances of his preaching before Lord Hertford " the last sermon that I shall ever preach " :

Lord *Hertford* had just taken and furnished a magnificent *Hotel* [Hôtel de Brancas] and as every thing, and anything gives the fashion of the moment at Paris, it had been the fashion for every one to go to see the English Ambassador's new hotel.—It occupied the curiosity, formed the amusement, and gave a subject of conversation to the polite circles of Paris, for a fortnight at least.

Now it fell to my lot, that is to say, I was requested to preach, the first day service was performed in the chapel of this new hotel.—The message was brought me when I was playing a sober game of Whist with the *Thornhills*, and whether it was that I was called rather abruptly from my afternoon's amusement to prepare myself for this business, for it was to be on the next day ; or from what other cause I do not pretend to determine, but that unlucky kind of fit seized me, which you know I can never resist, and a very unlucky text did come into my head,—and you will say so when you read it.

[1] *Walpole Corr.* (Yale), VII, 262 ; RSE, VII, 79.   [2] RSE, VI, 105.

" And Hezekiah said unto the Prophet, I have shewn them my vessels of gold, and my vessels of silver, and my wives and my concubines, and my boxes of ointment, and whatever I have in my house, have I shewn unto them : and the Prophet said unto Hezekiah, thou hast done very foolishly." [1]

The impropriety of preaching upon Isaiah's rebuke to Hezekiah for showing the royal treasures to the Babylonian ambassadors and his prophecy that they would subsequently be carried off to Babylon had apparently not struck Sterne in advance—or had it? It did not, at any rate, go unnoticed by the congregation, " a concourse of all nations, and religions too " ; nor did his fanciful explanation of why the Babylonian ambassadors had come to visit Hezekiah go unnoticed by David Hume. For Sterne had urged :

as the Chaldeans were great searchers into the secrets of nature, especially into the motions of the celestial bodies, in all probability they had taken notice at that distance, of the strange appearance of the shadow's returning ten degrees backwards upon their dials ; and had enquired and learned upon what account, and in whose favour such a sign was given ; so that this astronomical miracle, besides the political motive which it would suggest of courting such a favourite of heaven, had been sufficient by itself to have led a curious people as far as Jerusalem, that they might see the man for whose sake the sun had forsook his course.[2]

That evening at dinner, Sterne goes on, David Hume and he indulged in " a little pleasant sparring at Lord *Hertford's* table . . .; but there was nothing in it that did not bear the marks of good-will and urbanity on both sides. . . ." For " David was disposed to make a little merry with the *Parson* ; and, in return, the Parson was equally disposed to make a little mirth with the *Infidel* ; we laughed at one another, and the company laughed with us both. . . ."

The report got abroad, however, that Sterne had given offence by his sermon and had quarrelled with Hume. Sterne indignantly denied both charges. As to the sermon, " Lord Hertford did me the honour to thank me for it again and again " and " *David Hume* favoured it with his grace and approbation." As to the quarrel, it was " absolutely false. Mr. *Hume* and I never had a dispute—I mean a serious, angry or petulant dispute, in our lives :—indeed I should be most exceedingly surprised to hear that *David* ever had an unpleasant contention with any man ;—and if I should be

---

[1] Sterne, *Letters*, p. 219.
[2] " The Case of Hezekiah and the Messengers. Preached before his Excellency the Earl of Hertford. At Paris, 1763," in *Sermons of Mr Yorick* (Oxford 1927), i, 195–6. In publishing the sermon in 1766, Sterne erred in dating it in 1763. On 15 May 1764 he had written to his daughter : " I have preached at the ambassador's chapel —Hezekiah—(an odd subject your mother will say)." See Sterne's *Letters*, p. 212.

made to believe that such an event had happened, nothing would persuade me that his opponent was not in the wrong : for, in all my life, did I never meet with a being of a more placid and gentle nature ; and it is this amiable turn of his character, that has given more consequence and force to his scepticism, than all the arguments of his sophistry.—You may depend on this as a truth."

It may possibly have been at the same dinner—although Sterne was a frequent guest of the Hertfords—that another incident involving the two men of wit and goodwill took place. In the *Sentimental Journey* it is told how a " prompt French marquis " was confused over the identity of the two Scottish Humes, the historian and the dramatist. The marquis inquired politely of David whether he was Hume the poet. " No, said Hume—mildly— *Tant pis*, replied the Marquis. It is Hume the historian, said another—*Tant mieux*, said the Marquis. And Mr. Hume, who is a man of excellent heart, return'd thanks for both."

The parson and the infidel continued their good relations. In 1765 when he was about to publish the third volume of *Sermons of Mr. Yorick*, Sterne wrote to a friend concerning possible subscribers : " As so many men of genius favour me with their names also, I will quarrel with Mr. H[um]e, and call him deist, and what not, unless I have his name too." Sad to say, Hume's name does not appear on the lists. In 1768, however, following the death of Sterne, Hume contributed five guineas to the fund for Mrs Sterne and Lydia ; and five years later he admitted that " the best Book, that has been writ by any Englishman these thirty Years (for Dr Franklyn is an American) is Tristram Shandy "— but the Scot felt impelled to tone down the compliment, adding— " bad as it is."

The pleasant life in Paris of the Embassy Secretary was brought to an end in November 1765. The Duke of Richmond embarked at Dover on 30 October. He arrived in Paris on 6 November, but the critical illness of the Dauphin prevented his being presented to the French king before the 17th. By 27 December he had already received permission to return to England on leave and, on 5 February 1766, resigned his office. In less than three months Richmond and his brother, Lennox, had managed to make themselves as universally unpopular in France as Hertford and Hume had been popular. Lady Sarah Bunbury wrote in November 1766 : " My two brothers and their wives are arrived in town from Paris, where I hear they behaved very ill, especially the Lennoxes, who shut themselves up, saw no French, kept late hours, and laugh'd at everybody." [1] Britain unhappily had lost her two " Ambassadors of Good Will."

With the arrival of the Duke of Richmond, Hume had removed from the elegance of the Hôtel de Brancas, despite the invitation of the Comte de Lauraguais to keep his apartment (which would be especially marked for his privacy, *l'hôtel de Hume*). Prior to leaving for London to give an account of his commission to the King, Hume resided first, at the Hôtel de Beaupréau, rue de l'Université, and then at the Hôtel du Parc royal, rue du Colombier, where Horace Walpole also removed after the departure of Lady Hertford. The London press,[2] in the meantime, speculated that Hume was " to assume a public character at a Northern Court " and again that he would be named Embassy Secretary at the Court of Lisbon ; but of these rumours Hume was unaware or, at least, he did not concern himself with them.

He was, however, mightily concerned with where to settle down permanently and on this question was of many minds. Dublin, of course, was unthinkable. London was never seriously considered, as he had made clear to Blair :

> There is a very remarkable Difference between London and Paris, of which I gave warning to Helvetius when he went over lately to England, and of which, he told me, on his Return he was fully sensible. If a man have the Misfortune, in the former place, to attach himself to Letters, even if he succeeds, I know not with whom he is to live, nor how he is to pass his time in a suitable Society. The little Company, there, that is worth conversing with, are cold & unsociable or are warmd only by Faction and Cabal ; so that a Man, who plays no part in public Affairs, becomes altogether insignificant and if he is not rich, he becomes even contemptible : Hence that Nation are relapsing fast into the deepest Stupidity, Christianity & Ignorance. But in Paris, a man that distinguishes himself in Letters, meets immediately with Regard & Attention.

The real choice lay between Edinburgh, where Blair was living in Hume's " house " in James's Court, and Paris. From Edinburgh, Blair offered sound advice :

> You are now in the full possession of that *Otium cum Dignitate*, which is the point towards which every wise man as he begins to advance in Years ought to tend. Few People have been more fortunate than you ; You have enjoyed in France the full Blaze of your Reputation & Fame ; You have tasted all the pleasures of a Court & of Publick Life ; and after receiving every Tribute due to Letters & to merit, You retire, before it was too late, to your own Philosophic Base & Tranquillity. All your Friends rejoice that you still return an Attachment to Edinburgh. We hope it will increase ; and truly, if you

---

[1] *Walpole Letters*, SUPP. VOL. III, 8–9n.
[2] *Lloyd's Evening Post*, 30 Oct. and 22 Nov. 1765.

are to quit Paris this place has Several advantages which you will not easily meet elsewhere ; particularly your having a set of Friends & Connexions already formed and ready to receive you with open arms.[1]

All of Hume's Scottish friends concurred in opposition to his giving up Scotland, Adam Smith going so far as to call him " light-headed."

And light-headed Hume seems to have been. The " house " in James's Court he let to one Nairne, but on condition that Blair did not want to retain it and that he himself did not decide to return there. Later he committed himself completely to leasing it but, before the letter was posted, changed his mind once more. Finally he gave Blair warning to remove by Whitsunday 1766. But the story of Hume's light-headedness is not yet complete. " On this Subject of my future Abode," he confessed shamefacedly, " I have not these four Months, risen and gone to bed in the same Mind. When I meet with Proofs of Regard & Affection from those I love & esteem here, I swear to myself, that I shall never quit this Place ; An hour after, it occurs to me, that I have then for ever renounced my native Country and all my antient Friends ; and I start with Affright."

Yet why, he temporised, need an irrevocable decision be forced at the moment ? A house in Paris, in any event, would provide him with more time to consider plans for the future and might also make it possible for him to make the frequently discussed trip to Italy in the company of D'Alembert and Julie de Lespinasse. Indulging pleasant thoughts, he imagined himself taking Mme de Boufflers to Italy and even settling on some Greek island sacred to the memory of classical passion. Out of such musings, a decision was born.

On the advice of Mme Geoffrin, Hume leased a house in the Faubourg St Germain, thereby incurring the displeasure of Mme de Boufflers for not having consulted her. On second thought, he found that this house was too small and proposed to lease another in the Quartier Palais-Royal, which Baron d'Holbach promised to furnish for him while he was in England ; but before Hume's letter reached the proprietor, the house had already been leased to another. Was ever a philosopher so frustrated ? In mock despair Hume informed Blair of his dilemma : " I have taken a House at Paris ; but I will have one also in Edinburgh ; and shall deliberate in London which of them I shall occupy. . . . Nothing is so agreeable to an irresolute Man, says the Cardinal de Retz, as

[1] HL, I, 497–8 ; RSE, III, 55.

a measure which dispenses him from taking an immediate Resolution. I am exactly in the Case."

The arrival at Paris, on 16 December, of Jean-Jacques Rousseau added to Hume's confusion ; but it also provided him with the necessity of escorting " this nice little man," who called himself Hume's " pupil," to London as soon as possible. And in the neutral territory of London he could continue to debate whether to set up permanent residence in Paris or in Edinburgh.

CHAPTER 35

JEAN-JACQUES ROUSSEAU

" This nice little man."

JEAN-JACQUES ROUSSEAU, having found asylum in 1762 with the genial Earl Marischal Keith at Môtiers-Travers in Neuchâtel, had politely declined the invitation of David Hume to go to England. Though he had a tremendous reputation in England, Rousseau liked neither the country nor the people. " The happy land where David Hume and the Marischal of Scotland were born " was more of a temptation ; but Keith's visit there in 1763 dispelled all thoughts of living among so many bigots and in such an insufferable climate. Moreover, Hume was a philosopher, and Rousseau was not overfond of philosophers—though, to be sure, he had not read any of Hume's philosophy. He was, however, able to draw an astute comparison of the intellectual and temperamental differences between Hume and himself, acknowledging to Mme de Boufflers that :

Mr Hume is the truest philosopher that I know and the only historian that has ever written with impartiality. He has not loved truth more than I have, I venture to believe ; but I have sometimes put passion into my researches, and he has put into his only wisdom and genius. Pride has often led me astray by my aversion for what was evil or what seemed so to me. I have hated despotism in the republican and intolerance in the theist. Mr Hume has said : here is what makes intolerance, and here is what makes despotism. He has seen from all points of view what passion has let me see only from one. He has measured and calculated the errors of men while remaining above their weaknesses. [1]

The rage for Hume in Paris confirmed Rousseau's original hesitancy about going to England in his company ; and it is with noticeable relief that, after receiving the information about Hume from the Marquise de Verdelin in 1764, he considered the issue closed once and for all. " Hume," he commented, " wrote me a fine letter to offer me his friends and his friendship, should I wish to retire into England ; I scarcely foresaw then that one day he would be *à la mode* in Paris. But henceforth it doesn't matter. I lose a true friend for whom I shall grieve all my life and whom I shall never replace." Sharing Rousseau's antipathy to the

---

[1] Rousseau, VIII, 71.

English and to popular philosophers, Mme de Verdelin applauded the decision. " Mr Hume," said she, " is the darling of all the pretty women here ; that is probably why he is not one with me." [1] Rousseau, it is manifest, was content to regard Hume as a well-intentioned man of genius ; he was also content to keep him at a distance.

David Hume, likewise in a letter to Mme de Boufflers, recognised the vast differences between Rousseau and himself :

All the writings of that author appear to me admirable, particularly on the head of eloquence ; and if I be not much mistaken, he gives to the French tongue an energy, which it scarce seems to have reached in any other hands. But as his enemies have objected, that with this domineering force of genius there is always intermingled some degree of extravagance, it is impossible for his friends altogether to deny the charge ; and were it not for his frequent and earnest protestations to the contrary, one would be apt to suspect, that he chooses his topics less from persuasion, than from the pleasure of showing his invention, and surprizing the reader by his paradoxes. . . . If I dared to object any thing to M. Rousseau's eloquence, which is the shining side of his character, I should say, that it was not wholly free from the defect sometimes found in that of the Roman orator ; and that their great talent for expression was apt to produce a prolixity in both.

In regard to " The Profession of Faith of the Savoyard Vicar " in *Émile*, Hume made the further point : " I am not in the least surprized that it gave offence. He has not had the precaution to throw any veil over his sentiments ; and as he scorns to dissemble his contempt of established opinions, he could not wonder that all the zealots were in arms against him. The liberty of the press is not so secured in any country, scarce even in this, as not to render such an open attack of popular prejudices somewhat dangerous." [2] In short, Hume regarded Rousseau as not only a man of genius, but also an extreme individualist.

With all this distant and cool appraisal of one another, this recognition of disparate mentalities and personalities, there did not seem in 1764 to be any likelihood of the two men ever becoming fast friends. Hume was willing to be the protector of Rousseau— or of any persecuted man of letters—if protection was demanded. Rousseau was a persecuted man of letters and had, moreover, developed a phobia of persecution, but he was averse to seeking a protector, even a Hume, unless in dire peril. In the latter part of 1765 the force of renewed persecution drove Rousseau, though hesitant up to the last moment, straight into the arms of Hume. Hume's arms were open to receive him. Earlier in the year

[1] Rousseau, XI, 150 ; XIII, 231.   [2] HL, I, 373-4.

Hume had come forward with a benevolent scheme on his behalf. Colonel Edmonstoune had suggested that he should do something for Rousseau " without his knowing it," such as to " print his works in England for his benefit." And Lord Marischal had informed Hume of Rousseau's refusal of a pension from the King of Prussia and of his persistent refusal of all gifts. " Jean-Jacques," remarked Keith, " is too virtuous a man for this world, which seeks to turn his scrupulousness into ridicule." [1] So Hume was forewarned that any benevolent scheme must be cloaked in secrecy. An occasion was presented when the distinguished mathematician, Alexis-Claude Clairaut, gave Hume a letter from Rousseau describing his poverty and distress. Circulating this letter among Rousseau's friends in Paris, Hume suggested that they should contribute funds for the purpose of secretly augmenting the copy money to be paid to him for his *Dictionnaire de Musique*. The sudden death of Clairaut on 17 May, however, brought about the collapse of the scheme.

Mme de Verdelin, by that time, had come under the personal spell of Hume and became convinced that he was truly *le bon David*. Visiting Rousseau at Neuchâtel on the 1st of September, she was distressed at his unhappy condition. Aroused by his *Lettres de la Montagne*, the bigots were upon him again ; and Lord Marischal, now at Potsdam, was no longer able to protect his " wild philosopher." Mme de Verdelin was able to wring from him a reluctant consent that, should it become necessary, he would accept Hume's protection in England. Less than a week after her departure, the exile's house was stoned, and on 8 September he hurriedly left for L'Ile Saint-Pierre in the Lake of Bienne. Expelled thence after a few weeks by order of the Senate of Berne, the unfortunate man set off for Berlin to rejoin Lord Marischal. At Strasbourg he stopped short for final reconsideration.

At the instance of Mme de Verdelin, in the meanwhile, Hume had renewed his efforts to get Rousseau to England. An abode in the country but not too far from the booksellers of London was his thought, and he enlisted the assistance, first, of Horace Walpole and then of John Stewart and Gilbert Elliot. He planned to make a secret contribution to the rental out of his own pocket. Thus assured, Hume addressed a tactful letter to Rousseau dated 22 October : It opened :

I shou'd not have dropped an epistolary Commerce with you, for which I was beholden to our Friend, Lord Mareschal, and which did me so much honour and pleasure, had I not been afraid of being in the Number of those troublesome People, who, on pretence of being your Admirers, never cease persecuting you with their Letters. But a Conversation which I lately had with a Lady, who is much your Friend, the Marquise of Verdelin, revived in me the Hopes, that I might be of some Service to you in your present Situation ; and that you woud deign to accept of my good Offices. Your singular and unheard-of Misfortunes, independant of your Virtue and Genius, must interest the Sentiments of every human Creature in your Favour : But I flatter myself, that in England you woud find an absolute Security against all Persecutions, not only from the tolerating Spirit of our Laws, but from the Respect, which every one there bears to your Character.

The letter concluded with the information, useful to a man of letters, that " As the English Booksellers can afford higher Prices to Authors than those of Paris, you will have no Difficulty to live frugally in that Country, on the Fruits of your own Industry. I mention this Circumstance, because I am well acquainted with your Resolution, of laying Mankind under Obligations to you, without allowing them to make you any return." The letter was addressed in the hand of Mme de Verdelin *à Monsieur Rousseau à l'Ile Saint Pierre au Canton de Berne en Suisse.*[1]

Rousseau received Hume's letter at Strasbourg, Mme de Verdelin pressing him to accept the offer. " Mr Hume," she wrote, " charges me to assure you that you will be cherished, protected by the King, loved and respected by the last peasant." As for Hume himself, she continued, all Rousseau's friends in Paris regard him as " the most gentle, the most sympathetic, and the most gay of creatures inhabiting England." [2] Rousseau hesitated, however, until he had obtained the consent of Lord Marischal. Then, on 4 December, he finally wrote to Hume :

Your goodness affects me as much as it does me honour. The worthiest response that I can make to your offers is to accept them, and I do accept them. I shall leave in five or six days to throw myself into your arms. That is the advice of my Lord Mareschal, my protector, my friend, my father : that is the advice of Mme de Verdelin, whose enlightened goodwill guides me as well as consoles me : finally I dare to say that it is the advice of my heart which is happy in being indebted to the most illustrious of my contemporaries, a man whose goodness surpasses his fame. I sigh for a solitary and free retreat where I may finish my days in peace. If your benevolent solicitude procures it for me, I shall enjoy at once the only blessing that my heart desires and the pleasure of having it from you.

On 9 December Rousseau left Strasbourg in a post-chaise.

---

[1] Extracts taken from fascimile of English draft in HL, at 1, 526.
[2] Rousseau, xiv, 265.

Travelling through France on a special royal passport procured for him by Mme de Verdelin, Rousseau arrived at Paris on the evening of 16 December and lodged in the house of Mme Duchaine, bookseller, rue Saint-Jacques. Within a few days, however, the Prince de Conti extended to him the protection of the Temple with elegant quarters in the Hôtel de Saint-Simon. All Paris was curious to see the celebrated refugee. Bribes were offered Hume to parade his " pupil " at set times. " It is impossible to express or imagine the Enthusiasm of this Nation in his favour," wrote Hume to Blair in sheer delight. " I am perswaded, that were I to open here a Subscription with his Consent, I shoud receive 50,000 Pounds in a fortnight. . . . Voltaire and every body else, are quite eclipsed by him. I am sensible, that my Connexions with him, add to my Importance at present. Even his Maid, La Vasseur, who is very homely and very awkward, is more talkd of than the Princess of Monaco or the Countess of Egmont, on account of her Fidelity and Attachment towards him. His very Dog, who is no better than a Coly, has a Name and Reputation in the World." In actuality Rousseau was accompanied only by his dog, Sultan ; his mistress, Thérèse Le Vasseur, was still in Switzerland, and did not reach Paris until after his departure.

Prior to Rousseau's arrival, Hume had become uneasy over the repeated warnings of the *philosophes* that Rousseau had a suspicious mind, saw persecution where there was none, and always quarrelled with his benefactors. Going straight to Mme de Verdelin, Hume demanded the truth. " I do not want," he told her, " to serve a man merely because he is celebrated. If he is virtuous and persecuted, I would devote myself to him. Are these stories true ? " Reassured of Rousseau's uprightness, Hume proceeded with his plans.[1]

On meeting Rousseau personally, Hume was strongly attracted. " He dotes on his nice little man," it was said ; Mme de Verdelin was convinced that Hume would have thrown anyone out of the window who spoke ill of Rousseau.[2] Gone was Hume's cool and distant appraisal. Whatever his opinion of the writings of Rousseau, the *man* was now his dear friend and would remain so for life. " The Philosophers of Paris fortold to me, that I coud not conduct him to Calais without a Quarrel : but I think I cou'd live with him all my Life, in mutual Friendship and Esteem," he later

---

[1] Rousseau, xv, 185, 255. It is not absolutely certain that this conversation took place before 16 Dec. [2] *Ibid.*, xvi, 93 ; xv, 186.

confided to Blair. His first impressions of Rousseau, also in a letter to Blair, bear out this enthusiasm :

As to my Intercourse with him, I find him mild, and gentle and modest and good humoured ; and he has more the Behaviour of a Man of the World than any of the Learned here, except M. de Buffon. . . . M. Rousseau is of small Stature ; and wou'd rather be ugly, had he not the finest Physiognomony in the World, I mean, the most expressive Countenance. His Modesty seems not to be good Manners ; but Ignorance of his own Excellence : As he writes and speaks and acts from the Impulse of Genius, more than from the Use of his ordinary Faculties, it is very likely that he forgets its Force, whenever it is laid asleep. I am well assurd, that at times he believes he has Inspirations from an Immediate Communication with the Divinity : He falls sometimes into Ecstacies which retain him in the same Posture for Hours together. Does not this Example solve the Difficulty of Socrates's Genius and of his Ecstacies ? I think Rousseau in many things very much resembles Socrates : The Philosopher of Geneva seems only to have more Genius than he of Athens, who never wrote any thing ; and less Sociableness and Temper. Both of them were of very amorous Complexions : But a Comparison in this particular turns out much to the Advantage of my Friend : I call him such ; for I hear from all hands that his Judgement and Affections are as strongly byass'd in my favour as mine are in his : I shall much regreat the leaving him in England.

In his capacity of philosopher of human nature, Hume was doing his utmost to comprehend the complex personality of Rousseau. It is clear that on an intellectual plane he was doing well enough, but it is not so clear that he would be able to adapt himself to the personality of the man. For, despite the stories told him by the friends of Rousseau, there is little evidence in the latter's correspondence that he had any warmth of feeling for Hume. He simply did not see that under the bulky exterior, behind the placid countenance, beyond the vacant, scholarly stare, there dwelt a man of feeling. Few casual acquaintances knew this side of Hume, but his intimates did. Mme de Boufflers had gained insight into the man of feeling when in the summer of 1764 he had expressed himself on jealousy in friendship. " I confess with shame," he had told her, " that I am but too subject to this sentiment. . . . I never doubt of my friend's probity or honour; but often of his attachment to me, and sometimes, as I have afterwards found without reason. If such was my disposition even in youth, you may judge that, having arrived at a time of life when I can less expect to please, I must be more subject to inroads of suspicion." The difference between Hume and Rousseau in respect to jealousy lay in the fact that while the former strove earnestly and success- fully to control the emotion, the latter was wont to cherish it. Suspicion of Hume was already in the mind of Rousseau, but smothered under the protestations of common friends. Yet it was not easy for him to forget that Hume was a philosopher of Britain, the friend of the *philosophes* of France, a man who actually liked the *salons* and gay society. After ten days of the society of Paris, Rousseau in desperation sent a piteous plea to M. Jean-Jacques de Luze of Neuchâtel, who was to accompany patron and " pupil " to England. " I do not know how much longer I can endure this public scene," he complained. " Could you, for charity's sake, hasten our departure a little ? " [1] The departure was hastened, not merely for sake of charity, but out of necessity : the Duc de Choiseul had issued an official order for Rousseau to move on.

Doting on Rousseau as he did and as everyone recognised that he did, Hume was not without some embarrassment over his charge. Two incidents were to prove of future significance. The first concerned Horace Walpole, the second Baron d'Holbach ; the one was to have its influence on Rousseau, the other on Hume.

To Walpole, David Hume, like all philosophers, was simply ridiculous ; Jean-Jacques Rousseau, most eccentric of all philosophers, was a " mountebank " and a " hypocrite " and vain of persecution. A man who out of pure ostentation had turned down a pension from the King of Prussia was worthy only of contempt. So the Walpolian ingenuity, perhaps even before 16 December, concocted a feigned letter from that king to the notorious " hypocrite." This " pleasantry " he first tried out one evening at Mme Geoffrin's. Gratified with its reception, he wrote it out the next day, the French later being touched up by Helvétius, the Duc de Nivernais, and President Hénault. Shortly afterwards Walpole repeated it at the dinner-table of Lord Ossory. In its final form the ironical letter reads :

My Dear Jean-Jacques,

You have renounced Geneva, your native soil. You have been driven from Switzerland, a country of which you have made such boast in your writings. In France you are outlawed : come then to me. I admire your talents, and amuse myself with your reveries ; on which however, by the way, you bestow too much time and attention. It is high time to grow prudent and happy ; you have made yourself sufficiently talked of for singularities little becoming a truly great man : show your enemies that you have sometimes common sense : this will vex them without hurting you. My dominions afford you a peaceful retreat : I am desirous to do you good, and will do it, if you can but think it such. But if you are determined to refuse my assistance, you may expect that I shall say not a word about it to any one. If you persist in perplexing your brains to find out new misfortunes, chuse such as you like best ; I am a king and can make you as miserable as you can wish : at the

[1] Rousseau, XIV, 351.

same time, I will engage to do that which your enemies never will, I will cease to persecute you, when you are no longer vain of persecution.

Your sincere friend,
Frederic.[1]

Sardonic wit that he was, however, Walpole was gentleman enough to refrain from meeting Rousseau when all Paris wanted to, " thinking it wrong," as he was to acknowledge, " to go and make a cordial visit to a man, with a letter in my pocket to laugh at him." So far as Hume was concerned, Walpole was also circumspect. Hume happened to have been present at Lord Ossory's when Walpole repeated his jest and perhaps had indicated annoyance over its cruelty. For when Walpole presented a copy of the letter to a lady, he expressly warned her not to show it to Mr Hume " because he dotes on his nice little man ; you would embarrass us." [2] So, although Walpole and Hume were living in the same hotel, Hume never saw a copy of the letter until after he reached London. By that time, Walpole had given out numerous copies, and it was not long before the letter found its way into print. Walpole delighted in the publicity and vaingloriously informed his English correspondents that he had succeeded Hume and Rousseau as the lion of Paris.

While the *philosophes* enjoyed the satire, the friends of Rousseau were scandalised. Mme de Boufflers and the Prince de Conti scolded its perpetrator roundly ; the only effect, beyond boring him immoderately, was that he did suppress two other " pleasantries " about Rousseau that his prolific mind had invented. From London, Hume, though deeply distressed, attempted to smooth things over. Early in February 1766 he wrote to Mme de Boufflers in answer to her inquiry : " I suppose, that by this time you have learned it was Horace Walpole who wrote the Prussian letter you mentioned to me. It is a strange inclination we have to be wits, preferably to every thing else. He is a very worthy man ; he esteems and even admires Rousseau ; yet he could not forbear, for the sake of a very indifferent joke, the turning him into ridicule, and saying harsh things against him. I am a little angry with him ; and I hear you are a great deal : but the matter ought to be treated only as a piece of levity." [3]

The incident concerning Baron d'Holbach occurred on the eve of Hume's departure from Paris. In company with the Abbé Morellet, Hume had dined at the home of Helvétius, thence

---

[1] Hume, *Concise Account* (London 1766), pp. 20-1.   [2] Rousseau, xvi, 93.
[3] For a discussion of the interpretation of the *affaire*, see Appendix F.

proceeding to the Hôtel de Saint-Simon for a visit of two hours with Mme de Boufflers and Jean-Jacques. To his " pupil " Hume was all tenderness and complaisance. The final call, at about nine in the evening, was at Baron d'Holbach's. Full of kindly feelings, Hume babbled on about his hopes, not only to free " the little man " from persecution, but also to make him happy forever. The Baron listened quietly but was not impressed by his guest's fervour. " I am sorry to dispel the hopes and illusions that flatter you," he remarked gravely ; " but I tell you that it will not be long before you are grievously undeceived. You don't know your man. I tell you plainly, you're warming a viper in your bosom." David and the Abbé expostulated in vain. And David left the house with the Baron's words ringing in his ears, " You don't know your man, David, you don't know your man." [1]

Coming events cast their shadows before. The Walpole letter would come to the attention of Rousseau, and Rousseau, recalling his latent suspicions of Hume, would see in it a conspiracy of his patron with the *philosophes.* Facing such a fantastic accusation, Hume would recall the words of the Baron and would acknowledge them as truth. Whatever happened in England, the seeds of misunderstanding were already planted in fertile soils.

Preparations for the trip were finally completed. As a cautionary measure, 2 January 1766 was given out publicly as the date of departure, two days in advance of actual departure. Before leaving Paris, Jean-Jacques received a farewell note from Mme de Verdelin, pronouncing her benediction upon the newly consecrated friendship : " I have just seen D. Hume. I commended to him your welfare. He is worthy of the trust. The more I listen to him, the more I admire his candour. His soul is made for yours." [2]

The morning of the 4th, young Robert Liston, who was dying of curiosity to see the famous Jean-Jacques but diffident of disturbing him, posted himself near the Hôtel de Saint-Simon :

After waiting an hour or two in a Coffee-house opposite, I saw Mr. Hume come out and go toward the chaise. Now, thought I, now is the time. I run out and get as near as possible. But behold ! no Rousseau appeared. David observed me, and expressed some surprise at seeing me there.

" I am just come to have a peep at Jean-Jacques," says I : " I beg you'll not take any notice of me, but let me stare in full liberty."

" No, no, you shall go in and I'll present you to him."

" I'd rather not, I've nothing to say to him, and he's so shy."

[1] Morellet, *Mémoires* (Paris 1821), i, 105–06 : Marmontel, *Mémoires* (Paris 1891), ii, 257.   [2] Rousseau, xv, 5–6.

" Well, but we'll perhaps be long before we're ready : you shall at least go in, and sit in an antichamber where you'll see him at your ease." Saying this he pulled me in by the arm.

I waited in a parlour and when said famous personage came through carrying out a bundle to his chaise, I made him a low bow which he returned. Mr. Hume in the inner room, while Rousseau was absent, had told the Countess of Boufflers (a very famous woman and a great protectress of men of learning) that I was in the antichamber, and my motives for coming. She came out immediatly, commended my curiosity, made me some compliments, and insisted upon introducing me to Jean-Jacques. So when he came back she and Mr. Hume together presented me to him. I can't enter into the particulars of our Conversation,—but upon the whole he received me very well. I was about an hour there, saw him dine, and had the Honour to help him into the Chaise. He said he would be glad to crack with me when I came to England, &c.

His person is very thin & delicate looking, his face, and especially his sharp black Eyes promise every thing he has shown himself possessed of. His manners simple and affable.[1]

The travellers used two post-chaises, Hume's and de Luze's, Rousseau and Sultan alternating from one to the other. To avoid mishaps the carriages kept close together and proceeded leisurely. The party arrived at Calais on the 8th, having spent nights en route at Senlis, Roye, Arras, and Aine.

At Senlis the travellers were forced to share an inn-room with three beds. In the middle of the night Rousseau heard—or fancied or dreamed that he heard—Hume calling out in French in a loud voice, " Je tiens Jean-Jacques Rousseau, Je tiens Jean-Jacques Rousseau," over and over again. De Luze slept undisturbed. Shivering in mortal terror, Rousseau broke out into a cold sweat. The innocent phrases of Mme de Verdelin had somehow failed to soothe his tortured spirit ; the seeds of suspicion had taken root. Rousseau was not able to forget that night at Senlis.[2]

Detained at Calais by contrary winds, Hume seized the opportunity to broach a delicate subject, one that had been in the back of his mind since 1762. Would Jean-Jacques accept a pension from the King of England ? The fact that he had refused one from Frederick the Great, argued Hume, need prove no obstacle, because in England, unlike Prussia, he would be completely free and independent. Jean-Jacques was reluctant to commit himself, but finally told David that if the offer was actually made, he would

1 In NLS, MS 5517, f. 22. Reprinted in Mossner, " Rousseau Hero-Worship," in *Modern Language Notes*, LV (1940), 449–51.
2 There is some question as to whether the incident took place at Senlis or at Roye. Twice Rousseau (xv, 227 ; xvi, 90) names Roye ; but De Luze as quoted by Du Peyrou (Rousseau, xvi, 105–06) indicates that only at Senlis did all three sleep together. Hume himself recognised that Rousseau referred to Senlis (see NHL, p. 151).

have to get the approval of his " father," Lord Marischal. To Hume, of course, this could only mean tacit acceptance and he rejoiced to have the future welfare of his " pupil " assured so soon.

Hume was also pleased to find that Rousseau was engaged in a new literary enterprise. " I exhorted him on the road," he informed Mme de Boufflers, " to write his Memoirs. He told me, that he had already done it with an intention of publishing them. At present, says he, it may be affirmed, that nobody knows me perfectly any more than himself : but I shall describe myself in such plain colours, that henceforth every one may boast that he knows himself and Jean-Jacques Rousseau." Hume's study of the personality of Rousseau, however, had progressed to the stage where he could not accept the last statement. So, he added critically, " I believe that he intends seriously to draw his own picture in its true colours : but I believe at the same time that nobody knows himself less."

On the evening of 9 January the three travellers finally embarked. The crossing was rough and took twelve hours. Hume, as always at sea, was desperately sick and sought the refuge of his cabin. Rousseau, though somewhat squeamish, stayed on deck in the icy blasts during most of the night. Everyone was relieved to be at Dover in the morning. In a transport of joy on reaching the land of freedom, Jean-Jacques silently threw his arms around David's neck, covering his face with kisses and bathing it in tears.

London was not reached until the 13th, the nights en route having been spent at Canterbury and Dartford. London proved another Paris, although Hume drew the nice distinction between the " Enthusiasm " of Paris and the " Curiosity " of London. English curiosity was especially aroused by Rousseau's outlandish costume, a caftan, which he had assumed, he told Hume, because " he has had an Infirmity from his Infancy, which makes Breeches inconvenient for him." The London crowds gaped at the little, stooped foreigner dressed in a fur cap and a long purple robe, trimmed and lined with dark fur. As a special favour to Hume, Rousseau sat to a portrait in oils by Allan Ramsay. The King himself suggested that engravings should be made, and Hume and Ramsay distributed them among Rousseau's friends in Paris. The painting itself was presented to Hume by the artist. At about the same time, Ramsay also painted the portrait of Hume now in the Scottish National Portrait Gallery in Edinburgh.

George III desired to get an informal glimpse of the much-persecuted philosopher concerning whose pension overtures had already been made to him. So Hume arranged to produce Rousseau at the Drury Lane Theatre. At the last moment the plan almost miscarried because Rousseau was afraid that Sultan might run off and get lost. At Hume's suggestion he was locked up, but his master could not bear to hear him howl. With some difficulty Hume remained calm. " I caught him in my arms," he wrote to the Marquise de Barbentane, " and told him, that Mrs Garrick had dismissed another company in order to make room for him ; that the King and Queen were expecting to see him ; and without a better reason than Sultan's impatience, it would be ridiculous to disappoint them. Partly by these reasons and partly by force, I engaged him to proceed."

Garrick placed Rousseau in a box opposite the King and Queen. " I observed their Majestys to look at him," said Hume, " more than at the Players." Indeed, everyone wanted to see Jean-Jacques. " The crowd was so great at getting into the Theatre," according to a newspaper account, " that a great number of Gentlemen lost their hats and wigs, and Ladies their Cloaks, bonnets, &c." After the performance at a supper given in his honour by Garrick, Rousseau complimented the actor, saying, " Sir, you have made me shed tears at your Tragedy, and smile at your Comedy, though I scarce understand a word of your language." [1] So enthralled had Rousseau been by Garrick's performance that he had hung over the front of the box ; and Mrs Garrick, fearful that he might fall down into the pit, had felt obliged to hold on to his clothes.

The crowds and the turmoil of London were making Rousseau increasingly fretful. Princes, lords and ladies, men of letters, admirers all, found their way to the house of Mrs Adams, York Buildings, Buckingham Street, next door to John Stewart's. Over at the Misses Elliots' in Lisle Street, Leicester Fields, David's customary lodging-house in London, were staying his Scottish friend, William Rouet, and the young François Tronchin, son of Rousseau's arch enemy in Geneva. Rousseau reacted violently to the very name of Tronchin. " He looks upon Tronchin's being here," noted Rouet, " as a spy set by Geneva upon him : and his being accidentally lodged where Hume always used to lodge, (and where he is to come as soon as Rousseau is fixed in the country,) confirms him in this foolish conceit." [2] Here was further reason for Rousseau to leave London !

[1] *Lloyd's Evening Post*, 24-7 Jan. 1766.   [2] *Caldwell Papers*, PT. II, VOL. II, 63-4.

519 JEAN-JACQUES ROUSSEAU

To find a suitable residence, however, was not so easy. The French farmer's house at Fulham, which Stewart and Elliot had previously arranged for, proved to be small and dirty—" as dirty as a Frenchman's in France," Stewart had warned. Numerous other situations were offered, but each had to be carefully investigated. Hume was determined that Rousseau should not go to a distant and solitary place where he would have little opportunity to learn English and where he would be out of contact with the booksellers. A translation of some documents regarding Rousseau's adventures of 1765 was projected, and Hume was trying to hurry it along. So when Rousseau found the offer of an ancient monastery in Wales romantically appealing, Hume exerted all his influence, even using the name of Mme de Boufflers, to get it rejected. With Rousseau becoming feverish in the great city, however, Hume was compelled on 28 January to settle him temporarily at Chiswick, six miles out in the country on the Thames, where he boarded with a grocer.

Thérèse Le Vasseur, even in her absence, was proving an obstacle to the settlement. Rousseau insisted on equal rights for his mistress, and that she should be permitted to sit at the table with him ; but that was beyond the forbearance of some of the respectable English who would have been honoured to board the distinguished philosopher. " This woman forms the chief encumbrance to his settlement," complained Hume to Mme de Boufflers. " M. de Luze, our companion, says, that she passes for wicked, and quarrelsome, and tattling, and is thought to be the chief cause of his quitting Neufchatel. He himself owns her to be so dull, that she never knows in what year of the Lord she is, nor in what month of the year, nor in what day of the month or week ; and that she can never learn the different value of the pieces of money in any country. Yet she governs him as absolutely as a nurse does a child. In her absence his dog has acquired that ascendant. His affection for that creature is beyond all expression or conception."

The loyalty of Rousseau to Thérèse was not perfectly returned. At Paris where she paused in her journey from Switzerland, she accepted the offer of Hume's friend, James Boswell, who in 1764 had forced his presence upon Jean-Jacques, to escort her to London. In a letter to Mme de Boufflers, Hume accurately predicted the future : " I learn that Mademoiselle sets out post, in company with a friend of mine ; a young gentleman, very good-humoured, very agreeable, and very mad. He visited Rousseau in his mountains, who gave him a recommendation to Paoli, the King of

Corsica ; where this gentleman, whose name is Boswell, went last summer, in search of adventures. He has such a rage for literature, that I dread some event fatal to our friend's honour. You remember the story of Terentia, who was first married to Cicero, then to Sallust, and at last, in her old age, married a young nobleman, who imagined that she must possess some secret, which would convey to him eloquence and genius." On arriving at London on 12 February, Boswell left Thérèse with Hume overnight. The next day, after solemnly swearing to her that he would not reveal their *affaire*—at least while she and Rousseau were alive— Boswell escorted her to Chiswick and delivered her over to the philosopher.[1] Although he shortly became cool to Boswell, there is no positive evidence that Rousseau was ever aware of this very real injury to his honour. If he actually was, however, his subsequent actions might be held more accountable.

Offers to settle Rousseau poured in from most of the counties of England but were rejected for one reason or another. The effervescent Mrs Alison Cockburn urged Hume to bring Rousseau to Scotland : " Sweet old man, he shall sit beneath an oak and hear the Druid's songs. The winds shall bring soft sounds to his ears, and our nymphs with the songs of Selma shall remember him of joys that are past. O bring him with you ; the English are not worthy of him ; I will have him ! " [2] But Hume had not forgotten either the Scottish bigotry or the Scottish climate. A visit to the Surrey hills at the house of Colonel Webb having seemed to please his " pupil," Hume entered into negotiations to purchase the house and grounds—but Rousseau had changed his mind. During the same trip, David and Jean-Jacques visited " The Rookery " near Dorking, the home of Daniel Malthus, where they saw his three-weeks-old son, Thomas Robert, the future economist. Obliged finally to withdraw opposition to Rousseau's settlement in the distant country, Hume permitted him to accept the offer of a suitable house at Wootton in Staffordshire near the border of Derbyshire. The offer came from a wealthy landed gentleman, Richard Davenport of Calveley, hitherto unknown to Hume but a friend of Garrick, Sterne, and others of his acquaintance. Rousseau was joyful over the prospects.

General Conway, through whose good offices the pension was being procured, wished to show an especial mark of distinction to Rousseau by inviting him and Mlle Le Vasseur for dinner before their departure for Wootton. Hume wrote a note to that effect

[1] *Boswell Papers*, vii, 67.   [2] RSE, iv, 30.

on 17 March, and Rousseau answered the same day, declining under pretext of ill health. The real reason was that he was ashamed of displaying Thérèse in such company. The following day Davenport's coach brought the two in from Chiswick to Hume's lodgings in Lisle Street.

Rousseau was in a strange mood, silent and intensely alert. Before dinner he thought that he had detected his host in a complicated manoeuvre to gain possession of a letter that he had been writing. During dinner he sulked, and Hume was forced to give up all attempts at conversation. After dinner, when they were left alone, Hume's disconcerting stare and his enforced silence made Rousseau all the more nervous and irritable. Finally he burst forth—but let the story be given as Hume told it to Blair :

He had resolv'd to set out with his Gouvernante in a Post chaise ; but Davenport, willing to cheat him and save him some Money, told him, that he had found a Retour Chaise for the Place, which he might have for a Trifle, and that luckily, it set out the very day in which Rousseau intended to depart : His Purpose was to hire a Chaise, and make him believe this Story. He succeeded at first ; but Rousseau, afterwards ruminating on the Circumstances, began to entertain a Suspicion of the Trick. He communicated his Doubts to me, complaining that he was treated like a Child, that tho' he was poor he chose rather to conform himself to his Circumstances than live like a Beggar, on alms, and that he was very unhappy in not speaking the Language familiarly, so as to guard himself against these Impositions. I told him, that I was ignorant of the Matter, and knew nothing more of it than I was told by Mr Davenport ; but if he pleas'd I shou'd make Enquiry about it. *Never tell me that,* reply'd he, *if this be really a Contrivance of Davenports, you are acquainted with it, and consenting to it ; and you cou'd not possibly have done me a greater Displeasure.* Upon which he sate down very sullen and silent ; and all my Attempts were in vain to revive the Conversation and to turn it on other Subjects : He still answered me very dryly & coldly. At last, after passing near an Hour in this ill-humour, he rose up and took a Turn about the Room : But Judge of my Surprize, when he sat down suddenly on my Knee, threw his hands about my Neck, kiss'd me with the greatest Warmth, and bedewing all my Face with Tears, exclaim'd, *Is it possible you can ever forgive me, my Dear Friend : After all the Testimonies of Affection I have receivd from you, I reward you at last with this Folly & ill Behaviour ; But I have notwithstanding a Heart worthy of your Friendship : I love you, I esteem you ; and not an Instance of your Kindness is thrown away upon me.* I hope you have not so bad an Opinion of me as to think I was not melted on this Occasion ; I assure you I kissd him and embrac'd him twenty times, with a plentiful Effusion of Tears. I think no Scene of my Life was ever more affecting.

To Mme de Boufflers, Hume repeated the incident, requesting her to tell it only to the ladies in her circle because " I scarce know a male who would not think it childish."

In his own later and substantially different version of the

scene, Rousseau indicates that he had been thinking less of the stratagem of the retour chaise, than of Hume's supposed manoeuvre over the letter, and consequently of his possible treachery. He shivered (" je sens un frémissement inexplicable ") and was forced, he told Mme de Verdelin, to lower his eyes dizzily before the penetrating glances of Hume (" son regard sec ardent moqueur et prolongé "). Swept by a violent emotion even to the verge of fainting, he burst into tears of remorse. Throwing himself into the arms of his patron, he cried out : " No, David Hume is not a traitor ; that is impossible. If he is not the best of men, he must be the blackest." Hume did not get angry but calmly soothed Rousseau, patting him on the back and saying, " My dear Sir ! What is the trouble, my dear Sir ? " More and more aroused because Hume did not demand to know why he had been called a traitor, Jean-Jacques went to bed sick at heart. In the morning, apparently reconciled, he left for Wootton. David and Jean-Jacques were never to see one another again.[1]

Totally unaware of the terrible thoughts seething in the mind of his " nice little man," Hume was relieved at having him so well settled. Unbeknown to Jean-Jacques, Davenport had originally offered the house at Wootton, together with a staff of servants, entirely free ; but on Hume's objection that Rousseau would never accept such generosity, he had good-humouredly agreed to take thirty pounds a year in board. If it turned out that Rousseau was happy at Wootton, Davenport further intended to leave him in his will the life-rent of the house. The matter of the pension was also about to be settled favourably, as Lord Marischal had given his consent. All in all, Hume had good reason to feel entirely satisfied with what he had been able to do for his " pupil."

Hume was not, however, so confident as he had been that he could live all his life with Jean-Jacques without friction. He had discovered, as the result of inquiries instituted before leaving Paris, that Rousseau was not so indigent as he made himself out to be ; but he was willing to regard this affectation as but " one weakness more." The weakness, however, had disconcerting consequences. While still at Chiswick, Rousseau suddenly decided that he would receive no more letters because the postage had cost him more than twenty-five *louis d'or* a year at Neuchâtel, and most of the mail came only from unknown correspondents. So when Hume, who had been receiving his letters in London, brought out a " cargo " of them to Chiswick, Rousseau impatiently directed him to take them

[1] Rousseau, xv, 157 ; HL, ii, 391.

back to the post office. David expostulated that the postal clerks would then open them and learn Jean-Jacques's secrets, which might prove embarrassing to him and to his friends. Thus it was Hume's very solicitude over Rousseau's letters that provided the basis for the absurd charge that he was tampering with them.

The wide difference between Rousseau and himself on the subject of religion had become evident to Hume. " Happening to meet with Hume in the Park " soon after his arrival in London, writes Lord Charlemont, " I wished him Joy of his pleasing Connexion, and particularly hinted that I was convinced He must be perfectly happy in his new Friend, as their Sentiments were, I believed, nearly similar—' Why no, Man,' said He, ' in that you are mistaken. Rousseau is not what you think him. He is indeed a very sensible, and wonderfully ingenious Man, but our Opinions are by no means the Same. He has a hankering after the Bible, and is indeed little better than a Christian in a Way of his own.' " [1]

Hume's experience with Rousseau's recurrent moods and emotional instability had proved enlightening. Could anyone, no matter how well-intentioned, really fathom the man ? To Blair, soon after the departure of Jean-Jacques, David unburdened himself : " This Man, the most singular of all human Beings," he wrote, " has at last left me ; and I have very little hopes of ever being able for the future to enjoy much of his Company : tho' he says, that, if I settle either in London or Edinburgh, he will take a Journey on foot every Year to visit me." The letter continues with a piece of masterly analysis :

He was desperately resolv'd to rush into this Solitude, notwithstanding all my Remonstrances ; and I foresee, that he will be unhappy in that Situation, as he has indeed been always, in all Situations. He will be entirely without Occupation, without Company, and almost without Amusement of any kind. He has read very little during the Course of his Life, and has now totally renounc'd all Reading : He has seen very little, and has no manner of Curiosity to see or remark : He has reflected, properly speaking, and study'd very little ; and has not indeed much Knowlege : He has only felt, during the whole Course of his Life ; and in this Respect, his Sensibility rises to a Pitch beyond what I have seen any Example of : But it still gives him a more acute Feeling of Pain than of Pleasure. He is like a Man who were stript not only of his Cloaths but of his Skin, and turn'd out in that Situation to combat with the rude and boisterous Elements, such as perpetually disturb this lower World.

Hume was right. For at Wootton, in " the Peak of Derby, situated amidst Mountains and Rocks and Streams and Forrests "

[1] Lord Charlemont, " Anecdotes of Hume," in RIA, MS -12/R/7, f. 519.

—to use Hume's description—Rousseau found the seclusion he had been pining for. " There has been a frost ever since I have been here," he exulted to Hume in a letter of 29 March ; " it has snowed every day ; the wind is cutting ; nevertheless, I had rather live in a rabbit-hole of this warren than in the most superb apartment of London." Rousseau was not interested in learning English and sat silent before the visitors who came to pay their compliments. He boasted that he would employ the same tactics even when he knew enough English to be able to carry on a conversation, or he would speak French until the visitors left in despair. Rousseau wanted to be alone because he had carried with him to Wootton the dark suspicions against Hume that could not be suppressed and he wanted time to think about them.

These dark suspicions were, therefore, soon replaced in the morbid thinking of Rousseau by the clear outlines of an international conspiracy against him, a conspiracy headed by David Hume. There is little doubt that Rousseau would have arrived at this conclusion without outside aid ; but the English press inadvertently played into his hands. Rousseau's was a famous name and anything concerning him made good " copy." Friends, as well as the usual busybodies, saw to it that he was supplied with all the requisite clippings.

The vanity of Rousseau was no little hurt by the fact that the press accounts of him were .not consistently favourable. Newspaper stories of his travels through Switzerland and France and of his stays in Paris and London were inaccurate and disposed to give too much credit to the influence and patronage of Hume. The notorious King-of-Prussia letter was printed with no indication of the real author. In advance, Rousseau had first suspected that it was from Geneva, then from Voltaire ; but now on reading it, he was as positive as if he had actually watched him writing it, that it was from D'Alembert. As for Walpole—why, he had only permitted his name to be used as a screen to protect Rousseau's enemies, the *philosophes !* *A Letter from Mr. Voltaire to Mr. Jean Jacques Rousseau* was published, which contained a shrewd prophecy of Rousseau's reception in " the country of fine women and true philosophers " ; what particularly excited the attention of Rousseau was the omission of Hume's name, from which omission he concluded that Hume was in league with Voltaire. Anonymous squibs came out by the score, some of which Rousseau was convinced could only have come from Hume, or at least from information supplied by Hume.

Before the end of March Rousseau's letters to his friends were already full of veiled statements of the treachery of his patron. The first fully developed account of the " conspiracy " appeared on 10 April in a letter to Mme de Verdelin. But already three days previous Rousseau had broken out publicly by writing to the editor of the *St. James's Chronicle*, where the King-of-Prussia letter had first appeared, complaining that that letter had really been fabricated in Paris and adding darkly, " what rends and afflicts my heart . . . the imposter has his accomplices in England."

From then on nothing could halt Rousseau's campaign against Hume, not even the admonitions of his " father " and Mme de Verdelin. Both were deeply shocked at his accusations. What possible motive could Hume have to injure him? What about the well-known character of *le bon David*? Was it not clear that all the evidence of Hume's " treachery " could be interpreted in a favourable as well as in an unfavourable light? Above all, how could Hume's success in obtaining a pension of £100 a year from the King of England be interpreted as defamation? All arguments were in vain. The campaign against Hume, a series of " slaps in the face," proceeded according to plan.

The first " slap in the face " of his patron was the breaking off of correspondence with him. This step failed to arouse Hume because of their prior agreement not to burden one another in that respect. The second " slap in the face " was the open letter in the *St. James's Chronicle*. This step equally failed to arouse Hume because, as an honest man, he simply had no notion of what Rousseau was hinting at so obliquely. The " third slap in the face " was a letter of 12 May to General Conway, declining the pension in terms of the utmost ambiguity and complaining of a grievous calamity that had overtaken him. Finally Hume was aroused, not because of the rudeness in writing to Conway instead of to himself, but because of the seeming irresponsibility of declining a pension which had previously been accepted. Of the alleged grievous calamity Hume, of course, could make nothing at all.

Yet even after this third " slap," embarrassing as it was to the King of England, General Conway, Lord Marischal, and himself, Hume strove to maintain his equanimity. To Mme de Boufflers, however, he could admit his vexation : " Was ever any thing in the world so unaccountable? For the purpose of life and conduct, and society, a little good sense is surely better than all the genius, and a little good humour than this extreme sensibility." To Rousseau, Hume addressed on 17 May a calm and conciliatory letter, encouraging him to reconsider the refusal of the pension and apologising in the name of Horace Walpole for the offensive King-of-Prussia letter. A month later on 19 June, having had no response, he wrote again with a new proposal about the pension. The King had originally stipulated that the pension should remain secret, a provision that both Lord Marischal and Hume had imagined would be entirely satisfactory to Rousseau. After further study of the letter of refusal, however, General Conway and Hume came to the conclusion that Rousseau was piqued over the secrecy. With Conway's consent, therefore, Hume inquired whether Rousseau would accept a public pension. The General only insisted that acceptance be made in advance, " that His Majesty may not be exposed to a Second Refusal."

Still no reply from Rousseau. " Were he not the most unaccountable Man in the World," protested Hume to Davenport, " I shoud be very much scandalized and very much offended at this long Silence." Finally at the insistence of Davenport, Rousseau wrote to Hume on 23 June " the last letter you will receive from me," charging him with the lie direct : " You brought me to England, ostensibly to procure a haven for me, but actually to dishonour me."

To such a baseless and cruel accusation, how was an honourable man to react ? Stupefaction gave way to indignation, indignation to anger, and the anger became tinged with fear. " You and you alone," Hume implored Davenport, " can aid me in the most critical Affair, which during the Course of my whole Life, I have been engaged in." Hume was angry at the utter falsity of the charge ; he was fearful of the eloquent writer making it, a man who corresponded with friends all over Europe and who was engaged in writing his memoirs for purposes of publication. The clouds of vicious scandal might envelop even truth and the integrity of a lifetime be shattered by a lie !

In this spirit Hume recalled the warnings of Baron d'Holbach and his own innocent exultation of 6 March that they had not been fulfilled.[1] Now he could only admit his tragic and fearful mistake : " You are quite right, Monsieur le Baron, Rousseau is a monster " ; " the Blackest and most atrocious Villain that Ever disgraced human nature " ; " the lying, the ferocity, of the Rascal." [2]

---

[1] Hume's letter is not extant, but is referred to in Holbach's reply of 16 Mar. (RSE, v, 74).

[2] Hume wrote two letters to Holbach, 27 June and 1 July, neither of which is extant. The first quotation is found in Marmontel, *Mémoires*, II, 258 ; the other two in a letter of 7 July from Mme de Meinières to Hume (RSE, III, 47).

On 26 June, the day of receiving the accusation, Hume wrote twice to Rousseau's host, both at Wootton and at Davenport. He besought that gentleman to deliver an enclosed letter to Rousseau, after reading it himself, and to engage him to reply. Charitably assuming that he had been calumniated by a third party, Hume demanded to know the particulars and to be given the opportunity to refute them. " As an innocent Man ; I will not say, as your Friend ; I will not say, as your Benefactor ; but I repeat it, as an innocent Man, I claim the Privilege of proving my Innocence, and of refuting any scandalous Lye which may have been invented against me."

Davenport found Rousseau's accusation " an heap of confusion of which I can make neither head nor tail ; his letter to you," he goes on, " is perfectly astonishing, never any thing, was, so furious, so—I protest I dont know what to call it." After a long conference with Rousseau, Davenport extorted the promise of a specification of the charges but departed even more confused. " I am Really Sorry for him," he benignly acknowledged to Hume, " he's uneasy, frets perpetually & looks terribly—Tis almost impossible to conceive the odness of his extreme Sensibility, so that I conclude when he's Guilty of an error, his nerves are more in fault, than his heart. Things vex him, to the utmost extent of vexation which would not even move such a dull Soul as mine is. In Short I perceive his disorder is Jealousy, he thinks you are fond of some Savant Hommes, who he unfortunately thinks his Enemy's." [1]

Little imagining that Rousseau would—or, rather, could—specify charges against him and convinced that " this is a deliberate and a cool plan to stab me," Hume looked to his defences. The true facts must be placed on record to be available if needed. There was now no possibility of suppression of the break between " pupil " and patron. London and Paris were already ringing with rumours. So Hume carefully gathered together the documents of the case and connected them into a brief narrative. Lord Hertford and General Conway urged immediate publication. Hume hesitated but considered private publication with distribution of a few copies to those primarily implicated.

" I have never seen anything like it," wrote Mme de Boufflers acidly to Rousseau after receiving a copy of his " outrageous letter " to Hume. " All your friends are in consternation and reduced to silence. . . . Mr. Hume a dastard ! a traitor ! Great God ! . . . Madame la Maréschale de Luxembourg and I

[1] RSE, IV, 54–5 ; printed in NHL, Appendix A.

impatiently await your explanations of this incomprehensible conduct. I pray you, Sir, do not defer them, so that we may at least know how to excuse you, if you cannot be completely vindicated. The silence into which we are forced blackens you more than anything else." [1]

Always unexpected, Rousseau had already on 10 July answered Hume's demands for particulars. Though opening, " I am sick, Sir, and little able to write," the letter goes on in a very small and precise hand for eighteen folio pages. On 15 July, Hume informed Blair :

> I receiv'd a Letter from him, which is perfect Frenzy : It woud make a good eighteen-penny Pamphlet ; and I fancy he intends to publish it. He there tells me, that D'Alembert, Horace Walpole and I had from the first enterd into a Combination to ruin him ; and had ruin'd him : That the first Suspicion of my Treachery arose in him, while we lay together in the same Room of an Inn in France : I there spoke in my Sleep and betray'd my Intention of ruining him : That young Troncin lodg'd in the same House with me at London ; and Annie Elliot [the housekeeper] lookd very coldly at him as he went by her in the Passage : That I am also in a close Confederacy with Lord Lyttleton, who he hears is his mortal Enemy : That the English Nation were very fond of him on his first Arrival ; but that Horace Walpole & I had totally alienated them from him. He owns, however, that his Belief of my Treachery went no higher than Suspicion while he was in London ; but it rose to Certainty after he arrivd in the Country : For that there were several Publications in the Papers against him, which coud have proceeded from no body but me or my Confederate Horace Walpole. The rest is all of a like Strain, intermix'd with many Lyes and much Malice. I own, that I was very anxious about this Affair but this Letter has totally reliev'd me.

This " last mad letter " brought immediate relief to Hume because it excluded his first fear of " a deliberate and a cool plan " to stab him. Rousseau, he now recognised, was not a villain but a madman. " I am the most unhappy of human beings if you are guilty ; I am the vilest if you are innocent," Rousseau had written Hume. But he had misconceived the issue, which was not truly one of morality. The issue was not of Rousseau's sincerity, for of course he was sincere. Granted his extreme sensibility, his persecution mania, his candid admission that " I know only what I feel," the malignant whisperings of Thérèse Le Vasseur, the course of publications in the English journals, Hume's emotional inarticulateness in expressing affection, the basic inability of the two philosophers to understand one another in social intercourse— granted all these facts, Rousseau's letter is consistent with the complete logical consistency of dementia. It remains one of the

---

[1] Rousseau, xv, 350-1.

most brilliant and fascinating documents ever produced by a disordered mentality.

Upon receipt of Rousseau's letter of 10 July, Hume owned to Davenport, " I am really sorry for him ; so that, tho' I intended to be very severe on him in my Answer, I have been very sparing; as you may see. . . . I am afraid indeed you have a very bad Pennyworth of him ; but if I may venture to give my Advice, it is, that you wou'd continue the charitable Work you have begun, till he be shut up altogether in Bedlam, or till he quarrel with you and run away from you. If he show any Disposition to write me a penitenial Letter, you may encourage it ; not that I think it of any Consequence to me, but because it will ease his Mind and set him at rest."

Hume's last letter to Rousseau, dated 22 July, did not accept the latter's challenge as laid down : " If you are guilty, do not write to me any more ; that would be useless, and surely you will not deceive me. If you are innocent, deign to justify yourself." Hume confined himself to straightening out the facts of the much disputed " Conversation between us the Evening before your Departure." Rousseau, after relating how he had relapsed into giddiness when attempting to outstare Hume, had demanded : " The external features and the demeanour of *le bon David* denote a good man : but where, Great God, did this good man get those eyes with which he transfixes his friends ? " Hume rested content to remind his lost friend that many studious men are subject to " Reveries or Fits of Absence, without being exposed to such Suspicions." In writing these words, did Hume, one wonders, recall D'Alembert's prophecy that his unsociable stare would one day play him a nasty trick ? Lady Stanhope, when she heard of the incident, remarked to Hume, " I thought I saw you in one of your brown studies." [1]

The question of publication by Hume remained unsettled. His most intimate friends were opposed—Hugh Blair, Mme de Boufflers, Adam Smith, Lord Marischal. The last advised, " It will be good and humane of you, and like *le bon David* not to answer ; which you say is your own opinion." The Parisian group, though at first in agreement, ultimately changed their counsel, as D'Alembert, the spokesman, informed Hume on 21 July : " The public is now too much concerned with your quarrel, and things have advanced too far for you not to give them the plain unvarnished facts." Hume, therefore, completed his narrative

[1] RSE, vii, 45.

and had three copies made, one for D'Alembert, one for Lord Hertford, and one for himself. " It is nothing to dispute my Style or my Abilities as an Historian or a Philosopher," he wrote in explanation of this step ; " My Books ought to answer for themselves, or they are not worth the defending : To fifty Writers, who have attacked me on this head, I never made the least Reply : But this is a different Case : Imputations are here thrown on my Morals and my Conduct."

The King and Queen read the narrative at their own request and, according to Hume, entertained " the same sentiments that must strike everyone." D'Alembert, who had been granted discretionary powers, elected to publish. In October there appeared in Paris, under the joint editorship of D'Alembert and Suard, *Exposé succinct de la contestation qui s'est élévée entre M. Hume et M. Rousseau, avec les pièces justicatives.* An anonymous preface extolled the character of *le bon David* and a signed postscript by D'Alembert denied Rousseau's charge that he had been implicated in the King-of-Prussia letter. An English translation was brought out at London in November as *A Concise and Genuine Account of the Dispute between Mr. Hume and Mr. Rousseau ; with the Letters That Passed between Them during their Controversy. As Also, the Letters of the Hon. Mr. Walpole, and Mr. D'Alembert, Relative to This Extraordinary Affair.*[1]

The original documents were sent to the British Museum by Hume with a note of explanation to Dr Maty, the librarian : " As M. Rousseau had wrote to several of his Correspondents abroad, that I never dared to publish the Letters, which he had wrote me ; or if I published them, they wou'd be so falsify'd, that they wou'd not be the same, I was obliged to say in my Preface that the Originals wou'd be consigned to the Museum : I hope that you have no Objection to the receiving them. . . . I own," he added, " that I never in my Life took a Step with so much Reluctance as the consenting to that Publication : but as it appeared absolutely necessary to all my Friends at Paris, I cou'd not withstand their united Opinion." After the lapse of three months Maty replied that the trustees of the Museum did not think it proper to accept the manuscripts.[2]

" Thanks to God," exclaimed Hume to Mme de Boufflers in

---

[1] The MS which Hume sent D'Alembert is NLS 5722. For a careful exposition of the alterations made by D'Alembert and of the relations between the French and English printed versions, see P. M. Meyer, " The Manuscript of Hume's Account of His Dispute with Rousseau," in *Comparative Literature*, IV (1952), 341–50.

[2] Now in RSE.

December, " my affair with Rousseau is now finally and totally at an end, at least on my part : for I never surely shall publish another line on that subject." No more he did. In November George Deyverdun, an unknown young Swiss living in London, informed Hume that he had written the two satires in the *St. James's Chronicle* which Rousseau had insisted came from Hume.[1] Disregarding Deyverdun's offer to make public acknowledgment, Hume forwarded a copy of the letter to Davenport with the request that it be turned over to Rousseau.[2]

The world was now free to come to its own conclusions with respect to the quarrel between the two famous men. In general, the world agreed that Hume had acted the part of a benevolent and virtuous friend and many would have been willing to go along with the opinion of the Marquis de Chastellux that " David Hume can do no wrong."[3] From both friends and the public, however, there arose considerable criticism of Hume's alleged cruelty in having printed the *Concise Account.* " I forsaw," he ruefully acknowledged, " that many wou'd doubt of the Propriety of my Conduct : But I was told, that many, from want of Information, believed me to have been a Calumniator and a false perfidious Friend. You will own, that there was no Proportion between the one blame & the other."[4]

In retrospect Hume regarded " this whole Adventure . . . as a Misfortune in my Life." Yet only two actions of his in the whole unhappy affair did he have any real reason to regret, both of which occurred after the rupture so painstakingly brought on by Rousseau. The first was his intemperate language in immediate reaction to the " outrageous letter " of 23 June. Hume's justification is that, at the moment, he regarded the accusation of perfidy as a deliberate attempt to stab him, to ruin him in the eyes of the world ; and to the charge of traitor, he, therefore, returned *monster, villain,* and *rascal.* The second action of Hume's, and in a sense the necessary sequel of the first, was the publication of the *Concise Account.* His justification of this step has just been seen. Assured of his innocence, the world may charitably wish that Hume had preserved silence—but would the world be so

---

[1] RSE, IV, 74. Deyverdun, a friend of Gibbon, states that he had never met Hume. They were shortly to become acquainted, however, when Hume became Under-Secretary of State to Conway, in whose office Deyverdun was employed as a minor clerk.

[2] An unpublished note (HL, II, 116–17), prepared for a possible second edition of the *Concise Account* alludes to Deyverdun's letter but without naming him.

[3] RSE, IV, 22.   NHL, p. 156.

assured had he not published? The question is by no means academic.

David Hume was proud of his reputation for goodness of character and jealous of any aspersions cast upon it. As a philosopher he might conceivably have been expected to hold himself above mere worldly opinion; but as a man he recognised that there are limits to benevolence. *Le bon David*, after all, was no saint. He might well have credited himself, however, with having attained " the sentiment of benevolence in an eminent degree," a state which as philosopher he regarded as the highest mark of merit which can be earned by a human being.[1] After the event, it is certain that Hume was remorseful, and it is significant that in *My Own Life* no mention is made of the quarrel.

Jean-Jacques Rousseau, for his part, never gave up his intuition of an international conspiracy and his sense of persecution. " If I knew that Mr Hume would not be unmasked before his death," he protested to Mme de Verdelin in August 1766, " I should find it difficult to retain belief in Providence." [2] Rousseau's letter of 10 July had worked up to an impassioned and heartrending series of " Yes, Mr Hume, you have me." Alone at Wootton during the succeeding months, he was slowly coming to the conviction that he was actually suffering imprisonment. It was only a question of time until he would be prepared to make a frantic break for freedom. Always he remained unaware that the trammels in which he was caught were the trammels of his own mind and that from them there was no escape.

---

[1] *Phil. Wks.*, IV, 179.   [2] Rousseau, XVI, 35.

CHAPTER 36

UNDER-SECRETARY OF STATE

" I am now, from a Philosopher, degenerated into a petty Statesman."

HAVING left France at the completion of his diplomatic mission primarily to report to the King, Hume was early disillusioned. " I find," he informed Mme de Boufflers in February 1766, " that I might have spared myself the trouble of a journey to London, and that other foreign ministers, of a higher rank, have, without scruple, remained in the place of their mission." For some months after his arrival reports circulated that he would return to Paris as Embassy Secretary or as Chargé d'affaires, and also that he would receive a " Commission of Importance to Genoa." [1] The subject of these reports remained unconcerned but was becoming noticeably restive in London.

The " miserable affair " with Rousseau had detained him in the city during the summer, pending the publication of the *Concise Account*. Week after week, and on one pretext or another, the projected visit to Paris had been postponed ; but, in any event, Hume wished first to see his friends in Scotland. Hugh Blair wrote urging his return to Edinburgh : " We would even be content to bear a little persecution for the sake of it. *Usque ad aras*, is the word." Mrs Alison Cockburn roguishly inquired : " But what shall we do with you ? You are spoiled, it's impossible for me to retain you. I am a Christian, I neither paint nor fricassy. My wit is much abated, but I can play at quadrille and sleep with you. Will that do ? " [2]

Despite all the friendly persuasion, however, it was not until the middle of September that Hume was finally able to leave London and to go down to Ninewells. A few weeks later he was back at the " house " in James's Court, which his sister had taken over from Blair the previous Whitsunday. At Edinburgh Hume met with a royal welcome, the tone of which was happily caught by Mrs Cockburn : " I am truly glad to get David home again ; he's a very old friend, and I've long had a habit of liking him and being diverted with him." [3]

[1] *Lloyd's Evening Post*, 28 Feb., 7 Apr., 27 June 1766.
[2] RSE, III, 56 ; IV, 30.
[3] *Letters and Memorials of Mrs. Alison Cockburn*, ed. T. Craig-Brown (Edinburgh 1900), p. 58.

In the warm glow of friendship and relaxation from politics and controversy, Hume basked content. The announcement of Mme de Boufflers that the Prince de Conti was fitting up an apartment for him in the Temple fell on deaf ears. The reading of books had more appeal than the writing of books. Imperceptibly Hume drifted back " to the same view as formerly of burying myself in a philosophical retreat. I returned [to Edinburgh]," he acknowledges in his autobiography, " not richer, but with much more money and a much larger Income by means of Lord Hertford's Friendship, than I left it ; and I was desirous of trying what Superfluity coud produce, as I had formerly made an Experiment of a Competency."

London could hold little temptation to a man who believed that there he was " hated as a Scotsman and despisd as a Man of Letters." [1] Yet back in London he was shortly, the reluctant victim of a sense of gratitude and obligation to Lord Hertford. For Hertford had resigned as Lord Lieutenant of Ireland to become Lord Chamberlain at the Royal Court. His brother, General Conway, had moved from the Southern to the Northern Department of the Secretary of State, the Duke of Richmond inheriting the Southern. The resignation of William Burke, who followed his " cousin " Edmund into opposition early in February 1767, left vacant the Under-Secretaryship in the Northern Department. Hertford at once nominated David Hume, and Conway, who had been favourably impressed with his dispatches as Chargé d'affaires and who had become friendly with him over the matter of Rousseau's pension, was more than willing. Hertford himself wrote the letter of invitation to Hume, and Lady Hertford was prevailed upon by Horace Walpole to write a second letter, " more pressing than her Lord's." [2]

" I sate down," confessed Hume to Mme de Boufflers, " once or twice, to excuse myself ; but I own could not find terms to express my refusal of a request by persons, to whose friendship I had been so much obliged." He further explained that " I foresaw also, that a place was offered me of great credit and confidence ; that it connected me with General Conway, one of the best men, in every respect, of this country ; and that my continuance in place was likely to be very short, both because of the usual fluctuations of power in this country, and because the General, I know, was only waiting an opportunity of returning from the civil, to his usual military line."

[1] NHL, p. 155.   [2] Walpole, *Memoirs of George III*, II, 294–5.

So it was that on 20 February 1767 [1] David Hume was in London once again, " a banished man in a strange country," as he ruefully remarked, " a Philosopher, degenerated into a petty Statesman. . . ." Despite his misgivings, however, his tenure of office, which was to last for eleven months, did not prove unhappy. He had work to do, but not too much. He had hosts of friends and admirers, and few outspoken enemies. The Rousseau *affaire* inexorably played itself out to the conclusion that Hume himself had foreseen.

After the appearance of the *Concise Account* the public press had flamed anew. Shortly before leaving Edinburgh Hume had told Mme de Boufflers : " Agreeably to the license of this country, there has been a great deal of raillery on the incident, thrown out in the public papers, but all against that unhappy man. There is even a print engraved of it : M. Rousseau is represented as a Yahoo, newly caught in the woods ; I am represented as a farmer, who caresses him and offers him some oats to eat, which he refuses in a rage ; Voltaire and D'Alembert are whipping him up behind ; and Horace Walpole making him horns of *papier maché*. The idea is not altogether absurd." This print of *The Savage Man*, unknown to Hume, had been designed by his young madcap friend Boswell. Not all of the squibs, however, were against Rousseau. Some of those against Hume were so scurrilous that William Rouat at London thought it best not to forward copies to Edinburgh. He did, however, ask Baron Mure to tell Hume this fact—" that a certain lady, of very high rank and distinction, parted with child last week, and told Sir John Pringle, that this was entirely owing to the brusquerie of a puppy at her table, throwing out some impertinent reflections against Mr. Hume, and in favour of R[ousseau]. This he told me as a truth ; and indeed, it is literally true. What misfortunes do these disputes among philosophers involve poor mortals in ! " [2]

Rousseau, as Hume was informed in London by General Conway, had recently permitted Davenport to apply in his name for the royal pension, but on the express condition that Hume would have nothing to do with its granting. Conway would make no move, however, without Hume's full approbation, which was immediately forthcoming. The transaction was soon concluded, the General officially informing Davenport on 18 March. Yet before he received the initial payment, Rousseau took his own capricious course of action, the full story of which is related by Hume to Turgot.

---

[1] *Caldwell Papers*, PT. II, VOL. II, 108.   [2] *Ibid.*, p. 104.

I know not, whether you have heard of the late Incidents which have happened to the poor unfortunate Rousseau, who is now plainly delirious and an Object of the greatest Compassion. About three Weeks ago, he ran off, without giving the least Warning, from Mr Davenport's, carrying only his Gouvernante along with him, leaving most of his Baggage, and above thirty Guineas of Money : There was also a Letter found on his table, abusing his Land-lord, and reproaching him as an Accomplice with me in the Project of ruining and affronting him. He took the Road towards London ; and Mr. Davenport begged me to find him out, and to discover how his Money and Baggage might be sent after him. He was never heard of for a fortnight ; till at last a most extravagant Letter of his was delivered to the Chancellor, dated at Spalding in the County of Lincoln. He there tells the Magistrate that he was on his Road to Dover, in order to leave the Kingdom (tho' Spalding is entirely out of the Road). But he dares not proceed a Step farther, not stir out of the House ; for fear of his Enemies : He entreats therefore the Chancellor to send him an authorized Guide to conduct him : and this he demands as the last Act of Hospitality from the Nation towards him. A few days after, I learned from Mr Davenport that he had received a new Letter from Rousseau dated still at Spalding, in which he expresses great Contrition, speaks of his miserable and unhappy Condition, and marks his Intention of returning to his former Retreat at Wootton. I was then hopeful, that he had now recovered his Senses ; when behold ! a few hours after, General Conway received a Letter from him dated at Dover above two hundred Miles distant from Spalding : This great Journey he had made in about two days. Nothing can be more frenzical than this Letter : He supposes himself to be a Prisoner of State in the hands of the General at my Suggestion, entreats for Leave to depart the Kingdom, represents the Danger of assassinating him in private, and while he owns that he has been rendered infamous in England during his Life he fortells that his Memory will be justifyed after his Death. He says that he has composed a Volume of Memoirs, chiefly with regard to the Treatment he has met with in England, and the State of Captivity, in which he has been detained ; and if the General will fairly give him Permission to depart, this Volume, which is deposited in safe hands, shall be delivered to him, and nothing ever appear to the Disgrace of the Nation or of its Ministers. He adds, as if a Ray of Reason then broke in upon his Soul, speaking of himself in the third Person : *He abandons forever the project of writing his life and his memoirs : he will never let slip, orally or in writing, a single word of complaint about the misfortunes that he met with in England ; he will never speak of Mr Hume, or will speak of him only with honour : and when pressed to explain some indiscreet accusations that he sometimes made at the height of his sufferings, he will blame them without farther ado on his melancholy disposition, which inclined him to distrust and suspicion, by this unhappy bent, the product of his misfortune, now completes them.*[1]

Le bon David was all compassion. " This poor Man," he advised Turgot, " is absolutely lunatic and consequently cannot be the Object of any Laws or civil Punishment." Would all the good people in Paris band together to protect him from further persecution and to settle him, if possible, in " any safe and quiet Retreat, under a discreet Keeper " ? Hume also applied in similar

[1] HL, ii, 137–8. The passage in italics is my translation.

terms to Mme de Boufflers. The very day that Hume was writing his letters of compassion Rousseau landed joyfully at Calais, having experienced, as he put it, " many bizarre adventures."

So did Jean-Jacques Rousseau pass out of the life of David Hume. Hume, however, did not pass out of the life of Rousseau, for, although the posthumous *Confessions* stops short just before the period of the quarrel (perhaps in fulfilment of the mysterious offer in the last letter to General Conway), Rousseau never changed his mind about the patron who had " betrayed " him. During the course of the years, indeed, he intuited new evidence of Hume's iniquity. This was the matter of the Allan Ramsay portraits, in which Hume's diabolical intentions had for long eluded him. The malice of Hume regarding the portraits is canvassed in that extraordinary anatomy of self which was published only after his death, *Rousseau Juge de Jean-Jacques*. David " desired this portrait." avows Rousseau the Judge, " as ardently as a deeply smitten lover desires that of his mistress. Through importunities he extorted the consent of Jean-Jacques. That same Jean-Jacques was made to wear a deep black cap and a deep brown garment; he was posed in a dark spot; and, in order to paint him seated, he was forced to stand up, stooped over, supported by one hand on a low table, in an attitude where highly strained muscles altered the very contours of his face." And the purpose of this manoeuvring which resulted in "This terrible portrait," "The face of a frightful Cyclops"? Why, to distribute engravings throughout Europe so that Hume would become known as handsome and Rousseau as ugly![1] Fortunately, knowing nothing of all this fantasy, David had hung the two Ramsay portraits in his parlour at Edinburgh, where they remained for the rest of his life.

The " petty Statesman " at London in 1767, the new Under-Secretary of State, Northern Department, accepted his office stoically and unenthusiastically. " Upon Trial, my Situation appears far from disagreeable," he explained to Turgot, " and I find, that to a Man of a literary turn, who has no great undertaking in view, Business, especially public Business, is the best Ressource of his declining Years. . . . After the Course of hard Study in which I have been engaged, Business is rather a Relaxation than a Labour to me." [2] David Hume, indeed, belonged to a long line of men of letters, who during the course of the eighteenth century relaxed as Under-Secretaries of State. The list includes Matthew

---

[1] Rousseau, xv, 125, 129, 301 ; xix, 129, 196, 317 ; *Œuvres* (Geneva 1782–9), xxi, 248, 252–3, 257–8. See Textual Supplement on Ramsay's three Rousseau portraits. [2] See Textual Supplement on Hume's self-mockery.

Prior, Joseph Addison, Thomas Tickell, Nicholas Rowe, Hume's friend Robert Wood, and Richard Brinsley Sheridan.

Nowhere does Hume mention the salary of his office, for the simple reason that there was no salary.[1] The Under-Secretaries and the chief clerks divided among themselves, in an unknown proportion, certain fees, gratuities, and post-office rights. It has been surmised that an Under-Secretary of the period might have received, in this manner, from £300 to £500 annually. If David Hume's passbook [2] with Messrs James and Thomas Coutts, bankers in the Strand, is sufficient evidence in itself, his earnings totalled £501 10s during his eleven months in office.

The reward was perhaps sufficient as the duties, though responsible, were hardly arduous. To Blair, Hume wrote that " My way of Life here is very uniform, and by no means disagreeable. I pass all the Forenoon in the Secretary's House from ten till three, where there arrives from time to time Messengers, that bring me all the Secrets of this Kingdom, and indeed of Europe, Asia, Africa and America. I am seldom hurry'd ; but have Leizure at Intervals to take up a Book, or write a private Letter, or converse with any Friend that may call for me : And from Dinner to Bed-time is all my own. . . . I am far from complaining," he continued. " I only shall not regreat when my Duty is over : because to me the Situation can lead to nothing : at least, in all Probability ; and reading and sauntering and lownging and dozing, which I call thinking, is my supreme Happiness, I mean my full Contentment."

This description of the duties of the Under-Secretary is necessarily vague because the relations of the two departments of state were not clearly defined. In general, however, the Northern Department handled diplomacy with those European powers to the north of France, including Russia. American affairs were handled by the Southern Department until 1768, at which time a separate department was established. Home affairs, as well as foreign affairs, were divided between the two departments of state, those of Scotland coming under the Northern Department.

After Lord Shelbourne took over the Southern Department in March 1767, there is reason to believe that he occasionally

---

[1] M. A. Thomson, *The Secretaries of State, 1681–1782* (Oxford 1932), pp. 137–8 ; Sir John Tilley and Stephen Gaselee, *The Foreign Office* (London 1933), p. 21.
[2] NLS, MS 3028. The above sum represents the total of deposits identified only by " Cash Rcd. p. Recpt." Such items begin in Mar. 1767, within a month of his taking office. In Oct. 1767 Hume informed his brother that his income was " over 1100 Pounds a Year."

consulted Hume over problems of diplomacy with France. Hume's continued interest in France and his ambition to maintain friendly relations between Britain and France is expressed in a letter to Trudaine de Montigny :

> You judge right, My Dear Friend : It will never be in my purpose, and I believe, still less in my Power, to enter into the Prejudices entertained by the vulgar Part of my Country-men, and to feel an antipathy against the French Nation : I know them too well to be capable of such a Sentiment. Happily, both Nations are at present seriously disposed to cultivate Peace with each other. May they long continue so : But it is a melancholy Reflection what trivial Matters will often set them a quarrelling, and by that means, spread the Flame from one End of the Globe to the other. The last War, for Instance, proceeded from the most frivolous Causes. . . . It was fomented by some obscure designing Men, contrary to the Intentions of the two Kings, the two Ministries, even the Generality of the two Nations. The Explication of a few Points might have prevented that horrible, destructive, ruinous War ; more pernicious to the Victors than to the Vanquished. Perhaps the Endeavours of a Person even in my Station might have had some Effect, and might have prevented so great a Mischief. It wou'd be an extreme Pleasure for me to find myself so useful ; or even to flatter myself, that I had contributed something to so good an End.

" It is the duty of the Under Secretaries," wrote Charles Jenkinson in 1761, " to prepare materials and to get everything ready for the busyness they see likely to arise, and get all inclosures, which are oftentimes much longer than the despatches, properly prepared against the time they are wanted." [1] Jenkinson also makes it clear that the Under-Secretaries opened all mail, circulated it among the ministers affected, and sent it to the King, sometimes even before the Secretary of State himself had seen it. Frequently they drafted his replies. To them, certainly, was left a good deal of discretion and responsibility. The few of Hume's letters that have survived refer to such miscellaneous affairs as payments to the Elector of Mainz for supplies delivered to the Allied Army during the last war, negotiations with the Dutch envoy regarding the East India Company, the murder of the collector of customs at Ayr, and the dividends of the East India Company. In these letters [2] Hume writes primarily as a subordinate carrying out the directions of his chief and secondarily as a valued assistant bringing fresh matters to the attention of his chief.

As the trusted assistant and the good friend of General Conway, David Hume was in a position of influence, especially as far as Scotland was concerned. He took pride and found amusement in assuming the role of patron to the Scottish church. " You do

[1] *Jenkinson Papers*, p. 4.   [2] NHL, pp. 158–9 ; 167–8 ; 180.

extremely right in applying to me," he told Robertson, " whenever it is the least likely I can serve you or any of your friends." The statement was no more than the truth, since, even before his appointment, he had used his influence with General Conway to steer Scottish church patronage into the proper channels, that is to say, to the Moderate Party. In 1767 he was able to do favours for Blair, Robertson, and several other clerical friends. But it was in connexion with the annual " letter from the throne " addressed to the General Assembly at Edinburgh in May 1767 that he had the opportunity to give national recognition to the merits of the Moderate leaders. For the King's letter, signed by General Conway, was the composition of David Hume.

" Tell Robertson," the Under-Secretary instructed Blair, " that the Compliment at the End of General Conway's Letter to him was of my composing, without any Orders from him. He smild when he read it ; but said it was very proper, and signd it. These are not bad Puffs from Ministers of State, as the silly World goes." The " Compliment " or " Puff " reads as follows :

> You may be assured that the Presbyterian Church of Scotland, as by law established, will always meet with Our support to the full enjoyment of their rights and privileges ; and We are convinced, that the same wise conduct, which has so often manifested itself in your former meetings, will be exerted on the present occasion, and that cordiality, unanimity, and brotherly love will attend all your proceedings, and be the means of securing a happy and satisfactory conclusion of this present meeting of the General Assembly.[1]

Blair responded : " I suppose you writ the Kings Letter, and I make the Commissioners Speeches—but this *entre nous*— Robertson has got Mr Conways Letter ; and is very well pleased with the Close of it. He enjoined me to keep the Secret strictly, of its Composition." In reference to Hume's patronage, Blair added, " What a party you will make among the Ministers of this Church, if you continue a while in office ! " [2]

Whether officially or unofficially, Hume's influence was always at the command of friends or deserving acquaintances. One of the clerks in General Conway's office proved to be George Deyverdun, the young Swiss whose gratuitous attack upon Rousseau in the *St. James's Chronicle* had caused Hume no little embarrassment. Deyverdun had literary ambitions, editing with Gibbon—to whose influence he owed his clerkship—a periodical entitled *Mémoires littéraires de la Grande Bretagne*. Much interested, Hume introduced his subordinate to Horace Walpole and also

---

[1] *Edinburgh Evening Courant*, 23 May 1767.   [2] RSE, III, 61.

contributed to the final issue of the periodical, that which appeared in 1769, some strictures [1] on Walpole's *Historic Doubts on the Life and Reign of King Richard the Third* (1768). The strictures were not appreciated by the amateur historian, who was already displeased with Hume for having printed a letter of his in the *Concise Account*. Although Hume continued to be an occasional visitor at Strawberry Hill, Walpole grew more and more intolerant of him [2] and, indeed, of all Scots.

Hume's patronage of Deyverdun led to closer relations with Edward Gibbon. Through Deyverdun, Gibbon forwarded to Hume part of a manuscript "History of the Swiss Revolution," written in French, begging that he would condescend to glance over the pages. "Give me leave, Sir, to add," wrote Gibbon, "that I must beg you to consider this liberty as a proof of my respect ; and that I shall consider your severity as a mark of your esteem. If you advise me to burn what I have already wrote, I shall immediately execute your sentence, with a full persuasion that it is just. Let me say, however, I have perhaps vanity enough to make so unlimited a sacrifice to no man in Europe but to Mr. Hume." [3]

Reading the work with "great pleasure and satisfaction," Hume objected only to the language in which it was written :

> Why do you compose in French, and carry faggots into the wood, as Horace says with regard to the Romans who wrote in Greek ? I grant that you have a like motive to those Romans, and adopt a language much more generally diffused than your native tongue : but have you not remarked the fate of those two ancient languages in following ages ? The Latin, though then less celebrated, and confined to more narrow limits, has in some measure outlived the Greek, and is now more generally understood by men of letters. Let the French, therefore, triumph in the present diffusion of their tongue. Our solid and increasing establishments in America, where we need less dread the inundation of Barbarians, promise a superior stability and duration to the English language.[4]

Another friend, or rather, friendly rival, seeking the aid of Hume was Tobias Smollett, who, broken in health and spirits, was planning to go into "perpetual exile" in Italy. Smollett had spoken to Hume about the possibility of an appointment to an Italian consulship ; but, after conferring with Lord Shelburne, Hume politely replied that the consulships of Nice and Leghorn

[1] *Mem. litt. de la Grande Bretagne*, 1769, II, 25–6.
[2] Walpole's defence of his part in the Rousseau-Hume controversy and his reply to Hume on the *Historic Doubts* appeared posthumously in his *Works* (London 1798–1825), VOLS. II and IV.   [3] RSE, v, 40.   [4] HL, II, 170–1.

were pre-engaged. To another friend, however, Hume laid bare the fact that Smollett was *persona non grata* to Shelburne. "How can I take on me," his lordship had demanded of Hume, "the Patronage of a Person so notorious for libelling as Dr Smollet? I shoud disoblige everyone whom he has abus'd." [1] In the autumn of 1768 when Smollett was prepared to depart, he wrote to Hume in farewell : "I sincerely wish you all health & happiness. In whatever part of the earth it may be my Fate to reside, I shall always remember with pleasure & recapitulate with pride, the friendly intercourse I have maintained with one of the best men, & undoubtedly the best writer of the age. . . ." [2] In return Hume deprecated the proposed "exile" and expressed the hope that Smollett would continue to rely upon his services and would some day return to his native country. This friendly exchange was the last between the two men of letters.

Adam Ferguson, a non-expatriate Scot who was held in great affection by the Edinburgh men of letters, had been manoeuvred into the Professorship of Natural Philosophy in 1759, and four years later—where he more properly belonged—into the Professorship of Moral Philosophy. The first fruits of academic life, a proposed "Treatise on Refinement," had met with Hume's qualified approval, but, when developed into an *Essay on the History of Civil Society*, with his dismay. [3] Some chapters of the completed manuscript had been put into Hume's hands soon after his return from France. "I sat down to read them," he told Blair, "with great Prepossession, founded on my good Opinion of him, on a small Specimen I had seen of them some Years ago, and on yours & Dr Robertson's Esteem of them : But I am sorry to say it, they have no-wise answer'd my Expectation. I do not think them fit to be given to the Public, neither on account of the Style nor the Reasoning : the Form nor the Matter. My Concern for his Reputation obliges me to tell you my Opinion. . . ." He concludes, "I shall be agreeably disappointed if the Success prove contrary to my Opinion."

Blair admitted that Hume's opinion staggered him. "But what is to be done ? " he asked hopelessly. "Robertson & I have given our opinion already ; We cannot retreat. You know too the Nature of the Author ; not overmuch given to Submit." [4] In short, as no one dared to deter him, Ferguson rushed into print at

[1] NHL, p. 174.   [2] RSE, vii, 40.
[3] There is some question as to whether these two works of Ferguson are really the same. See HL, i, 304, 308.   [4] RSE, iii, 56.

Edinburgh before the close of 1766. When copies of the book reached London the following February, Hume found himself " agreeably disappointed " and hastened to forward the good news to the author and to Blair and Robertson. To the last he remarked : " Ferguson's book goes on here with great success. A few days ago I saw Mrs Montague, who had just finished it with great pleasure : I mean, she was sorry to finish it, but had read it with great pleasure. I asked her, whether she was satisfied with the style ? Whether it did not savour somewhat of the country ? Oh yes, said she, a great deal : it seems almost impossible that anyone could write such a style except a Scotsman."

Blair was self-satisfied. " I must take a Little Credit to my Critical Sagacity. Did not I foretell you all this," he reminded Hume, " when you was overwhelmed with doubts of fear ? " [1] Duly impressed with the universal acclaim, Hume attempted to reread the book. " But to my great Mortification and Sorrow," he was compelled to tell Blair, " I have not been able to change my Sentiments. We shall see, by the Duration of its Fame, whether or not I am mistaken." Though reaching a seventh edition during the lifetime of the author, the *Essay on the History of Civil Society* has not survived as one of the classics of the eighteenth century.[2] Hume nowhere specifies his disapproval of Ferguson's reasonings, but the inevitability of progress and the principle of perfection were notions which Hume surely found untenable and which he had repudiated in the *philosophes*.

While in France Hume had met Isaac de Pinto, the Dutch economist and philosopher. Convinced that Pinto's services to the East India Company deserved to be rewarded, Hume took up his cause and ultimately secured his new friend a pension.[3]

Several acts of patronage, none of which turned out successfully, originated in Hume's continued contacts with the *philosophes*. On Diderot's recommendation, he got a certain M. Neuville placed as the French master in the school of the Reverend John Gardner, in Kensington Square, London, and Mme Neuville as governess to Sir John Colebroke's daughter. But a year and a half later Neuville was dismissed for not meeting his bills. Hume's only excuse was that he had taken Diderot at his word.

When Turgot asked Hume to recommend a Professor of English at Parma, Hume at once thought of Robert Liston, formerly tutor

---

[1] RSE, iii, 60.
[2] Though Duncan Forbes produced a new edition in 1967. See bibliography for two unpublished Ferguson dialogues edited by me.
[3] See Textual Supplement for more on Hume's patronage of Pinto.

to the Elliot boys in Paris. Liston was willing, but Turgot replied that the Court of Parma insisted that the professor be a Catholic. "They will have nothing but a Papist," announced Hume disgustedly to Elliot. "Such Fools ! Let the Pope excommunicate them on the one hand : I will do so on the other." To Liston himself Hume was kindly : "I hope the Disappointment gives you no Uneasyness. The Course of Studies, into which the Proposal has led you, will not be disagreeable, nor in any respects a Loss to you ; and you have too much Prudence to set your Heart upon an Uncertainty. I did indeed think, that the Scheme woud have suited you very well, both in respect of Talents and Inclination." [1] The later Sir Robert Liston lived up to Hume's early expectations and had a brilliant diplomatic career.

The same confidence that Sir Gilbert Elliot had placed in Hume to supervise the education of his boys in Paris was now placed in Hume and Elliot by Mure. In a letter to Hume the Baron—John Home had observed in 1761 that "Muir is degenerated into a Baron & wears a wig that would amaze you"—wrote : "You know Sir Gilbert and you may dispose of my two youths. I trust them to you as my two best Friends, and the most capable to direct a matter of this kind." [2] Hume sent the boys to study under Graffini, a Frenchman who had set up school at Norlands, near Kensington, under the patronage of Lord Hertford and Lord Bute. But Graffini was something of an impostor. His claim to be known to D'Alembert and Helvétius proved to be false, and Hume branded him as "an empty, conceited Fellow ; full of Chimeras and Pretensions. . . ." Furthermore, Hume disapproved of Graffini's method of teaching Latin by means of word lists without grammar. "In a living Language," explained Hume to Mure, "the continued application of the Words and Phrazes teaches at the same time the Sense of the Words and their Reference to each other ; but a List of Words got by heart, without any connected Sense, easily escapes the Memory, and is but a small Part of the Language." Still he hesitated to remove the boys from the school, pointing out that, as they are "so very young, their time is not very precious" and they are in excellent health and morals. The boys prospered from Graffini's French, however, and after a year their pronunciation of that language was purer than of English. The pedagogical problem was finally solved with the resignation of Graffini as head master.

To the Mure boys we owe a graphic glimpse of Hume in

[1] HL, ii, 181 ; NLS, MS 5513, f. 94.   [2] NLS, MS 1005, f. 3 ; RSE, vi, 64.

London dressed in the height of Parisian fashion—" the philosopher's ponderous uncouth person equipped in a bright yellow coat spotted with black." To them also we owe an intimate glimpse into character. Having been taken to see St Paul's Cathedral and having been informed that the daily service was not attended and that even on Sundays the congregation was small, the boys sought to curry favour with the philosopher by remarking " how foolish it was to lay out a million . . . on a thing so useless." To their surprise, however, they met with instant rebuff : " Never give an opinion on subjects which you are too young to judge. St. Paul's," remonstrated Hume, " as a monument of the religious feeling and sentiment of the country, does it honour, and will endure. We have wasted millions on a single campaign in Flanders, and without any good resulting from it." [1]

Lord Charlemont also testifies to the genial non-dogmatic quality of Hume's religious scepticism. Charlemont once asked Hume what he thought of the immortality of the soul. " Why Troth, Man," replied the philosopher, " it is so pretty and so comfortable a Theory, that I wish I cou'd be convinced of it's Truth—But I can na help doubting." On another occasion, when in a particularly jovial mood, Hume dropped in to see Charlemont. " What has put you into this good Humour, Hume ? " inquired his host. " Why, Man," replied he, " I have just now had the best thing said to me I ever heard. Damn'd cutting indeed, but excellent. I was complaining in a Company, where I spent the Morning, that I was very ill treated by the World, and that the Censures past upon me were hard and unreasonable—That I had written many Volumes, thro'out the whole of which there were but a few Pages that contained any reprehensible Matter, and yet for those few Pages I was abused and torn to pieces. ' You put me in Mind,' said an honest Fellow in the Company, whose Name I did not know, ' of an Acquaintance of mine, a Notary public, who having been condemned to be hang'd for Forgery, lamented the Hardship of his Case, that after having written many Thousand inoffensive Sheets, He shou'd be hang'd for one Line.' " [2]

John Crawford, nicknamed " Fish " on account of his restless inquisitiveness, had become Hume's friend in Paris. " One of the gayest young gentlemen and the greatest gambler that ever belonged to Scotland," as he is described by his footman,[3] Crawford

[1] *Caldwell Papers*, PT. I, 38.
[2] Lord Charlemont, " Anecdotes of Hume," in RIA, MS—12/R/7, f. 515.
[3] John Macdonald, *Memoirs of an Eighteenth Century Footman, 1745–1779*, ed. John Beresford (London 1927), p. 82.

was in hot water with his father. Reconciliation was brought about through Hume's sound advice to the young rake. " Fish " repaid his indebtedness by proposing the philosopher for " a certain very infamous society in Pall Mall," which, however, had " too much taste & sense in it for one black ball to appear " against him. The club was Almack's and Crawford had been one of the original members since it was instituted in 1764 as a centre for high play in gambling.[1] Lord Bolingbroke and Lord Ossory, as well as Crawford, sponsored Hume. While still at Edinburgh, Hume accepted membership in order to be assured of " good Company " if " any Accident " brought him to London. How much David Hume indulged in gambling at Almack's during the succeeding two years remains unknown, but he probably could have made out very well had he been so inclined. General Scott of Balcomie, it is said,[2] offered to stake him to £1,000 annually in return for his winnings at whist. The proposal was rejected in disdain, Hume replying that " he played for his amusement but would never act as a pickpocket or for hire. . . ."

After staying at Almack's for some time, Crawford took over Sir James Gray's house in Clifford Street and began lavish housekeeping. His French cook attracted the best company, including David Hume. One of these dinners, attended by Hume, the Duke of Roxburgh, the Earl of March, the Duke of Ossory, the Duke of Grafton, David Garrick, and a Mr James, is of literary memory. " Tristram Shandy " was mentioned, and all present were concerned about his illness. Crawford's footman, John Macdonald, was dispatched to make inquiries. John found Sterne "just a-dying. I waited ten minutes ; but in five he said : ' Now it is come.' He put up his hand as if to stop a blow, and died in a minute." The gentlemen at Crawford's table, notes John, " were all very sorry, and lamented him very much." [3]

Hume's friendship with his chief, General Conway, became as intimate as that with Lord Hertford. Welcomed into the family circle of General Conway and Lady Ailesbury, Hume was charmed with their only child, Anne, in 1767 an attractive and vivacious girl of eighteen. To Hume is given the credit for having opened up to Anne the career of sculptor. Sauntering along a London

---

[1] RSE, IV, 43 ; Norman Pearson, " ' Fish ' Crawford," in *Nineteenth Century*, LXXV (1914), 389–401.

[2] By George Norvell, MS letter, 1 Mar. 1788, in Keynes Library, King's College, Cambridge. For another version by Norvell, see Hill Burton, II, 7–8*n*.

[3] Macdonald, *Memoirs*, p. 91. See NHL, p. 175 for Hume's advice to Crawford to ignore physicians.

street one day the philosopher and the young lady encountered an Italian boy carrying a tray of plaster figures on his head. Goodhumouredly Hume tried to draw the boy out concerning his wares, rewarding him finally with a shilling. When Anne twitted him on his humanity, the philosopher retorted, " Be less severe, Miss Conway. Those images, at which you smile, were not made without the aid of both science and genius. With all your attainments, now, you cannot produce such works." No girl to be dared in vain, Anne shut herself up in her room and was soon able to produce a recognisable head of her friend. Admitting the likeness, Hume reminded her that it was one thing to work in clay and quite another to handle the chisel. Nothing daunted, Anne returned to her room and in the course of time showed Hume, to his astonishment and pleasure, the same bust cut in stone.[1] The marriage of Anne Conway in 1767 to the Hon. John Damer proved to be unhappy and, in later life, Mrs Damer turned to a career as sculptor.

Friendship with the Conways and the Hertfords kept Hume in high-society circles. Both families had houses in London and estates in the country. Lord Hertford's country seat was Ragley in Hertfordshire and General Conway's was Park Place at Henley-on-Thames. Lady Mary Coke, daughter of the Duke of Argyll, had been Hume's acquaintance since 1758 and was now his friend. Her journals provide a sketch of a week spent at Park Place in July 1767 with General Conway and Lady Ailesbury, David Hume, and, for part of the time, Horace Walpole. The days were passed pleasantly in long walks through the steep hills, in playing at bowls, and in visits to neighbouring estates. The evenings were devoted to Pope Joan, a card-game, at which Lady Mary lost five guineas at one sitting and won thirteen at another. Walpole recited passages from his tragedy of the *Mysterious Mother*, and Hume gave vent to his spleen against Shakespeare. " Wou'd you have thought it possible," inquires Lady Mary, " that a Man of Genius shou'd not be able to discover the Beauties of that admirable Writer ? We are all against him."

Lady Mary probed into the religious beliefs of the " Great Infidel "—" 'tis the only thing I dislike in him. I have had some conversation with him, but I have no hopes of converting him from his erroneous way of thinking, & thank God, his infidelity does not invalidate my belief." On Sunday she was the only one of the

[1] This anecdote is related without citation of authority by G. and P. Wharton (pseudonyms for Mrs K. B. Thomson and J. Thomson), *The Queens of Society* (London 1890), ii, 166–9.

party that went to church, getting wet and hearing a dull sermon for her pains. " Upon the whole," she concluded, " I think the others were wiser that did not go. . . ." A dinner of a " Noble haunch of Venison " was almost completely devoured since " Mr Hume has a violent stomach, & Mr Conway eats heartily." The party broke up when the General was summoned to London for a Cabinet Council and Hume accompanied him.[1]

In August and September 1768 Hume made extended visits in the country, his first call being at Oakley Park, the seat of Lord Bathurst near Cirencester. " I am here," he told Crawford with undisguised pride, " at a kind of classical Place, celebrated by Pope, Swift &c [a]nd with a classical Man, who livd in Intimacy with these two wits and with Prior, Gay, Arbuthnot, Bolingbroke & every Person celebrated in his time. Both the Place and the Man are very agreeable, and the Weather is fine ; my Appetite good ; the Table plentiful, and the Wine excellent. Nothing is wanting to make the time pass as cheerfully as possible." [2] From Oakley Park, Hume moved on to Ragley to visit the Hertfords. There he met Thomas Lyttelton, who was later to succeed his father, the " good Lord Lyttelton," and to earn for himself the name of the " bad Lord Lyttelton." Professing to admire Hume greatly, Lyttelton was astonished at his hypersensitivity over the honour of his native country. Lyttelton innocently asked Hume " at what time of the year the harvest was housed in Scotland " ? But Hume conceived the question " to convey a suspicion, that there was no harvest, or at least no barns, in his country : and his answer was slight and churlish." [3]

Scot of Scots that he was, David Hume lived during his stay in London, 1767–69, with the Misses Elliot, who had removed to Brewer Street, Golden Square. There he dwelt among Scots, including James Macpherson, and there he kept a servant, one William Boyd.[4] There he received his Scottish friends : the older group of John Armstrong, Gilbert Elliot, and James Oswald ; and the younger group of Robert Adam, John Home, Andrew Stuart of Torrance, and Alexander Wedderburn. From there, too, he sallied forth on the never-ending round of visits and dinners. " I continue my parasitical Practices," he only half-ashamedly acknowledged, " that is, of dining at all the great Tables that remain in London."

[1] *Letters and Journals of Lady Mary Coke, 1756–1774* (Edinburgh 1889–96), II, 311–17.
[2] NHL, pp. 184–5.
[3] *Letters of the late Thomas Lord Lyttelton* (London 1780), p. 87.
[4] Macdonald, *Memoirs*, p. 93.

An innocent witticism indavertently led to strained relations with Oswald of Dunnikier. This " strangest Story you ever heard of " Hume recounts to Adam Smith :

> I was dining with him above two Months ago, where among other Company was the Bishop of Raphoe [John Oswald, brother of James]. After dinner, we were disposed to m[ak]e merry ; I said to the Company that I had been very ill us'd by Lord Hertford : For that I always expected to be made a Bishop by him during his Lieutenancy, but he had given away two Sees from me, to my great Vexation & Disappointment. The Right Reverend, without any farther Provocation, burst out into the most furious, and indecent, and orthodox Rage, that ever was seen : Told me that I was most impertinent ; that if he did not wear a Gown I durst not, no, I durst not have us'd him so ; that none but a Coward woud treat a Clergyman in that manner ; that henceforth he must either abstain from his Brother's House or I must, and that this was not the first time he had heard this stupid Joke from my Mouth.[1]

Keeping his temper, Hume immediately asked the Bishop's pardon, pointing out that in reality the joke was against himself— " as if I were capable of such an Expectation as that of being a Bishop." The angry cleric was not to be appeased, however, and Hume took advantage of the first opportunity to leave. What hurt him most in the affair was, not the " orthodox Rage " of the Bishop, which he had encountered previously, but Oswald's total silence and indifference. Smith, in reply, was indignant. " The Bishop is a brute & a beast," he protested, but excused Oswald's coldness on the grounds of his ill health.[2] Oswald died in 1769, but happily before that time the two old friends had become reconciled.

In the spring of 1768 three of Hume's clerical cronies were up from Edinburgh—Blair, Carlyle, and Robertson. The last was received in London with the applause due the author of the *History of Scotland*. The purpose of his visit was to arrange for the publication of the *History of Charles V* early in 1769 ; Hume was to see it through the press. Blair, known only for his Ossianic *Dissertation*, was totally eclipsed by Robertson ; his famous *Lectures on Rhetoric and Belles Lettres* was not to appear until 1783. Carlyle, back in London again in 1769 for Scottish church business, managed to see much of the town. He reports an evening of friendly " tittle-tattle " concerning the activities of the royal family : " It was truly amusing to observe how much David Hume's strong and capacious mind was filled with infantine anecdotes of nurses and children." [3]

Carlyle also reports the opening of John Home's tragedy of

---

[1] HL, ii, 142. [2] RSE, vii, 37. [3] Carlyle, p. 545.

The Fatal Discovery on 23 February 1769. So alarmed was Garrick over the anti-Scottish violence of the London mob that he had insisted that John should give up the original title of *Rivine* (one of Macpherson's Ossianic poems) and permit an Oxford student to attend the rehearsals at the Drury Lane as the ostensible author. After the opening night David commented tersely to Blair, " The *fatal Discovery* succeeded, and deserved it : it has feeling tho' not equal to Douglas, in my Opinion. The Versification is not enough finish'd. Our Friend escaped by lying conceal'd." Carlyle fills in the details. John, who had too much vanity and love of praise to remain concealed during the whole run of the play, soon disclosed himself as the author. " The house," observes Carlyle caustically, " evidently slackened after the town heard that John was the author." [1]

Four days after " Our Friend escaped by lying conceal'd," David Hume and many of his Scottish friends had further reason to feel national humiliation and outrage. The sad occasion was the verdict in the Douglas Cause, Scotland's *cause célèbre* of the eighteenth century. The vast Douglas fortune was at stake and, if the point at issue was simple, the determination of the facts was not. Briefly, the death in 1761 of Archibald, third Marquess of Douglas, left the inheritance in dispute, the Marquess having died childless. The two claimants were Archibald Steuart-Douglas, son of Lady Jane Douglas, sister of the Marquess, and the Duke of Hamilton, otherwise the nearest male heir. The precedence of a true and lawful son of Lady Jane was unquestionable, but the guardians of the young Duke of Hamilton contended that Archibald Steuart-Douglas was not her true and lawful son.

The substance of the Hamilton case was that Lady Jane, when in her fifty-first year and past the age of child-bearing, had purchased the infant from French parents and had brought him up as her own. The boy's legitimacy had been investigated by the guardians of Hamilton during Hume's residence in Paris, his interest being especially aroused because two of the guardians, Baron Mure and Andrew Stuart of Torrance, were his intimate friends. From Paris Hume wrote in November 1763, " Andrew Stuart is here at present : I meet with nobody here that doubts of the justice of his cause."

The Court of Session at Edinburgh on 15 July 1767 decided in favour of the Hamiltons by the narrow margin of the vote of the Lord President. " The Triumph of Reason over Prejudice,"

[1] Carlyle, pp. 534–5.

exulted Hume to Mure on that occasion, " was very signal even in that small Majority among your Judges ; but things having once taken a Turn, such strong Reason, aided by time, must certainly overcome weaker Prejudices." The case, as Hume anticipated, was appealed to the House of Lords, where on 27 February 1769 the decision was reversed.

Hume's indignation was unbounded. " I was present at it," he informed Mure, " and surely never was present at more scandalous Proceedings." The villain in the piece, according to Hume, was the Lord Chief Justice Mansfield—" when I heard his Judgement, I then knew that no thing farther cou'd be said, and saw the whole Mystery, which is, in the most egregious Degree, a Mystery of Iniquity." Soon after the Edinburgh decision, Hume had ventured to hope that Mansfield " will now probably think twice before he indulges his Propensity to Douglas." Even some of Lord Mansfield's friends suspected his " Propensity to Douglas," Bishop Warburton, for instance, querying, " whether he could conceive, if Lady Jane's Husband had it in his design to make the world believe that the Birth was an imposture, he could contrive any means of doing it more effectually than the means he employed " ? [1]

The day following the " iniquitous " decision, Hume was still greatly agitated. " Contrary to custom, he was quite out of humour," noticed Lady Mary Coke, who met him at Lady Hertford's, " & said several peevish things. He has hurt himself with the part he has taken in that Affair." [2] With few exceptions (notably, Boswell, Carlyle, and Ferguson), Hume's Scottish friends favoured the Hamiltons, and nearly all were as bellicose as he. Yet the only crumb of comfort that they were able to salvage from the whole affair was the fabulous generosity of William Pulteney,[3] one of the wealthiest men in the realm. As a token of his personal esteem and in compensation for a legal career placed in jeopardy, Pulteney sent Andrew Stuart a bond of annuity of £400 a year. Hume wrote to thank Pulteney for his generosity, but to Mure he confided his misgivings over Stuart's fate : " Pulteney's Behaviour to him is noble, but is not sufficient ; and yet I know not what farther can possibly be done, to throw the Infamy where it ought so justly to be laid."

[1] Warburton, copy of MS letter of 8 Feb. 1773 to Thomas Balguy, in collection transcribed by James Crossley and now in the University of Texas library.
[2] *Letters of Lady Mary Coke*, iii, 33.
[3] Son of Sir James Johnstone of Westerhall, William Johnstone had changed his name to Pulteney on marrying the heiress of Bath.

Andrew Stuart had, indeed, staked his career on the success of the Douglas Cause. He had gone so far as to call out Edward Thurlow, one of the barristers for the appellants, and to exchange shots with him. Now all seemed lost with Mansfield's cry of " Subornation of Perjury " against Stuart's chief witnesses and, by implication, against Stuart himself. After several years of brooding over the injustice that he felt had been done him and the Cause, Stuart published in January 1773 *Letters to the Right Honourable Lord Mansfield from Andrew Stuart, Esq.* Though alarmed at the " Imprudence of the Attempt," Stuart's Edinburgh friends met in solemn conclave at the home of Baron Mure and voted their full approbation. To Stuart, Hume at once penned his shortest letter on record : " Non debet fieri ; factum valet." [1] Then, ironically assuming the name of a common acquaintance whom neither one respected, he wrote to congratulate Stuart at length on what he recognised as a literary masterpiece :

> I am sorry to tell you, honoured Sir, that David Hume, whom perhaps you look on as your Friend, goes about railing at you in every Company : Son of a Whore and Son of a Bitch are the best Appellations he can afford you. He says, that it is intolerable, that this damnd Fellow, who was bred to nothing but drawing of Bonds and Leases, or at best Settlements and Entails, which are the sublime of his former Profession, shoud turn Author, and at once surpass him and all his Brethren : I am told that he has engag'd the Principal [Robertson], who, I hear, has the same Opinion of your Performance, to speak the same Lan[guage.] Such is the base Envy and Malignity of these low Minds !

Before the end of February, Hume was able to note with evident relief : " Andrew has easd his own Mind, and no bad Effects are to follow : Lord Mansfield is determined absolutely to neglect them." Andrew's final consolation was that, for sustained irony and vituperation, the *Letters to Lord Mansfield* was generally regarded as worthy of the pen of a Junius.

The position of a Scot in London, particularly so sensitive a Scot as David Hume, had been becoming increasingly intolerable. The tumult over John Wilkes, which had subsided during his exile abroad, recommenced with his return early in 1768. The struggle over his election between the House of Commons and the electors of Middlesex continued throughout that year and the following, the mob on the street demonstrating for " Wilkes and Liberty." But the cry of " Wilkes and Liberty " meant antagonism to Lord Bute and to all Scots ; and in the continuation of the

[1] NHL, p. 200.

North Briton David Hume was singled out on several occasions for attack.[1] Beginning in January 1769 and for another three years the " Letters of Junius " continued the anti-Caledonian poison.[2]

In this uncongenial atmosphere David Hume was growing more and more short-tempered. The coincidence of Wilkes, Junius, the Douglas Cause, and the London mob was too much for him to bear with equanimity. His letters abound with imprecations against " the rascally Mob "—" Licentiousness, or rather the frenzy of liberty, has taken possession of us "—" Every Event here fills me with Indignation, which I cannot command and care not to conceal ; and yet to a Philosopher & Historian the Madness and Imbecillity & Wickedness of Mankind ought to appear ordinary Events."

Hume had always held strong opinions on contemporary politics and had always expressed himself forcefully. His political persuasions are not, however, simple to determine. It is easy to say that he was becoming more conservative with age and more irascible with the continued onslaught against Scotland. That is true, but by no means the whole truth. In politics Hume, like most men, was not perfectly consistent. He was, to be sure, a friend of the " King's Friends "—but he served under the Whig Ministry of Lord Chatham, 1766–68, and was the friend of such political liberals as Lord Shelburne and Colonel Barré. He opposed " Wilkes and Liberty "—but he advocated the Whig theory of the state, even republicanism. The last essay that he wrote—" Of the Origin of Government," which was not completed before 1774—does not alter his basic position on the proper balance between authority and liberty : " Liberty is the perfector of civil society," but it cannot exist without authority.

On the most critical political issue of the last period of his life, and one that is a sure touchstone of political belief, Hume was on the side of the Colonies and against Lord North and the " King's Friends " with a consistency that perhaps cannot be found in any of his leading contemporaries. In 1766 he had rejoiced over the repeal of the Stamp Act, and, as early as 1768, was longing to see America " totally & finally " in revolt. Some years later he recalled a conversation at Lord Bathurst's where American affairs were being discussed and some of the company " mention'd former Acts of Authority exercised over the Colonies. I observ'd

[1] e.g., Nos. 47, 61, 73.
[2] Strange to say, Hume nowhere mentions " Junius " in his extant letters. Strahan does, however, when writing to Hume.

to them," remarks Hume drily, " that Nations, as well as Individuals, had their different Ages, which challeng'd a different Treatment. For Instance, My Lord, said I to the old Peer, you have sometimes, no doubt, given your Son a Whipping ; and I doubt not, but it was well merited and did him much good : Yet you will not think proper at present to employ the Birch : The Colonies are no longer in their Infancy." Hume adds, however, that the Colonies were " still in their Nonage " and that Dr Franklin wished to go too fast in emancipating them from Britain. Yet in 1775, when even Edmund Burke in the famous *Conciliation* speech was still not thinking of giving up the Colonies, Hume could state categorically : " I am an American in my Principles, and wish we woud let them alone to govern or misgovern themselves as they think proper." [1] Nor are his views on America to be dismissed as mere spleen against the English ; rather, they are calmly and shrewdly reasoned and perfectly consistent with his recognition that a revolution in France was inevitable.[2]

Throughout his residence in London Hume looked forward to Edinburgh rather than to Paris. With Mme de Boufflers a certain coldness had set in since her complaint that he had not informed her of the quarrel with Rousseau the *first* among his Parisian friends. There is no doubt that she was hurt and angry at Hume's failure to return to France. " Your letter, dear Madam," he wrote in March 1767, " for the first time in my life, gave me uneasiness and no less surprise." He still expressed hopes of their eventual reunion, but made no efforts to bring it about—as she became only too well aware. Two months later he wrote again, " I find you are desirous to hear no more of me, which, I own, is one of the greatest surprizes, and none of the least afflictions I have met with in the course of my life." To this she responded with impersonal inquiries concerning English politics.

After his resignation from office, Hume ventured to express the hope of a visit to France, for which Mme de Boufflers happily began to make extensive preparations. Later his excuses are of the flimsiest : " The truth is, I have, and ever had a prodigious reluctance to change my place of abode : and though this disposition was more than counterbalanced by my strong desire of enjoying your society, it made me perhaps yield more easily to the obstacles which opposed my journey. For this reason," he proceeds warily, " I shall say nothing of my future intentions ;

[1] See Textual Supplement for item in American periodicals, 17 August 1776.
[2] HL, II, 184, 242, 287–8, 300–1, 303.

lest I expose myself to the same reproach of irresolution, in case I do not fulfil them." In her reply Hume found " more sharpness . . . than I ever thought should have passed between us." After which rebuke the correspondence lapsed until 1772, when, writing from Edinburgh, Hume was completely forthright : " for my part, I have totally and finally retired from the world, with a resolution never more to appear on the scene in any Shape "—but the blow was softened by the offer to meet her at London if she crossed the Channel.

General Conway demitted office on 20 January 1768, at which time Hume's commission expired. Yet, despite his ever-increasing dissatisfaction with English politics, Hume remained in London until August 1769. For this delay he had the perennial excuse about his reluctance to change places of abode ; but that, in itself, would hardly have been sufficient reason to remain so long in an uncongenial environment. Two other reasons have more validity, the first of which is the new pension of £200 given him by George III at the request of General Conway and Lord Hertford. " The King has given me a considerable augmentation of my pension," wrote Hume to the Marquise de Barbantane, " expressing at the same time his expectation that I am to continue my History. This motive, with my habits of application, will probably engage me for some years." [1]

That Hume was impatient to continue the *History* is certainly not true, although the previous autumn he had received His Majesty's permission to inspect the papers in the various government archives. There is no doubt that he was disgusted with the high success of Mrs Catherine Macaulay's strictly Whiggish *History of England* and with the similar attempt of John Wilkes to exploit party prejudices. No doubt also he was sensitive over the efforts of Lord Bute to induce Robertson to turn to the field of English history. Whatever the reasons, Hume simply never got down to the arduous research involved, and after returning to Scotland could announce to Strahan " that I am fully determin'd never to continue my History, and have indeed put it entirely out of my power by returning to this Country, for the rest of my Life." Nor did he succumb either to Strahan's lure of money—" you may demand what you please for it. It shall be granted "—or to Strahan's lure of flattery—" It is the only thing wanting to fill up the Measure of your Glory as the Great Historian and Philos-

[1] On 19 January 1768 Hume wrote to Adam Ferguson sardonically probing the possibility of continuing his *History*. See Textual Supplement.

opher of the Eighteenth Century." Hume's definitive refusal to
Strahan is reported to have been in the following terms : " I must
decline not only this offer, but all others of a literary nature for
four reasons : Because I'm too old, too fat, too lazy, and too
rich." [1]

Man of letters to the end, however,—" as there is no happiness without occupation "—Hume was always interested in the
dissemination of enlightenment. The Abbé Morellet was planning
a new *Dictionnaire de Commerce* and sent him some copies of the
prospectus, which he distributed among friends and among the
members of Almack's. Hume may also have been the author of
a letter to the editor of the *Gentleman's Magazine* with an English
translation of the prospectus.[2] Another minor literary venture was
the signed " Advertisement " to the English translation of 1770
of Baron Manstein's *Memoirs of Russia, Historical, Political, and
Military, from the Year MDCCXXVII to MDCCXLIV*. In the
" Advertisement " Hume explained that " The following Memoirs
were sent me from Berlin by the Earl Marshal, with a desire that
they should be published in England."

These minor projects were not, to be sure, reasons to delay
Hume's return to Edinburgh. His second motive for remaining
overlong in London was the correcting a new edition of the
History, " which I oversee as anxiously, as if any body were concern'd about it, or ever woud perceive the Pains I take in polishing
it and rendering it as accurate as possible." After which fit of
petulance he breaks down and confesses, " I can only say, that I
do it for myself and that it amuses me."

The last sentence is crucial to the understanding of Hume's
latest period. He was finished with public life and with the
writing of books. His reputation would stand or fall on his
publications, which, however, he would endeavour to leave in as
perfect a form as possible ; to Gibbon he confided that " he always
laboured to reduce the superlatives and soften the positives." [3]
" It is one great advantage that results from the Art of printing,"
he consoled himself, " that an Author may correct his works, as
long as he lives." Revision would provide him with intellectual
amusement ; his friends in Scotland, with social amusement.
Belatedly, after a stay of twenty-nine months, he left London,
and by the end of August 1769 was back in Edinburgh, having
" done with all Ambition."

[1] RSE, VII, 63 ; *New Evening Post*, 6 Dec. 1776. [2] *Gent.'s Mag.*, XXXIX (1769), 473–5.
[3] D. M. Low, *Edward Gibbon : 1737–1794* (London 1937), p 20.

PART V

" SAINT DAVID OF SCOTLAND "

1769-1776

CHAPTER 37

AUTUMNAL SERENITY

" I returned to Edinburgh . . . very opulent, healthy, and though
somewhat stricken in Years, with the Prospect of enjoying long my Ease and
of seeing the Encrease of my Reputation."

In Edinburgh, " The Guid Toun," David Hume settled down
comfortably and serenely. By October 1769 he could remark, " I
. . . am here, Body & Soul, without casting the least Thought
of Regreat to London, or even to Paris. I think it improbable,"
he continued, " that I shall ever in my Life cross the Tweed,
except perhaps a Jaunt to the North of England, for Health or
Amusement." Before leaving London he had come to the conclusion that in his new affluence he would require larger quarters,
and had actually taken one of Allan Ramsay's houses in the
vicinity of the castle. Upon the representations of Mrs Alison
Cockburn, however, he gave it up, as being poorly situated on the
north side of a high hill. " I woud as soon be the Soul of an
unburryed Sinner wandring about the river Styx," protested that
amiable lady, " as live in these houses." For her own part, Alison
had two proposals to make. The first was that David should take
a house in the new southern extension of the city in George Square.
" You have no notion of our city now," she cautioned, " it has
expanded itself prodigiously." Her second proposal was to secure
for David a wife without putting him " to any trouble about
resolveing." [1] On both scores, however, the philosopher decided
to see for himself.

The New Town of Edinburgh, as differentiated from the
extension to the south, was slowly arising to the north of the old.
The Nor' Loch had already been drained and was to be turned
into a public park with gardens. Beyond it lay a magnificently
broad Princes Street, and beyond that the site of the New Town.
To connect the Old Town with the New, the North Bridge was
in the course of construction. The situation of the New Town
charmed Hume at first sight, and he soon came to an audacious
decision : there he would feu land and build his house.

During the exciting period of planning and of building, Hume

¹ RSE, IV, 32.

found James's Court " very chearful, and even elegant, but too
small to display my great Talent for Cookery, the Science to
which I intend to addict the remaining Years of my Life." To
Gilbert Elliot he boasted of his culinary prowess : " I have just
now lying on the Table before me a Receipt for making *Soupe a la
Reine,* copy'd with my own hand. For Beef and Cabbage (a
charming Dish), and old Mutton and old Claret, no body excels
me. I also make Sheep head Broth in a manner that Mr
[" Ambassador "] Keith speaks of it for eight days after, and
the Duc de Nivernois woud bind himself Apprentice to my Lass
to learn it. . . . All my Friends encourage me in this Ambition ;
as thinking it will redound very much to my Honour." His
cellar well stocked with the best French wines, and his scritoire
with the best French recipes, Hume patiently instructed his " lass,"
the faithful old Peggy Irvine, in the art of sophisticated cookery.
Henry Mackenzie recalls an excellent *bouillé,* and James Boswell
an elegant supper, including three sorts of ice-cream at the home of
the " northern Epicurus." Colonel Edmonstoune dryly observes,
" I dined with the philosopher . . . and got myself tipsy."

English travellers to Scotland during the eighteenth century
frequently noticed the similarity in manners and customs between
the Scots and the French. Captain Topham remarked that " The
air of mirth and vivacity, that quick penetrating look, that spirit
of gaiety which distinguishes the French, is equally visible in the
Scotch. It is the character of the nation ; and it is a very happy
one, as it makes them disregard even their poverty." As in France,
so in the streets of Edinburgh, kisses were exchanged when friends
met after long absence. When Baron Mure heard of Hume's
impending return in 1769 he wrote : " I rejoice to hear that
you . . ., my dear David, are soon to be with us. I shall long to
embrace you. . . . There are daily fewer men on whom one
would chuse to confer that mark of kindness." Mrs Elizabeth
Montagu, the London bluestocking, was astonished at the pleasant
contrast afforded with English " ignorance or brutality." The
Scots, she discovered, " live in ye french way, *des petits soupers fins,*
& they have ye easy address of the french. The lettered sage &
rural Gentleman is in Scotland a polite man." [1]

Yet David Hume's *petits soupers fins,* however luxurious in
quality, were never limited in quantity. " Ye ken I'm no epicure,"
he once assured Mrs Cockburn, when he arrived unexpectedly for

[1] Capt. E. Topham, *Letters from Edinburgh* (Dublin 1776), I, 82 ; *Caldwell Papers,*
PT. II, VOL. II, 155 ; Montagu, MS (uncat.), EM 1776, in Huntington Library.

dinner, " only a glutton." The Edinburgh *literati*—" David Hume
and the Rest of the Ministers," according to Mrs Mure—must
all have had prodigious appetites for Lord Kellie suggested that
they be named the *Eaterati*.[1] Nor was the English poet William
Mason being intentionally unkind when he sang :

> Let D**d H*e, from the remotest North,
> In sea-saw sceptic scruples hint his worth ;
> D**d, who there supinely deigns to lye,
> The fattest Hog of Epicurus' sty ;
> Though drunk with Gallic wine and Gallic praise,
> D**d shall bless Old England's halcyon days.[2]

" I hope," advised Gibbon to a friend visiting Edinburgh, " you
will not fail to visit the Stye of that fattest of Epicurus's Hogs, and
inform yourself whether there remains no hope of its recovering
the use of its right paw." [3] David's right paw, however, confined
itself almost exclusively to minor corrections of his published works,
recipes for the table, and letters to absent friends.

Adam Smith was absent, although his home town of Kirkcaldy
across the Firth of Forth was within sight of James's Court. " I
am mortally sick at Sea, and regard with horror, and a kind of
hydrophobia the great Gulph that lies between us," acknowledged
Hume shortly after his return to Edinburgh. " I am also tir'd of
travelling, as you ought naturally to be, of staying at home. I
therefore propose to you to come hither, and pass some days with
me in this Solitude. I want to know what you have been doing,
and propose to exact a rigorous Account of the Method, in which
you have employed yourself during your Retreat. I am positive
you are in the wrong in many of your Speculations, especially
where you have the Misfortune to differ with me." Buried in the
manuscript of the *Wealth of Nations*, Smith came to Edinburgh
infrequently, but Hume always kept a room in readiness for him.

On one occasion David did cross the Firth of Forth in the
company of Lady Wallace, who was later to become his tenant at
James's Court. When a stiff breeze blew up and that normally
vivacious person gave voice to the fear of drowning, Hume casually
observed that they might soon be food for fishes. " And who will
they begin with ? " cried out Lady Wallace in distress. " Why,
Madam, those of them that are gluttons will begin with me ;
those that are epicures with your ladyship." When this same lady

[1] Carlyle, in NLS, MS Acc. 1237 ; *Lives of the Lindsays* (London 1849), II, 321n.
[2] Mason, *An Heroic Epistle to Sir William Chambers on his Book of Gardening* (1773).
[3] Gibbon, *Private Letters*, I, 190.

asked Hume what to say to people who inquired concerning her age, he promptly returned : " Madam, say you are not yet come to years of discretion." [1]

On the floor below the philosopher in James's Court lived a Mrs Campbell, with whom he frequently played whist. In a mischievous mood one Sunday evening he knocked at the door uninvited to find her entertaining a party of pious elderly ladies at tea. Demurely he accepted a cup and chatted amiably with the ladies. After the removal of the teatray, however, he turned to his hostess and gravely inquired, " Well, Mrs Campbell, where are the cards ? "

" The cards, Mr Hume ! Surely you forget what day it is."

" Not at all, Madam. You know we often have a quiet rubber on a Sunday evening."

After vainly endeavouring to make him retract this calumny, Mrs Campbell fairly had to turn him out of the door, remonstrating, " Now, David, you'll just be pleased to walk out of my house, for you're not fit company in it tonight." [2]

While still at James's Court, Hume received a letter from Colonel Edmonstoune requesting him to hand on an enclosed guinea to a former maid of his. " I am sorry to tell you," wrote Hume in reply, " that your Nymph, whom I have not seen for many Years, has, by all accounts, degenerated very much from the primitive Innocence, in which you found her, and, I hope, left her : She has indeed, I believe, become a common Prostitute. . . . I commend your Humanity ; though perhaps, it is misplac'd on the present Occasion. Not but dissolute People are a proper Object of Compassion ; but no Assistance or Relief does them any Service. However, I keep your Guinea . . . till I shall see you. But why is that so seldom ? Why do you never come to Town ? What are you employ'd about, farming, reading, procreating, or nothing at all ? " The letter concludes, " Were I not occupyd very much in building, I shoud have attended Baron Mure, and rejoicd at your Fire Side." [3]

By the autumn of 1770 Hume was engaged in the building of " a small House," as he informed Strahan ; " I mean a large House for an Author : For it is nearly as large as Mr Millar's in Pall-mall. It is situated in our new Square," that is, St Andrew Square, one block north of Princes Street. During the following winter and spring, Hume actively supervised the erection of the

[1] Hill Burton, II, 458–9 ; *Scots Haggis*, p. 78.
[2] *Caldwell Papers*, PT. I, 41n.   [3] NHL, pp. 191–2.

dwelling-house, coach-house, and stables. As the North Bridge was not yet open, he customarily took the short cut to the New Town across the bog left by the draining of the Nor' Loch. On one of his daily trips to St Andrew Square during this period, Hume slipped from the path and fell into the bog, where he struggled in vain to extricate himself. In time, he was able to attract the attention of an old fishwife who, as she recognised " Hume the Atheist," doubted the propriety of helping him.

" But, my good woman," expostulated the helpless man, " does not your religion as a Christian teach you to do good, even to your enemies ? "

" That may well be," she replied, " but ye shallna get out o' that, till ye become a Christian yoursell : and repeat the Lord's Prayer and the Belief." Much to her astonishment Hume readily complied and was forthwith pulled out of the bog. Henceforth he was ever ready to acknowledge that the Edinburgh fishwife was the most acute theologian he had ever encountered.[1]

At Whitsunday 1771 Hume removed from James's Court ; but, not wishing to sell his old " house," he leased it to James Boswell, evidently for a period of four years.[2] After two years, however, Boswell, requiring larger quarters, removed to another " house " on the same stair and sub-let Hume's to Lady Wallace. Boswell's removal involved Hume in a lawsuit brought before the Baillie Court by one Adam Gillies, a mason.

An incident of minor eighteenth-century racketeering, the lawsuit is not without personal interest. In a letter of mandate, dated 19 February 1774, Hume authorised John Watson, a procurator, to appear for him in court. The pertinent facts in the case are these. Mrs Boswell, on leaving Hume's " house," had called in Gillies to replaster the kitchen. " The Fellow, having thus got into the house, went about teizing Lady Wallace, and telling her, that this and the other thing was wrong, and ought to be mended," but she found nothing wrong. Gillies then went to Hume, saying that Lady Wallace wanted the stone pavement under the coal bunker to be repaired ; and Hume, having confidence in her judgment, consented. Gillies further proceeded to make other unauthorised repairs, charging them to Hume's account. And when Hume refused to pay for more than the contracted work, Gillies had him summoned to court.

Gillies's libel was duly answered by the defence with a

[1] *Caldwell Papers*, PT, II, VOL. II, 177, *n*1.
[2] See below, Appendix G, p. 621.

memorial drawn up by Hume himself, acting as his own lawyer. After the questioning of witnesses at several preliminary hearings, the presiding Baillie on 5 April found " the Defender David Hume liable for the Sum of one pound fifteen Shillings & one penny, Sterling, the amount of the account libelled on " and found him also " liable to the pursuer in Fifteen Shillings, Sterling, of Expences." No man to take defeat without a struggle, Hume petitioned for a review and for a dismissal of all charges except those actually contracted for. This document, again drawn up by Hume himself, reads in part :

He is sorry to observe that he is brought in for a Debt which he never contracted, 'tis not so much as alledg'd by the Pursuer that he ever was employed by me to do the work mentioned in his accountt. The only answer he could make to this was, that the Work was necessary to be done, but this your Petitioner apprehends is no good answer, because by the same Rule he may go thro' every house in Edinburgh, & do what he thinks proper to be done, without the Landlords consent or approbation, & give the same reason for what he did, That the work was necessary & that the house was the better of it, a Doctrine quite new &, as your Petitioner apprehends, altogether untenable.

In the Defences, your Petitioner denied that ever he had employed, the Pursuer to do the Work for him & if he did it without his knowledge or his orders he certainly cannot complain, if your Petitioner tells him he is not Bound to pay him, for by the same rule if the House had been in danger of falling down & the Pursuer had taken it in his head to take it down & rebuild it, he might have pursued your Petitioner for payment of this new Building, a thing altogether Incongruous.

The reply in behalf of Gillies ridicules the petition—" it is always a sign of a Bad cause when a person goes into Suppositious cases in place of the reall question before the Court "—asks for its rejection, and demands that the defender be found " lyable in Seven shillings sixpence as the expense of this answer." However ethically sound Hume's position may have been—and there seems little doubt of it—Hume was overlooking the fact that the Baillie Court had the " power of valuing and selling ruinous houses within the borough, in order that they may be rebuilt, in the case the proprietor shall refuse to rebuild or repair them." [1] He seems also to have forgotten that the Baillies almost invariably ruled in favour of the tradespeople and against the gentry.

No further documents appear in the records, and in view of the fact that those previously cited are to be found among the " Unextracted Baillie Court Processes " [2] it is to be assumed that

[1] Arnot, *Edinburgh*, p. 499.
[2] Bundle No. 396 (50) ; in City Chambers, Edinburgh. See also " Burgh Court Diet Book," VOL. LVIII, under dates of 10, 15, 22 Mar. and 7 Apr. 1774.

Hume gave up his lost cause and paid Gillies before the costs mounted any higher. That he continued to seethe with indignation is also a safe assumption.

Prior involvement with the law had come to Hume through his newly feued land on St Andrew Square. The plot of ground had cost him dear, a total of £165 4s 11d, together with an annual " feu duty " of £2 18s.[1] Hume was willing to invest so much money because the plans of James Craig, which had been officially adopted by the Town Council for the laying out of the New Town, displayed the south side of Princes Street as open. So in order to safeguard their view of the proposed gardens and of the Old Town in the background, Hume and the other purchasers agreed to limit the height of buildings behind them on the north side of Princes Street. To their dismay, however, the Town Council soon began to issue permits for the erection of buildings on the south side—commercial buildings at that, including a coach-yard and wrights' shops.

The indignant feuars in St Andrew Square, including David Hume, Andrew Crosbie, and Sir William Forbes, protested at once, raising an action before the Court of Session to prohibit building on the south side of Princes Street. The protestors stated that their prime objectives were " to maintain their privileges, and to prevent the town of Edinburgh from defacing a plan which is an ornament to the kingdom, by preventing buildings, which . . . would be a disgrace to the ancient, or any, royalty." [2]

The " Haill Fifteen," as the Lords of Session were popularly known when sitting together, summarily dismissed the action in October 1771. An appeal to the House of Lords, however, brought reversal the following April, Lord Mansfield making partial atonement (in the eyes of Hume) for his adverse decision in the Douglas Cause by caustically condemning the conduct of the Town Council. In this way David Hume shared in the honour of safeguarding Princes Street for posterity.

The new dwelling-house of David Hume on the south-west corner of St Andrew Square was entered from the side street running down to Princes Street. Unnamed on Craig's map or on any other early map of New Town, this short street is tradition-

---

[1] " Council Records," VOL. XCI, ff. 75–7, and " Chartulary Extended Royalty No. 2," f. 145, in City Chambers, Edinburgh ; " P.R.S., Edinburgh," VOL. CCCXII, f. 87, in SRO.
[2] " Session Papers," VOL. CXXXI, No. 2, in Signet Library, Edinburgh ; Arnot's *Edinburgh*, pp. 316–18. See too Dr C. A. Malcolm's entertaining account of *Princes Street, Edinburgh*, issued in 1938 by the Life Association of Scotland.

ally associated with the philosopher. The story of its naming is
a good one.

Nancy Ord, the third daughter of Robert Ord, Lord Chief
Baron of the Court of the Scottish Exchequer, was a lovely and
charming young English woman and a favourite of David's.
Nancy had a keen sense of humour and one day roguishly chalked
on the outside of her friend's house " St David's Street." Peggy
Irvine discovered the sign and excitedly protested to her master.
Upon inspection David forbade her to touch it : " Never mind,
lassie, many a better man has been made a saint of before." The
jest took hold and Hume's Street, thereafter, was " commonly
called " St David's Street, later acquiring official sanction as
St David Street.[1]

If Nancy Ord actually " canonised " David, it was not for
the first time, either in jest or in earnest. Sir Harry Erskine
thought him a saint in his nature, and Lady Elliot-Murray could
not help but agree. In the ephemeral ballads of 1757 over John
Home's *Douglas*, he had been called " Scotland's St David."
Chastellux compared him to the St Michael of Michael Angelo
or of Raphael. Voltaire called him his " St David." [2] From *le bon
David* to St David was no great jump, and David Hume had no
reason to be affronted by " St David's Street." Doubtless he
understood Nancy's intentions perfectly because the philosopher
and the girl held one another in the deepest affection.

" I am engagd in the building a house, which is the second
great Operation of human Life," Hume had written to Baron
Mure in October 1770 : " For the taking a Wife is the first,
which I hope will come in time "—and there is reason to believe
that the statement was somewhat more than jocular. Henry
Mackenzie, who took great pride in the company of Hume, states
that, " I was frequently of his party at Chief Baron Ord's, whose
family were great favourites of his, and he certainly at one time
meant to pay his addresses to Miss Nancy Ord, at that time one
of the most agreeable and accomplished women I ever knew."
Elsewhere Mackenzie explicitely states that the " disparity of age "
prevented David from proposing to Nancy.[3]

To a man of sixty, a first marriage must seem a momentous
step and if to a woman about half his age, an almost impossible
one. Nevertheless, it was contemplated seriously. David Hume

---

[1] Hill Burton, ii, 436 ; there are several other versions. See below, Appendix H,
p. 621.   [2] Quoted by the Comte de Creutz, RSE, iv, 22, 47.
[3] Mackenzie, *Anecdotes and Egotisms*, pp. 77, 170, 176.

had never been a determined bachelor ; but, though a man of warm passions, he was customarily a man of caution. Earlier in life, we have some reason to believe, he had paid his addresses to a young lady in Edinburgh of good family and great personal attractions. His suit was unfavourably received ; some years afterwards, however, when he had attained celebrity, it was hinted to him by a common friend that the lady had changed her mind. " So have I," replied the philosopher. As late as 1766 " Fish " Crawford could tease his older friend about " the young beauty for whom you had formerly some passion." [1] Hume's passion for the two countesses of Italy and France may also remind us that he was attracted by external beauty when in conjunction with vivacity of manners and attainments of the mind.

David Hume, his many feminine admirers were convinced, was the sort of a man who should marry, and few of them would have been greatly surprised had he actually done so. Considerable comment was caused, nevertheless, when the report of his engagement to Nancy Ord reached Paris. " Is it true that M. Hume has married a devout woman ? " inquired Mme du Deffand of Horace Walpole in June 1770. Three months previous Mrs Alison Cockburn had heard, she wrote to David, " that Mr Hume is about to quit his immortal muse for a mere mortal, for a wife." Pretending to be highly indignant, she protested, " Can a man quit the applause of the whole world—and become the property of one female ? O fy—let us not hear of it." Then her curiosity got the upper hand—" Or in the Boswalian Manner let us have every Circumstance. . . ." [2]

At the very time that Hume was perhaps most seriously considering a belated marriage, he first began to feel the infirmities of age. " I have now no object but to

> Sit down and think, and die in peace—

What other project can a man of my age entertain ? " he wrote in January 1772 to Mme de Boufflers, whose agitation over the report of his marriage to Nancy Ord had been noticed by friends. Nevertheless, he continued to enjoy the company of attractive and vivacious women, and in his autobiography was to write with studied understatement that, " as I took a particular Pleasure in

---

[1] *Caldwell Papers*, PT. II, VOL. II, 178, *n2* ; RSE, IV, 43.   [2] RSE, IV, 33. See Textual Supplement for Hume's three known letters to Nancy Ord, published by John V. Price in *David Hume and the Enlightenment*, ed. W. B. Todd (Edinburgh and Austin 1974), 128–35.

the Company of modest women, I had no Reason to be displeased with the Reception I met with from them."

" My Sisters and I," writes Mrs Ann Murray Keith, daughter of Ambassador Keith, " were of that Circle which D. Hume lived intimately with, & a most pleasant Companion he was ! his Conversation never turned on those subjects which give offence in his writing. He was one of the sweetest tempered Men & the most benevolent that ever was born. His early Studies had turned very much on the dreadful effects of Enthusiasm, & that led him too far in his endeavours to correct the errors which had excited his horror. There was a simplicity & pleasantness of Manners about him that were delightful in Society. He was a Charm in domestic life ! In short he was one of the most worthy & agreeable Men I ever knew." [1]

At North Merchiston one afternoon for tea with Mrs Adam, David unexpectedly found himself alone with two or three young ladies of his acquaintance. While he was conversing amiably with them, the chair on which he was sitting began to give way under his weight, gradually bringing him to the floor. At first alarmed for his safety, the company were amused when the philosopher struggled to his feet and instructed them : " Young ladies, you must tell Mr Adam to keep strong chairs for heavy philosophers." [2]

Hume's " Charm in domestic life " had, however, its momentary lapses. One night, playing cards at Abbey Hill with Mrs Mure, he got into a warm discussion over the niceties of the game and lost his temper. Taking up his hat and calling to a Pomeranian dog that always accompanied him, " Come away, Foxey," he walked out of the house in the middle of the rubber. The family were to start the next morning for Caldwell ; and David, who lived a good mile distant, was at the door before breakfast, hat in hand, with an apology. It was Mrs Mure who was wont to refer to the Edinburgh literary circle as " David Home and the Rest of the Ministers." [3]

Lady Balcarres, an old crony of Mrs Cockburn, had long been a great favourite of David Hume. During his autumnal years at Edinburgh, he was a constant morning visitor at her home. In a reminiscent mood one day, she jested with him about a Christmas visit to Balcarres Castle on the Fife coast. The incident and its sequel are related by her daughter, Lady Anne Lindsay :

[1] NLS, MS 3524, f. 71.   [2] Adam, *Sequel*, pp. 21–2.
[3] *Caldwell Papers*, PT. I, 39 ; NLS, MS Acc. 1237.

When we were very young girls, too young to remember the scene, there happened to be a good many clever people at Balcarres at Christmas, and as a gambol of the season they agreed to write each his own character, to give them to Hume, and make him shew them to my father, as extracts he had taken from the Pope's library at Rome.

He did. My father said, " I don't know who the rest of your fine fellows and charming princesses are, Hume ; but if you had not told me where you got this character, I should have said it was that of my wife."

" I was pleased," said my mother, " with my lord's answer ; it shewed that at least I had been an honest woman."

" Hume's character of himself," said she, " was well drawn and full of candour ; he spoke of himself as he ought " ; but added, what surprised us all, that, " plain as his manners were, and apparently careless of attention, vanity was his predominant weakness. That vanity led him to publish his opinions, but that he thought he had injured society by disseminating them."

" Do you remember the sequel of that affair ? " said Hume.

" Yes, I do," replied my mother, laughing : " you told me that, although I thought your character a sincere one, it was not so—there was a particular feature omitted, that we were still ignorant of, and that you would add it ; like a fool I gave you the manuscript, and you thrust it into the fire, adding, ' Oh ! what an idiot I had nearly proved myself to be, to leave such a document in the hands of a parcel of women ! ' "

" Villain ! " said my mother, laughing and shaking her head at him.

" Do you remember all this, my little woman ? " said Hume to me.

" I was too young," said I, " to think of it at the time."

" How's this ? Have not you and I grown up together ? " I looked surprised.

" Yes," added he, " You have grown tall, and I have grown broad." [1]

The self-character that Hume so judiciously tossed into the fire may possibly survive in that " Character of —— written by himself," which, although not in his own hand, has been corrected by him. In any event, it is deserving of comparison with the character in *My Own Life* and with that drawn by Adam Smith :

1. A very good man the constant purpose of whose life is to do mischief.

2. Fancies he is disinterested because he substitutes vanity in place of all other passions.

3. Very industrious, without serving [either] himself or others.

4. Licentious in his pen, cautious in his words, still more so in his actions.

5. Would have had no enemies had he not courted them, seems desirous of being hated by the public but has only attained the being railed at.

6. Has never been hurt by his enemies, because he never hated any one of them.

7. Exempt from vulgar prejudices, full of his own.

8. Very bashful, somewhat modest, no way humble.

9. A fool capable of performances which few wise men can execute.

10. A wise man guilty of indiscretions which the greatest simpletons can perceive.

[1] *Lives of the Lindsays*, II, 321n.

11. Sociable though he lives in solitude.
12. Mirthful though he possesses little wit and still less humour.
13. An enthusiast without religion, a philosopher, who despairs to attain truth.
14. A moralist who prefers instinct to reason.
15. A gallant who gives no offence to husbands and mothers.
16. A scholar without [the] ostentation [of learning].[1]

Lady Anne Lindsay also remarks on the frequent dinners "monopolised by the divines, wits, and writers of the present day. . . . Our friend David Hume, along with his friend Principal Robertson, continue to maintain their ground at these convivial meetings. To see the lion and the lamb living together, the deist and the doctor, is extraordinary ; it makes one hope that some day Hume will say to him, ' Thou almost persuades me to be a Christian.' " Alison Cockburn goes a little further in suggesting that " David did not know he was a Christian." The reason she gives was his " total want of fire, of ethereal fire." Further instances of the tendency to " canonise " David ! Alison notes, however, that David was wont to refer to women as " the weak pious sex."

Hume allowed himself a wider latitude of expression with the stronger sex, and not always did the lamb remain on friendly terms with the lion. In the Reverend John Warden, for instance, Hume found another Bishop of Raphoe. The scene of the encounter was Lord Kames's, where also was William Smellie, the printer. The conversation went along pleasantly enough until Dr Warden happened to mention a sermon published by Jonathan Edwards with the curious title of *The Usefulness of Sin.* " The usefulness of sin ! " echoed David. " I suppose," he went on musingly, " Mr Edwards has adopted the system of Leibniz that all is for the best in this best of all possible worlds." Then he burst out " But what the devil does the fellow make of hell and damnation ? "

Dr Warden, to the amazement of all, took his hat and left the house despite Lord Kames's attempts to conciliate him.[2] Kames and Hume, it will be recalled, were on perfectly friendly terms during this period.

With Professor John Bruce, who held the Chair of Logic at Edinburgh, Hume was also on good terms. The Professor asked him to revise the syllabus of his lectures. In going over the proof-sheets, Hume came to the section entitled " Proofs of the Existence of the Deity." After a moment's pause, he said, " Right ; very well." But at the next section, which was entitled " Proof of the

[1] RSE, xiii, 38. The words in brackets were added by Hume.
[2] Smellie, *Memoirs* (Edinburgh 1811), i, 357-8.

Unity of the Deity," he cried out, " Stop, John, stop. Who told you whether there were *ane* or *mair* ? " The same professor met him one day on the staircase of the university library, where the inscription *Christo et Musis has aedes sacrarunt cives Edinenses* drew from the sceptic an irreverent observation on the juncture which the piety, rather than the classical purity, of the good town had made between the worship of the heathen and their own.[1]

One Sunday forenoon, going forth to his walk, the philosopher met Sir James Hunter Blair, an eminent banker in Edinburgh, on his way to church with his lady. They asked Hume to turn and accompany them. " What," replied he, " go to church with you ! with publicans and money changers, the same who were driven with scourges out of the temple ! No, no, I'll never be seen entering a church in such company." [2]

David Hume was justly proud of his new house, the building of which he had personally supervised. " I wish you saw (as I hope you will)," he wrote to Strahan, " my new House and Situation in St Andrews Square :   You woud not wonder that I have abjurd London for ever." To another correspondent he boasted that " our New Town . . . exceeds anything you have seen in any part of the world." The new house, of course, was managed by Peggy Irvine, who as housekeeper directed a staff of servants. The family itself was small : David and sister Katherine, to whom may be added David's little Pomeranian dog, Foxey. The brother and sister kept a plentiful table, entertained widely, and achieved a reputation for gracious hospitality. One of the first of their guests was a distinguished visitor from America, a man whom Hume held to be " the first philosopher, and indeed the first great man of letters, for whom we are beholden to her." [3]

" Thro' Storms and Floods I arrived here on Saturday night, late and was lodg'd miserably at an Inn," wrote Benjamin Franklin to Strahan ; " But that excellent Christian David Hume, agreeable to the Precepts of the Gospel, has received the Stranger and I now live with him at his House in the new Town most happily." Hume also wrote to Strahan : " I was so happy as to prevail on the Doctor to be my Guest during his Stay here. . . . He got over from Ireland in a short Interval between two Hurricanes by a particular Providence. At least I hope that he considers it in that light." Franklin had arrived at Edinburgh on

[1] Brougham, *Men of Letters*, 1, 238.   [2] *Caldwell Papers*, PT. 1, 40, n1.
[3] The following account of Franklin at Edinburgh is based largely on J. B. Nolan, *Benjamin Franklin in Scotland and Ireland 1759 and 1771* (Philadelphia 1938).

26 October 1771, and it was the following day that Hume offered him the hospitality of St David's Street. On 21 November Franklin finally left for London, having spent the entire period with Hume, with the exception of five days with Lord Kames at Blair Drummond and two or three more at Glasgow. The visit was marked by one long round of dinners in the Edinburgh literary circle.

Another American, Henry Marchant, a jurist from Rhode Island, was also in town ; and on 31 October Principal Robertson brought him after breakfast " to see Dr. Franklin, who lodged with the Celebrated Mr. David Hume in an Elegant House in the New Part of the City." The young American was greatly impressed with the Scottish philosopher : " Mr. Hume is a Gentleman I should think of about sixty years very large & heavy built. His Face is by no Means an Index of the Ingenuity of his Mind, especially of his delicacy & vivacity. But in Truth he is a very pleasant Gentleman in Conversation." The topic of discussion was the trade of Europe and America, and the group did not break up until the early afternoon. A few days later Hume invited Marchant to dine with him and Franklin. " Being only with ourselves," observes Marchant, " we set with much free Sociability till after Tea in the Evening." Unhappily Marchant had no eye for Boswellian details, but he does express surprise that Hume's servant, who lighted him home, refused to accept a gratuity. The practice of vails, which Hume had so obstinately opposed earlier in life, had finally been abolished.

A Boswellian glimpse of Hume and Franklin is supplied by Henry Mackenzie. " One day," he writes, " when the Doctor was detailing the natural advantages of America, and prophesying what a country it would become, ' You have forgotten one little article, Doctor,' said David, ' among your projected manufactures, the manufacture of men ' "—a prophecy which has certainly come true.[1]

On the morning of 5 November, Marchant attended medical lectures at Edinburgh University and in the evening, supped at Hume's with Franklin and the faculty. " We were introduced," he notes, " to the President & to all the Members ; And here I found all the Doctors whose Lectures I had heard in the Morning." The following day the two Americans left for Blair Drummond and Glasgow.

On 18 November, the day after his return to Edinburgh,

[1] Mackenzie, *Anecdotes and Egotism*, p. 170.

Franklin was the guest of honour at a dinner at St David's Street. The party included Marchant, Lord Kames, and Professors Black, Ferguson, and Russell. Marchant managed to produce a classic of understatement in his diary, " in such good company, I could not fail of being entertained." Lord Kames, the following day, gave a dinner for Franklin and Hume at his house in New Street. Then, on the eve of Franklin's departure, they were all the guests of Adam Ferguson.

Mrs Ann Murray Keith, who had occasion, she says, " to know a good deal " about Franklin's " temper & Heart " during his prolonged visit with Hume in 1771, found him a " Sly old Fellow." She adds that " I do not think he was either very gratefull or very agreeable " to his host, but fails to cite any evidence.[1] Certainly there is none on the part of either, though it may be suspected that being men of strong opinion, they indulged in animated disputes. Franklin's letter of thanks to Hume is not extant, but its friendly tone is reflected in Hume's acknowledgement of 7 February 1772 that, " I was very glad to hear of your safe Arrival in London, after being expos'd to as many Perils as St Paul, by Land and by Water : Though to no Perils among false Bretheren : For the good Wishes of all your Brother Philosophers in this place attend you heartily and sincerely, together with much Regret that your Business wou'd not allow you to pass more time among them." [2]

At London, soon after, Franklin spoke of David Hume as one " who entertain'd me with the greatest Kindness and Hospitality " and, through Strahan, sent him word " to be affectionately remembered to you and to your worthy Sister, who was so kind to him." In 1774 Franklin was deprived of the office of Deputy Postmaster-General of the Colonies after a vigorous attack by the Solicitor-General, Alexander Wedderburn. Torn between two friendships, Hume wrote to Adam Smith : " Pray, what strange Accounts are these we hear of Franklin's Conduct ? I am very slow in believing that he had been guilty in the extreme Degree that is pretended ; tho' I always knew him to be a very factious man, and Faction, next to Fanaticism, is, of all passions, the most destructive of Morality. . . . I hear that Wedderburn's Treatment of him before the Council, was most cruel, without being in the least blameable. What a Pity ! " Perhaps it was this factiousness of Franklin's that led Mrs Keith to imagine that he was ungrateful and disagreeable to Hume.

[1] NLS, MS 3524, f. 60.   [2] NHL, pp. 191–2.

With the departure of Franklin from St David Street, life there settled down to normal routine, shortly to be broken, however, as Hume informed Adam Smith, by " the Misfortunes of my Family." The deep and abiding affection between David and his sister Katherine is to be read between the lines of his apology for not having invited Smith over for Christmas. " My Sister," explains David, " fell dangerously ill of a Fever ; and though the Fever be now gone, she is still so weak and low, and recovers so slowly, that I was afraid it woud be but a melancholy House to invite you to. However, I expect, that time will re-instate her in her former Health, in which case, I shall look forward to your Company."

Family ties were always binding to David Hume, and with the Ninewells group he generously shared his late affluence. The original government pension of £200 in 1763 had been doubled at the termination of the Embassy Secretaryship, and in 1769 another £200 had been added. Unlike the earlier grants, however, this last was not free from tax deductions and produced only about £156 annually.[1] Under the persuasion of Lord Hertford and General Conway, therefore, Hume made some feeble effort to get another government sinecure, but nothing came of it. He needed no more money, being able to live well on less than half of his income. He was happy to provide an additional allowance to his sister, over and above her room and servants, and he took a particular pride and delight in financing and generally supervising the education of his nephews.

As Joseph Home, eldest son of John Home of Ninewells, showed little inclination to letters, his uncle purchased for him in 1770 a Cornetcy in the Second Regiment of Dragoon Guards for the sum of £1,000, to which he added £262 10s five years later for the difference between the Cornetcy and a Lieutenancy.[2] Hume also paid Joseph's expenses of about £100 a year and in 1775 treated him to a visit to France of eight or nine months' duration. In a letter of introduction to Mme de Boufflers, the fond uncle humorously stretched a point in favour of his nephew : " He is a piece of a scholar too, and passes for a prodigy of learning in his regiment. I doubt not but he will make a figure in that respect among the young officers " of France.

With his second nephew David Home, who had a real call

---

[1] This figure and those in the following paragraph are based upon NLS, MS 3028.

[2] For Hume's concern, generosity and advice over " Josey's " misfortune, see letter of 12 October 1771, in " David Hume : Some Unpublished Letters, 1771–1776," ed. Geoffrey Hunter, *Texas Studies in Literature and Language* (1960), II, 133–4.

to letters, the philosopher developed a close affinity. He paid for David's education at Glasgow University under Professor John Millar and proudly watched his progress in law. Always the man of letters even during his last illness, Hume advised him about his course of summer reading.[1] The young David was later to justify his uncle's faith and expressed his appreciation by changing his surname to Hume—no doubt to his father's disgust.

John Home of Ninewells had earlier become John Home of Ninewells and Fairney-castle ; in 1767 he moved to Edinburgh for his children's education. During David's absence as Under-Secretary of State, the family dwelt at James's Court and later were always welcome at St David Street. By 1776, however, they were also housed in New Town, Edinburgh, at Butters Land. The Earl of Home, a not infrequent visitor at St David Street, introduced to his kinsman a young English medical student named Sylas Neville, who was at first reluctant to meet the philosopher " on account of the badness of his principles." After meeting him, however, Neville altered his opinion : " His manner is easy & agreeable as might be expected in a man who has seen so much of life & is so well acquainted with the world. But at first one would not take him for that first-rate genius which he really is. He often talks very vulgar Scotch." [2] A young American medical student at Edinburgh, Benjamin Rush, had gained the impression that the philosopher's disposition was entirely benevolent and blameless.[3]

The pleasant pattern of Hume's last years in Edinburgh was customarily varied with country visits during the late summer, visits to the family home at Ninewells, to Mure at Caldwell, to Elliot at Minto, to Edmonstoune at Newton ; visits with General Conway and Lady Ailesbury (sister to the Duke of Argyll) to the Argyll estates at Roseneath on the Gareloch and at Inveraray Castle on Loch Fyne. The " Congress at Inveraray " of August 1771 was so well attended that, though fifty beds had been prepared, " even David Hume for all his great figure as a Philosopher, and Historian, or his greater as a fat man, was obliged by the *adamantine peg-maker* to make one of three in a bed." Perhaps it was on a less crowded visit to Inveraray that David Hume, at the express invitation of the parish minister, went to church in the company of Lady Elizabeth Hamilton. The sermon was on the subject of unreasonable scepticism. " That's at you, Mr. Hume,"

---

[1] For extract from letter of 20 May 1776, see Textual Supplement.
[2] *Diary of Sylas Neville, 1767–1788*, ed. Basil Cozens-Hardy (London 1950), pp. 192, 202. [3] See Textual Supplement.

commented his companion. At the close of his discourse the minister said, " And now, my friends, I will address a few words to the chief of sinners."—"That's to your Ladyship," retorted Hume.[1] From Ninewells in the autumn of 1772 Hume drove over in his chaise to Minto. Sir Gilbert unfortunately was not at home and, after a short stay, Hume went on to Edinburgh. Soon after, Lady Elliot-Murray wrote to inform him of the sequel:

Enter Sir Gilbert. Where is Mr. Hume?—Answer : He is gone. When did he come?—About one o'clock. And when did he go away?—About five. What ! have you quarrelled?—Yes. He and I had some little difference about his *byeuks*, and I tried to persuade him to burn them all, and write the other way ; for, as I said, I was sure he would be a shining light, and equal the author of the " Pilgrim's Progress," or Mr. Ebenezer Erskine, if he would only take the right side ; and he flew in a passion and went away in a huff ! How could you think he would be persuaded by you ? Pooh ! though I am but a simple woman, before it be long he may be convinced I can see farther into a millstone than he can do ; and if he had taken my advice, he might have rested his bones here this night in quiet, in place of rumbling along in the dark in a post chaise ; and so in other matters too, I might perhaps do him a service if he would be ruled by me. My dear, how can you be so wild ? And, my dear, where is the harm in telling one's mind, when you think you can do good by it, to a good worthy creature that is only a little mistaken or so ? Good by it, what a chimera ! but come, there is some other reason than this for his going away ? None that I know ; except a fine flim-flam letter that he received from the French Ambassador, saying, he expected to have the exquisite joy of beholding him at Edinburgh tomorrow. Ah, now I understand it. But when does he come back ? Why he either comes back with Mons. De Guigne, or after he has done the last duties to him at Edinburgh. So you see, if you do not come, you will have brought me in for the lesser excommunication ; for you will have been the cause of my deceiving my husband, and telling him a lie : although, for that matter, neither you nor I *lukelly* have any thing to fear now-a-days, for either the greater or lesser excommunication.[1]

These country excursions from the pleasure of urban life were themselves, to be sure, strictly in the line of pleasure. The sum of happiness achieved by the aging philosopher may perhaps be estimated from the statement in his autobiography : " . . . were I to name the period of my Life which I shoud most choose to pass over again I might be tempted to point to this last Period." This picture of Hume's autumnal serenity, however, although essentially true in focus, is somewhat distorted in detail. For the last years of his life were no little ruffled by a resurgence of controversy, the most acrimonious and personal of his entire career.

[1] Daniel Wray to Lord Hardwicke, quoted by John Nichols, *Illustrations of the Literary History of the Eighteenth Century* (London 1817–58), i, 141–2 (see Horace, *Odes*, iii, xxiv) ; Mackenzie, *Anecdotes and Egotisms*, p. 97.   [2] RSE, vi, 75.

CHAPTER 38

DISTURBERS OF THE PEACE

" That bigotted silly Fellow, Beattie."

IT was *An Essay on the Nature and Immutability of Truth ; in opposition to Sophistry and Scepticism*, a work which went through five editions between its first appearance in 1770 and the death of Hume in 1776, that was chiefly responsible for disturbing the philosopher's tranquillity. The author, James Beattie, was a follower of the " Common Sense Philosophy " which had been instituted in Scotland in 1764 by Thomas Reid, and which two years later had been applied by James Oswald in *An Appeal to Common Sense in Behalf of Religion*. Hume had exchanged amicable letters with Reid, but had completely ignored Oswald. Beattie was not to be ignored, however, for, unlike Hume's other " friendly Adversaries " at Aberdeen, who treated the aging philosopher with the respect due a serious thinker, it was Beattie's intention to arouse the emotional prejudices of his readers.

James Beattie was Professor of Moral Philosophy and Logic at Marischal College, Aberdeen, occupying a chair that had been given him at the early age of twenty-five, when, by his own account, he had never so much as inquired into the subject of metaphysics. Within a very few years, however, he had inquired so relentlessly as to convince himself that the great succession of British philosophers (Hobbes, Locke, Berkeley, and above all, Hume) were wrong and that he himself had arrived at ultimate truth. By 1767 his animus against Hume was so strong that he composed a prose allegory entitled " The Castle of Scepticism " in which Hume is portrayed as the despotic governor of the castle who enslaved and tortured all that could be enticed to enter.[1] Though the lampoon was ultimately suppressed by Beattie, its tone of satire, oddly enough, carried over into the *Essay on Truth*.

The emotional approach to philosophy taken by Beattie is outlined in a university lecture which he gave in the same year :

---

[1] MS in Aberdeen University Library. See Mossner, " Beattie's ' The Castle of Scepticism ' " : An Unpublished Allegory against Hume, Voltaire, and Hobbes, in University of Texas *Studies in English*, XXVII (1948), 108–45.

I shall . . . propose a Criterion which I hope will be of use in enabling you to detect those Scepticall & Sophisticall Reasonings which by contradicting common sense involve the whole of Science in confusion & error.

If therefore a philosopher advance a doctrine in contradiction to the general opinion both of the learned & unlearned in all ages ;—If the arguments by which the new doctrine is supported, however unanswerable they may be accounted, do never produce a serious & steady conviction of the truth of what they are intended to prove—If we think after reading the arguments with attention, that the Doctrine would be attended with fatal consequences to Science to Virtue & to Religion ;—Then let us pronounce all such Reasoning absurd in its own nature even previously to its being logically confuted.[1]

On the application of this doctrine in the *Essay on Truth* Beattie comments in a letter to Thomas Gray : " I have frequently given a little into declamation, and something of a flippant drollery, both which I know are unsuitable to a philosophical enquiry. I did this, partly to amuse myself, and partly to render my subject not altogether unentertaining." [2]

The propensity to declamation on the part of Beattie inspired such rhetoric as this : " When one has long drudged in the dull and unprofitable pages of metaphysics, how pleasing the transition to a moral writer of true genius ! Would you know what that genius is, and where it may be found ? Go to Shakespeare, to Bacon, to Johnson, to Montesquieu, to Rousseau ; and when you have studied them, return, if you can, to HUME, and HOBBES, and MALEBRANCHE, and LEIBNITZ, and SPINOSA " ; and the reference to the writings of the modern sceptic as " Those unnatural productions, the vile effusion of a hard and stupid heart, that mistakes its own restlessness for the activity of genius, and its own captiousness for sagacity of understanding." [3] So far from being contrite for his use of abusive language in a philosophical discourse, Beattie spiritedly defended it in a postscript to the second edition ; by 1776, however, he somewhat grudgingly and ostentatiously toned down a few passages.

Beattie had hit the right tone for popular success. In Scotland, where the Edinburgh booksellers had refused at first to bring out his invective against Hume, it had been published only by " a species of pious fraud " ; but it sold widely.[4] In England it had a

---

[1] " A Compendious System of Pneumatology, Comprehending Psychology, Moral Philosophy, & Logic. Taken at the Lectures of Mr. Js. Beattie P. P. At the Marischal College & University of Abdn. By J. Rennie. Anno 1767," pp. 452–3 (MS in Glasgow University Library).

[2] MS letter of 1 May 1770 in Beattie Papers (B. 24), Aberdeen University Library.

[3] Beattie, *Essay on Truth*, 4th edn. (London 1773), pp. 437–9 ; 482. In the 1776 edition, the second quotation above deletes " and stupid."

[4] Margaret Forbes, *Beattie and His Friends* (London 1904), p. 45.

tremendous vogue, Dr Johnson and Edmund Burke having proclaimed it true philosophy. At London in 1773, Beattie received the adulation of many who were pleased with the buffeting that he had administered to Hume and who were persuaded—as the Archbishop of Canterbury reported that George III was persuaded—that he had " cut Mr. Hume up by the roots." He was received by the King and awarded a pension of £200 annually —exactly one-third of the pension enjoyed by the vanquished philosopher. " I never stole a book but one," His Majesty confessed to Beattie, " & that was yours. . . . I stole it from the Queen to give it to Lord Hertford to Read." [1] At Oxford Beattie was awarded the degree of Doctor of Civil Law.

Beattie's popular victory over Hume is symbolised in Sir Joshua Reynold's allegorical painting entitled " The Triumph of Truth." Standing to one side in the painting and clad in a doctor-of-law's gown and bands, the *Essay on Truth* under his arm, James Beattie is complacent over the symbolism : Truth, in the garb of an angel, is depicted as pushing down into the bottomless pit three cringing demons, the first of which is recognizable as David Hume, the second is a caricature of Voltaire, and the third is unidentifiable. That Reynolds desired the first demon to be taken for Hume is tacitly admitted in a letter that he wrote to Beattie : " Mr Hume has heard from somebody, that he is introduced into the picture, not much to his credit ; there is only a figure covering his face with his hands, which they may call Hume, or anybody else ; it is true it has a tolerable broad back. As for Voltaire, I intended he should be one of the group." [2] Oliver Goldsmith, however, was disturbed by the pomposity of the allegory and expostulated : " It very ill becomes a man of your eminence and character . . . to degrade so high a genius as Voltaire before so mean a writer as Dr. Beattie ; for Dr. Beattie and his book together will, in the space of ten years, not be known ever to have been in existence, but your allegorical picture, and the fame of Voltaire will live for ever to your disgrace as a flatterer." The criticism applies equally to the painter's debasement of Hume.

At Edinburgh the distinguished ministerial friends of Hume (William Robertson, Alexander Carlyle, and Hugh Blair) were scandalised that the philosopher—no matter how he might be

[1] *James Beattie's London Diary, 1773*, ed. R. S. Walker (Aberdeen 1945), pp. 42, 86.
[2] Forbes, *Life of Beattie*, I, 331–2. The often-repeated remark that the third demon is Gibbon is palpably absurd. Before the publication of the first volume of the *Decline and Fall* in 1776, there was no reason to associate Gibbon with Hume and Voltaire.
[3] James Northcote, *Life of Sir Joshua Reynolds* (London 1818), I, 300.

mistaken in his philosophy—should be subjected to contumely worthy only of the Warburtonian school. Blair wrote to Beattie in protest : " In some places I cannot help thinking you are too severe on Mr Hume ; & perhaps indeed from my partiality to the Worthy, humane, good natured man, I wish you had been less so. . . . I have not altogether those formidable Views which you entertain of the Consequences of Scepticism. It may prove dangerous to be sure, and it is right to combat it : the Ballance should always be kept hanging in the right side ; but a little fluctuation, now and then, to the sceptical side, tends perhaps to humble the Pride of Understanding, and to check biggotry ; and the consequences as to practice, I am enclined to think, are not very great." [1]

Dr John Gregory, Professor of the Practice of Physic at Edinburgh, and a man of piety, explained to Mrs Montagu how Hume's friends found it possible at once to reprobate his philosophy and to love the man. Beattie's " Zeal for his Cause," he wrote, " has made him treat Mr Hume sometimes with a degree of Severity which I think had better been spared. I detest Mr Hume's Philosophy as destructive of every principle interesting to Mankind & I think the general Spirit that breathes in his History unfavourable both to Religion & Liberty, tho in other respects one of the most animated, entertaining & instructive Historys I have ever read. But I love Mr Hume personally as a Worthy agreeable Man in private Life, & as I believe he does not know & cannot feel the mischief his writings have done, it hurts me extremely to see him harshly used." [2]

A report circulated in 1772 that Lord Hailes, who as Sir David Dalrymple of Newhailes had been antagonistic to Hume when he was Keeper of the Advocates' Library, was intending to bring Beattie to Edinburgh University. The entire faculty, mostly friends of Hume, took to arms. John Home, the dramatist, wrote to Colonel Edmonstoune to bring all possible pressure to bear to resist the appointment of " Mr Battie, the Author of a most illiberal book written to abuse our friend David, & calculated if the times were violent to bring him to the stake." [3] Happily the report proved exaggerated, and no serious effort was made to call Beattie from Aberdeen. Dr Gregory could, however, inform Beattie with certain truth that " Edinburgh is perhaps the only

[1] MS in Beattie Papers (C. 33), Aberdeen University Library.
[2] Letter of 3 June 1770 in MSS MO (uncat.), Huntington Library.
[3] Letter of 18 Feb. 1772, in NLS, MS 1005, f. 15.

spot in Britain where you might be said to be in an enemy's country." [1]

Beattie's extraordinary success, outside Edinburgh, was a symptom of the times. It was due, not to the *Minstrel*, but to his attack on Hume in the *Essay on Truth*. Seeing nothing of the constructive side of Hume's philosophy of human nature and mistaking him for a complete sceptic, anxious only to subvert Christianity, the age would have rejoiced to see him demolished by any means. Beattie was, however, chastened in 1774 by Joseph Priestley. Adam Smith, writing from London in 1775, assured Hume that all his friends there had been " much diverted with Priestly's answer to Beatie," but that he had been advised against answering by Bishop Hurd, so that " a most incomparable controversy " had been lost.[2] Beattie's flimsy pretensions to philosophy were not fully exposed until 1783. Kant noted that he had missed the whole point of Hume's argument, and was, moreover, mischievously over-zealous and even impudent. " I should think," wrote Kant, " that Hume might fairly have laid as much claim to common sense as Beattie and, in addition, to a critical reason (such as Beattie did not possess), which keeps common sense in check and prevents it from speculating, or if speculations are under discussion, restrains the desire to decide because it cannot satisfy its own arguments." [3]

But what of Beattie's victim ? Hume was undoubtedly angry. He is reported to have said about the *Essay on Truth*, " Truth ! there is no truth in it; it is a horrible large lie in octavo." Dr Gregory told Beattie : " The hero of the piece is extremely angry, and so are all his friends, who are numerous." Beattie himself exulted, or pretended to exult, in the fact : " Mr Hume's censure I am so far from being ashamed of, that I think it does me honour. It is, next to his conversion, (which I have no reason to look for) the most desirable thing I have to expect from that quarter. I have heard from very good authority, that he speaks of me and my book with very great bitterness (I own, I thought he would rather have affected to treat both with contempt) ; and that he says, I have not used him like a gentleman. He is quite right to set the matter upon that footing." [4]

Hume kept his long-standing resolution not to answer

---

[1] Forbes, *Beattie and his Friends*, p. 66. The record of Lord Hailes's efforts to bring Beattie to Edinburgh is to be found in Newhailes, 24, 361–2, 366, 422–4. Hailes's letters to Beattie on this subject are amongst the Beattie MSS at Aberdeen University.
[2] See Textual Supplement. [3] Kant, *Prolegomena*, Introd.
[4] *Gentlemen's Mag.*, XLVII (1777), 159*n* ; Forbes, *Life of Beattie*, I, 173–4, 171.

opponents directly. But in October 1775 he took the extra-ordinary step of drawing up a short "Advertisement" to be prefixed to the second volume of all future editions of *Essays and Treatises*:

Most of the principles, and reasonings, contained in this volume, were published in a work of three volumes, called *A Treatise of Human Nature*: A work which the Author had projected before he left College, and which he wrote and published not long after. But not finding it successful, he was sensible of his error in going to the press too early, and he cast the whole anew in the following pieces, where some negligences in his former reasoning and more in the expression, are, he hopes, corrected. Yet several writers, who have honoured the Author's Philosophy with answers, have taken care to direct all their batteries against that juvenile work, which the Author never acknowledged, and have affected to triumph in any advantages, which, they imagined, they had obtained over it : A practice very contrary to all rules of candour and fair-dealing, and a strong instance of those polemical artifices, which a bigotted zeal thinks itself authorized to employ. Henceforth, the Author desires, that the following Pieces may alone be regarded as containing his philosophical sentiments and principles.[1]

This "Advertisement," commented Hume to Strahan, "is a compleat Answer to Dr Reid and to that bigotted silly Fellow, Beattie."

Complete answer it is not, nor is it an answer at all, but the petulant retort of an ageing man, tired of controversy and sick in body. The long and unhappy career of the youthful *Treatise* from 1739 to 1775, reaching the climax in the latest spate of abuse from Beattie, must have persuaded Hume to make a public repudiation. Happily, few philosophers of our day have taken the "Advertisement" seriously; and the *Treatise of Human Nature*, so maligned by its author, is considered a masterpiece.

A minor sequel to the Beattie affair was the anonymous publication of *A Specimen of the Scots Review* by the Reverend Thomas Hepburn in 1774. The first author taken up is "that great necromancer and magician David Hume, Esq. both because he has been the cause of many useless books being published, and because all the writings against him have brought empty fame, and more solid pudding, to the authors." Those authors, Hepburn avers, "have done more harm to philosophy, religion, and truth, by this argument [of common sense], than any sceptic has ever done." Hume was much diverted by Hepburn's *Specimen*. "I wish," he told his cousin, the dramatist, "he would continue, tho at the hazard of my getting a rap over the knuckles from time to time : for I see in this hero the spirit of Drawcansir, who spares neither friend nor foe. . . . I should desire my compliments to

[1] *Phil. Wks.*, III, 37–8.

him, were I not afraid that he would interpret the civility as paying blackmail to him."

The *Specimen* also castigates the truculence of the editors of the *Edinburgh Magazine and Review*, a truculence which was to involve David Hume in a thoroughly distasteful incident, the rejection by an upstart editor of a Humean review upon the book of a distinguished colleague. The prime mover of this new periodical, established in 1773, was Gilbert Stuart, a young Scot who had earlier obtained the patronage of Hume. For unknown reasons, however, Stuart suddenly turned against his native country and its men of letters, using the pages of the periodical for a series of violent attacks. Among the victims were Lord Kames and Lord Monboddo, but the chief victim was the Reverend Dr Robert Henry, who had recently been called to the New Grey Friars Church in Edinburgh. Henry was an historian and quite naturally had turned to Hume for advice and assistance. And it was through the repeated urgings of Hume that Strahan and Cadell in 1771 brought out the first volume of Henry's *History of Great Britain from the First Invasion of it by the Romans under Julius Caesar. Written on a New Plan.*

Though Stuart had praised this first volume, in 1773 he was perversely determined to castigate the second. Taking alarm at the treatment afforded Scots authors in the *Edinburgh Magazine and Review*, and knowing that Hume fully approved of his work, Henry cannily solicited his friend to prepare a review for the very citadel of the enemy. Hume was willing and mentioned the matter to Stuart. "David Hume," confided the latter to a correspondent, " wants to review Henry : but that task is so precious that I will undertake it myself. Moses, were he to ask it as a favour, should not have it : yea, not even the man after God's own heart." [1] Yet outright refusal to consider a review by so distinguished an historian as Hume was hardly to be made, and Stuart's scheme was Machiavellian. Hume was to be permitted to submit his review. If it proved unfavourable, so much the better, as Stuart could later add to the flames. When, however, the review turned out to be favourable, Stuart set about to reduce it to absurdity. The task was not difficult.

Following a descriptive opening and a long series of illustrative

[1] Isaac Disraeli, *Calamities of Authors* (London 1812), II, 60-1. The complete story of this episode is told by Mossner, " Hume as Literary Patron : A Suppressed Review of Robert Henry's *History of Great Britain*, 1773," in *Modern Philology*, XXXIX (1942), 361-82. The original proof sheets of Hume's review are in the William Andrews Clark Memorial Library, University of California at Los Angeles.

quotations, Hume's review had ended on a critical and personal note. Henry's name as historian was linked with that of the " celebrated " Dr Robertson, and both men were praised for their happy combination of profane learning with spiritual guidance of the people. " These illustrious examples, if any thing," it concluded, " must make the infidel abashed of his vain cavils, and put a stop to that torrent of vice, profaneness, and immorality, by which the age is so unhappily distinguished."

Stuart seized the opportunity of altering this final paragraph : for the name of Dr Robertson, Hume's friend, was substituted that of Dr MacQueen, his enemy ; the tone of honest commendation was altered to one of ironical adulation ; a continuation of the article was promised for a subsequent issue. Thus mutilated, the proof sheets were returned to Hume. They drew an indignant protest :

> I wish you woud check your Printer with some Severity for the Freedoms he uses ; I suppose to divert himself. He has substituted the Name of Dr MacQueen, whom certainly I did not think of, instead of Dr Robertson, to whose Merit I meant to do some Justice. The last Paragraph, which seems to be entirely his own, is also too high a Praise for a new Author like Dr. Henry. But, if you want a few sentences to fill up the Page, I have added them, and beg that you woud take care, that the Printer throw them off faithfully.[1]

The new final paragraph, which replaced Stuart's irony, associates Hugh Blair by allusion with Henry and Robertson as one who, " with the same hand, by which he turns over the sublime Pages of Homer and Virgil, Demosthenes and Cicero, is not ashamed to open with Reverence the sacred Volumes ; And with the same Voice by which, from the Pulpit, he strikes Vice with Consternation, he deigns to dictate to his Pupils the most useful Lessons of Rhetoric, Poetry and polite Literature."

This sincere tribute from the " Great Infidel " to his clerical friends was totally misunderstood by Stuart. " It is precious and would divert you," he chuckled. " I keep a proof of it in my cabinet, for the amusement of friends. This great philosopher begins to doat." Stuart's anger now turned against Hume, who, he said, " has behaved ill in the affair, and I am preparing to chastise him. You may expect a series of papers in the Magazine, pointing out a multitude of his errors, and ascertaining his ignorance of English history. It was too much for my temper to be assailed both by infidels and believers." [2] As for Hume's review of Henry, that was totally rejected, and Stuart printed his own

---

[1] NHL, p. 202.   [2] Disraeli, *op. cit.*, pp. 66–7, 70.

devastating blast in the February and March 1774 numbers of the *Edinburgh Magazine and Review*. His " chastisement " of Hume was later engineered through comments on other historical works, particularly John Whitaker's *History of Manchester*. It was on this note of savage attack on himself that David Hume's kindly intended patronage of a new friend and his well-meant tribute to two old friends ended. Even at this late stage of his career his intimacy with the Moderate Clergy of Edinburgh was misrepresented by those incapable of understanding the sympathy and tolerance of great minds.

Other contemporaries who simply could not fathom the character of *le bon David* as related to his sceptical philosophy include Thomas Gray, Dr Johnson, and James Boswell. Each in his own way reacted violently to the " Great Infidel " who was yet a good man. With Gray the philosopher had had some friendly contacts at the time of his patronage of John Home and James Macpherson. In 1775, however, Hume was stunned to learn Gray's true opinion of him as it appeared in William Mason's biography of Gray. Five years previously Gray had written to Mason :

> I have always thought David Hume a pernicious writer, and believe he has done as much mischief here as he has in his own country. A turbid and shallow stream often appears to our apprehensions very deep. A professed sceptic can be guided by nothing but his present passions (if he has any) and interests ; and to be masters of his philosophy we need not his books or advice, for every child is capable of the same thing, without any study at all. Is not that *naïveté* and good humour, which his admirers celebrate in him, owing to this, that he has continued all his days an infant, but one that unhappily has been taught to read and write ? That childish nation, the French, have given him vogue and fashion, and we, as usual, have learned from them to admire him at second hand.[1]

Boswell, for his part, did not accept Gray's interpretation.[2] " I cannot agree with him. Hume had certainly considerable abilities. My notion is that he had by long study in one view, brought a *stupor* upon his mind as to futurity. He had pored upon the earth, till he could not look up to heaven. He was like one of the Bramins who, we are told, by a rigid perseverance in maintaining a certain posture, become unable to change it. Or may we not with propriety compare him to the woman in the Gospel, who

---

[1] Mason, " Memoirs of his Life and Writings." prefaced to *Poems of Mr. Gray* (York 1775), pp. 384–5.
[2] Boswell, MS letter in NLS, MS 3278, f. 54. A full account of the relations between Hume and Boswell and Johnson is to be found in Mossner, *The Forgotten Hume*, Chs. 7–8.

' was bowed down, and could in no wise lift herself up,' till healed
by our Saviour who described her as one ' whom Satan hath
bound lo these eighteen years.' " This was a late condescension
on the part of that same James Boswell who in 1758 had found
Hume " a most discreet, affable man as ever I met with, and has
really a great deal of learning, and a choice collection of books.
He is indeed an extraordinary man, few such people are to be met
with nowadays." The younger James had complacently concluded
that " Mr. Hume, I think, is a very proper person for a young man
to cultivate an acquaintance with. . . ." [1]

Cultivate the acquaintance of "the greatest Writer in Brittain"
James Boswell certainly did, tricking him in 1763 into a correspondence. Three years later Boswell intruded himself into
Hume's patronage of Rousseau, and, after the outbreak of the
quarrel, published verses and designed a print concerning it. " I
am really the *Great Man* now," he boasted in 1768 ; " I have had
David Hume in the forenoon and Mr. Johnson in the afternoon
of the same day visiting me." [2] Yet the man who was to succeed
in seating Dr Johnson amicably side by side with the infidel Whig
statesman, John Wilkes, was unequal to the greater task of bringing
Johnson and Hume together. He never forgot Hume's remark
of 1762 that Johnson had once left a company upon his entering
it and he, almost certainly, remained unaware that the two had
been dinner guests in 1763 at the table of the Royal Chaplain
at St James's.[3] So when in 1773 Boswell played host to Johnson
at James's Court—though not in the house he was renting from
Hume [4]—David Hume alone among the distinguished men of
letters of Edinburgh was not invited.

The persistent terror that coloured the life of James Boswell
was of the final annihilation of James Boswell. Against this horror
he found some solace in the religious dogmatism of Dr Johnson.
From Johnson, whom he first met in 1763, Boswell learned to be
rough with the religiously heterodox and especially to bedevil all
defenders of the Scottish philosopher. On one occasion he even
goaded that philosopher himself into the taunt that " it required

[1] Boswell, *Letters*, I, 2.   [2] *Ibid.*, I, 160.

[3] That Johnson was once the guest of Hume is suggested by the cataloguer's
description of an undated and otherwise unknown letter of Hume's (No. 1185 in
Puttick & Simpson's catalogue for 30 July 1886) : " the Doctor [Johnson] to be my
guest." Johnson received his LL.D. only in 1765, and the meeting took place—if it
did—during the period 1766 to 1768, or, just conceivably, in 1776, when Hume was
also in London. I remain somewhat sceptical.

[4] Mossner, " Dr. Johnson *in partibus Infidelium ?* " in *Modern Language Notes*,
LXIII (1948), 516–19.

great goodness of disposition to withstand the baleful effects of Christianity." Curiously, however, there were times when Boswell felt that Johnson's abuse of Hume went too far, was " much too rough." One such time was when Johnson was instructing Boswell that Hume was full of intellectual conceit. " But why attack his heart ? " interjected the young Scot. " Why, Sir, because his head has corrupted it. Or perhaps it has perverted his head. I know not indeed whether he has first been a blockhead and that has made him a rogue, or first been a rogue and that has made him a blockhead." [1]

The paradox of the virtuous infidel, nevertheless, tormented Boswell from the time of first meeting him until long after his death. " Were it not for his infidel writings," he admitted to his fiancée, " every body would love him. He is a plain, obliging, kindhearted man." And again : " David is really amiable. I allways regret to him his unlucky principles and he smiles at my faith. But I have a hope which he has not or pretends not to have." [2] This curious paradox in the mind of Boswell rose to a crisis on three occasions : in 1775, in 1776 when Hume lay dying, and in a dream of 1784.

The first of these occasions belongs to the present period of Hume's life. At a church service in November 1775 the sermon was on the text, " O death, where is thy sting ? " and the lesson emphasised the consolations of Christianity. " A strange thought struck me," notes Boswell, " that I would apply to David Hume, telling him that at present I was happy in having pious faith, But in case of it's failing me by some unexpected revolution in my mind, it would be humane in him to furnish me with reflections by which a man of sense and feeling could support his spirit as an Infidel. I was really serious in this thought. I wonder what David can suggest."

Several weeks later, of a Sunday, and fortified with two church services, the man of little faith ventured to call upon the sceptical philosopher. David was just finishing dinner with his sister and youngest nephew. " He had on a White nightcap and a hat above it. He called for a fresh bottle of port, which he and I drank, all but a single glass that his Nephew took. I indeed took the largest share." Boswell drew Hume out expertly, over his bottle, through the leading literary themes of the day and elicited from him biographical information. " I had really a good chat with him this afternoon. I thought also of writing his life." Boswell did

---

[1] *Boswell Papers*, VII, 189 ; VI, 178.   [2] *Ibid.*, VIII, 227 ; Boswell, *Letters*, I, 160.

not, however, have the courage to broach the topic uppermost in his mind. That he was thinking about it is evident from his final reflection : " It was curious to see David such a civil, sensible, comfortable looking man, and to recollect this is the Great Infidel. Beleif or want of Belief is not absolutely connected with practice. How many surly men are teachers of the Gospel of peace ! " [1] The following year when Hume was on his deathbed Boswell was to take the last opportunity to investigate the moral enigma that he, like so many others, found in the virtuous infidel. The interview was to prove revealing—and for Boswell's peace of mind, quite catastrophic.

" Old age is but sorrow," Hume informed Mrs Stewart of Gillan, a close friend during his last years in Edinburgh ; " perhaps even youth is not much better ; but extreme old age is certain misery . . . may it be my fate for my own sake & for that of all my friends, to stop short at the threshold of old age, and not to enter too far into that dismal region. . . ." [2] Happily, therefore, his wish was granted and it was to be his fate not to enter " too far into that dismal region."

[1] *Boswell Papers*, XI, 5, 40–2.   [2] NHL, p. 228.

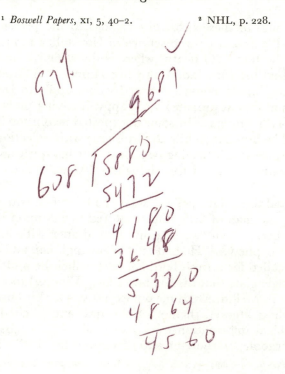

CHAPTER 39

DEATH COMES FOR THE PHILOSOPHER

" I now reckon upon a speedy Dissolution."

DISTURBED by occasional flare-ups of controversy, Hume's autumnal felicity was more seriously disturbed by increasing ill health. In 1772 he had begun to go into a slow and gradual decline, which he did his best to conceal from friends. Three years later the progress of the decline had become so rapid that within a year he lost seventy pounds in weight. The symptoms of high fever at night, severe diarrhoea, and internal haemorrhages he recognised as those from which his mother had long suffered and which had eventually caused her death. With this recognition and with the knowledge that he had the same constitution as his mother, he reconciled himself to the inevitable. The philosopher might well have recalled with Bishop Butler that " Things and actions are what they are, and the consequences of them will be what they will be."

Thus reconciled in his own mind, Hume continued, so far as possible, his normal activities. Up to the very end he was writing kindly and lively letters to absent friends, was revising the *Essays and Treatises* and the *History of England*, was concerned with filling vacancies in the faculty of Edinburgh University and in the Church of Scotland, was voraciously reading the new books as they fell from the press—was, in short, very much himself.

Two books that Hume had been anxiously awaiting were Edward Gibbon's *Decline and Fall* and Adam Smith's *Wealth of Nations*. Eagerly he read them in the spring of 1776 and then penned letters of congratulation to the authors. That to Gibbon combines praise with nationalistic coyness : " Whether I consider the Dignity of your Style, the Depth of your Matter, or the Extensiveness of your Learning, I must regard the Work as equally the Object of Esteem ; and I own, that if I had not previously had the Happiness of your personal Acquaintance, such a Performance, from an Englishman in our Age, woud have given me some Surprize : You may smile at this Sentiment ; but as it seems to me that your Countrymen, for almost a whole Generation, have given themselves up to barbarous and absurd Faction, and have totally neglected all polite Letters, I no longer expected any valuable Production ever to come from them." To Smith Hume wrote : " It was a Work of so much Expectation, by yourself, by your Friends, and by the Public, that I trembled for its Appearance ; but am now much relieved." Then after challenging his friend on some of the economic issues, he went on, " But these and a hundred other Points are fit only to be discussed in Conversation ; which, till you tell me to the contrary, I shall still flatter myself with soon. I hope it will be soon : For I am in a very bad State of Health and cannot afford a long Delay."

In his increasing weakness, Hume began to shy at invitations to visit friends, complaining about the heat or the cold of the room assigned him, of his reluctance to give up his own bed and mattress, of the inconveniences of travel. His friends, in turn, pleaded with their " dear obstinate David," their " obdurate Philosopher," their " Girl, for you are never two minutes of one mind." They were, however, always gentle and indulgent, for they knew, although they would scarcely admit it even to themselves, that their David was not to be long with them.

In March 1776 the Edinburgh circle were shocked by the loss of Baron Mure, following hard after that of Lord Alemoor. " The Baron was the oldest and best friend I had in the world," lamented David. " Poor David Hume," wrote Blair soon after that event. " He is declining sadly. I dread, I dread, and I shudder at the prospect. We have suffered so much by the loss of Friends in our Circle here of late, that such a blow as that would be utterly overwhelming. . . ." [1] All of Hume's friends had suggestions to offer : to stay at home, to go to England, to go abroad. Hume remained satisfied with his local physicians, Drs Joseph Black, William Cullen, and Francis Home, and was encouraged by them not to move and to " dye with much greater tranquillity in St. David's Street than anywhere else."

At London, however, Sir John Pringle, who since his resignation of the Edinburgh professorship in 1745 had become renowned as the founder of modern military medicine and as the President of the Royal Society, was incessantly urging his friend to come to that city. As early as the spring of 1775 he wrote : " I have frequently of late heard of your having fallen through your clothes, & being troubled with heats at night. Now though I have a very good opinion of our Edinburgh practice, yet, as I have so great a concern for you, I could not help desiring, indeed earnestly requesting that you would come up here this summer, & try what

[1] NLS, MS 1005, ff. 21-2.

we can do for you here." [1] He continued to prescribe for Hume during the following year, and finally, in April 1776, with the aid of pressure from other friends at London and Edinburgh, succeeded in persuading him to make the trip. " Have you no reason against it," inquired Hume of Dr Black, " but an apprehension that it may make me die sooner ?—that is no reason at all."

On 18 April three days before leaving Edinburgh, Hume penned *My Own Life*, in which he admits that the " Disorder in my Bowels " is " mortal and incurable. I now reckon upon a speedy Dissolution. . . . It is difficult to be more detached from Life than I am at present." As a prominent man, and moreover one who held notoriously unorthodox views on religion and immortality, Hume was well aware that the manner of his death would be of interest to the general public. He was a philosopher and was determined to die philosophically, and to convince the public that he had faced death in accordance with his principles—without hope and without fear. *My Own Life*, consequently, is, in part, autobiography and, in part, manifesto. Never was the philosopher more ironical than in making his preparations for dying.

Hume's detachment from life had already appeared in the new will which he had drawn up on 4 January and to which he added a codicil on 15 April. In the terms of this will to which the Earl of Home was witness, John Home of Ninewells was the principal heir and executor, or, in case of his prior death, his second son, David. To his sister Katherine, Hume bequeathed £1,200, the life rent of the " house " in James's Court, and a hundred books of her choice. Special arrangements were made for Hume's three nephews and two nieces. All servants received a year's wages except Peggy Irvine, who received three. A few miscellaneous gifts were listed for relatives and friends and £200 apiece for D'Alembert, Adam Ferguson, and Adam Smith. To Edinburgh Infirmary went £50.

A codicil, dated the same day as the original will, stated :

If I shall dye any where in Scotland, I shall be bury'd in a private manner in the Calton Church Yard, the South Side of it, and a Monument be built over my Body at an Expence not exceeding a hundred Pounds, with an Inscription containing only my Name with the Year of my Birth and Death, leaving it to Posterity to add the Rest.

(This was designed by Hume's friend, Robert Adam. Years later, Adam Smith commented, " I don't like that monument. It is the greatest piece of vanity I ever saw in my friend Hume.")

[1] RSE, vi, 96.

A further codicil of 15 April provided £100 for rebuilding the Bridge of Chirnside, with the proviso that none of the stones for the bridge be taken from the quarry of Ninewells except from that part of it which had been already opened. To David's nephew Joseph was assigned the sum of £50 to build " a good sufficient Drain and Sewer round the House of Ninewells," with the proviso that if the work was not completed within one year the money should be paid to the poor of the parish of Chirnside.

Hume was anxious about the disposition of his manuscripts, particularly those still unpublished. He was determined to ensure the publication of the *Dialogues concerning Natural Religion*, which had been composed in the early 1750s, somewhat revised in the early 1760s and now revised again and polished in the final months of his life. He was not unwilling to have published the two suppressed essays, " Of Suicide " and " Of the Immortality of the Soul," but he would not insist. The aforementioned letter to Gibbon shows Hume's anxiety to see how that ticklish subject, the early history of Christianity, had been treated. " I think you have observ'd a very prudent Temperament, but it was impossible to treat the Subject so as not to give Grounds of Suspicion against you, and you may expect that a Clamour will arise." Gibbon's treatment of religion evidently interested Hume partly for its bearing on the issue of publishing his own manuscript works on religion.

The *Dialogues* were Hume's pride, as he admitted to William Strahan : " Some of my Friends flatter me, that it is the best thing I ever wrote. I have hitherto forborne to publish it, because I was of late desirous to live quietly, and keep remote from all clamour." Publication, however, proved a difficult problem. In his original will, Hume had left all his manuscripts to Adam Smith with the specific request that the *Dialogues* be published, but when Smith demurred, he qualified this request and on 3 May granted discretionary powers. Dissatisfied, Hume then decided to publish the work immediately but his precarious health prevented this. Finally, he added a new codicil to his will on 7 August,[1] leaving all his manuscripts to Strahan, desiring him to bring out the *Dialogues* within two years and leaving the two suppressed essays to his discretion. Hume desired *My Own Life* to be prefixed to the first posthumous edition of his works. A final, decisive afterthought to the codicil ordained " that if my Dialogues from whatever Cause, be not published within two

[1] RSE, ix, 24.

Years and a half of my Death . . . the Property shall return to my Nephew, David, whose Duty, in publishing them as the last Request of his Uncle, must be approved by all the World." So was settled a most vexing problem for a dying man of letters.

The trip to England, if it did nothing to improve Hume's health, proved highly rewarding in demonstrating the affection in which he was held by friends. On the 20th of April Hume informed Strahan that " My Body sets out to-morrow by Post for London ; but whether it will arrive there is somewhat uncertain. I shall travel by slow Journies." Accompanied by his manservant, Colin Ross, who had been bequeathed to him by the late Baron Mure, and well supplied with cushions to bolster his gaunt frame, the philosopher unenthusiastically set out on his last journey from St David Street.[1]

Two days later, while he was resting in an inn at Morpeth, Colin, who was standing at the gate, saw a carriage draw up in which were John Home, the dramatist, and Adam Smith. The meeting was only partly fortuitous, because the two were hastening from London to Edinburgh in order to be with their friend. "David, I am afraid, loses ground," Adam Ferguson had informed John at London. "I hope we shall see you *here soon*, and that your attentions will contribute to preserve what we can ill spare." John had immediately made arrangements to return to Edinburgh and Adam had joined him. At Morpeth it was agreed that Adam should go on to Scotland to care for his ailing mother and that John should accompany David to London, and perhaps Bath, if the waters were indicated.

The boredom of the journey was now alleviated by the lively personality of the dramatist, who was astonished to find his friend never " more chearful, or in more possession of all his faculties, his memory, his understanding, his wit." When David first entered the chaise, he noticed a pair of pistols and dryly remarked that, as he had very little at stake, he would leave fighting the highwaymen to his companion. To prevent the post-boys from driving over five miles an hour was not easy, as they resented being passed by every traveller on the road. One in particular, who was hardly to be held back, whipped his horses as soon as he was dismissed to full speed. " *Pour se dédommager*," commented David laconically.

[1] The following account of the journey is largely based upon Home-Mackenzie, I, 168–82.

In the chaise the friends conversed easily on politics and personalities. David reviewed aspects of his own career, particularly his experiences in France. Taking a broad survey of the state of the world, he lamented "that the two most civilised nations, the English and French, should be on the decline ; and the barbarians, the Goths and Vandals of Germany and Russia, should be rising in power and renown." Half seriously, David remarked that he had set out to England only to please his friends and that they were answerable for shortening his life by one week apiece. "For," he said, "you will allow Xenophon to be good authority ; and he lays it down, that suppose a man is dying, nobody has a right to kill him." He talked calmly of the new piece of ground that he had just bought in the Calton Hill cemetery and thought it nonsensical that John should want to change the topic of conversation. He acknowledged that he was ready to go anywhere that Sir John Pringle and the whole faculty at London might want to send him, except that he would not submit to being " boated " or sent abroad—he preferred to die at home.

In the various inns on the road David ate tolerably, taking no liquid but water and supping on an egg. In periods of rest, the friends played whist or picquet ; and, when alone, David read constantly, chiefly in the classics. London was reached the first of May, and David put up at Mrs Perkins's a few doors from the Misses Elliot.

Sir John Pringle took over the care of the patient. He declared that he saw nothing alarming in the case, that it was only a stricture in the colon, that the Edinburgh physicians were all wrong, that the Bath waters would almost certainly effect a cure. To Mrs Perkins's lodgings came all those friends of Hume who were then in London, including Strahan and Gibbon. " I had the melancholy pleasure," writes the latter, " of seeing Mr. Hume in his passage through London, his body feeble, his mind firm." After a few days of rest and relaxation David and the faithful John proceeded to Bath.

On the road a perennial subject of friendly dispute arose : if Adam Ferguson, John, and David were all princes of adjacent states, how would they rule their kingdoms ? David held forth at length on how he would cultivate the arts of peace, and his friends the arts of war. As a final stroke of policy for self-protection, he would give one of them a subsidy to fall upon the other, and, after a long war, would end by being master of all three kingdoms. At this typical thrust of David's the two cronies broke into fits of laughter, impressing the people passing their chaise that they were the merriest of travellers.

In an inn at Spine Hill, near Newbury, they found a fishing party consisting of Lord Sandwich, the First Lord of the Admiralty, and several other officials, and " two or three Ladies of Pleasure." Writing back to that shrewd politician at London, William Strahan, the historian moralised :

> I do not remember in all my little or great Knowledge of History (according as you and Dr Johnson can settle between you the Degrees of my Knowledge) such another Instance ; and I am sure such a one does not exist : That the First Lord of the Admiralty, who is absolute and uncontrouled Master in his Department, shou'd, at a time when the Fate of the British Empire is in dependance, and in dependance on him, find so much Leizure, Tranquillity, Presence of Mind and Magnanimity, as to have Amusement in trouting during three Weeks near sixty Miles from the scene of Business, and during the most critical Season of the Year. There needs but this single Fact to decide the Fate of the Nation. What an Ornament woud it be in a future History to open the glorious Events of the ensuing Year with the Narrative of so singular an Incident.

At Bath Dr John Gustard took over the patient and found neither the haemorrhage of Dr Black nor the stricture in the colon of Sir John Pringle, but a simple bilious complaint which the waters scarce ever failed to cure. The learned patient complained about having to give up dying from two disorders with Greek names for a plebeian biliousness. The distinguished surgeon and anatomist, John Hunter, however, chancing to come to Bath, expressed the desire to examine Hume and felt with his fingers, wrote the latter to his brother, " a Tumour or Swelling in my Liver." The empirical philosopher was no little relieved to have tangible evidence of his disorder. " This Fact," he observed, " not drawn by Reasoning, but obvious to the Senses, and perceived by the greatest Anatomist in Europe, must be admitted as unquestionable, and will alone account for my Situation."

Soon afterwards Hume was able to feel the tumour by himself, finding it to be " about the Bigness of an Egg " and " flat and round." " The devil's in it if this do not convince you," he admonished " Fish " Crawford. " Even St Thomas, the infidel apostle, desired no better authority than the testimony of his fingers. They tell me that I have gained a great deal by this change of the seat of war, from the bowels to the liver ; but however able the generals, I expect little from this campaign, still less from our American hostilities." Henceforth Hume remained quietly amused as the doctors continued the great debate as to the major seat of his disorder. Actually, so far as the evidence goes, modern medical science might agree that, although cancer of the bowel cannot be ruled out, Hume probably died of chronic ulcerative colitis, following an acute bacillary dysentery. .

To Hugh Blair the philosopher wrote cheerfully of " the agreeable Surprise, which John Home put upon me. . . . Never was there a more friendly Action, nor better placed : For what between Conversation and Gaming (not to mention sometimes squabbling) I did not pass a languid Moment ; and his Company, I am certain, was the chief Cause, why my Journey had so good an Effect. . . ." He also teased the clergyman by intimating artfully that he might accept an invitation of two lady acquaintances at Bath to meet the Countess of Huntington " for her or my Conversion. I wish," he added, " I may have Spirits to humour this Folly." Sober Hugh fell into the trap, replying hastily : " I do not approve . . . of the Methodistical Company you speak of. I would not wish you to have any thing to do with that Tribe either in Joke or Earnest. You can have no sort of Intercourse with them that will not be misrepresented. You are too Conspicuous a Figure to be let pass without their fathering some foolish Story on you." [1]

The Bath waters proving unavailing and even injurious, Hume was anxious to return home ; but it was not until nearly the end of June that John and he passed through London and took the North road to Scotland. From Doncaster on the 27th David penned his last note to Blair :

> Mr. John Hume, alias Home, alias the Home, alias the late Lord Conservator, alias the late Minister of the Gospel at Athelstoneford, has calculated Matters so as to arrive infallibly with his Friend in St David's Street on Wednesday Evening. He has ask'd several of Dr Blair's Friends to dine with him there on Thursday, being the 4th of July ; and begs the favour of the Doctor to make one of the Number.

The farewell dinner was attended by most of the philosopher's friends, although scandal has it that Dr Robertson was absent, preferring to accept a previous invitation to a turtle feast.[2] It is an interesting coincidence that this gathering of the faithful took place on a momentous day in the history of the world, the day on which the Declaration of Independence was signed at Philadelphia. Unlike most of his friends, David Hume would have honestly rejoiced when the news from America reached Edinburgh a few days before his death.

[1] RSE, III, 63. [2] [Pratt], *Supplement to the Life of David Hume, Esq.*, pp. 36–7.

Finding Hume in " a very shattered Condition," his Edinburgh " grand Jury of Physicians," sat on him. Though they were willing to concede that he had a small tumour of the liver, they declared that the opinion of the English physicians was " absurd and erroneous " and that the real cause of his distemper was a haemorrhage as before—" an illness," retorted the patient, " that I had as Lief dye of as any other." When the sanguine doctors spread the word among his friends that they had cured him, he found the intelligence very agreeable, " as it is perfectly new." Having had his laugh at the doctors, Hume settled down to making final revisions of his works, reading the latest books, and parting with his friends.

One friend, though not of the intimate circle, came to visit the dying man more out of morbid curiosity than out of sympathy. James Boswell was determined to find out whether the philosopher facing immediate death had not changed his mind on the question of futurity. On Sunday, 7 July, he hastened to St David Street and found Hume alone in a reclining posture in his drawing-room. " He was lean, ghastly, and quite of an earthy appearance. He was drest in a suit of grey cloth with white metal buttons, and a kind of scratch wig. He was quite different from the plump figure which he used to present. He had before him Dr. Campbell's *Philosophy of Rhetorick.*[1] He seemed to be placid and even cheerful. He said he was just approaching to his end. I think these were his words."

Boswell, though characteristically striving to maintain an air of mystery—" I know not how I contrived to get the subject of Immortality introduced "—at once plunged into the reason for his visit, to draw out the philosopher on the subject of immortality. " He said he never had entertained any beleif in Religion since he began to read Locke and Clarke. I asked him if he was not religious when he was young. He said he was. . . . He then said flatly that the Morality of every Religion was bad, and, I really thought, was not jocular when he said ' that when he heard a man was religious, he concluded he was a rascal, though he had known some instances of very good men being religious.'[2] . . . I had a strong curiosity to be satisfied if he persisted in disbelieving a future state even when he had death before his eyes. I was persuaded from what he now said, and from his manner of saying it, that he did persist. I asked him if it was not possible that there might be a future state. He answered It was possible that a piece

---

[1] Just published.   [2] This opinion was to be published, *Dialogues*, p. 221.

of coal put upon the fire would not burn ; and he added that it was a most unreasonable fancy that we should exist for ever. . . . I asked him if the thought of Annihilation never gave him any uneasiness. He said not the least ; no more than the thought that he had not been, as Lucretius observes. . . . I tried him . . ., saying that a future state was surely a pleasing idea. He said No, for that it was allways seen through a gloomy medium ; there was allways a Phlegethon or a Hell. ' But,' said I, ' would it not be agreable to have hopes of seeing our friends again ? ' and I mentioned three Men lately deceased, for whom I knew he had a high value : Ambassadour Keith, Lord Alemoor, and Baron Muir. He owned it would be agreable, but added that none of them entertained such a notion. I believe he said, such a foolish, or such an absurd, notion ; for he was indecently and impolitely positive in incredulity. ' Yes,' said I, ' Lord Alemoor was a believer.' David acknowledged that *he* had *some* beleif. . . .

" The truth is that Mr. Hume's pleasantry was such that there was no solemnity in the scene ; and Death for the time did not seem dismal. It surprised me to find him talking of different matters with a tranquillity of mind and a clearness of head, which few men possess at any time. Two particulars I remember : Smith's *Wealth of Nations*, which he recommended much, and Monboddo's *Origin of Language*, which he treated contemptuously. I said, ' If I were you, I should regret Annihilation. Had I written such an admirable History, I should be sorry to leave it.' He said, ' I shall leave that history, of which you are pleased to speak so favourably, as perfect as I can.' . . . He said he had no pain, but was wasting away."

" I left him," concluded Boswell, " with impressions which disturbed me for some time." [1] Although Hume had been amusing himself somewhat at Boswell's expense, there is no reason to suspect that he had not been telling the strict truth about his own beliefs. There is, likewise, no reason to suspect that he was in any way disturbed by the interview.

Other busybodies, less morbid than Boswell, but equally impertinent, intruded themselves into the privacy of the dying man. A pious woman, wife of a tallow-chandler, lectured him on the evils of scepticism and prayed that he would see the errors of his ways. After inquiring into her mode of life, Hume replied : " Good woman, since you have expressed so earnest a desire that I should be inspired with *inward light*, I beg you will supply me with

[1] *Boswell Papers*, XII, 227–32.

outward light also." The woman retired, happy with an order for two stone-weight of candles.

A few of Hume's good friends, such as William Strahan, took occasion to express the hope that he would reconsider his religious scepticism. Most of his friends thought that he would recover or, at least, continued to say so. " I shall tell your friend Colonel Edmonstoune," said Dr Dundas to the philosopher one day, " that I left you much better, and in a fair way of recovery." To which Hume returned, " Doctor, as I believe you would not choose to tell any thing but the truth, you had better tell him that I am dying as fast as my enemies, if I have any, could wish, and as easily and cheerfully as my best friends could desire."

On the 6th of August Colonel James Edmonstoune came to say farewell. " Poor Edmonstoune and I parted to-day," wrote David to his cousin John, " with a plentiful effusion of tears ; all those *Belzebubians* have not hearts of iron." The next day the Colonel wrote to " My Dear Dear David : My Heart is very full. I could not see you this Morning ; I thought it was better for us both. You can't die, you must live in the Memory of all your friends and Acquaintances and your Works will render you immortal. I could never conceive that it was possible for any one to dislike you or hate you, he must be more than savage who could be an Enemy to a Man of the best Head and Heart and of the most amiable Manners." [1] The Colonel then applied to Hume, as it was later to be described by Adam Smith, " as to a dying man, the beautiful French verses in which the Abbé Chaulieu, in expectation of his own death, laments his approaching separation from his friend the Marquis de la Fare." [2]

On that same day Hume drew up the codicil to his will which made the final disposition of his manuscripts, about which he still felt considerable anxiety. The codicil also bequeathed gifts to several of his friends :

I leave to my Friend, Mr John Home of Kilduff, ten dozen of my old Claret at his Choice ; and one single Bottle of that other Liquor called Port. I also leave to him six dozen of Port, provided that he attests under his hand, signed *John Hume*, that he has himself alone finishd that Bottle at two Sittings : By this Concession, he will at once terminate the only two Differences, that ever arose between us, concerning temporal Matters.

I leave to my Friend Dr Hugh Blair a Copy of all my Writings at present in the Press ; as also a Copy to Mr Adam Smith, to Mr John Home, and to Coll. James Edmondestone, all of them Persons all very dear to me ; and whose Affection to me, I know by repeated Proofs, to have been mutual.

[1] RSE, v, 7.   [2] See Textual Supplement.

I leave to Mrs Anne Ord, Daughter of the late Chief Baron, ten Guinèas to buy a Ring, as a Memorial of my Friendship and Attachment to so amiable and accomplished a Person.[1]

The following day, the 8th of August, Hume had just received the letter from Edmonstoune when Adam Smith entered the room.[2] The two friends read it together. Adam found the spirit of life so strong in David that he ventured to entertain some faint hopes. " Your hopes are groundless," replied the philosopher serenely. " An habitual diarrhoea of more than a year's standing would be a very bad disease at any age ; at my age it is a mortal one. When I lie down in the evening I feel myself weaker than when I rose in the morning ; and when I rise in the morning weaker than when I lay down in the evening. I am sensible, besides, that some of my vital parts are affected, so that I must soon die."

" Well," said Adam, " if it must be so, you have at least the satisfaction of leaving all your friends, your brother's family in particular, in great prosperity."

David replied, according to Adam's account, " that he felt that satisfaction so sensibly, that when he was reading, a few days before, Lucian's *Dialogues of the Dead*, among all the excuses which are alleged to Charon for not entering readily into his boat, he could not find one that fitted him : he had no house to finish, he had no daughter to provide for, he had no enemies upon whom he wished to revenge himself. ' I could not well imagine,' said he, ' what excuse I could make to Charon, in order to obtain a little delay. I have done every thing of consequence which I ever meant to do, and I could at no time expect to leave my relations and friends in a better situation than that in which I am now likely to leave them : I therefore have all reason to die contented.'

" He then diverted himself with inventing several jocular excuses, which he supposed he might make to Charon, and with imagining the very surly answers which it might suit the character of Charon to return to them. ' Upon further consideration,' said he, ' I thought I might say to him, " Good Charon, I have been correcting my works for a new edition. Allow me a little time that I may see how the public receives the alterations." But Charon would answer, " When you have seen the effect of these, you will be for making other alterations. There will be no end of such

---

[1] RSE, IX, 24.

[2] Smith's account of Hume's last illness, in the form of a letter to Strahan, was appended to *The Life of David Hume, Esq ; Written by Himself* (London 1777) ; it is reprinted (with some omissions) in HL, II, 450-2.

excuses ; so, honest friend, please step into the boat." But I might still urge, " Have a little patience, good Charon, I have been endeavouring to open the eyes of the public. If I live a few years longer, I may have the satisfaction of seeing the downfall of some of the prevailing systems of superstition." (According to Dr Cullen,[1] writing of this incident to Dr Hunter on 17 September 1776, Hume " thought he might say he had been very busily employed in making his countrymen wiser and particularly in delivering them from the Christian superstition, but that he had not yet compleated that great work.") But then Charon would lose all temper and decency. " You loitering rogue, that will not happen these many hundred years. Do you fancy I will grant you a lease for so long a term ? Get into the boat this instant, you lazy, loitering rogue."

In reporting this conversation, Adam Smith goes on to observe, " But though Mr Hume always talked of his approaching dis-solution with great cheerfulness, he never affected to make any parade of his great magnanimity. . . . At his own desire . . . I agreed to leave Edinburgh, where I was staying partly upon his account, and returned to my mother's house . . . at Kirkaldy, upon condition that he would send for me whenever he wished to see me. . . ."

As long as the state of his health would permit, Hume had been making a round of farewell visits to friends, no longer in his chaise, but in a sedan chair. Mrs Anne Murray Keith writes that " I was not in Edinburgh when he dyed, but my Sisters got a farewell Visit from him ten Days before his Death. I fancy he saw they could not have stood any thing that came too near the Subject, so he avoided any thing particular, & endeavoured to make the Conversation as Cheerfull as possible. He payed the same Compliment to all those Ladies with whom he lived in intimacy." [2]

Mrs Katherine Mure, recently bereaved of her husband, came to take her farewell of David. He had an inscribed copy of his *History* ready to present to her. In thanking him she took the privilege of an intimate friend to express approval of that work and disapproval of his philosophical works. " O David," said she, " that's a book you may weel be proud o ; but before ye dee, ye should burn a' your wee bookies." To which, raising himself

[1] William Cullen, MS letter in Library of the Royal College of Surgeons of England (Hunter-Baillie Collection, Letter-book, 1, 140); Thomson in his *Cullen*, 1, 608, omits the words " the Christian." [2] NLS, MS 3524, f. 71.

on his couch, David replied with some vehemence, half offended, half in joke, "What for should I burn a' my wee bookies?" But feeling too weak for further discussion of the point, he shook his head and bade her farewell.[1]

On the 12th of August Hume sent Strahan "the last Correction I shall probably trouble you with : For Dr Black has promised me, that all shall be over with me in a very little time : This Promise he makes by his Power of Prediction, not that of Prescription." The letter concludes, "And indeed I consider it as good News : For of late, within these few weeks, my Infirmities have so multi-plyed that Life has become rather a Burthen to me." Writing the following day to apprise Sir John Pringle of his "near approach-ing Dissolution," Hume proceeds : " One would little regret Life, were it not the Experience of such good Friends, as you, whom one must leave behind them. *Mais, helas ! on ne laisse que des mourans :* as Ninon l'Enclos said on her Death-bed. Death appears to me so little terrible on his Approaches, that I scorn to quote Heroes and Philosophers as Examples of Fortitude : a Woman of Pleasure, who, however, was also a Philosopher, is sufficient."

The invalid was now able to see fewer and fewer even of inti-mate friends.[2] Boswell, who called twice for further probing on the question of annihilation, was turned away at the door. On the 20th of August Hume penned his last letter to Mme de Boufflers, expressing sympathy to her for the loss of the Prince de Conti :

> Tho' I am certainly within a few Weeks, Dear Madam, and perhaps within a few days, of my own Death, I coud not forbear being struck with the Death of the Prince of Conti, so great a Loss in every particular. My Reflection carried me immediatly to your Situation, in this melancholy Incident. What a Difference to you in your whole Plan of Life ! Pray, write me some particulars : but in such terms that you need not care, in case of Decease, into whose hands your Letter may fall.
>
> My distemper is a Diarrhoea, or Disorder in my Bowels, which has been gradually undermining me these two Years ; but, within these six months, has been visibly hastening me to my End. I see Death approach gradually, without any Anxiety or Regret. I salute you, with great Affection and Regard, for the last time. [2]

Hume's last exchange of letters was with Adam Smith, an exchange which was accidentally delayed on both sides by being sent by the carrier instead of by the post. Writing on 15 August

---

[1] *Caldwell Papers*, PT. I, 39–40.
[2] See Textual Supplement for Adam Smith's comment.
[3] HL, II, 335, corrected from Plate 41 in C. J. Smith, *Hist. and Lit. Curiosities* (London 1847).

and still worried about the fate of the *Dialogues*, Hume inquired :
" Will you permit me to leave you the Property of the Copy,
in case they shoud not be published in five Years after my
Decease ? Be so good as to write me an answer soon. My State
of Health does not permit me to wait Months for it." But Smith
disappointed his dear friend yet once again. To Hume's plea that
he publish the *Dialogues* if Strahan would not do so, Smith expostulated : " It would then be said that I had published, for the sake
of an Emolument, not from respect to the memory of my friend,
what even a printer for the sake of the same emolument had
not published." [1] To this Hume replied on 23 August, when
he was so feeble as to have to dictate the letter to his nephew
David. Dropping the issue of the *Dialogues*, Hume acceded to
Smith's request for permission to make any additions he pleased
to *My Own Life*. The letter closes : " I go very fast to decline,
& last night had a small fever, which I hoped might put a quicker
period to this tedious Illness, but unluckily it has in a great measure
gone of. I cannot submit to your coming here on my account
as it is possible for me to see you so small a Part of the day
but Dr Black can better inform you concerning the degree
of strength which may from time to time remain with Me." That
strength was fast waning. Although he retained his other faculties
intact, he lost the power of speech on the evening of the 24th.

At a dinner party on Sunday, 25 August, Dr William Cullen
gave David Hume for a toast, saying " I won't give him up yet.
Here is to his easy passage." [2]

About four o'clock that afternoon death came for the philosopher at his home in St David Street.

The burial took place on Thursday, 29 August, during a heavy
rainfall. A large crowd had gathered in St David Street to watch
the coffin being carried out. One of the crowd was overheard to
remark, " Ah, he was an Atheist." To which a companion
returned : " No matter, he was an *honest* man."

[1] RSE, vii, 39.   [2] Neville, *Diary*, p. 247.

CHAPTER 40

THE DIGNITY OF HUMAN NATURE

"A manly steady virtue, . . . calm sunshine of the mind."

"THUS died our most excellent, and never-to-be-forgotten friend," wrote Adam Smith to Strahan in the letter [1] published early in 1777 along with Hume's *My Own Life*; "concerning whose philosophical opinions men will no doubt judge variously, every one approving or condemning them according as they happen to coincide, or disagree with his own; but concerning whose character and conduct there can scarce be a difference of opinion. His temper, indeed, seemed to be more happily balanced, if I may be allowed such an expression, than that perhaps of any other man I have ever known. Even in the lowest state of his fortune, his great and necessary frugality never hindered him from exercising, upon proper occasions, acts both of charity and generosity. It was a frugality founded not upon avarice, but upon the love of independency. The extreme gentleness of his nature never weakened either the firmness of his mind, or the steadiness of his resolutions. His constant pleasantry was the genuine effusion of good nature and good humour, tempered with delicacy and modesty, and without even the slightest tincture of malignity, so frequently the disagreeable source of what is called wit in other men. It never was the meaning of his raillery to mortify; and therefore, far from offending, it seldom failed to please and delight even those who were the objects of it. To his friends, who were frequently the objects of it, there was not perhaps any one of all his great and amiable qualities which contributed more to endear his conversation. And that gaiety of temper, so agreeable in society, but which is so often accompanied with frivolous and superficial qualities, was in him certainly attended with the most severe application, the most extensive learning, the greatest depth of thought, and a capacity in every respect the most comprehensive. Upon the whole, I have always considered him, both in his life-

---

[1] Reprinted in HL, II, 452. Hume's *Life* (with Smith's letter and Strahan's preface) was published at London on 11 Mar. 1777 and went through three editions. The *Life* (with Smith's letter) had previously appeared at Edinburgh in the January number of the *Scots Mag*. See W. B. Todd, "The First Printing of Hume's *Life* (1777)," in *Library*, Fifth Series, VI (1951), 123-5.

time, and since his death, as approaching as nearly to the idea of a perfectly wise and virtuous man, as perhaps the nature of human frailty will admit." In this last sentence Adam Smith was deliberately echoing the last sentence of Plato's *Phaedo*.[1]

Public interest in the death of Hume centred around the philosophical tranquillity he had displayed in the last weeks of life, the press being flooded with defences of and attacks upon his conduct. On the part of the narrowly pious there was evidenced a certain disappointment, on the one hand, that the philosopher had shown no signs of fear, and, on the other hand, that he had not taken to the consolations of religion. For Gibbon and the " enlightened," on the contrary, Hume's death was " the death of a philosopher." It was in this tense atmosphere that Adam Smith composed his famous letter in order to explain some of the controversial passages in *My Own Life* and, at the same time, to express unequivocally his own unstinted admiration of his friend, not merely as a philosopher, but as a man. There can also be little doubt that Smith was writing under deep emotional stress : he was genuinely troubled over Hume's determination to publish the *Dialogues* and he was guiltily aware that his own prudent refusal to take any responsibility for them had caused his friend great disappointment. Smith's letter to Strahan was thus written to defend the memory of Hume and to salve his own conscience. It was also written courageously and with full awareness of the consequences.

With the appearance of *My Own Life* and of Smith's letter to Strahan, the attacks on Hume grew even more frantic. After ten years Smith was still embittered over the public reaction to his friendly effort. " A single, and as I thought, a very harmless Sheet of paper," he complained, " which I happened to write concerning the death of our late friend, Mr. Hume, brought upon me ten times more abuse than the very violent attack I had made upon the whole commercial system of Great Britain," [2]

James Boswell's morbid curiosity on the day of Hume's burial had led him to inspect the open grave and then to skulk behind a wall as the procession of mourners followed the corpse to the grave. Nor was Boswell the only busybody ; during the week following the interment, the crowds were such that the Ninewells

---

[1] For this reference to Plato, I am indebted to D. D. Raphael, " Adam Smith and ' The Infection of David Hume's Society '," in *Journal of the History of Ideas*, xxx, (1969), 248.

[2] Scott, *Adam Smith*, p. 283. For a discussion of the posthumous controversy over Hume, see below, Appendix I, pp. 621–3.

family found it necessary to assign two guards to watch the grave at night lest it be desecrated. Somewhat later, Boswell suggested to Dr Johnson that he should " knock Hume's and Smith's heads together, and make a vain and ostentatious infidelity exceedingly ridiculous." When told by Boswell that Hume had professed to be " quite easy at the thought of Annihilation "—" He lied," the moralist retorted : " He had a vanity in being thought easy. It is more probable that he lied than that so very improbable a thing should be as a Man not afraid of death ; of going into an unknown state and not being uneasy at leaving all that he knew. And you are to consider that upon his own principle of Annihilation," continued Johnson with weasel argument, " he had no motive not to lie." [1]

The illogic of Johnson did not offend the unphilosophical mind of Boswell, yet he remained uneasy. Surely so good a man as the David Hume he had known *must* have been a Christian—at least in secret ! It was not until 8 January 1784 that Boswell, to his own personal satisfaction, resolved the enigma that he had found in Hume. " Awakened after a very agreeable dream," wrote the biographer in his journal, " that I had found a Diary kept by David Hume, from which it appeared that though his vanity made him publish treatises of skepticism and infidelity, he was in reality a Christian and a very pious Man. He had, I imagined, quieted his mind by thinking that whatever he might appear to the World to show his talents, his religion was between GOD and his conscience. (I cannot be sure if this thought was in sleep.) I thought I read some beautiful passages in his Diary. I am not certain whether I had this dream on thursday or friday night. But after I awaked, it dwelt so upon my mind that I could not for some time perceive that it was only a fiction." [2] With this catharsis, Boswell's attitude towards Hume softened and in his published works he toned down some of the roughest passages from his journals.

Unlike Boswell's, Lord Monboddo's antipathy to Hume was worked off briefly with the witticism that that philosopher had died confessing, not his sins, but his Scotticisms.

The unauthorised publication in 1777 of Hume's suppressed essays under the title of *Two Essays* kept his name in the public eye, as did also the publication two years later by his nephew David of the *Dialogues concerning Natural Religion*. This latter work, so long and so highly cherished by the author, belongs

[1] Boswell, *Letters*, i, 264 ; *Boswell Papers*, xii, 34 ; xiii, 23.
[2] *Boswell Papers*, xvi, 20-1.

among the classics of philosophy. It shows that Hume rejects all attempts to base religion upon metaphysics. It shows further that a religion based upon matters of fact and scientific method still finds it difficult, if not impossible, to rise beyond human nature and the world of nature into the realm of the supernatural. Philo's last words on the subject are Hume's last:

> If the whole of natural theology . . . resolves itself into one simple, though somewhat ambiguous, at least undefined proposition, *that the cause or causes of order in the universe probably bear some remote analogy to human intelligence :* If this proposition be not capable of extension, variation, or more particular explication : If it afford no inference that affects human life, or can be the source of any action or forbearance : And if the analogy, imperfect as it is, can be carried no farther than to the human intelligence ; and cannot be transferred, with any appearance of probability, to the other qualities of the mind : If this really be the case, what can the most inquisitive, contemplative, and religious man do more than give a plain, philosophical assent to the proposition, as often as it occurs ; and believe that the arguments, on which it is established, exceed the objections which lie against it ? Some astonishment indeed will naturally arise from the greatness of the object : Some melancholy from its obscurity : Some contempt of human reason, that it can give no solution more satisfactory with regard to so extraordinary and magnificent a question. . . .[1]

These words out of the grave, as it were, are an addition made to the *Dialogues* in Hume's final revision of 1776.

The voice of Hume has continued to speak, and increasingly to be heard, down to the present day. " Every nation has, 'tis true, a particular library of good books written in their own language," observes the Abbé Dubos, " but there is besides a common one for all nations—*the library of mankind.*" There can be no doubt that the contribution of David Hume to the library of mankind is substantial. There can, likewise, be no doubt that in his life he followed admirably his own caution : *Be a philosopher ; but amidst all your philosophy, be still a man.*

The cool appraisal with which he closed *My Own Life* has never been successfully impugned :

> To conclude historically with my own Character—I am, or rather was (for that is the Style, I must now use in speaking of myself ; which emboldens me the more to speak my Sentiments) I was, I say, a man of mild Dispositions, of Command of Temper, of an open, social, and cheerful Humour, capable of Attachment, but little susceptible of Enmity, and of great Moderation in all my passions. Even my Love of literary Fame, my ruling Passion, never soured my humour, notwithstanding my frequent Disappointments. My Company was not unacceptable to the young and careless, as well as to the

---

[1] Hume, *Dialogues*, pp. 227–8.

Studious and literary : And as I took a particular Pleasure in the Company of modest women, I had no Reason to be displeased with the Reception I met with from them. In a word, though most men any wise eminent, have reason to complain of Calumny, I never was touched, or even attacked by her baleful Tooth : And though I wantonly exposed myself to the Rage of both civil and religious Factions, they seemed to be disarmed in my behalf of their wonted Fury : My Friends never had occasion to vindicate any one Circumstance of my Character and Conduct : Not but that the Zealots, we may well suppose, wou'd have been glad to invent and propagate any Story to my Disadvantage, but they coud never find any which, they thought, woud wear the Face of Probability. I cannot say, there is no Vanity in making this funeral Oration of myself ; but I hope it is not a misplac'd one ; and this is a Matter of Fact which is easily cleard and ascertained.

This is Hume's own quiet way of leaving the final appraisal of his character to posterity, just as he left it to posterity " to add the Rest " to the inscription on his tombstone. His biographer, at least, cannot shirk the challenge. And it is perhaps not unfitting to suggest that Hume, in the final correction [1] made to the *Enquiry concerning the Principles of Morals* only thirteen days before his death, had said the last word on himself both as man and as thinker. Thus completed his epitaph would read :

DAVID HUME
1711–1776

" Upon the whole, then, it seems undeniable, *that* nothing can bestow more merit on any human creature than the sentiment of benevolence in an eminent degree ; and *that* a *part*, at least, of its merit arises from its tendency to promote the interests of our species, and bestow happiness on human society."

[1] *Phil. Wks.*, IV, 179.

APPENDICES

APPENDIX A

HUME'S *MY OWN LIFE* [1]

18 of April 1776

It is difficult for a man to speak long of himself without Vanity : Therefore I shall be short. It may be thought an Instance of Vanity, that I pretend at all to write my Life : But this Narrative shall contain little more than the History of my Writings ; as indeed, almost all my Life has been spent in literary Pursuits and Occupations. The first Success of most of my writings was not such as to be an Object of Vanity.

I was born the 26 of April 1711, O.S. at Edinburgh. I was of a good Family both by Father and Mother. My Father's Family is a Branch of the Earl of Home's or Hume's ; and my Ancestors had been Proprietors of the Estate, which my Brother possesses, for several Generations. My Mother was Daughter of Sir David Falconar, President of the College of Justice : The Title of Lord Halkerton came by Succession to her Brother.

My Family, however, was not rich ; and being myself a younger Brother, my Patrimony, according to the Mode of my Country, was of course very slender. My Father, who passed for a man of Parts, dyed, when I was an Infant ; leaving me, with an elder Brother and a Sister under the care of our Mother, a woman of singular Merit, who, though young and handsome, devoted herself entirely to the rearing and educating of her Children. I passed through the ordinary Course of Education with Success ; and was seized very early with a passion for Literature which has been the ruling Passion of my Life, and the great Source of my Enjoyments. My studious Disposition, my Sobriety, and my Industry gave my Family a Notion that the Law was a proper Profession for me : But I found an unsurmountable Aversion to every thing but the pursuits of Philosophy and general Learning ; and while they fancyed I was poring over Voet and Vinnius, Cicero and Virgil were the Authors which I was secretly devouring.

My very slender Fortune, however, being unsuitable to this plan of Life, and my Health being a little broken by my ardent Application, I was tempted or rather forced to make a very feeble Trial for entering into a more active Scene of Life. In 1734, I went to Bristol with some Recommendations to eminent Merchants ; but in a few Months found that Scene totally unsuitable to me. I went over to France, with a View of prosecuting my Studies in a Country Retreat ; and I there laid that Plan of Life, which I have steddily and successfully pursued : I resolved to make a very rigid Frugality supply my Deficiency of Fortune, to maintain unimpaired my Independency, and to regard every object as contemptible, except the Improvement of my Talents in Literature.

During my Retreat in France, first at Reims, but chiefly at La fleche in Anjou, I composed my *Treatise of human Nature*. After passing three Years very agreeably in that Countrey, I came over to London in 1737. In the End of 1738, I published my Treatise ; and immediatly went down to my Mother and my Brother, who lived at his Countrey house and was employing himself, very judiciously and successfully, in the Improvement of his Fortune.

[1] RSE, ix, 23.

611

Never literary Attempt was more unfortunate than my Treatise of human Nature. It fell *dead-born from the Press* ; without reaching such distinction as even to excite a Murmur among the Zealots. But being naturally of a cheerful and sanguine Temper, I very soon recovered the Blow, and prosecuted with great Ardour my Studies in the Country. In 1742, I printed at Edinburgh the first part of my Essays : The work was favourably received, and soon made me entirely forget my former Disappointment. I continued with my Mother and Brother in the Countrey ; and in that time, recovered the Knowlege of the Greek Language, which I had too much neglected in my early Youth.

In 1745, I received a Letter from the Marquess of Annandale, inviting me to come and live with him in England : I found also, that the Friends and Family of that young Nobleman, were desirous of putting him under my Care and Direction : For the State of his Mind and Health required it. I lived with him a Twelvemonth : My Appointments during that time made a considerable Accession to my small Fortune. I then received an Invitation from General St clair to attend him as Secretary to his Expedition, which was at first meant against Canada, but ended in an Incursion on the Coast of France : Next Year, to wit 1747, I received an Invitation from the General to attend him in the same Station in his military Embassy to the Courts of Vienna and Turin. I there wore the Uniform of an Officer ; and was introduced at these courts as Aide-de-camp to the General, along with Sir Harry Erskine and Capt Grant, now General Grant. These two Years were almost the only Interruptions which my Studies have received in the Course of my Life : I passed them agreeably and in good Company : And my Appointments, with my Frugality, had made me reach a Fortune, which I called independent, though most of my Friends were inclined to smile when I said so : In short I was now Master of near a thousand Pound.

I had always entertained a Notion, that my want of Success, in publishing the Treatise of human Nature, had proceeded more from the manner than the matter ; and that I had been guilty of a very usual Indiscretion, in going to the Press too early. I therefore cast the first part of that work anew in the Enquiry concerning human Understanding, which was published while I was at Turin. But this piece was at first but little more successful than the Treatise of human Nature. On my return from Italy, I had the Mortification to find all England in a Ferment on account of Dr. Middletons Free Enquiry ; while my Performance was entirely overlooked and neglected. A new Edition, which had been published at London of my Essays, moral and political, met not with a much better reception.

Such is the force of natural Temper, that these disappointments made little or no Impression on me. I went down in 1749 and lived two Years with my Brother at his Country house : For my Mother was now dead. I there composed the second Part of my Essays, which I called Political Discourses ; and also my Enquiry concerning the Principles of Morals, which is another part of my Treatise, that I cast anew. Mean-while, my Bookseller, A. Millar, informed me, that my former Publications (all but the unfortunate Treatise) were beginning to be the Subject of Conversation, that the Sale of them was gradually encreasing, and that new Editions were demanded. Answers, by Reverends and Right Reverends, came out two or three in a Year : And I found by Dr Warburtons Railing that the Books were beginning to be esteemed in good Company. However, I had fixed a Resolution, which

I inflexibly maintained, never to reply to any body ; and not being very irascible in my Temper, I have easily kept myself clear of all literary Squabbles. These Symptoms of a rising Reputation gave me Encouragement as I was ever more disposed to see the favourable than unfavourable Side of things ; a turn of Mind, which it is more happy to possess than be born to an Estate of ten thousand a Year.

In 1751, I removed from the Countrey to the Town ; the true Scene for a man of Letters. In 1752, were published at Edinburgh, where I then lived, my Political Discourses, the only work of mine, that was successful on the first Publication : It was well received abroad and at home. In the same Year was published at London my Enquiry concerning the Principles of Morals, which, in my own opinion (who ought not to judge on that subject) is of all my writings, historical, philosophical, or literary, incomparably the best : It came unnoticed and unobserved into the World.

In 1752, the Faculty of Advocates chose me their Librarian, an Office from which I received little or no Emolument, but which gave me the Command of a large Library. I then formed the Plan of writing the History of England ; but being frightened with the Notion of continuing a Narrative, through a Period of 1700 years, I commenced with the Accession of the House of Stuart ; an Epoch, when, I thought, the Misrepresentations of Faction began chiefly to take place. I was, I own, sanguine in my Expectations of the Success of this work. I thought, that, I was the only Historian, that had at once neglected present Power, Interest, and Authority, and the Cry of popular Prejudices ; and as the Subject was suited to every Capacity, I expected proportional Applause : But miserable was my Disappointment : I was assailed by one Cry of Reproach, Disapprobation, and even Detestation : English, Scotch, and Irish ; Whig and Tory ; Churchman and Sectary, Free-thinker and Religionist ; Patriot and Courtier united in their Rage against the Man, who had presumed to shed a generous Tear for the Fate of Charles I, and the Earl of Strafford : And after the first Ebullitions of this Fury were over, what was still more mortifying, the Book seemed to sink into Oblivion. Mr Millar told me, that in a twelvemonth he sold only forty five Copies of it. I scarcely indeed heard of one Man in the three Kingdoms, considerable for Rank or Letters, that cou'd endure the Book. I must only except the Primate of England, Dr Herring, and the Primate of Ireland, Dr Stone ; which seem two odd Exceptions. These dignifyed Prelates separately sent me Messages not to be discouraged.

I was, however, I confess, discouraged ; and had not the War been at that time breaking out between France and England, I had certainly retired to some provincial Town of the former Kingdom, have changed my Name, and never more have returned to my native Country. But as this Scheme was not now practicable, and the subsequent Volume was considerably advanced, I resolved to pick up Courage and to persevere.

In this Interval I published at London, my natural History of Religion along with some other small Pieces : Its public Entry was rather obscure, except only that Dr Hurd wrote a Pamphlet against it, with all the illiberal Petulance, Arrogance, and Scurrility, which distinguishes the Warburtonian School. This Pamphlet gave me some Consolation for the otherwise indifferent Reception of my Performance.

In 1756, two Years after the fall of the first Volume, was published the second Volume of my History, containing the Period from the Death of

Charles I, till the Revolution. This Performance happened to give less Displeasure to the Whigs, and was better received. It not only rose itself; but helped to buoy up its unfortunate Brother.

But though I had been taught by Experience, that the Whig Party were in possession of bestowing all places, both in the State and in Literature, I was so little inclined to yield to their senseless Clamour, that in above a hundred Alterations, which farther Study, Reading, or Reflection engaged me to make in the Reigns of the two first Stuarts, I have made all of them invariably to the Tory Side. It is ridiculous to consider the English Constitution before that Period as a regular Plan of Liberty.

In 1759 I published my History of the House of Tudor. The Clamour against this Performance was almost equal to that against the History of the two first Stuarts. The Reign of Elizabeth was particularly obnoxious. But I was now callous against the Impressions of public Folly; and continued very peacably and contentedly in my Retreat at Edinburgh, to finish in two Volumes the more early part of the English History; which I gave to the public in 1761 with tolerable, and but tolerable Success.

But notwithstanding this Variety of Winds and Seasons, to which my Writings had been exposed, they had still been making such Advances, that the Copy Money, given me by the Booksellers, much exceeded any thing formerly known in England : I was become not only independent, but opulent. I retired to my native Country of Scotland, determined never more to set my Foot out of it ; and retaining the Satisfaction of never having preferred a Request to one great Man or even making Advances of Friendship to any of them. As I was now turned of fifty, I thought of passing all the rest of my Life in this philosophical manner ; when I received in 1763 an Invitation from Lord Hertford, with whom I was not in the least acquainted, to attend him on his Embassy to Paris, with a near Prospect of being appointed Secretary to the Embassy, and in the mean while, of performing the functions of that office. This Offer, however inviting, I at first declined ; both because I was reluctant to begin Connexions with the Great, and because I was afraid that the Civilities and gay Company of Paris woud prove disagreeable to a Person of my Age and Humour : But on his Lordship's repeating the Invitation, I accepted of it. I have every reason, both of Pleasure and Interest, to think myself happy in my Connexions with that Nobleman ; as well as afterwards, with his Brother, General Conway.

Those who have not seen the strange Effect of Modes will never imagine the Reception I met with at Paris, from Men and Women of all Ranks and Stations. The more I recoiled from their excessive Civilities, the more I was loaded with them. There is, however, a real Satisfaction in living at Paris from the great Number of sensible, knowing, and polite Company with which the City abounds above all places in the Universe. I thought once of settling there for Life.

I was appointed Secretary to the Embassy, and in Summer 1765, Lord Hertford left me being appointed Lord Lieutenant of Ireland. I was *chargé d'affaires*, till the Arrival of the Duke of Richmond towards the End of the Year. In the beginning of 1766, I left Paris and next summer, went to Edinburgh, with the same view as formerly of burying myself in a philosophical Retreat. I returned to that place, not richer, but with much more money and a much larger Income by means of Lord Hertford's Friendship, than I left it ; and I was desirous of trying what Superfluity coud produce, as I had formerly made an Experiment of a Competency. But in 1767, I received from Mr Conway an invitation to be Under-Secretary ; and this Invitation both the Character of the Person, and my Connexions with Lord Hertford, prevented me from declining. I returned to Edinburgh in 1769, very opulent (for I possessed a Revenue of 1000 pounds a year) healthy, and though somewhat stricken in Years, with the Prospect of enjoying long my Ease and of seeing the Encrease of my Reputation.

In spring 1775, I was struck with a Disorder in my Bowels, which at first gave me no Alarm, but has since, as I apprehend it, become mortal and incurable. I now reckon upon a speedy Dissolution. I have suffered very little pain from my Disorder ; and what is more strange, have, notwithstanding the great Decline of my Person, never suffered a Moments Abatement of my Spirits : Insomuch, that were I to name the Period of my Life which I shoud most choose to pass over again I might be tempted to point to this later Period. I possess the same Ardor as ever in Study, and the same Gaiety in Company. I consider besides, that a Man of sixty five, by dying, cuts off only a few Years of Infirmities : And though I see many Symptoms of my literary Reputation's breaking out at last with additional Lustre, I know, that I had but few Years to enjoy it. It is difficult to be more detached from Life than I am at present.

To conclude historically with my own Character—I am, or rather was (for that is the Style, I must now use in speaking of myself ; which emboldens me the more to speak my Sentiments) I was, I say, a man of mild Dispositions, of Command of Temper, of an open, social, and cheerful Humour, capable of Attachment, but little susceptible of Enmity, and of great Moderation in all my Passions. Even my Love of literary Fame, my ruling Passion, never soured my humour, notwithstanding my frequent Disappointments. My Company was not unacceptable to the young and careless, as well as to the Studious and literary : And as I took a particular Pleasure in the Company of modest women, I had no Reason to be displeased with the Reception I met with from them. In a word, though most men any wise eminent, have found reason to complain of Calumny, I never was touched, or even attacked by her baleful Tooth : And though I wantonly exposed myself to the Rage of both civil and religious Factions, they seemed to be disarmed in my behalf of their wonted Fury : My Friends never had occasion to vindicate any one Circumstance of my Character and Conduct : Not but that the Zealots, we may well suppose, wou'd have been glad to invent and propagate any Story to my Disadvantage, but they coud never find any which, they thought, woud wear the Face of Probability. I cannot say, there is no Vanity in making this funeral Oration of myself ; but I hope it is not a misplac'd one ; and this is a Matter of Fact which is easily cleard and ascertained.

APPENDIX B

THE HUMES OF NINEWELLS

The chief authorities for the genealogical table opposite, as also for the unwritten history of the Humes of Ninewells, are :

A. *Unpublished Documents*

" Papers which belonged to Sir Patrick Hume Lord Polwarth and Earl of Marchmont," Miscellaneous Papers, Bundle 129, in H.M. General Register House, Edinburgh (see especially " Ninewells Papers 1680–1716 " and " The Tutors of John Home of Nynewells to the Lady Nynewells, 1715 ").
" Parochial Registers. Co. of Edinburgh, B. 1708–1714," in New Register House, Edinburgh : vol. 685 (1), No. 15.

B. *Published Documents*

Accounts of the Lord High Treasurer of Scotland, ed. Sir James Balfour Paul, vol. vii (Edinburgh 1907).
Calendar of the Laing Charters, A.D. 854–1837, belonging to the University of Edinburgh, ed. John Anderson. Edinburgh 1899.
Historical Manuscripts Commission, London : vols. x (1885), lvii (1902).
Register of the Great Seal of Scotland, ed. John Maitland Thomson : A.D. 1546–80 (Edinburgh 1886) ; A.D. 1580–93 (Edinburgh 1888). A.D. 1609–20 (Edinburgh 1892).
Register of the Privy Council of Scotland : First Series, ed. David Marson, vols. iii, vi, vii, ix, xiv ; Third Series, ed. P. Hume-Brown and Henry Paton, vols. i, iv, v, vii, x, xi, xiii, xiv. (Edinburgh 1880–1933).
Register of the Privy Seal of Scotland, ed. David Hay Fleming, vol. ii (Edinburgh 1921).
Scottish Record Society, Edinburgh : vols. ii, xxvi, xxvii, xxviii, xxxi, xxxv, lx, lxii.

C. *Genealogical Histories*

Burke's Landed Gentry. London 1939.
Robert Chambers, *The Book of Days,* 2 vols. London 1863–4.
Drummond, *Histories of Noble British Families.* (London 1846), vol. ii.
Alexander Nisbet, *Heraldic Plates.* Edinburgh 1892.
The Scots Peerage, ed. Sir James Balfour Paul. (Edinburgh 1904–14), vol. iv.
Patrick W. Montague-Smith, " Ancestry of David Hume, the Philosopher," *The Genealogists' Magazine* 13 (1961), 274–9.

APPENDIX C

RANKENIAN CLUB

WHEN the history of the Rankenian Club comes to be written, the following will be among the chief published authorities :

[Anon.], " Memoirs of Dr. Wallace of Edinburgh," *Scots Magazine*, XXXIII (1771), 340–44.

Boswell, *Private Papers*, VOL. XV.

George Chalmers, *Life of Thomas Ruddiman* (London 1794).

Alexander F. Tytler, *Memoirs of the Life and Writings of the Honourable Henry Home of Kames* (Edinburgh 1807), 2 vols.

Hogg's *Instructor*, VIII (1852), 44.

Morren, Nathaniel, *Annals of the General Assembly of the Church of Scotland* (Edinburgh 1840), 2 vols.

Ross, Ian Simpson, *Lord Kames and the Scotland of his Day* (Oxford 1972).

It would seem indisputable that both Lord Kames and Sir Alexander Dick in the information that they provided Boswell were confusing the Rankenian Club, at least in part, with Thomas Ruddiman's classical club, which was founded at about the same date.

APPENDIX D

WILLIAM WARBURTON

MORE than a century ago Hill Burton (I, 109) remarked in the main section of the review of Hume's *Treatise* in the *History of the Works of the Learned* " a tone of clamorous jeering and vulgar raillery that forcibly reminds one of the writings of Warburton." The name of William Warburton had been suggested as author by earlier writers and has again been brought up in recent years, but no evidence has been produced. I myself have no direct evidence to offer, only certain circumstantial evidence.

In a note appended to an article in the October 1741 issue of the *History of the Works of the Learned* (p. 257), the editor goes out of his way to state :

" These articles, on the Physico-Theology of Dr. Morgan, were communicated by a Correspondent, who chuses, I find, to be concealed, with Regard to his Name, Profession, and Abode ; all I can say of him is, that by the Similitude of the MSS I believe him to be the Person who drew up the Account of the Treatise of Human Nature, which was printed in the Months of November and December 1739."

The apology of the editor for the Morgan review would correspond with his having earlier apologised, as it were, for the Hume review by the addition of the final conciliatory paragraph. A tone of contemptuous sarcasm characterises both reviews. An instance of it in that of Morgan may be cited because of an instructive allusion : " Readers, cast away Lord Shaftsbury,

Archbishop King, and the divine Bard who undertook to vindicate the Ways of God to Man ; and attend only to the Solution of our illustrious Physico-Theologer, who utters this ensuing Oracle. . . ." The allusion to Alexander Pope as the " divine Bard " of the *Essay of Man* would have come pat from the pen of the man who had but recently defended Pope's orthodoxy publicly, and, to no small extent, by the use of the authorities just cited. It is perhaps also worth noting that the only autobiographical comment in the Hume review would fit the facts of Warburton's career perfectly. For the writer there remarks that, " It is above twenty Years since I looked over that Piece of Dr. *Berkeley's.* . . ." The *Treatise concerning the Principles of Human Knowledge,* here referred to, appeared in 1710 and might well have been first read by Warburton, say about 1718, in which year he was aged twenty-one.

APPENDIX E

CANCELS IN *FOUR DISSERTATIONS*

THE two cancels in the " Natural History of Religion " occur at signatures C 12 and D. Although no copy of *Five Dissertations* is extant, the original text can be reconstructed from the variants noted by T. H. Grose on the now lost proofsheets (*Phil. Wks.,* IV, 331–32). The " prudent " alterations made by Hume are as follows :

PASSAGE I

1756 Proofsheets :

Thus the deity, whom the vulgar Jews conceived only as the God of *Abraham, Isaac,* and *Jacob,* became their *Jehovah* and Creator of the world.

1757 :

Thus, notwithstanding the sublime ideas suggested by *Moses* and the inspired writers, many vulgar Jews seem still to have conceived the supreme Being as a mere topical deity or national protector.

PASSAGE II

1756 Proofsheets :

Were there a religion (and we may suspect Mahomatanism of this inconsistence) which sometimes painted the Deity in the most sublime colours, as the creator of heaven and earth ; *sometimes degraded him so far to a level with human creatures as to represent him wrestling with a man, walking in the cool of the evening, showing his back parts, and descending from heaven to inform himself of what passes on earth.* . . . [*my italics*—E.C.M.]

1757 [*the following is substituted for my italics above*—E.C.M.] :

sometimes degraded him nearly to a level with human creatures in his powers and faculties. . . .

APPENDIX F

THE ROUSSEAU–HUME *AFFAIRE*

THE desire to implicate Hume in the King-of-Prussia letter has been the motivating principle of a long line of Rousseau apologists. The nineteenth-century minstranslation that made Hume acknowledge his complicity is retained in the twentieth-century *Correspondance générale*, providing the editor with the opportunity for denouncing Hume's later " prevarications ". The case is worth citation in full. Hume wrote to the Marquise de Barbentane, 16 February 1766 [HL, II, 16] : " Please tell Madame de Boufflers that I received her letter the day after I wrote mine. Assure her that Horace Walpole's letter was not founded on any pleasantry of mine : the only pleasantry in that letter came from his own mouth, in my company, at Lord Ossory's table ; which my Lord remembers very well." This appears in French [*Corr. gén.*, XIV, 16] as " Dites à Mme de Boufflers que la seule plaisanterie que je me sois permise relativement à la prétendue lettre du roi de Prusse, fut faite par moi à la table de Lord Ossory." This false confession was detected by Hill Burton in 1846 [II, 322*n*], but went unnoticed by some Rousseauists until the publication of Greig's edition of Hume's *Letters* in 1932.

The desire to implicate Hume in Walpole's letter has not, however, entirely been given up. Roddier,[1] for instance, who acknowledges the fact is seemingly content to build up a new case against Hume without facts. Hume, he argues, loved pleasantry and sociability. Several of his compatriots were in Paris, and he doubtless met them frequently and doubtless also joined in the pleasantries at the expense of Rousseau. His denials and those of Walpole carry no weight because the British will stick together to preserve the social amenities. Now, on the basis of this seemingly unimportant—and —certainly unsubstantiated—hypothesis, Roddier proceeds to interpret Hume's later conduct. It is to be understood in the light of a certain sense of guilt that he felt concerning Rousseau. The peccadillo was small enough, to be sure, but the guilt was there nevertheless. When Rousseau made the first vague accusations against him, it was this consciousness of guilt that distressed Hume so greatly. When Rousseau later specified the charges without directly involving him in the pleasantries giving rise to Walpole's letter, Hume was vastly relieved : that was the one point on which his conduct had not been perfectly commendable. He could, therefore, affect righteous indignation and even brutal anger. Thus is Hume convicted of cruelty and inhumanity. Thus is Hume not *le bon David*.

Roddier proceeds to an even more subtle slander, that of guilt by association : Hume's " jesuitism ". E.g. (263) " un séjour en France au collège des jésuites de la Flèche " ; (279) " son long séjour chez les jésuites de la Flèche " ; (281) " une force d'argutie digne d'un ancien élève des jésuites ". Nevertheless, Roddier must be credited (283) with conciliatory intent : " Le grief d'indiscrétion est, en effet, de beaucoup le plus sérieux que Rousseau puisse avoir contre Hume. N'allons point cependant tout de suit sux extrêmes, et prenant argument de cette grave faiblesse, ne nous

[1] Henri Roddier, *J.-J. Rousseau en Angleterre ou XVIII Siècle* (Paris 1950), 259–306. Part of this present appendix is repeated from my *The Forgotten Hume* (New York 1943), 217–18.

pressons pas tant de transformer le ' bon David ' en un franc scélérat." It is also to be conceded that, with the exception of the chapter on the Hume–Rousseau *affaire*, Roddier's scholarship is exemplary.

A minor point in Rousseau's 10 July 1766 letter to Hume may now be disposed of once and for all. In the first footnote to that letter, Rousseau had written : " J'en dirai seulement une qui m'a fait rire ; c'était de faire en sorte, quand je venois le voir, que je trouvasse toujours sur la table un Tome de l'Heloïse ; comme si je ne connoissois pas assez le gout de M. Hume pour être assuré que, de tous les Livres qui existent, l'Héloïse doit être pour lui le plus ennuyeux." As a matter of fact, Hume and Lord Elibank, as early as 9 April 1761 (Hume–Elibank, p. 450) had been discussing the book. Hume wrote : ". . . I sometimes thought Julie & her Lover a little too recherchés in their Sentiments ; but I only say *sometimes* and a *little* ; . . ." On 27 March 1766 Hume further remarked : " I think this Work his Masterpiece ; tho' he [Rousseau] himself told me, that he valu'd most his *Contrat sociale* ; which is as preposterous a Judgement as that of Milton, who preferd the Paradise regained to all his other Performances " (HL, II, 28).

APPENDIX G

HUME'S REMOVAL FROM JAMES'S COURT

THE date of Hume's removal from James's Court has hitherto been put as Whitsunday 1772, but that it was actually the previous year is made certain by the fact that Boswell moved into Hume's house there at Whitsunday 1771. This information was given me by the courtesy of Professor F. A. Pottle of Yale University ; it is corroborated by further facts in the text above. The incorrect dating was presumably based upon a letter from Hume to Strahan dated " 5 of March 1772," wherein he says, " I remove in little more than two Months " (HL, II, 261). This letter, however, is in obvious answer to Strahan's of 1 March 1771 (RSE, VII, 62) and should be corrected to read " 1771."

APPENDIX H

NAMING OF ST DAVID STREET

CERTAIN circumstantial evidence, hitherto unnoticed, affords good reason for accrediting the popular tradition. In two of the documents cited above in the text concerning Hume's plot of land, the street in question is described as " the street *called* St. David's Street," and the street " *commonly called* St. David's Street " [my italics]. As the other streets mentioned are cited in the customary manner, the inference seems plain that " St. David's Street " was not at this time an official name, but of popular origin. Hume's first known use of St David Street as an address, 22 December 1773, occurs in the second of the above documents (" Council Records," VOL. 91, f. 77, in City Chambers, Edinburgh).

A. S. Crockett, Director of Highways, Lothian Regional Council, has most courteously faulted the Nancy–David story but I feel his rationale is no more conclusive than mine. While perfectly willing to accept the Humean sceptical conclusion of suspense-of-judgement, I shall nevertheless retain the personal anecdote in the text.

APPENDIX I

POSTHUMOUS CONTROVERSY OVER HUME

ATTACKS[1] on the life and character of David Hume, particularly on his equanimity while dying, continued during the quarter-century following his death. In addition to numerous comments in the newspapers and periodicals, the following works of three well-known clergymen may be cited by way of example :

[George Horne]. *A Letter to Adam Smith LL.D. on the Life, Death, and Philosophy of his Friend David Hume, Esq.* " By One of the People called Christians." Oxford 1777.

— — *Letters on Infidelity.* " By the Author of *A Letter to Dr. Adam Smith.*" Oxford 1784.

William Agutter. *On the Difference between the Deaths of the Righteous and the Wicked, Illustrated in the Instance of Dr. Samuel Johnson and David Hume, Esq.* A Sermon Preached before the University of Oxford, 3 July 1786. London 1800.

John Wesley. *On the Deceitfulness of the Human Heart.* A Sermon preached at Halifax, 21 April 1790. *Works* (London 1878), VII.

Hume's old antagonist of the Advocate's Library period (Ch. 19, above) continued the assault with a translation of " My Own Life " into Latin prose and Adam Smith's Letter to Strahan into Latin verse. Hailes's irony in these pamphlets, however, was so subtle that many contemporary and modern readers failed to detect it. I must confess that I was one of the deluded until the misreading was called to my attention by Robert Hay Carnie of Bedford College, University of London, who provided ample evidence to prove his case.

[Sir David Dalrymple of Newhailes, Lord Hailes]. *Davidis Humei, Scoti, Summi apud suos philosophi, De vita sua acta, Liber singularis ; nunc primum latine redditus.* [Edinburgh] 1787.

— —*Adami Smithi, LL.D. Ad Gulielman Strahanum, Armigerum, De rebus novissimis Davidis Humei, Epistola nunc primum latine reddita.* [Edinburgh] 1788.

Among the friendly writers on Hume at Edinburgh may be singled out Henry Mackenzie, who published the sympathetic fiction referred to in Ch. 8, above : Henry Mackenzie. " Story of La Roche," in *The Mirror* (Edinburgh), 19, 22, and 26 June 1779.

One of the most curious and malicious of the posthumous attacks on the character of the philosopher happily never saw the light of publication. Someone signing himself " Ebenezer Hume " wrote to the publisher Thomas Cadell in London on 9 February 1778, enclosing extracts from an alleged 300 lines of verse entitled " Natural Religion : A Poetical Essay. The only Poetical Work of a late celebrated Historian." The covering letter explains that " a very noted Person a particular Friend of mine not long since Dead, intrusted

[1] See Mossner, " Philosophy and Biography : The *Case of* David Hume " in *Philosophical Review*, LIX (1950), 184–201. Reprinted in V. C. Chappell (ed.), Hume : " A Collection of Critical Essays " (New York 1966), 6–34.

me with a small Work which he call'd a jeu d'esprit of his, but enjoined me not to make any public use of it while he lived, as he laid no Stress upon that kind of writing." Now, however, as " such a Work and *such* a *Title*, might suit the growing Taste of the Times," the letter-writer proposes various means of bringing it out through Cadell's publishing house. Cadell was not interested and simply endorsed the cover " refused." The manuscripts of both letter and verse-fragments are in the Pierpont Morgan Library in New York City.

The poem is not Hume's : (1) The year before his death Hume had told Boswell that he had never written any verses (*Boswell Papers*, XI, 41) ; (2) the casual giving-away of a manuscript is most unlike Hume ; (3) " The Manuscript was originally left with me without being stop'd," wrote " Ebenezer Hume "—a practice never followed by Hume elsewhere ; (4) the poem is a summary of Deism, a system of religion reprobated by Hume ; (5) the poem ridicules some of the principal dogmas of Christianity, a freedom which Hume had not taken.

If, then, " Natural Religion : A Poetical Essay " is not Hume's, why was the attempt made to palm it off as his, and who was the projector ? Numerous hackwriters were interested in Hume for the sole purpose of selling a few columns of print on the basis of his notoriety. There seems to be more than that involved, however, in the present affair : this is a deliberate attempt to malign the reputation of Hume by putting his name—for few would have failed to do so from the hints provided—to ridicule of that feature of Christianity most sacred to all believers, that

> It was from all Eternity decreed
> That for Man's Guilt a guiltless God should bleed
> Tale too absurd too monstrous too profane
> Credit with aught but Ideotism to gain.

The posthumous assailant of the character of the philosopher requested Cadell to favour him " with a Line directed to the Post Office here," that is, at Edinburgh. This mysterious direction, together with the fact that no " Ebenezer Hume " is known among the philosopher's acquaintance nor is listed in the Edinburgh directories for the period, suggests that the assailant was using a pseudonym for the purpose of concealing his identity. That he was someone who hated Hume and wished to sully his name goes without saying. His eagerness to print is indicated in the proposals made to Cadell : " I am ready to sell the Copy, or print it myself under the Sanction of your Publishing it, or else I am willing to go halves with you in the Chance of it." That he was someone known to the Edinburgh circle of Hume's friends and, therefore, fearful of being recognised and exposed, is perhaps a warranted conjecture. But without further evidence, any attempt at identification would be unwarranted guesswork.

TEXTUAL SUPPLEMENTS

TEXTUAL SUPPLEMENTS

From p. 39, n. 2 :

The figure " 2 " following David's name in the Matriculation Book most likely represents his year at the University, a conclusion that is borne out by the fact that on another sheet, Scot's for 1710, " an " (anno) follows the numeral. On the 1723 sheet the symbols, " 1 ", " 2 ", " 3 " or " 4 " accompany the signatures of some of the students, though not of the majority. It is thus established that the numerals were not mandatory. It is perhaps a fair inference that David was admitted to the University with advanced standing, that he was one of the *Supervenientes* excused from the Humanity class. John's situation is less clear. On the evidence of the Justin,[1] John, who was two years older than David, would seem to have been two years ahead of him at the University, an inference that unhappily is not corroborated by the Matriculation Book. A further complication arises from the intention of many students, including the two Humes, not to take degrees and hence not to be confined to a required succession of classes. And, as some students, curiously enough, matriculated several times during their academic careers, no new evidence is to be inferred from the fact that the Ninewells boys matriculated only once. It is also difficult to say with any confidence for which class of several possibilities the Justin was required reading.

From p. 95, n. 1 :

Curiously enough the influence—if indeed there was any—may have been in the other direction. For Hume's well-known tri-partite division of human reason into knowledge, proofs and probabilities may have derived from the Chevalier Ramsay's *Voyages de Cyrus* (1727) or from Andrew Baxter, who quoted the relevant passage in his *Enquiry into the Nature of the Human Soul* (1733).[2]

---

[1] *Justini Historiae Philippicae*, 4th edn., Lugd. Batavorum, 1701. The volume was mine, but I have presented it to the Edinburgh University Library where it started and where it should end. I am following Hume's own usage of the anglicized form of Justinus.

[2] See John Laird, *Hume's Philosophy of Human Nature* (London 1932), p. 90, n. 1 ; *Treatise* BK. I, PT. III, SEC. XI in *Phil. Wks.*, I, 423-4.

From p. 97, n. 1 : (extract from Hume's letter to Michael Ramsay, 29 September 1734)

" I am resolved before the post go away to tell you of the Library to which I am admitted here in Rheims. I was recommended to the Abbé Noel-Antoine Pluche, which most learned man has opened his fine Library to me. It has all Advantages for Study and particularly holds an Abundance of Writings of both the French and English along with as complete a selection of the Classics as I have seen in one place. It is my Pleasure to read over again today Locke's *Essays* and The Principles of Human Knowledge by Dr. Berkeley which are printed in their original state and in French copy. I was told by a student from the University who attends to the order of the Library that his Master received new works of Learning & Philosophy from London and Paris each month, and so I shall feel no want of the latest books."

From p. 102, n. 2 : (extract from Hume's letter to " Jemmy " Birch, 1735)

" As to a celebrated Professor, I do not know, if there is such to be met with at present in any part of France, especially for the Sciences, in which generally speaking the French are much inferiour to our own Countreymen.[1] But as you know there is nothing to be learnt from a Professor, which is not to be met with in Books, & there is nothing requir'd in order to reap all possible Advantages from them, but an Order & Choice in reading them ; in which, besides the small Assistance I can give you, your own Judgement wou'd alone be sufficient ; I see no reason why we shou'd either go to an University, more than to any other place, or ever trouble ourselves about the Learning or Capacity of the Professor." [2]

From p. 104, n. 1 : (Hume's letter to Michael Ramsay, 26 August 1737)

Tours, August 26, 1737

My Dear Friend,

I have quitted La Fleche two days after receiving yours. I am now at Tours in my way to Paris, where I do not intend to stay any considerable time, unless some extraordinary Accident intervene : So that I propose to see you in London about 3 or 4 Weeks hence. You may be sure that this Meeting will afford me a very great Satisfaction. & 'tis with the utmost Concern I hear you will leave the City a little after my Arrival. Nothing can be more useful & agreeable than to have an intimate Friend with one at any critical Time of Life such as that which I am just going to enter upon. & I must certainly esteem it a great Loss to be depriv'd of your Advice, as well in points that regard my Conduct & Behaviour, as in those of Criticism & Learning. I can assure you I have great Confidence in your Judgement even in this last particular, tho' the State of your Health & Business have never permitted you to be a regular Student, nor to apply yourself to any part of Learning in a methodical manner, without which 'tis almost impossible to

[1] Presumably because of the strong Newtonian influence in the Scottish universities and at Newton's own Cambridge.
[2] " Hume at La Flèche, 1735," as above, p. 100, n. 1.

make any mighty Progress. I shall submit all my Performances to your Examination, & to make you enter into them more easily, I desire of you, if you have Leizure, to read over once le Recherche de la Verité of Pere Malebranche, the Principles of Human Knowledge by Dr Berkeley, some of the more metaphysical Articles of Bailes Dictionary; such as those [of] Zeno, & Spinoza. Des-Cartes Meditations would also be useful but don't know if you will find it easily among your Acquaintances. These Books will make you easily comprehend the metaphysical Parts of my Reasoning and as to the rest, they have so little Dependence on all former systems of Philosophy, that your natural Good Sense will afford you Light enough to judge of their Force & Solidity.

I shall be oblig'd to put all my Papers into the Chevalier Ramsay's hands when I come to Paris; which I am really sorry for. For tho' he be Freethinker enough not to be shockt with my Liberty, yet he is so wielded to whymsical Systems, & is so little of a Philosopher, that I expect nothing but Cavilling from him. I even fortify myself against his Dis-approbation & am resolv'd not to be in the least discouraged by it, if I shoud chance to meet with it. All Counsels are good to be taken, says the Cardinal de Richelieu. The good are good of themselves. The bad confirm the Good & give new Force to them. This is more especially true in works of Learning & Philosophy, where frivolous Objections & bad Reasoning give us alwise greater Assurance in the Truth.

I come now to that Article of your last Letter, wherein you seem to doubt either of my present Friendship [for] you or of its Continuance. I cannot imagine upon what such a Doubt may be founded. You know my Temper well enough not to expect any Romantic Fondness from me. But Constancy, Equality, Fidelity & a hearty Good will you may justly look for, & shall ne[ver] be disappointed. You speak of my superior Progress in the Sciences. I know not how far there may be a Foundation for what you say. I must flatter myself that there is some Ground for it in order to support my Courage in that dangerous Situation, in which I have placed myself. But however that may be I have enough of Science to know, that a Man who is incapable of Gratitude & Friendship is in a very disconsolate Condition, whatever Abilities he may be endow'd with & whatever Fame he may acquire.

I mist the Post at Tours, so that I finish this Letter at Orleans tho I have nothing farther to add, but farther Assurance of my Good will & Friendship. I know this will be more satisfactory to you than any Descriptions of Fields & Buildings, which I have met with in my Road: Besides that I will be able in a short time to satisfy your Curiosity in this particular, if you have any. Adieu
Orleans, August 31, 1737 [1]

From p. 118, n. 3:

Despite the essential rationalism of the *Essay on Man*, it was held by Hume in qualified esteem. But may he not have had Pope slyly in mind when he deplored in the Introduction to the *Treatise*: " Amidst all this bustle [in contemporary controversy] 'tis not reason, which carries the prize, but eloquence; and no

---

[1] [Hume–Poland, pp. 133-4.]

man needs ever despair of gaining proselytes to the most extravagant hypothesis, who has art enough to represent it in any
favourable colours. The victory is not gained by the men at arms,
who manage the pike and the sword ; but by the trumpeters,
drummers, and musicians of the army " ? Be that as it may, the
" man at arms " sent to the " musician " the gift of the *Treatise*.
On the flyleaf of each of the three volumes is inscribed in Hume's
hand : " To / Alexander Pope, Esq / at / Twickenham." Like
the *Treatise* itself, the inscription is anonymous.[1] One of Pope's
couplets in the *Essay on Man* was to draw a demurrer from Hume
in an essay of 1741.[2] (Kant's virtually unqualified admiration
of Pope as a philosopher is well known.)

From p. 133, n. 3 : (extract from Hutcheson's letter to Henry
Home)

" I perused the first volume, & a great part, indeed almost all the second.
And was every where surprised with a great acuteness of thought and reasoning
in a mind wholly disengaged from the prejudices of the Learned as well as
those of the Vulgar. I cannot pretend to assent to his tenets as yet, these
metaphysical subjects have not been much in my thoughts of late ; tho' a
great many of these sentiments and reasonings had employed me about 10 or
12 years ago . . . This book will furnish me matter of a good deal of
thought next vacation, now coming on in less than 6 weeks. I shall have the
greatest pleasure in communicating to the Ingenious Author whatever occurs
probable to me on these subjects. I have for many years . . . been . . .
more and more . . . running into the Old Academy, despairing of Certainty
in the most important subjects, but satisfied with a sort of Probable knowledge
which to an honest mind will be sufficient for the Conduct of Life. I should
be glad to know where the Author could be met with if a lazy Umbratick,
very averse to motion, ever takes a ramble in a vacation." [3]

From p. 138, n. 1 : (extract from letter from William Mure of
Caldwell to his sister Agnes, dated " Richmond June 5th 1740 ")

" We have been here now these ten days, and pass our time in a very
agreeable way, we have our countrey man Mr. Hume the author of the
Metaphysical books that you heard so much of last summer as a party in our
retirement, he is a very sensible young fellow and extreamly curious in most
parts of learning and how much soever he has shown himself a Sceptick upon
subjects of speculation and enquiry, he is as far from it as any man with
regard to the qualities of a well natured friendly disposition and an honest

[1] Minor corrections (a letter or a single word) have been made : seventeen in
Vol. I, five in Vol. II, none in Vol. III. The volumes are in the Donald F. and Mary
Hyde Library at Four Oaks Farm, Somerville, New Jersey.
[2] See p. 142 and Textual Supplement.
[3] Ian S. Ross, " Hutcheson on Hume's *Treatise* : An Unnoticed Letter," in
Journal of the History of Philosophy, iv (1966), pp. 69–70.

heart which are no doubt of greater consequence to the intrinsick worth of a character than any abstract opinion whatever. As he is very communicative of all his knowledge we have a great deal from him in the way of dispute and argument, and not a little too in the way of plain information we reason upon every point with the greatest freedom, even his own books, (which we are working at at present) we canvass with ease, and attack him boldly wherever we can get the least hold of him, and question or contradict his most favourite notions; all this goes on with the greatest good humour, and affords us entertainment both within doors, and in the feilds at our walks in this delightful country, which is the finest that one can possibly imagine, and has the preference by people that has travel'd throw most of Europe, to any they ever saw. We make use of our Philosopher too in another way less becoming the dignity of his Character, as we keep family within ourselves, he provides the necessaries of household Oeconomy and manages all the affairs of house keeping. From these few hints you may imagine we spend our time here in a pleasant enough manner, much more to all our satisfaction than in the continued noise and hurry of the town." [1]

The " well natured friendly disposition " and the " honest heart " appraisement of 1740 recall to mind once more the " It is not Pod, it is Me " appraisement of a decade or so earlier. The portrait of Hume in the twin capacities of " our Philosopher " and of manager of " all the affairs of house keeping " foreshadows the familiar portrait of *le bon David* of later years in Edinburgh.

From p. 143, n. 2 :

" That Politics may be reduc'd to a Science " opens with a denial of Pope's :

> For Forms of Government let fools contest ;
> Whate'er is best administer'd is best.[2]

" It is a question with several, whether there be any essential difference between one form of government and another ? and, whether every form may not become good or bad, according as it is well or ill administered ? Were it once admitted, that all governments are alike, and that the only difference consists in the character and conduct of the governors, most political disputes would be at an end, and all *Zeal* for one constitution above another, must be esteemed mere bigotry and folly. But, though a friend to moderation, I cannot forbear condemning this sentiment, and should be sorry to think, that human affairs admit of no greater stability, than what they receive from the casual humours and characters of particular men."

---

[1] J. C. Hilson, " An Early Account of David Hume," in *Hume Studies*, I (1975), 78–80.

[2] *Essay on Man*, III, 303–4. That Pope later denied the interpretation that Hume, and many others, gave to the couplet is irrelevant.

From p. 160, n. 1 :

A Letter from a Gentleman was evidently composed with a copy of Principal Wishart's charges, whether in print or otherwise, in front of him. Hume was " obliged to cite from my Memory, and cannot mention Page and Chapter so accurately as the Accuser. I came hither [i.e. Weldehall] by Post, and brought no Books along with me, and cannot now provide myself in the Country with the Book referred to."

The charges brought against Hume number six : (1) " Universal Scepticism " ; (2) " Principles leading to downright Atheism, by denying the Doctrine of Causes and Effects " ; (3) " Errors concerning the very Being and Existence of a God " ; (4) " Errors concerning God's being the first Cause, and prime Mover of the Universe " ; (5) " denying the Immateriality of the Soul, and the Consequences flowing from this Denial " ; (6) " sapping the Foundations of Morality, by denying the natural and essential Difference betwixt Right and Wrong, Good and Evil, Justice and Injustice ; making the Difference only artificial, and to arise from human Conventions and Contracts."

Hume's answer to this last charge was his first defence of his system of morality since Book III, " Of Morals ", of the *Treatise*.

" I come now to the last Charge, which, according to the prevalent Opinion of Philosophers in this Age, will certainly be regarded as the severest, *viz.* the Author's destroying all the Foundations of Morality :

He hath indeed denied the eternal Difference of Right and Wrong in the sense in which *Clark* and *Woolaston* maintained them, *viz.* That the Propositions of Morality were of the same Nature with the Truths of Mathematics and the abstract Sciences, the Objects *merely* of Reason, not the *Feelings* of our internal *Tastes* and *Sentiments*. In this Opinion he concurs with all the antient Moralists, as well as with Mr. *Hutchison* Professor of Moral Philosophy in the University of *Glasgow*, who, with others, has revived the antient Philosophy in this Particular.

When the Author asserts that Justice is an *artificial* not a *natural Virtue*, he seems sensible that he employed Words that admit of an invidious Construction ; and therefore makes use of all proper Expedients, by *Definitions* and *Explanations*, to prevent it . . . By the *natural Virtues* he plainly understands *Compassion* and *Generosity*, and such as we are immediately carried to by a *natural Instinct* ; and by the *artificial Virtues* he means *Justice*,

Loyalty, and such as require, along with a *natural Instinct*, a certain Reflection on the general Interests of Human Society, and a Combination with others. In the same Sense, Sucking is an Action natural to Man, and Speech is artificial. But what is there in this Doctrine that can be supposed in the least pernicious ? Has he not expressly asserted, That Justice, in another Sense of the Word, is so natural to Man, that no Society of Men, and even no individual Member of any Society, was ever entirely devoid of all Sense of it ? "

From p. 180, n. 1 :

Something of a mystery arises concerning the time of composition of the essay " Of National Characters ". There is reason to doubt that Hume left it with Lord Tinwald before departing for the Continent in February 1748. It has recently been plausibly, but not entirely convincingly, argued that Hume wrote it in Turin after becoming acquainted with the general theses of Montesquieu's *Esprit des Loix*. It was published on 18 November 1748 in both *Three Essays Moral and Political* and *Essays Moral and Political*. See Paul E. Chamley, " The Conflict between Montesquieu and Hume : A Study of the Origins of Adam Smith's Universalism " in *Essays on Adam Smith* (Oxford 1975), 274–305.

" I shall be very much mortify'd," wrote Hume with tongue in cheek to his Jacobite friend, Lord Elibank, " if you do not approve, in some small degree, of the Reasonings with regard to the original Contract, which, I hope, are new & curious, & form a short, but compleat Refutation of the political Systems of Sydney, Locke, and the Whigs, which all the half Philosophers of the Nation have implicitely embrac'd for near a Century ; tho' they are plainly, in my humble Opinion, repugnant to Reason & the Practice of all Nations." [1]

From p. 210, n. 1 :

From the Hague Hume made a short excursion to Delft to carry out a business commission for Lord Elibank. " I was carry'd into a very spacious, clean, cold House, & after waiting a little, the Master came to me, who was not quite of a piece with his House. I cou'd have almost been tempted to renew the

[1] Hume–Elibank, 437.

ill-bred Jest of Diogenes, who, in a visit of this kind, spit in the Master's Face, saying It was the only dirty Place he saw. The Gentleman spoke extreme good Dutch, very bad Latin, & scarce any French: So that our Conversation was not very long . . . Then he observes: ' The Boats cannot move along the Canals because of the Ice: And at the same time we have not the Pleasure of Scating, because the Snow, being mixt with the Ice, renders it too rough & uneven for that Amusement.' " [1]

At the Maas River the travellers were obliged to make use of an iceboat to cross the more than half-mile span of melting ice. Hume was boyishly delighted: " The Operation is after this Manner. You place Yourself on your Ice boat, which is like an ordinary Boat except only that it runs upon two Keels, shod with Iron. Three or four Men push you along in this Boat very cleverly, as long as the Ice will bear you: But whenever that fails, plump, down you go into the Water of a sudden: You are very heartily frighten'd: The men are wet, up to the Neck sometimes: But keeping hold of the Boat; leap in; row you thro the Water; till they come to Ice, which can bear. There they pull you up; run along with you; till you sink again: And so they renew the same Operation."

From p. 248, n. 3:

The decision of the Duke of Argyll is reported cursorily in a letter from London dated 9 January 1752 from Andrew Fletcher to his father Lord Milton.[2] " Yesterday I laid before His Grace the Letters &c concerning the Affair pendant at Glasgow: His Grace desires me to acquaint you that Mr David Home cannot be recommended to a Proffessorship there and that for many reasons which must easily occur to your Ldship."

From p. 264, n. 1:

Though stigmatizing slavery on humanitarian grounds, Hume also rejected the claim that slavery is a spur to population growth. Quite the contrary: " Wherever there are most happiness and virtue, and the wisest institutions, there will also be most people." The slave state is uneconomical and survives only with the continual importation of more slaves. This trail-breaking study in demography ends on a typically modest note: " The humour

---

[1] Hume–Elibank, 438–9.   [2] MS in NLS.

of blaming the present, and admiring the past, is strongly rooted in human nature, and has an influence even on persons endued with the profoundest judgment and most extensive learning."

From p. 268, n. 3 : (extract from Hume's letter to Lord Elibank)

" I would fain use the Liberty to interpose, and disswade your Lordship from publishing the Letter, which you do me the Honor of addressing to me. It is indeed very sharp & satirical & pleasant, but is too much so ; and will so much the more hurt the old Gentleman, that he professes a very high Regard for your Lordship, and woud be very ambitious of standing well in your Opinion.

Besides, my Lord, all Authors, as well as Poets, are of the *genus irritabile*. Mr Wallace has his Pen in his hand, prim'd & cockd & charg'd ; and is always ready for a Contest . . . If he were provokd by the Publication of your Letter, he woud reply in an angry & perhaps an abusive Strain ; and might descend to Personalities, which, tho' in reality they coud only hurt himself, yet woud be disagreeable to your Lordship. There was one Circumstance, which Wallace mentioned to me of your Lordship, which gave me the more Pleasure, that I had both made the Remark myself, and heard it from others as a Singularity, viz, that, notwithstanding your great Fire & Imagination, you are certainly the most civil, attentive, and best bred Man in the World. Dare I venture to entreat you, that in one Instance more you will sacrifice your Passion to your Politeness ? Especially as poor Wallace has certainly offended merely from Ignorance, and wou'd have spoke very differently, had he been acquainted with the real Matter of Fact.

I am not so assuming as to insist upon my own Practice in like Cases. We men of Ph[l]egm & Tranquillity (which we call Wisdom) have little merit in our Patience. But your Lordship will own, that it wou'd not be proper for a Person of your Rank, who are only an Author by Chance, to enter into such Altercations as often serve to discredit Literature, nor show as great Jealousy of a casual Production, as appears in Authors by Profession . . . I find so much Tranquillity, as well as Leizure, by keeping to this general Resolution, that I shall probably uphold it to the End of my Life." [1]

Lord Elibank did not publish. Peace prevailed. " Wisdom " had won the day.

From p. 270, n. 1 :

This philosophical approach does not partake of the narrowness of the nineteenth century, which made economics in Carlyle's view the " dismal science." " The spirit of the age ", wrote Hume, " affects all the arts ; and the minds of men, being once aroused from their lethargy, and put into a fermentation, turn themselves on all sides, and carry improvements into every art and science." Thus, he concludes, " *industry*, *knowledge*, and *humanity*, are linked together by an indissoluble chain." [1]

[1] Hume–Elibank, 444–5. [1] *Phil. Wks.*, III, 301–2.

From p. 319, n. 1 : (further discussion of the *Dialogues concerning Natural Religion*)

Although there are some passages of Cleanthes advocating the argument from design (" the chief or sole argument for a divine existence "), that Hume as Philo would find acceptable, and even a few passages of Demea, Hume has stipulated that " In every Dialogue, no more than one person can be supposed to represent the author." [1] An added factor of import, though one seldom taken into consideration because of the very art—and artfulness, as Hume later acknowledged—of the dialogue itself, is that Philo is allotted somewhat more than twice as much space as the other two interlocutors combined.[2] The presence of the youthful Pamphilus must not be allowed to becloud the issue : he takes no part in the debate (" My youth rendered me a mere auditor of their disputes "), and his concluding judgment that " Philo's principles are more probable than Demea's; but that those of Cleanthes approach still nearer to the truth " is but a delicious ironical imitation of the last sentence of Cicero's *De Natura Deorum*.[3]

From p. 320, n. 3 :

While paying judicious lip-service in the *Dialogues concerning Natural Religion* to the concept of a God, Hume is, in reality, undermining that belief. The sheerly negative thrust of the *Dialogues* is observable in two passages artfully put in the mouths of Cleanthes and Demea. Cleanthes is thus encouraged to demolish the *a priori* argument put forward by Demea :

" I shall begin with observing that there is an evident absurdity in pretending to demonstrate a matter of fact, or to prove it by any arguments *a priori*. Nothing is demonstrable, unless the contrary implies a contradiction. Nothing, that is distinctly conceivable, implies a contradiction. Whatever we conceive as existent, we can also conceive as non-existent. There is no Being, therefore, whose non-existence implies a contradiction. Consequently there is no Being, whose existence is demonstrable. I propose this argument as entirely decisive, and am willing to rest the whole controversy upon it." [4]

After this metaphysical setback, Demea is driven to plead the common argument from the hopes and fears of mankind :

[1] HL, I, 173.
[2] Greig, p. 236 and n. 3 : Demea, 12%; Cleanthes, 21%; and Philo, 67%.
[3] For the Ciceronian imitation I am indebted to Peter Gay, *The Enlightenment : An Interpretation* (London 1967), I, 414–15, n. 8.   [4] *Hume, Dialogues*, p. 189.

" It is my opinion, I own . . . that each man feels, in a manner, the truth of religion within his own breast; and from a consciousness of his imbecility and misery, rather than from any reasoning, is led to seek protection from that Being, on whom he and all nature is dependent. So anxious or so tedious a ·e even the best scenes of life, that futurity is still the object of all our hopes and fears. We incessantly look forward, and endeavour, by prayers, adoration, and sacrifice, to appease those unknown powers, whom we find, by experience, so able to afflict and oppress us. Wretched creatures that we are! What resource for us amidst the innumerable ills of life, did not religion suggest some methods of atonement, and appease those terrors, with which we are incessantly agitated and tormented." [1]

Both Cleanthes and Demea are obviously playing into the hands of the sceptic. Always Hume's authentic voice, Philo will speak out—as indeed he should—after Hume's death with the ultimate ironical phasing out of the " religious hypothesis," including, it is hardly necessary to specify, the Christian dispensation.[2]

From p. 399, n. 1 :

Hume would have had no difficulty in recognizing himself as " an ingenious and agreeable philosopher, who joins the greatest depth of thought to the greatest elegance of expression, and possesses the singular and happy talent of treating the abstrusest subjects not only with the most perfect perspicuity, but with the most lively eloquence." [3]

From p. 402, n. 3 :

Hume's friend, the artist Allan Ramsay, on a brief visit to Edinburgh in September 1760 provides a pleasing picture of the life of the historian during this productive period. Writing to Mrs Elizabeth Montagu, Ramsay reveals: " . . . by much drinking with David Hume and his associates, I have learnt to be very historical; and am nightly confirmed in the belief, that it is much easier to tell the *How* than the *Why* of any thing; and that it is moreover better suited to the state of man; who, we

---

[1] *Ibid.*, p. 193.
[2] See Ch. 40, below. My final interpretation of the *Dialogues* was presented at Edinburgh University in 1976 in a conference memorializing the 200th anniversary of Hume's death. This essay is now published (see p. 320, n. 3).
[3] *The Theory of Moral Sentiments*, edd. D. D. Raphael and A. L. Macfie (Oxford 1976), p. 179.

are all satisfied, from self-examination, is any thing rather than a rational animal." [1] Hume's associates, no doubt, included the friendly Moderate Presbyterian clerics.

From p. 414, n. 1 :

Some years later when in Paris, Hume was informed that Lord Elibank was about to publish a pamphlet blistering his account of Queen Mary in the *History of England*. In great distress, Hume threw caution to the winds. " You have always display'd such an unaccountable Violence in this silly Controversy about Queen Mary, and the polemical Spirit is so contagious, that, unless you allow this Work to lie bye you some time or make it be review'd by some Person of Temper, I am sure, that we are no longer Friends . . . Forgive me, My Lord, for suspecting a Person of your Lordships Education and remarkable Politeness of such a Fault : I never shou'd, if, in this Affair, I had ever found you reason with tolerable Temper : But surely, it will appear singular, that two Persons, who have always lived in great Intimacy, and who, methinks, wou'd not quarrel even about a living Mistress, shou'd break up their Friendship, on account of an old Strumpet, who has been dead and rotten near two hundred Years. I hope that it will not prove so." The friendship was not disrupted, but it took several exchanges of letters for the quarrel to cool off. Elibank did not, however, rush into print. [2]

From p. 426, n. 1 :

" Pray did your Lordship know when at Paris, Madame la Comtesse de Boufflers ? " inquired Hume of Lord Elibank, in evident perturbation. " My Reason for asking is that I had from her last Night a long Letter, the most obliging I ever receivd, and liker a Dedication than a Letter of Civility. I dare not say, that it is full of good Sense & Elegance & Spirit ; because she has so much bribd me with her Praises that I dare not trust my own Judgement on that head : But I imagine, if I dare depend upon my Impartiality, that she is a Lady of great Merit ; and tho there may seem to be an Affectation in writing to a Stranger, she

---

[1] Marcia Allentuck (ed.), " David Hume and Allan Ramsay : A New Letter," in *Studies in Scottish Literature*, ix (1972), 265.
[2] Hume–Elibank, p. 456.

excuses it so handsomely, that I can venture almost to acquit her of that Failing."[1]   Had Hume been aware that "on one occasion" the Comtesse "had lovingly spent an entire day trying to equal in French translation *one* paragraph of [his] elegant *History*," his composure might more easily have been restored: her hyperboles were no more than the truth.[2]

From p. 469, n. 2:

"I do not believe there is one Englishman in fifty, who, if he heard that I had broke my Neck to night, would not be rejoic'd with it. Some hate me because I am not a Tory, some because I am not a Whig, some because I am not a Christian, and all because I am a Scotsman. Can you seriously talk of my continuing an Englishman? Am I, or are you, an Englishman? Will they allow us to be so?"

From p. 485, n. 3:

While in Paris, Hume wrote to Millar on 26 August 1765, revealing that he was still harbouring the thought of composing the much requested ecclesiastical history: "You are again anxious after my ecclesiastical History. The Reports that you hear should be put aside as you know the facts of the matter and my resolve never to undertake a History which wou'd expose me again to Impertinence & Ill-manners. The Prejudices of all factions have not so far subsided that a History wrote with a Spirit of Impartiality could withstand the Rage & Clamor.

I have, however, been gathering most of the Works of Authors in France and England of the History of the Church, and I should be glad if I have the Leizure to read over them. An Account of some Periods in ecclesiastical History might be put beyond Controversy, and if one Volume were successful then the others might be composed: But I do not think it so near a Prospect."[3]

From p. 494, n. 3:

Alison Cockburn as usual came up with her customary feminine logic as to why Hume should go with Lord Hertford to

---

[1] Hume–Elibank, 450.
[2] Laurence L. Bongie, *David Hume, Prophet of the Counter-Revolution* (Oxford 1965), p. 65, citing *Nouveaux mélanges extraits des manuscrits de Mme Necker* (Paris, An X, 1, 202).
[3] Michael Morrisroe, Jr., "Hume's Ecclesiastical History: A New Letter," in *English Studies* 53 (1972), 1–3.

Ireland. " I wish you to go with him. I wish to break the hearts of all the French women, if they have any hearts ; but I suspect, for all the adulation you have met with amongst them that I am infinitely more your affectionate friend and servant . . . " [1]

From p. 500, n. 2 :

Adam Smith and his young pupil, the Duke of Buccleuch, had been in France and Switzerland since early in 1764. A stay of eighteen months in Toulouse and the Languedoc proved so tedious, despite Hume's letters of introduction to the local dignitaries, that Smith was driven to begin composition of a new book. *The Wealth of Nations* was to be his main occupation until its publication in 1776. At Ferney, just outside the boundary of Geneva, Smith had several agreeable conversations with the great Voltaire. Smith and his party arrived in Paris too late to meet the great Rousseau. On 4 January 1766 Hume left Paris, escorting him to England for sanctuary. But throughout most of 1766 in Paris Smith made the acquaintance of the *philosophes*, above all, of the *Physiocrates*. In the Parisian *salons* he was almost as well received as Hume himself.

From p. 537, n. 1 :

Sir Gavin de Beer in " Quelques considérations sur le séjour de Rousseau en Angleterre " in *Geneva* (1955), n.s. III, 37, has reproduced not one, but three Rousseau portraits by Allan Ramsay. The first is Hume's (now in the Scottish National Portrait Gallery), the other two, Davenport's (now, Lt.-Col. W. H. Bromley Davenport).

From p. 537, n. 2 :

Still he could mock himself plaintively : " I wou'd advise you," he warned a friend, " to be civil to me, and not treat me with Disdain, as a Scholastic, and a Philosopher, and a man of another World, and a Speculatist, and a Recluse : I assure you I scorn all those Epithets, and aspire to the Character of a Politician and a Man of Business, Names of much greater Dignity and Respect, in this Part of the World." [2]

[1] RSE, IV, 29.
[2] MS letter of 3 April 1767 in Yale University Library.

From p. 543, n. 3:

While still in France Hume had made the acquaintance of Isaac de Pinto, the Dutch Jewish economist and philosopher. Pinto had been instrumental during the peace negotiations of the Treaty of Paris early in 1763 in supplying the Duke of Bedford with information concerning the boundaries of the jurisdiction of the British East India Company in India. The information is said to have saved the Company a revenue of upwards of £700,000 annually. Pinto was seeking the reward of a pension from the Company for his important services and was dunning Hume and other British officials for their support. Hume became convinced that Pinto was in the right and affably wrote letter after letter on his behalf—apparently six or seven in all.

Hume's first letter on behalf of Pinto, dated from Paris, 14 March 1764 and addressed to Richard Neville, Minister Plenipotentiary until the arrival of Lord Hertford, is both humorous and circumspect:

" Manifold have been the persecutions, dear Sir, which the unhappy Jews, in several ages, have suffered from the misguided zeal of the Christians, but there has at last arisen a Jew capable of avenging his injured nation, and striking terror into their proud oppressors; this formidable Jew is Monsr. de Pinto, and the unhappy Christian, who is chiefly exposed to all the effects of his cruelty, is your humble servant. He says, that you promised to mention him to me; I do not remember that you did: he says, that he has done the most signal services to England, while the Duke of Bedford was Ambassador here; I do not question it, but they are unknown to me: he says, that he is poor, and must have a pension for his reward; I wish he may obtain it, but I cannot assist him: he sends me letters, which I transmit to you, but I cannot oblige you to answer them: he says, that Lord Hertford must get justice done him, if the Duke of Bedford neglects him; I do not believe that the Duke of Bedford neglects anybody that has done him service: he grows angry; I exhort him to patience.

This, dear Sir, is a very abridged account of the dialogue which passes every day between M. Pinto and me, that is, every day he can break in upon me, and lay hold of me: when he catches Lord Hertford, he is very copious on the same subject; but when he seizes poor Lord Beauchamp, his Lordship has good

T t

reason to curse the day he was born mild and gentle, and made incapable of doing or saying a harsh thing.

But to be serious with regard to the man, I imagine, from what he tells me, and from a letter of yours which he showed me, that he had endeavoured to be useful to the Duke of Bedford and you during the negotiations of the peace : perhaps he was useful in some particulars, but to what extent you best know, and I am certain, that you neither forget nor neglect him, tho you have not answered his multiplied letters. I should not think, that it at all lay upon me to solicit you in his behalf, or even to write to you about him, had I not been forced by his constant teazing, which I could no otherwise get rid of. If the Duke of Bedford thinks him entitled to no reward, you would do this family a great service by telling him so at once : if the Duke intends to do him service, he would be very happy to have the encouragement of some hint in his favour. I only beg of you to excuse my meddling at all in this affair ; which, I am sensible, does not belong to me, and which I should have avoided, had it not been in this manner extorted from me."

Pinto's campaign continued in England in 1767, and as Under-Secretary of State Hume was in a position of influence to see that justice was done, recruiting General Conway and Lord Hertford, among others, to the support of the Dutchman. Ultimately, it was chiefly Hume's letters that won for his new friend a pension of £500 for life. Pinto had written earlier a rebuttal to " Of Public Credit," one of the *Political Discourses*, but, though acknowledging its merit, Hume never saw fit to alter the text of his discourse.[1]

From p. 554, n. 1 :

Finally, an item dated 17 August 1776, just eight days before his death, appeared in several American periodicals : " David Hume, Esq., Dr. Smith and Sir James Stewart, have all given the king their opinions, that if a reconciliation does not speedily take place with America, that country is lost." [2]

---

[1] The full story is recounted by Richard H. Popkin : (1) " Hume and Isaac de Pinto," in *Texas Studies in Literature and Language*, XII (1970), 417–30 ; (2) " Hume and Isaac de Pinto, II. Five New Letters," in *Hume and the Enlightenment*, ed. W. B. Todd (Edinburgh and Austin 1974), 99–127.

[2] E.g. *Pennsylvania Gazette* (1776), *Connecticut Gazette and Universal Intelligencer* (1777).

From p. 555, n. 1 :

The day before Conway's demission, Hume wrote to Adam Ferguson instancing an act of patronage for the Scottish church and sardonically probing the possibility of continuing his *History*.[1]

" There has been a long Silence between us ; but not Forgetfulness ; at least, not on my part. Hepburn's affair is finished : It is my last Work, and cost me some Effort : I think I have therein very well discharged my Duty of Head of the Church of Scotland ; and have contributed to promote a Divine of singular Piety and Orthodoxy. We go out to morrow or next day ; which is an Event far from being disagreeable to me. I shall now be restord to my literary Leisure ; and am tempted, by the Importunity of Friends, to think of continuing my History for two or three Reigns more. It is well if I find Pleasure in the Occupation ; but I can discover no Reason why I shoud be at any Pains about it. Andrew Millar, very naturally, thinks Money will be a great Temptation to me : Others, equally silly, talk to me of Fame : Some, with no less Reason, of Truth. You may judge, from my past Experience, how sanguine I must have become with regard to all these Objects. The Devil is in it, if I have not learned by this time, how little disposd the World is to receive Truth ; of how little Value their Opinion is ; and what a moderate Fortune is sufficient for all the Necessaries of Life."

From p. 567, n. 2 :

In a playful letter of the summer of 1770 to Nancy Ord, Hume relates the aftermath of a game of cards at her house.

Edinburgh 16 of August 1770.

Madam

It has been the Maxim of all Legislators and Judges from Solon to Sheriff Cockburn to pardon the Criminals who confess and discover their Accomplices ; and I doubt but you and all the Ladies at Dean will follow so clement and equitable a Maxim. You must know then, that two pretended Gentlemen (of which one was Mr Nairne with the demur and sanctify'd Look, a very suspicious Circumstance) travelling yesterday in a Chaise to Melville, one of them offers a Shilling to pay the Toll : The Bar-keeper scruples the Piece : On Examination, it is found to be one of my Lord Chief Baron's Counters : The Pockets of the Fclon are searchd, and found to contain five more, which he had plainly purloind from your Home. Mr Nairn however and his

---

[1] MS letter of 19 January 1768 in the Theatre Collection, Modern Humanities Research Center, University of Texas. Hitherto unpublished. The Reverend Thomas Hepburn appears later in Chap. 38 as the somewhat quixotic " defender " of Hume.

Companion, a great fat man, are not immediatly put in Arrest; but dreading the Rigors of Justice, Mr Nairne's Companion is contented to give up the stolen Goods, which are sent by the Bearer: He protests that he has neither drunk nor embezzled any of them. He pleads hard for Mercy; but is very willing, that Mr Nairne should be hang'd by way of an Example. He is even willing to bear false Witness against him, which must be allowd very commendable and meritorious, and seems fully to entitle him to a Pardon. Thus you see the Danger of admitting Thieves and Pick-pockets and Sharpers to game with you. If the chief Baron winks at such Enormities, I assure you I will not during my Administration. I even prohibit all of you from going to Chappel for fear of meeting there with Mr Nairne: As to his Companion, he does not commonly haunt that place so much, which is a better Sign of him; as your hypocritical Thief is commonly the most irreclaimable. I am Madam with great Regard

> Your most obedient and most humble Servant
>
> David Hume

Three years later Hume entrusted Nancy with choosing wall paper for the drawing-room of his new house on St David Street —which may perhaps be taken as an indication that the house was being prepared for a wife.

Finally, in the summer of 1776, and highly conscious of his own fatal illness, he wrote from Bath, where he had gone to try the efficacy of the waters. The letter is a declaration of love:

Bath 10 of June 1776

Dear Madam

I know it will affect you to hear, that the favourable Accounts of my Health, which I desired my Nephew to communicate to you, have vanished into Smoke; the Waters began to disagree with me; all the bad Symptoms recurred; and are found to proceed from a Vice in my Liver, for which the Physicians pretend there may be a Remedy, but for which I believe there is none. In short, you are likely to lose, at no great Distance of time, one of the Persons in the World, who has the greatest Regard and Affection for you. My Dear Miss Nancy, hear this Declaration with Sympathy and Cordiality. I know what an egregious Folly it is for a Man of my Years to attach himself too strongly to one of Yours; but I saw in you so much other Merit, beside that which is the common Object of Affection, that I easily excused to myself the Imprudence; and your obliging Behaviour always kept me from being sensible of it. It is the best placed Attachment of my Life; and will surely be the last. I know, that the Tear will be in your Eye when you read this; as it is in mine when I write it.

I bid you not Adieu; because I intend to set out from this [place] in eight or ten days; and may reach my own House in ten or twelve more. It will not be long after, till I kiss your hand. My Compliments to your Sisters; I wish I coud say to your father ; [1] and that he coud be sensible of the sincere Regard which I bear to him. I am Dear Miss Nancy, Your most affectionate Friend and humble Servant.

David Hume

Nancy was remembered in a codicil to David's will. She never married.[2]

From p. 575, n. 1 : (extract from Hume's letter to his nephew, David Home, 20 May 1776)

" You will now enter on a Course of Summer Reading, and Exercise, which you will intermingle properly together. I cou'd wish to see you mix the Volumes of Taste and Imagination with more serious Reading ; and that sometimes Terence and Vergil and Cicero, together with Xenophon, Demosthenes, Homer and Lucian (for you must not forget your Greek) shoud occupy your Leizure together with Voet, Vinnius, and Grotius. I did not observe you to be very fond of the Poets, and surely one may pass through Life, though not so agreeably, without such Companions : But the Familiarity with them give Taste to Prose Reading and Compositions ; and one wou'd not allow so agreeable a Vein to dry up entirely for Want of Exercise.

I believe I recommended to you already the Perusal of Mr. Smith's new Book if it falls in (as I believe it does) with Mr Millar's Course of Lectures. It is a book of Science and deep Thought and as some of its Positions and Reasoning may seem to admit of Doubt, it will, on that account prove a better Exercise to your Thoughts & Researches." [3]

From p. 575, n. 3 :

A young American medical student at Edinburgh University 1766–8, Benjamin Rush, was apprised by members of the Hume circle that the philosopher was " a gentleman of the most amiable private Character, and much beloved by every Body that knows him. He is remarkably charitable to the poor, and has provided handsomely for several poor Families that were related to him. He never swears, nor has any one ever accused him of any immoralities of any kind." Rush was instrumental in persuading the Reverend John Witherspoon, Hume's old witty opponent, to

[1] Robert Ord died July 1776.
[2] The three letters above (16 August 1770 ; 12 April 1773 ; 10 June 1776) are Hume's only known letters to Nancy Ord. The holographs are in the collection of John V. Price of E. U., as are the papers of the Ord family. Copies in the hand of John Hill Burton, Hume's biographer of 1846, are in NLS MS 9427, f. 24v. Burton apparently suppressed them from his biography. They were published by Price, before acquiring the originals, in " Hume and Nancy Orde. Three Letters," in *David Hume and the Enlightenment*, ed. W. B. Todd (Edinburgh and Austin 1974), 128–35.
[3] Hume–Poland, p. 138.

accept the presidency of the College of New Jersey in 1768. The following year Rush visited Paris and brought back a letter from Diderot to Hume.[1]

From p. 581, n. 2 : (extract of letter from Adam Smith to Hume, 1775 [9 May])

" Your friends here have been all much diverted with Priestly's answer to Beatie. We were in great hopes that Beatie would have replyed and we are assured he has a reply ready written ; but your old friend Hurd, whom my Lord Mansfield, has with great judgement, made a Bishop, wrote to Beatie, I am assured, and advised him against answering ; telling him that so excellent a work as the immutability of truth required no defence. We by this means have lost a most incomparable controversy. Priestly was perfectly prepared to carry it on thro' at least twenty rejoinders. I have some hopes still of getting somebody to provoke Beatie to draw his Pen again." [2]

From p. 599, n. 2 :

O, Toi qui de mon Ame
Es la chère Moitié
Toi qui joins la délicatesse
Des sentimens d'une Maîtresse
A la Solidité d'une sûre Amitié
David, il faut bientôt que la Parque cruelle
Vienne rompre des si doux Noeuds
& malgré nos Cris et nos voeux
Bientôt nous assuirons une absence éternelle.
Adieu, Adieu.
J. E.

From p. 602, n. 2 :

" Poor David Hume is dying very fast," Adam Smith informed Alexander Wedderburn, " but with great chearfulness and good humour and with more real resignation to the necessary course of things, than any whining Christian ever dyed with pretended resignation to the will of God." [3]

[1] *The Autobiography of Benjamin Rush* (Princeton 1948), 49, 69.
[2] Hume–Poland, p. 140.
[3] Letter 163, 14 August 1776, in *Correspondence of Adam Smith*, edd. Mossner and Ross (Oxford 1976).

AUTHORITIES CITED

AUTHORITIES CITED

THE following lists are restricted to works actually cited in the text or notes, except that items in Appendix B are not repeated. A fuller bibliography may be found in T. E. Jessop, *A Bibliography of David Hume and of Scottish Philosophy from Francis Hutcheson to Lord Balfour* (London 1938). A revised and enlarged edition is awaiting publication. *Fifty Years of Hume Scholarship*, Ed. Roland Hall, (Edinburgh 1978).

I. DAVID HUME

MANUSCRIPTS

Calendar of Hume MSS in the Possession of the Royal Society of Edinburgh, compiled by J. Y. T. Greig and Harold Beynon. Edinburgh 1932. [IX, 4 (see under Mossner in Sect. II, *C*, below), 5, 7, 24 ; XIII, 38.]

" Draft of Preface to a volume of D. Hume's History in David Hume's own hand found among my father's papers." Keynes Library, King's College, Cambridge.

Four Dissertations : " This Book is to be considerd as a Manuscript and to be deliverd to Mr Strahan according to my Will." NLS, MS 509.

"Journal, 1746." Fragments in (1) BM Add. MS 36638, P. 4510 ; (2) Pierpont Morgan Library ; (3) Newhailes, 541.

Historical Memoranda. Huntington Library, MS HM 12263 ; NLS, MSS 732, 733, 734, MS 3803.

Legal briefs, 1774, concerning lawsuit with Adam Gillies. City Chambers, Edinburgh, Bundle No. 396 (50).

Review of Robert Henry's *History of Great Britain*, 1773. Corrected proof sheets in William Andrews Clark Memorial Library. [See under Mossner, in Sect. II, below.]

Will of 1776 in " Registers and Records of Scotland " in NRH.

PUBLICATIONS

(a) Letters

Letters of David Hume, and Extracts of Letters referring to him, ed. Thomas Murray. Edinburgh 1841.

Letters of David Hume to William Strahan, ed. G. Birkbeck Hill. Oxford 1888.

The Letters of David Hume, ed. J. Y. T. Greig. Oxford 1932. 2 vols. [Cited as HL.]

New Letters of David Hume, edd. R. Klibansky and E. C. Mossner. Oxford 1954. [Cited as NHL.]

Letter from David Hume, Esq., to the Author of the " Delineation of the Nature and Obligation of Morality." [n. p., n. d., published after Hume's death.]

Extract of undated letter, No. 1105, in Puttick & Simpson's catalogue, London, 30 July 1886.

" Dawida Hume'a Nieznane Listy W Zbiorach Muzeum Czartoryskich (Polska)," ed. Tadeusz Kozanecki, in *Archiwum Historii Filozofii I Mysli Spoleczhej* 9, 127–41. [Cited as Hume–Poland.]

" David Hume: Some Unpublished Letters, 1771–1776," ed. Geoffrey Hunter, in *Texas Studies in Literature and Language*, II (1960), 127–50.

" The Eighteenth-Century Marian Controversy and an Unpublished Letter by David Hume," ed. Laurence L. Bongie in *Studies in Scottish Literature*, I (1964), 236–52.

" Hume and Friends, 1756 and 1766: Two New Letters," ed. J. C. Hilson and John V. Price, in *The Yearbook of English Studies* 7 (1977), 121–127.

" Hume at La Flèche, 1735: An Unpublished Letter," ed. E. C. Mossner, in University of Texas *Studies in English*, XXXVII (1958), 30–33.

" Le Bon David Again: Three New Hume Letters," ed. Ian S. Ross, in *Texas Studies in Literature and Language*, x (1969), 537–45.

" More Unpublished Letters of David Hume," ed. J. C. Hilson, in *Forum for Modern Language Studies*, VI (1970), 315–26.

" New Hume Letters to Lord Elibank, 1748–1776," ed. E. C. Mossner, in *Texas Studies in Literature and Language*, IV (1962), 431–60. [Cited as Hume–Elibank.]

Morrisroe, Michael, Jr., " Did Hume read Berkeley? A Conclusive Answer," in *Philological Quarterly*, 52 (1973), 310–15.

—— " Hume's Ecclesiastical History: A New Letter," *English Studies*, 53 (1972), 1–3.

Popkin, Richard, " Hume and Isaac de Pinto, II. Five New Letters," in *Hume and the Enlightenment : Essays presented to Ernest Campbell Mossner*, ed. William B. Todd. Edinburgh and Austin, 1974, pp. 99–127.

(b) Other publications

An Abstract of a Treatise of Human Nature, 1740 : A Pamphlet hitherto unknown by David Hume. Reprinted with an Introduction by J. M. Keynes and P. Sraffa. Cambridge 1938. A BL copy with MS corrections by Hume has been discovered.

" Advertisement " to the English translation of Baron Manstein's *Memoirs of Russia, Historical, Political, and Military, from the Year MDCCXXVII to MDCCXLIV.* London 1770.

A Concise and Genuine Account of the Dispute between Mr. Hume and Mr. Rousseau ; with the Letters that Passed between Them during their Controversy. As Also, the Letters of the Hon. Mr. Walpole, and Mr. D'Alembert, Relative to This Extraordinary Affair. London 1766.

David Hume : A Letter from a Gentleman to his friend in Edinburgh, edd. E. C. Mossner and John V. Price. Edinburgh 1967.

David Hume : Writings on Economics, ed. Eugene Rotwein. Edinburgh 1955.

Dialogues concerning Natural Religion, 2nd edn. with Supplement. Ed. with introduction by Norman Kemp Smith. Edinburgh and London 1947. [Cited as *Dialogues*.]

The Natural History of Religion (ed. A. Wayne Colver) and *Dialogues concerning Natural Religion* (ed. John V. Price). Ed. A. Wayne Colver. Oxford 1976. [Definitive ed.]

Essays and Observations, Physical and Literary, Read before a Society in Edinburgh and Published by Them. Edinburgh 1754. [Hume was co-editor and presumptive author of the introduction.]

Essays on Suicide, and The Immortality of the Soul, Ascribed to the late David Hume, Esq. Never before published. With Remarks, intended as an Antidote to the Poison contained in these Performances. London 1783. [Anon. and unauthorised.]

History of England. Ed. of Edinburgh 1792. 8 vols.

—— Abridged and with an introduction by Rodney W. Wilcup. Chicago and London 1975.

The Life of David Hume, Esq. : Written by Himself. London 1777. [Includes a letter from Adam Smith to William Strahan concerning Hume's last days.]

Petition of the Grave and Venerable Bellmen, Or Sextons, of the Church of Scotland, To the Honourable House of Commons. [London 1751. Anon. Reprinted in *The Scotch Haggis*, Edinburgh 1822. Also in John V. Price, *The Ironic Hume*. Austin 1965. Appendix B.]

The Philosophical Works of David Hume, edd. T. H. Green and T. H. Grose. London 1874–5. 4 vols. [Cited as *Phil. Wks.*] Reprinted 1964. Scientia Verlag. Aalen.

Recueil Philosophique ou Mélange de Pièces sur la Religion & la Morale, ed. Jacques André Naigeon. Paris 1770. [Fr. translation of Hume's essays " Of the Immortality of the Soul " and " Of Suicide " by Baron d'Holbach.]

" Sixteen notes on Walpole's *Historic Doubts*," in *Mémoires Littéraires de la Grande Bretagne* (1769), II, 25–6.

Hume : Theory of Politics, ed. F. M. Watkins. Edinburgh 1952. [With an appendix by R. Klibansky discussing marginalia in the BL copy of Hume's *Treatise*.]

A True Account of the Behaviour and Conduct of Archibald Stewart, Esq ; late Lord Provost of Edinburgh, In a Letter to a Friend. London 1748. [Anon. Reprinted in John V. Price, *The Ironic Hume*. Austin 1965. Appendix A.]

Two Essays. London 1777. [Anon. and unauthorised : " Of Suicide " and " Of the Immortality of The Soul."]

II. OTHER AUTHORITIES

(A) EIGHTEENTH CENTURY

MANUSCRIPTS

(a) Personal Letters and Writings

(i) Letters to Hume

EDINBURGH UNIVERSITY : Robert Wallace (Laing II, 96).

ROYAL SOCIETY OF EDINBURGH [described in *Calendar of Hume MSS*] : Jean d'Alembert, III, 6, 14, 21 ; Hugh Blair, III, 51, 53–6, 60–1, 63 ; Comtesse de Boufflers, III, 65, 66, 70, 71, 72, 74, 75, 76, 78, 79, 83 ; George Campbell, IV, 11 ; Marquis de Chastellux, IV, 20, 22 ; Alison Cockburn, IV, 28, 30, 32, 33 ; General Conway, IV, 39 ; John Crawford, IV, 43 ; Comte de Creutz, IV, 47 ; Peter Crocchi, IV, 48 ; Richard Davenport, IV, 54–5 ; Mme du Deffand, IV, 72 ; Alexander Dick, IV, 75 ; Denis Diderot, IV, 78–80 ; James Edmonstoune, v, 3, 7 ; Lord Elibank, v, 8 ; Gilbert Elliott, v, 13 ; Lady Elliot-Murray, VI, 75 ; Mme Geoffrin, v, 36 ; Edward Gibbon, v, 41 ; Claude-Adrien Helvétius, v, 52 ; President Hénault, v, 55 ; Earl of Hertford, v, 59, 61 ; Lady Hervey, v, 68 ; Baron d'Holbach, v, 72, 74 ; Earl of Holdernesse, III, 79 ; Earl Marischal Keith, v, 99, 100, 102–3, 110 ; Mme de Meinières, III, 47 ; Andrew Millar, VI, 31 ; William Mure, VI, 64 ; Alexander Murray, VI, 70 ; Richard Price, VI, 85 ; Sir John Pringle, VI, 96 ; Allan Ramsay the Younger, VI, 103–4 ; Michael Ramsay, VI, 105 ; Michael Ramsay the Younger, VIII, 27 ; Thomas Reid, VII, 3 ; Mme Dupré de St Maur, IV, 85 ; Adam Smith, VII, 37, 39 ; Tobias Smollett, VII, 40 ; Lady Stanhope, VII, 45 ; John Stewart, VII, 49–50 ; Andrew Stuart, IV, 67 ; Elizabeth Stuart, VIII, 73 ; Robert Wood, VII, 101.

(ii) Other Letters

ABERDEEN UNIVERSITY : (in Beattie Papers) James Beattie (1 May 1770, 17 Dec. 1776) ; Hugh Blair (14 May 1770).

BRITISH LIBRARY : (in Hardwicke Papers) Thomas Birch, Add. MS 35400, ff. 110v., 111r.

EDINBURGH UNIVERSITY : Alexander Carlyle, MS Do. 4.41/96 ; Michael Andrew Ramsay, Laing MSS, II, 301 ; Alexander Stenhouse, Laing MSS, II, 451/2.

DR R. H. GRIFFITH LIBRARY, UNIVERSITY OF TEXAS : William Warburton, as transcribed by James Crossley, II, 32.

HUNTINGTON LIBRARY : John Gregory (MSS MO uncat., 3 June 1770) ; Elizabeth Montagu (EM 1776 uncat., 20 Oct. 1766).

KEYNES LIBRARY, KING'S COLLEGE, CAMBRIDGE : George Norvell (1 Mar. 1788).

LIBRARY OF THE ROYAL COLLEGE OF SURGEONS OF ENGLAND : William Cullen (17 Sept. 1776. Hunter-Baillie Collection, Letter-book, VOL. I).

NATIONAL LIBRARY OF SCOTLAND : Hugh Blair, MS 1005 ; James Boswell, MS 3278 ; Joseph Grant, MS 3005 ; Henry Home, MS 2956 ; John Home, MS 1005 ; Mrs Ann Murray Keith, MS 3524 ; Robert Liston, MSS 5513, 5517 ; Mrs William Mure, MS Acc. 1237.

SCOTTISH RECORD OFFICE, EDINBURGH : (in Adam Box) Robert Adam (15 Nov. 1755) ; (in Abercairny Papers) Andrew Baxter (13 June 1723) ; Wm. Hamilton of Bangour (29 July 1739) ; James Oswald (17 Dec. 1741, Jan. 1742, 6 Mar. 1742) ; Josiah Tucker (15 Feb. 1764) : G.D. 24.

PIERPONT MORGAN LIBRARY : " Ebenezer Hume " (8 Feb. 1778, containing 300 lines of verse entitled " Natural Religion," allegedly by David Hume).

(iii) *Other Writings*

ABERDEEN UNIVERSITY : (in Beattie Papers, B. 18) James Beattie, " The Castle of Scepticism." [See under Mossner in Sect. II, below.]

BRITISH LIBRARY : Thomas Birch, " Journal," Add. MS 4478c, f. 417r.

EDINBURGH UNIVERSITY : (in Laing MSS) : George Chalmers, " MS Notes on David Hume," II, 451/2 ; Robert Wallace, " An Address to the Reverend the Clergy of the Church of Scotland By a Layman of their Communion on occasion of composing acting & publishing the Tragedy called Douglass," II, 620² ; " A Letter from a Moderate Free-thinker to David Hume Esquire concerning the Profession of the Clergy. In Which It is shewed That Their Vices Whatever They Are Are Owing to Their Disposition and Not to the Bad Influence of Their Profession," II, 97 ; " The necessity or expediency of the churches inquiring into the writings of David Hume Esquire and calling the Author to answer before the spiritual Courts," II, 97 ; " Observations on the Account of the Miracles of the Abbe Paris," II, 620²⁰.

GLASGOW UNIVERSITY : J. Rennie, " A Compendious System of Pneumatology, Comprehending-Psychology, Moral Philosophy, & Logic. Taken at the Lectures of Mr. Js. Beattie P. P. At the Marischal College & University of Abdn. By J. Rennie, Anno 1767."

HISTORICAL MANUSCRIPTS COMMISSION : Lord Hailes, " A Volume of Anecdotes, etc. collected by Lord Hailes," 4th Report. London 1874.

NATIONAL LIBRARY OF SCOTLAND : John Home of Ninewells, " Tack of John Home of Ninewells to Peter Johnson," MS 582, f. 77.

ROYAL IRISH ACADEMY : Lord Charlemont, " Anecdotes of Hume," MS— 12/R/7, ff, 497–531.

(*b*) *Official Letters and Documents*

ABERDEEN UNIVERSITY : " Minutes of the Philosophical Society in Aberdeen, 1758–1771."

CITY CHAMBERS, EDINBURGH : " Burgh Court Diet Book from 13 May 1773 to 31 August 1779," VOL. LVIII (1774) ; Chartulary Extended Royalty No. 2 " ; " Council Records," VOLS. LXIV, LXV, XCI.

EDINBURGH UNIVERSITY : " Library Accounts 1697–1765 " ; " Matriculation Book 1627–1703 " ; " Scholarium Matricula ab Anno MDCCIV."

GLASGOW UNIVERSITY : " Act against Infidels and Immorality " in " Assembly Register, 1755 " ; " Minutes of the University Meetings."

NATIONAL LIBRARY OF SCOTLAND : (Advocates' Library) " Library Accounts 1727–65," " Minutes of the Faculty, 1751–83," " Register of the pro- ceedings of the Curators & Keeper of the Library in relation to their Office Beginning Anno 1725," " Treasurer's Accounts 1738–1792 " F.R.

134, 2, 118, 43 ; (Select Society) " Minutes and Procedure of the Select Society," " Rules and Orders of the Select Society " (MS 23.1.1.) ; J. P. Wood, " List of Advocates, 1687–1751," MS 37.2.8.

NEWHAILES [microfilms deposited in NLS and University of Virginia Library] : General St Clair MSS, bound Vols. 2–8.

SCOTTISH RECORD OFFICE, EDINBURGH : " Parochial Register : Chirnside " ; " Parochial Registers Co. of Edinburgh : B. 1708–14 " ; " P. R. S., Edinburgh," VOL. CCCXII, f. 87.

PRESBYTERY OF DUNS, ARCHIVES : " Minutes of the Presbyterie of Chyrnside (1713–1734)."

PUBLIC RECORD OFFICE, LONDON : Lord Halifax (letter of 2 July 1765), SP 78/267 ; Lord Hertford (letter of 15 Oct. 1763), SP 78/258 ; General St Clair (letters of 11 May 1748, 9 June 1748), SP 80/180 ; " War Office Papers, 1746," SP 41/17.

SIGNET LIBRARY, EDINBURGH : " Session Papers," VOL. CXXI.

EIGHTEENTH-CENTURY NEWSPAPERS AND PERIODICALS

Annual Register
Bibliothèque britannique, ou histoire des
    ouvrages des sçavans de la Grande-
    Bretagne
Bibliothèque raisonnée des ouvrages des
    savans des savans de l'Europe
Caledonian Mercury
Critical Review
Daily Advertiser
Edinburgh Evening Courant
Edinburgh Review
Gazette and London Daily Advertiser
Gelehrte Erlanger Zeitungen
Gentleman's Magazine
Göttingische Zeitungen von gelehrten Sachen
Historical Register
History of the Works of the Learned
Journal britannique

London Chronicle
Lloyd's Evening Post
London Evening Post
London Review
Mémoires littéraires de la Grande
    Bretagne
The Mirror
Monthly Review
Neuen Zeitungen von gelehrten Sachen
New Evening Post
North Briton
Nouvelle bibliothèque, ou histoire
    littéraire des principaux écrits que se
    publient
St. James's Chronicle
Scots Magazine
The Weekly Magazine, or
    Edinburgh Amusement

GENERAL BIBLIOGRAPHY

GENERAL BIBLIOGRAPHY

Accounts of the Lord High Treasurer of Scotland, VOL. III. Edinburgh 1907.
Adam, William. *Sequel to the Gift of a Grandfather.* [Priv. ptd.] 1836.
Adams, William. *Essay on Mr. Hume's Essay on Miracles.* London 1751.
" A.G.T.V.O.C." [Pseud.] *Inquiry into the Grounds and Nature of the Several Species of Ratiocination. In which, the argument made use of in the Philosophical Essays of D. Hume, Esq. is occasionally taken notice of.* London [1754].
Agutter, William. *On the Difference between the Deaths of the Righteous and the Wicked, Illustrated in the Instance of Dr. Samuel Johnson and David Hume, Esq. A Sermon Preached before the University of Oxford, 3 July 1786.* London 1800.
Album Studiosorum Academiae Rheno-Traiectinae. Utrecht 1886.
Allentuck, Marcia. " David Hume and Allan Ramsay : A New Letter," in *Studies in Scottish Literature*, XI (1972), 265–6.
Anderson, George. *A Remonstrance against Lord Viscount Bolingbroke's Philosophical Religion.* Glasgow 1756.
— — *Estimate of the Profit and Loss of Religion.* Edinburgh 1753. [Anon.]
— — *Infidelity a Proper Object of Censure.* Glasgow 1756. [Anon.]
[Anon.] " An Account of the Life and Writings of the late David Hume," in *Annual Register*, XIX (1776), 27–30.
— — *Admonitions from the Dead in Epistles to the Living.* London 1754.
— — *Advertisement.* Edinburgh 1758. [A broadside satirising Hume's projected removal from Edinburgh to London.]
— — *A Journey through part of England and Scotland along with the Army under the Command of his Royal Highness the Duke of Cumberland.* 3rd edn. London 1747.
— — "Attaque des Anglais contre la ville de L'Orient en Octobre 1746. Relation de David Hume," in *Bulletin archéologique de l'Association Bretonne*, Series 3, VI, 144–68.
— — *The City Cleaned, and Country Improven.* Edinburgh 1760.
— — " Memoirs of Dr. Wallace of Edinburgh," in *Scots Magazine*, XXXIII (1771), 340–4.
— — " Strictures on the Account of the Life and Writings of David Hume," in *Weekly Magazine*, XXXVIII (1777), 289–92.
Argenson, Marquis d'. *Mémoires.* Paris 1857–8. 5 vols.
Arnot, Hugo. *History of Edinburgh.* Edinburgh 1788.
Baldensperger, Fernand. " La première relation intellectuelle de David Hume en France : une conjecture," in *Modern Language Notes*, LVII (1942), 268–71.
Balfour, Andrew. *Letters Writ to a Friend.* Edinburgh 1700.
Balfour-Melville, B. *The Balfours of Pilrig.* Edinburgh 1907.
Basson, A. H. *David Hume.* Harmondsworth 1958.
Beattie, James. *An Essay on the Nature and Immutability of Truth ; in opposition to Sophistry and Scepticism.* 4th edn. London 1773.
— — *James Beattie's London Diary, 1773*, ed. R. S. Walker. Aberdeen 1946.
— — *The Minstrel.* London 1799. 2 vols.
Beattie, James Hay. *Essays and Fragments in Prose and Verse*, ed. James Beattie. [Priv. ptd.] London 1794.

de Beer, Sir Gavin, " Quelques Considérations sur le Séjour de Rousseau en Angleterre," in *Geneva*, n.s. tome III (1955), 1–38.

Belloy, Pierre-Laurant-Buyrette de. *Le Siège de Calais*. Paris 1765.

Bengesco, Georges. *Bibliographie de Voltaire*. Paris 1882–90. 4 vols.

Bisset, Robert. *Life of Edmund Burke*. London 1798.

Black, George F. *The Surnames of Scotland*. New York 1946.

Blacklock, Thomas. *Poems on Several Occasions*. Edinburgh 1754.

—— *Poems ; to which is Prefix'd, an Account of the Life, Character, and Writings, of the Author, by the Reverend Mr. Spence, Late Professor of Poetry, at Oxford*. 3rd edn. London 1756.

Blair, Hugh. *A Critical Dissertation on the Poems of Ossian, The Son of Fingal*. London 1763. [Anon. Appendix to this dissertation appeared in *Works of Ossian*, 3rd edn., 1765, II, 445–60.]

—— *Observations upon a Pamphlet, intitled An Analysis of the Moral and Religious Sentiments contained in the Writings of Sopho, and David Hume, Esq*. Edinburgh 1755. [Anon.]

Bolingbroke, Lord. *Works*, ed. David Mallet. London 1754. 5 vols.

Bonar, John. *An Analysis of the Moral and Religious Sentiments contained in the Writings of Sopho and David Hume, Esq. ; Addressed to the consideration of the Reverend and Honourable Members of the General Assembly of the Church of Scotland*. Edinburgh 1755. [Anon.]

Bongie, Laurence L. *David Hume : Prophet of the Counter-Revolution*. Oxford 1965.

Boswell, James. *Boswell's Life of Johnson*, ed. G. Birkbeck Hill ; rev. and enlarged by L. F. Powell. Oxford 1934–50. 6 vols. [Cited as *Johnson*.]

—— *Letters*, ed. C. B. Tinker. Oxford 1924. 2 vols.

—— *Private Papers of James Boswell from Malahide Castle*, edd. G. Scott and F. A. Pottle. [Priv. ptd.] New York 1928–34, 18 vols. [Cited as *Boswell Papers*.]

[Boyle Lectures.] *A Defence of Natural and Revealed Religion*, edd. Letsome and Nicholl. London 1739. 3 vols.

Braly, Earl. " The Reputation of David Hume in America." [Unpublished doctoral dissertation in the University of Texas Library.]

Brougham, Henry Peter. *Lives of Men of Letters and Science, who flourished in the time of George III*. London 1845–6. 2 vols.

Brown, John. *An Estimate of the Manners and Principles of the Times*. London 1757–8. 2 vols.

Brunet, Oliver. *Philosophie et Esthétique chez David Hume*. Paris 1965.

Burbure, F. R. F. Marchant de. *Essais historiques sur la ville et le collège de la Flèche*. Angers 1903.

Burdy, Samuel. *Life of the late Reverend Philip Skelton*. London 1816.

Burton, John Hill. *Life and Correspondence of David Hume*. Edinburgh 1846. 2 vols. [Cited as Hill Burton.]

Butler, Joseph. *The Analogy of Religion, Natural and Revealed, to the Constitution and Course of Nature*. London 1736.

—— *Fifteen Sermons Preached at the Rolls Chapel*. London 1726. [The first three are generally known as " Sermons on Human Nature."]

Cafron G. and R. Yve-Plessis. *Vie privée du Prince de Conty*. Paris 1907.

Cain, Roy. " David Hume and Adam Smith : A Study in Intellectual Kinship." [Unpublished doctoral dissertation in the University of Texas Library.]

Caldwell Papers, ed. William Mure. Glasgow 1854. 2 vols. [Vol. II in two parts.] [Cited as *Caldwell Papers*.]

Campbell, George. *A Dissertation on Miracles : Containing an Examination of the Principles advanced by David Hume, Esq ; in an Essay on Miracles.* Edinburgh 1762.

Campbell, John. *Lives of the Lord Chancellors,* 5th edn. London 1868. 10 vols.

Carlyle, Alexander. *The Autobiography of Alexander Carlyle of Inveresk,* ed. John Hill Burton. London and Edinburgh 1910. [Cited as Carlyle.]

Chalmers, George. *Life of Thomas Ruddiman.* London 1794.

Chambers, Robert. *A Biographical Dictionary of Eminent Scotsmen.* Glasgow 1855. 5 vols.

— — *Domestic Annals of Scotland.* 2nd edn. Edinburgh 1859–61. 3 vols.

Chamley, P. E. " The Conflict between Montesquieu and Hume : A Study of the Origins of Adam Smith's Universalism," in *Essays on Adam Smith.* Oxford 1975.

Cockburn, Alison. *Letters and Memorials,* ed. T. Craig-Brown. Edinburgh 1900.

Cockburn, Henry. *Memorials of His Time,* ed. H. A. Cockburn. Edinburgh 1909.

Cohen, Ralph. " The Critical Theory of David Hume." [Unpublished doctoral dissertation in Columbia University Library.]

— — " David Hume's Experimental Method and the Theory of Taste," in *ELH,* xxv (1958), 170–89.

— — " Poetic Unity and Association of Ideas," in *Philological Quarterly,* xxxvi (1957), 465–74.

— — " The Transformation of Passion : A Study of Hume's Theories of Tragedy," in *Philological Quarterly,* xli (1962), 450–64.

Coke, Lady Mary. *Letters and Journals, 1756–1774,* ed. J. A. Horne. Edinburgh 1889–96. 4 vols.

Collé, Charles. *Journal et Mémoires,* ed. Honoré Bonhomme. Paris 1868. 3 vols.

Comber, Thomas. *Vindication of the Great Revolution in England.* London 1758.

Craig, Maurice James. *The Volunteer Earl : Being the Life and Times of James Caulfeild, First Earl of Charlemont.* London 1948.

Cudworth, Ralph. *A Treatise concerning Eternal and Immutable Morality.* London 1731.

— — *The True Intellectual System of the Universe.* London 1678.

Daiches, David. *The Paradox of Scottish Culture : The Eighteenth-Century Experience.* London 1964.

Dalzel, Andrew. *History of the University of Edinburgh.* Edinburgh 1862. 2 vols.

Decisions of the Court of Session (1733–1754), ed. Patrick Grant of Elchies. Edinburgh 1813.

Deffand, Mme du. *Correspondance complète,* ed. Sainte-Aulaire. Paris 1867. 3 vols.

— — *Correspondance complète,* ed. Lescure. Paris 1865. 2 vols.

Dempster, George. *Letters to Sir Adam Fergusson, 1756–1813,* ed. Sir James Fergusson. London 1934.

Denina, Carlo. *Essay on the Revolutions of Literature.* [Engl. transl.] Glasgow 1763.

Dewey, John. *Logic, the Theory of Inquiry.* New York 1938.

Dick, Alexander. " Journal of a Tour, 1736," in *Gentlemen's Magazine,* N.S. xxxix (1853), 23–6, 159–65, 263–6, 579–83.

Dickson, W. K. " David Hume and The Advocates' Library," in *Juridical Review,* xliv (1932), 1–4.

Diderot, Denis. *Lettres à Sophie Volland,* ed. André Babelon. Paris 1938. 2 vols.

Disraeli, Isaac. *Calamities of Authors.* London 1812. 2 vols.

Diverrés, P. *L'Attaque de Lorient par les Anglais, 1746.* Rennes 1931.

Dobson, Austin. " The Portraits of Carmontelle," in *At Prior Park.* London 1912.

Doddridge, Philip. *Letters to and from Philip Doddridge,* ed. T. Stedman. Shrewsbury 1790.

Dorat, Claude-Joseph. *Œuvres choisies.* Paris 1827.

Douglas, John. *The Criterion : or Miracles Examined.* London 1752.

Douglas Tracts. [The numerous controversial tracts of 1756–7 over John Home's *Douglas,* cited in Chaps. 24 and 26, are to be found in the collections in the Bodleian Library, Harvard College Library, Huntington Library, and NLS.]

Dubos, J.-B. *Critical Reflections on Poetry, Painting and Music.* [Engl. transl. by Thomas Nugent.] London 1748. 3 vols.

Dutens, Louis. *Memoirs of a Traveller, Now in Retirement.* [Engl. transl.] London 1806. 4 vols. in 2.

Edwards, Jonathan. *Remarks on the Essays, on the Principles of Morality, and Natural Religion.* Edinburgh 1758.

Elibank, Lord. *Inquiry into the Original and Consequences of the Public Debt.* Edinburgh 1753.

Elliot, G. F. S. *The Border Elliots.* Edinburgh 1897.

Elliott, Robert C. " Hume's ' Character of Sir Robert Walpole ' : Some Unnoticed Additions," in *Journal of English and Germanic Philology,* XLVIII (1949), 367–70.

Epinay, Mme d'. *Mémoires et correspondance.* Paris 1818. 3 vols.

Fénelon, François de Salignac de la Mothe. *Traité de l'existence et des attributes de Dieu.* Paris 1713.

Ferguson, Adam. *Essay on the History of Civil Society.* Edinburgh 1767.

— — *An Essay on the History of Civil Society, 1767,* ed. Duncan Forbes. Edinburgh 1966.

Ferguson, Robert. *Scots Poems.* Edinburgh 1925.

Fitzgerald, Percy. *Life and Times of John Wilkes.* London 1888. 2 vols.

Fleming, Caleb. *Three Questions Resolved . . . . With a Postscript on Mr. Hume's History of Religion.* London 1757. [Anon.]

Flew, Antony. *Hume's Philosophy of Belief : A Study of his first Inquiry.* London 1961.

Forbes, Margaret. *Beattie and His Friends.* Westminster 1904.

Forbes, William. *An Account of the Life and Writings of James Beattie, LL.D.* Edinburgh 1806. 2 vols.

Fortescue, John W. " A Side-Show of the Eighteenth Century," in *Blackwoods Magazine,* CCXXXIII (1933), 330–45.

Fountainhall, Lord. *Historical Notices of Scottish Affairs.* Edinburgh 1848.

— — *Historical Observes.* Edinburgh 1840.

— — *Journals.* Edinburgh 1900.

Fraser, William. *The Annandale Family Book, of the Johnstones, Earls and Marquises of Annandale.* Edinburgh 1894.

Gay, Peter. *The Enlightenment : An Interpretation.* VOL. I, " The Rise of Modern Paganism " ; VOL. II, " The Science of Freedom." New York 1967–9.

Gerard, Alexander. *An Essay on Taste.* London 1759.

— — *The Influence of the Pastoral Office on the Character Examined ; with a View, especially to Mr. Hume's Representation of the Spirit of that Office.* Aberdeen 1760.

Gibbon, Edward. *Memoirs,* ed. O. F. Emerson. Boston 1898.

—— *Private Letters, 1753–1794,* ed. R. E. Prothero. London 1896. 2 vols.

Goodall, Walter. *Examination of the letters said to have been written by Mary Queen of Scots, to James, Earl of Bothwell.* Edinburgh 1754. 2 vols.

Grant, Alexander. *Story of the University of Edinburgh.* London 1884. 2 vols.

Gray, Thomas. *Poems of Mr. Gray with Memoirs prefixed,* ed. Wm. Mason. York 1775.

—— *Works,* ed. Edmund Gosse. New York 1885. 4 vols.

Greig, J. Y. T. *David Hume.* London 1931. [Cited as Greig.]

Grimm, Friedrich Melchior. *Correspondance littéraire,* ed. M. Tourneaux. Paris 1882–5. 16 vols.

Hailes, Lord. *Adami Smithi, LL.D. Ad Guelielmum Strahanum, Armigerum, De rebus novissimis Davidis Humei, Epistola, nunc primum latine reddita.* [Edinburgh] 1788. [Anon.]

—— *Davidis Humei, Scoti, Summi apud suos philosophi, De vita sua acta, Liber singularis ; nunc primum latine redditus.* [Edinburgh] 1787. [Anon.]

Hamilton of Bangour, William. *Poems on Several Occasions.* Edinburgh 1760.

Hardy, Francis. *Memoirs of the Earl of Charlemont.* London 1810.

Harris, George. *Life of Lord Chancellor Hardwicke.* London 1847. 3 vols.

Helvétius, Claude-Adrien. *De l'Esprit.* Paris 1758.

Henderson, G. D. *Chevalier Ramsay.* Edinburgh 1952.

Henderson, Robert. " A short account of the University of Edinburgh, the present Professors in it, and the several parts of Learning taught by them," in *Scots Magazine,* III (1741), 371–4.

Hepburn, Thomas. *A Specimen of the Scots Review.* Edinburgh 1774. [Anon.]

Higgs, Henry. *Bibliography of Economics, 1751–1755.* Cambridge 1935.

Home, Henry (Lord Kames). *Elements of Criticism.* Edinburgh 1762. 3 vols. [Anon.]

—— *Essays on the Principles of Morality and Natural Religion.* Edinburgh 1751. [Anon.]

—— *Essays upon Several Subjects Concerning British Antiquities.* Edinburgh 1747.

—— *Objections against the Essays on Morality and Natural Religion Examined.* Edinburgh 1756. [Anon.]

Home, John. *Works,* ed. Henry Mackenzie. Edinburgh 1522. 3 vols. [Cited as Home-Mackenzie.]

Hopkins, Mary A. *Hannah More and Her Circle.* New York 1946.

Horne, George. *A Letter to Adam Smith LL.D. on the Life, Death, and Philosophy of his Friend David Hume, Esq.* " By One of the People called Christians." Oxford 1777. [Anon.]

—— *Letters on Infidelity.* " By the Author of *A Letter to Dr. Adam Smith.*" Oxford 1784. [Anon.]

Hume, Baron David. *Lectures, 1786–1822,* ed. G. C. H. Paton. Edinburgh 1939.

Hunt, Erica. *Chirnside Past and Present.* Edinburgh 1975.

Hurd, Richard. [see also under Warburton]. *Moral and Political Dialogues.* London 1761.

Hutcheson, Francis. *An Essay on the Nature and Conduct of the Passions and Affections. With Illustrations on the Moral Sense.* London 1728. [Anon.]

—— *An Inquiry into the Original of our Ideas of Beauty and Virtue ; In Two Treatises.* London 1725. [Anon.]

—— *Philosophiae moralis institutio compendiaria.* Glasgow 1742.

Index Librorum Prohibitorum. Rome 1911.

Jacobi, F. H. *David Hume über den Glauben, oder Idealismus und Realismus. Ein Gespräch.* Breslau 1787.

Jeffner, Anders. *Butler and Hume on Religion.* Stockholm 1966.

The Jenkinson Papers, 1760–1766, ed. Ninetta S. Jucker. London 1949.

Jenyns, Soame. *Works,* ed. C. H. Cole. London 1790. 4 vols.

Jesse, John. *George Selwyn and His Contemporaries.* London 1882.

Johnson, Samuel. *Johnson's Journey to the Western Islands of Scotland,* ed. R. W. Chapman. London 1934.

Journals of the House of Lords (1760–4), VOL. XXX.

Justini Historiae Philippicae. 4th edn. Lugd. Batavorum [Leiden] 1701. Ed. Georg Graevius.

Kames, Lord [see under Henry Home].

Kay, John. *Edinburgh Portraits.* Edinburgh 1885. 2 vols.

Keill, John. *Introductio ad veram physicam.* Oxford 1702. [Engl. transl.] London 1720.

King, William. *An Essay on the Origin of Evil,* with John Gay's anon. *Dissertation concerning the fundamental principle and immediate criterion of virtue.* [Transl. and ed. by Edmund Law. London 1731.]

Laird, John. *Hume's Philosophy of Human Nature.* London 1932.

Leechman, William. *Sermons,* ed. James Wodrow. London 1789. 2 vols.

Leland, John. *View of the Principal Deistical Writers.* 2nd edn. with additions. London 1755–6. 3 vols.

Leroy, André-Louis. *David Hume.* Paris 1953.

Letters to Henry Fox, Lord Holland, ed. the Earl of Ilchester. London 1915.

"L.F." "Gresset et Frédéric II," in *Les Annales Fléchoises et la Vallée du Loir,* II (1904), 232–5.

Lindsay, Lord. *Lives of the Lindsays.* London 1849. 3 vols.

Linière, R. de. "Notes on the manor-house of Yvandeau at La Flèche," in *Les Annales Fléchoises et la Vallée du Loir,* IX (1908), 244–5.

Livingston, D. W. and J. T. King, edd. *Hume: A Re-evaluation.* New York 1976.

Low, D. M. *Edward Gibbon: 1737–1794.* London 1937.

Lyttelton, Thomas. *Letters.* London 1780.

Macdonald, John. *Memoirs of an Eighteenth Century Footman, 1745–1779,* ed. John Beresford. London 1927.

Macdonald, Norman D. Newspaper clipping of letter of 6 Sept. 1932 in Edinburgh Room of the Edinburgh Public Library. [Newspaper not cited.]

Mackenzie, Henry. *Anecdotes and Egotisms,* ed. H. W. Thompson. London 1927.

— — "Story of La Roche," in *The Mirror.* Edinburgh 1779, 19, 22, and 26 June.

— — *Works.* Edinburgh 1808. 8 vols.

Macky, John. *A Journey through Scotland.* London 1723.

Maclaurin, Colin. *An Account of Sir Isaac Newton's Philosophical Discoveries.* London 1748.

Macpherson, James. *Fragments of Ancient Poetry, Collected in the Highlands of Scotland, and Translated from the Galic or Erse Language.* Edinburgh 1760. [Anon., with anon. preface by Hugh Blair.]

— — *Works of Ossian,* 3rd edn. London 1815. 2 vols.

MacQueen, Daniel. *Letters on Mr Hume's History of Great Britain.* Edinburgh 1756. [Anon.]

Maitland, William. *History of Edinburgh*. Edinburgh 1753.

Malcolm, C. A. *Princes Street, Edinburgh*. Edinburgh 1937.

Marmontel, Jean François. *Mémoires*, ed. Maurice Tourneaux. Paris 1891. 3 vols.

Mason, William. *An Heroic Epistle to Sir William Chambers on his Book of Gardening*. London 1773.

Mathieson, W. L. *The Awakening of Scotland : A History from 1747 to 1797*. Glasgow 1910.

Meikle, Henry W. " The Chair of Rhetoric and Belles-Lettres in the University of Edinburgh," in *University of Edinburgh Journal* (1945), 89–92.

Meyer, Paul H. " The Manuscript of Hume's Account of His Dispute with Rousseau," in *Comparative Literature*, IV (1952), 341–50.

— — " Voltaire and Hume's ' Descent on the Coast of Britanny '," in *Modern Language Notes*, LXVI (1951), 429–35.

Montesquieu, Baron de. *Correspondance*, ed. André Morize. Bordeaux 1914. 2 vols.

— *Two chapters of a celebrated French work, intitled, De l'esprit des loix, translated into English*. Edinburgh 1750.

Morellet, André. *Eloges de Mme Geoffrin*. Paris 1812.

— — *Mémoires*. Paris 1823. 2 vols.

Morgan, Alexander, and R. K. Hannay. *University of Edinburgh : Charters, Statutes, and Acts of the Town Council and the Senatus, 1583–1858*. Edinburgh 1937. [Cited as Morgan–Hannay.]

Morren, Nathaniel. *Annals of the General Assembly of the Church of Scotland*. Edinburgh 1840. 2 vols.

Morrisroe, Michael, Jr. " Hume's Rhetorical Strategy : A Solution to the Riddle of the *Dialogues concerning Natural Religion*," in *Texas Studies in Literature and Language*, XI (1969), 963–74.

— — " The Rhetoric of the *Dialogues* of David Hume." [Unpublished doctoral dissertation in the University of Texas Library.]

— — " Rhetorical Methods in Hume's Works on Religion," in *Philosophy & Rhetoric*, 2 (1969), 121–38.

Mossner, E. C. " Adam Ferguson's ' Dialogue on a Highland Jaunt with Robert Adam, William Cleghorn, David Hume, and William Wilkie'," in *Restoration and Eighteenth Century Literature*. Chicago 1963, 297–308.

— — " An Apology for David Hume, Historian," in *PMLA*, LVI (1941), 657–90.

— — " Beattie's ' The Castle of Scepticism ' ; An Unpublished Allegory against Hume, Voltaire, and Hobbes," in University of Texas *Studies in English*, XXVII (1948), 108–45.

— — *Bishop Butler and the Age of Reason : A Study in the History of Thought*. New York 1936.

— — " The Continental Reception of Hume's *Treatise*, 1739–1741," in *Mind*, LVI (1947), 31–43.

— — " Hume and the Legacy of the *Dialogues*," in *David Hume : Bicentenary Papers*, ed. George Morice. (Edinburgh 1977), 1–22.

— — " David Hume's ' An Historical Essay on Chivalry and modern Honour '," in *Modern Philology*, XLV (1947), 54–60.

— — " Dr. Johnson *in partibus Infidelium ?*," in *Modern Language Notes*, LXIII (1948), 516–19.

— — " The Enigma of Hume," in *Mind*, XIV (1936), 334–49.

— — " The Enlightenment of David Hume," in *Introduction to Modernity*

(Austin 1965), 43–62. Reprinted in *Rivista Critica di Storia della Filosofia*, XXII (1967), 388–99.

—— "The First Answer to Hume's *Treatise*, an Unnoticed Item of 1740," in *Journal of the History of Ideas*, XII (1951), 291–4.

—— *The Forgotten Hume : Le bon David*. New York 1943.

—— "Hume and the Ancient–Modern Controversy, 1725–1752 : A Study in Creative Scepticism," in University of Texas *Studies in English*, XXVIII (1949), 139–53.

—— "Hume and the French Men of Letters," in *Revue International de Philosophie*, VI (1952), 222–35.

—— "Hume and the Scottish Shakespeare," in *Huntington Library Quarterly*, III (1940), 449–51.

—— and Harry Ransom. "Hume and the ' Conspiracy of the Booksellers ' : The Publication and Early Fortunes of the *History of England*," in University of Texas *Studies in English*, XXIX (1950), 162–82.

—— "Hume as Literary Patron : A Suppressed Review of Robert Henry's *History of Great Britain*, 1773," in *Modern Philology*, XXXIX (1942), 361–82.

—— "Hume's Epistle to Dr. Arbuthnot, 1734 : The Biographical Significance," in *Huntington Library Quarterly*, VII (1944), 135–52.

—— "Hume's *Four Dissertations* : An Essay in Biography and Bibliography," in *Modern Philology*, XLVIII (1950), 37–57.

—— "Hume's ' Of Criticism '," in *Studies in Criticism and Aesthetics, 1660–1800*, edd. Howard Anderson and John S. Shea. Minneapolis 1967, 232–48.

—— "Of the Principle of Moral Estimation : A Discourse between David Hume, Robert Clerk, and Adam Smith : An unpublished MS by Adam Ferguson," in *Journal of the History of Ideas*, XXI (1960), 222–32.

—— "Philosophy and Biography : The Case of David Hume," in *Philosophical Review*, LIX (1950), 184–201. [Reprinted in *Hume : A Collection of Critical Essays*, ed. V. C. Chappell. Garden City, N.Y. 1960, pp. 6–34.]

—— "Rousseau Hero-Worship," in *Modern Language Notes*, LV (1940), 449–51.

—— "Was Hume a Tory Historian ? Facts and Reconsiderations," in *Journal of the History of Ideas*, II (1941), 225–36.

Nangle, Benjamin C. *The Monthly Review, First Series 1749–1789. Indexes of Contributors and Articles*. Oxford 1934.

Neville, Sylas. *Diary, 1767–1788*, ed. Basil Cozens-Hardy. London 1950.

Nichols, John. *Illustrations of the Literary History of the Eighteenth Century*. London 1817–58. 8 vols.

—— *Literary Anecdotes of the Eighteenth Century*. London 1812–15. 9 vols.

Nidditch, P. H. *An Apparatus of Variant Readings for Hume's Treatise of Human Nature*. Sheffield 1976.

Nobbs, Douglas. "The Political Ideas of William Cleghorn, Hume's Academic Rival," in *Journal of the History of Ideas*, XXVI (1965), 575–86.

Nolan, J. B. *Benjamin Franklin in Scotland and Ireland 1759 and 1771*. Philadelphia 1938.

Northcote, James. *Life of Sir Joshua Reynolds*. 2nd edn. London 1818. 2 vols.

Northumberland, Duchess of. *Extracts from the Diaries*, ed. J. Greig. London 1926.

Notices and Documents illustrative of the Literary History of Glasgow. Glasgow 1831.

Noyes, Charles E. " Aesthetic Theory and Literary Criticism in the Works of David Hume." [Unpublished doctoral dissertation in the University of Texas Library.]

Oswald, James. *An Appeal to Common Sense in Behalf of Religion.* Edinburgh 1766–72. 2 vols.

Passmore, John. *Hume's Intentions.* London 1968.

Pearson, Norman. " ' Fish ' Crawford," in *Nineteenth Century*, LXXV (1914), 389–401.

Pemberton, Henry. *A View of Sir Isaac Newton's Philosophy.* London 1728.

Petrie, Charles. "The Elibank Plot, 1752–3," in *Transactions of the Royal Historical Society*, 4th Series, XIV (1931), 175–96.

Plarr, V. G. "Unpublished Letters to William Hunter," in *Chambers's Journal*, 6th Series, IX (1906), 56–7.

Pope, Alexander. *Works*, ed. Wm. Warburton. London 1751. 9 vols.

Popkin, Richard. "David Hume and the Pyrrhonian Controversy," in *Review of Metaphysics*, VI (1952–3), 65–81.

—— "David Hume: His Pyrrhonism and his Critique of Pyrrhonism," in *Philosophical Quarterly*, I (1950–1), 385–407.

—— "Hume and Isaac de Pinto," in *Texas Studies in Literature*, XII (1970), 417–30.

—— "Hume and Isaac de Pinto, II. Five New Letters," in *Hume and the Enlightenment*, ed. W. B. Todd. Edinburgh and Austin 1974, pp. 99–127.

Pouilly, Lévesque de. *Théorie des sentiments agréables.* Paris 1736.

Pratt, Samuel Jackson. *Curious Particulars and Genuine Anecdotes respecting the late Lord Chesterfield and David Hume, Esq.* London 1788. [Anon.]

—— *Supplement to the Life of David Hume, Esq.* London 1777. [Anon.]

Price, John V. *David Hume.* New York 1968.

—— "Hume's ' Account of Stewart ' : An important presentation copy," in *The Bibliotheck*, VI (1973), 199–202.

—— *The Ironic Hume.* Austin 1965.

Price, Richard. *Review of the Principal Questions and Difficulties in Morals.* London 1758.

Prior, James. *Life of Edmond Malone.* London 1860.

Rae, John. *Life of Adam Smith.* London 1895.

Ralph, James. *The Case of Authors by Profession.* London 1762.

Ramsay, Andrew Michael. *Philosophical Principles of Natural and Revealed Religion, Unfolded in a Geometrical Order.* Glasgow 1748–9. 2 vols.

Ramsay of Ochtertyre, John. *Scotland and Scotsmen in the Eighteenth Century*, ed. Alexander Allardyce. Edinburgh and London 1888. 2 vols. [Cited as Ramsay.]

Raphael, D. D. "Adam Smith and ' The Infection of David Hume's Society '," in *Journal of the History of Ideas*, XXX (1969), 225–48.

Register of the Privy Council of Scotland. Edinburgh. XIV (1898) ; 3rd Series, I 1908), II (1921), V (1912), XIII (1932).

Reid, Thomas. *An Inquiry into the Human Mind, on the Principles of Common Sense.* Edinburgh 1764.

Richmond, H. W. *The Navy in The War of 1739–48.* Cambridge 1920.

Ridpath, George. *Diary*, ed. Sir James Balfour Paul. Edinburgh 1922. [Cited as Ridpath.]

Ritchie, T. E. *Account of the Life and Writings of David Hume.* London 1807.

Roberts, William. *Memoirs of the Life and Correspondence of Mrs. Hannah More.* London 1834.

Robertson, William. *History of Scotland.* London 1759. 2 vols.

Roddier, Henri. *J. J. Rousseau en Angleterre au XVIIIe Siècle.* Paris 1950.

Rogers, Samuel. *Table-Talk*, ed. A. Dyce. New Southgate 1887.

Rose, Hugh, and Lachian Shaw. *A Genealogical Deduction of the Family of Rose of Kilravock*, ed. C. Innes. Edinburgh 1848.

Ross, Ian S. "Hutcheson on Hume's *Treatise*: An Unnoticed Letter," in *Journal of the History of Philosophy*, IV (1966), 69-70.

— — *Lord Kames and the Scotland of his Day.* Oxford 1972.

Rousseau, Jean-Jacques. *Collection complète des œuvres.* Geneva 1782-9. 33 vols.

— — *Correspondance Générale*, edd. Théophile Dufour and P.-P. Plan. Paris 1924-34. 20 vols. [Cited as Rousseau.]

Russell, Bertrand. *Nightmares of Eminent Persons.* New York 1955.

Rutherforth, Thomas. *Credibility of Miracles Defended against the Author of Philosophical Essays.* Cambridge 1751.

Sainte-Beuve, C.-A. "La Comtesse de Boufflers," in *Nouveaux Lundis* for 19 Jan. 1863.

Schazmann, Paul Emile. *La Comtesse de Boufflers.* Lausanne 1933.

Schilpp, Paul Arthur. *Albert Einstein : Philosopher-Scientist.* Evanston 1949.

The Scotch Haggis : Consisting of Anecdotes, Jests, Curious and Rare Articles of Literature. Edinburgh 1822. [Reprints, without naming the author, Hume's *Bellman's Petition.*]

The Scots Peerage, ed. Sir James Balfour Paul. Edinburgh 1904-14. 9 vols.

Scott, Hew. *Fasti Ecclesiae Scoticanae.* Edinburgh 1915-28. 7 vols.

Scott, Walter. Review of *Works of John Home*, in *Quarterly Review*, XXXVI (1827), 167-216.

Scott, William R. *Adam Smith as Student and Professor.* Glasgow 1937.

— — *Francis Hutcheson : His Life, Teaching and Position in the History of Philosophy.* Cambridge 1900.

Scottish Record Society. Edinburgh. VOLS. II (1898), XXVII (1905), XXXI (1908), LXII (1930).

Sharp, L. W. "Charles Mackie, the First Professor of History at Edinburgh University," in *Scottish Historical Review*, XLI (1962), 23-45.

Sherbo, Arthur. "Some Early Readers in the British Museum," in *Transactions of the Cambridge Bibliographical Society*, VI (1972), 56-64.

Sheridan, Thomas. *British Education ; or, The Source of the Disorders of Great Britain.* London 1756.

Shields, Alexander. "Life of Renwick," in *Biographia Presbyteriana.* Edinburgh 1827.

Smart, Alastair. *The Life and Art of Allan Ramsay.* London 1952.

Smellie, William. *Literary and Characteristical Lives of John Gregory, Henry Home, David Hume, and Adam Smith.* Edinburgh 1800.

— — *Memoirs.* Edinburgh 1811.

Smith, Adam. *An Inquiry into the Nature and Causes of the Wealth of Nations.* London 1776. 2 vols. New definitive edn. Edd. Campbell, Skinner and Todd. Oxford 1976.

— — *The Theory of Moral Sentiments.* London 1759. New definitive edn. Edd. Raphael and Macfie. Oxford 1976.

Smith, Norah. "Hume's 'Rejected' Essays," in *Forum for Modern Language Studies*, VIII (1972), 354-71.

Smith, Norman Kemp. *The Philosophy of David Hume : A Critical Study of Its Origins and Central Doctrines.* London 1941.

Smollett, Tobias. *Works*, ed. George Saintsbury. London 1895. 12 vols.

Stanhope, Philip. *History of England.* London 1836-54. 7 vols.

Sterne, Laurence. *Letters*, ed. L. P. Curtis. Oxford 1934.

— — *Sermons of Mr. Yorick.* Oxford 1927. 7 vols. in 2.

—— *Works*, ed. W. L. Cross. New York 1904. 12 vols.

Stewart, Dugald. *Biographical Memoirs of Smith, Robertson, and Reid*. Edinburgh 1811.

Stewart, John B. *The Moral and Political Philosophy of David Hume*. New York 1963.

Stona, Thomas. *Remarks upon the Natural History of Religion by Mr. Hume*. London 1758. [By " S.T."]

Sugg, Redding S., Jr. " Hume and the British Romantics." [Unpublished doctoral dissertation in the University of Texas Library.]

Thomson, John. *Life, Lectures and Writings of William Cullen*. Edinburgh 1932. 2 vols.

Thomson, Mark A. *The Secretaries of State, 1681–1782*. Oxford 1932.

Thorpe, Thomas. *Autograph Catalogue*. London 1833.

Tilly, Sir John and Stephen Gaselee. *The Foreign Office*. London 1933.

Tindal, Matthew. *Christianity as old as the Creation ; or, the Gospel, a Republication of the Religion of Nature*. London 1730.

Tindal, Nicholas. *Continuation of Mr. Rapin's History of England*, VOL. XI, London 1763.

Todd, William B. " The First Printing of Hume's *Life* (1777)," in *Library*, 5th Series, VI (1951), 123–5.

—— ed. *Hume and the Enlightenment*. *Essays presented to Ernest Campbell Mossner*. Edinburgh and Austin 1974.

Topham, Edward. *Letters from Edinburgh*. Dublin 1776.

Trinius, J. A. *Freydenker Lexicon*. Leipzig 1759.

Tytler, Alexander F. *Memoirs of the Life and Writings of the Honourable Henry Home of Kames*. Edinburgh 1807. 2 vols.

Tytler, William. *An Historical and Critical Inquiry into the Evidence Produced by the Earls of Murray and Morton against Mary Queen of Scots. With an Examination of the Rev. Dr Robertson's Dissertation and Mr Hume's History with respect to that Evidence*. Edinburgh 1760. [Anon.]

[Voltaire?]. *A Letter from Mr. Voltaire to Mr. Jean Jaques Rousseau*. London 1766.

Voltaire. *Le Caffé, ou L'Ecossaise, comédie par Mr. Hume pasteur de l'Eglise d'Edimbourg. Traduite en Français*. London [Geneva] 1760. [Anon. The comedy, of course, was not the work of John Home.]

—— *Œuvres complètes*. Paris 1883–7. 52 vols.

Wallace, Robert. *A Dissertation on the Numbers of Mankind in Antient and Modern Times*. Edinburgh 1753.

Walpole, Horace. *Letters*, ed. Mrs. Paget Toynbee. Oxford 1903–5. 16 vols. [Cited as *Walpole Letters*.]

—— *Memoirs of the Reign of King George III*. London 1894. 4 vols.

—— *Works*. London 1798–1825. 9 vols.

—— *The Yale Edition of Horace Walpole's Correspondence*, ed. W. L. Lewis. New Haven 1937– . [In progress. Cited as *Walpole Corr.* (Yale).]

Warburton, William. *Letters from a late eminent Prelate to one of his Friends*. New York 1809.

—— *Remarks on Mr. David Hume's Essay on the Natural History of Religion, Addressed to the Rev. Dr. Warburton*. London 1757. [Anon. Compiled by Hurd from the notes of Warburton.]

—— [See also under Pope.] *A Selection from Unpublished Papers*, ed. Francis Kilvert. London 1841.

Watts, Isaac. *Logick : Or, The Right Use of Reason in the Enquiry after Truth*. London 1729.

Wesley, John. " On the Deceitfulness of the Human Heart. A Sermon preached at Halifax, 21 April 1790," in *Works*, VOL. VII. London 1878.

Wharton, G. and P. [pseudonyms for Mrs. K. B. Thomson and J. Thomson]. *The Queens of Society*. London 1890.

Wilkie, William. *The Epigoniad ; a Poem*. Edinburgh 1757. [Anon.]

— — *The Epigoniad ; A Poem* . . . " *The Second Edition, Carefully Corrected and Improved. To Which is Added a Dream. In the Manner of Spenser*." London and Edinburgh 1759.

Witherspoon, John. *Ecclesiastical Characteristics ; Or, The Arcana of Church Policy*. 5th edn. Edinburgh 1762. [Anon.]

— — *The Moderator, No.* II. Edinburgh 1757. [Anon.]

— — *Works*, 2nd edn., revised and corrected. Philadelphia 1802. 4 vols.

Wodrow, Robert. *Analecta*. Glasgow 1843.

INDEX

EXPLANATORY NOTE

The multifarious Homes and Humes mentioned in this index are identified by a key date, or by a relationship to David Hume, in parentheses following each name. Hume himself is referred to throughout as DH. His works are mentioned without naming the author, and are cited by the short titles adopted under the entry "Hume, David (1711–76), (**22**)."

   The entry for DH *is necessarily lengthy, and is subdivided as follows:* (**1**) Childhood and family relations, (**2**) Physical characteristics, (**3**) Health, (**4**) Career, (**5**) Finances, (**6**) Travels, (**7**) And Scotland, (**8**) Education, (**9**) Reading, (**10**) Religion, (**11**) As political theorist, (**12**) As historian, (**13**) As philosopher, (**14**) As man of letters, (**15**) Conviviality and wit, (**16**) Friendships (principal), (**17**) Relations with women, (**18**) Controversies, (**19**) Estimates of his character, (**20**) Soubriquets and pseudonyms, (**21**) Miscellaneous comments of, (**22**) Works published by him, (**23**) Works, published, unauthorised, (**24**) Works, printed but left unpublished, (**25**) Works, published but still unlocated, (**26**) Works, ms, located, (**27**) Works, ms, unlocated, (**28**) Works, projected.

   Short titles of books and pamphlets are listed alphabetically where authorship is unknown; in other cases they may be found under the name of the author. Periodicals are indexed alphabetically.

   Numerals following an asterisk indicate mere passing or unimportant references.

INDEX

Grose, T. H.: his study of variants of DH's "Five Dissertations," 618.

Grotius, Hugo, *De Jure Belli ac Pacis*, 41.

Guerchy, C.-L.-F. de Regnier, Comte de, 435, 439, 445.

Guibert, Comte de, 454.

"Guidelianus": *see* Edmonstourne of Newton, James.

Guines, Duc de, 576.

Gustard, Dr John, 595.

Haddington, Thomas, 7th Earl of, 150.

Hailes, Sir David Dalrymple of Newhailes, Lord: Curator of Advocates' Library, 252; member of Select Society, 282; DH considers as author of anon. *Philosophical Essays* [Balfour], 296; wishes to bring Beattie to Edinburgh U., 580; translates DH's *Life* into Latin prose and Smith's *Letter to Strahan* into Latin verse, 621; *89, 234.

Haldane, John: his *Players Scourge*, 368.

Halifax, George Montagu-Dunk, 2nd Earl of, 492, 493.

Halkerton, Lord: title in Falconer family, 7.

Hamilton, Lady Elizabeth, 575.

Hamilton, Baillie Gavin: presides over Edinburgh Council meeting considering DH's candidacy, 156; takes advice of ministers on offer to Hutcheson, 157; informs Council of Hutcheson's refusal, 157; no backer of DH for Edinburgh for Edinburgh professorship, 302; letter to Strahan on prospects of publishing *History* quoted, 302-3; sets up shop in London, 304; boycotted in London booksellers he returns to Edinburgh, 304; but refuses Millar's offer to buy rights in *History*, 304; attributes failure to "Cry of Clergy," 305; DH quoted on his unbusinesslike procedures, 312; *Life* quoted on, 312; DH persuades him to accept new Millar offer, 314; DH refuses to consider him as publisher for vol. ii, 314; DH's attitude towards, 316; his offer of publication on *History of Scotland* rejected, 396.

Hamilton, James George, 7th Duke of, 550-1.

Hamilton, Balfour and Neill (publishers), 295.

Hamilton of Bangour, William: "Braes of Yarrow" in *Tea-Table Miscellany*, 56; "To H[enry] H[ome] in the Assembly" quoted, 59; as Jacobite, 60, 181; "To a Gentleman going to travel" quoted, 61; permitted to read "Of Miracles," 112; his *Ode on the Battle of Gladsmuir* quoted, 178; DH's sympathy for in Rebellion, 181; his verses in DH's hand, 378.

Hanover, House of, 25, 302, 430.

Hardwicke, Philip Yorke, 2nd Earl of:

may have been shown "Five Dissertations" by Warburton, 324; his alleged threat to prosecute publisher, 327, 330; *438, 499.

Harrogate: DH visits in 1763, 432.

Hawke, Adm. Edward, 209.

Hawley, Gen. Henry, 178.

Hay, Matthew, 410-11.

Hay of Drumelzier, William, 57.

Hay of Locharret, Sir William, 8.

Hay, Thomas, 158.

Haymarket Theatre, 108.

Heineccius: his *Methodical System of Universal Law* published by Noon, 114.

Helvétius, Claude-Adrien: DH evades proposal to translate his *De l'Esprit* and to sponsor him for Royal Society, 423; as friend of DH, 475, 480; warned about London by DH, 504; touches up King-of-Prussia letter, 513; *485, 514, 544.

Helvétius, Mme, 480.

Hénault, President: admires DH, 423; receives DH, 441; permitted by Mme du Deffand to attend *salon* of Mlle de Lespinasse, 453; friend of DH, 475; congratulates DH, 493; touches up Walpole's King-of-Prussia letter, 513.

Henry VII, King of England, 302, 412.

Henry, Rev. Robert, 583, 584, 585.

Hepburn, Rev. Thomas, 582.

Herd, David, 375.

Herring, Thomas, Archbishop of Canterbury: likes *History*, 305, 309; Boswell on his invitation to DH to visit Lambeth quoted, 309.

Hertford, Francis Seymour Conway, 1st Earl of: entertained at Strawberry Hill with Mme de Boufflers, 431; first meeting with DH, 434; appointed Ambassador to France, 434; his offer to DH of personal secretaryship, 435; possible reasons for choice, 435-6; Mme de Boufflers's possible connexion with offer, 437; DH accepts, 437-8; comment of others on, 438; his voyage to France, 439-440; his arrival in France overshadowed by that of DH, 441; DH considers asking for replacement, 443; takes DH to masquerade, 444; DH fears to embarrass by supporting Murray, 466; his great esteem for DH, 489; his character, 490; home life in the Hôtel de Brancas, 490-1; his appointment of DH criticised, 491; his campaign to have DH appointed Embassy Secretary, 492; his appointment to Ireland as Lord Lieutenant, 493-4; unable to take DH as conjunct secretary, 494; his embarrassment at having to withdraw invitation to DH for social visit there, 495-6; Sterne preaches sermon before him, 501-2; urges DH to publish *Concise Account*, 527; copy given him by DH,

Hume, David (*contd.*)

"Of National Characters," 234, 260; anecdote of his reception by pious lady, 245; anecdote of his avoidance of Bible, 246; Wallace's unpublished refutation of his character of the clergy, 260; quoted, 261, 262; published refutations of same, 262; friendships with liberal clergy, 274; irreligion charged against *History*, 305; preface to VOL. II quoted on "proper office of religion," 306; and on various sects, 307; *Dialogues* and "Natural History of Religion" important contributions to philosophy and psychology of religion, 319; consults Elliot concerning, 319–20; DH not provoked to become Scottish Voltaire, 355; shocked by dogmatic atheism of *philosophes*, 485, 486; difference in his position and Rousseau's, 523; as patron of Church of Scotland, 539–40; Boswell's version of his last remarks on quoted, 597–8; *see also* Church of Scotland *and* DH (22).

(**11**) As political theorist: quoted on political impartiality, 139; his "character of Walpole," 143–4; as "revolution Whig," 179–80; opinion of Jacobite Rebellion, 177, 179–80; on "Political Whigs" and "Religious Whigs," 186; on policies of "Broad Bottomed" Ministry, 190–1; on expedition to Brittany, 198–9; on St Clair, 199; on Jacobitism, 236–8; as critic of economic theory, 270–1; his *History* accused of being Jacobite, 310; of being Tory, 310, 311; DH's comments on, in *Life*, quoted, 311; quoted on "touchstones of party men," 413.

(**12**) As historian: Mackie's history courses at Edinburgh U., 44–5; DH's "Essay on Chivalry," 46–7; "Of the Study of History," in *Essays*, 141; advertisement to *Treatise* intimates intention to turn to history, 175; first attempt at writing history during Annandale period, 175; *Account of Stewart* is historical narrative at its best, 183; expedition to Brittany valuable experience for, 202, 204; DH quoted to that effect, 208; *Tudors* progressing well in 1757, 390; future course of *History* undecided, 390; DH quoted on reception of *Tudors*, 398; signs contract for *Early History*, 402; DH disgruntled at its being branded Jacobite, 403; considers writing on reigns of William III, Anne, and George I, 420; rumours of his intent to write "Ecclesiastical History," 420.

(**13**) As philosopher: in early years, 51; early statement of intentions, 63; his statement on successive stages of composition of *Treatise*, 73; projection 73–4;

planning, 74; composition, 74; his debt to Newtonians, 74; his differences with, 75; philosophical scepticism, 75; debt to "sentimentalists," 76; debt to ancients, 78; debt to five modern philosophers, 78–80; influence of John Gay's associationism on, 80; anticipates argument in "Of Miracles" in discussion with Jesuit at La Flèche, 101; quoted on differences with Hutcheson on origin of moral sense, 149; expedition to Brittany valuable to, 203, 204; tenets applied in realm of religion in *Dialogues* and "Natural History of Religion," 319; considered as bigoted by *philosophes*, 485, 486; *see also* DH (22), (23), (24), (25).

(**14**) As man of letters: importance of style, 3, 63; as causing quarrel with Miller, 90; concern over style of *Treatise*, 119; criticism of Leechman's style, 148; failure of *Treatise* due to "manner," 140; letter to Reid on quoted, 298.

DH's early passion for literature, 49–51; *Enquiry* (*Understanding*) represents new plane of philosophical expression, 175; little leisure for literary work, 175; Boswell on his literary success, 223; popularity of later works, 223–4; controversies aided sales, 225; Continental reception, 225, 227–8; compared to Montesquieu, 229; recognised by Montesquieu, 229; success accompanied by frustrations, 230–1; as editor of *Essays and Observations*, 258; preface quoted, 257–8; literary reputation in Scotland, 229–30; as a critic, 376; as no poet, 378.

(**15**) Conviviality and wit: family background for, 28; dinners in honour of Stewart's wine, 183; in Army, 203; plays whist, 203, 402, 546; his "infantine" wit, 233, 277, 549; as literary wit, 234–9; as host in Edinburgh, 245–6; 560–1; arguments with John Home (poet) over wine, 276, 599.

(**16**) Friendships (principal): *see* Abercromby, Alembert, Armstrong, Boufflers, Carlyle, Clephane, Cockburn, Conway, Crawford, Diderot, Edmonstoune, Elliot, Erskine, Ferguson, Geoffrin, Hertford, Holbach, John Home (poet), Jardine, Kames, Keith, Lespinasse, Henry Mackenzie, Meinières, Millar, Montigny, Mure, Orde, Oswald, Allen Ramsay (Younger), Michael Ramsay, Robertson, Smith, St Clair, Strahan, Andrew Stuart, Wedderburn; *see also* DH (17).

(**17**) Relations with women: youthful thoughts on love, 47–8; as sexually normal, 83; favourite of ladies in

The Humes of Ninewells

Hay of Yester

Home of Home

Sir Alex. Home of Home
d. 1424
m.
Jean
dau. of Sir Wm. Hay of Locharret or Yester

Thomas of Tynninghame

Thomas of the Brumhouse

George of Ninewells *

Sir Alex.
d. 1491
The 'founder of Dunglass'

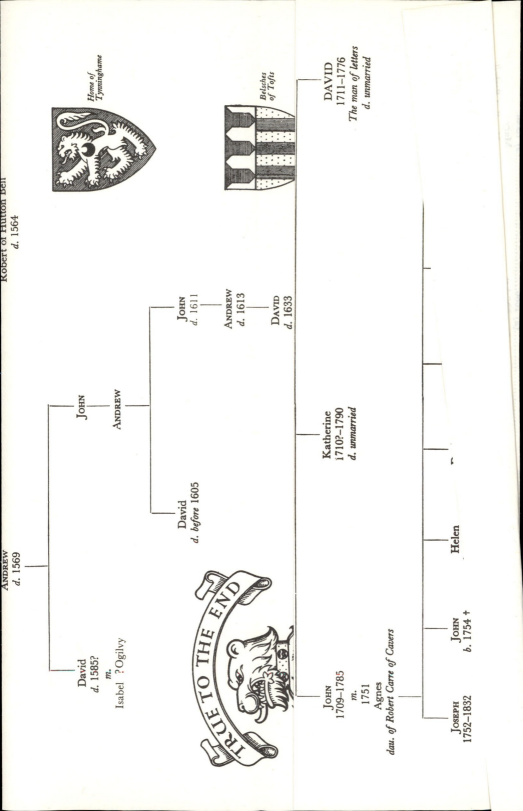